AF865083

SOTHIS PRESS

Sothis Press aims to completely reimagine the public domain book with an emphasis on universal access to captivatingly designed print editions. We believe that technology will enable every single book ever published to be perpetually accessible in beautiful print form. Sothis is beauty in ubiquity.

www.sothis.press
1 Waterhouse Square, London, ECIN 2ST

The Law Notes

April 1907 to March 1908

Edward Thompson Company

SOTHIS PRESS

ISBN 978-1-0365-2126-4

The Law Notes is in
the public domain.

This edition is published by
Sothis Press © 2023. The company
is registered in England and Wales.
The Company Number is 14900389.

Law Notes.

VOLUME XI.

APRIL, 1907, TO MARCH, 1908.

EDWARD THOMPSON COMPANY, LAW PUBLISHERS,
NORTHPORT, LONG ISLAND, NEW YORK.
1908.

INDEX TO VOLUME XI.

1

Law Notes

APRIL, 1907.

PUBLISHED BY EDWARD THOMPSON COMPANY.
NORTHPORT, LONG ISLAND, N. Y.

CONTENTS.

An index to volume 10 of LAW NOTES, *which was completed by the March number, has been prepared and will be sent free to subscribers on application to the publishers.*

WHATEVER doubts there may be as to the advisability of attempting a general codification of the common law, experience has demonstrated that certain portions of the law are well adapted to statement in the form of a code. The English Bills of Exchange Act, a codification of the law merchant as applied to negotiable instruments, has been in successful operation since 1882, and our own Negotiable Instrument Law, first enacted in New York in 1897, is now in force in some thirty of the United States. The Negotiable Instrument Law is based on the English Act, but unlike that enactment starts from the generalization of a negotiable instrument rather than from the special conception of particular negotiable instruments — bills of exchange and promissory notes. The American law is, as its extensive adoption indicates, an excellent piece of legislation, although it is not free from blemishes. We owe it to the Commission on Uniform State Laws, a body made up of commissioners from the several States appointed by their respective governors. The commission owes its existence to a suggestion from the American Bar Association, and its work has been done under the auspices of that body. In England the results of the Bills of Exchange Act were so satisfactory that the experiment of codification has been extended to other branches of mercantile law. The subject of sales was put in the form of a code by Sir Frederick Pollock and enacted into a statute in 1894. We are glad to see that the Commissioners on Uniform State Laws have adopted the same course, and, after experimenting without success on the subject of divorce, have returned to the field of commercial law. In the present session of the legislature of New York a Sale of Goods Act, prepared by the commission, has been introduced. The history of the bill is thus given by the New York *Commercial Bulletin:* "The original draft of this Act was prepared in 1902–3 by Prof. Samuel Williston, of Cambridge, Mass., at the request of the Commissioners on Uniform State Laws in national conference. It was printed in the summer of 1903 and sent with a request for criticism to teachers of the law of sales and to other experts on the subject. Some criticisms were received, and with the light of these criticisms and his own further reflection, the draftsman presented to the conference of Commissioners on Uniform State Laws, at its meeting at St. Louis in 1904, a number of suggested amendments. The draft was then gone over carefully, section by section, by the conference. Doubtful points and changes in wording were discussed and voted upon. The draft was then recommitted to the committee on commercial law, with instructions to embody the changes adopted by the conference and to present a revised draft at the meeting of the conference in August, 1905. Another draft was presented, in accordance with these instructions, at the meeting of the conference at Narragansett Pier in August, 1905. This draft included for the first time a number of sections on the transfer of property by means of documents of title. These sections are numbered sections 27–40 in the present draft. Because of these sections it was thought best once more to recommit the draft. At the meeting of the conference in St. Paul in August, 1906, another draft was adopted and recommended to the legislatures of the several States for passage." The care with which the enactment has been prepared appears from the above recital of its history. If it passes the New York legislature that State will have the honor of being the pioneer in adopting the Sale of Goods Act, as it was the pioneer in the adoption of the Negotiable Instrument Law in 1897.

THE statement in succinct and intelligible form of the law of negotiable instruments has proved a convenience to the business world. Instead of the principles of that law having to be extracted laboriously from thousands of cases it is now accessible to the banker or merchant in a few printed pages. The same benefits may be expected to flow from the codification of other branches of commercial law whose rules must be continually applied in the dealings of the business world. Again, the advantage to be derived from uniformity was never more apparent than in the United States at the present time. Long ago Lord Mansfield and Judge Story quoted as applicable to commercial law the aspiration of Cicero: "There will not be one law at Rome, another at Athens, one now, another hereafter, but among all nations and in all time a law single and the same will obtain." Uniformity, at least as regards commerce, is vastly more important in this era of railroads and telegraph lines than ever before. The numerous separate States of the Union are essentially one community for purposes of business. A comparatively small number of great cities supply the merchants of the whole country, and the convenience is obvious of having "single and the same" the law which regulates the transactions between the various parts of our immense territory. In the nature of things it is not to be expected that, even if the law on negotiable instruments and the sale of goods could be absolutely the same to-day in the half a hundred jurisdictions which compose the Union, such uniformity will continue. Cicero's *lex alia nunc, alia post hac,* is but a dream. As Mr. Justice Holmes has observed: "However much we may codify the law into a series of seemingly self-sufficient propositions, those propositions will be but a phase in a continuous growth." But though we may not hope to arrest the process of development, yet we may to some extent influence the direction of that development. In a country whose business life is as closely knit together as is ours the tendencies will be toward a greater uniformity in law as the needs of the communities advance under like influences. If, to the great convenience of our trading and commercial circles, we can introduce a present uniformity into the law, we may safely hope that it will be many years before any revolutionary diversities will appear to mar the symmetry of our work.

SINCE the Spanish-American war and the acquisition of foreign territory under the Treaty of Paris there have been evidences of an increased interest in and study of international law. The Treaty of Paris forced the United States to take a place among the world powers and brought with it the necessity of a more extended knowledge of the rules which regulate the intercourse of those powers with one another. The need has been recognized, and the study of international law is the object of a new society under the presidency of Secretary Root, which numbers among its members Chief Justice Fuller, Justices Day and Brewer of the Supreme Court, Secretary Taft, ex-Secretaries Foster and Olney, Judge Gray of Delaware, and other distinguished men. Its object is "to develop public interest in international law, and to promote the establishment of international relations on the basis of law and justice." In connection with the formation of this society we should note the appearance of the *American Journal of International Law,* a quarterly devoted to the subject indicated by its title. Mr. Hannis Taylor, one of the accomplished editors of the *American Law Review,* whose elaborate text-book on international law is evidence of his fitness for the task, has added to the *Review* a department devoted to this subject. The introductory article in the *Journal* is contributed by Secretary Root. He calls attention to the need of information on the subject of international law on the part of the body of the people under a government where, as in ours, representatives of the people, elected by them and responsible to them, control the administration. Of Mr. Root's article the New York *Sun* observes: "Well timed and useful is Mr. Root's suggestion that the more clearly the people of a country understand their own international rights the less likely are they to take extreme and extravagant views of them, and the less ready to fight for something to which they are not entitled. On the other hand, the more distinctly and generally the people of a given country become alive to their own international obligations and duties, the less likely will they be to resent the just demand of other countries that those obligations and duties be observed. There is ample recent justification also for another suggestion of Mr. Root's, that the more familiar the people of a given country become with the rules and customs of diplomatic self-restraint and courtesy between nations, which long experience has shown to be indispensable for preserving the peace of the world, the greater will be their willingness to refrain from discussing publicly international controversies in such a spirit as to hinder peaceful settlement by wounding sensibilities or arousing anger and prejudice on the other side." The readiest way, it is suggested, to promote the habit of reading and thinking about international affairs on the part of the public is through the newspapers. Let editorial writers acquire an interest in these matters from the *American Journal of International Law,* or from other sources, and through the columns to which they contribute a more or less intelligent acquaintance with such questions may be handed on to the people.

FROM time to time we have mentioned in these columns the excellent work which is resulting from the changed point of view toward criminals on the part of the State. The idea of prevention and reformation where possible is taking the place of the mere punishment of wrongdoers. The State is realizing in earnest its position as *parens patriæ* and is seeking to meet the resulting obligations. A new class of reformatories, juvenile courts, the probation system, and indeterminate sentences are some of the practical effects of this effort. An admirable address on the movement, especially in its relations to the juvenile court, was made by Judge Julian W. Mack in Louisville, Ky., in February last. The speaker touched the keynote of the system, the substitution of the idea of delinquency for that of crime, as follows: "The essentially new principle in Anglo-American jurisprudence that has been brought in in this juvenile court legislation has to do with the so-called delinquent child, the child whether of good or of bad parents, good or bad homes, that has broken the law. I don't say a sinner, because the child is much more often sinned against than sinning, and yet whether the parent be directly or indirectly at fault, the child has been allowed to drift the wrong way." When the ill-trained or neglected child has drifted into some petty infraction of law he is no longer held to the responsibility of an adult. The juvenile court instead of asking the delinquent "have you done a certain thing," asks "what are you, how have you become what you are; and, having determined that, we don't ask how you should be punished, but what can the State, the great parent, do to its child to help that child along into good citizenship." Even the first wrong steps of the child, its truancy from school, must be controlled. All this demands special machinery, truant and probation officers, the building perhaps of institutions. To meet these demands, money and an aroused public opinion are necessary. "The people," says Judge Mack, "must realize that unless we begin to have social justice we cannot stop the wrong in the child." When we consider the good results that have been achieved by these courts, results established by experience, we may be sure that the juvenile court is an institution which has "made good," and that the constitutional objection which has been raised against such courts in particular instances must be obviated, not by abandoning the idea, but by modifying the structure or practice of the court into harmony with the Constitution — or even by modifying the guaranties of the Constitution itself.

A FURTHER experiment in these new reform ideas, from Chicago, is noticed in the Boston *Advertiser*. "This Chicago system," says our contemporary, "is, briefly stated, a parole system, under which the accused men are fined and the fine held in abeyance during good behavior, reports at a night session of the court being made bi-weekly. In this the system does not differ essentially, perhaps, from our own probation system, which has been found to be of great value in treating such cases. The distinguishing feature of the Chicago idea is that in the place of paid probation officers to keep track of the culprits there is a voluntary committee of business men who visit the men under suspended fine, and note the progress of reform. That this service of business men is practical as well as philanthropic is indicated in the statement that an average of $250 a week has been added to the revenue of the business men in the district through the increased earning capacity of the workingmen." These statistics show, if we receive them at their face value, that the system which demands outlay in time and money may be the cheapest in the long run. But it cannot be that the average income of every "business" man in the district was thus increased, and in the absence of particulars the figures mean little. Another and very questionable experiment is reported as being agitated in the juvenile court of Omaha, Neb. It is to pay children for their attendance on school, and thus relieve the parents from the temptation or necessity to place them in factories. "Regular weekly appropriations," an exchange tells us, "are to be taken from churches, friendly societies, women's clubs, and other organizations. The plan is to make it unnecessary for children to work for the support of their parents or for younger brothers and sisters. Working children are to be placed in school, and the exact amount of their earnings will be paid to them by the courts." A poor substitute this for an adequate compulsory school law, and one would imagine the juvenile courts could hardly compete with the factories as to rates of wages. But all these experiments are interesting in this novel line of development.

A YOUNG man summoned for jury duty in a Chicago court explained to the judge that he was a believer in labor unions and therefore in a contest in which one of the parties was a union man he must favor the union man, regardless of what the law might be. In the view of this singularly candid individual the labor unions form an *imperium in imperio*, who claim and receive from him an allegiance paramount to that due the Nation or the State. The misguided young man was lectured severely by the judge, but we are inclined to think that many a union man, without thus candidly stating his position, would have undertaken the performance of jury duty and then unconsciously perhaps have had ears only for the union side of the argument. The young man deserved some credit for his candor and for his ability to know himself. While labor organizations have been the means by which the workingman has attained a large part of the freedom which he enjoys, and while they were and are essential to the protection of the rights of workingmen, the spirit in which they are frequently conducted betrays no consideration wider than the advantage of the union. In the new-found strength of organization they are too ready to go rough-shod to their aims without considering that they have duties as well as rights. Their attitude is, it is sad to think, but a natural result of that of capital toward them. But other times, other manners. We are arriving at a period in our history when capital is to be held to a strict accountability for the powers which it wields, and the position of labor should, and we believe will, reflect the changed attitude of the State. Not very hopeful of improved conditions, however, are the comments of the labor press on the Moyer case. It will be remembered that Moyer, Haywood, and Pettibone of the Western Federation of Miners were arrested in Denver, Colorado, for the murder of ex-Governor Steunenburg, of Idaho. With the consent of the governor of Colorado they were hurried by a special train to Idaho. They sought to secure their release upon the ground that they had been illegally turned over to the authorities of Idaho. The courts, including the Supreme Court of the United States, decided adversely to their contention — as would have been anticipated by any one familiar with the course of decision on this topic. Now the socialists and labor press are raising an absurd outcry and declaiming about a conspiracy to deprive the accused men of their constitutional rights. They wish "to ascertain by what authority or through what influence, if any, the United States Supreme Court can set aside the Constitution of the United States and legalize the crime of kidnapping." Such stuff would be ludicrous if it were not for the fact that the labor press is probably read by many ignorant persons, who receive its utterances as oracular, and firmly believe that the "money power" has bribed the Supreme Court and that the accused men are to be done to death in despite of justice and law.

THE Court of Appeals of the State of New York has affirmed the decision of the Appellate Division of the Supreme Court, holding that George W. Perkins, vice-president of the New York Life Insurance Company, was not guilty of grand larceny by reason of his part in the company's contribution of $50,000 to the Republican national campaign fund. The decision was reached by a bare majority of the court, Chief Judge Cullen and Judges Chase and Werner dissenting. The warrant on which Perkins was arrested was framed on a statute denouncing as grand larceny the taking of the property of another in any manner whatever. The facts were that the president of the New York Life promised on behalf of the company $50,000 toward the campaign fund. He then asked Mr. Perkins to pay the amount by his, Perkins's, check, it being understood that the insurance company was to reimburse him. Reimbursement was made by a check payable not to Perkins personally, but to the order of J. P. Morgan & Co. The court, in an opinion written by Judge Gray, declares that the act of Perkins lacked the felonious intent which is essential under the statute. "Under the statute," it was said, "the crime of larceny no longer necessitates a trespass; but it does need as an essential element that the 'intent to deprive or defraud' the owner of his property or of its use shall exist. The intent, by necessary implication, as from its place in the penal statute, must be felonious; that is to say, an intent without an honest claim of right. It is not now essential, as it was under the Roman and early English law, that the intention of the taker shall be to reap any advantage from the taking. The statute makes the crime to consist in the intent to despoil the owner of his property. That is necessary to complete the offense, and if a man, under the honest impression that he has a right to the property, takes it, it is not larceny, if there be a colorable title. The charge of stealing property is only substantiated by establishing the felonious intent. The act of the president of the insurance company, which the relator may be regarded as abetting — that is, the contribution of corporate funds for the purpose of a political campaign — was not *malum prohibitum*, or a prohibited wrong; for it was not until two years later that it was made a misdemeanor by the law of 1906. . . . The act not being *malum prohibitum* nor *malum in se*, the innocent motive of indirectly promoting the corporate affairs, through the supposed advantage of the continuance in power of the Republican administration, purged the act of immorality, and it lacked the criminal intent. The company had not the right, under the law of its existence, to agree to make contributions for political campaigns any more than to agree to do other things foreign to its charter, but it had capacity to make agreements, if not prohibited or inherently wicked. Its act would affect the interests of those concerned with the conduct of the corporate business and effect a private wrong, but it would not be a public offense, or illegal in the sense of violating any public interest. . . . That the relator may have made a mistake of law, which will not relieve him from liability in a civil action, may be true, and he expressly disclaimed in his letter any intention to dispute such a liability; but this was a case where the intent, or good faith, was in issue, and then knowledge of the law is material. The relator came to the aid of the president of the company, who as such had agreed to contribute money to the campaign fund, and advanced the moneys temporarily. Having done so, for no other reason than for the supposed advantage of the company, his claim to be reimbursed from the treasury of the company is openly presented and it is paid. But within the spirit if not the letter of section 548 of the Penal Code, that was not larceny." Chief Judge Cullen, in his dissenting opinion, declared that the indirect method in which the money was reimbursed cast suspicion on Perkins's good faith, "and might be considered by the magistrate as militating against him." He added: "The concealment of the payment as described would warrant the magistrate in finding that the parties were conscious of wrongdoing in making it and feared exposure."

While the Thaw case was dragging its unsavory length along a somewhat similar trial in Virginia was begun and finished. The Strothers brothers were indicted for the murder of William Bywaters. Bywaters, who was a trusted cousin of the Strothers family, seduced the sister of the young men and then persuaded her to submit to a criminal operation. The relations of Bywaters with the young woman were discovered and he was compelled under protest to marry her. After the ceremony, as he was attempting to escape from the house and desert his wife, he was killed by her brothers. During the trial Judge Harrison repudiated the idea of an "unwritten law" in Virginia. The jury, however, rendered a verdict of not guilty. In discharging the jury the judge thanked the jurors and remarked: "It is an established precedent in the State of Virginia that no man tried for defending the sanctity of his home shall be found guilty." The jury had the power, whether or not it had the right, to take into consideration all the baseness of the man killed and all the circumstances which palliated the killing. The jurors chose to exercise this power, and by their verdict cleared the slayers. They expressed correctly the sentiments of their time and people on the matters involved. The Boston *Herald* observes: "Should not Virginia at once write upon her statute books what is now recognized and accepted as the law? Should she not specify the causes and the circumstances that justify men and women in executing private vengeance and protecting honor? Written law is brought into contempt when it is superseded by unwritten law." This contrast of written and unwritten law, as every one who is familiar with the uses of the latter much-abused term must admit, will hardly bear analysis. The real contrast is between positive law, whether written or unwritten, and the somewhat nebulous conception of a "higher law" — a law which, by necessity, admits of no exact definition, and of which the individual must be the judge. If the tribunal before which the individual is called to answer for his act refuses to recognize his defense, he becomes perhaps a martyr in the sight of those who share his convictions. If the tribunal shares his feelings and prejudices he is cleared of the charge. The jury is a tribunal which pre-eminently reflects the sentiments of its time and place. Perhaps it owes to this fact its deep root in the affections of the American people. Certainly no body better adapted to weigh the exact force of those facts which are claimed to justify individual revolt could be devised. And its strength lies in the fact that it reflects its time and locality. Its verdicts are the strong growth of natural conditions, not an exotic, a pale reflection of something foreign to the habits and life of the people. But by the very conditions of its being, the jury will faithfully reflect every advance in popular sentiment. The diffusion of education, of truer and larger ideals, must affect the community generally and its true representative — the jury. Suppose that at a given stage of society it is sought to embody in statutory definition every phase of fact which will justify individual revolt, the inevitable tendency will be to arrest development at this point. If the resort to "private vengeance" is made a statutory right, men will seek it more readily than when it is felt to be the last refuge against overwhelming outrage, a refuge which will protect the avenger or fail him, not according to general rules, but according to all the facts of the individual case. If the right of individual revolt against the letter of written law is in existence it seems far better that it should remain as it is, unwritten and hedged about by the sense of responsibility for overstepping the vague and perhaps arbitrary lines accorded by popular sentiment. One such limitation is seen in the recent Mississippi case of Mrs. Birdsong. Here a woman undertook to avenge her own wrongs against her betrayer. She was found guilty. Perhaps behind the figure of the avenger there must appear the image of weakness and innocence betrayed, which lends an element of altruism to the crime. And more than human depravity in the creature on whom vengeance is wreaked may count for much.

OUR British cousins seem to have followed with unusual interest the progress of the Thaw case. Even American lawyers might well be startled by some of the proceedings in that notorious trial, and we may well believe that Englishmen find food for thought here, and are surprised by the changes which that venerable instrument, trial by jury, has developed in the western hemisphere. The *Manchester Guardian* turns for enlightenment to the works of that distinguished philosopher Mark Twain, and finds in "Roughing It" a dictum as to the jury, which appears to agree with the result of its present-day studies. Mark declares the jury to be "the most ingenious and infallible agency for defeating justice that human wisdom could contrive." He illustrates the truth of his proposition by describing from the stores of his experience "one of those sorrowful farces in Virginia, which we call a jury trial." Every man capable of reading had read about the crime and very one not dumb or idiotic had talked about it. But in forming the jury all those who had talked of the case or had read of it were excluded, according to principles which, Mr. Twain declares, would have been followed by any court in America. A minister, a banker, a merchant of high standing, an intelligent manufacturer, were all excluded. We are only surprised that the panel contained no lawyers. Each of the rejected citizens "said the public talk and newspaper reports had not so biased his mind but that sworn testimony would overthrow his previously formed opinions and enable him to render a verdict without prejudice and in accordance with the facts. But of course such men would not be trusted with the case. Ignoramuses alone could mete out unsullied justice. When the peremptory challenges were all exhausted a jury of twelve men was impaneled — a jury who swore they had neither heard, read, talked about, nor expressed an opinion concerning a murder which the very cattle in the corrals, the Indians in the sage brush and the stones in the streets were cognizant of! It was a jury composed of two desperadoes, two low beerhouse politicians, three barkeepers, two ranchmen who could not read, and three dull, stupid human donkeys! . . . The verdict rendered by this jury was Not Guilty. What else could one expect?" The *Guardian* should not have neglected the veracious account of the trial of Mr. Lycurgus B. Jones, as reported in verse by Bret Harte, in forming an opinion of the American administration of law. And American lawyers seeking light on the British court room should attentively study Bardell *v.* Pickwick.

ESTIMATES OF DISTANCE.

DR. COLEGROVE says: "We regularly refer all of our perceptions of memory to common standards. The memories of these perceptions, therefore, will not be accurate, but, like the perceptions from which they arose, will be shortened. Distance recalled after reading two minutes is found to be shorter than the same distance as perceived, and the perceived distance is shorter still than the same objectively measured." ("Memory," pp. 222, 223.)

In a magazine article by the same authority he describes some experiments made to find how accurately mental standards of length coincide with the external units they represent. Lines from one inch to five inches in length were used, and the subjects seemed to exhibit a general tendency toward under-estimation of lengths. ("Notes on Mental Standards of Length," *Journal of Psychology*, January, 1899, p. 292.)

Our impression as a layman would be that in everyday life distances are abbreviated in recollection because we do not spontaneously recall fully the various landmarks, each of which would add something to the remembered perception of distance. In fact, Dr. Abercrombie says that "in our judgment of distance by sight we are greatly influenced by the eye resting on intermediate objects." ("The Intellectual Powers," pt. ii., § 7.)

In Sir William Parry's account of his polar voyages he says: "We had frequent occasion, in our walks on shore, to remark the deception which takes place in estimating the distance and magnitude of objects, when viewed over an unvaried surface of snow. It was not uncommon for us to direct our steps towards what we took to be a large mass of stone at the distance of half a mile from us, but which we were able to take up in our hands after one minute's walk."

Is it not true that adults or aged persons think of distances observed in childhood as longer than they really were? If this is correct, the impression produced and retained of the degree of effort then required to traverse the distance we have in mind may constitute the explanation. Mr. Spencer, speaking of our conception of time, reminds us that a gnat whose wings make ten or fifteen thousand strokes per second, each stroke implying a separate nervous action "probably as appreciable by the gnat as is a quick movement of his arm by a man," must have a magnified sense of duration; and he remarks that "it requires a greater number of a child's movements than of a man's movements to measure a day." ("Principles of Psychology," § 91.)

Other and more occult influences may affect our conceptions of childhood experiences. Mr. Ruskin, in his later years, thought that even the English weather had degenerated from what it was in his earlier years. (*Spectator*, lvii. 1038.)

> "In the jolly winter
> Of the long ago
> . . . . .
> Then, as I remember,
> Snowballs to eat
> Were as good as apples now,
> And every bit as sweet!"
>
> JAMES WHITCOMB RILEY: *Old Man's Nursery Rhyme.*

Direct evidence as to distance, not established by actual measurement, is matter of opinion based upon opportunity and capacity for observation and accuracy of observation. Bird *v.* Long Island R. Co., 11 N. Y. App. Div. 134, 42 N. Y. Supp. 888. And "it is a matter of common experience that eye measurements are unreliable." Riordan *v.* New York, etc., R. Co., 41 N. Y. Misc. 399, 84 N. Y. Supp. 1046. "But few witnesses can state with any degree of accuracy the number of feet a car or other object is from them, when called upon to state it without measurement, or without particular thought, at the time the object was seen, as to the number of feet it was away." Geist *v.* Detroit City R. Co., 91 Mich. 446, 51 N. W. Rep. 1112, *per* Morse, C. J.

In a report of personal experiences in the Manchurian campaign which was written by Captain L. Z. Soloviev of the Thirty-fourth East Siberian Rifle Regiment, translated for the United States Army War College, and printed by the War Department for distribution among officers of the army, he says that determination of the range by eyesight for the purpose of effective rifle fire was very difficult in battle and gave the Russian officers much trouble. The use of regulation range finders was unsatisfactory for lack of time. Firing by volleys to find the range gave good results when the local conditions were favorable. He deems it " most important that during peace time frequent exercises should take place in estimating distances by the eye, taking advantage of each favorable occasion and not treating it as a tedious formality."

" Under the most favorable circumstances it is impossible to measure distances on the water with accuracy," said Mr. Justice Davis in The Great Republic, 23 Wall. Jr. (U. S.) 20, 29. In at least sixty collision cases in admiralty courts, which the writer has at hand, the same want of confidence in such estimates, especially when the observation was made at night, has been expressed. A computation made by the court from facts established with reasonable certainty will probably be more accurate. The Bristol, 11 Fed. Rep. 156, 158. See also The Doris, 108 Fed. Rep. 552, 554. And there is much less liability to mistake in the estimate of a vessel's officers as to the bearing of another vessel off their bow than of the number of feet between the vessels. The Helen Keller, 50 Fed. Rep. 143. There is no doubt, however, that seamen would tell more accurately the distance of one vessel from another than persons unaccustomed to the sea. The Fenham, 6 Moore P. C. N. S. 501, 508.

Excitement of a witness is always detrimental to precision of observation of events or to judgment on existing conditions. Computations of distance must, in the nature of things, be essentially conjectural and at random when formed in the alarm of actual collision and shipwreck and under the confused and terrified state of mind and memory attending such a mischance. The Brig Emily, Olc. Adm. (U. S.) 132, 8 Fed. Cas. No. 4,453, *per* Betts, D. J. See also The Favorita, 18 Wall. (U. S.) 598, 602; The Great Republic, 23 Wall. (U. S.) 20, 29; The Relief, Olc. (U. S.) 104, 20 Fed. Cas. No. 11,693.

In the estimates made by onlookers of the distance at a given moment between a moving train and a person in its pathway, with disaster impending, differences of judgment are probable, and no estimate can be regarded as certain. Sheehan *v.* St. Paul, etc., R. Co., (C. C. A.) 76 Fed. Rep. 201, 207. Witnesses for the plaintiff, who was struck by an electric car, " in the excitement of the moment might have misjudged or easily mistaken the distance the car traveled or the point at which it stopped " after the accident. Beers *v.* Metropolitan St. R. Co., 88 N. Y. App. Div. 9, 84 N. Y. Supp. 785, *per* Hooker, J.

Estimates of all sorts — distance, speed, periods of time, etc. — may be made more certain, or perhaps conclusive, by reference to independent data. Thus, estimate of time may be rectified by association with distance:

Cominius. Though thou speak'st truth,
Methinks thou speak'st not well. How long is't since?
Messenger. Above an hour, my lord.
Cominius. 'Tis not a mile; briefly we heard their drums:
How couldst thou in a mile confound an hour,
And bring thy news so late?
Messenger. Spies of the Volsces
Held me in chase, that I was forced to wheel
Three or four miles about, else had I, sir,
Half an hour since brought my report.
Coriolanus, Act I., Sc. 6.

Of course, the process is reversible, and distance may be ascertained by co-ordination with a known period of time and rate of speed. Thus, in a collision case, the circumstances were such that the means of measuring distance between the vessels were afforded a reasonable degree of accuracy by the length of time three torchlights were burning, the time being ascertained by experiment. The Golden Grove, 13 Fed. Rep. 674, 696. It is to be remarked, however, that estimates of short periods of time unaided by collateral facts are notoriously unreliable, probably less to be depended upon than an estimate of distance by a fairly competent observer; and judgments of speed of moving objects are universally regarded as mere guesses with more or less approximation to the truth.

Confirmation of an estimate of distance is illustrated in the Mangrove Prize Money Case, 188 U. S. 720. It appeared that the Indiana fired a shot across the bow of the Panama and sent a prize crew aboard. The officer who fired the gun testified that he estimated the range at forty-five hundred yards, and that, the shot being accurate, the distance from the Panama was about forty-eight hundred yards. " This was the estimate formed by the expert on the spot at the time," said Mr. Justice Holmes, " for the purpose of immediate action, when it was necessary to be accurate. Whatever it was, it was verified by the result of the shot, so that really the only question is whether it is remembered correctly, which there is no reason to doubt."

" The testimony of even disinterested and unimpeached witnesses on the subjects of measurements, distances, dates, and the like, which is based merely on memory, estimate, or casual observation, must yield to that which is based on actual measurement or reference to definite data." Bussee *v.* State, (Wis. 1906) 108 N. W. Rep. 64, 65, *per* Dodge, J. In all cases actual measurements of distance must prevail over estimates with the naked eye. Koepke *v.* Milwaukee, 112 Wis. 475, 88 N. W. Rep. 238; Ryan *v.* Manhattan R. Co., 121 N. Y. 126, 23 N. E. Rep. 1131; Perkins *v.* Delaware Tp., 113 Mich. 377, 71 N. W. Rep. 643; Good *v.* Dodge, 10 Fed. Cas. No. 5,531. Where such measurements are made under possibly changed conditions the party offering them will produce a better impression if he causes them to be made in the presence and with the knowledge of the opposite party. Goldsmith *v.* London, 11 Ontario 26, 31.

When it is found that a witness estimating a distance of say half a mile makes ten feet in a rod and fifty rods in an eighth of a mile, the circumstance is likely to excite attention. See The Schooner Alaska, 7 Ben. (U. S.) 183, 1 Fed. Cas. No. 130. In a case in Nova Scotia where a locomotive fireman testified that he commenced to blow the whistle " eighty rods below a crossing and continued up to the crossing," Chief Justice McDonald said: " On cross-examination, however, it appears that the evidence of this witness on the point in question is worthless, as he did not know what space a rod covered — how many yards or feet." Robertson *v.* The Halifax Coal Co., 20 Nova Scotia 517, 525. This conclusion is not sound. Cannot a person estimate gallons, or a gallon measure, by his eye just as accurately without knowing how many cubic inches constitute a gallon, as he can if he does know? It is quite probable that the majority of grocers and others in the habit of using such measures, and peculiarly qualified to make an accurate estimate of quantities by gallons, do not know how many cubic inches there are in a gallon. There is no reason for excepting linear measurements — estimates of distance — from the same considerations. Almost as well might a witness be declared incompetent to testify that he was eating bread because he cannot give a recipe for making it. In Ward v. Chicago, etc., R. Co., 85 Wis. 601, 608; 55 N. W. Rep. 771, 773, Judge Orton said: "It does not follow that a witness may not be able to form a reasonably intelligent opinion of the distance or space of a mile if he cannot readily know or tell how many feet or rods there are in a mile. He may be able to form an opinion of what is a foot in length, height, or depth, or of what is a rod or a mile. A knowledge of these main spaces is acquired by observation and practical test, while their minute subdivisions depend much upon the tables to be learned and remembered."

CHARLES C. MOORE.

PLAYING TO THE GALLERY.

"Tears, idle tears, I know not what they mean."

MAYBE the poet didn't know what tears mean, but the jury lawyer knows; and he doesn't consider them exactly idle, either. A number of years ago, when Gen. Luke E. Wright, the present Ambassador to Japan, was prosecuting attorney down in Memphis, he prosecuted for murder a man whom his distinguished father, sometime justice of the Supreme Court of Tennessee, defended. Judge Wright wept freely during his argument to the jury, as he described the virtues of his oppressed client and the wicked machinations of his client's oppressors. The judge's display of emotion affected the jury deeply — that is, it did until Gen. Wright, in summing up, said: "Gentlemen of the jury, the tears of the learned counsel for the defense wouldn't make so much of an impression upon you if you knew, as I know, that he never weeps for less than a thousand dollars." History records that the defendant was convicted, but it is silent as to the subsequent interview between the State's attorney and the defendant's counsel.

Perhaps Gen. Wright — one of the ablest trial lawyers this country has ever known — chose the most effective method possible of checkmating a play to the gallery by adversary counsel. Certain it is that the reviewing courts seem reluctant to reverse for bits of acting indulged in by lawyers or their clients. In fact, they are apparently inclined to look with tolerance, and almost with approval, on displays of that nature made by zealous advocates.

In State v. Danforth, 73 N. H. 215, it was sought to reverse a conviction for rape on the ground that the prosecuting attorney, in the presence of the jury, kissed a child that had been born to the prosecuting witness. The appellate court refused to reverse, however, saying: "If the counsel for the State kissed the child in the presence of the jury, a charge which counsel denies and which is not found to be true, such act had no tendency to prove that the defendant was the father of the child — the point in controversy — or that counsel thought so. As evidence, the act was clearly immaterial. Being immaterial, the verdict cannot be affected by the bad taste of such an exhibition unless the spectacle clearly tended to prejudice the jury against the defendant. If what the jury saw tended to create in their minds sympathy for the child, it is not clear how the result of sympathy so evoked could prejudice them against the defendant in this proceeding, however the fact might be in a proceeding for bastardy. It could not aid the child to convict the father for rape."

In Ferguson v. Moore, 98 Tenn. 342, an action for breach of promise to marry and for seduction under the promise, Mr. Justice Wilkes held that it was not only the privilege, but was possibly the duty, of the plaintiff's counsel to shed tears in addressing the jury. On this point he said: "It is next assigned as error that counsel for plaintiff, in his closing argument, in the midst of a very eloquent and impassioned appeal to the jury, shed tears and unduly excited the sympathies of the jury in favor of the plaintiff, and greatly prejudiced them against defendant. Bearing upon this assignment of error we have been cited to no authority, and after diligent search we have been able to find none ourselves. The conduct of counsel in presenting their cases to juries is a matter which must be left largely to the ethics of the profession and the discretion of the trial judge. Perhaps no two counsel observe the same rules in presenting their cases to the jury. Some deal wholly in logic and argument, without embellishments of any kind. Others use rhetoric and occasional flights of fancy and imagination. Others employ only noise and gesticulation, relying upon their earnestness and vehemence instead of logic and rhetoric. Others appeal to the sympathies — it may be the passions and peculiarities — of the jurors. Others combine all these with variations and accompaniments of different kinds. No cast-iron rule can or should be laid down. Tears have always been considered legitimate arguments before a jury, and while the question has never arisen out of any such behavior in this court, we know of no rule or jurisdiction in the court below to check them. It would appear to be one of the natural rights of counsel, which no court or constitution could take away. It is certainly, if no more, a matter of the highest personal privilege. Indeed, if counsel has them at command, it may be seriously questioned whether it is not his professional duty to shed them whenever proper occasion arises, and the trial judge would not feel constrained to interfere unless they were indulged in to such excess as to impede or delay the business of the court. This must be left largely to the discretion of the trial judge, who has all the counsel and parties before him, and can see their demeanor, as well as the demeanor of the jury. In this case the trial judge was not asked to check the tears, and it was, we think, an eminently proper occasion for their use, and we cannot reverse for this."

In State v. Burns, 119 Iowa 663, a prosecution for seduction, wherein it appeared that a child had been born to the prosecuting witness, error was predicated of the remarks of the prosecuting attorney in his closing argument that the defendant "ought to have married the prosecuting witness; that he ought to have said to her, 'That child is blood of my blood, flesh of my flesh,' and married her, and then his old gray-haired father and mother would have had no cause to mourn." The appellate court refused to reverse, saying: "The comments thereon may or may not have been logical and just, but that is something that the court cannot assume to control. Within reasonable limits, the language of counsel in argument is privileged, and he is permitted to express his own ideas in his own way, so long as they may fairly be considered relevant to the case which has been made. No lawyer has the right to misrepresent or misstate the testimony. On the other hand, he is not required to forego all the embellishments of oratory, or to leave uncultivated the fertile field of fancy. It is his time-honored privilege to

> 'Drown the stage in tears,
> Make mad the guilty and appall the free,
> Confound the ignorant, and amaze, indeed,
> The very faculties of eyes and ears.'

Stored away in the property room of the profession are moving pictures in infinite variety, from which every lawyer is expected to freely draw on all proper occasions. They give zest and point to the declamation, relieve the tediousness of the juror's duties, and please the audience, but are not often effective in securing unjust verdicts. The sorrowing 'gray-haired parents' upon the one hand, and the broken-hearted 'victim of man's duplicity' upon the other, have adorned the climax and peroration of legal oratory from a time 'whence the memory of man runneth not to the contrary,' and for us at this late day to brand their use as misconduct would expose us to just censure for interference with ancient landmarks."

In a prosecution for assault with intent to commit murder, where the prosecuting attorney, during his argument, advanced toward the defendant, pointing his finger at him, and addressed him personally, saying, "You sought this trouble with him [the prosecuting witness] and made a cowardly attack upon him," it was held that there was no such misconduct as would justify a reversal of the judgment of conviction. People v. Wheeler, 65 Cal. 77. But in Hamilton v. State, 97 Tenn. 452, 457, which was a prosecution for homicide, the court said: "Pointing the finger or shaking the fist or any other unseemly demonstrations toward the prisoner, are entirely out of place, and should be promptly corrected by the trial judge." It must be observed, however, that this is a mere dictum, as no such misconduct on the part of the prosecuting attorney was assigned as error, and, though there was a reversal, it was on another ground.

In Washington v. State, 124 Ga. 423, which was a prosecution for seduction, the court refused to reverse a judgment of conviction on the ground that during the argument for the State the prosecutrix wept in the presence of the jury. In that case, however, the defendant failed to object at the trial to the weeping and did not ask the court to take any action in reference to the matter.

In Dowdell v. Wilcox, 64 Iowa 721, which was an action by the widow of a Civil War veteran to recover possession of two horses and a wagon which had been taken under an execution issued against her deceased husband during his lifetime, the plaintiff's counsel appealed to the prejudice of the jury in her behalf, and denounced the judgment creditors as leeches and oppressors of poor women and widows. The plaintiff sat near her counsel, facing the jury, and, when he made sympathetic appeals to the jury because her husband had been a soldier and she was a widow, she wept or pretended to weep. On appeal, this conduct was assigned as error, but the court said: "We do not think the judgment should be reversed for this alleged misconduct of counsel and plaintiff. Indeed, we are not prepared to say that there was a departure from what ought to be regarded as fair and legitimate in the trial of a cause to a jury. Great latitude is allowed in appealing to the sympathy of the jury in the arguments of the counsel. That, and the widow in tears, are a kind of stage performance which courts cannot very well, and perhaps ought not to attempt to, control."

In State v. Laxton, 78 N. Car. 564, a prosecution for rape, it appears that the mother of the prosecutrix, and other members of her family, sat within the bar during the delivery of the argument for the State, and occasionally wept when reference was made to the enormity of the crime and its consequences to the prosecutrix, and that they withdrew while the prisoner's counsel was addressing the jury. The appellate court refused to reverse the judgment of conviction, on the ground that it was within the sound discretion of the trial court to determine whether the demonstrations made by the relatives of the prosecutrix should have been checked.

It seems that in a criminal prosecution the prosecuting attorney may use his histrionic powers to reproduce the details of the crime, in illustration of his argument. Thus, in Todd v. State, (Tex. Crim. 1898) 44 S. W. Rep. 1096, wherein the defendant was convicted of murder, the court refused to treat seriously an assignment of error based on the action of the prosecuting attorney in illustrating the "hip-pocket movement" by drawing a plug of tobacco from his pocket. In fact, the incident seemed to appeal to the court's sense of humor. Said Henderson, J., in delivering the opinion: "We do not believe that the remarks of the district attorney complained of were of such a character as requires a reversal of this case. The suggestion by him as to the facility with which the 'hip-pocket' movement is resorted to by those charged with homicide, and in that connection reaching for his own hip pocket as if to draw a weapon, and, instead thereof, pulling therefrom a plug of tobacco, it occurs to us was rather humorous than otherwise, and clearly not of a character to prejudice appellant." In Owens v. Com., (Ky. 1900) 58 S. W. Rep. 422, which was a prosecution for homicide, it appears that the commonwealth attorney lay down on the floor, during his argument, "and holloed at the top of his voice, 'Dan Owens, come here, and strike me with that club,' and called upon others to come and strike him with a 'board heart.'" The Court of Appeals held that this theatric exhibition afforded no ground for reversing the conviction, saying: "This was an unusual position for counsel to assume in arguing to a jury, still the court cannot attempt, in a matter of the kind, to regulate counsel in his effort to demonstrate a proposition, or to call vividly before a jury facts which he believes the testimony establishes. The court cannot regulate counsel in the argument of a case in the manner of gestures and attitudes, nor direct when he shall modulate his voice or increase its tone."

The last two cases cited offer suggestions of numerous possibilities, particularly in criminal prosecutions. No matter what the crime charged might be — always excepting certain offenses mentioned only by lawyers, and not in polite society — the prosecuting attorney might stage a little drama for its reproduction. In that way he could illustrate his argument and appeal to the jurors through the medium of their eyes as well as their ears. If satisfactory "supes" for the drama were not obtainable, the prosecutor might arrange beforehand to have members of the "profession" pose for moving pictures, so that the ends of justice might not be defeated. By the same token, if the prosecuting attorney were not an orator, he might write out his speech and have it delivered into a phonograph by an elocutionist. The phonograph and the vitascope (or some similar 'graph and 'scope) would make a great combination. Jury duty would be sought instead of avoided. The expenses of the trial could be met by charging an admission fee. And then the right to reproduce the trial on the vaudeville stage by means of the phonograph and the vitascope might be sold. And then, too, it would be possible — But the possibilities are so many and so obvious that it is useless to discuss them further.

The only trouble is that the prosecuting attorney might be unwilling to do anything that would subject him to the criticism of being a machine politician. J. C. M.

THE ENGLISH BAR.*

I am advised by our strenuous and indefatigable secretary that usage requires your president to receive the members of the association at their annual meeting with an address of welcome in which some subject of interest to the profession may be presented. It is certainly delightful to welcome so

* Address delivered at the thirtieth annual meeting of the New York State Bar Association, held at the city of Albany, N. Y., on the 15th and 16th of January, 1907, by Joseph H. Choate, president of the association.

large a gathering of the active and prominent members of the bar of the State as are assembled here to-day. I am sure that our meetings and discussions and our published reports are of great value to the profession.

I seize upon the first opportunity to thank you for the great honor done me in electing me as your president after a long absence from the country, during which I was wholly withdrawn from your ranks.

In selecting a subject for my address, it has occurred to me that some account of the English bar, as it was my great privilege to meet its members under the pleasantest circumstances, might possibly be of interest and advantage on an occasion like the present.

You will, of course, understand that I make no reference to the other branch of the profession, which is so distinct — the attorneys and solicitors — upon whose learning, efficiency, and skill the whole of the social and business life of England very largely depends; but I speak only of the bar proper, and of it especially as represented by its leading members, with whom I had much personal intercourse. These are really a group by themselves, generally university men of generous culture, not deficient in means to sustain them during the long and dreary waiting for briefs after their call to the bar, and then working their way to the front by force of character, courage, and ability, and universally recognized as the worthy representatives of the whole body of our great profession.

Let me say in the first place as to the English bench and bar both, that I always found them full of interest in, and sympathy with, their brethren in America. Their fraternity with us was always cordially acknowledged, as that of two great branches of the same stock. In view of our common history and language and our identical system of jurisprudence, which relies upon the same authorities, English and American — freely interchanged — for the establishment of the same principles of justice, I found no perceptible difference in what I may call the cardinal features of the profession between them and us. Their hospitality on all occasions was most cordial, alike in their private houses, in the Inns of Court, and in that great banquet which they gave to the bench and bar of the United States in 1900, which was promoted by that great advocate and jurist, Lord Russell of Killowen, the Lord Chief Justice, and which took place on the very eve of his untimely death.

While I was made to feel entirely at home among them, by the general resemblance and identity of our pursuits and surroundings, it was in the changes that time and circumstances have wrought in us rather than in them that I was most interested — and in the observation of which I think we have something to learn.

When Jeremiah Evarts, the father of my great master in the law, and himself a truly great and righteous man, had graduated from Yale, and was considering the law as a profession for life, he was greatly disturbed by the question whether, as the one side or the other of every lawsuit was necessarily wrong, he could honestly and conscientiously engage in a pursuit in which about half the time he would necessarily be struggling to maintain injustice, and he consulted Judge Ellsworth, afterwards Chief Justice of the United States, who solved his doubts by advising him that any cause that was fit for any court to hear was fit for any lawyer to present on either side, and that neither the judge nor counsel had the right to prejudge the case until both sides had been heard, and he told him of Sir Matthew Hale, one of the most righteous lawyers and judges in English history, who began with the same misgivings, but modified his views when several causes that he had condemned and rejected proved finally to be good.

That, I think, was true of all the functions of the American lawyer in those old days. His relation to the business of his clients was strictly professional, just as much so as that of the physician or the surgeon.

And so it is to-day of the English barrister. Whether he tries or argues a cause, or revises a pleading or a contract, or gives an opinion on the facts submitted, he acts without any interest in the matter, or any relation to it other than the purely professional one. The rigid rules of the profession by which he is bound absolutely forbid him to take a contingent interest or share in any controversy in which he acts professionally, and the slightest violation of this rule would compel his disbarment. And so the whole community knows that in proportion to his skill and capacity and judgment they may absolutely confide in his professional conduct, and that no private or personal interest in the subject of the controversy can bias him to mislead or confuse the counsels of the court. In the same way his compensation is not dependent upon the amount involved or upon the result of the controversy, but upon his own eminence and reputation. So that when I told some leading barristers that our Court of Appeals had decided that the amount involved and the result as to winning or losing were material factors in the measurement of the lawyer's compensation, they fairly scouted the idea.

There is no doubt that two important changes in our system have seriously detracted from this strictly professional attitude of the American advocate, and laid him open to question. I mean the fact that we have not maintained the distinction between the two branches of the profession, but every one of us is a barrister, a solicitor, and an attorney, and where three or four of us combine to form a firm, each is properly held responsible for all that is done by any of the firm. But the chief cause of detraction from our absolute independence and disinterestedness as advocates is that fatal and pernicious change made several generations ago by statute, by which lawyers and clients are permitted to make any agreements they please as to compensation — so that contingent fees, contracts for shares, even contracts for half the result of a litigation, are permissible, and I fear not unknown. How can we wonder, then, if the community implicates the lawyer who conducts a cause with the morale of the cause and of the client? If he has bargained for a share of the result, what answer can we make to such a criticism? And how can we blame the community when it suspects that such practices are frequent or common, and even sanctioned by eminent members of the profession, if they confound us all in one indistinguishable crowd, and refuse to accord to any of us that strictly professional relation to the cause which the English barrister enjoys? And how can the courts put full faith in the sincerity of our labors as aids to them in the administration of justice, if they have reason to suspect us of having bargained for a share of the result?

If you ask me whether there is no way out of this confusion of condemnation or suspicion for the individual lawyer, I say emphatically there is.

True, we cannot go back on the habits of generations, or repeal statutes which have imbedded such practices in the social habits of the people. But the individual advocate can persistently refuse to follow such practices, or to take a contingent fee or a share in the controversy, and I am old-fashioned enough to wish that every member of the profession who aspires to leadership would take such a stand, and to believe that if he did so it would promote his reputation and success in true professional distinction.

For a whole generation, yes, for two generations, we had before us a noble example of this moral distinction — alas, he is no longer with us — I refer to the late James C. Carter, who so long and so gloriously led us, and who I believe never touched a contingent fee or a share in a controversy of which he had thconduct, and was for all the world exactly like the best examples of the leaders of the English bar.

In another respect the English barristers have a great advantage over us, and one that tends to promote and increase the reasonable enjoyment of life, and that is in more frequent recreation and relaxation and more stated and prolonged holidays — holidays established by custom which has the force of law. In all the time of my busy practice in New York, we were steadily engaged in court from the first Monday of October to the last Friday of June, with hardly an appreciable break — a few days at Thanksgiving, the week from Christmas to New Year's, and the legal holidays, very few in number. With these scanty exceptions, it was one perpetual grind of work for nine successive months, and the few lucky ones were those who had the temperament and the physique to stand the strain.

But in England the courts come in with appropriate and appointed ceremonies on the twenty-fourth of October, and work for eight weeks, which brings them to Christmas and a two weeks' holiday — when every barrister drops his briefs absolutely and quits London for the country or for the Continent, which can be reached in a few hours. Then they return and work for eight or ten weeks more, which brings them to the Easter recess, another real holiday of ten or twelve days, with the same advantages. Another eight or ten weeks of work, and Whitsuntide arrives, a third intermediate holiday, of which we know nothing and which we ought to borrow at once. And then a fourth term of eight or ten weeks of work brings them up to the twelfth of August, when the law is off on grouse, and courts and barristers, King, Lords and Commons, disappear for the long vacation of ten or eleven weeks, which brings them back new men for the beginning of the working year again.

Thus, with the same or only a little more vacation in the aggregate these frequently recurring holidays of substantial amount, which are thoroughly availed of, relieve both judges and barristers of that protracted and unremitting strain and pressure which I used to find it so hard to bear.

The amount of litigation in proportion to the population must, I think, be much less in England than in New York. Otherwise it would be quite impossible for the thirty-five judges of the High Court and the Lords Justices of Appeal, and the judicial committee of the House of Lords to dispose of the whole of the principal business of England without any serious accumulation of arrears, while in the State of New York, with its eight millions of people, we have ninety-seven justices of the Supreme Court, seven judges of the Court of Appeals, and ten federal judges. Doubtless the county courts in England dispose of more business and give greater relief to the High Court than is afforded by similar subordinate tribunals to our Supreme Court; but, for all that, the volume of business must be vastly greater here than there.

It is an essential part of our system to bring justice home to every man's door, and it is made very cheap here, especially for the losing party, while in England litigation, for the party who unsuccessfully and without merits prosecutes or defends a lawsuit, is a seriously expensive business, for in the exercise of the discretion vested in them the judges in the adjustment of costs are inclined to charge the beaten party with the whole expense of the litigation, including the counsel fees paid by the other side.

Here again comes in another unfortunate result of our system of contingent fees which has resulted in blocking our calendars with thousands of experimental and speculative lawsuits, in arrears in at least one of our departments for two or three years, which it is quite impossible for our judges to cope with.

Everything in the system of English judicature seems to be arranged with a view to the despatch rather than the accumulation of business. They have nothing like our dismal Code of Civil Procedure with its many thousand sections, which itself in the whole history of its growth and development has been, and is to-day, a prolific cause of litigation and delay, and affords, I should think, an opportunity for a distinct and separate motion every week from the commencement of the cause till its trial. Instead of that they have a few simple rules of practice made by the High Court and always under its control, and these are very simply administered, usually before a master, after the cause is at issue — and the barrister is generally relieved of any attention to that part of the practice which acts so thoroughly upon the nerves of any lawyer who is engaged in great affairs.

Our pernicious and dilatory habit of waiting for counsel, who are engaged elsewhere when the cause is reached or called on the day assigned, is practically unknown, and the consequence is that in an important cause several counsel must be retained, so that if one is not ready, another shall be, and the cause proceed.

Of course the solicitors and attorneys prepare briefs, and relieve the barrister of a vast amount of that kind of work out of court, for which counsel with us are largely responsible. I am sure, however, that every conscientious barrister, from the moment of receiving his retainer, is ready to hold consultations and advise on every important step, but as a rule they are not troubled with interviews with parties and witnesses in preparation for the trial. In fact, direct communication between the barrister who is to try the case and the witnesses is theoretically disallowed, and seldom happens.

But it is in the actual conduct of the case in court that the barristers derive great assistance and support from the prompt and efficient system that prevails. The judges being appointed by the government, practically selected by the Lord Chancellor from barristers who have been long in active practice in the courts, are already fully qualified for the performance of judicial duties from the moment they enter on their exalted office, and are not only presumed to know the law, but generally do actually know it. Such a thing as a judge having to be educated upon the bench, so expensive and so detrimental when it does happen, is utterly unknown there, and as a result the judge takes charge and holds control of the case from beginning to end. Questions of evidence and motions for nonsuit which with us are often occasions of prolific argument are promptly decided. The judge is presumed to know the law of evidence, and it rarely happens that such a question has to be more than stated in order to have it disposed of. Perhaps I was myself as great an offender as anybody in the consumption of time in the discussion of questions of evidence, having often argued them by the hour; and I well remember one case with Mr. Roscoe Conkling where we spent an entire day in the argument of a motion to nonsuit, and even then the court adjourned till the next morning to decide it.

In cases tried without a jury, including equity, probate, and admiralty causes, when the judge has heard the evidence and the arguments, he is generally ready to decide it, and the pernicious habit which once prevailed, and I fear still prevails with us, of taking two weeks, often extended to four, to hand up briefs, when the judge will have largely forgotten the case, and will have to study them at his subsequent leisure, is practically unknown, and the proceedings upon appeal in cases reserved are greatly facilitated by the appeal being heard on the judges' minutes, and report of the points reserved.

If you ask me how the leaders find their way to the front, I should say exactly as they do with us. They are eliminated by a process of natural selection, for merit and fitness, from the whole body of the bar. I have known the leaders of the bar on both sides of the Atlantic, and in this respect the same rule prevails. There is every variety among them of physical, mental, and moral qualities. No two are ever alike in personal characteristics, except in one vital and essential quality, which is common to them all, I mean the power and the will to hold on and hold out, under all circumstances and against all counter-inducements, until the goal is reached. This indomitable tenacity of purpose, with brains, health, and character, insures success and leadership there as here.

A very striking story told me by one of the gentlemen named illustrates what I mean. Some forty years ago on the Northern Circuit three able and ambitious young men had tried hard for a few years, by assiduous attendance, for business in the courts, and almost hopeless of success, they met and seriously discussed the question whether they should not give it up, and seek some other service in the Colonies, or in some of the many avenues of employment which are open there as here to barristers who despair of the future in the direct line of the profession — but they held on, for life or for death, and in thirty years or thereabouts from the time of their discussion, one had become Lord Chief Justice of England, as Lord Russell of Killowen; the second, Lord High Chancellor, as Lord Herschel; and the third, speaker of the House of Commons, who, after an arduous and honorable term of service in that high office, now lives in retirement as Viscount Selby.

The question of emoluments is always an interesting one to lawyers, and if things remain as they were when I went to England eight years ago I should say that for professional leaders in the same relative position the earnings here and there were about the same. There is a well-worn story of Sir Roundell Palmer, who as attorney-general contested against Mr. Evarts the Alabama claims before the Geneva tribunal of arbitration, that in one year he realized fifty thousand pounds, but that was adding his compensation as attorney-general to his large and lucrative practice, which is not permitted any longer to the attorney-general or the solicitor-general. But such earnings there or here represent a prodigious and killing amount of work; and the story is that an old friend, desiring an interview with Sir Roundell, called at his chambers one Thursday morning, and asked if he could see him. The clerk replied that if he must he could do so, but he would advise him not to, for he hadn't been in bed since Sunday night. So I have heard of a great chancery barrister many years later realizing in one year twenty-eight thousand pounds, and during my stay in London thirty thousand pounds a year was the highest sum I heard ascribed to the most successful leaders of the day. Such earnings anywhere represent the absolute devotion of the highest professional qualities and the sacrifice of everything else to the largest interests of the commercial world. These figures compare very favorably with the best I ever knew or heard of while I was actually engaged in steady practice. Since my return, I have heard of fabulous sums received by lawyers, either as shares agreed upon, or from great corporations or estates, as rewards for very moderate services. For the credit of the profession, I decline to believe such stories, for in the long run nothing is so damaging to us as a profession as the spirit of commercialism — the Wall street notion that money is the only thing worth striving for, an idea which when it once gets hold of a man unfits him for true leadership, and when it once gets hold of the profession is sure to demoralize it.

I have no time to discuss here to-day the much vexed question of the comparative merits of legal education here and in England — but from what I have seen of the leading English barristers, what splendid men they are physically, mentally, and morally, how learned and broadly educated, accomplished, and thoroughly equipped, I should say that the system which has produced such men, the combined results of education at the universities and the great Inns of Court, ought not hastily to be exchanged for another as a training for the English bar.

Perhaps some day the Inns of Court will combine their splendid resources to create and maintain a great university of law, to which men of all nations, races, and languages will resort to legal training; but although this was strongly urged upon them, I believe by Lord Russell and other prominent benchers, the time for such a serious change has not yet come.

Those splendid Inns of Court to which I have so often referred — for it is impossible to speak of English law or English lawyers without constant reference to them — afford to our brethren who belong to them and to whom they belong a home around which their affections centre, and places and occasions of social and fraternal intercourse utterly unknown to us.

As the sole authority through which admission to the bar can be obtained, as seats of study and learning in preparation for professional life, as the custodians and guardians of all the history and traditions of the law, they command the loyal affection and devotion of all their members. As the great nurseries of the common law and of equity, and identified in their annals with the whole progress of justice and of civilization in England, established already for centuries, while we were yet a component part of the English nation, I regard them as the common property and the common pride of all lawyers the world over who speak the English tongue. There our predecessors in the bar of England have been working out by patient industry and with ever advancing knowledge those principles which underlie the liberties of England and America alike, and the debt of gratitude we owe them for that long service cannot be overstated. What are those absolute principles which thus lie at the foundation of our common civilization? "That there is no such thing as absolute power; that King, Lords and Commons, Presidents, Congress, courts, and people are alike subject to the law; that before its supreme majesty all men are equal; that no man can be punished or deprived of any of his rights except by the edict of the law pronounced by independent tribunals which are themselves subject to the law; that every man's house is his castle, and though the winds and the storms may enter it, the King or the President cannot; that our government on both sides of the water is, in the sublime words of the great Sidney, 'a government of laws and not of men.'"

You will not wonder then that in common with all other lawyers I felt an immediate and personal interest in those cradles of the law in which, before America was discovered, those ultimate principles of right and justice which our fathers brought over with Magna Charta and the Petition of Right were brought into being, and already in the way of final establishment.

Those graceful and magnificent halls, rich in beauty and teeming with great traditions, about which the memories of all that has been great and noble in our profession for five centuries still linger, cannot but have an ennobling and inspiring influence upon all who frequent them. The footsteps of American lawyers on arriving in England naturally turn first to them, and often as I haunted them I always met and heard of my countrymen there before me. Their unbounded hospitality often gladdened my long stay among them. On Grand Night in each term of court, when the benchers of each Inn assemble within those noble walls to entertain their friends and their members and students, with the portraits of the great judges and lawyers of the past whom they claim as their own looking down upon them, and the shields and arms of their treasurers for centuries surrounding them, they seemed to me to represent and embody the living spirit of our law, holding now for the time being, and for transmission to future generations, all the rich heritage of the past. And when as a tribute to the American bar and in demonstration of their fraternal sympathy and affection they made me too a bencher of the Middle Temple, to represent you all, and in the same spirit bade me farewell at Lincoln's and Gray's Inns, I felt that my professional life had not been wholly in vain.

My conclusion, from a fair knowledge of both countries, is that in the law, as in every other element of our common civilization, each nation has yet much to learn from the other, and that to that end we ought studiously on both sides to cultivate more frequent and constant intercourse and a better knowledge of each other, and no profession can do so much as ours to bring about this happy consummation.

I also became thoroughly convinced that for each country its own system of legal administration and of professional life as it stands to-day is better than any abrupt or violent effort at reform would be. That system for each nation has been slowly evolved out of social usage and common law and statute in the course of centuries, and any sudden changes would be more likely to mar than to mend it. But we may hope on both sides, by the friendly interchange of ideas from time to time, to gain much in the way of progress and improvement.

Cases of Interest.

Carrier's Liability for Smallpox Caught from Agent. — In Missouri, etc., R. Co. *v.* Raney, 99 S. W. Rep. 589, the Texas Court of Civil Appeals affirmed a judgment for damages against a carrier because of smallpox communicated by a ticket agent to a person purchasing a ticket. The court held that the knowledge of the ticket agent that he was infected with the disease was the knowledge of the carrier, and that the carrier was liable for all the natural and probable consequences of his act in selling tickets when he knew himself to be so infected. And it was further held that one of the natural and probable consequences of such act was the communication of the disease by the purchaser to his wife. Losses in business on account of the plaintiff's patrons being kept away through fear of contracting the disease were held to be not too remote to furnish a basis for the recovery of damages.

Anti-Trading-Stamp Ordinance Held Invalid. — In Denver *v.* Frueauff, 88 Pac. Rep. 389, the Colorado Supreme Court follows the lead of most of the other jurisdictions in which the question has arisen in declaring void an ordinance forbidding the giving of any trading stamp or other device which shall entitle the purchaser of property to receive from any person or corporation other than the vendor any property other than that actually sold. Such an ordinance, the court holds, is not justifiable as an exercise of the police power, nor is it authorized by a constitutional provision prohibiting lotteries and gift enterprises, such provision applying only to transactions in which the element of chance is involved.

Juvenile Court Law of Utah Upheld. — In Mill *v.* Brown, 88 Pac. Rep. 609, the Utah Supreme Court holds that the State statute of 1905 establishing juvenile courts is constitutional, except as to one section giving the juvenile courts power to punish parents who cause or contribute to the delinquency of their children, which section is held to deny the parent the right of trial as for any other crime. The remainder of the act is upheld. The court holds that the act is not a criminal law, but has for its object the surrounding of delinquent children with proper environments, and therefore violates no constitutional provisions because not providing for trial by jury, for arraignment and plea, for a warrant to bring a child before the court, for notice to his parent, or because of the manner of trial and examination, and the child being required to be a witness.

Licorice Trust Held Illegal. — In U. S. *v.* McAndrews & Forbes Co., 149 Fed, Rep. 823, Judge Hough, of the federal Circuit Court for the Southern District of New York, holds that a secret arrangement between two corporations, which together produce about eighty-five per cent. of all the licorice paste consumed in the United States, whereby they cease competition, fix from time to time the prices at which each shall sell, and apportion the customers between them, and also by concerted action secure contracts with their chief if not only competitors, which enable them to control either the output of such competitors or the prices at which and the persons to whom they shall sell, and in pursuance of which scheme they are enabled to and do advance the price to all purchasers nearly fifty per cent. within a few months, is an illegal combination and conspiracy in restraint of interstate commerce within the meaning of the Sherman Anti-Trust Law.

Larceny by Changing Baggage Checks. — In Aldrich *v.* People, 79 N. E. Rep. 964, the Illinois Supreme Court affirmed a conviction for a rather novel form of larceny. The appellant's scheme was to check a trunk containing nothing but rubbish, and thereafter to change the check on his trunk for one on another promising-looking trunk, and rely on the transportation company to do the rest. It was contended by the appellant that, as the property was obtained with the consent of the transportation company, the taking did not amount to larceny, even though such consent was obtained by means of a trick or device and with the intention of stealing the trunk. But the court held that if he received and converted the property to his own use, and there was a felonious intent on his part to steal the property in the trunk throughout the entire scheme, he was guilty of larceny.

Boycott — Restraint of Interstate Commerce. — In Loewe *v.* Lawlor, 148 Fed. Rep. 924, Judge Platt, sitting in the United States Circuit Court for the District of Connecticut, held that the action of members of a labor union in attempting to compel a hat manufacturer to unionize his factory by leaving his employment and preventing others from taking employment therein, and also, with the assistance of members of affiliated organizations, by declaring a boycott upon his goods in other States into which such goods had been shipped for sale at retail, did not have such relation to interstate commerce as to constitute a combination or conspiracy in restraint of such commerce in violation of the Sherman Anti-Trust Act. Judge Platt, while deeming the question very uncertain, sustained a demurrer to the complaint in order that it might be decided by the Supreme Court before the case was tried on its merits.

New York Stock Transfer Tax Law Invalid. — In People *v.* Meusching, 79 N. E. Rep. 884, the New York Court of Appeals held that a State law imposing a tax on transfers of stock of domestic and foreign corporations of two cents "on each share of $100 of face value or fraction thereof" measured the tax by the number of shares transferred, regardless of the face or actual value thereof, and was unconstitutional because the tax imposed did not operate alike on all stock, but, without any basis for classification, bore lightly on some stocks and heavily on others. In the course of the opinion Vann, J., said: "Two corporations may be doing the same kind of business upon the same amount of capital, with assets of the same value, and shares aggregating the same face value, but, if a share in one has but half the face value of a share in the other, still the sale of the same number of shares in each would be taxed the same amount, in manifest disregard of justice and principle."

The Panama Canal Case. — In Wilson *v.* Shaw, 27 Sup. Ct. Rep. 233, the United States Supreme Court holds that the United States acquired a perfect title to the Panama Canal zone under the treaty of November 18, 1903, with the Republic of Panama, and that the contention that title was not acquired in accordance with Act of Congress of June 28, 1902, by treaty with the Republic of Colombia, is sufficiently answered by the fact that Congress subsequently ratified the treaty. Such title, it is held, is not rendered the less perfect because of the omission from the treaty of some of the technical terms used in ordinary conveyances of real estate; nor does the failure to define the exact boundary of the zone affect the title of the United States, the description being sufficient for identification, and the boundaries having been practically identified by the concurrent action of the two nations alone interested. The court holds that the United States has power to construct a canal in the territory acquired by virtue of the treaty in question. The opinion of the court was delivered by Mr. Justice Brewer.

RIGHT OF STATE TO PROHIBIT EXPORT OF WATER. — In McCarter *v.* Hudson County Water Co., 65 Atl. Rep. 489, the New Jersey Court of Errors and Appeals upheld the constitutionality of a recent statute making it unlawful for any persons or corporation to transport through pipes, conduits, etc., the waters of any fresh-water lake, pond, or stream of New Jersey into any other State. The suit was brought to restrain the defendant from supplying one of the boroughs of New York city with water from the Passaic river. The court held that neither under the common law nor the statutes of New Jersey was there any right in the riparian owner, as such, to divert the water of lakes or streams in order to make merchandise of it, or for any other than riparian uses except as to a limited class of purposes beneficial to the people of the State of New Jersey; that the State in its sovereign capacity controlled the fresh-water lakes and natural streams, subject to the interests of riparian owners; and that the legislature might prohibit the abstraction of such water, save for riparian uses and for purposes authorized by legislative grants. It was held that the statute was not violative of the interstate commerce clause of the Federal Constitution, because water abstracted contrary to the statutory prohibition could not legitimately enter into interstate commerce.

FRAUD—PREVENTING SALE OF OPTIONS.—In Rogers *v.* Virginia-Carolina Chemical Co., 149 Fed. Rep. 1, the Circuit Court of Appeals, Third Circuit, recently rendered an interesting decision as to what constitutes actionable fraud. The plaintiffs alleged that, having secured options of great value for the purchase of certain deposits of phosphate, they entered into negotiations with the defendant for the sale of such options; that the defendant in pursuance of a fraudulent scheme to prevent the plaintiffs from selling the options to others, so that after the expiration of such options the defendant could purchase the property directly from the owners, made false and fraudulent representations of its desire and intent to purchase the options, whereby the plaintiffs were induced to enter into a contract giving the defendant the exclusive right for a stated time to purchase the options; and that the plaintiffs were thereby prevented from selling their options to others to their great damage. On demurrer it was held that the declaration stated a cause of action. The court said: "There is a *prima facie* presumption of fairness and honesty in the dealings of mankind, and, where one man makes a promise to another as an inducement for a change of position or other action on the part of the latter, he, if not expressly, impliedly avers that he has an existing intent to fulfil his promise, and such implied averment of existing intent is of matter of fact, and, if false and fraudulent, is a fraudulent representation, which may or may not, according to the circumstances, furnish the basis for an action *ex delicto*."

PATENT MEDICINE TRUST HELD ILLEGAL. — In Jayne *v.* Loder, 149 Fed. Rep. 21, the Circuit Court of Appeals, Third Circuit, held that an agreement intended to maintain the retail price of patent and proprietary medicines entered into by the Proprietors' Association of America, the National Wholesale Druggists' Association, and the National Association of Retail Druggists, was an illegal combination and conspiracy in restraint of interstate commerce in violation of the Sherman Anti-Trust Act. By this agreement it was provided that wholesalers should refrain from selling such medicines at any price to "aggressive cutters" of prices or brokers; an aggressive cutter being defined as a dealer who was so designated by seventy-five per cent. of the local trade at any given place. In pursuance of such concerted plan, proprietors thereafter sold only at fixed and uniform prices to those wholesalers who agreed to maintain prices and not to sell to aggressive cutters or brokers. A list of prices was furnished by a committee of the wholesalers, and a list of aggressive cutters was supplied by the secretary of the retailers' association. If a wholesaler violated the agreement and sold to an aggressive cutter, he was at once reported and his name listed among the aggressive cutters, notice of that fact being sent to all retailers who were members with a suggestion that they act for the protection of their interest. If he was subsequently reinstated, a notice of that fact was also sent to the retailers. The court said: "If co-operation and concerted action such as this does not make out a combination and conspiracy in restraint of trade, it is difficult to see what would be effective to do so."

WALL-PAPER TRUST DECLARED ILLEGAL. — In Continental Wall Paper Co. *v.* Voight, 148 Fed. Rep. 439, the Circuit Court of Appeals for the Sixth Circuit held the so-called "wall-paper trust" to be an illegal combination in restraint of trade and interstate commerce. The trust was formed to control the output of ninety-eight per cent. of the wall-paper mills of the United States, and to this end made contracts with them to buy their entire output at an agreed price. The trust was nominally to make all sales to wholesalers and others, either directly or indirectly, at a uniform price, subject to an agreed scale of discounts, varying according to an arbitrary classification of buyers. The difference between the price at which the manufacturers sold to the trust and the price at which it sold constituted the dividends to be distributed among the trust's shareholders, who were composed exclusively of those controlling the combining manufacturers; the stock being distributed in proportion to the size of the manufacturer's product the year before the trust was formed. The contract provided against the enlargement of plants, and the only two manufacturers of wall-paper machinery in the United States were induced to become parties by agreeing not to sell except to members of the combination. An agreement was also made with Canadian manufacturers to prevent cutting of the price. Each member was required to deposit his shares with the trust, to be held as security to prevent breach of the contract. Contracts were then made with jobbers and wholesalers binding them to buy only of the trust at specified prices, and not to sell at less than the prices fixed by the trust, on pain that if they did not enter into such contracts they could not buy at all. The court held that this constituted a clear violation of the Sherman Anti-Trust Act.

Book Reviews.

THE LIFE OF JUDGE JEFFREYS.

By H. B. Irving, M. A. Longmans, Green & Co., New York. 1906. 380 pp.

As a piece of special pleading and in the point of interest, Mr. Irving's work takes high place in that "literature of rehabilitation" which attempts to shed a kindlier light on such sacred and profane bogies as Judas Iscariot, Benedict Arnold, *et id omne genus.* But, however, ingenious and interesting, such works are not often convincing and rarely obliterate the impression which history has left on the public mind. By using chiaroscuro effects, as it were, by throwing into strong relief the sinister aspects of the contemporaries of Jeffreys, and the distorted moral sense of his time, the author seeks to minimize, if not conceal, those traits which made the "hanging Chief Justice" and Kirke's "Lambs" protagonists in the bloody drama enacted in Western England as a close to the Monmouth uprising. The petty jealousy which made Roger North belittle the vigorous mental ability that Jeffreys unquestionably possessed does not extenuate the equally unquestionable perversion of that same ability. Party loyalty is the excuse which is urged for the sentence found at his demand, and on scant circumstantial evidence, against Lady Lisle, a venerable noblewoman whose seventy years of age would seem sufficient evidence of her nonparticipancy in the Monmouth revolt and the head and front of whose offending appears to have been her indiscriminate charity, shown to loyalist and rebel alike.

We are also asked on similar grounds and because of the custom of the times to excuse his treatment of Prideaux, who was delivered to the tender mercies of Jeffreys that the Chief Justice might collect a ransom as a part of his remuneration. When we read how Jeffreys contemptuously declined £7,000 and then £10,000, finally receiving £15,000 with £240 off for cash, by dint of threatening to make Prideaux's offense a hanging matter, although he "had done nothing," to quote Mr. Irving, "that could be construed into an overt act of sympathy" with Monmouth, we are moved to believe that the Justice of which Jeffreys was chief was not only blind but dumb and fettered. Not only were English judges not always so subservient to mere custom, but Gascoigne even went so far as to refuse obedience to the royal will which sought to control him in the exercise of his judicial function at a time when such a refusal was a parlous matter, while Sir William Jones dared declare himself a bulwark against the encroachment of the royal prerogative on the liberty of the subject.

The book contains three excellent reproductions of portraits which show Jeffreys as a man of such prepossessing appearance and bearing that it is hard to believe him as black as history has painted him.

The publishers have presented the work in an attractive and handsome form.

HISTORY OF ROMAN PRIVATE LAW.

History of Roman Private Law, Part I. Sources. pp. 168. By E. C. Clark, LL.D. Cambridge University Press. G. P. Putnam's Sons, New York. 1906.

This little book on "Sources" forms the first section of a contemplated History of Roman Private Law. Its writer is well known as the Regius Professor of Civil Law in the University of Cambridge and as author of Practical Jurisprudence. That a satisfactory presentation of the history and development of Roman private law in the light of modern research is highly desirable will be readily admitted. Professor Clark is competent to do the work, and it is to be hoped that he will give himself heartily and seriously to the task. In his preface he says, quoting the famous words of Livy, "Whether I shall be doing what is worth while in writing a new history of Roman Law at this time of day, I scarcely know." Any misgiving on this point should be resolved, as he has resolved it, in favor of the undertaking. The work is quite worth the doing provided only it is well done. Any estimate of the merit of the work at this stage would be premature. It is enough to say that if the treatise is completed according to the plan indicated in this introductory portion it will undoubtedly be a welcome addition to the English literature of Roman law.

THE LAW OF TORTS.

The Law of Torts. By Francis M. Burdick, Dwight Professor of Law in Columbia University School of Law. Banks & Co., Albany, N. Y. pp. lxxx + 501.

This book shows a creditable range of observation in the writer, a feature which is manifested in the number of instructive cases which are either referred to or discussed. From every other point of view from which a legal treatise may properly and honestly be judged, the book is worse than a disappointment — it is a failure. The printer's work is such as must cause the author chagrin and mortification, as it will certainly cause the reader vexation and amazement. Many of these pages, one may safely say, were never seen by a proofreader. The right-hand running head throughout the section on Malicious Prosecution is "Malicious Persecution." If the author has not discovered any new category of wrong, the compositor certainly has. On a single page the eye is arrested by three gross typographical errors in the three black-letter catchlines. The cross-references are vague and inaccurate. The citations have not been verified and corrected.

But these offenses against the art of modern book-making are relatively venial. Turning to matters of graver moment, we find, to begin with, that the author has been exceedingly unhappy in the arrangement of his material. The sequence is controlled by no consideration either of historical development or of the theoretical affinities of the subject-matter. A discussion of torts following an order conceived according to the sorts of harm inflicted, as this purports to be, would no doubt present some valuable features. We apprehend, however, that under such a treatment trespass on the person, whether done by the wrongdoer directly or through some independent agent, would somehow get together with negligent injuries to the person; and trespass to property would not be found far removed, as is the case in this book, from torts involving negligent damage to property.

The undue expansion of Chapter III. on "Harms That Are Not Torts" is productive of confusion. Much matter is gathered here that can be intelligently understood only in connection with the discussion of specific torts which is found in the second part of the book. It is as if a writer on the syntax of a language should gather into an introductory chapter a great variety of exceptions to the particular rules which he proposed to expound in a subsequent part of his treatise. The result is embarrassing to the reader and leads to unnecessary repetitions and cross-references.

The style in which the book is written is very much lacking in precision. An illustration of this catches the eye on page 348, where it is said that trover lies "even for property which the plaintiff had no legal right to possess" — a sufficiently striking statement to any student who may have learned that possession or the right of possession is an indispensable prerequisite to the maintenance of this action. Professor Burdick really means something quite different from that which his language literally imports, but it is necessary for the reader to refer to the case cited by him to ascertain what that meaning is.

In many places it will be found that it is not so much the style as it is the writer's thought that is lacking in precision. Thus, turning to the rudimentary topic of trespass, a subject which ought not to be beyond the capacity of any writer on torts to state with reasonable accuracy, we find this remarkable proposition: "It has been said that trespass does not lie for an assault upon a ship or other insensate thing, but that it does for beating and wounding a beast" (p. 343). The real import of the authorities to which the author here refers is to be found in a distinction — which he fails to perceive — in regard to the common-law remedies; that is to say, the action of trespass *vi et armis* in the form of a count for assault and battery has once or twice been maintained for the unlawful beating of live things, but this form of action has been held not to be at all proper where forceful damage is done to other sorts of chattels, i. e., inanimate things. As stated by Professor Burdick, the proposition becomes one of substantive law and is sufficiently blundersome. He hastens to put us on the track of a different rule, saying: "The better view seems to be, however," etc. There is nothing the matter with the decisions so far as the actual rulings of the courts are concerned. The trouble is in Professor Burdick's interpretation of the cases.

Equally inaccurate is the statement on page 343, that liability for damage done by domestic animals is held by some courts to depend on the question whether the owner has a valuable property in them. Neither in this paragraph nor in the next, which also treats of liability for harms done by domestic animals, is there any trace of reference to knowledge of vicious propensity — a factor which is usually conclusive on the question of liability.

On page 344, again, it is said: "And if one sets fire upon his land, he is liable in trespass if it escapes and harms another's goods." This, of course, does not state a principle that ever did or ever could prevail at common law. The remedy for consequential damage done by fire is the action on the case. The American authority cited by Professor Burdick sustains his text, however, and merely shows that some mistakes have been made by courts which writers of law books have no right to perpetuate.

It is needless to multiply instances of erroneous and misleading statements. The book shows abundant evidence of being made up by the putting together of propositions that have been decided on one occasion or another, without sufficiently weighing their significance and the principles involved. Too often in these pages do we see that inevitable mark of the lack of analysis which consists in representing the different courts as being in conflict, when a little advertence to the actual facts decided would show either that the supposed conflict does not exist or that the decisions belong to a different stage of development. The little topic of trespass *ab initio* (p. 346) afforded good opportunity to any writer who might be disposed to do so, to go somewhat beneath the surface, but instead Professor Burdick contents himself with repeating a few platitudes that have been handed down from the time of Coke, and giving citations to some modern cases.

As a whole, the work proves how futile it is for any one to attempt to state the law of civil liability in any of its branches without having first mastered the principles underlying the common-law actions.

News of the Profession.

The Georgia State Bar Association will hold its next annual meeting at Tybee Island on May 30 and 31.

The Wisconsin State Bar Association held its annual meeting in Milwaukee on March 12 and 13. Particulars of the meeting will be given in this column next month.

Death of Ontario Judge. — Hon. John J. O'Meara, junior judge for the county of Carlton, died in Ottawa on February 15 of pneumonia, at the age of forty-seven.

Nebraska's New Federal Judge. — The new federal judgeship for the District of Nebraska recently created by Act of Congress has been filled by the appointment of Thomas C. Munger of Lincoln.

First Woman Lawyer in Tennessee. — On February 21 Miss Marion Griffin, of Memphis, was admitted to the Tennessee bar, being the first woman to achieve that distinction.

Additional Federal Judge for Alabama. — During February a bill was put through Congress authorizing the appointment of an additional United States district judge for the Northern District of Alabama.

American Bar Association to Meet in Portland. — The executive committee of the American Bar Association has announced that the next meeting of the association will be held in Portland, Me., on August 26, 27, and 28.

Massachusetts Lawyer a Suicide. — Milton Druce, an attorney of Fall River, Mass., aged forty-six, committed suicide on February 10 by shooting himself with a pistol. Continued ill-health was assigned as the cause.

New Federal Judgeship in Ohio. — During February Congress passed a bill providing for an additional United States judge for the Southern District of Ohio. J. J. Adams, of Zanesville, has been selected for the place.

Distinguished Toronto Lawyer Dead. — Mr. Christopher Conway Robinson, a prominent member of the Toronto bar, died suddenly of heart disease on March 4, in his fiftieth year. Mr. Robinson was recognized as an authority on the subject of railway legislation.

Virginia Lawyer Dies on Train. — John H. Lewis, a prominent attorney of Lynchburg, Va., died on a train February 23, while returning to his home from a professional trip to a neighboring city. Mr. Lewis was sixty-six years of age. The cause of his death was heart failure.

Well-known Chicago Lawyer Dies. — Robert E. Jenkins, a well-known member of the Chicago bar, sixty-one years of age, died in that city on March 5. He was for seven years treasurer of the Chicago Bar Association and was at one time president of the Chicago Law Institute.

Judge Dallas Resigns Law Professorship. — Hon. George M. Dallas, of the Federal Circuit Court, on February 28 resigned his position as professor of the law of torts in the University of Pennsylvania Law School, which he had held since 1891. His place in the faculty is taken by Francis H. Bohlen.

Justice of the Peace Blown to Pieces. — Robert Cortese, a justice of the peace of Paterson, N. J., was killed on February 8 by the explosion of an infernal machine which had come to him in the form of an express package. Cortese had made enemies among the Italians of Paterson by his vigorous and fearless pursuit of criminals.

For Uniform Divorce Laws. — The work of the National Divorce Congress is beginning to bear fruit. In at least two States — New Jersey and Wisconsin — bills have already been introduced looking to the adoption of the changes recommended by the Congress, and in many others the question is said to be receiving careful consideration.

Louisiana State Bar Association. — On February 4 a meeting of the Louisiana State Bar Association was held in New Orleans, at which W. S. Parkinson was elected president to succeed E. T. Merrick; H. H. Randolph and W. S. Benedict were re-elected to the office of vice-president and secretary. It was decided to hold the annual convention at Shreveport during May.

Kaffenburg's Disbarment Affirmed. — On March 5 the New York Court of Appeals affirmed the order disbarring from practice "Abe" Kaffenburg, thus driving the last nail into the coffin of the once-noted firm of Howe & Hummel. Kaffenburg was disbarred because of his activities in connection with the Dodge-Morse divorce case, which was also the cause of Hummel's downfall. Howe died some years ago.

Federal Judge Finkelnburg Resigns. — Hon. G. A. Finkelnburg, of the Federal District Court at St. Louis, has tendered his resignation, to take effect April 1. Failing health is given as the reason for his retirement. Judge Finkelnburg is sixty-nine years of age and has been on the federal bench only about two years. Col. David P. Dyer, United States district attorney at St. Louis, is slated to succeed him.

Senator Spooner to Practice in New York. — On March 3 Senator John C. Spooner, of Wisconsin, announced that he had tendered his resignation to take effect May 1. Mr. Spooner has served for sixteen years in the United States Senate and has come to be universally regarded as the greatest constitutional lawyer in that body. It is stated that he will practice law, in New York city, though still retaining his residence in Wisconsin.

Former Member of Nevada Supreme Court Dies. — Hon. Rensselaer R. Bigelow, ex-justice of the Supreme Court of Nevada, died in San Francisco February 18, aged fifty-three years. A native of New York, he emigrated to Nevada while a young man, and in 1882 was appointed district judge. Eight years later he was promoted to the Supreme Court. After serving out his term he removed to San Francisco, where he resided until his death.

International Congress of Maritime Law. — The next international congress for the framing of a universal code of maritime law will be held in Venice in September next. The conference will discuss questions relating to the limitation of shipowners' responsibilities, discrepancies existing between the bottomry laws and maritime privileges of various countries, and the principles of freight legislation. Fifteen governments have already expressed their intention of adhering to the recommendations of the congress.

Establish Supreme Court for Saskatchewan. — During September the legislature of the Province of Saskatchewan passed a bill providing for the establishment of a Supreme Court. The court is to consist of a chief justice and four associate justices, and will sit in Regina to hear appeals. For the benefit of such of our readers as do not know where Saskatchewan is, we have looked it up in the atlas and can authoritatively state that it is situated in Canada, northwest of Manitoba. One rather peculiar thing about the new court is that Regina, the place where the sittings are to be held, is the capital of the adjacent Province of Assiniboia.

Death of John Cunneen. — John Cunneen, ex-attorney-general of New York and one of the most distinguished members of the Buffalo bar, died in that city on February 21, of pneumonia. Mr. Cunneen was born in Ireland in 1848 and came to this country when he was fourteen. For several years he worked on a farm, attending school during the winter months, and later he taught school, at the same time studying law. He was admitted to the bar in 1874 and sixteen years later took up his residence in Buffalo. In 1902 he was nominated for the office of attorney-general on the Democratic ticket and was the only Democrat elected, having received the indorsement of the Prohibition party. At the expiration of his term he resumed the practice of the law in Buffalo and was in active practice up to the time of his death.

Maine State Bar Association. — The annual meeting of the Maine State Bar Association was held in Augusta on February 13. The only set address was that on "The Desirability of Establishing a System of Superior Courts," by the president, Hon. Orville D. Baker, of Augusta. The balance of the time was spent on committee reports, elections, and other routine business, and the discussion of matters of local interest. Among the latter was the question whether the State should aid in the passage of uniform laws relating to negotiable instruments, divorce, and sales. A special committee was appointed to provide a reception for the American Bar Association when it meets at Portland in August. The following officers were elected: President, Orville D. Baker, of Augusta; vice-presidents, L. B. Deasey, of Bar Harbor, George C. Wing, of Auburn, and Fred H. Appleton, of Bangor; secretary and treasurer, Leslie C. Cornish, of Augusta.

English Notes.

Death of a County Judge — His Successor. — Judge Mansel Jones, of the Sheffield County Court, died February 2 of paralysis in his sixtieth year. He was called to the bar in 1859, and became county judge in 1902. The vacancy has been filled by the appointment of Mr. William Denman Benson, who was called to the bar at the Inner Temple in 1874 and became a member of the South Wales Circuit.

A Radical High-Sheriff. — In one of the counties of England recently the high sheriff applied to the King's Bench judges for permission to substitute a motor car for the horse-drawn vehicle used by the judges on their ceremonial drives from their circuit lodgings to the Assize Court. After giving the matter the gravest and most anxious consideration, the judges decided that they could not countenance so radical an innovation.

Lord Thring Dead. — Lord Thring, who drafted more important acts of Parliament than any other lawyer whom England has produced, died February 4 at his country house, Alderhurst, Englefield Green, Surrey. He was born in 1818, and was called to the bar at the Inner Temple in 1845. He devoted himself more to the study of law than its practice, and from 1853, when he drafted the Succession Duty Bill, to 1886, when he drafted the Home Rule Bill, his hand helped to give shape to most of the important measures before Parliament. In 1860 he was appointed counsel to the Home Office, and in 1868 to the newly created post of Parliamentary counsel to the treasury, which he held until 1886. He was made a K. C. B. in 1873, and a peer in 1886.

Lord Davey's Death. — On February 20 Lord Davey, since 1894 a Lord of Appeal in Ordinary of the House of Lords, died at his residence in London. Lord Davey was born in 1833, was called to the bar at Lincoln's Inn in 1861, and became a K. C. in 1875. For a number of years he was the recognized leader of the chancery bar. In 1886 Mr. Gladstone appointed him solicitor-general in the home rule administration. In 1893 he was appointed a Lord Justice of the Court of Appeal, but within less than a year thereafter was promoted to the House of Lords to fill the vacancy caused by the appointment of Lord Russell of Killowen to the office of chief justice. While it can hardly be said that his reputation as a judge equaled his reputation at the bar, yet his work on the bench was in every way worthy of the highest court in England.

New Old Bailey Opened. — On February 27 the new Central Criminal Court, erected on the site of the historic Newgate prison, commonly known as the Old Bailey, was dedicated by King Edward, who was accompanied by Queen Alexandra. The streets traversed by the royal procession were decorated with bunting and lined by large crowds. The Lord Mayor and the sheriffs in their robes of office met their Majesties at Temple

Bar, where the Lord Mayor presented to the King the city sword, symbolical of handing over the defense of the City to his Majesty while he remained within the boundaries. In a pavilion in front of the portico of the new Sessions House an address was presented to the King. In his reply the King referred to the "barbarous penal code" administered within the walls of the old building and said he rejoiced at the fact that this was being "gradually replaced in the progress toward higher civilization by laws breathing a more humane spirit and aiming at the nobler purpose of reforming criminals by showing mercy to first offenders, which often proves the means of reshaping their lives." The King then declared the building open. Their Majesties subsequently inspected the interior of the court house, the cornerstone of which was laid in 1902. The building cost $1,500,000. The site has been occupied by prisons since the year 1180, and for over a century Newgate was the scene of all the public executions until the Private Executions Act of 1868 ended such spectacles.

ANOTHER CRIMINAL APPEAL BILL. — The agitation for a court of criminal appeal, which gained great impetus from the disclosures in the Beck case and, more recently, in the case of George Edalji, will not down. In the King's speech to Parliament during February, announcement was made of a bill for the establishment of such a court to be introduced into the House of Commons by the Attorney-General. In reference to the opinions of judges and other presumably competent critics, the Lord Chancellor agreed to a number of material changes in the ill-starred measure he introduced into the House of Lords last session, and the hope is expressed in some conservative quarters that in the new bill further right will be given to such criticism. The chief argument on which the opponents of a criminal appeal court have relied is that right of appeal on questions of fact will necessarily impair the sense of responsibility under which juries act when they know themselves to be the final judges of the facts. This idea seems to have such deep roots in the minds of English lawyers, and especially of the judges, that a bill will have small chance of enactment into law which goes further than to grant an absolute right of appeal on questions of law and to give the Home Office the right to refer questions of fact to the court. The Home Office has recently issued a summary of twenty-three bills providing for appeal in criminal cases which have been introduced since 1843. Of these none except the one introduced at the last session ever succeeded in getting through either house. That one was passed by the House of Lords on July 13, but was dropped in the House of Commons.

THE VALUE OF SHORTHAND TO A LAWYER. — In the preface to a recently published book on "Easy Shorthand," by Sir Edward Clarke, K. C., one of the most distinguished of England's lawyers, the author says: "In court, while a junior, I of course had to take notes in longhand, as others might require to use them, but as a leader I have always taken them in a mixture of longhand and shorthand, which is very rapidly written and very easy to read. And I have found it most useful to be able to take down the exact words used by a witness, or by an opposing counsel in his speech, or by the judge in his summing up or judgment, or by a speaker to whom I had to reply in the House of Commons. Again, shorthand has been very valuable in enabling me to copy rapidly extracts from books, or to note down quotations made in conversation or in speeches, or good sayings or good stories, which can be set down on any scrap of paper that is handy, and made valuable use of afterwards. But perhaps to me the most important advantage of writing shorthand has been in the preparation of speeches and the drafting of letters. No speech should ever be made without preparation, nor any important letter without a draft. The use of shorthand in the preparation of speeches gives a vigor and freshness of diction which is apt to be lost in the laborious process of longhand writing; while the process of drafting a letter in shorthand and copying it afterwards actually takes less time than the deliberate production of an undrafted letter, and has additional advantages of giving opportunity for correction, and leaving a copy in the writer's hands."

THE DIFFICULTY OF GETTING JURIES IN NOTED CASES. — Commenting on the fact that the length of time consumed in obtaining a jury in the Thaw case in New York seemed to have struck the lay press of England and Ireland as very remarkable, the Irish correspondent of the *Law Times* says: "As a matter of fact the law in these countries and that in the United States are very similar in this respect, and in many of the state trials in Ireland during the last century the swearing of a jury was just as difficult and lengthy an operation as it was in the Thaw case. Where a case has excited great public, political, social, and religious interest, and where, as a consequence, challenges for cause are numerous, the swearing of a jury may be prolonged for an indefinite period. Each challenge is a miniature trial in itself, which may necessitate the swearing of triers, the examination and cross-examination of witnesses, and the argument of counsel. In the case of Reg. *v.* Robert Kelly, on the 30th October, 1870, in which the accused was indicted for the murder of Head Constable Talbot, swearing of the jury took the most of the first day. In Reg. *v.* Parnell and others, in which the late Mr. Parnell and other Irish members of Parliament were prosecuted for conspiracy in connection with the alleged inciting of tenants not to pay rent, the trial lasted from Tuesday, the 28th Dec., 1880, till Tuesday, the 25th Jan., 1881, before Mr. Justice Fitzgerald and Mr. Justice Barry. The jury were impaneled under the old system, and, although the panel which finally came before the court contained only twenty-four names, the various discussions that took place — chiefly as to the right of the traversers to challenge six jurors peremptorily — occupied half a day. After a trial occupying twenty-nine days, the jury disagreed and were discharged. There was no further trial."

THE EDALJI INQUIRY. — "The great satisfaction with which the public has welcomed the decision of the Home Secretary to appoint an inquiry into the Edalji case is a convincing proof of the necessity of the course which Mr. Gladstone has taken," says the *Law Journal*. "We do not, however, share the belief that this case proves conclusively the need for the establishment of such a Court of Criminal Appeal as the government have sought to bring into existence. Many of the criticisms which have been directed against Mr. Edalji's conviction have been concerned with the way in which his case was presented. Another point which may be urged is that the trial of the case, having regard to the strong local feeling which had been excited by the outrages, ought to have been removed to some place where less excitement and prejudice prevailed. A further question to be considered is whether so serious a case ought ever to be tried before a chairman of quarter sessions without any real legal training. It is not at all certain that a Court of Criminal Appeal, dealing with the case as it was presented at quarter sessions, would have arrived at a different result. All human tribunals, even a Court of Criminal Appeal, must remain liable to err; however acute the tribunal, the testimony of false, biased, or inaccurate witnesses must sometimes mislead. One or two striking miscarriages of justice, such as the Beck case, do not dispose of the arguments that may be brought against the establishment of a Court of Criminal Appeal with practically an unlimited jurisdiction on questions of fact. The Home Office has not wholly failed to prove that it can deal satisfactorily with them, though the exercise of its functions in the revision of convictions might certainly be improved by the power to refer such cases as Mr. Edalji's to a judicial tribunal."

Obiter Dicta.

Against Public Policy. — In the recent case of American Mut. L. Ins. Co. *v.* Mead, 79 N. E. Rep. 526, the Appellate Court of Indiana has held that a man has no insurable interest in the life of his mother-in-law. The temptation is regarded as being already sufficiently great.

Some Judicial Knowledge. — In an opinion handed down on March 8, United States Judge Hough, of New York, held that vermouth was not a wine. His honor took judicial notice of the fact that, in this country at least, that liquid is regarded solely as a constituent element of the seductive cocktail.

suit originated in a justice's court. The plaintiff was the owner of a kid of the alleged value of $1.00. The defendant was the owner of a mule, and the record discloses that 'her name was Maud.' The cause of controversy was the death of the kid at the hands (or, to speak more accurately, at the mouth and forefeet) of the mule." The record not disclosing that the owner of the mule knew that she was vicious and dangerous, the court held that he was not liable. Had "Si" been the defendant, the case might have had a different termination.

A Letter Head. — A correspondent contributes to our museum the following letterhead which was formerly used by a justice of the peace for Levy county, Fla.:

HEADQUARTERS FOR EVERYTHING WANTED.

Notary Public,
State of Florida at large
Justice of the Peace,
for Levy County.
Special attention in the execution of Pension papers, Deeds, Mortgages &c.
Manager of Grist and Saw Mills and Cotton Ginnery.

OFFICE OF

IRA J. CARTER, P. M.

DEALER • IN • GENERAL • MERCHANDISE,

Dry Goods, Groceries, Hardware & Crockery.

BUY AND SELL BEEF, STOCK CATTLE AND SEA ISLAND COTTON.

HIGHEST CASH PRICE PAID FOR CHICKENS, EGGS AND ALL COUNTRY PRODUCE.

Remember my P. O. and Shipping Directions.

Drugs, Medicines, Stationery, Toilet Articles, Cigars, Tobacco &c.
Agent for:
School Books for Levy and Alachua Counties, Newspapers, Periodicals and Delinators.

If you have not in stock goods ordered, don't enter my order for goods to follow.

A Love Affair. — In Simmons *v.* State, (Tex. Cr. App.) 40 S. W. Rep. 968, the defendant was convicted of a misdemeanor because, having contracted to "work for Love," he "thereafter voluntarily escaped from said Love." The Appellate Court reversed the judgment holding that, "if the appellant, with the consent or approval of Love, was permitted to go at large, it was not an escape." There are some cynical persons who would regard that as a pretty lucky escape.

Reus Ipse Dicat. — A correspondent wishes to know the origin and use of the phrase "*reus ipse dicat*" (let the defendant himself tell) used by Judge Garrison in Bien *v.* Unger, 64 N. J. L. 600. We have been unable to find any previous or subsequent use of the term and are inclined to believe it a coinage of Judge Garrison's which has never gotten into circulation. Perhaps some of our readers can throw light on the question.

There Are Others. — A considerable amount of facetious comment has been indulged in by the lay press on the fact that the will of the late Chief Justice Paxson, of Pennsylvania, has recently been declared invalid for lack of subscribing witnesses. However, such occurrences are not nearly so common as the deaths of doctors, and are certainly not more frequent than the cases of preachers "lighting out" with other men's wives or the fund for foreign missions. Let us not lose heart.

Ejusdem Generis. — A correspondent calls attention to the following annotation in Wilson's Texas Criminal Code: "Note 1. — *Constitutionality of Occupation Taxes.* — The occupation tax imposed on liquor dealers by the Act of 1873 was held constitutional. Harris *v.* State, 4 App. 131. So also was the tax on lawyers, imposed by the Acts of 1873 and 1876. Languille *v.* State, 4 App. 321. So also was the tax on dogs. *Ex parte* Cooper, 3 App. 489. So also the tax on the Police Gazette, etc."

Our Old Friend Maud in Court. — Readers of the Sunday "comic supplements" may be interested in the following from the reported case of Harvey *v.* Buchanan, 121 Ga. 384: "This

A Victory for "Temperance." — Out in Indiana a circuit judge has recently held that the saloon business is prohibited by the common law and that the legislature of Indiana has no power to license it. A local newspaper speaking of the judge's opinion, which was greeted with "an outburst of approval," said: "Judge Artman was afterward heartily congratulated personally by the temperance leaders in attendance." This must make the future look dark and joyless to the Hoosier booze artists, but thanks to the genius of the giants who framed our national Constitution, the right of the ungodly to import the oil of joy in original packages can never be taken away.

Boy Beats Western Union. — A young man with a tenacity of purpose which may hereafter cause him to be heard from further is Hyman Sandman, an ex-messenger boy of the Western Union Telegraph Company at Worcester, Mass. Back in 1905 Hyman put in a claim against the company for lunches and overtime work amounting to $1.55. The manager refused to allow it, and immediately there began a great legal battle which was only ended on March 13, when in an entry of settlement of judgment in the Superior Court at Worcester, the company agreed to pay the small plaintiff $25 and the costs of the suit. The company fought the boy all along the line and threw in his way every obstacle that a soulless corporation could devise, but he held firm to his purpose and rendered a service to generations of messenger boys yet unborn.

A New Field for Lawyers. — Probably no votary of the jealous mistress was ever retained in a stranger case than one which has recently enlisted the services of Traverse A. Spraggins, of Jersey City. Into his office came one Wing Kee, who for twenty-three hours every day purifies and imparts lustre to the collars and cuffs of Jersey City's gilded youth. The Celestial narrated how he had become enamored of an American girl who daily passed his laundry, and offered the attorney a fee of $500 if he would prevail upon the lady to throw in her lot with the adoring Wing. At last accounts Lawyer Spraggins was still in doubt as to the proper procedure to adopt in his client's behalf, feeling no doubt that the matter called for diplomacy of the most delicate character. Meanwhile Wing Kee has added an extra half hour to his day's work in order to make his store of this world's goods more attractive to the charmer.

Pure Stock. — If any one doubts that this is an Anglo-Saxon country, we would call his attention to the following list of cases taken from the calendar of the Haralson (Texas) Superior Court, January term, 1907:

Montfort, admr., v. Janoosky.
" " " Grunik.
" " " Kasaya.
" " " Wohl.
" " " Conet.
" " " Sillay.
" " " Bukaza.
" " " Miko.
" " " Bohn.
" " " Resofozky.
" " " Bodnar.
" " " Oehschlager.
" " " Prinz.
" " " Kegyosy.
" " " Sczency.
" " " Jesik.
" " " Horine.

One Way to Win a Case. — The following extract is from a brief recently filed on a petition for rehearing in the Appellate Court of Indiana: "The opinion of the court in this case is so sane, so sound, so scholarly, so able and exhaustive, that it is subject to no criticism and needs no further argument or authorities to support its unanswerable propositions or conclusions. The correctness, the soundness, the justness and ability of the opinion are its strongest supports and place it beyond the reach of the cobwebs of criticism. It has been said of one of the masterpieces of English literature, the Letters of Junius, that no words could either be added to or taken from the sentences without weakening and impairing them. We believe, in all candor, that this proposition applies in all of its force to the decision and opinion in this case, when viewed, considered, and tested as a masterpiece of judicial literature." After further complimenting the court for considering the case "with candor, impartial justice, and with breadth, learning, and ability, rarely equaled and perhaps never excelled, at least in these recent years, in the decisions and opinions of any of the most distinguished courts of the country," the writer closes with the assertion that "the opinion will take its place as a leading case in the great courts of the country, and will stand as a monument to the industry, the learning and ability of the court, and to disturb it would be like destroying landmarks or assailing the temple of justice." It would be a callous court indeed that could reverse itself in the face of such warm and disinterested approbation.

An Awe-Inspiring Dun. — Every day the collection agencies are making it more disagreeable to owe money. From time to time we have published some of the ablest efforts of these agencies to harrow the souls of delinquents, but the following, which was sent in by a Massachusetts correspondent, seems to be about the nerviest that has yet come under our observation. The "complaint" was sent to a local justice of the peace with the following instructions:

Dear Sir:

We send you the enclosed complaint for collection.

After dating and signing the same with your office address, and anything else you may choose to add, mail it to the party. If they pay in ten days accept $1.60 as full payment, you retain 60 cents for your trouble and send us $1.00. If they do not pay within 10 days and it becomes necessary for you to follow it up with another letter, make them pay full amount of $2.60 and you can retain $1.60 for your trouble and send us $1.00 and give us the name and address of the party from whom you collected.

Yours truly,
HALL-WELLS COLLECTION BUREAU.

The "complaint" is as follows:

COMPLAINT AGAINST JOHN DOE.	Amount due,	$1.60
	Fees,	
	Cost,	1.00
	Total amount due,	$2.60

The above claim has been placed in the hands of the Justice of the Peace in your town to collect from you $1.60 with costs, making the total amount due $2.60.

The evidence is as follows:

About six months ago the Humbug Company of New York expended large sums of money in advertising their goods. In response to one of their advertisements, they have your written order for $3.20 worth of their goods to be sold for a premium. The Company honored said order and sent you their first instalment of 16 handkerchiefs, value at 10c. each, on their regular terms to be sold and paid for within fifteen days, or the goods were to be returned. The result has been that you have kept the goods many months beyond the stipulated time, without paying for or returning them. You have repeatedly ignored all letters notifying you that the contract had expired and that no further delay would be tolerated, also telling you that action would be taken for recovery of their value.

It is the law of every State that any person receiving or making use of any article is liable for payment of same, and under this law can begin action.

Please make note of the fact that these goods were not sold, only consigned to you, and therefore remain the sole property of the Humbug Company, New York, until paid for.

A failure to settle for goods shipped out on consignment constitutes an act of embezzlement, punishable by law, but using the United States mails for obtaining goods illegally is fraud and is punishable by imprisonment; minors are not exempt. Ask your Postmaster to read to you Section 505, page 237, Postal Laws and Regulations.

It is our purpose to see that justice is done and to punish all offenders and when necessary to send the Constable with writs of execution.

Now, therefore, take notice that this account must be settled at the office of the Justice of the Peace mentioned below, on or before ten days after the date affixed below on this complaint. The law is severe in suppressing all wrong-doing. Unless you pay the amount due the law will be enforced.

The total amount due including cost is $2.60. If the claim is paid within ten days from date, we will accept $1.60. If not, additional cost will be added for prosecution of the claim.

HALL-WELLS COLLECTION BUREAU,
550 Pearl St., New York.

Dated this.......... day of.............., 1906.

Please call at my office at once and pay the above claim and avoid extra cost.

.... Justice of the Peace.
Town......................

Correspondence.

THE THIRTEENTH JUROR.

To the Editor of LAW NOTES.

SIR: In the March issue of LAW NOTES, page 224, you make the following statement: "Bills have been introduced in some of our legislatures to add a thirteenth citizen to the jury, who should hear the evidence, but who should take part in the verdict only in case one of the regular jurors was unable to serve. The plan has never, we believe, been enacted into law." I beg to correct an erroneous belief by referring you to section 1089 of the Penal Code of California, which provides for the appointment of one or two additional jurors, to be known as "alternate jurors," whenever, in the opinion of the trial judge in felony causes, the trial is likely to be a protracted one. Such alternate jurors must attend at all times upon the trial and shall take the place of regular jurors in case of death or sickness before the final submission of the case. This section has been on our statute books since 1895. LEO H. SUSMAN.

SAN FRANCISCO.

[Our attention has also been directed to this statute by Alfred Daggett, Esq., of Visalia, California. — *Editor* LAW NOTES.]

Law Notes

MAY, 1907.

PUBLISHED BY EDWARD THOMPSON COMPANY.
NORTHPORT, LONG ISLAND, N. Y.

CONTENTS.

A SHORT time ago we noted the decisions of Judges Evans and McCall adverse to the validity of the federal Employers' Liability Act, and published in another department of our columns the opinion of Judge Evans in full. Since that time several federal judges have considered the act and pronounced it to be a constitutional exercise of the power of the national government over commerce. Judge Emory Speer, sitting in the United States Circuit Court in Georgia, has sustained its validity in an elaborate opinion. He holds the employees of interstate carriers to be as much instrumentalities of commerce as machinery and commodities. The question will probably be soon determined by an authoritative decision of the Supreme Court. If it is upheld, its chief effect will be to abrogate in cases tried in the federal courts the fellow-servant rule and to substitute for the common-law rule of contributory negligence the discarded doctrine of comparative negligence. The fellow-servant rule, while recognized universally in the absence of statute, is, as every one knows, of recent origin. Its effective father in American law was Chief Justice Shaw, who announced it in 1842 in the great case of Farwell *v.* Boston, etc., R. Co., 4 Metc. (Mass.) 49. Twelve years before, the first locomotive on the first railroad in the United States had been put in operation, and it is no reflection on the genius of Shaw for adapting his decisions to the needs and conditions of society as it existed around him to declare that no one could then have foreseen the development of railroads and the effect of that development on the life of the country. At any rate, the experience of more than half a century has demonstrated that the fellow-servant doctrine is not adapted to the conditions of labor under such vast employers as railroads have come to be, and the rule has been abrogated as to them by statute in a number of States. The tendency of the times is toward such legislation, and the seal of approval has been placed upon it by this Act of Congress. Though the courts will not look at the motives with which a statute was passed, it may be permissible for us to see in the act less a tender consideration for the good of interstate commerce than for the personal well-being of the employees of interstate carriers. Under the fiction of acting under the commerce clause, the fellow-servant law, so far as Congress can alter it, is to be changed — as the English Court of King's Bench drew to itself jurisdiction by the fiction of trespass. The English court having laid hands on the jurisdiction administered an admirable quality of justice, and Congress has given us a statute whose provisions are wise and make for justice. But the precedent tends to obscure that principle of local self-government on which our progress in history is founded. Reforms from a distant central government have never been very successful. They fail in making themselves a part of the life of the people as do reforms of indigenous growth. To all this class of objections it might be objected that the federal government is in a very different position from central governments of the past. Aristotle limited the population of an effective state to one hundred thousand citizens. The introduction of the principle of representation confuted his theories. The close community of sentiment between the most distant parts of our country, made possible by quick means of communication and constant commercial intercourse, by the wide distribution of newspapers and other means for the interchange of ideas, is rapidly wiping out mere geographical distance as a barrier between the several States and tending toward homogeneity among our population. That for the present at any rate there are limitations to this process, our misunderstanding with Japan warns us.

DEAN AMES, of Harvard, in whose admirable summary of the Law of Bills and Notes it is strenuously contended that negotiable instruments are specialties, would be shocked by a recent decision of the Supreme Court of Georgia. The payee of a note signed "D. C. N. Buckhalter, Agt.," brought action on the note against Mrs. Lula H. Buckhalter, and the court held that he might, the suit being between the original parties, give evidence to charge Mrs. Buckhalter as principal although her name nowhere appears upon the paper. Buckhalter *v.* Perry, (Ga. 1907) 56 S. E. Rep. 631. Whether or not a negotiable instrument can be considered a "specialty" (and it seems to us that early attempts to place it in that class failed), the rule has been universally admitted that "in suits upon negotiable instruments no evidence is admissible to charge any person as a principal thereto, unless his name is in some way disclosed upon the instrument itself." The Supreme Court of Georgia admits this rule, but it recognizes an exception in cases between immediate parties. The existence of this exception is a mooted question. To recognize its existence is to weaken the great principle which lies at the foundation of negotiable paper that it must carry its claim to credit on its face, without necessity of resorting to extrinsic evidence, and to weaken it unnecessarily, since the payee may recover against the undisclosed principal upon the original consideration. Peutz *v.*

Stanton, 10 Wend. (N. Y.) 271. But this course arrives at justice between the parties, and that is the immediate object before the court rather than the development of a neat and logical doctrine of negotiable paper. The point in Buckhalter *v.* Perry, judging from the opinion in the case, seems to have been unruled upon in Georgia, as no precedent from the State is cited. The court was therefore at liberty to adopt the opposite rule excluding parol testimony, a rule approved by the English and by most American courts when the name of the principal does not appear in any way. 1 Am. and Eng. Encyc. of Law (2d ed.) 1052–1053. It is the rule adopted not only in the English Bills of Exchange Act (see § 23), but in the American Negotiable Instrument Act, § 18, with certain exceptions which do not affect this case, § 42. Considering the great convenience of uniformity in the commercial law, the suggestion is made that courts before adopting a ruling upon a point in the law of bills and notes which is not covered by their own decisions, and upon which there is a diversity of authority, might profitably select that one of the divergent views which has been adopted in the Negotiable Instrument Act, if, as is usually the case, that enactment has merely codified a line of previously existing authorities. In this way we shall bring nearer that desirable time when one and the same commercial law shall obtain throughout the land, and in England and her colonies likewise.

The retiring president of the Wisconsin Bar Association, Mr. L. J. Nash, dealt interestingly with the question of the amendment of our Federal Constitution at the last meeting of the association. Constitutions must grow and change, he declared, and this growth must be provided for. While the provision for amending the Constitution seemed sufficient in 1789, it has proved insufficient. Partly, we may suggest, because the difficulty of obtaining the assent of the required number of forty-six States is so much greater than when the States only numbered thirteen. Some of the changes which he regards as desirable are stated as follows: "If the power of amendment actually existed to-day as a practical method of changing law, the mode of electing senators would be quickly changed, the authority to count and the method of counting electoral votes would be certain, the fiction of the electoral college would be abolished, the treaty-making power would be rearranged so that the country could not without a referendum be committed to the policy of annexing and governing millions of alien and nonassimilable races, and in a manner to enable the government in negotiating a treaty to dispense with the aid of an indicted mayor of a single city; some way would be found to annex the rotten boroughs of Delaware and Rhode Island to other States; Vermont and New Hampshire would be united, and Nevada would be joined to Utah or Idaho." A sweeping list this, and one not likely to beget confidence in Mr. Nash as of a calm and judicial temperament. He suggests that the States have led the way in constitutional development, and indicates that their example might be wisely studied by those who are planning to reform the national government. "If the work of providing a modern and effective method of amending the Federal Constitution were seriously entered upon, it would be found that the States have led the government in the development of constitutional law. Patriotic and courageous faith in the people is more than a beautiful sentiment. It requires us to believe that the people were as wise in what they withheld as in what they granted; that they intended to recall or enlarge their grants by amendment and not by 'construction;' that they expected their Constitution would be interpreted judicially and not otherwise, and that the people are as capable in 1907 as in 1787 of deciding wisely what their fundamental law ought to be." If the present method of amending the Constitution is too cumbrous for practical use, the first thing to be done would seem to be to propose a new method of amendment and by a determined effort to get that provision embodied in the Constitution under the present amendment clause. If this is the only alternative to amendment "by judicial construction," the sooner it is done the better.

Not so startling were the remarks of Judge John Barton Payne, of Chicago, on the same occasion, and yet he observes upon a tendency in contemporary life, whose realization may be of as great value as remedying the deficiencies noticed by Mr. Nash: "If we have a danger threatening at all, I should say that as a people we seem to lack respect for the law. Our desire to press human liberty to the front, our desire to accomplish great good at a moment's notice, has made us indifferent to the means used to accomplish the end. This is evidenced by the hasty legislation of our country. The effect is to make law and legislation the subject of sarcasm, wit, and trifling remarks. The legislative craze that now infests the country has for its object the enlargement of legislative power and the curtailment of the executive and judicial. If we were to enforce the laws as they stand we should be much nearer to happiness. After all, the man who is hunting happiness finds it is always in the next county or the next State. If there is such a thing as happiness then as a matter of fact it is here and now. If we don't live it we won't find it." This wild desire to reform the world in a moment and indifference to the means used marks other public officials besides legislators. But we think that "indifference" fails to convey the correct impression of the situation. We believe it is not so much indifference to means as a disproportionate sense of the importance of the object. This leads men to consider means justifiable and legal which their calm unbiased reason would scout, and questionable courses are adopted in the saddest, most earnest good faith. Perhaps we might find an illustration in the case decided by an Indiana trial judge noticed in the next paragraph.

A striking example of anarchy upon the bench is reported in a decision of an Indiana judge to the effect that the State law licensing retail traffc in intoxicating liquors is unconstitutional. But while the decision is in essence anarchy, it is anarchy suffering from some lamentable disease of personality, which has forgotten its own personal identity, and is posing in the best of faith with a benevolent smile as the friend and upholder of law and morality. It goes without saying that a court which pronounces a deliberate act of the legislature void because it does not tally with the ideas of morality supported by the court itself and by the section of society whose opinions the court reflects is striking at the very foundations of organized government. It affords, however, an interesting if extreme illustration of a type of thought not uncommon at the present day, and indicates a whirlpool which judges might well mark on their sailing charts. Not that many are like to steer with sails full set right into it as Judge Artman does, but that little insidious approaches are not so uncommon. When the constitutionality of State liquor laws has been discussed in our courts, the validity of the statutes has usually been questioned as conflicting with the powers of the general government over commerce, or as unduly limiting the citizen's rights of property. In considering these questions the courts have recognized that the liquor trade was a dangerous business, liable to great abuse, and productive under certain circumstances of pauperism and crime. The traffic was declared to be a valid subject of police regulation, and statutes limiting or prohibiting it within the legislative competence. The courts refused therefore to meddle with the duties of a co-ordinate department of government or to set aside such statutes. It is probably from such cases as these that Judge Artman collects a number of uncomplimentary statements about saloons and the evils of drink. He calls these statements of the reasons for refusing to meddle with legislative "holdings," and deduces therefrom support for his own course in setting aside a declaration of the legislative will, because opposed to his own views of morality. He says: "In view of these holdings, based, as they certainly are, upon good reason and sound common sense, it must be held that the State cannot under the guise of a license delegate to the saloon business a legal existence, because to hold that it can is to hold that the State may sell and delegate the right to make widows and orphans, the right to break up homes, the right to create misery and crime, the right to make murderers, the right to produce idiots and lunatics, the right to fill orphanages, poorhouses, insane asylums, jails, and penitentiaries, and the right to furnish subjects for the hangman's gallows. With due appreciation of the responsibilities of the occasion, conscious of my obligations under my oath to Almighty God and to my fellow man, I cannot by a judgment of this court authorize the granting of a saloon license, and the demurrer to the amended remonstrance is therefore overruled, the amended remonstrance is sustained, and the application is dismissed at the cost of the applicant." This is certainly a strenuous advance on the old mirage of a golden age by force of statute. It has so often been demonstrated that a fallen humanity will not be good in spite of the most ideal laws, that we were becoming somewhat discouraged. Who knows what good results may follow reform by the judiciary directly under a misinterpretation of the constitution and over the heads of the legislature?

It is instructive to observe how rarely our courts, vested for the first time in history with the full practical authority to declare legislation invalid, have attempted to base the exercise of their power on the vague conception of natural right underlying the written provisions of the constitution, a body of principles which constitute its "spirit" as distinguished from its written provisions. Three centuries ago Lord Coke declared in Dr. Bonham's Case, 8 Rep. 118, that "when an Act of Parliament is against common right and reason," "the common law will control it and adjudge it to be void." But this bit of Utopian speculation was necessarily barren in England, and when, as under our written constitutions, *mutatis mutandis,* it is an actuality, courts have conscientiously limited themselves to adjudging laws void when in conflict with the written provisions of the constitution. In one of the early cases affirming the police power over the liquor trade, Judge Hubbard, of the New York Court of Appeals, after observing that, apart from express constitutional limitation, an American legislature had the powers of the British Parliament and that the guaranties of the bill of rights are ample securities for private rights, proceeded: "I am opposed to the judiciary attempting to set bounds to legislative authority, or declaring a statute invalid upon any fanciful theory of higher law or first principles of natural right outside the constitution. If the courts may imply limitation, there is no bound to implication except judicial discretion, which must place the courts above the legislature and also the constitution itself. This is hostile to the theory of government." Wynehamer *v.* People, 13 N. Y. 378. If such reformers as Judge Artman obtain control of the courts, the legislatures and all their works will indeed be in danger of the judgment. What would be left of our poor constitutions were the members of our highest courts to adjudicate by the "spirit" of the instrument — meaning thereby the convictions of the majority of their members — which might be a little stimulant for the stomach's sake, prohibition, single tax, socialism, or what not?

An interesting case was decided last month by the New York Court of Appeals, involving the validity of the present apportionment law of that State, under which the legislature now in session was elected. The apportionment law was passed by the last legislature, and according to the stories current in the newspapers was the work of certain politicians who wished in this way to oust their rivals from districts which were safe for them as the law stood. The act thus passed is declared by the Court of Appeals to be void by reason of its failure to observe the constitutional requirements for apportionment. It follows that the present legislature, elected under the act, is a *de facto* body only and cannot claim the privileges of a *de jure* legislature. The decision of the court holding the act unconstitutional is written by Justice Chase, and Chief Judge Cullen adds an opinion, of much wider interest, explaining the effects of the court's holding. "That the violation of the Constitution," said the chief judge, "is too plain to be disregarded is the conclusion to which we have been forced by the reasons stated by my brother Chase, but at the same time we think it not only proper but our duty to say that in our opinion the fear that our decision may throw the government of the State into confusion is unfounded."

The suggestion that upon the announcement of the court's decision the present legislature ceases to be even a *de facto* body is pronounced to be "without force either in principle or under the authorities. An act of the legislature, if invalid, as violating the constitution, is invalid from the time of its enactment, not merely from the declaration of its character by the courts, but though the appointment or election of a public officer may be illegal, it is elementary law that his official acts while he is an actual incumbent of the office are valid and binding on the public and on third parties . . . In State *v.* Williams, 5 Wis. 308, it was contended that a statute of the State was invalid because approved by a governor whom the courts subsequently declared not to be entitled to the office. Nevertheless, it was held that as the statute was approved by an actual incumbent of the office of governor it was in all respects valid and effective. Of course, an officer who, though *de facto,* is not such *de jure,* may be ousted from the office he illegally holds by proceedings instituted to try his title to the office, and when adjudged a usurper he ceases from that time to be an officer *de facto.* But to have this effect the judgment must be rendered in a proceeding to oust him from office; it is not sufficient for the purpose that his title to office be declared bad in a collateral proceeding. It follows, therefore, that not only is the present legislature a valid legislature, but that each member thereof, so long as the particular house to which he belongs does not oust him, is as to all the world not only a *de facto* but a *de jure* member, and he is entitled to all the privileges of a member, the exemption of his person, the right of his salary, and the like, and his title to office cannot be challenged before any tribunal except the house itself. Thus there can be no vacancy in any particular district which the governor or other officer can call upon the electors to fill unless the house ousts the member and declares him not entitled to his seat. All this, however, does not show that our decision is a mere *brutum fulmen* and of no practical effect. While the courts cannot pass on the title of any present member of the legislature, they can control the action of administrative officers in the conduct of the next election that takes place. If the present legislature should pass a new apportionment bill in compliance with the provisions of the constitution, the next general election at which members of either house are to be elected will be held under the new statute. If the legislature fails to discharge this duty, then the election must be held in accordance with the apportionment under the constitution of 1895. In other words, while the courts cannot interfere with the present legislature, they can compel future elections to be held in compliance with the constitution."

The annual dinner of the Boston Bar Association last month was an interesting occasion, and some of the remarks of the speakers were suggestive. Mr. Justice Loring declared that a judge must sit on a jury case at least once a year to be thoroughly conversant with his duties. He regarded therefore as "a public calamity" the change which has been advocated in the structure of the Supreme Court by which it would become altogether a court of appeal and its members be removed from all *nisi prius* duty. "What you want," he said, "is to have the people behind a court, to have the sanction of public opinion. You want a court made up of the community, a court close to the people, and a court that impresses the people. You can never get such a court from a court of appeal." The opinion will certainly strike the reader who lives in a State where the highest court is purely a court of appeal as somewhat remarkable. "A court close to the people" has been one of the advantages claimed for the elective system of selecting judges. Perhaps the fact that Massachusetts maintains the system of appointing judges by the governor may help to explain Judge Loring's remarks. Chief Justice Aiken, of the Superior Court, warned the legal profession of the dangers of expert testimony. "The time has come," said he, "for a dissolution of copartnership of the lawyer and the doctor, with the doctor the retiring member of the firm." Every one will heartily assent to the proposition that expert testimony as at present used in our courts is something of a scandal. It is a luxury which only the rich can afford and which gives very little or no assistance to the jury in arriving at a verdict. The evils of the system were emphasized in the Thaw case, which recently ended in a mistrial, in New York. The prosecution had a number of experts, stars of the first magnitude in the medical heavens, who swore one way and doubtless rendered bills of a size corresponding to their eminence, while a brilliant constellation attached themselves to the fortunes of the defense. The hypothetical questions which were addressed to these distinguished gentlemen were said to contain more than 12,000 words — an amount of matter equal to nearly ten pages like this one. All this is a *reductio ad absurdum* of our present system. Surely some practical method might be devised of getting the authoritative opinions of experts, when such opinions are needed, without this cumbrous mass of absurdities, upon which any imaginable system would be an improvement. One obstacle in the way of improvement is that attitude of worship toward the jury as a blessing-in-itself, without regard to the ends it is supposed to accomplish, an attitude which has so seriously affected the handling of appeals by the courts. The interminable hypothetical questions, enlightening to nobody, are due to this cause. Truly we may say that trials are now made for the jury, not the jury for trials. And yet the poor jurors in these long-drawn-out modern court dramas suffer greater hardship than any one connected with the case, unless it may be the defendant.

It was certainly a judgment *ad hominem,* or rather *ad feminam,* which the Texas Court of Civil Appeals delivered recently in a suit against a railroad for the unlawful expulsion of a female passenger. Fort Worth R. *v.* Travis, 99 S. W. Rep. 1141. The lady claimed damages for physical and mental suffering, and the defendant sought to show that the plaintiff was a Christian Scientist and therefore above suffering. The judge excluded the evidence and the plaintiff had a verdict. The appellate court held the exclusion to be error; that the plaintiff's belief should have been submitted to the jury. "If," said the court, "she had such control of her feelings, or thought she had, as to render her insensible to pain when she willed to be, we see no reason why that circumstance should not have been considered by the jury in determining the extent of her suffering and the compensation to be made on account of it." But after all wasn't logic with the lady rather than with the court's law? Christian

Scientists, so far as we can understand their doctrines, profess to believe that all physical pain is due to "error," which error is the preposterous belief transmitted through numberless generations of mentally weakened ancestors that there is such a thing as matter and that that matter can have any influence on the entity mind. Now evidently it takes good hard thought, and plenty of it, even from the point of view of a Christian Scientist, to overcome this wretched popular prejudice. We doubt if even the most advanced member of the sect, upon unexpectedly stepping on a tack — not having on the delusion of shoes — could escape a momentary thrill of error. Of course a good stiff bit of thought afterwards could overcome the erroneous impression, but the pain would have been suffered. As a tortfeasor is liable for all the consequences of his unlawful act, he should be liable for all the extra exertion which he has compelled the lady to undergo, and, as action and reaction are equal, the only way to measure this is the pain she would have suffered but for her efforts. For we submit that the victim's duty to take measures to lessen her sufferings cannot apply to an act of mere thought. In so far as her sufferings were merely mental and caused by the acts toward her of other minds, do Christian Scientists deny that one mind can inflict pain on another? Lastly, the plaintiff in this case may have been an aspirant toward the heights of Christian Science, but she may not have attained the requisite proficiency to bar pain, and her own testimony or other proof that she actually suffered would not in any way be contradicted by her professed creed. We admit that yielding to the delusion so far as to bring suit will probably make the further toils of her ascent more difficult. But that is her business and not the court's.

SECRET SOCIETIES AND THE LAW.

If you are curious as to what transpires within the lodge room of a secret order upon initiation night there is one sure way of becoming informed, and that way lies through the taking of regular membership in the order. Though you may already be a brother in one or more such organizations, you can never be certain as to what may be expected upon a new venture. Even the chronic "joiner" never becomes expert enough to be enabled to determine which degree to take in evening clothes and which in his old suit. Your lifelong friend will suddenly cease in his confidences when the subject of his lodge is touched upon and will take on that innocent, and at the same time mysterious, air that only the member of a secret tribe can assume. And the cleverest wife cannot drag from her husband, though he may be a man most communicative in other affairs, the slightest hint of what goes on in that out-of-the-world haunt which he calls his lodge, though she must occasionally gain an inkling from the condition in which her spouse arrives home after the working of a degree.

Once in a great while, however, a few of the profound secrets of some fraternal institution are brought to light and made public through the medium of the court of law. A very recent decision of the Supreme Court of the State of Michigan, denying pecuniary solace for injuries received by the plaintiff at the hands of a degree team, which was conferring upon him the honor of initiation into the ranks of the Knights of the Modern Maccabees, a secret insurance society of wide repute, has suggested a search for other cases of similar character. Taking into consideration the fact that the secret orders in this country annually bring three hundred thousand new members into the fold, and the further fact that it is almost impossible for one to conceive of a situation or condition that has not been many times presented for the consideration of the courts, the results which such a search have produced are decidedly meagre.

There is magazine and statistical authority for the statement that the secret societies of the United States maintain upwards of seventy thousand lodges and can lay claim to more than six millions of members. It is stated that every fifth man one passes on the streets is identified with some fraternal organization whose secrets he has bound himself by the strongest and most solemn oaths never to divulge. The numbers given do not include the membership of military companies, labor organizations, nor of college fraternities. It is needless to say that the reports show no instance of a college man bringing action against his fraternity to recover damages for injuries received during the process of his being made a "Greek," though it is most common to hear or read of a serious accident, unintentional or otherwise, to a candidate for initiation into a Greek letter fraternity. Whatever he may have been before setting out upon his college career, or whatever he may prove to be after his *alma mater* turns him off upon the world, during his four years' course the real, *bona fide* college man rarely shows the yellow streak. If all of the freshmen in almost any large institution of learning were to institute such actions for trespass, negligence, false imprisonment, assault and battery, etc., as accrue during their freshman year, the upper-class men would undoubtedly be overwhelmed with judgments.

The recent Michigan decision, to which reference has already been made, is that of Kaminiski *v.* Knights of Modern Maccabees, decided in October, 1906. The plaintiff was injured while undergoing the ceremony of being officially received as a member of a branch of the defendant order, known as the Belle Isle Tent. He set forth in his complaint that by the rules and regulations of the defendant order, governing the initiation of new members, the initiation officers were required to put the candidates through certain motions, marches, and gymnastics, which, when properly conducted, were entirely harmless. The complaint went on to aver that the degree team, in putting Mr. Kaminiski through, made use of a certain ritualistic method of initiation adopted and promulgated by the defendant, in accordance with which the officers of the Belle Isle Tent recklessly, negligently, and carelessly grasped the plaintiff by his shoulders, tripped his knees forward, and threw his body backward, causing him to fall upon the floor of the room with great force and violence, resulting in serious and permanent injury.

An idea of what is planned by way of reception for secret society initiates may be gained from an examination of the following excerpt from the initiatory ceremony, which was introduced upon the trial: "Two of the soldiers pass out of the inclosure and capture Judas and take his sword. They wrap chain about his arms and remain outside of the inclosure until the general says: 'Let him stand aside and await his doom.' The other soldiers rush upon and seize the candidate (Kaminiski) and after a brief pause, the lights being turned on, the first soldier says: 'He is a rebel.' Second soldier: 'Let us kill him.'" Eager in the performance of their duty the loyal soldiers, or guards as they are sometimes called, rushed upon Kaminiski and proceeded to exemplify the quoted portion of the ceremony of initiation in the manner and with the results above described.

Although the plaintiff was probably unaware of it at the time, he agreed in his application for membership to be bound by the laws, rules, and regulations of the order, one of which provided that a subordinate tent and its officers should, in all matters, be the agent of its members and applicants for membership and that the Great Camp would in no case be liable for any fault or negligence on the part of a subordinate tent or any of its officers. The laws of the order empowered the subordinate tent to determine whether an accepted candidate should be initiated or merely "obligated" and granted to the subordinate tent authority to select the degree team to confer the initiatory work and to provide the necessary paraphernalia therefor. Whatever may have been the liability of the degree team or of the Belle Isle Tent, which appointed and directed the team in its work, the Supreme Court of Michigan considered it very clear that neither the team nor the tent was, in view of the facts stated, acting as the agent of the Great Camp at the time the injury complained of occurred, and that the Great Camp was, therefore, not responsible in damages.

The authorities present two instances in which a candidate suffered injury at the hands of, or rather at the horns of, a contrivance described as a mechanical or artificial goat. The more important of the two decisions is that of the United States Circuit Court of Appeals in the case of Jumper *v.* Sovereign Camp Woodmen of the World, which decision was made the subject of an editorial in the New York *Law Journal* shortly after being handed down.

It appeared from the facts of the case that M. F. Jumper, having been accepted for membership in the Order of Woodmen of the World, a secret society issuing insurance, presented himself for initiation to the local camp at Water Valley, Mississippi, known as the L. Q. C. Lamar Camp thereof, which was a branch of the sovereign camp, authorized and directed by such sovereign camp as to the manner and mode of conferring initiation. The customary blindfold was placed over the plaintiff's eyes, and, in the language of the complaint, "he was then and there carelessly and roughly assaulted and struck and beaten and wounded with some hard substance of considerable weight and force, upon pelvic bone of hip, so as to cause this plaintiff great bodily pain and suffering, and that he was so struck with great and unnecessary force, from which his hip bone was injured, fractured, and shattered, and which has caused him to be permanently injured, and to be unable to pursue his usual avocation, that of a railroad engineer." As a balm for the inhumane treatment complained of the plaintiff demanded damages of twenty thousand dollars. It was held that the defendant was not liable, for the reason that the plaintiff did not show that there existed between the Sovereign Camp (defendant) and the Water Valley Camp such relationship of master and servant or of principal and agent as would render the Sovereign Camp responsible for the acts of the lodge at Water Valley.

It may interest some to know that, in all probability, the Water Valley Lodge is the only lodge in the State of Mississippi in which the goat exercise is used. Even in that lodge its use is not treated as a part of the regular initiation, and it is never used on any subject until he has been pronounced fully initiated and congratulated upon being one of the obligated sovereigns of the camp. The night upon which the goat is brought out depends partly upon the number in attendance and somewhat upon the number of those who are to be the objects of its interesting treatment. In this particular case it was shown to have been operated during a recess from the regular business of the lodge when the lodge was standing at ease for the purpose of allowing the brethren to take part in the play.

A case which ought to hold the interest of prospective candidates for secret society membership is that of The State *v.* Webster Williams and others, in which the defendants were indicted for assault and battery and which came up before the Supreme Court of Georgia in June, 1876. The defendants and the prosecutrix, it seems, were members of a benevolent society in Hamilton, N. C., known as the "Good Samaritans." The organization had not only a ceremony of initiation, but a ceremony of expulsion as well. The prosecutrix having been remiss in some of her obligations and being unable to explain to the satisfaction of her fellow members, the defendants proceeded to perform upon her the ceremony of expulsion, which consisted in suspending her from the wall by means of a cord fastened around the waist. The prosecutrix had previously witnessed the expulsion of other members in this manner, and, for that reason, was probably the more energetic in her resistance. Resistance, however, availed her nothing, and she was expelled in accordance with the rites of the order.

The defendants' counsel contended that if his clients only intended to perform the usual ceremony of expulsion and were actuated by no other motive they were not guilty; that in order to commit a crime there must be an unlawful act, coupled with a vicious will. The holding of the court may best be found in the words of the judge, which follow: "When the prosecutrix refused to submit to the ceremony of expulsion established by this benevolent society, it could not be lawfully inflicted. Rules of discipline for this and all voluntary associations must conform to the laws. If the act of tying this woman would have been a battery had the parties concerned not been members of the Society of Good Samaritans, it is not the less a battery because they were all members of that humane institution."

In Kinver *v.* The Phœnix Lodge, I. O. O. F., a Canadian case, the plaintiff brought his action against the lodge into which he was initiated to recover for injuries which resulted from the initiation. The following is the plaintiff's recital of what occurred: "On the night of the initiation Mr. Connors, a member, adjusted the cap for me in the ante-room of the lodge; it blindfolded me. I was then taken, as I suppose, into the lodge room. My hands were then tied to my sides above the elbow, I think, and I think by a chain. I was shoved then from behind at the small of the back; it was a violent push. I felt something then catch my legs. My head struck first; the push knocked me over. My feet were lifted up. It bent me the wrong way backwards. My temple struck; it was injured and my eye was swollen. When I got to my feet I was led round a few times with the chain still on; no harm was done to me after that. Before the lodge was closed the Noble Grand (the head of the lodge) came to me and said, 'I am afraid we hurt you.' I said, 'You have hurt my back.'"

The Noble Grand, who did not witness the plaintiff's rough treatment, but who heard the noise which accompanied it, contributed the following to the testimony: "I have heard unusual noises at these celebrations before. I have seen a candidate taken and rolled on the floor when he was blindfolded and before the ceremony commenced, and before the conductor took charge of him. I would not consider rolling on the floor injurious; it occurs before the man is chained; possibly the conductor is a party to whatever is done to the candidate. Hearing the noise, I supposed some of his shopmates were having a little lark with him. I had heard the noise before, and never took any active steps to stop it."

As to what actually happened to the plaintiff, it appeared that a linen organ cover was rolled up and held before him. He was given a violent push by one or more of the members, which sent him tumbling forward for a distance of about seven feet, where he came in contact with the organ cover, which was held so as to catch him a little above the knees. The effect of this, of course, was to trip the plaintiff and throw him heavily upon the floor. It was held that the members of the lodge, in their rough handling of the plaintiff, their new brother, were acting as the agents of the lodge, and that the lodge must answer in damages.

JOHN E. BRADY.

THE ATTITUDE OF EQUITY TOWARD THE STRIKE AND BOYCOTT — USE OF THE INJUNCTION.

THERE has never been a time when decisions of courts relative to labor and labor organizations have been of greater interest or importance than at the present time. This is largely so because the power and position of organized labor, as, to a great extent, those of organized capital, remain as yet somewhat undetermined. As questions involving these things arise for consideration, by a gradual process of extension or restriction we attain unto a known state, which, in turn, aids in the solution of succeeding problems, perhaps under new conditions. There are, however, some phases of the organized labor movement that have been before the courts often enough to have reached a stage of finality. I wish to speak of these more settled phases first, and then pass to some that are not so well determined.

There is a long line of decisions to the effect that a combination of persons is illegal. Note a few expressions from well known cases:

In Com. v. Hunt,[1] the court said: "The general rule of the common law is that it is a criminal and indictable offense for two or more to confederate and combine together, by concerted means, to do that which is unlawful or criminal, to the injury of the public, or portions or classes of the community, or even to the rights of an individual."

In State v. Burnham,[2] this language was used: "Combinations against law or against individuals are always dangerous to the public peace and to public security; to guard against the union of individuals to effect an unlawful design is not easy, and to detect and punish them is often extremely difficult."

In Reg. v. Parnell,[3] we find this: "An agreement to effect an injury or wrong to another by two or more persons is constituted an offense, because a wrong to be effected by a combination assumes a formidable character; when done by one alone it is but a civil injury, but it assumes a formidable or aggravated character when it is to be effected by the powers of a combination."

In Com. v. Carlisle:[4] "There is between the different parts of the body politic a reciprocity of action on each other, which, like the action of antagonizing muscles of the natural body, not only prescribes to each its appropriate state and action, but regulates the motion of the whole. The effort of an individual to disturb this equilibrium can never be perceptible, nor carry the operation of his interest or that of any other individual beyond the limits of fair competition. But, the increase of power by combination of means being in geometrical proportion to the number concerned, an association may be able to give an impulse, not only oppressive to individuals, but mischievous to the public at large; and it is the employment of an engine so powerful and dangerous that gives criminality to an act that would be perfectly innocent, at least in a legal view, when done by an individual."

The Vermont court said in State v. Stewart:[5] "A combination of two or more persons to effect an illegal purpose, either by legal or illegal means, whether such purpose be illegal at common law or by statute, or to effect a legal purpose by illegal means, whether such means be illegal at common law or by statute, is a common-law conspiracy. Such combinations are equally illegal whether they promote objects or adopt means that are *per se* indictable, or promote objects or adopt means that are *per se* oppressive, immoral or wrongfully prejudicial to the rights of others. If they seek to restrain trade, or tend to the destruction of the material prosperity of the country, they work injury to the whole public."

The court uses this language in State v. Buchanan:[6] "Every conspiracy to do an unlawful act, or to do a lawful act for an illegal, fraudulent, malicious, or corrupt purpose, or for a purpose which has a tendency to prejudice the public in general, is at common law an indictable offense, though nothing be done in execution of it, and no matter by what means the conspiracy was intended to be effected, which may be perfectly indifferent, and makes no ingredient of the crime, and therefore need not be stated in the indictment. . . . There is nothing in the objection that to punish a conspiracy where the end is not accomplished would be to punish a mere unexecuted intention. It is not the bare intention that the law punishes, but the *act of conspiring*, which is made a substantive offense by the nature of the object intended to be effected."

In State v. Glidden,[7] it is said: "Any one man, or any one of several men, acting independently, is powerless, but when several combine, and direct their united energies to the accomplishment of a bad purpose, the combination is formidable. Its power for evil increases as its numbers increase. . . . The combination becomes dangerous, and subversive of the rights of others, and the law wisely says that it is a crime."

These are the authorities that are most frequently cited to support the contention that a combination is illegal. They should not, however, be construed as meaning that there should never be any combination, or that *all* combination is illegal.

1 4 Metc. (Mass.) 111, 121.
2 15 N. H. 396, 401.
3 14 Cox C. C. 508, 514.
4 Brightly N. P. 36, 39, 40.
5 59 Vt. 273, 286; 9 Atl. Rep. 559.
6 5 Har. & J. (Md.) 317, 352, 355.
7 55 Conn. 46, 75; 8 Atl. Rep. 890.

It is interesting to read in this connection the dissenting opinion of Judge Holmes, now of the United States Supreme Court, in the case of Vegelahn *v.* Guntner.[8] He says, in the course of that opinion: "It is plain from the slightest consideration of practical affairs, or the most superficial reading of industrial history, that free competition means combination, and that the organization of the world, now going on so fast, means an ever increasing might and scope of combination. It seems to me futile to set our faces against this tendency. Whether beneficial on the whole, as I think it, or detrimental, it is inevitable, unless the fundamental axioms of society, and even the fundamental conditions of life, are to be changed. One of the eternal conflicts out of which life is made up is that between the effort of every man to get the most he can for his services, and that of society, disguised under the name of capital, to get his services for the least possible return. Combination on the one side is patent and powerful. Combination on the other is the necessary and desirable counterpart, if the battle is to be carried on in a fair and equal way."

The combination of labor in the form of "unions," organized for the purpose of mutual benefit, has never come under the ban of the law. And while the "union," as such, has not come under the ban, yet upon a number of occasions it has been necessary for the law to step in and put its restraining hand upon some of the practices inaugurated by the "union." And of these I wish to speak next.

Whenever difficulty or disagreement arises between employer and employee, one of the first things thought of by the latter, as a means of enforcing his demands, is a strike. As to what constitutes "a strike," has been a subject of judicial discussion. In the very well reasoned case of Arthur *v.* Oakes,[9] Circuit Justice Harlan says: "What is to be deemed a strike, within the meaning of the order of the Circuit Court? In the opinion of the circuit judge, made a part of the record, we are informed that at the argument below the definition proffered to the court by the interveners as one recognized by the labor organizations of the country was as follows: 'A strike is a concerted cessation of or refusal to work until or unless certain conditions which obtain or are incident to the terms of employment are changed. The employee declines to longer work, knowing full well that the employer may immediately employ another to fill his place, also knowing that he may or may not be re-employed or returned to service. The employer has the option of acceding to the demand and returning the old employee to service, of employing new men, or of forcing conditions under which the old men are glad to return to service under the old conditions.'"

This may be the meaning of "a strike" accepted "by the labor organizations of the country," but that all do not agree with such a definition may readily be seen from the following, taken from the opinion in the case last above cited:[10] "The learned circuit judge said that a more exact definition of a strike was 'a combined effort among workmen to compel the master to the concession of a certain demand by preventing the conduct of his business until compliance with the demand,' and he said: 'It is idle to talk of a peaceful strike. None such ever occurred. The suggestion is an impeachment of intelligence.'"

Before some of the courts the question as to the legality or illegality of a strike has been raised. A reading of the expressions of the courts on that point materially aids one in arriving at a definition of "a strike." In this same case of Arthur *v.* Oakes,[11] the circuit judge went on to say: "All combinations to interfere with perfect freedom in the proper management of one's lawful business, to dictate the terms upon which such business shall be conducted, by means of threats or by interference with property or traffic, or with the lawful employment of others, are within the condemnation of the law. It has been well said that the wit of man could not devise a legal strike, because compulsion is the leading idea of it. A strike is essentially a conspiracy to extort by violence; the means employed to effect the end being not only the cessation of labor by the conspirators, but by the necessary prevention of labor by those who are willing to assume their places, and as a last resort, and in many instances an essential element of success, the disabling and destruction of property of the master; and so by intimidation and by the compulsion of force, to accomplish the end designed."

With this extreme characterization of a strike, Circuit Justice Harlan was unable to agree, for he says:[12] "We are not prepared, in the absence of evidence, to hold as matter of law that a combination among employees, having for its object their orderly withdrawal in large numbers or in a body from the service of their employers, on account simply of a reduction in wages, is not a 'strike,' within the meaning of the word as commonly used. Such a withdrawal, although amounting to a strike, is not, as we have already said, either illegal or criminal."

This same idea is well expressed in the case of Farrer *v.* Close,[13] where the court spoke thus: "I am, however, of the opinion that strikes are not necessarily illegal. A 'strike' is properly defined as 'a simultaneous cessation of work on the part of the workmen;' and its legality or illegality must depend on the means by which it is enforced, and on its objects. It may be criminal, as if it be part of a combination for the purpose of injuring or molesting either masters or men; or it may be simply illegal, as if it be the result of an agreement depriving those engaged in it of their liberty of action, similar to that by which the employers bound themselves in the case of Hilton *v.* Eckersley, 6 El. & Bl. 47, 66; or it may be perfectly innocent, as if it be the result of the voluntary combination of men for the purpose only of benefiting themselves by raising their wages, or for the purpose of compelling the fulfilment of an engagement entered into between employers and employed, or any other lawful purpose."

In practically all of the cases relative to this matter the court enters a discussion of the personal liberty of the employee, maintaining that if he were not allowed to cease work at any time he wished, he would in effect be deprived of his liberty. He may be under contract to remain in service for a longer period of time, and if he chooses to violate that contract he may be laying himself liable to a civil action for damages, but in the ordinary cases the equity side of the courts will not interfere and by injunction compel him to remain at work.

But there is another element that not infrequently enters into a strike. There are but few people living in cities to-day, who have not seen and known something of a strike. Very frequently the employees of a concern will walk out of their own accord, but it has likewise become a very common thing for a strike to be promoted and induced by those whose "business" it is to do so. There are the professional "agitators, organizers, and walking delegates, who roam all over the country as agents of some combination, who are vampires that live and fatten on the honest labor of the country, and who are busybodies creating dissatisfaction among a class of people who are quiet, well-disposed, and who do not want to be disturbed by the unceasing agitation of this class of people."

8 167 Mass. 92; 35 L. R. A. 722, 725.
9 63 Fed. Rep. 310.
10 Arthur *v.* Oakes, *supra.*
11 *Supra.*
12 Arthur *v.* Oakes, *supra.*
13 L. R. 4 Q. B. 602, 612.

In regard to the right of these "walking delegates" to instigate a strike, inducing employees to break their contracts and cease serving, it has been held that equity will restrain them from acting, upon application of the employer. This was the exact question in United States *v.* Haggerty.[14] That was a suit on the relation of the Guaranty Trust Company of New York against Haggerty and others, residents of Illinois, Pennsylvania, Ohio, and West Virginia, who had gone into a certain coal district in the latter State for the purpose of inducing miners to strike. In a very able opinion, District Judge Jackson, presiding over the Circuit Court, said: "I do not question the right of the employees of this company to quit work at any time they desire to do so, unless there is a contractual relation between them and the employer which should control their right to quit. At the same time I do not recognize the right of an employer to coerce the employees to continue their work when they desire to quit. But can it be said where a conspiracy exists to control the employees, as in this instance, either by threats, intimidation, or a resort to any other modes usually accompanying the action of strikers, that such action on their part is not only illegal, but a malicious and illegal interference with the employer's business? The question is its best answer."

The strike, then, according to the legal view, is merely a simultaneous cessation of work by the employees, and, as such, is not illegal or wrong. Courts will not interfere to prevent a strike of that nature, though equity will restrain a combination or conspiracy organized for the express purpose of inducing a strike, and especially restrain those who have no other interest in the controversy between the employee and his employer than to induce the strike.

The next thing to be noticed in connection with this subject is the manner of making the strike effective. In most industries, the labor is not of such a specialized character as to necessitate a discontinuance of the business whenever a strike has been declared. Frequently unskilled labor may be substituted, and the business continued, though perhaps under difficulties. It is because of this fact that the strikers find it necessary to employ some means to prevent the employment of others in their places, and in some way, if possible, force the employer to an acceptance of the terms upon which they will return to their work. If something of this kind were not done, a strike would merely mean the displacement of those dissatisfied, and the striker, instead of finding himself bettered, would find himself out of employment altogether. This brings me to what I term the counterpart of the strike, the boycott. Under this term I include everything used by the strikers to make the strike effective, whether it be to keep would-be employees away, or to interrupt other business relations.

Like the term "strike," "boycott" has also been judicially defined. In Brace *v.* Evans,[15] speaking of the boycott, it is said: "In popular acceptation it is an organized effort to exclude a person from business relations with others, by persuasion, intimidation, and other acts which tend to violence, and thereby coerce him, through fear of resulting injury, to submit to dictation in the management of his affairs."

In Park *v.* Druggists' Association,[16] the following definition is given: "A boycott means to refuse to sell or do business with a concern, and to prevent anybody else from doing business with a concern on any conditions."

The New York court, Jenks, J., speaking, has this to say in Mills *v.* Printing Co.:[17] "I think the verb 'to boycott' does not necessarily signify that the doers employ violence, intimidation, or other unlawful coercive means, but that it may be correctly used in the sense of the act of a combination, in refusing to have business dealings with another until he removes or ameliorates conditions which are deemed inimical to the welfare of the members of the combination, or some of them, or grants concessions which are deemed to make for that purpose."

In Oxley State Co. *v.* Coopers' I. U. of N. A.,[18] it is said: "The term 'boycott' has acquired a significance in our vocabulary, and in the literature of the law. . . . The term implies that a general proscription of all articles so manufactured, and the goods packed in them, would be inaugurated and maintained by the power of these assemblies, wherever they could reach. It is fair to presume . . . that the defendants were determined to use all means, short of violence, to make the proscription effective. That has been the history of such proceedings in the past, and such is the meaning imputed to the use of the word 'boycott.' It has become a word carrying with it a threat and a menace."

There is some difference of opinion as to the legality of the boycott, as will be seen from the following cases.

In the last case above cited[19] the facts were substantially as follows: The plaintiff was engaged in the cooperage business, and had introduced into its plant certain machines resulting in the displacement of about one hundred coopers. The defendants demanded a discontinuance of the use of the machines under penalty of a declaration of a boycott, not only against the plaintiff, but also against all concerns that bought products of the plaintiff. In the course of its opinion, the court said: "No one can question the right of the defendants to refuse to purchase machine-made packages, or of goods packed in them, or, by fair means, to persuade others from purchasing or using them. If that is all that is implied by a boycott, as insisted by defendants, it is difficult to see where they violate any law, although it might injure the complainant's business. It has been decided, however, that while such action would not be unlawful by an individual, a combination and conspiracy to accomplish the purpose would be an illegal act."[20]

The court used this language in Thomas *v.* Railway Co.:[21] "But the combination was unlawful, without respect to the contract feature. It was a boycott. . . . Boycotts, though unaccompanied by violence or intimidation, have been pronounced unlawful in every State of the United States where the question has arisen, unless it be in Minnesota, and they are held to be unlawful in England."[22]

Several jurisdictions take the opposite view, and this "minority" view, as it might be termed, seems best stated by the New York court. In Mills *v.* Printing Co.,[23] it is pointed out that "such a combination may be formed and held together by argument, persuasion, entreaty, or by the 'touch of nature,' and may accomplish its purpose without violence or other unlawful means (*i. e.*, simply by abstention)," and hence "it cannot be said that 'to boycott' is to offend the law."[24]

14 116 Fed. Rep. 510.
15 3 Ry. & Corp. L. J. 561.
16 175 N. Y. 1; 62 L. R. A. 632, 637.
17 91 N. Y. S. 185, 189.

18 72 Fed. Rep. 695, 699.
19 Oxley Stave Co. *v.* Coopers' I. U. of N. A., *supra*.
20 *Citing* Arthur *v.* Oakes, *supra*.
21 62 Fed. Rep. 818–821.
22 *Citing* State *v.* Glidden, 55 Conn. 46, 8 Atl. Rep. 890; State *v.* Stewart, *supra*; Steamship Co. *v.* McKenna, 30 Fed. Rep. 48; Casey *v.* Typographical Union, 45 Fed. Rep. 135; Toledo, A. A. & N. M. Ry. Co. *v.* Penn. Co., 54 Fed. Rep. 730.
23 *Supra*.
24 *Citing* Bohn *v.* Hollis, 54 Minn. 223; Sinsheimer *v.* United Garment Workers, 77 Hun 215; Cook, Trade and Labor Com., § 9, p. 43; Tiedeman, State and Federal Control, etc., vol. 1, p. 440 *et seq.*; Bowen *v.* Matheson, 14 Allen 499; Mogul S. S. Co. *v.* McGregor, L. R. 23 Q. B. 598; Marx, etc., Co. *v.* Watson, (Mo.) 67 S. W. Rep. 391; Ulery *v.* Exchange, 54 Ill. 233, 240; State *v.* Glidden, *supra*; Allen *v.* Flood, (1898) A. C. 1; Quinn *v.* Leathem, (1901) A. C. 495; Park *v.* Druggists' Assoc., *supra*.

In determining whether or not the boycott is illegal, it is well to examine what the various courts have held in regard to the means used to make it effective. That open violence is not a proper means for making the boycott effective, is so plain and fundamental as to require no citation of authority. Of the other means that might be, and frequently are, used, the most common are picketing, displaying placards and transparencies, and circulation of posters and circulars. Of these, I speak in the order named.

The term "picketing" is, I think, pretty generally understood to mean the stationing of men in and about the premises or place of business against which the boycott has been declared. Sometimes these pickets are so placed for the mere purpose of making silent observation for the sake of obtaining information. More frequently, however, their object is to persuade customers or would-be workmen from entering into relations with the company or person under the ban. Sometimes their entreaty is boisterous and persistent, and sometimes degenerates into a mere application of villainous and opprobrious epithets to those who do not heed them. Every one who has ever been in a community when a strike was in progress has seen examples of this. While it might be said that the placing of a mere watch about the premises does not constitute an illegal act, yet as a matter of fact even that sometimes amounts to an intimidation, which all the courts hold to be illegal, and it unquestionably amounts to intimidation when the pickets are guilty of using discourteous language toward those whom they would prevent from entering relations with the offending party. Note what some of the courts say.

In the case of Vegelahn *v.* Guntner,[25] the principal question was whether the patrol should be enjoined against. In the course of its opinion, the court said: "It was thus one means of intimidation, indirectly to the plaintiff, and directly to persons actually employed, or seeking to be employed, by the plaintiff, and of rendering such employment unpleasant or intolerable to such persons. Such an act is an unlawful interference with the rights both of employer and of employed. An employer has a right to engage all persons who are willing to work for him, at such prices as may be mutually agreed upon, and persons employed or seeking employment have a corresponding right to enter into or remain in the employment of any person or corporation willing to employ them. These rights are secured by the Constitution itself.[26] . . . Intimidation is not limited to threats of violence or of physical injury to person or property. It has a broader signification, and there may also be a moral intimidation which is illegal." And again: "The defendants contend that these acts were justifiable because they were only seeking to secure better wages for themselves, by compelling the plaintiff to accept their schedule of wages. This motive or purpose does not justify maintaining a patrol in front of plaintiff's premises, as a means of carrying out their conspiracy."

In the case of Frank *v.* Herold,[27] Vice-Chancellor Pitney has this to say in regard to maintaining a picket: "In my judgment, any conduct on the part of any person which tends to hinder or prevent another from working if he or she chooses to work is an unlawful infringement of the personal rights of that individual. It is urged that one person has a right to persuade another to work or not to work. That may be if the other person is willing to listen and be persuaded; but no person has a right to impose upon another his arguments or persuasions against the willingness of that other person to listen. No person has the right to invade my private residence, or to accost me as I am walking along the street, to urge or persuade me to a certain course of conduct, if I do not choose to stop and listen to him. . . . Applying these principles to the case in hand, the parties defendant are charged . . . with accosting, annoying, and molesting . . . operatives of the complainants while on their way to and from their work. Now these . . . operatives, in my judgment, have the right to walk the streets entirely unmolested . . . without having epithets cast at them, or in fact anything done to make it disagreeable for them to go to and from their work."

In the recent case of Underhill *v.* Murphy,[28] it was said: "The appellees not only picketed plaintiff's place of business, but . . . to protect his employees from violence, he had to take them to and from the places where they worked in a conveyance. . . . The acts of the defendant as truly destroyed the plaintiff's property when they broke up his business by force and intimidation as they would have done in the case of visible property by burning it or carrying it off. Among the inalienable rights . . . guaranteed as inherent in all men is 'the right of acquiring and protecting property.' The right to acquire and protect property is as sacred in the case of intangible property as tangible, and an injunction may be granted to protect intangible rights no less than those that are tangible."

Recurring again to Mills *v.* Printing Co.,[29] this is said about picketing: "'Picketing' may simply mean the stationing of men for observation. If, in the doing of this act solely for such purpose, there be no molestation or physical annoyance or let or hindrance of any person, then it cannot be said that such an act is *per se* unlawful. But 'picketing' may also mean the stationing of a man or men to coerce or to threaten or to intimidate or to halt or to turn aside against their will those who would go to and from the picketed place to do business or to work or to seek work therein, or in some other way to hamper, hinder, or harass the free dispatch of business by the employer. In that case picketing may well be said to be unlawful. . . . I may add that I am not prepared to say that all picketing which goes no further than 'persuasion and entreaty' of those who are about to work or to seek work or to do business in the picketed place is absolutely lawful. A wayfarer upon the public street should be free for peaceful travel. No man against my will has the legal right to occupy the public street to arrest my course or to join me on my way, be he ever so polite or gentle in his insistence. There may be no intimidation, and yet an interruption of peaceful travel. There may be annoyance without danger."

These cases would seem to indicate, then, that picketing is lawful so long as it does not constitute an intimidation, an annoyance, or an interruption of peaceful travel. It will be readily seen, however, that what can be accomplished by picketing is very little indeed.

Passing now to the matter of displaying placards, banners, and transparencies. This subject is so bound up with the matter of picketing that it is difficult to obtain a separate expression from the court in regard to it alone, for which reason I will mention but two cases. In the very recent case of Goldberg *v.* Stablemen's Union,[30] the facts were substantially as follows: The plaintiff was carrying on business as a vendor of groceries and general household goods. There was a reduction in wages, and upon a refusal to return to the old schedule a strike was declared, and a boycott inaugurated by the defendant. In carrying out the boycott the defendant maintained directly in front of the plaintiff's places of busi-

[25] *Supra.*

[26] *Citing* Com. *v.* Perry, 155 Mass. 117; People *v.* Gillson, 109 N. Y. 389; Coal Co. *v.* People, 147 Ill. 71; Ritchie *v.* People, 155 Ill. 98; Low *v.* Printing Co., 41 Neb. 127.

[27] (N. J. Ch.) 52 Atl. Rep. 152, 154.

[28] (Ky.) 78 S. W. Rep. 482.

[29] *Supra.*

[30] (Cal.) 86 Pac. Rep. 806.

ness pickets bearing placards and transparencies on which were printed: "Unfair firm; reduced wages of employees 50 cents per day. Please don't patronize." In granting an injunction the court said: "It is averred in the complaint that in the case at bar . . . with intent to threaten and intimidate employees and patrons and customers of plaintiff, the said defendants do keep immediately in front of plaintiff's place of business, and threaten to so keep there, representatives and pickets bearing the placards and transparencies above set forth, and that by said means they have intimidated patrons and customers of plaintiff from entering said place of business, and will, if not restrained, continue to so intimidate the said patrons. It cannot be successfully contended that the said acts of defendants committed immediately in front of plaintiff's place of business as aforesaid, could not, in the nature of things, have had the effect of intimidating plaintiff's patrons, . . . and such acts, having such effect, undoubtedly interfered with and violated plaintiff's constitutional right to acquire, possess, defend, and enjoy property." [31]

The above case being from one of the extreme western jurisdictions, I take the next from the extreme east. The case of Sherry *v.* Perkins [32] was a bill in equity to restrain the president and secretary of the Lasters' Protective Union from causing to be carried in front of the plaintiff's shoe factory a banner on which was the following inscription: "Lasters are requested to keep away from P. P. Sherry's. Per order L. P. U.;" and also a banner on which was the following: "Lasters on a strike, and lasters are requested to keep away from P. P. Sherry's until the present trouble is settled. Per order L. P. U." In the course of its opinion the court said: "The case finds that the defendants entered, with others, into a scheme, by threats and intimidation, to prevent persons in the employment of the plaintiff from continuing in such employment, and to prevent others from entering into such employment; that the banners, with their inscriptions, were used by the defendants as a part of their scheme, and that the plaintiff was thereby injured in his business and property. The act of displaying banners with devices, as a means of threats and intimidation, to prevent persons from entering into or continuing in the employment of the plaintiff, was injurious to the plaintiff, and illegal at common law and by statute. . . . It is not found that the inscriptions upon the banners were false, nor do they appear to have been in disparagement of the plaintiff's business. The scheme, in pursuance of which the banners were displayed and maintained, was to injure the plaintiff's business, not by defaming it to the public, but by intimidating workmen, so as to deter them from keeping or making engagements with the plaintiff. The banner was a standing menace to all who were or wished to be in the employment of the plaintiff, to deter them from entering the plaintiff's premises. Maintaining it was a continuous, unlawful act, injurious to the plaintiff's business and property, and was a nuisance, such as a court of equity will grant relief against." [33]

So it would appear from these cases, that the displaying of banners, transparencies, placards, or other devices, directly in front of one's place of business constitutes such an unlawful act as to warrant an injunction.

Passing now to the circulation of letters, posters and circulars, calculated to cause a withdrawal of customers, we find likewise a difference of opinion. There is, however, a majority and a minority holding. Of the latter, perhaps the best is the case of Casey *v.* Typographical Union, [34] which was a suit by the plaintiff, the proprietor and publisher of the *Commonwealth*, a daily and weekly newspaper, to restrain the publication and circulation of posters, handbills, and circulars printed and circulated in pursuance of a combination to boycott. In granting the injunction prayed for, the court said: "The editorial in the Bulletin of December 1st declares that the boycott 'is still on, and will be until the proprietor of the 'rat' sheet employs union men.' It requests all 'K. of L., assemblies, unions, and workingmen to bear in mind that Mr. Casey refused to employ or in any way recognize organized labor.' It asks their aid in compelling complainant to recognize the rights of labor by withdrawing their patronage from his paper, and if possible let him know why. It calls upon them not to patronize any merchants who advertise in complainant's newspaper, and if they see the paper in any place of business to refuse to buy goods unless the merchant immediately stops the 'rat' sheet. The communication sent by the union on the 3d of November to Messrs. Griffin, agents for the sale of complainant's paper, contains the following: 'This union will consider it a great favor for you to give up the agency of the *Commonwealth*. If you do not do so, we will have to consider you the enemy of organized labor.' These are fair samples, and they indicate the method by which the boycott was to be made effective. Yet counsel say that there were no threats; that the defendants were only exercising their constitutional right to freely speak and publish their opinions; that what defendants have done is a necessary and natural and proper incident of bitter, but yet lawful, competition, and that this was only fair argument and persuasion. These propositions are in direct conflict with decisions made long ago, and recognized in all subsequent cases."

In a very recent New York case, [35] where the court had under consideration publications of the same nature, it was held that "striking employees of a publishing company and the local unions of which they are members have the right to publish circulars setting forth the circumstances of the strike, and requesting that their friends shall withhold patronage from the company." The New York opinion, written by Judge Blanchard, is certainly well-reasoned, and, I believe, indicates an inclination on the part of the court to allow greater privileges to labor than had theretofore been allowed.

To sum up, then, the attitude of the courts toward the application of the injunction to prevent strikes and boycotts, we find:

First. An injunction will not issue to prevent a strike, even though there may be a combination in order to secure a simultaneous cessation of work of a great number of employees, but will issue to prevent persons, not parties to the controversy, from inciting a strike of employees otherwise satisfied with their employment.

Second. There is a division of opinion as to the right of an injunction to prevent boycotts, some courts holding that it should properly issue to prevent the use of means to make effective the boycotts, while others have refused to grant injunctive relief.

Third. There would seem to be a tendency on the part of courts to be a bit more liberal toward labor in the matter of combination than formerly, for the reason that changed industrial conditions, resulting in combination of capital, also require a combination in labor to insure equal ground to both.

W. F. MEIER.

[31] *Citing* Allis Chalmers Co. *v.* Reliable Lodge, 111 Fed. Rep. 264; U. S. *v.* Haggerty, *supra*; Frank *v.* Herold, *supra*.
[32] 147 Mass. 212; 17 N. E. Rep. 307.
[33] *Citing* Gilbert *v.* Mickle, 4 Sandf. Ch. 357; Spinning Co. *v.* Riley, L. R. 6 Eq. 551.
[34] 45 Fed. Rep. 135.
[35] Butterick Pub. Co. *v.* Typographical Union, 100 N. Y. S. 292.

UNIVERSAL CITATIONS FOR ALL OPINIONS.

UNDER the present system of reporting decisions the most annoying and confusing feature is the fact that the same case will be found cited sometimes to one book, sometimes to another, and frequently to three or four. Uncertainty as to whether the same opinion is referred to leads often to a needless examination of the same case twice. At other times the particular publication cited not being available, one must make a laborious search through complex and perhaps incomplete tables of parallel references. What is needed is one universal citation for every opinion.

The whole difficulty has arisen from the fact that often the official citation is not known until weeks, months, or even years, after the appearance of the decision in some unofficial series. Even when known, the citation, under the present method, by volume and page of the official reporter, furnishes no key to the position of the case in the unofficial series. This condition has now grown to a magnitude unbearable to the publishers and to their patrons.

The addition of a dozen ems type measure, which is necessitated by the giving of two citations, correspondingly increased when three or more citations are given, amounts in the aggregate every year to hundreds or even thousands of pages in the law books offered to the profession. To provide these "parallel citations" entails large expense on the publishers, who are obliged to provide expensive and complex tables of cases, and to keep the same constantly revised as the cases appear in the official series. It requires them to expend much time and labor in verifying all of these citations. It involves additional expense for composition and paper, and all this expense must in the end be borne by the buyer of the books. He, instead of profiting by it, only finds his labors magnified and the complexity of his search increased.

After many years' experience as a publisher, the writer has reached the conclusion that this difficulty, like many others, arises out of complexity and artificiality, and may be solved by a return to simplicity of methods.

Reported decisions are nothing more nor less than official documents which are publicly recorded. Like other public records they must be systematically kept, and common experience has fixed upon the numerical system as perhaps the best and simplest method of keeping impersonal data. Viewed thus, does it not seem strange that courts which file and docket their pending cases according to numbers should not record their precedents in a similar way? Especially since this will enable any one having studied a case in any publication, or indeed in manuscript, to cite it as though it had already appeared in the official volume. The reporting number or citation, being known when the case is filed, will attach and appear in any and all copies and publications thereof. The use of the name of the case and the volume and page of the report, although not necessarily discontinued, can be ignored, or not, according to circumstances.

The plan, while possessing the merit of simplicity, is not open to the objection of untried novelty. Some years ago the writer, then a member of the West Publishing Company, conceived the publication of the Federal Cases, comprising those variously reported, as well as unreported, federal decisions antedating the Federal Reporter. Until so published, this was probably the most inaccessible body of case law in America, and yet the plan of citing the cases therein, as for example, "Fed. Cas. No. 6833," though lacking official sanction, has proved entirely satisfactory. It is submitted that the numerical system would prove far more satisfactory when generally adopted as the official method of citation, and the writer invites and desires the co-operation of members of the bar in securing this reform.

All that is needed to effect it is a legislative enactment, or a rule of court, providing that in the future the decisions as handed down shall be consecutively numbered in the order in which they are rendered. This should begin at the close of any volumes of reports which at the time were in process of completion. It should be provided that the number so given should be the official mode of citing the case. Thus, "Ala. No. 432." It should be provided that the decisions should be reported and published in their numerical order, and the bound volumes of reports should bear appropriate labels showing the number of the first and last cases therein contained. The volumes should be paged according to the present method of paging, but the number of the case ought also to appear at the head of each page. Under this plan the decisions rendered without opinion, the "memorandum decisions," and the "decisions not to be reported" ought to appear, even if only by title, in their regular order and be numbered.

It seems certain that unofficial reporters covering but one State would at once adopt the official numerical system for their own publications. The unofficial reporters which cover more than one State, and the various series of selected cases, even now strive to segregate the cases of each State. No doubt they would follow the numerical order so far as possible. A simple numerical table in the front of each volume as published, and appropriate labels, would do away with the troublesome, complex, and necessarily more or less incomplete tables now furnished in other volumes.

Another advantage lies in the fact that the numerical system would make possible the giving of the official citation in all those works of permanent character which must now either leave out the official citations or leave out the new cases because not yet published in the official series. In short, each case would be marked and identified unchangeably and unmistakably by one citation, authentic, universal, and immediately available. JOHN B. WEST, *in Current Law.*

Cases of Interest.

STATUTE AGAINST COMBINATION OF EMPLOYERS UPHELD. — In Joyce *v.* Great Northern R. Co., 110 N. W. Rep. 975, the Minnesota Supreme Court holds that a statute declaring it unlawful for two or more employers of labor to combine or confer together for the purpose of preventing any person from procuring employment is not unconstitutional as being class legislation.

BARBER SHOP NOT A PUBLIC PLACE. — In Faulkner *v.* Solazzi, 65 Atl. Rep. 947, the Connecticut Supreme Court of Errors holds that a barber shop is not a "place of public accommodation" within the meaning of a statute authorizing the recovery of double damages for discrimination against negroes by the proprietors of places of public accommodation.

TRAILING BY BLOODHOUND. — In State *v.* Hunter, 56 S. E. Rep. 547, the North Carolina Supreme Court held that in an arson case evidence that a bloodhound followed tracks, which a witness testified were the defendant's tracks, and at a certain point on the trail appeared to catch the scent of something in the air, whereupon he broke off through the woods and finally treed the defendant, was competent to corroborate the testimony as to the identity of the tracks.

CANCELLATION OF MARRIED WOMAN'S DEED — IN PARI DELICTO. — In Burton *v.* McMillan, 42 So. Rep. 849, the Federal Supreme Court holds that the maxim *in pari delicto* should not be applied to a case where a married woman sues to set aside a deed of her separate property made by her under express or implied threats of the prosecution of her husband, and to save him from prosecution, whether the threatened prosecution was lawful or unlawful, when she was sick and nervous and when she does not appear to have had abundant opportunity for consideration and consultation with disinterested advisers. Citing 6 Am. & Eng. Encyc. of Law (2d ed.) 416, 417.

Practicing Medicine — What Constitutes. — In People v. Allcutt, 102 N. Y. Supp. 678, the New York Appellate Division, First Department, held that a person who held himself out by sign and card as a "doctor," with office hours, who prescribed no drugs, but consulted with his patients, diagnosed their ailments, prescribed diet, conduct, and remedies, and gave treatment by manipulation with the fingers, professing to cure without drugs all diseases that physicians could cure with drugs and many that they could not cure and who took payment for his services, was practicing medicine within a statute making it a misdemeanor to practice without a license.

Power of Corporation to Purchase Its Own Stock. — In Knickerbocker Importation Co. v. State Board of Assessors, 65 Atl. Rep. 913, the New Jersey Court of Errors and Appeals holds that the implied grant of power under the Corporation Act of New Jersey to corporations to purchase their own stock "for legitimate corporate purposes" does not authorize the acquisition by a corporation of its own stock for the purpose of creating so-called treasury stock. In the course of an instructive opinion, Dill, J., said: "Neither bookkeeping nor mere recitative language in resolutions of a board of directors creating values can be accepted as the equivalent of the proof of *bona fide* value required by our statute when stock is issued for property purchased."

Liberty of the Press — Account of Execution. — The right of the State to prohibit the publication by newspapers of any account of the details of the execution of the death penalty upon criminals was upheld by the Minnesota Supreme Court in State v. Pioneer Press Co., 110 N. W. Rep. 867. The defendant was indicted for publishing an account of an execution in violation of the statute, and demurred to the indictment, contending that the act was unconstitutional as infringing upon the liberty of the press. In affirming a judgment overruling the demurrer, the court held that the power to restrict the liberty of the press extended not only to matter of a distinctly blasphemous, obscene, seditious, or scandalous nature, but also to that of such character as naturally tended to excite the public mind and thus indirectly affect the public good, saying in part: "If, in the opinion of the legislature, it is detrimental to public morals to publish anything more than the mere fact that the execution has taken place, then, under the authorities and upon principle, the appellant was not deprived of any constitutional right in being so limited."

Strikers' Right to Picket. — The right of striking workmen to post pickets for the purpose of peaceably persuading others to quit work or to refuse employment is upheld by the Circuit Court for the western district of the northern Ohio district in Pope Motor Car Co. v. Keegan, 150 Fed. Rep. 148, and by the Circuit Court for the eastern district of Wisconsin in Allis-Chalmers Co. v. Iron Moulders' Union, 150 Fed. Rep. 155. In both cases, however, the courts hold that the right is subject to strict limitations, and that if the pickets are so numerous that their presence itself amounts to an intimidation, or their conduct is of such a threatening nature as to create fear and alarm among the persons solicited, thus virtually amounting to coercion, then the strikers are outside their legal rights. In the latter case Judge Sanborn, after reviewing the decisions at length, reaches the conclusion that the constant maintenance of pickets after repeated acts of violence, the use of abusive epithets, and the creation by the pickets of an unfriendly atmosphere surrounding workmen, constitute a criminal conspiracy.

Juvenile Courts — Constitutional Rights of Parents. — In People v. McLain, 80 N. E. Rep. 244, the Illinois Supreme Court has rendered an important decision as to the power of juvenile courts to commit delinquent children to State institutions. The court holds that, where parents provide their child with a comfortable and moral home, supply it with school facilities and moral training, and are ready to render it all the duties of parents, a commitment of such child to an institution for delinquent children on the sole ground that it has been found guilty of a misdemeanor in proceedings to which the parents are not parties, is an infringement of the parents' constitutional right of the pursuit of happiness and a deprivation of their property rights in the child's services without due process of law. The court is careful to point out that where the circumstances require it the right of the parent must be deemed "secondary to that of the general public as organized for the safety and welfare of mankind," but holds that the "extraordinary exigency which may justify the State in supplanting the father as the natural custodian and protector of his son" was not shown to exist in this particular case.

Extortion by Officer of Labor Union. — In People v. Weinsheimer, 102 N. Y. Supp. 579, the New York Appellate Division, First Department, sustained a conviction of the president of a local labor union of extortion. It was shown that the defendant refused to permit a resumption of work on a building until he was paid an amount of money which he demanded from the plumbing contractor, and that after such payment the work proceeded without interruption. The court held that it was sufficient to sustain a conviction that it appeared that the contractor would have sustained damage if the money had not been paid, without proof of the amount of such damages; and that it was immaterial whether the money paid over belonged to the contractor or the owner of the building. Evidence that before the contractor obtained the work and while it was being performed by another, who was subsequently compelled to surrender it, the defendant obtained an introduction to one of the owners of the building and requested a payment of $3,000 in consideration of a non-strike guaranty during the performance of the plumbing work on the building, was held to be admissible generally to show a preconceived plan and determination on the defendant's part to commit the offense and was not limited to the issue of motive or intent.

Political Contributions by Corporate Officers. — By a bare majority of four to three the New York Court of Appeals has held, in People v. Moss, 80 N. E. Rep. 383, that the contribution of corporate funds to a political campaign by officers of an insurance company does not *prima facie* constitute larceny under the New York statutes. The facts of the case, which have been made widely familiar through the newspapers, are as follows: President McCall of the New York Life Insurance Company, having promised to contribute up to $50,000 to the Republican campaign committee in 1904, requested George W. Perkins, one of the vice-presidents, to make the payment personally, promising that he would later be reimbursed from the funds of the corporation. Mr. Perkins made the payment, and subsequently, the president having brought the matter to the attention of the finance committee, which expressed itself as of the opinion that Mr. Perkins should be reimbursed from the funds of the company, thereafter President McCall, under his authority to pay out the company's money on executive order, caused such reimbursement to be made without further action on the part of the finance committee or trustees of the company. In proceedings for the arrest of Mr. Perkins for the larceny of such fund the proof showed that he had derived no personal advantage from the money, and that it was paid by him in the honest belief that he was benefiting the insurance company. Gray, J., writing the majority opinion, took the ground that, there being no evidence of an attempt to defraud, the facts did not establish *prima facie* the commission of larceny. With him concurred Judges O'Brien, E. T. Bartlett, and Hiscock, the latter delivering an opinion. Dissenting opinions were written by Cullen, C. J., and Werner, J., with whom Chase, J., concurred.

Book Reviews.

GOOD SCOTCH.

The Trial of Deacon Brodie. Edited by William R. Roughead, Writer to the Signet. Canada Law Book Co., Toronto.

This is the fifth and latest volume of the series devoted to Notable Scottish Trials. The preceding volumes report the trials of Madeleine Smith, Directors of the Bank of Glasgow, Dr. Pritchard, E. M. Chantrelle. The books are handsomely printed and illustrated.

It was in August, 1788, that Brodie was indicted and tried for theft, attended with house-breaking. He was found guilty and, according to the law of that time, suffered the death penalty. It was in the city of Edinborough that Deacon Brodie played his two-fold part — by day a substantial and respected citizen and member of the town council, by night a roysterer, gambler, and cracksman. The psychologic interest of his character and the dramatic elements of his career have led to the suggestion that he was the original Dr. Jekyll and Mr. Hyde. It is certain that Stevenson was interested in Brodie's career and actually wrote a play founded upon it. The report of the trial given in this volume is prepared from the original record, with additional particulars from contemporary sources. The story is well told, and to the lawyer it is notable as affording a singularly graphic view of the old-time practice in the Scottish criminal courts. The appendix contains an account of the judges and counsel engaged in the trial, and we lift therefrom the following anecdotes concerning this galaxy of legal talent:

Robert Macqueen, Lord Braxfield, who presided, was the last of the Scottish judges who rigidly adhered to the old "braid Scots." "Hae ye ony counsel, man?" said he to Margarot when placed at the bar. "Dae ye want tae hae ony appintit?" "No," replied Margarot, "I only want an interpreter to make me understand what your lordship says." Strong built and dark, with rough eyebrows, powerful eyes, threatening lips, and a low, growling voice, he was like a formidable blacksmith. His accent and his dialect were exaggerated Scotch; his language, like his thoughts, short, strong, and conclusive. Despising the growing improvement of manners, he shocked the feelings even of an age which, with more of the formality, had far less of the substance of decorum than our own. Thousands of his sayings have been preserved, and the staple of them is indecency, which he succeeded in making many people enjoy, or at least endure, by hearty laughter, energy of manner, and rough humor. He domineered over the prisoners, the counsel, and his colleagues alike. Devoid of even a pretense to judicial decorum, he delighted while on the bench in the broadest jests and the most insulting taunts, over which he would chuckle the more from observing that correct people were shocked. Yet this was not from cruelty, for which he was too strong and too jovial, but from cherished coarseness. Gerald, at his trial, ventured to say that Christianity was an innovation, and that all great men had been reformers, "even our Saviour himself." "Muckle he made o' that," chuckled Braxfield; "he was hangit." On another occasion he remarked to an eloquent culprit at the bar, "Ye're a vera clever chiel, man, but ye wad be nane the waur o' a hangin'." Of Braxfield's grim humor in its unprofessional aspect but a few samples are now tolerable. Among these, however, is the following: When a butler gave up his place because his mistress was always scolding him, "Lord," exclaimed his master, "ye've little tae complain o'; be thankfu' ye're no marriet till her." "Out of the bar or off the bench," says Stevenson, "he was a convivial man, a lover of wine, and one who shone peculiarly at tavern meetings." When Lord Newton, then Charles Hay, was one morning pleading before him, after a night of hard drinking — the opposing counsel being in the like case — Braxfield observed: "Gentlemen, ye maun just pack up yer papers and gang hame; the tane o' ye's riftin' punch, and the ither's belchin' claret; there'll be nae guid got oot o' ye the day."

Sir David Rae, Lord Eskgrove, was another of the judges. "A more ludicrous personage," says Cockburn, "could not exist. To be able to give an anecdote of Eskgrove, with a proper imitation of his voice and manner, was a sort of fortune in society. Scott in those days was famous for this particularly. Yet never once did he do or say anything which had the slightest claim to be remembered for any intrinsic merit. The value of all his words and actions consisted in their absurdity." In the trial of Glengarry for murder in a duel, a lady of great beauty was called as a witness. She came into court veiled, but before administering the oath Eskgrove gave her this exposition of her duty: "Young woman, you will now consider yourself as in the presence of Almighty God and of this High Court. Lift up your veil, throw off all modesty, and look me in the face." Cockburn also narrates that, having to condemn certain prisoners who had broken into the house of Luss and assaulted and robbed the inmates, Eskgrove first, as was his almost constant practice, explained the nature of the various crimes, assault, robbery, and hamesucken — of which last he gave them the etymology; he next reminded them that they had attacked the house and the persons within it, and robbed them, and then came to his climax — "All this you did, and God preserve us! joost when they were sitten doon tae their denner!" On condemning a tailor to death for stabbing a soldier, the learned judge aggravated the offense thus: "And not only did you murder him, whereby he was bereaved of his life, but you did thrust, or push, or pierce, or project, or propel, the lethal weapon through the bellyband of his regimental breeches, which were His Majesty's!" Lockhart states that in Scott's young days at the bar he was counsel for the appellant in a case before Eskgrove concerning a cow which his client had sold as sound. In opening his case Scott stoutly maintained the healthiness of the animal, which, he said, had merely a cough. "Stop there," quoth the judge; "I have had plenty healthy kye in my time, but I never heard o' ane o' them coughin'. A coughin' cow! that will never do — sustain the sheriff's judgment, and decern!"

Charles Hay, afterwards Lord Newton, one of the counsel for Brodie, was "a man famous for law, paunch, whist, claret, and worth." "In private life he was known as 'The Mighty.' He was a bulky man with short legs, twinkling eyes, and a large purple visage; no speaker, but an excellent legal writer and adviser. Honest, warm-hearted, and considerate, he was always true to his principles and his friends. But these and other good qualities were all apt to be lost sight of in people's admiration of his drinking. His daily and flowing cup raised him far above the evil days of sobriety on which he had fallen, and made him worthy of having quaffed with the Scandinavian heroes." On the bench he frequently indulged in a certain degree of lethargy, and on one occasion a young counsel, who was pleading before the division, confident of a favorable judgment, stopped his argument, remarking to the other judges on the bench, "My lords, it is unnecessary that I should go on, as Lord Newton is fast asleep." "Ay, ay," cried Newton, "you will have proof of that by and by," when, to the astonishment of the young advocate, after a most luminous review of the case, he gave a very decided and elaborate judgment against him. The following story, says Chambers, was once told of Lord Newton by Dr. Gregory to King George the Third, who laughed at it very heartily. A country client coming to town to see him, when at the bar, upon some business, found on inquiry that the best time for the purpose was at four o'clock, just before Hay sat down to dinner. He accordingly called at the counsel's house at that hour, but was informed that Mr. Hay was then at dinner, and could not be disturbed. He returned the following day earlier in the afternoon, when to his surprise the servant repeated his former statement. "At dinner!" cried the enraged applicant; "did you not tell me that four was his dinner-hour, and now it wants a quarter of it!" "Yes, sir," said the servant, "but it is not his *this day's*, but his *yesterday's* dinner that Mr. Hay is engaged with. So you are rather too early than too late." It is said that Newton often spent the night in all manner of convivial indulgences, drove home about seven o'clock in the morning, slept two hours, and, mounting the bench at the usual time, showed himself perfectly well qualified to perform his duty. His lordship was also so exceedingly fond of card-playing that it was humorously remarked, "Cards were his profession, and the law only his amusement."

John Clerk, afterwards Lord Eldin, was one of the counsel for George Smith, who was indicted jointly with Brodie. In appearance Clerk was singularly plain; he was also very lame, one of his legs being shorter than the other; and his inattention to dress was proverbial. It is related that when walking down the High Street one day from the court he overheard a young lady saying to her companion rather loudly, "There goes Johnnie Clerk, the lame lawyer," upon which he turned round and said, "Na, madam, I may be a lame man, but no' a lame lawyer." Clerk was of a convivial disposition, and the contrast between the crabbed lawyer and the good-natured *bon vivant* was strongly marked. He was a member of the Bannatyne Club, of which Sir Walter Scott was president. On one occasion, after the anniversary dinner, he is said to have fallen down stairs and injured his nose, which necessitated his wearing a patch upon the organ for some time afterwards. On a learned friend inquiring how the accident happened, Clerk replied that it was the effect of his studies. "Studies!" ejaculated the inquirer. "Yes," growled Clerk; "ye've heard, nae doot, about *Coke upon Littleton*, but I suppose ye never heard tell o' *Clerk upon Stair!*"

OUTLINES OF CRIMINAL LAW.

Outlines of Criminal Law. By Courtney Stanhope Kenney, LL.D. American edition by James H. Webb, B. S., LL.B. New York. The Macmillan Company. 1907. 404 pp.

The present edition omits certain portions of the original work dealing with modern English statutes and rules thought not to be of general importance to the American student, and is, in short, a revision of that work for use by American students and readers. The original edition embodies, as is stated in its preface, the substance of lectures delivered by its author, Mr. Kenney (changed to "Kinney" in the preface to the American edition), at the University of Cambridge, from time to time, throughout a quarter of a century. The position and experience of the author, who is also favorably known as the author of Selected Cases on the Law of Crimes and of Torts, as well as the knowledge of the student's requirements which the editor of the American edition, as instructor in the law department of Yale, may be presumed to possess, warrant the expectation that the present volume is peculiarly adapted to the needs of the American student and teacher of criminal law.

The opening chapters discuss, in the order named, The Nature of a Crime; The Mental Element in Crime; Exemptions from Responsibility; Inchoate Crimes; and Possible Parties to a Crime. The chapters on The Mental Element in Crime and Exemptions from Responsibility, the latter embracing the subjects of infancy, insanity, intoxication, corporations, mistake, and compulsion, are perhaps of more than usual interest. Notwithstanding the number and importance of the subjects treated, the significance of each as bearing on criminal responsibility is instructively stated. These chapters also very well illustrate the system of orderly arrangement of matter which is preserved throughout the volume; Roman numbers, Arabic numbers, and letters being employed to indicate the divisions and subdivisions of the text.

The greater portion of the book is devoted to specific crimes. The author uses for the order of treatment the classification of crimes adopted by Serjeant Stephen, which divides them into offenses against the persons of individuals, offenses against the property of individuals, and offenses against public rights. Offenses against the person are taken up in the order of those which are fatal and those not fatal, the latter being classified in turn as the nonsexual and sexual. The offenses against the property of individuals are arson, burglary, larceny, embezzlement, false pretenses, and forgery, each of which offenses is made the subject of a chapter. Several chapters are then devoted to crimes against the safety of the state, the most important of which are treason, perjury, crimes against sexual morality, offenses against international law, and statutory crimes such as bribery, official misconduct, and breaking prison. The order in which the various crimes are discussed is logical, and the amount of space given to each impresses one as being in proportion to its importance to the student.

Following the treatment of specific crimes are two chapters entitled respectively, Modes of Judicial Proof, and The General Rules of Evidence. The discussion at this point becomes more general, and is applicable to both civil and criminal cases. For the collegiate student of law, whose course would necessarily include a work on the law of evidence of far more exhaustive character than any treatment here possible, these chapters probably have less value than the portions of the work dealing with the substantive law of crime. The chapter on The General Rules of Evidence is of exceedingly wide scope, all the following subjects coming in for a share of attention: burden of proof; the manner in which testimonial proof is given; leading questions; the necessity that a witness speak only from his memory and not from his reason; the relevancy of evidence; the best evidence rule; hearsay evidence; competency of the witness; privileges of the witness; proof of documents. These chapters are valuable, however, as far as they go, and no doubt help the beginner to understand properly the following chapter on Rules of Evidence Peculiar to Criminal Law. The volume concludes with a chapter on Limitations on Criminal Jurisdiction, considered with reference to time and territory.

The style of the book is simple and precise. The language is that of the instructor endeavoring in the clearest manner possible to impart his ideas to his pupil. As might be expected in a work of this character, there are frequent illustrations of the principles stated, and in the present work the illustrations used are particularly apt and striking. The belief of Mr. Kenney, expressed in the preface to his first English edition, that his long experience as lecturer at Cambridge had afforded him an opportunity to ascertain "what principles and what illustrations are so successful in arresting the attention and impressing the memory of students" as to be worth putting before them in a manual for their use, is undoubtedly justified by the pages of this volume. The work should find favor in the particular field for which it is so well adapted.

TRIAL EVIDENCE.

Trial Evidence. A Synopsis of the Law of Evidence Generally Applicable to Trials. By Richard Lea Kennedy. St. Paul. Keefe-Davidson Co. 1906.

This law book is unique in not citing any reported cases. The American and English Encyclopædia of Law, and the leading works on Evidence are the sole authorities referred to. The text consists of condensed statements of those rules of evidence which are apt to arise at the trial — a practical codification of trial evidence. So far as tested these concise statements of the law are entirely accurate and in this form will be found useful to the trial lawyer. A special feature consists in leaving blank every other page for the noting of local decisions and statutes. The practitioner who will keep this little book at his right hand will find it profitable.

THE PENNSYLVANIA CONSTITUTION.

Messrs. T. & J. W. Johnson, of Philadelphia, have brought out a work which ought to be particularly welcomed by Pennsylvania lawyers — "Commentaries on the Constitution of Pennsylvania," by Thomas Raeburn White, of the Philadelphia Bar, and late assistant professor of law at the University of Pennsylvania. The author first states the principles by which the courts are guided in interpreting the constitution, and then, clause by clause, gives the construction placed by the courts upon particular provisions. The constitution as a whole is printed in the appendix together with references to the pages where the clauses are quoted and discussed.

News of the Profession.

The Minnesota State Bar Association held its annual meeting and dinner in St. Paul on April 2. Particulars will be given in this column next month.

Death of Prominent Maine Lawyer. — Hon. Thomas W. Vose, judge of the Bangor, Me., Municipal Court, died in that city March 23, aged seventy-nine years.

Lawyers of Three States to Meet in Memphis. — The State Bar Associations of Tennessee, Arkansas, and Mississippi will hold a joint meeting in Memphis on June 4, 5, and 6.

Sater, Not Adams, Got Ohio Judgeship. — In this column last month it was incorrectly stated that the new federal judgeship in Ohio had fallen to J. J. Adams. In fact the President appointed John E. Sater, of Columbus.

Well-known Colorado Lawyer Dead. — Judge Allen T. Gunnell, one of the best known members of the Colorado bar, died at his home in Colorado Springs on March 21 at the age of fifty-nine. He was at one time vice-president of the Colorado State Bar Association.

State Bar Associations to Meet. — The Mississippi State Bar Association is to hold its annual meeting in Vicksburg on May 14 and 15. The Maryland lawyers will gather at Ocean City July 3, 4, and 5. The Georgia Association will meet this year on May 30 and 31 in Savannah instead of Warm Springs.

Attorney-General of Mississippi Dies. — Hon. William Williams, attorney-general of Mississippi, died at Jackson, Miss., on March 22, after an illness of several weeks. Mr. Williams was but thirty-seven years old and was serving his fifth year in office. He was admitted to the bar in 1890.

The Officers of the Pennsylvania Bar Association for the Year 1907 are: president, Thomas Patterson, Allegheny; vice-presidents, Samuel W. Pennypacker, Montgomery; Francis J. O'Connor, Cambria; Frank M. Trexler, Lehigh; C. H. McCauley, Elk; Boyd Crumrine, Allegheny; secretary, William H. Staake, Philadelphia; treasurer, William Penn Lloyd, Cumberland (Mechanicsburg, Pa.).

Women Judges in Pennsylvania — Maybe. — A sensation was created in the Pennsylvania House of Representatives on March 18 when Representative Creasy, of Columbia, offered a bill providing that "women learned in the law are and shall be eligible to the office of judge in all courts of record in this commonwealth." The measure had not become a law at this writing.

Death of H. Clay Ewing. — H. Clay Ewing, who was attorney-general of Missouri from 1872 to 1874, and at one time a Supreme Court commissioner, died in Jefferson City, Mo., on March 22, aged seventy-nine. One of his greatest achievements as a lawyer was the conducting of the suit by the State of Missouri to set aside the sale of the Missouri Pacific Railroad property.

Nova Scotia's Chief Justice Retires. — Sir Robert Weatherbe, chief justice of Nova Scotia, resigned his position on March 19 on account of failing health. He is over seventy years of age and has been on the bench for nearly thirty years, having been appointed in 1878. In the year preceding his appointment he represented the Dominion of Canada before the fisheries commission which awarded $5,500,000 to Canada.

Vice-Chancellor Pitney Retires — His Successor. — On April 9 the venerable Vice-Chancellor Henry C. Pitney, of New Jersey, retired from the bench. Chancellor Magie has appointed James E. Howell, of Newark, to succeed him. Judge Howell has been practicing law in Newark since 1874, and was a member of the well-known firm of Cault & Howell. He is fifty-eight years old. His appointment has been received with favor by the New Jersey bar.

Made Attorney-General of Mississippi. — Governor Vardaman, of Mississippi, has appointed R. V. Fletcher to succeed the late Attorney-General Williams. For more than a year past Mr. Fletcher has held the office of assistant attorney-general, and owing to the ill health of his chief has been discharging practically all of the duties of the position to which he has now been promoted. Mr. Fletcher is a young man, being under forty years of age.

Death of J. Hubley Ashton. — J. Hubley Ashton, formerly assistant attorney-general of the United States and special counsel for the government in the Venezuela claims cases, died at his home in Washington, D. C., on March 14, aged seventy-one. Mr. Ashton was a native of Philadelphia and a graduate of the University of Pennsylvania. From 1861 to 1865 he was United States District Attorney for the Eastern District of Pennsylvania, and in the latter year was made assistant attorney-general, which office he held for three years. For several years Mr. Ashton was a professor of law in Georgetown University, but retired on account of ill health. He was one of the founders of the American Bar Association.

Maine Judge Resigns — His Successor. — On March 21 Hon. Frederick A. Powers, associate justice of the Supreme Judicial Court of Maine, tendered his resignation, to take effect March

31. Judge Powers was first appointed to the court on January 2, 1900, and received a re-appointment a few months ago. His resignation was a surprise to the bar of the State as well as a matter of regret, for he was regarded as one of the strongest members of the court. Governor Cobb filled the vacancy by appointing Leslie C. Cornish, of Augusta, one of the ablest and best-known lawyers in Maine. Judge Cornish is fifty-two years old, a graduate of Colby College and the Harvard Law School, and was admitted to the bar in 1880. Since his admission he has practiced his profession with marked success in Augusta. The appointment has been most favorably received throughout the State.

ILLINOIS SUPREME COURT JUDGE DEAD. — Hon. Jacob W. Wilkin, associate justice of the Supreme Court of Illinois, died April 3 in Danville, Ill., of Bright's disease. Judge Wilkin was seventy years old, having been born at Newark, Ohio, in 1837. His parents moved to Illinois in 1844 and he obtained his education at McKendree College at Lebanon, Ill. He served throughout the Civil War as a captain in the Federal army and was commissioned a major when mustered out. In 1879 he was elected a judge of the Fourth Circuit of Illinois and on being re-elected in 1885 was assigned to the Appellate Court of the Fourth District. Three years later he was promoted to the Supreme Court, where he served with distinction for eighteen years. He would have become chief justice of the court in June.

SOME FRENCHMEN FAVOR CAPITAL PUNISHMENT. — The proposed abolition of capital punishment in France appears to be encountering opposition in some parts of the country. At the close of the assizes at Bordeaux recently the jury of the Gironde department handed a resolution to the presiding judge in which they supported the appeal previously made by the jurymen of the Bouches du Rhône department in favor of the maintenance of capital punishment and the strict execution of sentences. They unanimously requested the presiding judge to transmit to the President of the Republic and the Minister of Justice their respectful request that capital punishment should be maintained and applied as the supreme and necessary penalty of French penal legislation.

TO HAVE NIGHT COURTS IN NEW YORK. — The movement towards keeping New York city "open all night" continues. As is well known there have been for many years a considerable number of places of refreshment and amusement open at all hours, and in the last few years business has been tending in the same direction. First came an all-night shoe store, then a day-and-night bank, and a month or so ago announcement was made of the formation of a corporation to supply legal services at all hours. Now the Board of Police Magistrates have unanimously declared in favor of night police courts to supply the demands of the city's large and growing nocturnal population. A bill looking to that end has been introduced into the State legislature and will probably meet with no opposition except from the professional bondsmen. The Boston magistrates have also been considering such a plan, but do not appear to think the present state of Boston's civilization demands night courts.

SOME CORRECT INFORMATION ABOUT SASKATCHEWAN. — In announcing in this column last month the establishment of a Supreme Court for the Canadian Province of Saskatchewan we undertook to inform our benighted readers where the said province was situated, and remarked in passing that it seemed peculiar that the sessions of the court were to be held at Regina, the capital of the adjacent Province of Assiniboia. To be perfectly candid, our knowledge regarding Saskatchewan was of an unusually vague and nebulous nature, and the statements were rashly made after a hurried glance at the atlas of the Century Dictionary. Many Canadian readers have sent in letters gently but firmly calling us down, and one encloses a very impressive map which proves conclusively that the amount of our ignorance about Saskatchewan is nothing short of scandalous. Apparently all that part of Canada has been shuffled about a whole lot since the Century Dictionary man was up there, and Saskatchewan now includes the most of what used to be Assiniboia as well as part of the former territory of Athabasca. Hereafter we are going to be mighty cautious about the geography of Canada.

WISCONSIN STATE BAR ASSOCIATION. — The twenty-ninth annual meeting of the Wisconsin State Bar Association was held in Milwaukee on March 12 and 13. At the same time the annual meeting of the District Attorneys' Association, a subsidiary organization, was also held. The address of President L. J. Nash to the Bar Association was on "Some Ideal States and Some Constitutional Ideals." A paper on "John Jay and the Treaty of 1794," was read by G. W. Hazleton, of Milwaukee, and Burr W. Jones, of Madison, discussed "The Homicide Problem in the United States." The annual address was delivered by John Barton Payne, of Chicago, who, without any particular text, discoursed on present-day conditions and some of the problems now confronting legislatures and courts. The meeting was closed with a banquet at which Howard L. Smith, of Madison, acted as toastmaster. Among those who responded to toasts were Hon. Joshua E. Dodge, of the Wisconsin Supreme Court, Frank M. Hoyt, of Milwaukee, Frank W. Hall, of Madison, and J. S. Anderson. Officers were elected for the ensuing term as follows: President, Burr W. Jones, of Madison; secretary, C. I. Haring, of Milwaukee; treasurer, John B. Sanborn, of Madison.

DELEGATES TO HAGUE CONFERENCE. — On April 12 announcement was made at the State Department at Washington of the personnel of the delegation from this country to the second Peace Conference which is to meet at The Hague on June 15. The delegates are Joseph H. Choate, ex-Ambassador to Great Britain; Gen. Horace Porter, ex-Ambassador to France; U. M. Rose, former president of the American Bar Association and now president of the Arkansas State Bar Association; David Jayne Hill, United States Minister to the Netherlands and former professor of international law at Rochester University; Brig.-Gen. George B. Davis, Judge Advocate-General of the United States Army and formerly professor of international law at the United States Military Academy; Rear-Admiral Charles S. Sperry, United States Navy, president of the Naval War College; William I. Buchanan, former Minister to Argentine and to Panama and chairman of the American delegation to the Rio conference. The secretary to the delegation is Chandler Hale, son of Senator Hale, of Maine, and formerly secretary of the United States embassy at Vienna. The expert in international law is James Brown Scott, solicitor of the Department of State, and the expert attaché is Charles Henry Butler, reporter of the United States Supreme Court. The delegation will sail from New York about May 15.

English Notes.

TO CLEAR UP ARREARS IN COURT OF APPEAL. — Owing to a great congestion of business in the Court of Appeal the Lord Chancellor has introduced a bill into the House of Lords to authorize the court, with the consent of the Lord Chancellor, to sit in divisions consisting of two judges.

SAFER TO STEAL THAN BUY ON CREDIT. — In the House of Lords recently Lord James of Hereford, in arguing for the restriction of the present power of the county courts to commit delinquent debtors to jail for contempt of court in not paying their debts, narrated an anecdote of two men who were discharged from prison at the same time. One said to the other: "What were you in for?" The reply was: "I got fourteen days for stealing a duck." "Why, that's odd," said the first one, "I have had forty days for not paying for one."

The Lord Justices Valiant Trenchermen. — In the course of a recent trial before Mr. Justice Darling the judge declined to make a requested ruling, saying that, if he did so, the Court of Appeal would say he was wrong. Counsel having expressed disagreement with this view, the judge said: "Well, you know the Court of Appeal as well as I do, perhaps better, for you see them at work, while I only meet them at luncheon." To which the barrister dryly replied: "Your lordship sees them at their best."

Insanity at Time of Trial. — In Scotland, during March, a man by the name of Brown was brought to trial on a charge of murder, and the public prosecutor took the position that the accused was insane and ought not to be tried. The defendant, however, maintained that he was innocent of the crime charged and that the Crown had no right to accuse him and then refuse to have him tried. No preliminary inquiry into his mental condition was held, and the trial jury found that the defendant was insane at the date, not of the crime, but of the trial. Thereupon he was consigned to an asylum for the criminal insane without having been found guilty of anything.

Tightening the Screws on Corporations. — The new Companies Act, now pending in Parliament, proposes to close up a good many openings for dishonesty in corporation management. One very healthy provision requires promoters either to issue a prospectus disclosing certain prescribed facts, or, in lieu of it, to file a statement containing all the facts which would have to be disclosed in a prospectus. Every company is also required to file an annual statement of its affairs — its assets and liabilities, and how their values are arrived at, in the form of a balance sheet. There are also sections imposing conditions on foreign corporations having a place of business in the United Kingdom.

The Edalji Inquiry. — Apparently the agitation over the case of George Edalji, the young lawyer convicted on a charge of maiming cattle, is not going to result in the expected public inquiry. The three members of the committee invited by the Home Secretary to conduct the inquiry — Sir Robert Romer, Sir Arthur Wilson, and Mr. Lloyd Wharton — all declined to undertake the task of acting as judge and jury to determine the guilt or innocence of Mr. Edalji. The chief objection urged by them was that the committee would have no power to compel the attendance of witnesses. Consequently the Home Secretary has modified the inquiry, and the committee is now examining the papers in the case with a view to advising the Home Secretary whether or not a free pardon should be granted to Edalji.

A Warning to Superstitious Editors. — The owners of "haunted" houses will doubtless learn with pleasure that, if the presence of the ghost diminishes the rental value of the premises, they can recover damages of the person who first discovered the said ghost and spread the tidings. At least an English jury has recently awarded a house-owner substantial damages against a newspaper publisher for disseminating the belief that his house was infested by restless spirits. The plaintiff brought an action for slander of title, alleging as special damage that by reason of the defendant's statement he had been unable to find a tenant for his house. The defendant being unable to produce either the ghost or satisfactory evidence of its presence in the house, the jury came to the conclusion that there wasn't any ghost — which was an unusually intelligent conclusion for a jury to arrive at.

Right of the Dog to One Bite. — The proverbial right of every dog to take one bite at a human being without creating any liability on the part of its owner appears to have been encroached upon by a recent decision in the English Divisional Court. It was not proved that the offending animal had actually bitten any one before it sank its teeth into the defendant's person, but in the trial court it was found that theretofore the dog had displayed symptoms of a desire to taste human gore, such as should have caused the owner to institute an inquiry into its mental state and take measures to protect the public against the possibility of a canine brainstorm. Consequently judgment was given in favor of the plaintiff and affirmed on appeal. The title of the case is Barnes *v.* Lucile. The ancient privilege of the dog to take one bite at cattle had already been taken away by an act which became effective on January 1, but humans were supposed to be still open to him.

Bench Changes. — Sir Richard Henn Collins has been promoted from Master of the Rolls to be a Lord of Appeal in Ordinary, in the place of the late Lord Davey. Lord Collins is sixty-four years old. He became a Queen's Counsel in 1883, was appointed a judge of the King's Bench Division in 1891, became a Lord Justice in 1897, and succeeded the late Sir A. L. Smith as Master of the Rolls in 1901. His successor as Master of the Rolls is Sir Herbert Cozens-Hardy, who has been a Lord Justice since 1901, three years prior to which time he had been appointed a judge of the Chancery Division. He is sixty-eight years of age. To close the gap thus created in the Court of Appeal Sir William Rann Kennedy has been promoted from the King's Bench Division to be a Lord Justice. He is sixty years old and has served in the King's Bench for fourteen years. The vacancy created in the King's Bench Division by this chain of promotions has been filled by the appointment of Mr. William Pickford, K. C. The new judge is fifty-seven years old, was called to the bar at the Inner Temple in 1874, and became a Queen's Counsel in 1893. From 1901 to 1904 he served as Recorder of Oldham, and in the latter year was made Recorder of Liverpool. At the bar he has long occupied a front place as a commercial lawyer. The *Law Journal* says of him that he "has the advantage of looking like a judge."

Rayner's Sentence Commuted. — Americans who are familiar with the supercilious manner in which the British are wont to comment on the administration of justice in this country cannot but find both satisfaction and amusement in the case of Horace George Rayner, who, on January 24, shot and killed William Whiteley, a millionaire merchant of London, and then fired a bullet into his own head. Rayner, it seems, claimed to be an illegitimate son of Whiteley, and it was brooding over the wrongs which he considered had been heaped upon him by his neglectful parent that led him to commit the crime. By dint of skilful surgical and medical attention the murderer's life was kept in him and finally he was patched up sufficiently to be brought before the bar of justice. Between the rising of the sun and the going down of the same a jury was impaneled, all the evidence was introduced, the lawyers summed up, a verdict of guilty was brought in, and the prisoner was duly sentenced to death. Comparisons with the interminable Thaw trial of course proved irresistible and the English newspapers promptly took occasion to thank God on the street corners that they were not as other men. But almost immediately an uneasy feeling began to pervade the British public that justice had been a bit too expeditious in this instance, and the Home Secretary was soon the recipient of a mammoth petition bearing hundreds of thousands of signatures, wherein he was requested to extend clemency to Rayner. In consequence it was announced on March 30 that, obedient to the popular clamor, the Home Secretary had recommended commutation of the sentence to life imprisonment. But, not satisfied with this concession, a considerable portion of the British public has kept up a clamor for a further reduction of the sentence to a few years of imprisonment, and their agitation bids fair to prove successful. All of which must needs bring a complacent smile to the American face.

Obiter Dicta.

WHAT IS IT, IF NOT SOCIAL? — In Schroeder v. State, 99 S. W. Rep. 1003, the Texas Court of Criminal Appeals holds that the persons assembled in a barroom do not constitute a "social gathering" within the meaning of a statute prohibiting the carrying of a pistol into a social gathering.

A NATURAL MISTAKE. — From Italy comes this story of a litigant who, having to go on a journey while his case was pending in court, instructed his lawyer to let him know the result by telegraph. After several days he received the following message: "Right has triumphed." He at once telegraphed back: "Appeal immediately."

A GENUINE LUXURY. — In rendering a judgment for the sum of two dollars a Buffalo, N. Y., judge recently remarked: "I am compelled to find for the plaintiff for a small amount — far too small to justify a litigation between two busy men; but they have both had the satisfaction of employing lawyers and trying the case a full day, and now the court hopes they will have the pleasure of paying them."

TAKE NO STOCK IN BRAINSTORMS. — In these days of "unwritten law" and "brainstorms," the following language used recently by the Pennsylvania Supreme Court in affirming a conviction of murder is worth noting: "Indulgent as the law of Pennsylvania is in favor of the accused, it has never tolerated, nor is likely to tolerate, a doctrine of transitory frenzy as a defense to murder." From which we take it that the great, original brainstorm was in luck in moving to New York before getting into action.

A CRIMINAL CONSPIRACY. — The members of the Lauderdale county (Ala.) bar who indulge in criminal practice appear to have fallen upon evil days. According to a dispatch, dated March 21, every prisoner who had come up for trial in the three preceding days of the then current term had pleaded guilty without employing counsel, and the conspiracy among the malefactors to take the bread out of the legal mouths was assuming alarming proportions. The lawyers down there are thoroughly disgusted with the behavior of the criminal classes.

A PUBLIC BENEFACTOR. — During the trial of a murder case in Jersey City, recently, one of the jurors, John G. Snyder, arose in the jury box and, addressing the judge, said: "May it please the court, I have noticed that the opposing counsel have engaged in a great deal of facetious repartee during the progress of this case. A murder trial is a very serious proceeding, and I would suggest that the lawyers be instructed to eliminate all witticisms at each other's expense." The witticisms which aroused Mr. Snyder's resentment were not reported in the press accounts, but it is good betting that there was plenty of cause for complaint.

A HOT ONE. — This from a correspondent who apparently feels rather deeply on the subject. The italics are his: "How much better is a *watered-stock corporation* lawyer than what you from your self-styled superior moral altitude are pleased to call "an ambulance-chaser"? Your infernal swindling *in-*

surance and *watered* corporation shysters are a damned sight worse than any other class of professional men anywhere, and you ought to, and *do*, know it as well as anybody else, if you only had the *decency* to admit it. Whenever any one dares to even *look* towards a corporation all such as you instantly cry out 'anarchist" and similar idiotic expressions."

Providential Intervention. — A correspondent sends in the following clipping from a West Virginia newspaper. Although outside the legitimate scope of our museum, it seems to be worthy of preservation:

Notice.

In my failure to secure a buyer for my entire stock of goods, I feel that it is the will of the dear Heavenly Father that I shall continue in the business instead of going on a farm. So I have already ordered, and am still ordering, more new goods, which will be on in a few days.

I respectfully beg a continuance of the patronage of my many friends and customers with whom I have had such pleasant dealings for many years.

Yours anxious to serve,

J. C. Loury,
Huntersville, W. Va.

A Puzzler. — A correspondent contributes to our museum an envelope bearing the following strange device:

Return in Five Days to

ATTORNEY-AT-LAW.
LIVINGSTON, TEXAS

To the first of our readers who fails to guess what the lawyer's name is we shall present a handsome gold-plated oil-stove.

Law Notes

JUNE, 1907.

PUBLISHED BY EDWARD THOMPSON COMPANY.
NORTHPORT, LONG ISLAND, N. Y.

CONTENTS.

SOME time ago a paragraph was going the rounds of the newspapers to the effect that the aged Senator Whyte, of Maryland, had just scored his eightieth success in defending clients under indictment for murder. The fact was the basis of much editorial moralizing and head-wagging. One paper observed that "it is not unfair to assume that the majority of these accused clients were guilty of some degree of the crime with which they stood charged." Another sighed that the senator had "done his full share of harm in the world" and had been "a great force in bringing the law into contempt." A third opined that such a record was rather a source of disgrace than of congratulation. Senator Whyte is amply able to defend his own conduct from such insinuations, and the comments are quoted as a typical expression of the attitude of the lay mind toward the problems of professional ethics, and the readiness to condemn the solution approved by the judgment and the practice of lawyers. In the first place it seems absolutely impossible to eradicate the notion which lies unformulated at the basis of such comments that a guilty defendant in a criminal case is not entitled to counsel, and that the lawyer who undertakes his defense degrades himself, and to that extent lowers his profession. It is our boast that we live under "a government of laws, not of men," and the accused is entitled to demand an acquittal or a conviction according to law. According to law he is entitled to counsel, and it is the duty of that counsel to see that before he is pronounced guilty every real and every technical requirement of the law is complied with. If we are indeed living under a government of law, the accused is entitled to the benefit of even the technicalities that the law has created. It is surely a monstrous paradox to say that by insisting upon compliance with the law to the crossing of the last *t* or the dotting of the last *i* one is undermining the respect for law. If for a moment we could conceive of counsel failing to avail themselves of technical defenses for their clients on the theory that substantial justice was being done, we should be but a little way from such substantial justice as was meted out in the attainder of Sir John Fenwick (whose case forms a stirring episode in Macaulay's History), because his friends had spirited away one of the two witnesses necessary for his conviction of treason.

THE *locus classicus* on the question of a lawyer's right to appear in a cause which he regards as bad is, as every one knows, contained in a conversation between Dr. Johnson and Boswell. The sturdy common sense of the "great moralist" solved the question in a way all the more impressive because he was not a lawyer. And yet in a recent issue of a great newspaper the fact that Johnson was no lawyer was referred to as if it detracted from the weight of his opinion. Truly a curious idea. But if the opinions of lawyers are desired, that of the late Lord Chancellor of England, Lord Halsbury, may perhaps have weight. He characterized as "ridiculous, impossible of performance, and calculated to lead to great injustice," the thesis "that an advocate is bound to convince himself by something like an original investigation that his client is in the right before he undertakes the duty of acting for him." To do so, he added, would be "usurping the office of the judge, by which I mean the judicial function, whether that function is performed by a single man or by the composite arrangement of judge and jury which finds favor with us." When the whole theory of our law, the conduct of trials, and the nature of an advocate's duties are remembered, all this seems too clear for any possible difference of opinion. The lawyer must, of course, stoop to no connivance at an unlawful or guilty method of defense, nor must he lie by stating or intimating to the jury his own individual opinion that the defendant is guiltless. Even though his client is guilty, it is his right and duty to present to the jury the evidence in the most favorable aspect for the prisoner, and to avail himself of all technical advantages. According to our system of administering justice, truth is struck out between the opposing arguments of counsel each of whom presents his side of the case as strongly as he can. The ultimate decision rests not with the counsel, but with court and jury. The system may admit of improvement, but as it is the advocate must act for his client with all the ability of which he is master. And by so doing he discharges his duty not only toward the client but to society at large.

THE impression seems general that the ethical code of the lawyer is in urgent need of revision, and that unless from the superior heights of other vocations benevolent warnings are uttered and a helping hand is extended he is like to sink down under the weight of his own immorality. Some of the leading members of his own profession are lending color to the benevolent efforts of those who would aid him in forming a new and higher ideal of conduct. In a recent speech before the Ethical Culture Society of New York Mr. Justice Brewer managed, it seems to us, to convey about as many misapprehensions of the honorable lawyer's position as is possible in the same number of words. Among other things he is represented in the New York *Times* as saying: "The old idea that a lawyer must be all that his client wishes is passing away. He has no right to barter his own integrity, to sell his honor or his conscience. A lie has no place in a court room, and half a truth is, as we all know, often the worst kind of a lie. A verdict won by a falsehood is a disgrace to the counsel, and equally so a verdict won by a trick. That success is really a defeat, for it makes a profession consecrated to the pursuit of justice an instrument of injustice." The plain inference which the lay members of the Society for Ethical Culture would draw from the eminent justice's words was that according to the "old idea" it is the approved practice for a lawyer to "barter his integrity," "to sell his conscience," "to lie," "to win verdicts by falsehood," and so forth, at the bidding of any scoundrel who should employ him. Of course the learned justice knows that this never was the case and never will be. The Rev. Mr. Chadband was at pains to point out that a "human boy" was not an elephant. Mr. Justice Brewer seems to assume that an elephant is a human boy, and rightly denies that this should be the case. If the fact is so it is indeed a sad one, and we do not wonder that the president of the Ethical Society should propose to form instanter a special branch of that virtuous organization for the reform of elephants and lawyers. Further on in the same address the learned justice says: "We must remember that the wisdom of the lawmaker can never keep pace with the ingenuity of trained minds seeking to evade legal limitations. The old saying that holes may be found in every law means simply that an ingenious lawyer can often find either in the statute itself or in the mode prescribed for its enforcement some way of escape from its penalties. It is this which provokes the frequent remark that the law so seldom reaches the rich, for the rich can pay for the brainiest, and the brainiest most certainly and quickly discovers the means of evasion. As against this, I appeal for a higher standard of professional ethics. I appeal to every lawyer to put his heart alongside his head, to mix his conscience with his brains. Let him have the courage to say to his client: 'It may be legal, but it is dishonest, and I will have nothing to do with it.' Is this asking too much of the profession?"

It is obvious that no honorable man, whether lawyer or laborer, will lend himself to assist in schemes of fraud and wrong. But statutes denouncing certain acts and passed in furtherance of a particular view of public policy may create merely *mala prohibita*, wrongs only because the statute declares them unlawful. What the meaning of such a statute is, what the exact acts prohibited are, and what the law permits to be done, are surely questions upon which a client may legitimately ask legal advice, and the lawyer as legitimately give it. To contend, for instance, that the conveyancer who devised the settlements of Mr. Thellusson's will, or he who to-day advises as to the limitations permissible under Thellusson's Act, is doing something dishonorable, is only to talk ridiculous nonsense. We will go further. A client has a right to the advice of his lawyer as to the "exact limits of the law," and the lawyer may advise him on the question, although the law may stop short of prohibiting transactions which the adviser, as an individual, heartily disapproves of. The law is established by the state for the guidance of external human action. The state says, in effect: We hold you blameless as a citizen if you conform your conduct to these rules. Every citizen has a right to know exactly what those rules are, to what they bind him and what they permit him to do. Having this knowledge it is his right as a citizen to select any course not forbidden by the law. Whether when he has selected his course in the light of full knowledge, the lawyer shall assist him to carry it out, requires the lawyer to apply the standard of individual conduct, as opposed to the external standard of the law. He will decide it as his standards are high or low, and according as he decides public opinion will determine his place in the community, his power for good or ill, as an individual. As an individual, the lawyer's conduct must conform to the same standards as that of other honest men; but to say, as the distinguished speaker appears to have done, that a lawyer has no right to advise as to the "exact limits" of a law, even though the law permits injustice, appears to us untrue. To lament an old standard of conduct which permitted lying and falsehood is, at any rate, to indulge in meaningless rhetoric and to create a false and misleading impression.

Mr. Justice Brewer's opinions on the ethics of lawyers have appeared at the same time with or caused numerous statements from others more or less eminent. His political opponent, Mr. Bryan, seems to agree with him at least in the estimate to be placed on their brothers of the profession. The eminent Democratic statesman, in addressing a body of Chicago lawyers, said: "I believe the day will come in this country when we will not have so many men who will sell their souls to make grand larceny possible. Perhaps some time it will not be less disgraceful for a lawyer to assist in a gigantic robbery than for a highwayman to go out and hold up the wayfarer. I knew of a case recently in which they had to go to New York to get lawyers to represent the people because all the lawyers available nearer at hand had been bought up." Mr. Julius Henry Cohen, in *The Independent*, goes these gentlemen one better. He says: "The client suspects, but shuts his eyes. The lawyer knows, and holds his tongue. Can he hold his conscience, too? If the State's attorney shall not prosecute before satisfying himself of the defendant's guilt, shall his adversary defend before satisfying himself of his client's innocence?"

This is the very nonsense exposed by Lord Chancellor Halsbury. It is the very point so exhaustively threshed out in the case of Reg. v. Courvoisier. In that case the accused was defended by Mr. Charles Phillips, to whom Courvoisier confessed his guilt at an early stage of the trial. The report of the case in Townsend's Modern State Trials examines the ethical question from every point of view and agrees with the doctrine stated by us in an earlier paragraph. In a paper entitled "The Mystery of Murder and Its Defense" contributed to the *Law Review* for March, 1850, by Samuel Warren, and reprinted in his "Miscellanies," the question of Phillip's conduct in this case and its bearing on the ethical obligations of the lawyer are again fully examined with the same result. But the absurdity of Mr. Cohen's rhetorical question is sufficiently apparent from the theory of the administration of justice in our courts considered in the light of common sense. Mr. Olcott, former judge and district attorney, is reported in the New York *Herald* as saying: "No lawyer is compelled to take a case if in his judgment his client be guilty of the crime charged. If a person is guilty of a crime it is obvious that the testimony he may give will be perjury, and a lawyer who will put such testimony on record I consider is guilty of subornation of perjury. If a lawyer is morally certain that a client is guilty he will still be fulfilling his duty if he refuses to take the case." Admitting the truth of Mr. Olcott's first proposition — though Erskine suffered loss of position rather than refuse Tom Paine's retainer — we must see more than one *non sequitur* in his second quoted sentence. The true limitations of a lawyer's professional privileges and his ethical obligations have perhaps never been better expressed than by a United States judge of the last century. Judge McCrary has observed: "There is, there must be, a limit beyond which the advocate cannot go. A lawyer should never be the tool of an unscrupulous client. If he is asked to aid a rascal in an effort to oppress and wrong another he must refuse. No fee should be sufficient to hire him for such a work." Perhaps all the lawyer's perplexities over ethical questions will disappear, now that Dr. Adler and the Ethical Culturists have extended from superior heights a kindly helping hand to him along with the other outcast classes.

AN interesting discussion of the relation of the federal government toward the crime of lynching is contained in the decision of the United States Circuit Court for the Northern District of Alabama in the late case of U. S. *v.* Powell. The case should be considered in connection with *Ex p.* Riggins, 134 Fed. Rep. 404, since it grew out of the same facts and involves the same questions. A negro named Maples, under indictment in the Alabama courts and in the custody of the State officials, was forcibly taken by a mob from the officers and lynched. Riggins and Powell were charged with participation in the lynching and indictments were found against them in federal courts under Rev. Stat. U. S., §§ 5508, 5509, the specific charge being that of conspiracy to deprive a citizen (Maples) of rights and privileges secured by the Federal Constitution and laws. Riggins, questioning the legality of his commitment, secured a writ of habeas corpus, and upon the hearing in the Circuit Court, before District Judge Jones, the writ was dismissed. Judge Jones filed an elaborate opinion in which the validity of the indictment from a constitutional point of view was carefully examined and upheld by acute and suggestive arguments. Riggins appealed to the Supreme Court, and that court quashed the writ on the ground that habeas corpus was not the proper remedy, but expressed no opinion on the constitutional questions involved. Riggins *v.* U. S., 199 U. S. 547. The same constitutional questions arise in Powell's case and are presented upon a demurrer to the indictment. Judge Jones renders the opinion here as in the Riggins case, reiterating and elaborating his arguments in the former decision. The demurrer is sustained, however, in deference to *obiter* observations of the Supreme Court in Hodges *v.* U. S., 203 U. S. 1 (noticed in these columns last January), and with less regret, perhaps, because the government has and used the right to appeal provided by recent congressional legislation. The view taken by the Circuit Court in these cases requires that a right not to be lynched be found in the Federal Constitution, since Congress has the power to legislate only in favor of individual rights secured by the Constitution of the United States. The court finds the action of the mob to be a violation of the right to due process of law secured by the Fourteenth Amendment. The obvious difficulty in this interpretation is the series of decisions under the "equal protection of the laws" clause of the same amendment, which hold in effect that Congress has no authority under this clause to legislate against the acts of individuals. These cases are distinguished upon a difference found in the nature of the duty enjoined by the two clauses. The right to the equal protection of the laws is said to be complete when fair laws are provided and are fairly executed. The obligation cast upon the States to afford due process of law, in the language of the decision in the Powell case, "condemns and forbids any course of procedure, unless it 'hears before it condemns, proceeds upon fixed principles, and not arbitrarily, and renders judgment only after trial.'"

THE rights and duties which arise under the due process clause of the Fourteenth Amendment are sketched in accordance with this interpretation as follows: "The force of this clause then puts upon the State, to be performed for the benefit of the citizen or person, the affirmative duty of affording him the enjoyment of all those rights and privileges which are included in and go to make the due administration of the State's established course of judicial procedure. What are these affirmative duties of the State, in such a case, and what constitutes their performance? Having put the accused in prison, upon an accusation of crime, in order to mete out its justice to him, the State must inform him of the nature and cause of the accusation. It must safely keep and protect him in prison, until it can give him the opportunity, as well as the right, to appear before its tribunal. When the State brings him there, it must compel his witnesses to attend, if they will not come. It must confront him with his accusers in open court, and give him the opportunity, as well as the right, to examine them there. The tribunal which it sets up to administer its justice in that case must hear him and his witnesses before it decides his fate. If he be acquitted, he is entitled to go forth unharmed. If he be found guilty, he must still be protected, and have opportunity to present whatever he can in arrest of judgment. If he be sentenced, even to death, he still has the right to live, in the peace of the State and of the United States, until the sentence is executed in the mode, and time, and by the authority prescribed by law. Hurtado *v.* California, 110 U. S. 516." The citizen, it is contended, may be deprived of the enjoyment of the rights thus outlined, by the actions of lawless men, who by themselves punishing the accused "can prevent enjoyment, in the constitutional sense, of due process of law at the hands of the State." Since the amendment gives Congress power to "enforce" its provisions by "appropriate" legislation, and since the action of the mob deprives a citizen of due process of law, a right guaranteed by the Constitution, it is declared that, in the opinion of the court, the indictment should be sustained.

It appears to us that this reasoning, while ingenious, is incorrect in two points. The guaranty of the amendment is only that the States shall "not deprive" the citizen of due process. That is, the State shall refrain from any acts which curtail the rights connoted under due process. It is hard to see how the *State* is chargeable with the acts of a lawless mob which overpowers its officers who are doing their best, as the representatives of the State, to resist the law-breakers and protect the prisoner. But let us grant this point in accordance with the reasoning of the court, and it follows that Congress may prevent infringement of this right which is guaranteed in the Constitution. The Fourteenth Amendment is the only place in the Constitution wherein the court finds a right secured to the citizen which is violated by the mob. The unanimous result of every decision of the Supreme Court on the Fourteenth Amendment is that it is directed solely against the States, though the State may infringe its provisions by the acts of any of its departments, legislative, judicial, or executive. Congress has authority to enforce it by "appropriate legislation." What is "appropriate legislation" under the amendment? Why, obviously such legislation as tends to prohibit the *States* from infringing the rights secured. The amendment imposes duties upon the States, not upon individuals, and the penal statutes "appropriate" to enforce the duties imposed must be such as bring home punishment to the States which have violated the amendment. The utmost limit of "appropriate" legislation is legislation which punishes the representatives of the State, and in no aspect of the case can the vicarious punishment of individuals be "appropriate" to enforce a duty from the State. If we concede that Congress might legitimately enact laws punishing negligence on the part of executive officers charged with the custody of a prisoner lynched, yet by no ingenuity of reasoning can the last clause of the Fourteenth Amendment be made to warrant legislation against individuals, purely as such. In *Ex p.* Virginia, 100 U. S. 339, an indictment against an individual under the Fourteenth Amendment was upheld, but on the distinct ground that he, as an official of the State, represented the State. The court, after declaring that the amendment was directed against States, not individuals, reconciled the seeming inconsistency by saying: "Whoever, by virtue of public position under a State government, deprives another of property, life, or liberty without due process of law * * * violates the constitutional inhibition; and as he acts in the name of and for the State, and is clothed with the State's power, his act is that of the State." The other cases in the Supreme Court upholding indictments under the sections of the Revised Statutes under which the indictments in the Riggins and Powell cases are framed are for violation of duties toward the federal government directly. See Logan *v.* U. S., 144 U. S. 263, and the cases reviewed therein. But we do not know that any contention is made, or is possible, that the action of the mob in murdering Maples is a violation of a duty guaranteed by the federal government elsewhere than in the Fourteenth Amendment.

Is freedom of the press embraced within the "liberty" protected by the Fourteenth Amendment from deprivation without due process of law? This was the interesting question raised by Senator Patterson before the Supreme Court of the United States upon a writ of error to the Supreme Court of Colorado. That court had adjudged him in contempt and subjected him to a fine for certain articles reflecting on the court in his Denver newspapers. The Supreme Court found it unnecessary to decide the question, dismissing the writ, apparently because the federal question, if any, was considered upon the facts as fictitious and unreal. See Wilson *v.* North Carolina, 169 U. S. 586. The court, by Mr. Justice Holmes, announced the familiar principle that criticism of pending cases, whether on trial before judges alone or a jury, was a contempt, but that "when a case is finished, courts are subject to the same criticism as other people." Surely the liberty of the press, which Lord Mansfield defined aptly and tersely in the Dean of St. Asaph's case as consisting "in printing without any previous license, subject to the consequences of the law," is not infringed by subjecting an editor to the consequences of contempt. Judge Harlan filed an interesting dissenting opinion. Throughout his judicial career he has always consistently upheld the old individualistic conception of government and, by consequence, a liberal interpretation of the guaranties of the Fourteenth Amendment. He declared: "I cannot assent to that view [the view of the majority] if it be meant that the legislature may impair or abridge the right of a free press of free speech whenever in its judgment the public welfare requires that it be done. The public welfare cannot override constitutional privileges, and if the rights of free speech and of a free press are in their essence attributes of national citizenship, then neither Congress nor any State since the adoption of the Fourteenth Amendment can, by legislation or by judicial action, impair or abridge them. In my judgment the action of the court below was in violation of the right of free speech and a free press as guaranteed by the Constitution. I go further and hold that the privileges of free speech and of a free press belonging to every citizen of the United States constitute essential parts of every man's liberty, and I protest against violation of that clause of the Fourteenth Amendment forbidding a State to deprive any person of his liberty without due process of law. It is, I think, impossible to conceive of liberty as secured by the Constitution against hostile action, whether by the nation or by the State, which does not embrace the right to enjoy free speech and the right to have a free press."

OUR readers will remember the case of the sailor in the United States navy who was refused admission to a dance hall in Newport, Rhode Island, to which he had purchased a ticket. The case attracted considerable comment at the time, and the President of the United States contributed to the fund raised to enable the excluded sailor, Fred J. Buenzle, to bring suit against the proprietor of the hall for damages for what was characterized as an unpatriotic discrimination against the brave fellows who were clad in the uniform of the American navy. The case has just been decided by the Superior Court of Rhode Island, and the written opinion of Judge Sweetland declares that the proprietors of the Sea View Dancing Pavilion had a right to exclude Buenzle, remaining liable for such damages as the plaintiff could show that he suffered from the breach of the contract evidenced by the ticket he had purchased. In other words, that the plaintiff was in the uniform of the navy was not considered as taking the case out of the familiar rule as to the purchasers of tickets to places of public amusement, operated under no statutory obligation not to discriminate against the class to which the plaintiff belonged. A ticket to such a place of amusement is a mere license, and its revocation exposes the proprietor to an action for breach of contract, not to a tort action. Mc-Crea *v.* Marsh, 12 Gray (Mass.) 211. In his opinion Judge Sweetland said: "From this review of the authorities the court decides that, in the absence of statutory provision, the defendants when they refused to admit the plaintiff to their dancing pavilion, for whatever reason that refusal was given, revoked the license granted by the ticket of admission and rescinded the contract implied in the sale and purchase of said ticket. For this act on the part of the defendants, whether the ticket be regarded as a license or as the evidence of a contract, the plaintiff is entitled to recover in the form of action which he has employed. His damages will be restricted to his actual damage, the price of the ticket, and the expenses directly connected with his attempt to attend the place of amusement of said defendants." The plaintiff having brought an action in assumpsit, his reference in the declaration to his constitutional and statutory rights was to be regarded as surplusage. But the court declared that the license required of the defendant for the conduct of his business, as one of a list enumerated in the statute, was "manifestly for police regulation, and cannot reasonably be held to change these businesses from private to public enterprises, and to interfere with what Mr. Cooley terms every man's civil rights to be left at liberty to refuse business relations with any person whomsoever, whether the refusal rests upon reason or is the result of whim, caprice, prejudice, or malice." Further, under the plaintiff's declaration, it was held immaterial "whether the defendants' business was a private enterprise or was properly devoted to a public use. The plaintiff was excluded, and is suing for damages for the breach of the contract implied in the ticket. His case in assumpsit stands in no different position, if the breach was of a contract to admit to a private place of entertainment or was of a contract to admit him to a place devoted to public use. His damages in an action *ex contractu* are his actual damages, whatever the nature of the place." The decision was on demurrer to the complaint, and though the demurrer is overruled, the decision is a practical victory for the defendant.

THE first meeting of the American Society of International Law convened at Washington last month under the presidency of Secretary Root, who gave to the society a most interesting discussion of the view of the administration on our recent misunderstanding with Japan over the San Francisco school question. The question, it seems, was much simpler than it was thought to be by men like ex-Secretary Olney and Judge Simeon E. Baldwin. It was a fortunate occasion for the president of the society to make clear, by a little patient explanation, the elementary underlying principles of our government against "somewhat widespread popular misapprehension." The gist of the secretary's speech is perhaps contained in this quotation: "Since the rights, privileges, and immunities, both of person and property, to be accorded to foreigners in our country and to our citizens in foreign countries are a proper subject of treaty provision and within the limits of the treaty-making power, and since such rights, privileges, and immunities may be given by treaty in contravention of the laws of any State, it follows of necessity that the treaty-making power alone has authority to determine what those rights, privileges, and immunities shall be. No State can set up its laws as against the grant of any particular right, privilege, or immunity any more than against the grant of any other right, privilege, or immunity. No State can say a treaty may grant to alien residents equality of treatment as to property but not as to education, or as to the exercise of religion and as to burial but not as to education, or as to education but not as to property or religion. That would be substituting the mere will of the State for the judgment of the President and Senate in exercising a power committed to them and prohibited to the States by the Constitution. There was, therefore, no real question of power arising under this Japanese treaty, and no question of State rights."

IN an address before the Harvard Law School Judge William J. Gaynor, of Brooklyn, has illustrated the right to criticise the conduct of cases already finished, and readers of his remarks will have no difficulty in supplying the title of the case he had in mind. His subject was "The Realities of Legal Practice," and adverting to his own State he said that in some of the counties "the trial of causes is entirely regular and normal," and "a mere dirty vulgar murder case is not turned into sensationalism or grotesqueness there." The judge "understands that he is no mere automaton, required to sit on the bench looking meek and wise or stupid, quite helpless and limited in his powers to rule on objections made by lawyers, while they do as they please. He understands that he is put there with ample power to control and shape the case, and exclude everything irrelevant, dilatory, and trifling from it, whether it be first objected to by the lawyers or not." If a medical witness, continued the judge, "is cross-examined for four days instead of for half an hour and the time taken up day after day with harangues, bickerings, long arguments of elementary propositions, trifling adjournments, and so on, it is because the trial judge permits it. Intelligent expedition is not haste. This is a matter for the judiciary and the bar to speak plainly about." The impressions which the Thaw case made upon Judge Gaynor seem very similar to those produced on the profession in England, if we may judge from the comments of the English professional journals. It is well to have some one to raise from a responsible position a protest in our own country against some features of that trial.

WHAT SHOULD A LAWYER CHARGE?

What should a lawyer charge for his services? The question concerns us all nearly — notwithstanding the fact that some of us find it more difficult to get an opportunity of charging than to fix the amounts of our fees. The matter was touched upon by the Hon. Joseph H. Choate in his recent address on the English bar, delivered before the New York State Bar Association (which was reproduced in April Law Notes). He said that English barristers neither approve nor follow the American plan of considering the amount in controversy in fixing their fees. In his expressive language "they fairly scout the idea." While he does not say so in so many words, the fair inference to be drawn from his remarks is that he considers that the English idea is preferable to the American.

Mr. Choate is always instructive and entertaining, and all Americans, and particularly all American lawyers, listen with interest and respect to whatever he has to say. No doubt it is permitted, however, to differ with him every now and then.

The right to take the amount in controversy into consideration has been upheld so repeatedly by the American courts that its existence cannot be doubted. Indeed, we do not understand that Mr. Choate and our English brethren question the legality of the practice. The only question is as to its propriety; and on this point our courts have spoken so unmistakably and convincingly that no lawyer on this side of the water need feel the slightest hesitancy on any ground in charging more where a large sum is involved than he would charge for the same services where the amount at stake was smaller.

There are good reasons for the American view — reasons so good that it is difficult to see the justice or propriety of any other view. Where the amount in controversy is large, the responsibility of the lawyer is greater than where the amount is small. Measured by the actual time he devotes to his client's interests, his labors may be no greater and no more severe in the one case than in the other; and he may devote the same earnest and conscientious attention to the one case as to the other case. But the strain upon him is bound to increase in the same ratio that the interests intrusted to him increase in financial importance; and he is justly entitled to compensation for that increased strain. Then, too, the benefit to the client should be taken into consideration. In all fairness, a business man should pay more for services that gain or save him a hundred thousand dollars than for services that concern only a tenth of that amount, irrespective of the amount of labor his lawyer performs. It might be urged also that the principle which we advocate governs the charges made by common carriers, brokers, and others acting in a responsible or fiduciary capacity. But we need not rely upon such an argument.

The courts have expressed themselves so emphatically and so clearly on this point that it would be useless to attempt to elaborate further than to quote them. Let us see what they have said.

In Eggleston *v.* Boardman, 37 Mich. 14, the court, in disposing of the contention that one day's work by a lawyer in an important cause was worth no more than the same services in a suit of less magnitude, said: "We cannot concur in this reasoning, the effect of which, if adopted, would be to establish a scale of compensation for professional services, when the amount to be paid was not specially agreed upon, dependent upon the skill and professional standing of the person employed, and the actual time by him devoted to the work, but without any reference to the real nature of the questions he was called upon to investigate, or the amount in controversy, and the increased care and responsibility arising therefrom. Whenever an attorney or solicitor is retained in a cause, it becomes his implied duty to use and exercise reasonable skill, care, discretion, and judgment in the conduct and management thereof. It would be very difficult to lay down any definite rule or principle, applicable alike to all cases, as to the care and skill required. Each case must be governed by its own peculiar facts and circumstances, and the amount in controversy must in every case play a very important part in the determination of this question. . . . It is very evident that the responsibility, the care, anxiety, and mental labor is much greater in a case where the amount in controversy is large than where it is insignificant, although perhaps the same questions might be raised in each case, or the more difficult questions arise in the case where the amount was of but slight consequence. Nor is this responsibility, care, and mental labor dependent alone upon the number of hours or days which may be given to the preparation and trial or argument of a case. This responsibility and mental anxiety is not so imaginative and shadowy that it should not be considered in arriving at a proper compensation to be allowed in fixing the value of the services rendered. . . . In all cases the professional skill and standing of the person employed, his experience, the nature of the controversy, both in regard to the amount involved and the character and nature of the questions raised in the case, as well as the result, must all be taken into consideration in fixing the value of the services rendered."

In Lombard *v.* Bayard, 1 Wall. Jr. (C. C.) 196, Grier, J., in fixing the compensation of a lawyer who had acted as auditor or master in the cause, said: "The services of men of learning, skill, and experience in their professions are not to be rated like those of day laborers. . . . Every gentleman of the bar well knows that there cannot be any one rule of charges in the nature of a horizontal tariff for all cases. Often, where the parties are poor and the matter in contest is small, counsel receive but very inadequate compensation for their exertion of body and mind; and for myself I know that for some of the most severe labor of my professional life I have been the least well paid. In other cases where the parties are wealthy, and the sum in controversy large, they will receive a tenfold greater compensation for perhaps a tithe of the same labor. In some cases the whole sum in dispute would be poor compensation. In others, five per cent. of it will be very liberal. Hence, in all cases, professional compensation is gauged not so much by the amount of the labor as by the amount in controversy, the ability of the party, and the result of the effort. And this is perfectly just."

In Ward *v.* Kohn, (C. C. A.) 58 Fed. Rep. 462, Sanborn, J., said: "In the absence of a contract price, attorneys are entitled to receive what they deserve for their services. The amount of their compensation must vary with the place in which their services are rendered, for the same services are of more value in a large and prosperous commercial city than in a small country town; with the character and standing of the lawyer who renders them, for the services of an attorney of ripe experience, great learning, eminent ability, and high reputation deserve and command better compensation than those of the tyro in the profession; with the importance of the matters involved in the litigation, for the same services deserve more compensation where life, liberty, character, or large amounts of property are at stake than where but a few dollars are in dispute; and with the results attained, for success earns a better reward than failure."

In Garfield *v.* Kirk, 65 Barb. (N. Y.) 464, it was held that the value of the property involved in a suit should be considered in fixing the lawyer's compensation for his services. The reasoning of the court was as follows: "It requires no greater labor to draw a complaint or answer, or to render any other specific service, in a case in which the amount involved is $1,000,000 than in one in which it is $100. And yet, every lawyer knows that the labor bestowed upon a case is, as a general rule, in proportion to the magnitude of the interest involved. While the labor in drawing a pleading may be no more, when the amount involved is large, than when it is small, yet the labor in the examination of authorities and documents preliminary to drawing it, and the care bestowed upon the pleading itself, would be much greater in one case than in the other. This extra care and labor must be compensated; and it may be measured with some degree of accuracy by the amount involved in the suit. The attorney who does the labor can estimate, himself, the value of his extra labor, but there is no way another lawyer can acquire the means of estimating the value of the services better than by being informed of the magnitude of the interests involved."

In Ottawa University *v.* Parkinson, 14 Kan. 159, the court, in holding that it was proper for a witness to consider the amount in controversy in giving his opinion as to the value of legal services, said: "It is claimed that the premises on which the witness based his estimate of the value of the services rendered are erroneous; that he had no right to consider 'the amount in controversy, and the legal questions involved, and the general importance of the case,' in making his judgment of the value of the services. But we think these were all proper and important elements in determining the value of the services. We know that an attorney is bound to fidelity to his client as much when the amount is one dollar as when it is a million. His obligation is not changed. But it is in the knowledge of every professional man that when great interests are confided to his care he is expected to use the utmost diligence in the preparation of the case. He is not expected to nor does he limit his services by the rule of ordinary care and skill that governs him in an ordinary case."

In Quint *v.* Ophir Min. Co., 4 Nev. 304, the court said: "To ascertain what may be a reasonable compensation for services rendered by an attorney, the amount involved and the character of the business transacted by him must be taken into account, because as he is liable in damages for any negligence, the law gives him a compensation proportionate to the responsibility imposed upon him." In Smith *v.* Chicago, etc., R. Co., 60 Iowa 515, it was held that while the labor of a lawyer in conducting a case wherein a large sum is involved may be no greater than would be required in conducting a case of trifling importance, the responsibility is greater, and that fact ought to be considered in determining the compensation to which he is entitled.

But why multiply authorities? Those which we have cited show abundantly that our courts consider that it is not only legal but just and proper that the sum involved should enter into the fixing of the amount of a lawyer's fee. Indeed, it has been said more than once that the client's financial condition or his ability to pay should be taken into consideration.

On that point the court said in Ward *v.* Kohn, 58 Fed. Rep. 462: "The wealth of a defendant cannot be considered in any case to enhance the fee for professional services above a reasonable compensation for the service actually rendered. It cannot be considered to make a fee extortionate or a compensation unreasonably large. But every judge and every gentleman of the bar knows that much severe professional labor is rendered by practicing attorneys without any compensation, and much more for compensation so small as to be entirely inadequate. It is as difficult to defend the poor as the rich from a groundless charge of murder. It requires as much learning, labor, and professional skill to recover or save from attack property of little value, that may be the entire estate of the poor man, as it does to recover thousands of dollars for the wealthy. The duty of the lawyer to defend the former and maintain his rights is as great as it is to the latter, and to the honor of the profession it may be said that it is performed with equal zeal and fidelity. But it is the general practice of the gentlemen of the bar to fix the fees for such services far below a fair compensation or to charge no fee at all — to measure their fees more by the inability of such a client to pay a fair compensation, or to pay at all, than by the value of the services they render. When, on the other hand, a client who has the means to pay what professional services are fairly worth employs an attorney, it is right and just that he should pay a fair and reasonable compensation for the service he obtains. In other words, the fees the attorney deserves from such a client should not be measured by the inadequate compensation and small fees the gentlemen of the bar usually receive from those who are unable to pay at all or to pay a fair compensation, but they should be measured by the fees usually obtained by attorneys for like services from those who are able to pay just compensation for the service rendered."

A similar opinion was expressed in Breaux *v.* Francke, 30 La. Ann. 336. But in Stevens *v.* Ellsworth, 95 Iowa 321, 63 N. W. Rep. 683, it was held that in fixing the compensation to which a lawyer is entitled the wealth of his client cannot be considered. In so holding the court said: "We think no court has ever said that, with the facts the same, a reasonable compensation for a professional service for a poor man is worth less than the same service for a rich man. It is likely true that less is often taken from the poor than from the rich, but the reason is not because of a difference in what the service is reasonably worth, but because of a disposition of professional persons to charge less in such cases, even to the extent, in some cases, of making it a gratuity or a mere trifle. The practice is to be commended, but not under a rule that they may, while thus giving to one, take, because of that fact, from another. If it is the rule that fees may be enhanced because of the wealth of the client, we do not see why, in a case where the client is poor, that fact may not be shown to lessen the compensation, and such a rule has never obtained."

In International, etc., R. Co. *v.* Clark, 81 Tex. 48, an action by a lawyer against a corporation to recover a fee, it was held that it was proper to refuse an instruction "that no greater fee would be reasonable against a wealthy man or corporation than a poor man for the same services." See also Hamman *v.* Willis, 62 Tex. 507. And in Robbins *v.* Harvey, 5 Conn. 335, it was held that the poverty of the client had no bearing upon the question of the compensation to which the lawyer was entitled.

Unless history belies him, Mr. Choate has not always believed in the English doctrine. It has been asserted repeatedly that he received a hundred thousand dollars for assisting to convince the Supreme Court of the United States that the federal government has no power to impose a tax upon incomes. No doubt he has charged smaller sums for other professional services which have made equal demands upon his time and energies without even thinking that he has undervalued his services.

Besides, we all remember the story (now become a classic) concerning the fee earned by Mr. Choate and that other eminent lawyer, Edward Lauterbach. As the story runs, in the early professional days of those two gentlemen they were associated in a suit which they pushed to a successful conclusion. At the end of the litigation Mr. Lauterbach consulted with his colleague as to the amount of the fee they should charge. At Mr. Choate's suggestion, the matter was left to his discretion. Shortly thereafter he handed to Mr. Lauterbach, as his share of the fee, a check which was for such a sum that it caused that gentleman to look at his associate in amazement and admiration and to exclaim: "Joseph! almost thou persuadest me to become a Christian."

J. C. M.

INTENT IN LAW.

Holland in his work "Elements of Jurisprudence," in substantiation of his theory that the law pays no regard to intent in contracts, but is rather concerned with external manifestations of intent, cites the instance of a man contracting with another, but not meaning to carry out the contract. Here, he says, not only will the party be unable to evade liability by setting up his intent not to be bound, but should he desire to hold the other party liable, the latter, even though he knew the former's intention not to perform, cannot set up that fact as destroying mutual intent. In other words, the law in contracts looks to the conformity or nonconformity with external requirements rather than to inward states of mind.

It is interesting to trace how far the principle of the law's regard for set standards rather than states of mind, pervades other departments of legal liability. In view of the fact that the more highly developed a system of jurisprudence is, the more impersonal its operation becomes, no less than the higher the form of government, the less it concerns itself with the enforcement of moral obligations, the extent to which the law's operations are affected by the presence or absence of intent becomes a matter of significance.

In crimes, intent is usually an element. In prosecutions for homicide, assault, larceny, burglary, or arson, the state of mind of the accused is always relevant. Hence in crimes, unlike the law of contracts, the state of mind, not simply an impersonal standard, becomes the determining test.

And it is curious to note that while justice is best promoted by disregarding states of mind and applying the external test with reference to contractual liability, in crimes discrimination between acts accompanied by intent, and acts not so accompanied, best insures justice. In other words, with reference to contracts the law's progress is indicated by a drift away from consideration of states of mind, while with reference to crimes the law's progress is evidenced by a drift away from the times when liability could be incurred irrespective of intent.

It should be observed, however, that the contract test of determining liability more from external standards than inward states, is approximated in criminal law by the imputation of criminal intent from gross negligence in causing injury. Recent decisions, for instance, have established that not only may a man be guilty of manslaughter where he is grossly negligent in throwing objects from an elevation upon a crowded thoroughfare, but that an officer in making a lawful arrest in an improper manner may be guilty of murder where he uses excessive force resulting in death. But it may be here remarked that the tendency to infer intent from gross negligence, far from indicating the law's arbitrariness, really illustrates, by affording more positive protection of rights, the growing definiteness of remedial law.

To some offenses not otherwise crimes, but made so by statute, such as indictable monopolies or nuisances, intent is not material; external acts irrespective of states of mind determine liability. But it remains true of ordinary crimes that the actor's state of mind largely determines criminal responsibility — the same act being harmless or criminal according as there is absence or presence of wrongful intent.

In civil actions, state of mind is not so important a factor as in criminal actions. In a large class of injuries to property — in trespass *quare clausum fregit*, trespass *de bonis asportatis*, trespass on the case, trover, replevin, and detinue — liability exists irrespective of intent. Yet in actions for assault and battery, fraud, and malicious prosecution, intent plays a vital part. To examine more in detail: —

To maintain assault and battery, intent must always appear. An act causing personal harm is only an assault where it is intended as such. However a man may harm another, if he is not doing an unlawful act, or a lawful act in an improper manner, there is no liability for the injury. And there is not observable in civil actions for assault any stretching of the tendency to impute intent from gross negligence as in criminal prosecutions: for an injury accompanied with negligence, an action on the case alone lies. No action for trespass *vi et armis* can be maintained without showing wrongful intent.

In actions for malicious prosecution, the defendant's state of mind also enters into recovery. If he honestly believed the charges he preferred, then the fact that he could have discovered their falsity does not subject him to liability. The law applicable to malicious prosecution bears no resemblance to the contract doctrine that external standards, not inward states, must prevail. But it should be noted that as in false imprisonment, lack of reasonable cause for suspicion may supply wrongful intent, so a tendency is observable away from inquiries as to inward states in actions for malicious prosecution — lack of probable cause here subjecting more and more to liability.

In an action for deceit the defendant is liable, if wilfully deceitful or grossly negligent. If he believes a statement to be false which proves true, he is not liable; so far intent is immaterial. But if he believes a statement true which proves false, he is not absolutely liable as in libel, unless grossly negligent in believing it; here intent is an element. The difference is pointed out by Pollock to lie in the inherent natures of the respective rights: libel is a violation of the absolute right to reputation; hence damaging words are enough without intent. But deceit is based on the defendant's wrongdoing — hence his state of mind becomes material.

However, this test obviously does not hold all around. If in every violation of absolute rights the mere injury itself is enough without intent, then in actions of assault and battery all inquiry as to intent would be precluded.

To consider next civil actions not based upon the intent of the wrongdoer. And first, in all civil actions for injuries to property, whether for mere trespass or for depriving the owner of his property, liability exists independent of wrongful intent. For an action of false imprisonment intent is not absolutely essential; lack of probable cause may supply it. Here is an analogous instance of liability irrespective of inward states — liability here hinging on the same impersonal standards obtaining in the law of contracts.

The test applied in contract law is further illustrated in actions for violation of personal safety by the absolute liability attaching to dangerous things. The owner of a wild animal or a large reservoir, for instance, must at his peril prevent the one from causing injury, the other from damaging property; and it is no answer to an action for injury resulting therefrom to set up that the owner was not negligent, or did not intend the injury: he is absolutely liable irrespective of negligence or intent. The principal, not otherwise responsible, may be liable for the acts of an independent contractor committed through being intrusted with dangerous instrumentalities; and the fact that the principal showed no negligence in the selection of such agent does not exempt him.

A common carrier is absolutely liable in the event of loss or damage to goods irrespective of intent or negligence: unlike a warehouseman, the carrier must answer where the goods have been stolen without fault or negligence on his part.

In all these cases the law obviously does not inquire into surrounding circumstances as a condition to liability: failure to comply with an external requirement, the prevention of injury in the case of dangerous things, or the prevention of injury to goods in the case of liability of common carriers, entails liability without regard to fault.

In libel, the defendant's state of mind is not relevant. Though he honestly believed the statement to be true, yet if it turns out to be false, he is liable; while a statement supposed to be false, if in fact true, entails no liability. Inward states then do not enter into the law of libel; conformity to external standards — uttering erroneous defamatory matter — characterizes the right of recovery in libel. And the rule applies equally to words libelous *per se* and words entailing no liability in the absence of special damages: if untrue in either case, they carry their consequences without regard to innocence of utterance.

To sum up. In all crimes, whether against the person, as in murder, or against property rights, as in larceny, as well as in civil actions for assault, fraud, and malicious prosecution, the law is concerned with states of mind equally with acts — with psychology quite as much as with external manifestations of volition. But actions for trespass to either realty or personalty, actions of trespass on the case for injuries occasioned by negligence, or by dangerous things, and actions of libel, trover, replevin, and detinue, may all be maintained without reference to the intent of the wrongdoer — the law here trenching not at all on psychology.

Unless the law will ever hold a defendant liable for deceit, where his statements are untrue regardless of his state of mind, the doctrine of conformity to externals as the test of liability, obtaining in the law of contracts, will never extend to all departments of legal liability. The mere fact that gross negligence in forming a belief may expose the defendant to liability for deceit, does not affect the general principle that liability for fraud turns primarily upon the question of intent.

The rule that gross negligence in forming a belief amounts to wilful misrepresentation must not be confounded with the salutary principle prohibiting an action for deceit where there is simple negligence in making false statements. Where gross negligence exists, it is tantamount to fraud; but for mere negligence in forming an opinion as to the truth or falsity of a statement, while there may be ground for rescinding a contract, there is not basis for an action of deceit.

Liability for negligence illustrates the growing stress upon external and impersonal requirements rather than inward states of mind. Whereas once the standard of care exacted by law was that degree which a man would be expected to exercise in the regulation of like affairs of his own, now the degree of care is that which a reasonably prudent man would be likely to display under similar circumstances. The individual drops out of legal consideration; the only inquiry of the law is as to whether there has been conformity or nonconformity to this standard of ordinary care.

For trespass, conversion, and all injuries to property a person is liable whether conscious or not that he trespassed or dealt with another's goods: though innocence of wilful wrong may mitigate the damages.

In slander of title, the innocence of the charges made will prove a defense. Such actions are now practically obsolete, however, and only possess interest as illustrating some circuitous and illogical aspects of the science of law. There seems to be no good reason why this distinction between slander generally and slander of title is observed. If a defendant is liable for defamatory matter, even though honest in his charges, he should be equally liable for damages to property rights, whether honest or not; for if the liability for defamatory words regardless of intent is based on infringement of an absolute right, then should a slanderer of title be held regardless of intent, since injury to property is also a violation of an absolute right. But the distinction is firmly established that in slander erroneous statements defamatory of another — the external test — is applied; while in slander of title the actor's knowledge or state of mind must be considered.

While in actions for slander of title intent is a subject of inquiry, yet for all injuries to property rights the rule does not so unqualifiedly hinge on intent, or state of mind. If a man believes his assertions that another's property is encumbered, lack of intent is a defense. But if a man appropriates the name designating another's business so as to deceive people of ordinary prudence, he is liable though innocent of fraudulent designs. Here, however, he is not held for fraud, but for damage to property rights. Manifestly the law applying here bears resemblance to the contract doctrine determining liability from external expressions rather than inward states of will.

It should be observed that even in cases of liability resting on inward states instead of external standards, the law sometimes holds defendant for gross negligence in the absence of positive knowledge or wilfulness. Fraud illustrates this tendency.

To sum up finally. In homicides, larceny, and crimes generally, and in civil actions for assault, malicious prosecution and fraud, the law concerns itself with states of mind. Whereas, the doctrine applicable to the law of contracts, that the law concerns itself with external manifestations rather than inward states of will, finds application also in civil actions for libel, false imprisonment, for keeping dangerous things, for negligence, and for all injuries to property, such as trespass, conversion, etc.

It should be added that even though in libel no inquiries are made as to actual states of will, belief in libelous statements, while not removing liability yet mitigates damages; and knowledge in cases of negligence, where external standards apply, makes the degree of care legally exacted greater than usual.

"Jurisprudence," says Pollock in writing of negligence, "is not psychology, and law disregards many psychological distinctions, not because lawyers are ignorant of their existence, but because for legal purposes it is impracticable or useless to regard them." Holland has pointed out that the older theory regarded inward states more, while the later drift of law is more towards establishing impersonal standards.

It seems eminently just that an owner of property should be able to obtain it from another, whether or not such other acquired the property innocently and for value. The law on this subject could never justly occupy itself with psychology. But it is equally clear that where a person is injured by another, justice must ever demand that the question whether the injury was intentionally or unintentionally caused must be considered. The law here must ever be concerned with psychology.

Perhaps in malicious prosecution and slander of title as well as in libel, negligence, false imprisonment, and trespass to property, the law in making the presence or absence of external requirements instead of states of will the test of liability, would better protect a man's right to immunity from baseless suits or injuries to title.

But in fraud or assault, the law could never justly abolish regard for state of mind by making external manifestations of that state the test of liability — to say nothing of the indispensable intent test of crimes.

It is clear, therefore, that the law will never reach the stage where it will disregard intent altogether and merely make external expressions of that intent the test as in contract. Even though disregard of intent and the application of impersonal standards in slander of title, for instance, might prove beneficial, yet entire disregard of inward states of mind would throw the law back to the times when a man was liable for injuries regardless of whether they were wilfully or unintentionally, negligently, or necessarily occasioned. Psychology, therefore, must always remain within the legitimate province of law.

And with reference to the growing emphasis on impersonal standards, it should be observed that the test applied to contracts in determining liability from external standards is one adopted to prevent fraud, not to rigidly bind men contrary to intent.

On close analysis, even in those instances where liability may be incurred regardless of intent — as in trespass to property, damage to reputation, or for contracts — the law does not absolutely exclude inquiry into intent, where such a course would further the ends of justice. However binding in form a contract may be, it may be rescinded or reformed in a proper case of mistake either of one of the parties or of both. However strictly a contract may have conformed to legal requirements, it would be unenforceable if entered into through jest. The law adopts impersonal standards to prevent fraud: it only abandons inquiry into intent where a person seeks to evade the consequences of acts fully intended.

It has already been shown that the law does not rigidly adhere to the uniform disregard of intent in formal contracts.

The law must ever be concerned with the true significance of men's dealings; and a proper appreciation of the meaning of a transaction can only be obtained by arriving at the intent of the parties. J. M.

THE CASE OF EUGENE CHANTRELLE.

Eugene Marie Chantrelle, a Frenchman born at Nantes in 1834, had received a regular medical training, but had never obtained any professional qualifications; and after a stormy and wandering youth he had settled down in England as a teacher of modern languages. About the year 1866 he proceeded in this capacity to Edinburgh, where he rapidly acquired a lucrative connection. Soon after his arrival he became unduly intimate with one of his pupils, a girl barely sixteen, whom he married in August, 1868, two months before the birth of their first child. From the first the marriage was most unhappy; the husband was repeatedly and ostentatiously unfaithful to his child wife. He "beat her, kicked her, caned her, cursed her." More than once she had to invoke the protection of the law, and she was only restrained from petitioning for a divorce by dread of the scandal and exposure. Chantrelle sank into habitual intoxication. His classes fell off, and pecuniary difficulties were added to the wife's other miseries. The only redeeming feature in her husband's conduct was his uniform kindness to the children, two little boys, ten and eight years old at the time of Mme. Chantrelle's death, and a baby born a few months before that event.

On New Year's Eve, 1877, Mme. Chantrelle was in the usual good health which she had enjoyed in spite of her wretched life. Her husband's behavior had been less brutal since the birth of the youngest child. The family dined happily together at their house in George street, and a bottle of champagne was opened in honor of the festive season. On New Year's Day she was unwell, but from purely natural causes. She had no appetite, suffered from sickness, and retired early to bed. About ten o'clock the servant of all work, Mary Byrne, came in to wish her good night and saw a tumbler three parts full of lemonade on a small table by the bedside. At her mistress's request she peeled an orange for her and left it there on a plate with a few grapes. An hour or so later, M. Chantrelle entered the apartment, stayed talking with his wife, and then retired to the adjoining bedroom, which he shared with the two boys. taking the baby with him for fear it might disturb the mother's rest.

The next morning Byrne came down shortly before seven, and while she was tidying up the kitchen she heard moans proceeding from her mistress's bedroom upstairs. Hastily entering, for the door was about a foot open, she found madame lying in bed with the bedclothes partially off her, unconscious, "awfully pale looking, her eyelids closed," and now and again "moaning very heavily." The girl roused her master, and between them they tried, though without success, to awaken the sleeper. At last, after considerable delay, Chantrelle went off to summon Mr. Carmichael, a general practitioner in the neighborhood, who arrived at 8.30, to find Mme. Chantrelle "profoundly and completely unconscious." There was a strong escape of gas in the room, though Byrne swore afterward that she had noticed nothing of the sort on her earlier entry. The doctor ordered the immediate removal of his patient into the front bedroom, set to work to promote artificial respiration, and, with Chantrelle's consent, despatched a card to Dr. (now Sir Henry) Littlejohn, the eminent toxicologist, begging him to come at once "if you would like to see a case of coal-gas poisoning." On his arrival in an hour's time the latter formed the gravest view of the case. At his suggestion Mme. Chantrelle was conveyed to the Royal Infirmary, where she died about four o'clock, without having recovered consciousness. A post-mortem examination conducted the next day by Drs. Maclagan and Littlejohn failed to reveal the cause of death, and the appearances discovered were not, in the opinion of the doctors, consistent with gas poisoning. The customary bright patches on the skin were wanting, the blood showed perfectly normal under the spectroscope, while in examining the lungs and the cavities of the body not the faintest odor of coal gas could be perceived.

The relations between Chantrelle and his wife were sufficiently notorious in Edinburgh, and immediately on quitting the house in George street, Dr. Littlejohn, who was surgeon to the police office, had sent to request the gas company to inspect the premises. One of the gas fitters noticed in the architrave of the window in Mme. Chantrelle's bedroom a place from which a gas bracket had been removed, and on opening the shutter he discovered a pipe loose between the architrave and the wall. On inspection the pipe was found to be broken, and from the hole the gas, when turned on at the meter, escaped freely; a piece of piping about two inches long was on the ledge at the foot of the shutter, and had evidently been wrenched off by bending backward and forward; the break was quite fresh, and could not have been caused accidentally. Dr. Littlejohn had been convinced that Mme. Chantrelle was suffering from the effects of narcotic poisoning, and when the post mortem proved nugatory he sought the cause in another quarter. Both on the nightgown of the deceased and on the sheets of the bed were certain stains caused apparently by vomited matter. These were cut out and submitted to examination, but not until the police had discovered, locked up in one of the rooms, enough drugs to stock a surgery, including various preparations of chloral and extracts of opium, both fluid and solid. On Saturday, January 5, immediately after his wife's funeral, during which he displayed the most edifying emotion, Chantrelle was arrested and lodged in the Calton prison. A fortnight later Drs. Littlejohn and Maclagan reported that a chemical analysis of the contents of the stomach and other organs of the deceased revealed no traces of poison, vegetable or mineral; but they found on the sheet and bedgown indisputable evidence of the presence of opium, accompanied in each case by portions of grapes and orange, substances which had been previously recognized in the contents of the stomach. Their analysis was confirmed by Messrs. Crum Brown and Fraser, professors respectively of chemistry and materia medica in the University of Edinburgh.

Chantrelle was tried before Lord Justice Clerk Moncrieff on May 7. The prosecution was conducted by the Lord Advocate, afterward Lord Watson; the Solicitor-General, Mr. J. H. Macdonald, now Lord Kingsburgh; and Messrs. Muirhead and Burnet, advocates depute. For the prisoner appeared Mr., afterward Lord, Trayner; Mr., now Lord, Robertson; and the present Lord Advocate, Mr. Thomas Shaw. As is well known, Scotch criminal procedure admits of no opening speech from counsel, and the jury have to wrestle as best they may with the apparently disconnected facts as they accumulate. The relevancy of much of the earlier evidence is liable to be missed, and when, as in the Ardlamont case, the Crown opens with a mass of complicated financial details, fifteen good men and true are bewildered in a fog, from which they do not always emerge.

In Chantrelle's trial, however, the evidence fell automatically into logical and consecutive order. Mary Byrne was clear as to the absence of any smell of gas when she entered her mistress's bedroom; she first noticed it on returning thither after her master had sent her off to see if the baby was crying, and as she opened the door she saw him coming from the window where the broken pipe was afterwards discovered. Byrne also swore that the lemonade in the glass had been nearly all consumed since she left it the night before and that one of the quarters, or "liths," of orange had disappeared from the plate. She was confident that the dark stains on the bed linen were not there when she said good night. Evidence was called that among the frequent threats of violence to his wife, Chantrelle had boasted that he knew of a way of poisoning her which defied detection. He had not only insured her life recently for £1,000 against accident, but he had made particular inquiries whether "accident" included death after partaking of unwholesome dishes, such as toasted cheese. The date of taking out the policy (November, 1877) coincided with the purchase of a particular extract of opium, of which no trace could be found among the drugs in his possession, and during the closing months of the year he was being dunned for small bills and in debt to the tune of over £100. Not the least pathetic incident in the trial was the evidence of the prisoner's ten-year-old son, a "strange unchildish elf," who nursed his baby brother, tried to comfort his mother, and was the good spirit of that unhappy household:

"My papa and mamma got on well sometimes. I don't know any reason why they did not get on well. He called her bad names. I have heard him swear at her. Mamma never used bad words to him. Mamma left the room when he used bad words and sometimes she cried. I also cried sometimes when he did so. I have seen him strike her. He struck her with his hand on the side of the head."

The Crown admitted that no traces of opium were to be found in the body, and relied entirely upon the analysis of the linen stains, but their medical witness insisted that it would have been idle to expect to find vestiges of so easily absorbed a narcotic twenty-four hours after it had been swallowed. The prisoner had been the last person with his wife on the evening before she died, and he had enjoyed full opportunity of dosing the fruit, and possibly the lemonade, with extract of opium. The "declaration" "emitted" by him in Scotch fashion consisted largely of groundless charges of infidelity against his wife. He insisted that she had been poisoned by an escape of gas which, so he said, completely filled her bedroom.

Mr. Trayner's speech was vigorous and ingenious, but unconvincing. He practically limited himself to contending that the prosecution had not made out their case. "He was not there to say that Mme. Chantrelle died from poisoning by coal gas; he was not there to say from what she died; but he was there to say she did not die from opium administered to her by the prisoner." Incidentally he labored to prove that the bulk of the medical evidence, as well as the facts of the case, were favorable to the gas hypothesis, and that the attempt to bring home the severance of the gas pipe to the prisoner had failed. But his main lines of defense were negative — that a majority of the common symptoms of poisoning by opium were absent, both during the unconsciousness of the deceased and on her post-mortem examination; that the length of time for which Mme. Chantrelle had survived was entirely contrary to the usual course of narcotic poisoning; that the tests to which the linen stains had been subjected were imperfect, and that, even if they satisfied the jury as to the presence of opium, they failed utterly to show that that substance had ever been in the mouth or stomach of the deceased. Finally, he made it a strong point that at any time between the death and the funeral the prisoner could have made away with the bed linen or obliterated the stains. It was the stock defense of a good advocate who has little or nothing in the way of fact to rely on and is driven to rebut hypothesis by hypothesis.

Lord Moncrieff compressed into an hour and twenty minutes a charge on which many English judges would have deemed a day well spent. Its deadly candor left little hope for the prisoner; every point in his favor received its meed of respectful consideration, but the combination of circumstances pointing in one direction was overwhelming. The jury were absent for little over the hour, and unanimously found "the panel guilty of murder as libeled." He received sentence of death, and then, as the macers were about to lift the trapdoor leading to the cells below, and before he could be checked by the court, Chantrelle had undone the main theory of the defense by volunteering his conviction that the bed stains could proceed from nothing but opium, "opium administered in a solid form" by some other person than himself.

As in all cases of circumstantial evidence, an agitation was raised to procure a commutation of the sentence, but it failed to move Mr. Secretary Cross. Chantrelle was hanged on May 31 within the walls of Calton prison. The exhortation of the worthy Scotch minister who attended him could produce no confession or act of contrition. "He dies and makes no sign." Of his guilt there is no ground for doubt, but, save in the selection of a vegetable poison which leaves no traces in the body of the victim, he was a most clumsy criminal. The manufacture of evidence is a snare which seldom fails to prove fatal to those who employ it, and the breaking of the gas pipe was a piece of almost incredible bungling. Had Chantrelle merely turned on the jet in the room where his wife was lying stupefied by opium, and then shut the door, he would have produced the desired symptoms without exciting the smallest legitimate suspicion. — *The Spectator* (London).

Cases of Interest.

Fire Policy on Automobile — Place of Origin of Fire. — In Preston *v.* Ætna Ins. Co., 103 N. Y. Supp. 638, the New York Appellate Division, First Department, held that where an accident to an automobile resulted in the leakage of gasoline from the tank, and fire was communicated to the escaped gasoline from burning lamps affixed to the outside of the vehicle, the fire loss on the machine was not one "originating within the vehicle" within a clause of a fire policy exempting the insurer from liability for fire so originating. Clarke, J., dissented.

Railroad Not Liable for Wreck Caused by Cyclone. — In Galveston, etc., R. Co. *v.* Crier, 100 S. W. Rep. 1177, the Texas Court of Civil Appeals held that where a cyclone struck a freight train with sufficient force to lift the cars from the trucks, hurl one of them a distance of 150 feet into a field beyond and spin it around like a top, and leave only the engine and three heavy iron tank-cars on the rails, the wreck was entitled to be regarded as an act of God, and the railroad could not be held liable for injuries sustained by a person riding in the caboose of the train.

Injunction Against Ticket Scalping. — In Pennsylvania Co. *v.* Bay, 150 Fed. Rep. 770, Circuit Judge Kohlsaat granted an injunction against the defendant and others restraining them from buying and reselling special nontransferable tickets to be issued in the future by the complainant. The court held that a railroad company had a present property interest in the right to issue such tickets and to have them maintained as nontransferable, and that equity had power to prevent a sale of such tickets in violation of their terms, there being no adequate remedy at law.

Automobile Accident — Owner's Liability — In Long *v.* Nute, 100 S. W. Rep. 511, the St. Louis (Mo.) Court of Appeals held that where an automobile was operated by a person employed for that purpose, it would be presumed that he was acting within the scope of his authority and about his employer's business; and that such presumption was not changed by the fact that the chauffeur, in operating the automobile, made a detour from the direct route between his employer's home and a place to which he was directed by his employer to go.

Public's Right to Use Beach for Bathing. — Under the common law, as modified by the colonial ordinance of 1641-47, littoral owners in Massachusetts take the fee to their portion of the land between high and low watermark, subject to the easement of the public for navigation and free fishing and fowling. In the recent case of Butler *v.* Attorney-General, 80 N. E. Rep. 688, the Massachusetts Supreme Court holds that while there is a right to swim or float in or on public waters as well as to sail on them, there is no right in the public to use for bathing purposes, as those words are commonly understood, the part of the beach or shore above law watermark, whether covered with water or not.

Prisoner Acquitted on Ground of Insanity — Habeas Corpus. — In Urquhart *v.* Brown, 27 Sup. Ct. Rep. 459, the United States Supreme Court holds that, where a jury in a murder case brings in a verdict of "not guilty by reason of insanity" and after such acquittal the court by virtue of statutory authority orders the defendant to be committed to prison pending further orders of the court, a federal court should not discharge him on habeas corpus, even though his detention by the State authorities be in contravention of the Federal Constitution, since he should be left to his remedy by writ of error from the United States Supreme Court to review the final action of the highest court of the State.

Admissibility of Telephonic Communications. — In General Hospital Soc. *v.* New Haven Rendering Co., 65 Atl. Rep. 1065, the Connecticut Supreme Court holds that a conversation by telephone between an agent of a corporation at its office, with a person in the office of another corporation speaking for it, though unaccompanied by evidence that the person speaking for the latter was authorized to use its telephone for the purpose of communicating messages from its office, other than the presumption arising from the use of the telephone in the course of business, is *prima facie* admissible for any purpose that a conversation otherwise had with a person at the office of the latter corporation, apparently in charge thereof as its representative, would be admissible.

Injunction Against Inducing Breach of Contract. — In Beekman *v.* Marsters, 80 N. E. Rep. 817, an injunction was granted restraining the defendant from acting as agent of a corporation with which plaintiff had a contract giving him an exclusive agency. The plaintiff had obtained from the Jamestown Hotel Corporation, conducting a hotel within the grounds of the Jamestown Exposition, a contract whereby he was made their exclusive agent for the New England States to solicit patrons for the hotel. The defendant persuaded the hotel corporation to break the contract in order to allow him also to act as their agent in the same territory. Loring, J., after reviewing at some length the English and American cases bearing on the subject, announced the judgment of the court that the injunction should be granted.

Riparian Owner's Right to Build Pier. — The common-law principle that the King owns the soil of the sea in his own right is held not applicable to the conditions existing in this country by the New York Court of Appeals in Trustees *v.* Smith, 80 N. E. Rep. 665. The question involved in the case was whether the holder under a crown grant made in 1697 of upland bounded on high-water mark had the right to build a pier in front of his premises in order to reach navigable water, which pier extended over lands under water granted by the crown to a town. The court held that the land granted to the town was to be held for the people, and that the riparian owner had a right to build his pier, provided it did not constitute a nuisance. Hiscock, Vann, and Werner, JJ., dissented.

Legislature's Right to Regulate Increases of Railroad Stock. — In State *v.* Great Northern R. Co., 111 N. W. Rep.

289, the Minnesota Supreme Court holds that a statute leaving it to the judgment and discretion of a commission whether or not to allow an increase of capital stock by railway corporations is unconstitutional as being a delegation of legislative power. The court holds that the legislature has an undoubted right to enact a statute regulating increases of capital stock by railroads; and that "in the exercise of this right it may pass a statute providing generally for what purposes and upon what terms, conditions, and limitations an increase of capital stock may be made, and confer upon the commission the administrative duty of supervising any proposed increase of stock. It may also delegate to the commission the duty of finding the facts in each particular case, and authorize and require it, if it finds the existence of facts that bring the case within the statute, to allow the proposed increase; otherwise to refuse it." But an attempt to authorize the commission in its judgment to allow an increase of stock for such purpose and on such terms or conditions as it may deem advisable is void as a delegation of legislative power.

RELIGIOUS EXERCISES IN PUBLIC SCHOOLS. — In Church *v.* Bullock, 100 S. W. Rep. 1025, the Texas Court of Civil Appeals holds that the holding of morning exercises in the public schools, consisting of the reading by the teacher without comment of nonsectarian extracts from the Bible, King James's version, and by repeating the Lord's Prayer, and the singing of appropriate songs, in which the pupils are invited, but not required, to join, does not constitute the public schools a place of worship, nor render them sectarian, nor convert them into a religious seminary, within the meaning of a constitutional provision that no one shall be compelled to attend or support any place of worship, and that no money shall be appropriated from the treasury for the benefit of any religious society or for the support of any sectarian school. The court said: "The laws of this State neither require nor forbid the use of the Bible in the public schools, and the court will not exercise its powers to declare its use unlawful, simply because there is apprehension that the school authorities may abuse its use by attempting to teach some sectarian or theological views or opinions of their own."

INJURY CAUSED BY MUTUAL MISUNDERSTANDING. — That the husband of a woman who, in response to a knock at the door, cries "Come in," is not legally responsible for injuries sustained by the knocker through entering the wrong door, is declared by the Virginia Supreme Court in Clark *v.* Fehlhaber, 56 S. E. Rep. 817. The plaintiff, as the shades of night were falling fast, called at the defendant's house for the purpose of interviewing his wife on a matter of feminine business. She entered a side door which was customarily used and, passing into a vestibule from which several doors opened, knocked at one of them. The defendant's wife, who was inside the house, without ascertaining the identity of the door whereon the plaintiff was knocking, extended a cheery invitation to "Come in." Accordingly the plaintiff opened the door, stepped in, and, after an abrupt and startling descent in obedience to the well-known law of gravitation, brought up with some violence against the floor of the cellar. Feeling naturally aggrieved and embittered by this untoward occurrence, the plaintiff began to cast about in her mind — as soon, at least, as she collected and reassorted her rudely scattered faculties — for some person on whom to wreak her vengeance. It probably did not take her long to decide upon the husband as the logical candidate, and in the lower court she actually recovered judgment against him, but the appellate court thought that "the injury was proximately occasioned by mutual misunderstanding, responsibility for which, if anybody was in fault, attached to both alike," and accordingly reversed the judgment and dismissed the case.

Book Reviews.

FOUNDATIONS OF LEGAL LIABILITY.

Foundations of Legal Liability: A Presentation of the Theory and Development of the Common Law. By Thomas Atkins Street. Three volumes. Edward Thompson Co., Northport, N. Y. 1906.

[The following appreciation of Foundations of Legal Liability appeared in the April number of *The Law Quarterly Review*, London. No legal periodical stands higher in the estimation of the profession, and the editorial qualities that find expression in its pages impart exceptional weight to its judgments. Most of our readers are, of course, aware that Sir Frederick Pollock is the editor of this quarterly. As no review of Mr. Street's work has appeared in LAW NOTES, our readers will no doubt be pleased to see what is thought of it by a competent and disinterested reviewer in the original home of the common law.—ED.]

"This is a work of considerable pretensions and unusual merit. It aims at searching out the foundations of the common law, and showing how stage by stage the simple principles of a primitive society have become adapted to the wants of a complicated and restless civilization; and on the whole is satisfactorily and well done. The author, whose name is unfamiliar to us, displays a wide and accurate range of reading and, what is even rarer, a power of analysis and independent thought which is fruitful in suggestions both ingenious and original. He has bestowed much care and labor in the production of an institutional work that should be widely used and with very beneficial results. The author's standpoint is that the common law has grown to its present dimensions through the operation of two paramount influences — the historical and the philosophical; and he aims to trace the course of both. He finds the foundations of the common law, where only they are certainly to be found, in the Year Books and in old English reports; and he does not lose touch of the English reports and trust to the vast volume of the American cases throughout his course till he lands in law of to-day; since, as he says, 'the utterances of the English courts are on the whole in closer and more direct succession to the original common-law doctrine than are the decisions of the American courts.' The result is, for English readers at any rate, that the book has a greater simplicity through discarding the perpetual jangle of rival jurisdictions, and a greater interest through the reader's attention being undistracted by the consideration of nonessential differences. American cases are, however, freely used, as they ought to be, and where they are of the greatest value. . . .

"Though we do not find in Mr. Street's work either that beauty of style (though his style is clear and strong and good), or that wide and accurate scholarship, or the penetrating philosophic instinct that pervades Pollock and Maitland's History of the English Law, yet we can think of no treatise which, since fate forbids us to hope for the continuation of that altogether admirable book, will carry on the student better through the period of the Year Books and the early reporters than this of Mr. Street. Mr. Justice Holmes's line of investigation, as shown in The Common Law, applied to the matter of Broom's Commentaries, is the nearest suggestion we can think of to convey to any one wishing to apprehend the scope of Mr. Street's book a conception of its range and method. Mr. Street takes an early case from a Year Book or from Dyer or Moore or Croke, preferentially the earliest case, and then traces the principle there adumbrated or in germ down through its various vicissitudes till he brings it to rest in the current opinion of to-day; or sometimes he works by the reverse process, and taking a doctrine full grown he strips it of its accretions and shows it once again in its rudiments.

"We fancy that Mr. Street is, comparatively at any rate, a young writer; for the quality of his writing improves as he goes on. His first volume, on Tort, is the least satisfactory of the three; though this, even if it stood alone, we should still highly commend. He starts with a discussion on trespass. The initial point in the law of tort, he tells us, is the idea of hurt or damage done by force. Later comes the moral element, and wrongdoing is presumed wherever personal rights of individuals are interfered with. Trespass is modified into case, which takes in negligence; then follow nuisance, conversion, defamation, and deceit. Deceit is the forerunner of assumpsit. It has as its essence the notion of damage done by deceitful artifice; and this gives rise to an action on the case in the nature of deceit where failure to perform a promise can be alleged; hence flows the action of assumpsit with its aspects both of tort and contract and destined to a dominating place in both provinces. . . .

"Mr. Street's second volume deals with Contracts. He starts with the real contracts, as originally the only kind recognized by the law, and proceeds to show the course of their development, through debt, with its *quid pro quo* and its exacting formalities gradually wearing away, till we come to the formless promissory obligations of modern law. All this is very well done. In the *Harvard Law Review* there is a series of very remarkable articles by Messrs. Ames, Langdell, Williston, Beale, and Ashley (to mention only some of a band of contributors of exceptional brilliancy), which probe deeply into the origin and history of contractual obligations. Mr. Street has wisely laid these under heavy tribute, and has greatly added to the value and interest of his book by doing so. He has also enabled English readers to become acquainted with trains of reasoning and conclusions of the highest importance for the correct understanding of this province of our law, which hitherto have been to a great extent inaccessible to them. The distinction between the English and the Roman contract, what is a 'cause' and what a 'consideration' and wherein they differ, is elaborately and well pointed out. The history of how the unilateral contract was superseded by the bilateral is also treated in detail. The steps which show the development of this stage of our law are best marked in the reports, too much neglected, of the Tudor period, but than which there are not any richer in the assertion of principle and indications of legal growth; and to these Mr. Street liberally resorts and with much advantage and some novelty. The Stuart reports, too, Mr. Street has treated in a way that makes plain, what is often forgotten, that when the Stuart judges passed from the region of politics to that of law their grasp of the principles of the common law was unsurpassed. Mr. Street keenly appreciates the influence of individual judges in working out the doctrines of the law. In his pages the masterful intellect of Holt, C. J., is shown most often dominating his colleagues for good and in the cause of breadth of doctrine; but sometimes, as in his struggle against the negotiability of promissory notes, the enemy of progress, and overpowering the courts only to be subdued by the intervention of the legislature. There, too, is a whole chapter devoted to a connected account of the efforts of Lord Mansfield to liberalize the law . . . Mr. Street's treatment of the Statute of Frauds is excellent; so is his treatment of the doctrine of representation both in contract and tort.

"Part III of the second volume deals with the History and Principles of the Law of Bills and Notes. This is as well done as any section of Mr. Street's work. The historical portion is clearly stated, and the reasons for the train of the decisions are given. There is added as an appendix what is practically a treatise on the Negotiable Instruments Law of the United States. . . .

"Mr. Street's third volume deals with Actions. There is a smack of antiquity, at this time of day, in writing upon actions. But Mr. Street correctly points out that accurate knowledge of substantive law is acquired more easily by a knowledge of the purport and scope of the old division of actions. . . . In adding to his treatise a volume upon the old forms of action we think Mr. Street has done well. Many a modern lawyer whose opinion and mode of doing his business are the admiration of wholly confiding clients, if furnished with a volume of Rolle or of Comyns and asked to explain any page of it would be utterly at a loss. It is not good that such reservoirs of our old law with their abundant stores of the most enduring principles should cease to be resorted to by the practicing lawyer. To the historical student of law they must ever be of the greatest value and interest; but it is not well that they should cease to be resorted to to illustrate the daily wants of the law; and a treatise like this of Mr. Street's, which will explain the meanings of forms now fallen into disuse and will elicit the permanent value that is latent in them, is of high value as a means of legal education, and should be carefully studied.

"There is an admirable index and table of cases which renders reference very easy. We should commend Mr. Street's rare reticence in his citation of cases. The vice of American text writers, indeed of text writers generally, is to swamp their works with redundant authorities; but Mr. Street has quite avoided this fault. His book deals with principles, not with authorities, though his principles are always adequately supported by authorities. A word should also be said for the sumptuous way in which the book is produced; type, paper, get-up generally, are all admirable."

23 *Law Quarterly Review* (April 1907), pp. 228-232.

MUNICIPAL CONTROL OF PUBLIC UTILITIES.

Municipal Control of Public Utilities: A Study of the Attitude of our Courts toward an Increase of the Sphere of Municipal Activity. By Oscar Lewis Pond, LL.B., Ph. D., Member of the Indianapolis Bar. New York. The Columbia University Press. The Macmillan Company, Agents. London: P. S. King & Son. 1906. 115 pp.

This book is one of a series of Studies in History, Economics, and Public Law, edited by the faculty of Political Science of Columbia University.

The purpose of the author, as stated in the introductory chapter, is to answer the legal questions raised by the contention that recourse to "repressive activity," as the author styles municipal regulation of public utilities, is inconsistent with constitutional guaranties, and the claim that the system of municipal government does not permit a municipal corporation "to enter into the field of what is denominated as private business." In order to accomplish this purpose the author discusses the nature of the city organization and the construction placed by the courts on the powers given to cities, the constitutional limitations on municipal activity, the powers of control possessed by cities over the operation by private individuals of those public utilities which it is deemed wise to leave in private hands, and how far the judicial construction of the law with regard to the taxation and sale of the property of cities aids or hampers the cities in the discharge of the new duties they may be called upon to assume. Succeeding chapters deal with The Two Capacities of Municipal Corporations; Construction of Municipal Charters; The Implied Powers of Municipal Corporations; What Are Municipal Purposes Within the Meaning of the Constitution; Exemption from Taxation of Municipal Property; Sale of Municipal Property Providing Public Utilities; Power to Grant Exclusive Franchises, and Municipal Regulation of Rates for Public Utilities.

The attitude of the courts, both state and federal, toward the question of municipal regulation, ownership, and operation of public utilities is stated in a clear and interesting manner. In the discussion of any question of governmental authority it is well to understand the scope and limitations of the power as preliminary to a consideration of the expediency of its exercise. As giving an introductory discussion of the legal aspects of municipal ownership the book is a distinct contribution.

In a final chapter, however, giving his conclusions, the author does not hesitate to indicate his view as to the expediency of the general adoption of this policy, and says that "while . . . the courts have naturally not been called upon to decide the expediency or inexpediency of the policy of municipal ownership and operation of public utilities, since they have regarded the decision of this question in concrete cases are not a judicial matter, but rather a question for the municipality concerned to decide for itself within the limits of the statutes, they have in a number of instances not hesitated to voice the feeling that the trend of modern thought was favorable to municipal ownership and operation."

The book lacks an index.

LAW OF CRIMES.

A Digest of Important Cases on the Law of Crimes. Compiled, Edited, and Arranged for the use of Law Students. By John R. Rood. George Wahr, Ann Arbor, Mich. 1906. xiii + 623 pp.

This digest was prepared for the use of teachers and students in pursuing a modified case system of studying law. Instead of being in the form of a classification of digest paragraphs, as the title indicates, it is a compilation of abridged reports of cases. These appear to have been carefully selected and well arranged. While the digest was compiled for the use of teachers and students, the practitioner will find the book useful for occasional reference.

News of the Profession.

THE OHIO STATE BAR ASSOCIATION will meet at Put-in-Bay July 8–11.

NEW FEDERAL JUDGE IN ALABAMA. — On April 9 President Roosevelt filled the vacant federal district judgeship in Alabama by appointing Oscar R. Hundley.

THE MISSISSIPPI STATE BAR ASSOCIATION held its annual meeting in Vicksburg on May 7, 8, and 9. Particulars will be given in this column next month.

WELL-KNOWN BOSTONIAN DEAD. — Augustus Strong Wheeler, one of the best-known members of the Boston bar, died in that city April 14, aged eighty-seven years. He was a member of the firm of Hutchins & Wheeler.

A WOMAN JUSTICE OF THE PEACE. — Mrs. Catherine Waugh McCulloch, of Evanston, Ill., has the proud distinction of being the first woman to be made a justice of the peace in this country. She took up the duties of her office during April.

YERKES RESIGNS AND RESUMES PRACTICE. — On April 13 announcement was made of the resignation of John W. Yerkes from the position of commissioner of internal revenue. Mr. Yerkes will resume the practice of law in New York city in association with the firm of Hamilton & Colbert.

WEST VIRGINIA'S FIRST WOMAN LAWYER DEAD. — Mrs. Leila J. Fraser, the first woman to obtain admittance to the bar of West Virginia, died April 29 at Mudlavia Springs, Ind. She was the wife of General James G. Fraser, of Governor Davidson's staff, and practiced law in partnership with her husband.

WOMAN ADMITTED BY FEDERAL SUPREME COURT. — On April 18 Miss Ida M. Moyers, of Washington, D. C., was admitted to practice before the United States Supreme Court, being the twenty-eighth of her sex to achieve that distinction. The first was Belva A. Lockwood, who was admitted on March 3, 1879, and for six years thereafter stood alone in her dizzy eminence.

MONTREAL LAWYER DEAD. — Mr. Meredith B. Bethune, member of the Montreal law firm of Bethune & Bethune, died suddenly on April 27 of heart failure. He was graduated from McGill University in 1869 with the degrees of M. A. and B. C. L., and being aditted to the bar in the same year, formed a partnership with his father which continued until the time of his death.

TWO TEXAS LAWYERS SHOT. — Down in Texas the lawyers seem to have been furnishing a good deal of target practice lately. On April 26 county attorney H. L. Robb was shot from a second-story window in Groveton — that is, the bullet was shot from the window — by R. D. Kinley, one of the leading lawyers of that section. On April 30 Carroll B. Short, a prominent attorney of Center, Tex., was shot and killed by Dr. Buck Paul.

WILLIAM H. ARNOUX DEAD. — William H. Arnoux, formerly judge of the New York City Superior Court, died at Vineyard Haven, Mass., on April 23, aged seventy-six years. He was a member of the firm of Arnoux, Ritch & Woodford up to the time of his retirement from practice in 1896. In 1889 he was elected president of the New York State Bar Association. He served as judge of the Superior Court from 1882 until 1895.

GOOD NEWS FOR CHICAGO JURIES. — It is reported from Chicago that hereafter jurors in that city will be made as comfortable as convicts, if not more so. On an upper floor of the criminal court building quarters for the accommodation of three juries are being constructed. There are three suites, each containing bedrooms, a sitting-room, dining-room, bath, and so on, with a gymnasium common to all, but to be frequented by members of only one jury at a time.

PROMINENT INDIANAPOLIS LAWYER DEAD. — Hon. Theodore P. Davis, one of the most prominent lawyers in Indiana and a former member of the Appellate Court of that State, died at his home in Indianapolis on April 25 of Bright's disease. Judge Davis was a native of Indiana, fifty-two years of age, and was admitted to practice in 1874. In 1893 he was elected to the bench of the Appellate Court and served one term of four years, at the end of which he resumed practice in Indianapolis in partnership with Frank E. Gavin.

INTERNATIONAL LAW ASSOCIATION. — The International Law Association will meet in Portland, Me., on August 29, 30, and 31, immediately following the annual meeting of the American Bar Association in the same city. Distinguished delegates will be in attendance from all the civilized countries of the world. This will be the second time in the twenty-five years of its existence that the association has met in the United States. The meeting last year was held in Berlin, and the year previous in Christiana, Norway.

DEATH OF OLD LOUISIANA LAWYER. — Hon. A. W. O. Hicks, for many years a prominent attorney of Texas and Louisiana, died April 29 in Shreveport, La., at the advanced age of ninety years. Judge Hicks was born in Cannon county, Tenn., moved to Shelbyville, Tex., in 1839, and resided there until 1866, when he went to Shreveport. He was a member of the first constitutional convention of Texas, and for many years served as county judge of Shelby County. After his removal to Louisiana he served two terms as judge of the first judicial court of Caddo Parish.

DISTRICT OF COLUMBIA LAWYERS DINE. — The annual banquet of the District of Columbia Bar Association was held at the New Willard hotel in Washington on April 17, with President William F. Mattingly acting as toastmaster. The banquet was given in honor of the local judiciary, and those who responded to toasts were Justice Harlan, of the United States Supreme Court; Chief Justice Shepard, of the District Court of Appeals; Chief Justice Clabaugh, of the District Supreme Court, and Chief Justice Peelle, of the Court of Claims.

JUDGE WALLACE RETIRES. — Hon. William J. Wallace, of the United States Circuit Court of Appeals, second circuit, has resigned. Judge Wallace reached his seventieth birthday on April 14 and has sat on the federal bench since 1874, when he was appointed judge of the northern New York district by President Grant. In 1882 President Arthur appointed him circuit judge for the second circuit, and on the creation of the Circuit Court of Appeals in 1891 Judge Wallace became a member of that tribunal. The degree of doctor of laws has been conferred on him by his *alma mater*, Hamilton College, and also by Syracuse University.

EX-CHIEF JUSTICE OF CALIFORNIA DIES. — Hon. Niles Searls, formerly chief justice of the California Supreme Court and one of the pioneer lawyers of that State, died at his home in Berkeley on April 27. Judge Searls was born in New York in 1824. After taking a course in law he migrated to Missouri where he remained until the gold fever of 1849 carried him to California. While in immediate contact with the gold fields he acquired a profound knowledge of mining law and customs and he was subsequently very influential in shaping the mining laws of California. His first judicial experience was as judge of the fourteenth district. Later he served two terms as State senator, after which he was appointed chief justice of the State Supreme Court. He had of late years been living a very retired life.

DEATH OF AN OREGON PIONEER. — Hon. Reuben Patrick Boise, one of the three men who framed the first code of laws for Oregon territory, and formerly a member of the Oregon Supreme Court, died at his home in Salem, Ore., on April 13, aged eighty-eight years. He was a native of Massachusetts, but emigrated to Oregon in 1850 and soon became prominent in the affairs of that territory. In 1857 President Buchanan appointed him a member of the territorial Supreme Court, and after the admission of Oregon to statehood Judge Boise was elected to the State Supreme bench. By preference he left that court to accept nomination for circuit judge of the third circuit, and in that position he served for many years. He is generally regarded as one of the strongest judges that ever sat on the bench in Oregon.

DEAN HUFFCUT A SUICIDE. — Ernest W. Huffcut, dean of the Cornell University Law School and legal adviser of Governor Hughes of New York, committed suicide on May 4 by shooting himself in the right temple. He was at the time on his way to New York city on the Hudson River steamboat Charles W. Morse. Insomnia resulting from overwork is supposed to have led to the suicide. Mr. Huffcut was a native of Connecticut and was forty-seven years of age. He was graduated from Cornell in 1884, and four years later took the degree of LL.B. in the Cornell Law School. He practiced law in Minneapolis for two years and then became a professor of law at the University of Indiana. From there he went to Northwestern University, where he remained until 1893. In that year he returned to Cornell as a professor of law, and in 1903 was chosen director of the law faculty and dean of the law school. He was a member of the American Bar Association and the New York State Bar Association, and had been since 1905 the New York commissioner for the promotion of uniformity of legislation. He was appointed legal adviser to Governor Hughes immediately after the latter's election in 1906 and had spent much of his time since then in Albany conferring with the Governor in regard to pending legislation.

RECOMMENDATIONS OF INSURANCE LAW COMMITTEE. — The insurance law committee of the American Bar Association met in Philadelphia on April 23 and 24 and decided on the following recommendations, which in elaborated form will constitute the report of the committee to the association at the annual meeting in August.

First. The appointment of State insurance commissioners for fitness and expert qualifications for the position, rather than as a reward for political services.

Second. That all companies created outside of the United States make deposits in at least one State. The chief motive for this recommendation was the action of certain German companies after the San Francisco fire which repudiated their policies.

Third. The repeal of the retaliatory tax laws.

Fourth. The repeal of the valued policy laws.

Fifth. The creation in each State of the office of fire marshal. This exists at present in only about one-third of the States.

Sixth. The enactment of a federal statute prohibiting the use of the mails by wildcat insurance companies and by any company not authorized by the law of the State of its origin.

Seventh. The apportionment and contingent distribution of deferred dividend surplus on policies now in force, as a precedent to the right to do business outside of the State in which the company is created.

AMERICAN SOCIETY OF INTERNATIONAL LAW. — On April 19 and 20 the first annual meeting of the American Society of International Law was held in Washington, D. C., with many distinguished lawyers in attendance. Among those who spoke or took part in the discussions were Secretary of State Elihu Root, Richard Olney, Brig.-Gen. George B. Davis, Rear Admiral Charles H. Stockton, Everett P. Wheeler, Hannis Taylor, Prof. John Bassett Moore, Dr. William Draper Lewis, Prof. Charles Noble Gregory, U. M. Rose, John W. Foster, and Oscar S. Straus. The president of the association, Hon. Elihu Root, delivered an address on "The Real Question under the Japanese Treaty and the San Francisco School Board Resolution." Some of the subjects discussed were immunity of private property on the high seas; trade in contraband; the transference of prize cases to an international tribunal; the Drago doctrine; the rights of foreigners in the United States in case of conflict between federal treaties and state laws; and the second Hague conference and the development of international law as a science. Officers were elected as follows: President, Elihu Root; vice-presidents, Chief Justice Melville A. Fuller, Justice David J. Brewer, Justice William R. Day, William H. Taft, Andrew Carnegie, Joseph H. Choate, John W. Foster, George Gray, John W. Griggs, W. W. Morrow, Richard Olney, Oscar S. Straus, and Horace Porter.

English Notes.

DEATHS OF PROMINENT LAWYERS. — Sir Samuel Hall, K. C., long a leading member of the chancery bar and later Vice-Chancellor of the County Palatine of Lancaster, died April 6, aged sixty-six. Mr. John Edmund Wentworth Addison, K. C., former judge of the Southwark County Court, died April 20 in London, aged sixty-nine.

PHONOGRAPH RECORD NOT INFRINGEMENT OF COPYRIGHT. — In the recent case of Newmark *v.* National Phonographic Co. (noted in the *Law Journal* for April 20, at page 259) Mr. Justice Sutton held that a phonographic record of a song was not a "copy" of a "sheet of music" within the meaning of the English Copyright Act of 1842.

ANNUAL MEETING OF BAR SOCIETY. — The annual meeting of the Bar Society was held in Lincoln's Inn on April 17, the Attorney-General presiding. Some of the matters discussed were the congestion in the Court of Appeal, the relations of the colonial bars to the bar of England, the change in the Long Vacation, and the desirability of having official stenographers attached to the criminal courts.

TO IMPROVE THE PORTION OF SCOTTISH WIDOWS. — A bill has recently been introduced in Parliament to give widows in Scotland the same rights that were secured to widows in England by the intestate estates act of 1890, by which the widow is entitled to the whole estate if it is under $25,000, and if it is over $25,000 has a first charge to that amount. By Scottish law the widow of an intestate without issue gets one-half of the movable estate and a third of the heritable, the residue going to the husband's relatives.

SENTENCE DOUBLED BY AN ECHO. — The new criminal court building in London, known as the "New Old Bailey," is not proving altogether satisfactory so far as its acoustic properties are concerned. There is in fact a decided echo. Recently Judge Rentoul was sentencing a prisoner, and immediately on his pronouncing sentence, "Six months' hard labor" was apparently repeated from the other side of the room. The prisoner, who seems to have been possessed of a very proper sense of humor, turned to the warder and inquired whether "these yer two sentences" were not to run concurrently.

PRESUMPTION OF SURVIVORSHIP. — The case of Wallis *v.* Brown, recently before the English Court of Probate, brought up the question of survivorship in death by a common disaster in a rather novel form. The point arose not, as in most of the cases, as the result of a shipwreck, but in consequence of a double murder and a suicide, one of the deceased having gone out of his mind and shot his wife, his sister-in-law, and himself. There was medical evidence, founded on the position of the bodies, which pointed to the inference that the wife had lived the longest of the three, and accordingly Mr. Justice Bargrave-Deane ruled that she had survived her sister.

RESPONDEAT SUPERIOR APPLIED TO AUTOMOBILE ACCIDENT. — A case of some interest to purchasers of automobiles is that of Perkins *v.* Stead, lately decided by one of the Divisional Courts. The defendant having purchased an automobile, the vendors supplied him with a chauffeur to drive him for a short distance on his way home. While the chauffeur was running the car he collided with the defendant's motor bicycle. The court held that the chauffeur was at the time of the accident the servant of the purchaser, who was entitled to direct him how to drive, and therefore the defendant was liable for damages caused by the chauffeur's negligence.

QUEER CASES BEFORE THE PRIVY COUNCIL. — Probably no other tribunal has such curious causes before it as the Judicial Committee of the Privy Council. The latest weird contest before it was a case from India in which one set of idol-worshipers sued another set of idol-worshipers with respect to a monopoly of the right to practice rites at the shrine of a certain god. An even stranger case before the same body was one in which Lord Justice Rigby, then at the bar, was briefed on behalf of no less a personage than the great god Vishnu. The argument was that a difference existed between the hundred and seventh and hundred and eighth incarnations. The question was whether certain property had belonged to the god in his physical capacity, or whether it became his upon his attaining immortality. The later incarnation sued the earlier, saying that the property belonged to the god's divine self, and had not been acquired by him before in the flesh.

A "SPOOK SUIT." — Considerable interest has been manifested in London over the libel suit brought by the Rev. T. Colley against J. N. Maskelyne, a well-known "illusionist." Mr. Colley is a great believer in "spirits" (not the alcoholic but the psychic kind) and offered to give £1,000 to anybody who could reproduce by artificial means certain spiritual doings which he had witnessed at seances. Maskelyne promptly took up the gauntlet, and there seems to be no reasonable doubt that he earned the promised reward. The Rev. Colley, however, refused to pay, by reason of which Maskelyne was incited to issue a pamphlet containing statements that Colley did not regard as complimentary, among them one to the effect that Colley had no right to the title of Archdeacon which he affected. Consequently he sued for libel, and Maskelyne counterclaimed for the £1,000 reward. At last accounts the reverend gentleman seemed likely to lose both ways. He fared very badly on cross-examination.

ANOTHER CRIMINAL APPEAL BILL. — On April 17 the Attorney-General introduced into the House of Commons a bill for the establishment of a court of criminal appeal. In his introductory speech he expressed the hope that he had smoothed away the difficulties and met the objections which caused the House of Commons at the last session to kill the Lord Chancellor's bill after it had passed the House of Lords. The measure calls for a new and distinct court of record, to consist of eight judges — the Lord Chief Justice and seven other judges of the High Court to be designated by him. The measure gives an absolute right of appeal on questions of law, but as to questions of fact the leave of the appellate court is required. The court is not empowered to order a new trial, but is given power to take further evidence and to refer to a special commissioner matters requiring prolonged examination of documents or accounts, or any scientific or local examination which cannot conveniently be conducted before the court.

WILLS OF ENGLISH LAWYERS. — The lawyer's traditional distaste for elaborate testaments, as illustrated by the fact that the late Lord Davey's will was scribbled on a sheet of rough foolscap, has been shared by many of England's most distinguished lawyers. Lord Mansfield found half a sheet of note paper ample for the disposal of all his worldly possessions; Sir James Fitzjames Stephen's will was a model of brevity, for it began and ended in thirteen words; and a dozen lines served to dispose of Lord Russell of Killowen's estate of nearly £150,000. The late Lord Grimthorpe showed a fine contempt for convention in scribbling three of his fourteen codicils on the backs of an old letter, a dinner invitation, and a circular respectively. Lord St. Leonards put his last testament away so carefully that nobody could ever find it; Lord St. Helier provided fees for lawyers by tearing a sheet out of his will; and Mr. H. C. Richards, K. C., also did his profession a good turn by leaving a will full of interlineations; while Serjeant Maynard deliberately left an ambiguously worded testament in order that certain legal questions which had puzzled him when living should be settled when he was dead.

"DEMENTIA AMERICANA" FROM AN ENGLISH VIEWPOINT. — The London *Law Journal* in a recent issue says editorially: "This new category of madness was evolved by the exigencies of the Thaw trial. The theoretical existence of this form of insanity, having failed to serve its intended purpose, is now strenuously repudiated by all parties; and its ingenious inventor, Mr. Delmas, appears to run considerable risk of being thrown over by his assistants in the defense, as was the leader who preceded him. 'Brainstorms' are in fact under a cloud; and there are evidences of returning reason in the great American public, whose divided opinions on the old topic of 'Killing no murder,' in its latest society phase, were fairly reflected in the disagreement of the jury. The provision of the American law which divides the crime of murder into degrees corresponding roughly with the heinousness of the offense, so that the death sentence is reserved for fatal attacks of a deliberate and brutal character, should make it easy for a jury not befogged by new-fangled theories of this character, supported and controverted by voluminous expert evidence, to come to a right decision on the guilt or innocence of Mr. Thaw in the killing of his rival, and it is to be hoped that, in the interests of sane public opinion, such a conclusion may still be arrived at."

Obiter Dicta.

Very Fastidious. — Over in Vienna the legal profession appears to be held to a much stricter etiquette than in this country. A lawyer was recently disbarred there for picking up cigar butts in the public streets, a practice which was pronounced "unseemly and derogatory to the dignity of his profession."

Arboreal Rights of Small Boys. — "The immemorial habit of small boys to climb little oak trees filled with abundant branches reaching almost to the ground is a habit which corporations stretching their wires over such trees must take notice of." Whitfield, C. J., in Temple *v.* McComb City Electric Light & Power Co., (Miss. 1907) 42 So. Rep. 874.

A Cool Client. — An Oregon attorney, representing a client whose title to a certain cold storage plant was under fire, closed an able argument before the Oregon Supreme Court recently with the following bit of pathos: "Your honors, there is more resting upon your decision than this cold storage plant; a human life is at stake. My client's life's efforts are in this cold storage; his life blood is in this cold storage; his body and soul are wrapped up in this cold storage."

There Is. — In our March number was published a letter from a Kentucky lawyer telling of a father, son, and grandson all practicing law at the Richmond, Ky., bar, and asking, "Is there another bar in America that has three generations actively engaged in the practice of the law?" We are reliably informed that the firm of S. K. & B. C. Williams, of Newark, Wayne county, N. Y., is composed of Stephen K. Williams, Byron C. Williams, and George E. Williams, who are respectively father, son, and grandson, and are all actively engaged in practice.

A Canny Cow. — The following letter, recently received by the trouble department of the M., K. & T. Railway Co. from a section foreman, will probably appeal to those prosperous readers of ours who handle the "cow cases" for soulless railroad corporations:

Dear Sir

in Reply to your letter of 4/7 in Regard to that Old Black Bob tail Cow that Cow Has lived on the Right a Way for the last Six years & She Walks Right over the Cattle gards Just as there Was none there & there is no guard that Will Stop Her. She is in on the Rite of Way Every Day & there is no train that Will Hit Hur for She is all time on the look out i Have notified the owner & he Says She Will take car of Herself So i Dont no What to Doo With Her

Yours truly.

A Lawyer's Card. — The following is the business card of a lawyer of Mammoth Springs, Ark.:

ILE BE DAMD

If I don't tend to your business right; defend you against the impositions of your enemies; collect your debts; secure your titles to your homes; write your mortgages and your contracts of any and all kinds; take your depositions; and, so long as you remain moral, sober and honest, and pay your Lawyer's fees, I'll pay your taxes and keep up your standing in the church, so I will. Respectfully,

J. M. BURROW

LAWYER NOTARY PUBLIC

An Editor's Opinion of Thaw's Lawyers. — The editor of The West Virginia *Bar* pays his respects to the galaxy of legal talent retained for the defense in a recent notorious murder trial, in the following trenchant language: "The Thaw case was distinguished for many peculiar things, but for nothing more than the aggregation of scrub lawyers he gathered in for his defense. With the exception of Delmas, they were hardly competent to conduct a case of assault and battery before a justice, and Thaw would have been elected to the chair the first week of the trial if they had conducted his defense. They were not only scrubs, but they acted scrubby to Delmas all through the trial, and are keeping it up. The Thaws will appreciate Delmas more when they have put some other fellow in his place."

Was Barred by Antiquity. — A somewhat difficult legal problem was recently presented to Justice Altstadt, of Omaha. A decidedly ungallant gentleman seventy years of age brought suit against a maiden lady, on whose head some sixty-five winters had sifted their snows, to recover an indebtedness amounting to $135. The defendant pleaded an accord and satisfaction, alleging that the plaintiff had agreed to accept in full satisfaction of his claim one kiss from the defendant's ruby lips, which said osculation had been promptly and fervidly delivered by the defendant. Justice Altstadt apparently dodged the difficulty by deciding that the defense was of an equitable nature of which his tribunal could not take cognizance, for he gave judgment in favor of the plaintiff for the full amount of the claim, reserving to the defendant the right to bring an independent action for the recovery of the kiss or the value of same. Perhaps the learned justice was of the opinion that even though there may have been an accord, there could not possibly have been any satisfaction.

A Gentle Hint. — A California lawyer calls attention to a scheme which he has found efficacious in bringing to time the kind of people that ignore letters from lawyers. It consists of a postal card on which is printed merely his name and address, the date, a file number, and the simple statement in bold type

I want to see you

He says: "I find it very useful as a saver of the time required to dictate and write a letter; also, it doesn't offend the P. O. people; but after a man has had one or two he comes along instead of having the postman conclude that he isn't paying his grocer. As regular clients often get the same thing when an appointment is needed, or there is something ready for them to sign, the "beat" has no kick coming. The case or claim number at the top offers a ready reference. It's all in getting them educated up to knowing enough to climb down when they are invited."

A HEINOUS OFFENSE. — The glory seems to be departing from Texas. From the not very remote time when the popular idea of a typical Texan was a fierce-looking gent carrying a full complement of guns and bowie knives, to the stage of civilization mirrored in the following information, is indeed a long stride of ethical progress:

In the Name and by the Authority of the State of Texas.

Hugh L. Humphries, County Attorney of the County of Potter, State aforesaid, presents in the County Court of said County, at the July Term, A. D. 1907, of said Court, that R. M. West, on or about the 21st day of April, A. D. One thousand nine hundred and seven, and before the filing of this information, in the County of Potter and State of Texas, did then and there unlawfully, willfully and maliciously wound a cat, the same then and there being a domesticated animal, the same then and there being the property of F. Scruggs,, with intent then and there, on the part of him the said R. M. West, to injure the said F. Scruggs, the owner thereof, against the peace and dignity of the State. HUGH L. HUMPHRIES,

County Attorney of Potter County, said State.

FULL PARTICULARS. — The following ingenuous certificate emanated from a Tennessee notary:

Sworn to and subscribed to before me this 19th day of June 1905. And I hereby certify the foregoing deposition was taken before me as stated in the caption except that the taking was adjourned over from the 18th to the 19th of June, 1905, as appears in the deposition, and that I am not interest in the cause, nor of kin, or counsel to either of the parties, and that I sealed them up and put them in the Post Office at Newcombe, Tenn., addressed to the Pulaski Circuit Court Clerk, at Somerset, Ky., without being out of my possession after they were taken. My name appears in the caption as Hamp Rosier. I am generally known and addressed this way. My full name, however, is David Hampton Rosier, and my notary seal is "D. H. Rosier." I answer to all of these names. There is no other person in this country by either one of the names except my little son D. H. Who is 9 years of age.

This June 19th 1905.

Hamp, alias D. H. Rosier,
Notary Public.

A FINE POINT OF LAW. — The following inquiry as to the jurisdiction of a justice of the peace was received by attorney G. D. B. Reynolds, of Troy, N. C.:

MY DEAR SIR, It with much pleasure i write you a fue lins to let you hear fromme i am well and hope these fue lins will find you the same. I suppose you reach home O K Mr Reynolds I have a fue questions to ask you in regards to law if you will give full perticklers it will be highly apreshated.

Have a J. P. a right to find a person for contimpt of cort in such a case as below the J. P. goes in to the evidents and bind the case over to supream cort and requare a bond of fifty dollars for his apearence and the J. P. fails to fix up bond and the defindent is dismiss by the cort and no bond is fix up and the in a fue days later isues a capers for the defindent and find him because he have fail to give bond, please ans in full if you are in a possition to do so as this have apeared to me and i would like get all the information i could in regards to the matter, and is thare any way that i can deal with him if it is not law Mr Reynolds i thank now that i shall spend a fue days in your town this summer waiting for your early reply i beg to remain,

Yours most respt,
Leon B. Sutton.

Correspondence.

KIDNAPPING BY THE STATE.

To the Editor of LAW NOTES.

SIR: In an editorial of the April issue of LAW NOTES, referring to the attitude of the Socialist and Labor press upon the decision of the Supreme Court of the United States upon the manner in which Moyer, Haywood, and Pettibone were abducted and taken to Idaho to answer an indictment for the murder of Ex-Governor Steunenburg, you state that the decision is such "as would have been anticipated by any one familiar with the course of decision on this topic." Has there ever been a case before the Supreme Court of the United States in which there was presented for decision the same identical question that was presented in the case of the State of Idaho *v.* Moyer *et al.*? Has the same court ever before held that sovereign States, through their official heads, can enter into and lawfully carry out a conspiracy to kidnap peaceable and law-abiding citizens, or, for that matter, any person, and take them into a foreign jurisdiction and among strangers to be tried for a crime, when they are not "fugitives from justice" within the meaning of the Constitution? If States can do this without running counter to the Constitution of the United States, why may they not be permitted through their legislatures to in effect abolish that part of the Constitution? You will probably agree that an express statutory enactment of any State providing for the extradition of persons not "fugitives from justice" would violate the United States Constitution, and would, therefore, be void. If this be true, then why should a State be permitted to do clandestinely and at the dead of night that which it could not do openly? And having thus forcibly kidnapped its victim, what other remedy, other than the return of the prisoner to the State from which he was taken, would he have? What other tribunals than the federal courts should pass upon the question of the legality of such proceeding? H. W. HOUSTON.

PARKERSBURG, W. Va.

Law Notes

JULY, 1907.

PUBLISHED BY EDWARD THOMPSON COMPANY.
NORTHPORT, LONG ISLAND, N. Y.

CONTENTS.

JUDGE WILLIAM J. WALLACE, of the Federal Circuit Court of Appeals for the second circuit, has retired from the bench after a service extending over thirty-three years as judge of the District Court, the Circuit Court, and the Circuit Court of Appeals. Judge Wallace takes with him in his retirement into private life the reputation of an able judge and the respect of the bar. The feeling of the bar toward him was indicated by a dinner in his honor presided over by ex-Judge Alton B. Parker, and attended by more than five hundred lawyers. Upon this occasion Judge Wallace expressed his opinion, an opinion entitled to peculiar weight from his long and eminent career on the bench, upon the tenure of the judicial office and the pay of the judges. Among other things, he said: "I believe that the selection by appointment and the life tenure have contributed more than all else to secure an independent, efficient, and honored judiciary; and I believe with these features moderate salaries will secure as fit men as any who can be tempted by larger pay. Many of the federal judges have accepted their places at large pecuniary sacrifice, and few of them would have accepted them if it had not been for the life tenure. There are as learned and able men among them as are any of the English judges. Great judges are few, and no bench in any state or nation has a larger proportion of them than has the federal judiciary. It has been proposed by the most conspicuous leader of one of the great political parties — I don't refer to him who presides over us — to substitute for the life term of the federal judiciary an elective term of, I think, seven years. No blow more fatal than this could be aimed at all that is valuable in our existing system. It has been provoked largely by the courage of these judges in restraining the lawless acts of trades unions, and in protecting the enforcement of State legislation which they believe to conflict with the guarantees of the Federal Constitution. It would be better to abolish these courts altogether. They would not be federal courts in any true sense, because the judges would be merely the selection of the localities of their jurisdiction, and consciously or unconsciously they would reflect the local influences of their environment." A feverish desire for experiment and change seems to have seized upon a portion of the people at this time, and one hears a demand for sweeping aside every obstacle to "new things," though tried and trusted institutions should be involved. Calm words proceeding from experience and ability should have an effect on this spirit.

A WORD about certain present-day characteristics of our national life in a wider field was spoken by Judge Wallace. He alluded to the race of the political parties "to capture the votes of the discontented, the prejudiced, the unthinking, and the fanatical believers in socialistic theories." The tendency is toward the formation of a majority who would, under the guise of protecting public interests, meddle with private enterprises and lawful occupations and who threaten the rights of the minority. And yet the excuses for this feeling of class discontent are few. "The majority in this country," the speaker observed, "more than in any other country in the world, are prosperous; but too many of them envy the greater prosperity of some of the minority, and through vindictiveness or greed propose to wrench it from them and appropriate it to themselves. They forget when wreaking vengeance on the predatory abuses of power by the unscrupulous managers of corporations they are striking down the property rights of multitudes of innocent investors in every community who are in no degree responsible for the wrongs that have been committed." One way in which this discontent is finding utterance is in the demand for greater federal activity in legislation at the expense of the States, a demand which has found aid and comfort in Secretary Root's warning to the States that if they failed to exercise the powers committed to them under our original scheme of government, they must be prepared to see the federal government step into their place. Mr. Root's utterance continues to call forth amazed comment. Former Justice Hatch, of New York, had this to say in a recent address: "Other utterances have proceeded from other public men which are in harmony with this utterance, but none before has been so bold as to stand up in the presence of forty-five States, holding a commission by their authority, and say that their reserved rights should be taken away unless they adopted certain lines of policy. If the Secretary's language could be construed as meaning that the courts shall find within the bounds of the Constitution constitutional authority for the proposed measure, we should have no criticism to make. But the admission that the power to be taken away is reserved to the States excludes such interpretation of the language. The existing rights of the States can only be taken away with the consent or neglect of the executive, and if so taken away it will be in violation of an oath to support and keep inviolate that instrument. It is the same oath which Lincoln took with such a solemn sense of obligation, and which he fulfilled with tremendous vigor. Let us hope that the energy of constitutional obligation has not died out." The Honorable Champ Clark, of Missouri, in addressing the Georgia Bar Association, was even more emphatic. He said: "I rejoice with exceeding great joy that no country lawyer made the sinister suggestion — the most sinister ever made by any prominent American — that if legislation does not furnish the federal government all the powers wanted, 'sooner or later constructions of the Constitution will be found to vest the power where it will be exercised.' Mr. Elihu Root, secretary of war under one President and secretary of state under another, attained the 'bad eminence' of suggesting that the courts be tampered with in order to strain or stretch the powers of the federal government in order to suit the ideas of himself and other *ultra*-Hamiltonians. Mr. Root is the head of the New York bar. His suggestion means that justice is to be corrupted at the fountain — a suggestion that should be repugnant to every lover of the Republic, without regard to political affiliations. His idea, if put into practice, would convert the courts into engines of oppression more hateful that autocratic power exercised openly by a Cæsar or a Napoleon."

An interesting point has been decided by the New York Supreme Court, Appellate Division, First Department, in the case of De Wolf *v.* Ford and Shaw, proprietors of a hotel. An employee of the hotel forced his way into Mrs. De Wolf's apartment after midnight, when she was in her nightrobe, and in the presence of her brother and a third person, used toward her threatening and insulting language. Mrs. De Wolf sued for damages, but the Appellate Division, speaking by Mr. Justice Ingraham and affirming the lower court, held that a hotel proprietor is not responsible in damages because a guest is insulted or his privacy invaded. The decision is based on Calye's Case, 8 Coke 32, decided about 1584, that is, three hundred and twenty-three years ago. In that case, which is reprinted in Smith's Leading Cases, it is held that the innkeeper's special liability is limited to movable property only, and does not extend to his person. Therefore, "if the guest be beaten in the inn, the innkeeper shall not answer for it; for the injury ought to be done to his movables which he bringeth with him." Mr. Justice McLaughlin filed a strong dissenting opinion, which raises some nice questions as to the power of the common law to respond to changed conditions of society without the aid of legislation. "The law," he declares, "is a progressive science, and it has been the boast of the members of the legal profession that it not only keeps abreast but is ahead of the varying changes which are constantly being made for the comfort and improvement of human society. For this reason I do not think a rule applied three hundred years ago in determining whether an innkeeper was liable, considering the advancement that has since been made and the changes that have taken place in the mode of living, is decisive of the question. To hold that the proprietor of a hotel is liable if a lady's handbag be stolen from her room while she is a guest, but is not liable if one of his employees, by his direction, invades the privacy of her room against her protest when she is disrobed and in the act of retiring, and uses vile and insulting language to her, is to my mind abhorrent. It is but another way of asserting that the law is powerless to punish the greatest outrage. It is generally supposed when one, as a guest, is assigned to a room in a hotel that this insures him the privacy of his home, as long as he pays the price charged for the room, conforms his conduct to the rules of the house, and behaves himself properly. It is not true, as I understand the law, that the proprietor of a hotel or his servant has the right, without the consent of a guest, at any time to enter his room. This is not the law, and if it is it ought not to be, because it is against good morals and the general law of decency, and whenever the proprietor of an inn, either himself or by his servants, commits such acts, he is liable in damages."

The general proposition that because the law considers an act, A, in violation of legal duty and so remediable by an action for damages, therefore the act B, which seems to contemporaneous notions more outrageous than A, must be likewise actionable, seems to lie at the basis of the reasoning of the dissenting opinion. This would place our common-law rights largely at the mercy of individual courts and judges. It would deprive them of all certainty and definiteness. A more conservative view was taken of an analogous question in Robinson *v.* Rochester Folding Box Co., 171 N. Y. 538, where the court, denying to a young woman any remedy for the unauthorized use of her portrait by the defendant in advertisements, declared that the case was one which was proper for legislation — a suggestion which the legislature availed itself of in a short time. The "members of the legal profession" who boast that the law "not only keeps abreast but is ahead of the varying changes which are constantly being made for the comfort and improvement of human society," are, we fear, carried away by enthusiasm for their great science. How law, which can only represent, and somewhat imperfectly at best, the needs of society under actual conditions, and must develop through experiment and adaptation to unforeseen needs, can anticipate those needs, would surely puzzle any of the boasters. It is as if the laws of railroads should be developed before steam was applied to the movement of trains of cars, or a complete doctrine of trusts and monopolies should precede the actual evolution of industry through these agencies. Even Lord Coke, who considered the common law to be "the perfection of human reason," a sort of body of truth existing somewhere *in nubibus* to be drawn upon as exigencies should require, would have drawn back at such a proposition.

In his speech at the Georgia Day celebration at the Jamestown Exposition the President went at some length into a discussion of the policies of his administration. On the subject of compensation to workingmen for injuries, he observed: "The present practice is based on the view announced nearly seventy years ago, that 'principles of justice and good sense demand that a workman shall take upon himself all the ordinary risks of his occupation.' In my view, principles of justice and good sense demand the very reverse of this view, which experience has proved to be unsound and productive of widespread suffering. It is neither just, expedient, nor humane; it is revolting to judgment and sentiment alike, that the financial burden of accidents occurring because of the necessary exigencies of their daily occupation should be thrust upon those sufferers who are least able to bear it, and that such remedy as is theirs should only be obtained by litigation which now burdens our courts. As a matter of fact, there is no sound economic reason for distinction between accidents caused by negligence and those which are unavoidable, and the law should be such that the payment of those accidents will become automatic instead of being a matter for a lawsuit. Workmen should receive a certain definite and limited compensation for all accidents in industry, irrespective of negligence. When the employer, the agent of the public, on his own responsibility and for his own profit, in the business of serving the public, starts in motion agencies which create risks for others, he should take all the ordinary and extraordinary risks involved, and, though the burden will at the moment be his, it will ultimately be assumed, as it ought to be, by the general public."

THESE remarks were uttered in defense of the National Employers' Liability Act, and were followed by a reference to "the extreme unwisdom of the railway companies in fighting the constitutionality" of the statute. There are two utterly different questions involved in national legislation on this subject. One is, of course, the question of the right of Congress to legislate on such matters, the raising of which, according to the President, marks the folly of the railroads. The other is the justice of the rules embodied in the legislation. That the President underestimates the importance of the first question seems apparent. It is quite as if one should contend that good laws adminstered by a despot were equally desirable with the same laws administered by a constitutional government. But leaving the matter of the right of legislation on one side, the substance of the legislation contended for is exactly in line with the laws of the principal countries of Europe. The President's programme, based as it is on the assertion of federal power, may strike the lawyer as in many particulars revolutionary. The natural hostility to untried and revolutionary plans should not blind us to the fact that this particular legislation, while to some extent experimental with us, has in one form or another been adopted in those older nations which we are inclined to consider the home of conservatism.

CAN a negro, by reason of the fact that he is an interstate passenger on a railroad train, demand a seat in a coach set apart for white passengers, when it is a rule of the railroad company, independent of local statute, that whites and negroes must ride in separate compartments? This question was presented to the Kentucky Court of Appeals in the recent case of Chiles *v.* Chesapeake, etc., R. Co., 101 S. W. Rep. 386. The plaintiff was traveling on a first-class ticket from Washington, D. C., to Lexington, Ky. At a point in Kentucky it became necessary for the plaintiff to leave the train on which he was traveling and to secure a seat in another train which was to convey him to Lexington. When he entered this train, he was required to find a seat in the coach set apart for first-class colored passengers. For "the mortification and humiliation" to which he was thus subjected, the plaintiff instituted a suit for damages, claiming that his rights as an interstate passenger had been infringed. A jury in the trial court found that the accommodations in the coach to which the plaintiff was compelled to remove were substantially the same as in the coach for whites, so that there was no discrimination against the plaintiff, and found a verdict for the defendant. Upon appeal to the Court of Appeals this verdict was affirmed. The sole question was the right of the carrier to require, without regard to statute, the separation of the races in its cars. This right was sustained by the court as an application of the carrier's power to establish reasonable rules and regulations for the transportation of passengers. The court examines the important cases on the subject including Westchester, etc., R. Co. *v.* Miles, 55 Pa. St. 209, 93 Am. Dec. 744, decided in 1867, characterized as "perhaps the leading case on the question;" The Sue, 22 Fed. Rep. 843; Murphy *v.* Western Atlantic R. Co., 23 Fed. Rep. 637; Houck *v.* Southern Pac. R. Co., 38 Fed. Rep. 226. "That there is a natural, well-marked difference between the white and colored races," said the court, "goes without saying. That this racial distinction in many places and with many persons develops into a deep-seated antipathy between the races, resulting too often in conflict and bloodshed, is a matter of common knowledge. . . . This racial distinction and the resulting classification is recognized by legislatures, authorized by courts, sanctioned by custom, and approved by an enlightened public opinion. It is not confined to any community, state, or nation, but is found wherever the two races abound in sufficient numbers to make noticeable the impassable chasm that separates them. In the home, the school, the church, the public place — in truth everywhere — it exists. These observations are not set down in any spirit of unkindness or hostility to the colored race, or with a view to create or encourage discrimination or repression that will place obstacles in the way of their improvement or advancement, but rather to note an irremovable and remediless condition that must be acknowledged and that will steadfastly be adhered to." The principles which underlie this decision seem to be incontrovertible. But the question is one which must ultimately come before the Supreme Court of the United States, and the decision of that court will be awaited with interest.

A STATUTE of Missouri enacts that the suicide of the insured shall be no defense to the company insuring him unless the suicide was contemplated at the time the insured made application for the policy, and that any stipulation to the contrary in the policy shall be void. In Whitfield *v.* Ætna L. Ins. Co., 205 U. S. 489, the Supreme Court upholds this statute as a legitimate exertion of power by the State, and holds that a stipulation in the policy that in case of suicide recovery shall be limited to one-tenth of the face value of the policy is nullified by the statute. To a suggestion of the insurance company that the statute "seemingly encourages suicide and offers a bounty therefor, payable not out of the public funds of the State, but out of the funds of insurance companies," the court replied: "There is some foundation for this suggestion in a former decision of this court, in which it was held that public policy, even in the absence of a prohibitory statute, forbade a recovery upon a life policy, silent as to suicide, where the insured, when in sound mind, wilfully and deliberately took his own life. Ritter *v.* Mutual L. Ins. Co., 169 U. S. 139. But the determination of the present case depends upon other considerations than those involved in the Ritter case. An insurance company is not bound to make a contract which is attended by the results indicated by the statute in question. If it does business at all in the State, it must do so subject to such valid regulations as the State may choose to adopt. Even if the statute in question could be fairly regarded by the court as inconsistent with public policy or sound morality, it cannot for that reason alone be disregarded; for it is the province of the State, by its legislature, to adopt such a policy as it deems best, provided it does not in so doing come into conflict with the constitution of the State or the constitution of the United States. There is no such conflict here. The legislative will, within the limits stated, must be respected, if all that can be said is that in the opinion of the court the statute expressing that will is unwise from the standpoint of the public interests."

WE all have somewhere in our hearts a sneaking sympathy for the hero of a story of our school days — the Athenian citizen who voted to ostracise Aristides for no better reason than that he was tired of forever hearing everybody call him "the Just." Of course we would not have imitated this unenlightened individual, but his point of view is appreciable under the pressure day after day of references which would imply a monopoly of all the virtues by some leading public men. We long for "a square deal" for the average statesman who has not been detected in dark conspiracy or labyrinthine lies. A somewhat similar feeling seems to have been aroused in the editorial breast of the New York *Sun* by "the persistent laudation [apropos of the Thaw case] of criminal procedure in England as compared with the conduct of prosecutions for crime in this country." To rebut the claim of superiority, the *Sun* gives this *résumé* of the celebrated Tichborne case, which was tried with all the advantages of the most experienced and distinguished judges and counsel. "The trial began in April, 1873. At that time there existed a special provision of law in England which permitted criminal trials of exceptional importance to be presided over by three judges instead of only one. Under this law the court consisted of Sir Alexander Cockburn, then Lord Chief Justice of England, and Justices Mellor and Lush. Sir Henry Hawkins, afterward for many years a distinguished judge himself, was the leading counsel for the prosecution, being assisted by Charles Bowen, one of the most accomplished lawyers in England, who subsequently became a lord justice of appeal, but died after a short and brilliant career on the bench. The claimant was defended by Dr. Kenealy, a fine classical scholar and eloquent speaker, who derived his title from his honorary degree as a doctor of laws. The case for the prosecution lasted through April, June, and July until July 21st, when Dr. Kenealy began his opening address in behalf of the defendant, concluding it just a month later, on August 21st. The evidence for the defendant then occupied the court until October 27, 1873, when an adjournment was taken in order to obtain evidence for the prosecution from South America and Australia; and it was not until December that all the evidence was finally put in. On the second day of that month Dr. Kenealy began his address to the jury. This continued during the remainder of the year 1873 and until January 14, 1874. On the following day Mr. Hawkins rose to reply and his speech lasted a fortnight. Then came the charge to the jury by the Lord Chief Justice. This address occupied eighteen sittings of the court; and as evidence of the keen interest which the case excited in the public mind the biographer of Lord Bowen states that 'the report of the judge's charge in the London *Times* occupied no less than 180 columns of that paper.' The case was finally submitted to the jury on February 28, 1874, having lasted through 188 actual working days!" This record certainly distances anything that the records of our American courts can show.

A FEW years ago there was quite a movement to enhance the dignity of the courts by dressing the learned occupants of the bench in grave and reverend silk gowns. The gowns as worn by our American judges are simple affairs of black silk, and a judge on this side the water cannot rival the joyous gayety of his old-world brother arrayed in scarlet and fine lace. Time was when even this simple black gown was anathema to the militant republicanism of the majority of our people. But the idea that differentiating the judge from the individual as much as possible would have the effect of increasing the awe with which the sight of him inspired the *hoi polloi* has gained ground considerably. Perhaps also it increases the essential dignity of the court. Every one feels that he must live up to his dress, and the ordinary man when he puts off his business sack coat and dons his Sunday frock coat and silk tile feels the obligation to be on his best behavior. If then we can increase the dignity of a twentieth century judge by dressing him in a garment cut by a fashion plate some six centuries out of date, by all means do so. But why pause with the plain black gown which our academic functions have taught us to consider only suitable for the fresh and verdant graduate? Why let our universities make gay their doctors with gorgeous hoods and gowns, while we retain simple black for the judges? If the wearer of black clothes can increase his dignity by cutting them according to an obsolete fashion, because he is thereby separated from the common herd, *a fortiori* he may enhance his dignity the more by gorgeous coloring, because he is thus even more removed from the workaday world. And yet none of our courts have had the courage to try an experiment founded on this absolutely exclusive reasoning. Try scarlet gowns and mayhap full-bottomed wigs, and the dignity of our courts will rise like the mercury of a thermometer on a summer day. Besides, even the district judges of New York have adopted black gowns, and these are the very baccalaureates of the bench. Let the higher courts rise to a proper sense of their dignity and don garments more seemly for the doctors of the profession. Unworthy of the twentieth century administration of justice is the behavior of Mr. Justice Marean, of the Supreme Court in Brooklyn, N. Y., who is stated to have "removed his gown in the afternoon" and to have expressed this reprehensible sentiment: "I believe that this attempt to make judges wear gowns is an attempt to add dignity to the court in an unworthy manner." Every order of men must contain its unprogressive elements.

THE advice given by a client to Sir Walter Scott in lieu of a fee was embodied by his genial counsel in the lines

"A terrier dog and a rusty key
Was Walter Scott's first Jedburgh fee."

In spite of the efforts of Scott his client, a burglar, was convicted. In grateful remembrance of his young advocate's efforts the convict made him the legatee of his professional experience that an old-fashioned rusty lock and a small noisy dog were the most efficient safeguards against gentlemen of his persuasion. The small dog appears to be equally effective against that latest product of our criminal classes, the professional murderer by bomb or poison. That past master of the craft, Harry Orchard, testified that the plan to murder Gen. Sherman Bell was defeated because "Bell had some little dogs that used to come out and bark at him whenever he came too near the house." The "little dogs" keeping off by their busy self-important barkings the dark and sinister figure of the messenger of murder make an impressive picture. Their conduct was none the less effective, even though we should agree with certain great authorities that their delight to bark and bite was the product of simple instinct, and does not entitle them to rank with the heroes of moral courage.

THE action brought in a New York court by Mrs. or Miss Randolph or Reilly against Stokes to recover compensation for the support of the plaintiff's illegitimate child, whose paternity she charges upon the defendant, was an unsavory case in any point of view. Among other evidence introduced was a number of letters written by the defendant to the plaintiff, in which the story of their relations is developed pretty fully. One would have thought that the nature of these letters would have excluded them from the columns of a respectable newspaper, and yet some of the New York papers reproduced them in full. The opportunity to place before the public these specimens of salacious correspondence, so that they might be available to all classes, ages, and sexes at one or two cents for the entire series, was seized upon with avidity. There was involved in the case no vital issue of life or death such as might excuse the republication of the malodorous details of the Thaw trial. The story was one of low intrigue, lust, and greed, such as one might find in those French novels "on gray paper with blunt type," to which Browning alludes. It can hardly be claimed that any public interest is involved in prostituting the columns of the press to the dissemination of such vile stuff. The newspapers which make the courts involuntarily *particeps criminis* in the corruption of the young should be dealt with rigorously, if there is any effective way to reach them. There is a class of newspapers whose reputation is a warning against all sorts of abominations. Is their example spreading to a higher order of journals?

TESTIMONY CONCERNING PUBLICATION OF WILLS.

IN New York, New Jersey, and several other States the statute prescribing the requisites for valid execution of a will requires that in the presence of the attesting witnesses the testator shall declare it to be his last will and testament. The weight of evidence that this formality, commonly called "publication," was or was not observed, is the subject of the following article.

Dr. Lushington remarked that the fact of publication or no publication of a will is one not likely to make a strong impression on the memory of an attesting witness. Hudson *v.* Parker, 1 Rob. Ecc. 14. And Chief Justice Denio, of New York, said the experience of every one will teach him that memory is not greatly to be relied on in determining the question. Peck *v.* Cary, 27 N. Y. 9, 29.

In some jurisdictions the fear that honest wills, executed in the most formal manner, might be defeated of probate because witnesses would not be likely to recollect a testamentary declaration, has led the legislature altogether to omit the requirement of publication. See Allen *v.* Griffin, 69 Wis. 529, 35 N. W. Rep. 21.

Chancellor McGill, of New Jersey, suggested that publication is a part of the transaction which addresses itself to mental understanding as distinguished from such physical acts as those of attending and signing, so that if the attention of a witness was to some extent diverted, for example, by absorption in a book, a testamentary declaration would be apt to escape his memory or remain there in such hazy and indeterminate form that interested parties could easily extinguish it by friendly persuasion. Swain *v.* Edmunds, 53 N. J. Eq. 142, 32 Atl. Rep.

It is highly probable that a testator's statement that the paper was his will would make an impression as strong as or stronger than most of the other constituent acts in executing a will, upon the mind of a witness who had no other reason to suppose that the instrument was a will; and it would make a much fainter impression upon the mind of a witness already possessed of knowledge or belief that it was a will.

In a case in the New York Surrogate's Court the validity of a will offered for probate depended upon the question whether the testator declared it to be his will when the attesting witnesses signed the instrument. The witnesses concurred in saying that he requested them to attest "an instrument in writing." They did not testify so positively that he did not declare it to be his will, but they were manifestly of opinion that he did not. The surrogate pronounced sentence rejecting the will. "If we speculate as to probabilities," he said, "it would appear strange if they should remember that the testator called the paper an instrument — a general term — and forget that he declared it to be his will — a special term, and clothing the document with a special interest." Wilson *v.* Hetterick, 2 Bradf. (N. Y.) 427, 430.

It is doubtless true that the term "will" is of a character to attract attention and impress the feelings and memory; for the reason, however, that it is associated with the idea of death, and not because it is a special term. "Indenture" and "single bill obligatory" are special terms, but they have no impressive associations, and it would be difficult to suppose that either term would survive in memory the general term "instrument in writing." Dr. James says: "When memory begins to decay, proper names are what go first, and at all times proper names are harder to recollect than those of general properties and classes of things." And he quotes Kussmaul as follows: "The concreter a conception is, the sooner is its name forgotten. This is because our ideas of persons and things are less strongly bound up with their names than with such abstractions as their business, their circumstances, their qualities." James, Principles of Psychology, pp. 683, 684.

But aside from this criticism of the particular reason given by the surrogate in the case last cited, the correctness of his decision is almost beyond dispute. In a later case in the New York Appellate Division, witnesses favorable to the proponent of a will, which was executed less than two years before probate, testified to their recollection that the testator used the word "document," and they had no remembrance that he designated it by any other word, although they showed good memories of other incidents attending the execution of the will. "We cannot doubt," said the court, "that they would have recalled the essential and momentous word 'will' which their surmises led them to expect, had the testator used that word or its substance, or in any manner conveyed it to their minds. And it would then, doubtless, have stood out in their memories more strikingly than any of the details which they so minutely recounted." Matter of Turrell, 47 N. Y. App. Div. 560, 62 N. Y. Supp. 1053, 28 Misc. (N. Y.) 106, *affirmed* 166 N. Y. 330, 59 N. E. Rep. 910. See also In Goods of Gunstan, 7 P. D. 102, 116.

In a case where one subscribing witness testified that the testatrix spoke of the instrument as her "will" and the other witness testified that the words "business letter" and not "will" were used, and there was no other testimony on that point, the court, in view of all the surrounding circumstances, concluded that the word "will" was used, and perhaps in another connection the words "business letter." *In re* Buchan's Will, 38 N. Y. Supp. 1124.

In still another case where a witness testified that the testatrix requested him to attest her signature, that she said nothing to impress his mind with the fact that it was an important document, and that if she had said it was her will he thought he would have remembered it, the surrogate accepted his recollection as correct. Matter of Shaffer, 2 How. Pr. N. S. (N. Y.) 494. See also McCord *v.* Lounsbury, 5 Dem. (N. Y.) 68. And in New Jersey probate of a will was denied upon positive testimony of the witness that the testatrix spoke only of "some writings" which she was changing. Darnell *v.* Buzby, 50 N. J. Eq. 725, 26 Atl. Rep. 676.

It will be observed that these are not cases of mere failure of memory, but on the contrary there is a lively memory of things said which creates a strong suspicion that publication of the instrument as a will was purposely avoided. But it is not necessary that the witness should recollect a substituted designation of the instrument, for it may not have been referred to by any term; the attestation clause is not alone sufficient to overcome the uncontradicted testimony of attesting witnesses who distinctly recollect that no declaration whatever was made. Matter of Nash, 76 N. Y. App. Div. 212, 78 N. Y. Supp. 449.

The "station in life" of a witness, to quote an expression in the English cases in connection with a discussion of the general subject, may be considered in weighing his testimony that a testamentary declaration was or was not made. Thus in a conflict of testimony, a New York surrogate credited the statement of a leading business man, "a man of character, intelligence, and large experience in affairs," who said that no declaration was made, rather than the contrary testimony of testator's servant who could neither read nor write. Matter of Shaffer, 2 How. P. R. N. S. (N. Y.) 494.

Other things equal, the testimony of subscribing witnesses is more to be depended upon than that of other witnesses present at the time. Matter of Higgins, 94 N. Y. 554.

Mere failure of recollection of a witness is the slightest kind of evidence that no publication was made, especially where there is a full attestation clause and a long time has elapsed. Hitch *v.* Wells, 10 Beav. 84; Matter of Voorhis, 125 N. Y. 765; Matter of Hunt, 110 N. Y. 278, and other cases too numerous to cite here.

Four months between the date when the will was executed and the date when an attesting witness testified was thought to be "a period too short according to ordinary experience and observation for a material fact in an important transaction to fade from the memory of a person who was under a special duty to remember it." Nevertheless in the same case where the testimony of the witness exhibited instances of failure and confusion of recollection regarding various circumstances attending the execution of the will, the court was thoroughly convinced that he was mistaken in his testimony that he did not hear the will published, in view of other testimony that publication was made. Robbins *v.* Robbins, 50 N. J. Eq. 742, 26 Atl. Rep. 673.

Since courts are unquestionably inclined to seize upon slight circumstances to impeach the accuracy of recollection of witnesses who are testifying, after a considerable time, that no publication was made, we subjoin a specimen description of testimony deemed too distinct and circumstantial to admit of any gap in memory, although five years had elapsed: "Both witnesses are intelligent — Mr. Zerbe exceptionally so. Still both have failed to recollect whether the testator declared the paper to be his will. One circumstance, however, is very persuasive that he did not, and that is that both witnesses say that at the time, and after the time, when they attested the paper they did not know what it was, and were curious to know what it was. This is a fact about which they cannot be easily mistaken. Mr. Zerbe says that he was surprised that [the testator] did not inform him what he was signing, because their relations had been of such a confidential nature, and because he had never before asked him to sign a paper without explaining it. He says he was curious for a week afterwards about what he had signed. If he was ignorant, it follows of course that no statutory declaration was made. Mr. Smith also says that he hesitated to sign because he did not know what the paper was. Now, assuming the desire of both these gentlemen to tell the exact truth, as they recall it — of which I have no doubt — I can conceive how they can be mistaken in respect to their knowledge of the character of the paper at and after the time when they had witnessed it." *In re* Clark, (N. J. 1900) 52 Atl. Rep. 222, 224, *per* Reed, V. C.

Absence of an attestation clause, and ignorance of all

persons present when the will was executed that the law required publication, go far toward supporting testimony that it was not made. Matter of Sarasohn, 47 Misc. (N. Y.) 535, 95 N. Y. Supp. 975.

Where a witness testifies that publication was not made and another witness of equal credibility testifies to the contrary, and the circumstances are such that the latter cannot possibly have been mistaken and must be guilty of deliberate perjury unless his testimony is true, his testimony will be accepted as correct if the trier of facts can perceive that the other witness, because of inattention or other reason, may possibly be mistaken. Swain *v.* Edmunds, 53 N. J. Eq. 142, 32 Atl. Rep. 369. This rule for weighing testimony is applied in all sorts of cases and with very great frequency.

The "best recollection" of a witness, who declines to affirm more positively, that the testator declared the paper to be his will, is sufficient to establish the fact in the absence of all evidence to the contrary and even if there is no attestation clause. Vernon *v.* Vernon, (N. J. 1905) 61 Atl. Rep. 409. However, the "impression" of a witness that a declaration was made hardly amounts to recollection and cannot be regarded when his testimony pretty clearly indicates that his impression is derived from conversations with proponent's lawyers wherein he was first informed what were the requisites for due execution of a will. Hopper's Will, Tuck. N. Y. Sur. 378, 394.

A witness who is a beneficiary in the will has a *prima facie* bias in favor of the proponent, and if his testimony conflicts with that of a disinterested witness, the testimony of the latter is usually, according to the general rule in similar situations, entitled to the greater credit. Matter of Shaffer, 2 How. Pr. N. S. (N. Y.) 494.

A witness's testimony to publication, if given in response to leading questions on direct examination, is practically nullified by complete failure of recollection on cross-examination when deprived of the benefit of suggestive interrogatories. Smith's Will, Tuck. N. Y. Sur. 227.

Where the testator purposely folded the will so as to conceal its contents from attesting witnesses, it is a circumstance corroborative of their testimony that no declaration was made. Matter of Shaffer, 2 How. Pr. N. S. (N. Y.) 494. See also *In re* Clark, (N. J. 1900) 52 Atl. Rep. 222; Matter of Turrell, 28 Misc. (N. Y.) 106, 59 N. Y. Supp. 780, *affirmed* 47 N. Y. App. Div. 560, 62 N. Y. Supp. 1053.

The fact that the hearing of a witness who testifies that no declaration was made was slightly defective, will be considered in weighing his testimony. Matter of Buchan, (Surrogate Ct.) 16 Misc. (N. Y.) 204, 38 N. Y. Supp. 1124.

Courts are not all indisposed to believe that a witness may at one time recollect what he had previously been unable to recall. But the validity of a will is too serious a matter to depend upon the vacillations of a repeatedly prompted and prodded memory. Where there was no attestation clause, and the evidence consisted solely of the testimony of two attesting witnesses, one of these had no recollection of publication in any form. The other attesting witness upon each of his three several examinations in the course of the trial utterly failed to prove the requisite declaration. At last he returned to the stand, and without giving any reason for having better recollection of the incident, testified with precision to an exact publication of the paper by the testator as his last will. "This last testimony," said the court, "becomes valuable only because it contradicts what he had three times previously said on the same subject. It is presented in a manner to suggest grave doubts of its accuracy. To accept it as sufficient proof of the publication by the testator, in the presence of two witnesses of the instrument claimed to be his last will, and thus deprive his heirs of their inheritance, is, in my view, impossible for a court of justice." Davenport *v.* Davenport, 67 N. J. Eq. 320, 58 Atl. Rep. 535, *per* Grey, V. C.

Little reliance can be placed upon the testimony of a witness who had forgotten all about the transaction, and who says his memory was refreshed by conversation with one of the parties to the probate proceeding, but cannot state the purport of that conversation. Hopper's Will, Tuck. N. Y. Sur. 378, 394. See also Matter of Barber, 92 Hun (N. Y.) 489, 37 N. Y. Supp. 235.

CHARLES C. MOORE.

STORIES FROM THE LAW REPORTS: THE LIABILITY OF A FALSE PROPHET.

Ellis v. Newbrough, 6 N. Mex. 181, 27 Pac Rep. 490.

IT is written: "I am the Lord thy God, who brought thee out of the land of Egypt, out of the house of bondage. Thou shalt not have strange gods in my sight. Thou shalt not make to thyself a graven thing, nor the likeness of any things, that are in heaven above, or that are in the earth beneath, or that abide in the waters under the earth. Thou shalt not adore them, and thou shalt not serve them. For I am the Lord thy God, a jealous God, visiting the iniquity of the fathers upon their children unto the third and fourth generation, to them that hate me, And shewing mercy unto many thousands, to them that love me, and keep my commandments" (Deut. 5: 6–10, Douay Version). And again: "But if thou forget the Lord thy God, and follow strange gods, and serve and adore them: behold now I foretell thee that thou shalt utterly perish." (Deut. 8:19, Douay Version.)

But is the founder of a new religious sect liable in damages for seducing a member of an old communion from the faith of his fathers and inducing him to join a community composed of the new sectarians? This question was answered in the negative in Ellis *v.* Newbrough, 6 N. Mex. 181, 27 Pac. Rep. 490. In that case the defendants, the leaders of the "Faithists," who had established a religious Utopia in New Mexico which they called the First Church of the Tae in the Land of Shalam, induced the plaintiff to abandon his home in far-off Georgia and cast his lot with the faithful seekers after the Life Everlasting. The plaintiff, according to his complaint, was persuaded by the false and fraudulent representations of the defendant to become a member of the community, whereupon he did to the new faith "consecrate his life, his labor, and all his worldly effects and prospects, together with those of his two children, placing all good faith and confidence in said community."

The plaintiff, after living in the community for more than two years, reached the conclusion that he had been led to follow false gods, and that he had been greatly damaged thereby, whereupon he brought his action, alleging that "he has sustained great damage in loss of time and labor and opportunity, and in the education of his children, and that he has suffered great anguish of mind in consequence of the dishonor and humiliation brought upon himself and his children by reason of his connection with said defendants in said community, to the damage of the plaintiff in the sum of $10,000."

The action seems to have been in form one of trespass on the case, but the complaint, which the court characterized as "unique and weird," sought relief on the ground of false and fraudulent representations knowingly made by the defendants to the plaintiff. The plaintiff charged the defendants with acts of tyranny, immorality, etc., but those were apparently minor grounds of complaint, his chief grievance being that he had been deceived into believing that all property should be held and enjoyed in common, whereas in fact the title thereto was vested solely in the prophet of the faith. Seemingly, the plaintiff was disappointed at not having bettered his worldly condition, and threw in the charges of improper conduct on the part of the defendants for the purpose of enlisting the sympathy or arousing the indignation of the court.

The court, however much it may have been distressed at seeing the plaintiff in such sad case, held that the law could afford him no remedy. It found that he had made no sacrifice of property to become a member of the organization, and held that, being a man of ordinary intelligence, he could not complain that he had been misled into accepting the somewhat extraordinary doctrines of a new religion, particularly in view of the fact that for several years he had practiced the faith without objection.

From a hasty examination of the religious writings used to convert the plaintiff it is difficult to determine which to admire the more — the imagination of the author or the credulity of the convert. The principal writing was entitled as follows: "Oahspe: A New Bible in the words of Jehovih and his Angel Embassadors. A sacred history of the dominions of the higher and lower heavens on the earth for the past twenty-four thousand years, together with a synopsis of the cosmogony of the universe; the creation of planets; the creation of man; the unseen worlds; the labor and glory of gods and goddesses in the ethereal heavens. With the new commandments of Jehovih to man of the present day. With revelations from the second resurrection, formed in words in the thirty-third year of the Kosmon era." A neat, illuminative, and modest title that. The book was written in an admirable spirit, too, as was shown by the declaration in the preface that "it blows nobody's horn; it makes no leader."

The Oahspe contained a very interesting account of the circumstances attending its origin. This account was summarized by the court as follows: "That once upon a time the world was ruled by a triune composed of Brahma and Buddha and one Looeamong; that the devil, entering into the presence of Looeamong, tempted him by showing the great power of Buddha and Brahma, and induced him (Looeamong) to take upon himself the name Kriste, so that it came to pass that the followers of Kriste were called Kristeyans; that Looeamong or Kriste, through his commanding general, Gabriel, captured the opposing gods, together with their entire command of 7,600,000 angels, and cast them into hell, where there were already more than 10,000,000 who were in chaos and madness. This Kriste afterward assembled a number of his men to adopt a Code. At this meeting it is said there were produced 2,231 books and legendary tales of gods and saviors and great men, etc. This council was in session four years and seven months, and at the end of that time there had been selected and combined much that was good and great, and worded so as to be well remembered of mortals."

This statement, condensed though it is, shows that the book threw some valuable sidelights upon sacred history. After having agreed upon a Bible — or "adopted a platform," as the court somewhat irreverently says — the council proceeded to the election of a god. The contest for this honorable position seems to have been a free-for-all one, the contestants including, in addition to "Kriste," heathen and Brahmin deities, to say nothing of others whose religious affiliations we are unable to classify. On the first ballot there were thirty-seven candidates, among them being such well-known divinities as Vulcan, Jupiter, and Minerva. It seems that the convention was deadlocked for quite a while. "The record tells us that at the end of seven days' balloting 'the number of gods was reduced to twenty-seven.' And so the convention or council remained in session 'for one year and five months, the balloting lasted, and at the end of that time the ballot rested nearly equal on five gods, namely, Jove, Kriste, Mars, Crite, and Siva,' and thus the balloting stood for seven weeks. At this point Hatsus, who was the chief spokesman for Kriste, proposed to leave the matter of a selection to the angels. The convention, worn out with speech-making and balloting, readily accepted this plan. Kriste, who, under his former name of Looeamong, still retained command of the angels (for he had prudently declined to surrender one position until he had been elected to the other), together with his hosts, gave a sign in fire of a cross smeared with blood, whereupon he was declared elected, and on motion his selection was made unanimous."

While the Oahspe was thus rich in historical learning concerning the birth of Christianity, it must not be supposed that it ignored matters of heathen and profane interest. It contained many bits of information of the kind in which encyclopædias and patent-medicine almanacs abound, such as the date of the birth of Confucius, the date of the discovery of America by Columbus, etc.

We should like to reproduce a number of the beauties of the Oahspe, but unfortunately are unable to do more than give a hint of its treasures by quoting the wonderful descriptions of certain lands with which our readers may or may not be familiar. A portion of the promised land was described thus: "Next south lay the kingdom of Himalawowoaganapapa, rich in legends of the people who lived here before the flood; a kingdom of seventy cities and six great canals, coursing east and west, and north and south, from the Ghiee mountain in the east to the West mountain, the Yublahahcoolaesavaganawakka, the place of the king of bears, the EEughehabakax (grizzly). And to the south, to the middle kingdom, on the deserts of Geobiathhaganeganewohwoh, where the rivers empty not into the sea, but sink into the sand, the Sonogallakaxkax, creating prickly Thuazhoogallakhoomma, shaped like a pear." Another country was described as follows: "In the high north lay the kingdom of Olegalla, the land of giants, the place of yellow rocks and high spouting waters. Olegalla it was who gave away his kingdom, the great city of Powafuchswowitchahavagganeabba, with the four and twenty tributary cities spread along the valley of Anemoosagoochakakfuela. Gave his kingdom to his queen, Minneganewashaka, with the yellow hair, long hanging down."

Evidently the author of those passages had read Gulliver's Travels and Hiawatha, to say nothing of the Chrononhotonthologos.

We must pass over in silence most of the plaintiff's evidence, but there is one thing we feel bound to mention before closing. It seems that at least one of the community's members had the habit of dropping into poetry, and that one of her lapses, which read as follows, was habitually sung by the faithful, in chorus, to the tune of Dixie:

"For all things are held in common,
Hooray! Hooray!
Thus everything belongs to all,
And peace abounds in Shalam;
Away, away, away out west in Shalam!"

The plaintiff contended that the singing of the lines to the tune of Dixie was such an act of disloyalty as entitled him to a verdict. The court, however, denied the soundness of this contention, saying: "The authoress of these beautiful and touching lines is Nellie Jones, a member of the society. She is not made a party to this action, however, and therefore no judgment can be rendered against her. The lines were, by direction of one of appellants, Dr. Newbrough, sung to the air of Dixie. We cannot give our assent, however, to the views of the able counsel for the appellee that causing these lines to be sung to the air or 'tune of Dixie' was of itself, such an act of disloyalty as to entitle the plaintiff to a verdict. The writer of this opinion, like the appellee, is himself a native of the land of Dixie, that

'Fair land of flowers,
And flowery land of the fair.'

And, as he reads these lines of Nellie Jones, memory carries him back to the days of his boyhood, and to the land of the 'magnolia and the mocking bird.'

"O, glorious Land of Shalam! O, beautiful Church of Tae! When the appellants, the appellee, Ada Sweet, and Nellie Jones, aforesaid, formed their inner circle, and, like the morning stars, sang together, it matters not whether they kept step to the martial strains of Dixie, or declined their voices to the softer melody of Little Annie Rooney, the appellee became forever estopped from setting up a claim for work and labor done; nor can he be heard to say that 'he has suffered great anguish of mind in consequence of the dishonor and humiliation brought on himself and children by reason of his connection with said defendants' community.' His joining in the exercises aforesaid constitutes a clear case of *estoppel* in Tae."

We must say that we sympathize with the plaintiff for failing to get relief in this respect, irrespective of the merit of his other contentions. There is no doubt that he felt very much aggrieved at the singing of the song to the air of Dixie. The sacrilege sank deep and rankled in his manly bosom. To demonstrate this, it is only necessary to quote one portion of his testimony: "*Q*. You all sang this with a good deal of lustiness? — *A*. No. sir; we sang it to the tune of Dixie."

J. C. M.

SUNDAY BASEBALL.

THE question whether the playing of baseball on Sunday shall be permitted is one of acute interest to the majority of American citizens. Baseball is the nation's pastime, and any and all matters concerning or affecting the game are sure to command ready attention. With each recurring baseball season the agitation respecting Sunday games is revived. The present season is no exception to the rule, and therefore a word or two concerning the subject may not be out of place at this time.

It may be asked why this word or two should appear in a legal publication. This is a pertinent query, but one not difficult to answer. The Sunday baseball question has two aspects, which may be characterized as the moral aspect and the legal aspect. With the moral aspect the legal profession have little to do, as a profession. But in their capacity as citizens and particularly as makers of the law, lawyers should be profoundly interested in the moral side of any public question. Without desiring to expatiate, however, at any great length upon the moral viewpoint, it may be said that there are many arguments, and some very strong ones, in favor of Sunday baseball. This nation, following in the footsteps of some older ones, is gradually changing its attitude towards Sunday observance, and we are already a great many years removed from the Puritanical idea of what the Bible means when it commands us to keep the sabbath day holy. We no longer deem it a sin to have our places of worship warmed and lighted. The modern beautiful and ornate church bears little resemblance to the plain, ugly meeting house of the seventeenth century. Nor do we longer feel that we blaspheme when we sing our hymns of praise with an instrumental accompaniment. In matters of recreation, we have advanced equally far. Walking and driving on Sunday are not now considered sinful. In place of the tract or book of sermons, we read nowadays the Sunday newspaper, the latest novel, or the current magazine. Who is there to-day that finds fault with any of these occupations, provided they are not allowed to conflict with a regular attendance at religious services? It is not at all surprising, therefore, that many can be found who advocate the modification of still more of our theories in the interest of the game of baseball. When properly played, and it is generally so played, it is the cleanest, healthiest, and manliest of all sports. And it is undoubtedly the most popular of all forms of amusement. Perhaps in this fact lies the greatest objection to its being indulged in on Sunday. For while dozens may witness a golf contest, and hundreds a tennis match, thousands upon thousands crowd into our baseball parks at every opportunity. And, of course, where so many people are gathered, there is bound to be considerable noise and more or less disturbance of the public peace and repose. But there are worse things than a hearty laugh or an exuberant shout. It should be remembered that ball games are not played at such hours of the day that these thousands of spectators are attracted from religious worship. The poles of this powerful magnet are not turned towards the churches. The saloons, the dance halls, and the gambling houses are the places which lose their patrons. Is it not better that men, and mostly young men, should laugh and shout in the open, even at some expense to the peace of society, than that they should lurk in the dark and secret byways leading to dens of vice? This is but one of the arguments which the advocates of Sunday baseball advance. There are a number of others equally plausible. But perhaps we can do no better than to sum up the situation, morally speaking, in the following language of Mr. Justice Gaynor, one of the most enlightened and respected members of the present New York Supreme Court bench: "This is one of a class of cases in which it is the duty of the judiciary to speak out plain, after the manner of judges in times past. I therefore deem it not at all outside of my judicial office to add to what I have already said, that it is practically the unanimous sentiment of the religious and God-fearing people of the community that it is far better for our grown boys and young men who have to work indoors all the week for a living to go into the fields on Sunday afternoon after attending church, and participate in or witness good, elevating, healthy physical exercise than to be driven instead to go to dance gardens, drinking places, pool rooms, and worse places; and there is no one trying to stir up any obscure or obsolete statute against that opinion except those who rule the police. Fathers and mothers would much rather know that their grown sons are at a ball or golf game on Sunday afternoon than not know where they are. Many of our boys and young men scarcely see the sun at all during the short days of the year except on Sundays, and have no other day for outdoor exercise from one end of the year to the other. This is something which our ministers of the gospel well know, and the significance of which they fully appreciate." (See People *ex rel.* Poole *v.* Hesterberg, 43 Misc. (N. Y.) 510.)

Looking at the Sunday baseball question from the legal aspect, the situation is somewhat puzzling at first, especially to a layman. The latter cannot understand why so simple a question as whether it is against the law to play a game of ball on

Sunday should give so much trouble. And yet, when he picks up his Monday newspaper he finds that games have been played the day before in some large cities and not in others; that contests have been engaged in in some communities without molestation, while in other parts of the same State similar contests have been stopped by the police; that players who have been arrested for participating in the game on Sunday have been punished in some courts and discharged in others. This general confusion as to right and wrong bothers the lay mind not a little. The lawyer would doubtless declare that the explanation lies in a conflict of laws between jurisdictions, such as exists in the case of marriage and divorce, corporations, and the like. This, however, is not strictly accurate. The confusion in this particular instance is attributable to either one of two things, namely, a difference in judicial interpretation of the law, or the connivance of public officials at wilful violations of the statutes.

In some States baseball playing on Sunday is expressly prohibited by statute. Thus, in *Indiana*, the statute forbids baseball on Sunday for an admission fee. (See State *v.* Hogriever, 152 Ind. 652.) But, in spite of the statute, Sunday games are played in many of the cities of the State. In *Ohio*, Sunday baseball is expressly prohibited. (Bates' Annot. Stat., § 703*a*.) And it has been held under this statute that arrests for its violation may be made on Sunday. (See *Ex p.* Carroll, 12 Wkly. Law Bull. 9.) Nevertheless, National League games are played in Cincinnati on Sunday, and American League games in Cleveland, apparently without a word of protest from any one. These two jurisdictions furnish noteworthy examples of wilful violation of the statutes.

In some other jurisdictions Sunday baseball is made illegal, not by express statutory provision, but by virtue of judicial interpretation of statutes. Thus, in *Michigan*, the statute reads that "no person shall . . . take part in any sport, game, or play on the first day of the week." This statute has been conceded to include baseball. See Scougale *v.* Sweet, 124 Mich. 311, wherein it was also held that playing ball on Sunday was a breach of the peace under another statute referring to the duty of the sheriff to disperse unlawful assemblages. Similarly, in *Nebraska*, it has been held, under a statute providing that if "any person of the age of fourteen years or upward shall be found on the first day of the week, commonly called Sunday, sporting, rioting, quarreling, hunting, fishing, or shooting, he or she shall be fined," etc., that playing baseball comes within the definition of "sporting." (See State *v.* O'Rourk, 35 Neb. 614.) This decision was followed and reaffirmed eleven years later, in Seay *v.* Shrader, 69 Neb. 245, wherein the court said: "Since that decision was rendered, the legislature has been in regular session no less than six times. It is fair to presume that if the law as there announced had been offensive to public sentiment, or the interpretation there put upon it had been generally regarded as erroneous, it would long since have been changed." Notwithstanding these positive decisions, however, baseball continues to be played on Sunday both in Michigan and in Nebraska.

In *Missouri* the situation is somewhat different. There the existing statute is held not to apply to baseball. The manner in which this result was reached is interesting. In the early case of State *v.* Williams, 35 Mo. App. 541, it was held that the game of baseball is included in the words "or games of any kind" in a statute providing as follows: "Every person who shall be convicted of horse racing, cock fighting, or playing at cards or games of any kind, on the first day of the week, commonly called Sunday, shall be deemed guilty of a misdemeanor," etc. The court said: "The statute was not aiming to prevent the doing of things immoral *per se*, or the tendency of which is immoral, as the inhibition is not against gambling or betting on the games, but merely against doing the act on that day, though it be not immoral or tending to immorality. The object of the lawmakers being thus apparent, and the language used to cover that object so apt, would it not be inexcusable technical refinement for the courts to say that the general words 'or games of any kind' did not include the game of baseball? That game is said to have become national, and it is well known that in some sections of the country and of this State it attracts vast crowds of people, rivaling in numbers those which assembled in the amphitheatres of Rome or gathered to witness the Olympian games of Greece. It is going further than we feel at liberty to venture, to say that the legislature did not intend to include such a game in the terms of the statute under consideration." This case, however, was impliedly overruled in St. Louis Agricultural, etc., Assoc. *v.* Delano, 108 Mo. 217, wherein the court, construing the same statute, held that it did not include athletic games and sports, saying: "These prohibitions are evidently leveled against sports and games that have a demoralizing tendency, and do not extend to mere athletic sports." The court further argued that the words "or games of any kind" fell under the rule which prescribes that where general words follow particular ones they are to be construed as applicable to things or persons of a like nature. In *Ex p.* Neet, 157 Mo. 527, the question came squarely before the Supreme Court whether the game of baseball was included within the prohibition of the statute. Regarding the statute, the court remarked that it had been on the statute books of Missouri in exactly the same words since 1835, and that playing a game of baseball on Sunday (or on any other day) could not have been in the minds of the lawmakers when this provision of law was first enacted, for the very simple reason that such a game was wholly unknown at that time. The court affirmed the principle laid down in St. Louis Agricultural Assoc. *v.* Delano, and disapproved State *v.* Williams. It then proceeded: "Baseball does not belong to the same class, kind, species, or genus as horse racing, cock fighting, or card playing. It is to America what cricket is to England. It is a sport of athletic exercise, and is commonly called a game, but it is not a gambling game nor productive of immorality. In a qualified sense it is affected by chance, but it is primarily and properly a game of science, of physical skill, of trained endurance, and of natural adaptability to athletic skill. It is a game of chance only to the same extent that chance or luck may enter into anything man may do. But when chance or luck is pitted against skill and science it is as fair an illustration of what will result as any test that could be applied. If the view of the Williams case had been adopted, this statute would have been elastic enough to cover every game that ever was or ever will be invented, no matter whether it was harmless, promotive of physical or mental development, or deleterious to both. It would prevent games of chess, backgammon, jacks, authors, proverbs, faro, keno, and poker alike, and when played on Sunday any one would have been as illegal as any other. Such a construction would have curtailed many of the pleasures of many of our people, without elevating them or improving their moral tone. Until the lawmakers expressly provide for such sweeping changes in the lives and customs and habits of our people, it is not proper for the courts by construction to impair their natural rights to enjoy those sports or amusements that are neither *mala in se* nor *mala prohibita* — neither immoral nor hurtful to body or soul. We therefore conclude that there is no law in this State which prevents playing a game of baseball on Sunday."

In *Illinois* apparently the only statutes bearing upon the question are paragraphs 428 and 429 of the Criminal Code, which provide a fine for any one who shall disturb the peace of society or of a private family by engaging in any amusement or diversion on Sunday. Evidently it has never occurred to any one in Illinois that Sunday baseball games disturb the peace of society, for the practice is common there, and an inspection of the State reports fails to show any decision in which the question has been passed upon.

In *New York* the law is probably in a more confused and perplexing state than in any other jurisdiction. Section 265 of the Penal Code prohibits "all shooting, hunting, fishing, playing, horse racing, gaming, or other public sports, exercises, pastimes, or shows upon the first day of the week, and all noise disturbing the peace of the day." The first case construing this statute in reference to baseball was People *v.* Dennin, 35 Hun 327, decided in 1885. It was therein held that three men who were playing ball on private grounds, without making any noise, were not guilty of violation of the statute. The court considered section 265, together with sections 259 and 262, relating to Sunday observance, and said: "From the three sections it is manifest that the thing done must be a serious interruption of the repose of the community on Sunday. The thing prohibited must be to a greater or lesser extent public." This decision was criticised in People *v.* Moses, 140 N. Y. 214, wherein it was said that the Dennin case was not correctly decided. The court said: "That playing ball by several persons in a place open to the view of the people who may be in the vicinity, or who may pass by, is condemned by the principles which lie at the bottom of the Sunday laws, and is an act of playing within the meaning of the statute, cannot be doubted." It is to be observed, however, that the question of baseball playing on Sunday was not in issue in the Moses case. In Matter of Rupp, 33 N. Y. App. Div. 468, decided in 1898, it was held (citing People *v.* Moses) that ball playing on Sunday is a misdemeanor and that an arrest therefor may be made without warrant.

In People *ex rel.* Bedell *v.* Mott, 38 Misc. (N. Y.) 171, decided in 1902, Judge Gaynor followed People *v.* Dennin, declaring that it was not overruled by People *v.* Moses, and held that ball playing on Sunday was not a crime when it did not amount to an interruption of the repose and religious liberty of the community. In 1904 the question again came before Judge Gaynor, at Supreme Court chambers, in the case of People *ex rel.* Poole *v.* Hesterberg, 43 Misc. 510. The case was a habeas corpus proceeding to test the legality of certain arrests for playing ball on Sunday. The learned justice adhered to his decision in the Bedell case and handed down an opinion which is so remarkable in many particulars that we feel justified in quoting from it at some length. He said: "No complaint was made in the present case by any citizen that the repose and religious liberty of the community or of himself were interrupted. The arrests were voluntarily made by the police, and the information is sworn to by a captain of police only. He does not allege that the repose and religious liberty of the community were interrupted. His action seems to be in defiance of the decisions of our courts. He sets himself above the law; a thing grown very common with the police in this city of late years, and of which there seems no sign of abatement by those who control the police. Men and women are being arrested daily on charges which the courts have decided over and over again do not constitute any criminal offense. It cannot be too often said to those who rule the police that our government, like all free governments, is a government of laws and not of men. Those who turn it into one of men and not of laws are more dangerous to society than any other class of law breakers, or all other law breakers combined. They would destroy our system of government and substitute one of arbitrary power and unlawful force. Ten years ago the police of the city of Brooklyn took it upon themselves to chase, club, and lock up all boys and men found playing ball on Sunday in the outskirts and remote places of the city, while many shows and places of evil resort were open, and train loads of people were being carried by to them; but on the protest of citizens they were stopped in their course by a police commissioner who came to understand the limitations of his powers and duty, and of those under him, under a free government such as ours. Since then ball playing and golf playing on Sunday have been unmolested here. It would seem that we are now on the eve of another similar movement by the police, for such movements come periodically, and for no reason whatever other than mere officiousness. . . . There are many minor offenses which should be left for redress to the coming forward of private accusers before the magistrates or other authorities, as our laws and the procedure of our courts contemplate. The accusatory method of enforcing the criminal laws is open to every citizen. The community can take care of itself in such matters without any police meddling. Baseball and golf, and other innocent and healthy games, are being played everywhere outside of the city on Sunday without being meddled with by constables or policemen. Such meddling is practically unknown except in this city, where, of all places, we should have humane, sensible, and intelligent government. The general sentiment of the community has to be consulted in respect of the enforcement of certain laws, and always has been in the Anglo-Saxon world as well as elsewhere, until recently in the city of New York. It is a maxim of the law that you cannot indict a whole community. The Anglo-Saxon sheds statutes which grow obsolete and obnoxious, the same as a snake sheds his skin. He has seldom bothered to repeal them, as every one acquainted with the history of laws very well knows. No citizen any longer makes a complaint under them, and thus they become dead-letter laws. It is not the business of the police to revive them. They are not employed and paid by the citizens for any such purpose."

A month later Justice Gaynor held in another case that a public game of baseball, *i. e.*, a game to which the public are invited and to which an admission fee is charged, is within the inhibition of the statute. He said: "The prohibition is only against public games and exercises, namely, those to which the public are invited, because the statute presumes that they interrupt the repose of the community." People *v.* Poole, 44 Misc. (N. Y.) 118.

In Dunham *v.* Binghamton, etc., Assoc., 44 Misc. (N. Y.) 112, Justice Forbes, at Binghamton, refused to dissolve an injunction secured by property owners against the playing of ball on Sunday on certain premises, declining, however, to pass upon the merits of the question.

This, then, is the situation in New York State: We have an *obiter dictum* by the Court of Appeals that Sunday baseball is illegal, but we have a positive declaration by the Supreme Court, not yet overruled, that Sunday baseball is not illegal except when an admission fee is charged to witness the game, or when the public peace is unduly disturbed. This contrariety of views is largely responsible for the fact that baseball is played on Sunday in some parts of the State and not in others. The magistrates before whom the cases of alleged violation of the law come for decision are at liberty to adopt either view, or to declare, as has been done in some cases, that the question is too unsettled to warrant them in rendering any decision whatever. It may be said that if the Missouri argument as to legislative intent has any force it is fully applicable to New York State. As far back as the New York Revised Statutes of 1828 we find the following prohibition: "There shall be no shooting, hunting, fishing, sporting, playing, horse racing, gaming, frequenting of tippling houses, or any unlawful exercises or pastimes on the first day of the week, called Sunday." Baseball was then not known, but when the Penal Code was enacted in 1881, professional baseball had been played for several years. The legislature, however, merely reworded the section, without any change evidencing an intention specifically to include baseball.

In closing, it may be well to add a word as to the validity of Sunday baseball legislation. Statutes which expressly prohibit the game, or which so result by judicial decision, have been uniformly upheld against constitutional objections. (See State v. Hogriever, 152 Ind. 652; State v. O'Rourk, 35 Neb. 614; State v. Powell, 58 Ohio St. 324.) If it is a valid exercise of legislative power to prohibit the playing of baseball on Sunday, it is, of course, perfectly possible for legislatures to permit the sport with well-defined limitations and restrictions.

AN ENGLISH VIEW OF AMERICAN CRIMINAL PROCEDURE.

THE disagreement of the jury in the Thaw case makes really very little difference. It would have made very little difference even if Thaw had been convicted of murder in the first degree and sentenced to be electrocuted. There is as wide a gulf between passing a verdict in the criminal courts of America and carrying it out as there is between passing a law and getting it enforced. I venture to say with all possible abruptness that the machinery does not exist in the United States for making a murderer of Thaw's wealth and social influence pay the penalty for his crime.

In the twelve years that I have known America at all intimately I only recollect one instance in which the criminal law worked with anything approaching the English standard of swiftness and precision. That was in the case of the man who shot President McKinley. Public opinion insisted on a speedy trial and a speedy execution, and public opinion had its way. Had the victim been a man of less prominence the odds would have been over seventy to one against his assassin ever being brought to the chair.

The odds I have quoted are not to be taken as a mere figure of speech. They are a literal and appalling fact. Since 1885 there have been 131,951 murders and homicides in the United States, and but 2,286 executions. In 1885 the number of murders was 1,808; in 1904 it had risen to 8,482. In 1885 the number of executions was 108; in 1904 it was 116. There was nothing that I am aware of to make 1904 a year of peculiar criminality. Indeed, the figures for 1905 and 1906 tell an even more sinister tale — Americans seem now to be killing one another at the rate of more than 9,000 a year. Looking over the statistics of the last twenty years one finds, roughly speaking, that while executions have remained virtually stationary, murders and homicides have multiplied fivefold.

There are over five times as many murders committed in the United States per million inhabitants as in Australia, more than fourteen times as many as in England and Wales, eight times as many as in Japan, nearly ten times as many as in Canada, and about twenty-five times as many as in Germany. Only one European country, Italy, has ever shown in this respect a worse record; only one country in the world to-day, Mexico, exceeds the American average; and the United States has the further distinction of being the only country where the proportion of murders to population is positively on the increase.

These are facts as undeniable as they are portentous. The immigrant and the negro help, of course, to swell the figures; but the darkies and the aliens may be eliminated altogether, and the white native-born Americans will still be responsible for more than three times as many murders in proportion to their numbers as stand to the discredit of any other civilized nation, except Spain and Italy. What is the explanation of so disturbing a phenomenon? Is it nothing more than the lawlessness of a raw, vigorous, and untrammeled community, but barely emerging from the backwoods stage of growth? Or is it the reflex action on matters of social conduct of that excessive individualism, that "State-blindness," as Mr. H. G. Wells has happily called it, the pervasive lack of a civic and social conscience, which have already wrought such confusion and degradation in the body politic?

Here, however, I am concerned not so much with the commission of crimes as with the failure to punish them. If the frightful increase of murders in the United States stands in need of explanation, the immunity of the murderers and their all but invariable escape from the full penalties of the law are facts of a yet wider and more ominous significance. Nine months ago an American judge, in an address to a lawyers' association, used these words: "I say that our administration of the criminal law has broken down. It is an unworkable machine. I know we convict men and send them to the penitentiary; but I state it here, as a fair statement of the administration of the criminal law in America, that if a man has the means to employ able counsel, so as to 'make a fight,' as we say, in the great majority of cases he can escape punishment for crime."

Mr. Taft, a former judge in the United States 'Criminal Court, and now secretary of war in Mr. Roosevelt's cabinet, has been even more emphatic. Addressing the Yale Law school, in 1905, he said: "I grieve for my country to say that the administration of the criminal law in all the States of the Union (there may be one or two exceptions) is a disgrace to our civilization." Justices Brewer and Brown, of the United States Supreme Court, have said the same thing in other words. The leading legal journal of the country is filled with similar admissions. No American lawyer of any standing would, I think, argue otherwise.

Take a few instances. Frank Steunenberg, a former governor of Idaho, was assassinated on December 30, 1905. It is hoped to bring his alleged murderers to trial next month. Not long ago a case was reported in the American papers in which a mob lynched a prisoner who had been held for two years under a charge of murder, though the question whether he had killed the victim had not been raised. A man named Patrick was convicted in New York in 1902 of murder, nearly two years after the crime was committed. It took three years to get the case argued before the Court of Appeals, where the sentence was confirmed in March, 1905. A further appeal to the United States Supreme Court occupied the whole of 1906. Three months ago came the news that the governor of New York had changed the sentence to imprisonment for life.

One could multiply such instances by the score, and the defects they point to can all, or nearly all, be traced back to one general cause. The criminal procedure of America to-day is very much as ours was in the time of the Stuarts. It is hopelessly entangled in technicalities, and neglects justice and common sense to chase after an impossible infallibility of form. In a criminal case, as it is conducted across the Atlantic, it is not the prisoner in the dock, but the judge on the bench who is really on trial. The counsel on both sides polish up a thousand little points of pleading and practice and evidence, and fire them off at the judge, who has to decide upon them off-hand. If he falls into a single error, no matter how trivial or how far removed from the question of the guilt or innocence of the accused, the appellate court will order a new trial of the case almost automatically.

That is the grand distinction between the American procedure and our own. In the English courts all such errors of form are brushed aside, unless they can be shown to have caused a miscarriage of justice. In the American courts any error, however technical and however little related to the fundamental issue, is held to presume prejudice. The appellate judge considers not whether the verdict he is reviewing is a just one on the facts of the case, but whether a single error of procedure was committed in reaching it. And if any such error is discovered he has then to satisfy himself not only that no prejudice to the rights of the accused arose from it, but also that none could have arisen in the mind of any juryman.

Thus it is that we find such absurdities as that of the United States Supreme Court, the highest tribunal in the land, reversing a judgment because the record failed to show that the defendant had been arraigned and had pleaded not guilty. Thus, only a few months ago a retrial was ordered in one case because the cross-examination of a witness extended somewhat beyond the examination in chief; and a conviction was set aside in another because the prosecuting attorney said some things in his speech to the jury that the appellate court thought he ought not to have said; and in a third case, by reason of some wholly immaterial error, a court felt constrained to reverse a judgment which in the same breath it declared to be absolutely just.

There are many other things, such as the sentimentalism of juries, the abuse of the pardoning power, the limited authority of the trial judge, and the ebullience of the press, that favor the accused in America. But most of all is he helped by the pernicious rule that any error which it is impossible to show affirmatively did not prejudice the defendant must lead to a reversal of judgment. Hence appeals and retrials multiply without end. Hence lawyers and criminals flourish while justice and society helplessly suffer. — "Anglo-American," in the *London Mail*.

Cases of Interest.

Street Along Water Front — Riparian Rights. — In Johnson *v.* Grenell, 81 N. E. Rep. 161, the New York Court of Appeals has recently held that the grantee of a lot abutting on a street extending along the margin of a river acquires title to the whole of the street, subject to the easement of travel thereon, and takes the riparian rights which follow a grant of uplands, there being no reservation in the grantor of title to the street.

Municipal Contracts — Patent Pavements. — In Saunders *v.* Iowa City, 111 N. W. Rep. 529, the Iowa Supreme Court holds that, under a statute requiring contracts for street improvements to be let to the lowest responsible bidder, the city council in its resolution and advertisement for bids may properly require the use of a certain patented pavement. The ruling is in line with the weight of authority on this vexed question. See 20 Am. and Eng. Encyc. of Law (2d ed.) 1166.

Employers' Liability Act Upheld. — Two federal district judges having declared that in their opinion the Act of Congress of June 11, 1906, known as the Employers' Liability Act, is unconstitutional and void, now comes three others who hold it to be valid. The cases are Snead *v.* Central of Georgia R. Co., 151 Fed. Rep. 608, decided by Judge Speer, of Georgia; Plummer *v.* Northern Pac. R. Co., 152 Fed. Rep. 206, decided by Judge Hanford, of Washington, and Kelley *v.* Great Northern R. Co., 152 Fed. Rep. 211, decided by Judge Morris, of Minnesota.

Inheritance Tax — Power of Appointment. — In Chanler *v.* Kelsey, 27 Sup. Ct. Rep. 550, the United States Supreme Court holds that a New York statute imposing an inheritance tax on the exercise by will of a power of appointment conferred by a deed executed prior to the passage of such statute, is not unconstitutional as authorizing the taking of property without due process of law, or as impairing the obligation of contracts. Mr. Justice Holmes wrote a dissenting opinion in which Justice Moody concurred.

Anti-Trading Stamp Act Unconstitutional. — In Leonard *v.* Bassingdale, 89 Pac. Rep. 879, the Supreme Court of Washington falls into line with the courts of numerous other States which have declared invalid statutes aimed against the use of trading stamps. The Washington statute makes it a misdemeanor to sell or exchange property under representation or inducement that an unidentified or chance prize or premium, or that a stamp, trading stamp, or other like device entitling the holder to receive such a prize, etc., or that the redemption of such stamp, etc., is to be part of the transaction, or to sell or exchange any trading stamp, etc., to aid such sale or exchange. The court holds that this act violates the constitutional provision that no person shall be deprived of life, liberty, or property without due process of law.

Assault and Battery by Parent on Child. — Children who are not being spoiled by the sparing of the rod will doubtless be interested in the case of State *v.* Koonse, 101 S. W. Rep. 139, wherein the Missouri Court of Appeals holds that if punishment inflicted by a parent upon a child is so excessive and cruel as to show that the parent was not acting in good faith for the child's benefit, the parent is guilty of an unlawful assault. Johnson, J., said: "The welfare of the child is the principal ground on which the parental right to chastise him is founded, and where the punishment inflicted is so excessive and cruel as to show beyond a reasonable doubt that the parent was not acting in good faith for the benefit of the child, but to satisfy his own evil passion, he no longer is to be considered as a judge administering the law of the household, but as a malefactor guilty of an unlawful assault on a helpless person intrusted to his care and protection."

Breach of Conditional Pardon. — In *Ex p.* Houghton, 89 Pac. Rep. 801, the Oregon Supreme Court holds that where the governor, in pursuance of statutory authority, issues a pardon conditioned that the person pardoned shall be and remain a law-abiding citizen and that in the event of his not remaining so the governor may revoke the pardon without notice or the intervention of any court, such conditions become binding on the person pardoned upon his acceptance of the pardon, and he may be rearrested and confined at the instance of the governor without any judicial investigation. The court said: "Where the pardon provides upon its face that the governor may summarily determine whether the conditions have been complied with, and, if he finds that they have not, may revoke the pardon and order the reconfinement of the offender, such stipulation becomes binding upon the convict, and authorizes his rearrest and commitment upon the terms and in the manner imposed. 24 Am. and Eng. Encyc. of Law (2d ed.) 595."

Liability of City for Damage by Mob. — A rather amusing case of destruction of property by a mob was decided by the New York Court of Appeals in Adamson *v.* City of New York, 80 N. E. Rep. 797. On the afternoon of an election day an unoccupied two-story frame dwelling owned by the plaintiff was demolished by a varying crowd of young men and boys, and its constituent elements were devoted to building bonfires. The plaintiff sued the city under a statute making a city or county liable for damages to a person whose property is destroyed or injured therein by a mob or riot. It was shown in evidence that there was no disturbance except such as was naturally incidental to prying the building apart and bearing away the parts thereof, and there was no evidence of any purpose to accomplish the destruction by violence. On the contrary, it appeared that as soon as a policeman came on the scene the crowd ran away. It was also shown that at the same time in other portions of the police precinct boys and men were stealing wood for bonfires. The court held that these facts did not show damage by a "mob or riot," and that the plaintiff was not entitled to recover.

Trained Nurse Not a Servant. — In Parkes v. Seasongood, 152 Fed. Rep. 583, Judge Brown, sitting in the Federal Circuit Court for Rhode Island, held that a trained nurse performing her usual duties and exercising the skill which is the result of training in that profession, does not come within the definition of a servant, but rather is one who renders personal service to an employer in the pursuit of an independent calling, and the employer is not liable as master for her acts. The action was brought by a hotel proprietor against a guest occupying rooms in the hotel for permitting a nurse in his employ to remain in such rooms and there give birth to an illegitimate child. The child was stillborn and its body was concealed in a closet outside the defendant's rooms. Its subsequent discovery caused a lively scandal in the hotel, which resulted in considerable damage to the landlord's business. The court held that the defendant could not be held liable as master and could not be charged with liability for the concealment of the body in a place not under his control, unless he actively caused or participated in such concealment.

Some Automobile Cases. — In Ward v. Brooklyn Heights R. Co., 104 N. Y. Supp. 95, the New York Appellate Division, Second Department, holds that where a person riding as a mere passenger in an automobile, and having nothing to do with the management or control of the machine, is injured by a collision with a street car, he is not chargeable with the negligence of the driver of the automobile.

In Hillhouse v. United States, 152 Fed. Rep. 163, the Circuit Court of Appeals, Second Circuit, holds that an automobile constitutes "household effects" within the provision of the tariff law admitting free of duty household effects used abroad not less than one year, and that the fact that the machine has undergone extensive repairs abroad just prior to the importation does not alter the rule, except that so much of it as is a new manufacture may be assessed with duty.

In Patterson v. Kates, 152 Fed. Rep. 481, the owner of an automobile was held not liable for an injury which occurred while the chauffeur was making a trip in the machine for purposes of his own use in no way connected with his duty.

Liability for Refusing Lodging to Sick Visitor. — A novel point was decided by the Minnesota Supreme Court in Depue v. Flateau, 111 N. W. Rep. 1. The plaintiff having called at the defendant's farm on a very cold afternoon was taken violently ill and requested the defendant to allow him to remain overnight. This the defendant refused to do, and assisted the plaintiff from the house and into his cutter, starting him on his way home, seven miles away. Shortly afterward the defendant was again taken ill, fell from his cutter, and was found next morning nearly frozen. His action for damages was dismissed in the lower court, but the Supreme Court reversed the order denying a new trial, holding that as the plaintiff was on the premises by express invitation, the defendant owed him the duty, on discovering his physical condition, to exercise reasonable care not to expose him to danger by sending him away. The court said: "Whenever a person is placed in such a position with regard to another that it is obvious that, if he does not use due care in his own conduct, he will cause injury to that person, the duty at once arises to exercise care commensurate with the situation in which he thus finds himself, and with which he is confronted, to avoid such danger; and a negligent failure to perform the duty renders him liable for the consequences of his neglect."

Removal of Snow from Sidewalks. — In State v. McCrillis, 66 Atl. Rep. 301, the Rhode Island Supreme Court holds that a municipal ordinance requiring owners, occupants, and persons having charge of property to remove the snow from adjacent sidewalks is not violative of the provision of the State Constitution declaring that all laws should be made for the good of the whole and the burdens of the State ought to be fairly distributed among its citizens, or that one forbidding the taking of private property for public uses without just compensation; nor does it violate the provisions of the Fourteenth Amendment to the Federal Constitution relating to equal protection of the laws and due process of law. In the course of the opinion Blodgett, J., said: "From the fact of his citizenship, every citizen is under obligation to render some unpaid service to the State which protects him, reasonable, of course, in view of the exigencies which require such a service from him, and a law which simply defines and enforces such an obligation is entirely within the scope of the legislative power." The decision is in line with what would seem to be the weight of authority, although there are some well-reasoned cases holding otherwise. The authorities on the point are collected in 27 Am. and Eng. Encyc. of Law (2d ed.) 155.

Book Reviews.

PRINCIPLES OF GERMAN CIVIL LAW.

The Principles of German Civil Law. By Ernest J. Schuster, LL.D. (Munich), of Lincoln's Inn, Barrister-at-Law. 8vo., pp. xliv, 684. Oxford: Clarendon Press. New York and London: Henry Frowde. 1907. $3.00 net.

This is a most excellent book and by no means deserving of any merely perfunctory notice. The perusal of its lucid and fascinating pages has, indeed, been to us at once a pleasure and a means of improvement. The work contains a systematic exposition of the principles of the German civil law. The arrangement of the matter has been made with special reference to the needs of English readers, and the author has so chosen his material as to afford a very easy and satisfactory approach to the body of the German law.

We are told in the preface that the book was written with three distinct ideas in view, viz.: (1) to assist the study of English law from a comparative standpoint; (2) to give an insight into the latest and most perfect attempt made in any country to systematize the whole of the private law; (3) to give some practical help to the increasing number of practitioners who, in the course of their daily work, have to deal with questions of foreign and private international law. Judged by any fair criterion and from either of these standpoints, the work is worthy of high commendation.

Some of us are, no doubt, inclined to think that much academic nonsense has been expended over the subject of comparative jurisprudence. We are all more or less familiar with that class of writers "who, partly by desultory reading and partly by hearsay, have acquired some vague notions about foreign law, and who have studied their own law by the same methods and with the same results." The labors of such writers naturally serve to bring this whole branch of study into disrepute. The sarcasm about the jurist who knows every system of law but his own has its origin in this prejudice, and is not altogether without justification. But our author rightly protests that such men have nothing in common with the true representatives of the science of comparative law. It is quite true that with stronger scholarship and growing knowledge this prejudice against comparative study must disappear, and even those who work solely for professional standing and success will more and more see that grasp of legal principle is of greater value than mere knowledge of cases and isolated rules. Well does our author observe that such grasp of principle is unobtainable unless law is looked upon as an organic whole of which every part is correlated to the other.

Dr. Schuster is thoroughly imbued with the scientific spirit and he is a sufficient master both of the English and the German systems of law to enable him to make comparisons that are really helpful. His usual method of exposition is to begin a topic with a historical statement based upon materials drawn from Roman, German, and perhaps English sources. This is followed by a succinct statement of the principles of English law now applicable to that topic. Then comes a fuller presentation of the German civil law. The result is an exposition of the law pertaining to the matter in hand which is in the highest degree intelligible and instructive.

The work is, of course, largely based on the German codes which became effective on Jan. 1, 1900; but Dr. Schuster has wisely chosen to write a systematic treatise on the German law of to-day, and not merely to give a translation of the codes with annotations of his own. The codes are naturally quite technical and their parts are so inextricably interdependent that a satisfactory exposition of the whole code system would be complicated and tedious. The systematic exposition here given of the more important provisions is much better adapted to the needs of the student, and the result is a much more readable book than would have been possible on the other plan. Happily for the peace of mind of the average reader the work is not burdened with many footnotes or with excessive bibliographical material.

We heartily recommend the book to teachers and to all lawyers and students who take an intelligent interest in law as a science. Here is found a systematic presentation of a great system of law, compressed, without any destructive effect upon the harmony of the whole, into the limits of one volume. The order in which the ideas underlying the system are arranged and the general method of exposition will be found to be full of suggestions to the student of the common law. There certainly are many lawyers in this country who find it necessary or at least highly desirable, for professional purposes, to acquaint themselves with the main outlines of the German law of to-day. So far as we know, this is the only satisfactory book in English from which such information can be obtained.

News of the Profession.

THE NEW JERSEY STATE BAR ASSOCIATION met in Atlantic City on June 14 and 15. Details of the meeting will be given in this column next month.

THE PENNSYLVANIA STATE BAR ASSOCIATION held its thirteenth annual meeting at Bedford Springs on June 25, 26, and 27. An account of the meeting will be given in this column next month.

WELL-KNOWN DENVER LAWYER DEAD. — Lewis B. France, reporter of the Colorado Supreme Court decisions from 1876 to 1889 and one of Denver's best known citizens, died in that city on June 7 at the age of seventy-four.

JESSE JAMES, LAWYER. — At the graduating exercises of the Kansas City School of Law, on May 31, Jesse James, son of the famous outlaw, was awarded the highest grade for the year's work.

DEATH OF J. WARNER MILLS. — J. Warner Mills, author of Mills's Annotated Statutes of Colorado and numerous other legal publications, died in Denver on May 17, aged fifty-five years. Mr. Mills was anative of Wisconsin and a graduate of the University of Wisconsin. He located in Colorado in 1877.

HUMMEL "DOING TIME." — On May 20 Abraham H. Hummel, of the notorious law firm of Howe & Hummel, was taken to the penitentiary on Blackwell's Island, N. Y., and began serving the sentence of one year's imprisonment imposed on him for conspiracy in connection with the Dodge-Morse divorce case. It is reported that he is lodged in cell 23.

DATES FOR BAR ASSOCIATION MEETINGS. — The annual meeting of the Colorado State Bar Association will be held at Colorado Springs on July 5 and 6. The Illinois lawyers will meet on July 11 and 12 at Galesburg. On July 8-10 the Texas lawyers will be in session at Beaumont, and the Washington Association will convene in Seattle on July 13.

NEW YORK SUPREME COURT JUDGE DEAD. — Justice James W. Dunwell, of the New York Supreme Court, Fourth Department, died at his home in Lyons, N. Y., on May 22, aged fifty-eight years. He was graduated from Cornell University in 1871, and three years later was admitted to the bar. In 1896 he was elected to the Supreme Court for a term of fourteen years.

DUNN ELECTED TO ILLINOIS SUPREME COURT. — On June 8 Hon. Frank K. Dunn was elected a member of the Illinois Supreme Court to fill the vacancy created by the death of Justice Jacob W. Wilkin. Judge Dunn is fifty-three years old, and a graduate of Kenyon College and of the Harvard Law School. During the last six years he has been judge of the sixth judicial circuit of Illinois.

DISTINGUISHED IOWA LAWYER DEAD. — W. A. Foster, one of the most widely known lawyers that Iowa has produced, died suddenly of heart disease at his home in Davenport, Ia., on May 27. His greatest successes at the bar were won in Chicago, where in the celebrated Cronin murder case he successfully defended John F. Beggs, the only one of the accused men to escape conviction. In the trial of the Haymarket anarchists he was special counsel for Spies.

DEATH OF WELL-KNOWN COLORADO JUDGE. — Hon. Allison H. De France, judge of the first judicial district of Colorado and one of the most prominent citizens of that State, died at his home in Golden on May 12 of heart disease. He was born in Pennsylvania in 1835, and went to Colorado in 1861. He was elected district judge in 1894 for a term of six years, and was twice re-elected. From 1887 to 1889 he served as a member of the Supreme Court Commission of that State.

FELL FROM ROOF AND KILLED HIMSELF. — Lucius H. Perkins, a prominent lawyer of Lawrence, Kan., fifty-one years old, fell from the roof of his house on June 1 and was killed. The fact that Mr. Perkins carried insurance on his life approximating $500,000, the greater part of which was written within the last year, caused the lay press to wag its head somewhat skeptically over his taking off, but the circumstances seem to show very clearly that his death was entirely accidental.

H. G. WARD SUCCEEDS JUDGE WALLACE. — On May 23 President Roosevelt appointed Henry Galbraith Ward, of New York, to be United States circuit judge for the second judicial circuit, in place of Judge William J. Wallace, resigned. Judge Ward was born in New York city in 1851. He was graduated from the University of Pennsylvania in 1870, and was admitted to the bar in Philadelphia in 1873. Since 1884 he has been practicing in New York. The new judge has had no previous judicial experience.

DEATH OF FORMER CHIEF JUSTICE OF UTAH SUPREME COURT. — Hon. James A. Miner, formerly chief justice of the Supreme Court of Utah, died in Salt Lake City, May 22, at the age of sixty-five. Judge Miner was a native of Michigan. In 1890 he was appointed a justice of the Utah Territorial Supreme Court by President Harrison, and on the admission of Utah to statehood he was elected a member of the State Supreme Court. He later became chief justice of the court, and held that position at the time of his retirement, in 1903.

CHIEF JUDGE GARRETSON, OF NEW JERSEY, DEAD. — Hon. Abram Quick Garretson, chief judge of the Supreme Court of New Jersey, died on June 3 of pneumonia at his home in Morristown. Judge Garretson was born in 1842, and was graduated from Rutgers College, after which he studied law in the Harvard Law School. He began practicing in 1865. From 1878 to 1883 he served as judge of the Court of Common Pleas of Hudson county, and thereafter he practiced in partnership with James B. Vredenburgh until he was appointed to the Supreme Court in 1900.

FEDERAL JUDGE TOWNSEND DIES. — Hon. William Kneeland Townsend, judge of the United States Circuit Court, second circuit, died suddenly, on June 1, at his home in New Haven, Conn. Judge Townsend was born in New Haven in 1849, and was graduated from Yale in 1871. Being admitted to the bar in 1874, he began the practice of his profession, and was at one time corporation counsel of that city. In 1892 he was appointed judge of the United States District Court, and was made circuit judge in 1902. He was the author of a number of legal treatises, and was lecturer on the law of contracts in the Yale Law School.

DINNER TO JUDGE WALLACE. — On May 29, at the Waldorf-Astoria Hotel in New York city, a dinner was given in honor of Judge William J. Wallace, who has recently resigned the presiding judgeship of the United States Circuit Court of Appeals for the second circuit. About five hundred members of the bench and bar of New York were present, and Hon. Alton B. Parker presided. Among the speakers were Judge Lacombe, of the United States Circuit Court of Appeals; Chief Justice Cullen, of the New York Court of Appeals, and Federal Circuit Judges H. H. Lurton, of Tennessee, and Le Baron B. Colt, of Rhode Island. Judge Wallace has associated himself with the well-known law firm of Butler, Notman & Mynderse, which will hereafter be styled Wallace, Butler & Brown.

LOUISIANA STATE BAR ASSOCIATION. — The annual meeting of the Louisiana State Bar Association was held in Shreveport on May 10 and 11. Mayor Bernstein delivered an address of welcome, to which response was made on behalf of the association by Judge E. W. Sutherlin. In his annual address President W. S. Parkerson, of New Orleans, discussed the new laws enacted in the state and nation, and took occasion to criticise President Roosevelt quite sharply on account of his inclination toward personal aggrandizement. Henry P. Dart, of New Orleans, read a paper on "Quarantine, National and State," and Judge A. A. Gunby, of Monroe, read one on "The Lawyer in Literature." The meeting was concluded by a banquet at the Inn Café, at which toasts were responded to by the following gentlemen: H. P. Dart, of New Orleans; J. H. Levy, of Shreveport; W. S. Parkerson, of New Orleans; B. R. Forman, of New Orleans; H. P. Wells, of Shreveport; P. Brabites, of New Orleans; Judge J. C. Pugh, of Shreveport; and Congressman J. T. Watkins, of Minden.

JOINT MEETING OF TENNESSEE AND ARKANSAS LAWYERS. — The State Bar Associations of Tennessee and Arkansas held a joint meeting in Memphis on June 4, 5, and 6. Hon. James H. Malone, of Memphis, made an address of welcome to the visitors, which was responded to by representatives of the two associations. Then followed the annual addresses of the presidents, Joseph W. House, of the Arkansas Association, and F. H. Heiskell, of the Tennessee Association. The three principal addresses of the meeting were "Constitutional Changes," by Yancy Lewis, of Dallas, Tex.; "Criminal Law Reform," by Chief Justice A. H. Whitfield, of the Mississippi Supreme Court; "The Growing Importance of the Fourteenth Amendment," by Hannis Taylor, of Washington, D. C. Papers read during the meeting were: "A Page from English State Trials," by Jesse Turner, of Van Buren, Ark.; "The Practice of the Law: a Trade or a Profession," by Albert W. Biggs, of Memphis; "Lawyers of Antiquity," by Eugene F. Ware, of Topeka, Kan.; "The Court Reporter," by T. D. Crawford, of Little Rock, Ark.; "Local Government," by Joshua W. Caldwell, of Knoxville, Tenn.; "The Progress of the Law as Compared with Other Professions," by N. W. Norton, of Forest City, Ark. The meeting closed with a banquet.

GEORGIA STATE BAR ASSOCIATION. — The twenty-fourth annual meeting of the Georgia State Bar Association was held at Tybee Island, near Savannah, on May 30 and 31. The president, Judge A. L. Miller, of Macon, called the meeting to order, and after the reception of committee reports the annual address was delivered by Congressman Champ Clark, of Missouri. Mr. Clark's subject was "The Country Lawyer as a Factor in Public Affairs." President Miller delivered "Some Friendly Suggestions to Young Lawyers." Other papers read during the meeting were: "The History of the Establishment of the Supreme Court of Georgia," by Hon. J. R. Lamar, of Augusta; "The Probate Court: Its Jurisdiction and Incidents, Ordinary and Extraordinary," by Hon. Henry McAlpin, of Savannah; "Land Litigation in Wiregrass Georgia," by E. K. Wilcox, of Valdosta; "Lynching and the Law's Delay," by John E. Pottle, of Milledgeville; "Convict Labor and Our Penal System," by Paul F. Akin, of Cartersville; "Defects in the Georgia Laws Relating to Liens of Mechanics and Materialmen," by Henry A. Alexander, of Atlanta. W. C. Bunn, of Cedartown, had prepared a paper on "The Development of the Law in Georgia with Regard to Child Labor in Factories," but was prevented by illness from attending, and the paper was read by J. G. Tyson, of Cedartown. The meeting concluded with the usual banquet. Officers for the ensuing year were elected, as follows: President, Samuel B. Adams, of Savannah; vice-presidents, James B. Lamar of Augusta, E. R. Black of Atlanta, Samuel S. Bennett of Camilla, Hewit A. Hall of Newman, J. E. Dean of Rome; secretary, Orville A. Parke, of Macon; treasurer, Z. D. Harrison, of Atlanta.

MISSISSIPPI STATE BAR ASSOCIATION. — The second annual meeting of the Mississippi State Bar Association was held in Vicksburg on May 7, 8, and 9. After President Murray F. Smith, of Vicksburg, had called the meeting to order, Col. R. V. Booth, president of the Vicksburg Bar Association, made an address of welcome, which was responded to by C. C. Dunn, of Meridian. Then followed the annual address of the president. The principal event of the second day was to have been the annual oration, but this had to be omitted from the programme by reason of inability to secure the attendance of the orator who had been invited to speak. Among the papers read during the course of the meeting were the following: "Needed Banking Legislation," by Chancellor Percy Bell, of Greenville; "The Constitutional and Legal Phases of Government Ownership of Railroads," by C. H. Alexander, of Jackson; "Uniformity of Legislation," by William O. Hart, of New Orleans. On the evening of the second day the annual banquet was held at the Hotel Carroll, at which President Smith acted as toastmaster. Toasts were responded to by the following gentlemen: Hon. E.

J. Bowers, of Bay St. Louis; Chief Justice A. H. Whitfield, of the Mississippi Supreme Court; T. A. McWillie, of Jackson; Hon. John M. Allen, of Tupelo; Hon. J. H. Price, of Magnolia; Hon. H. C. Niles, of Meridian, and Leroy Percy, of Greenville. The following officers were elected: President, C. H. Alexander, of Jackson; vice-presidents, J. S. Sexton of Hazlehurst, W. E. Baskin of Meridian, Judge W. D. Houston of Aberdeen; secretary and treasurer, Sidney Smith, of Lexington. The next meeting will be held in Meridian.

English Notes.

LIABILITY OF AUTOMOBILE OWNER FOR INJURIES. — A point of some importance to owners of motor cars was recently decided by the Court of Appeal in the case of Harris v. Fiat Motors (noted in the LAW JOURNAL for May 25, at page 340). The owner of a motor car had given express orders to his chauffeur not to allow any one else to drive the car. While out in the car with a friend the chauffeur went to the back of the vehicle to ascertain the cause of a noise in the working of the gear and intrusted the driving to his friend. During the time the friend was driving an accident occurred, and an action was brought to recover damages of the owner. The Court of Appeal holds that a servant may, when the circumstances create an absolute necessity, delegate his duties to another person, so as to make the latter in law the servant of the master.

LORD YOUNG DEAD. — Lord Young, until two years ago a judge of the Scottish Court of Session, died in London, May 22, aged eighty-eight years. He was called to the Scotch bar in 1840, and in 1869 was the recipient of the unusual honor of being called to the English bar by special resolution. Subsequently he was elected a Bencher of the Middle Temple. In 1862 he was Solicitor-General in Lord Palmerston's government and held the same office in the Gladstone ministry in 1868. In the following year he succeeded Lord Moncrief as Lord Advocate. He was appointed a judge of the Court of Session in 1874 and held the position until 1905, when he resigned. Lord Young was in his time a noted wit, and many of his sayings are still current, especially his classification of witnesses as "liars, damned liars, and experts." Another often quoted witticism of his is his definition of an "act of God" as "something which no reasonable man could ever expect."

TO ABOLISH PRIMOGENITURE. — A bill has recently been introduced into Parliament the object of which is to alter the descent of land in cases of intestacy, so that where a person dies without having made a will, or where his will does not completely dispose of all his landed property, all such property not disposed of shall be divided in the same way that personal property is at present. Clause 1 of the bill abolishes all existing modes or canons of descent and of devolution by special occupancy or otherwise of lands, whether operating by the general law or by any custom of any county, locality, or manor. Tenancy by the curtesy, dower, and freebench are also abolished, and the intestate's lands are to vest in and be dealt with by his legal personal representatives as if the land was personal estate. The existing rules of equity as to the administration of assets are left unaffected.

JUDICIAL STATISTICS FOR 1905. — The civil judicial statistics for 1905, recently issued, show a decrease in litigation, the first since 1899. The total number of legal proceedings was 1,473,919 as against 1,518,527 in 1904. Of matrimonial causes there were 921, of which 752 were petitions for divorce — thirty-two more than in the preceding year, but less than in 1902 or 1903. Of these petitions 429 were filed by husbands and 323 by wives. Decrees *nisi* were granted to husbands in 362 cases and to wives in 261 cases. Of the marriages dissolved 33.23 per cent. had lasted from five to ten years, 39.43 per cent. had lasted from ten to twenty years, while 10.89 per cent. had survived a score of years or more. The steady growth of imprisonment for debt is shown by the fact that 11,427 debtors were sent to prison during the year as against 11,096 for the previous year, and an average of 10,218 for the years ending with 1905.

THE EDALJI CASE. — The case of George Edalji, the young English lawyer convicted on a charge of maiming cattle, and recently pardoned by the Home Office, refuses to down. The action of Mr. Gladstone, the Home Secretary, in granting a free pardon but without compensation seems to have satisfied nobody, and Edalji's supporters are still clamoring for an investigation that will clear up the mystery which enshrouds the case and establish the authorship of the anonymous letters which have figured so prominently. Sir Arthur Conan Doyle, whose efforts were largely responsible for the reopening of the matter, has come out with a statement that he has recently received a letter and a post card in the same handwriting as the letters involved in the Edalji case. He offers a reward of £20 to anyone who will give him certain information as to the source of the letter and post card, and there is reason to believe that the time is not far distant when the whole affair will be made clear. Meanwhile strong and continuous pressure is being brought to bear on Mr. Gladstone to secure a further investigation. The following resolution recently sent to him by the Criminal Law and Prison Reform Department of the Humanitarian League is a typical expression of the prevailing sentiment: "That we cannot regard the report of the Edalji Committee as in any respect clearing up the various questions involved in the case, and we desire to repeat our demand for a public inquiry at which both Mr. Edalji and the public officials whose conduct has been called in question, and in some respects censured, should be represented."

AN ENGLISH VIEW OF JUVENILE COURTS. — A writer in the *Pall Mall Gazette* has this to say regarding juvenile courts:

Certain cranks are getting up an unnecessary agitation to establish in London a special court for the trial of juvenile offenders. One would imagine that we possessed an enormous infantile criminal population. As a matter of fact, only three child criminals, convicted in 1906, were under twelve years of age. Presumably the sentimentalists would have the children conveyed to the Police Court in miniature Black Marias drawn by Shetland ponies.

A magistrate who specialized in juvenile offenders would unquestionably be more severe to them than a magistrate who has before him in the ordinary course of his business murderers, blackmailers, and every sort of mature criminal. He would say to himself:

"You are a bad child. You are worse than most children. Such and such an evil must befall you."

Whereas, the ordinary magistrate regards a child — any child, however bad — as a pleasing change from the murderer and blackmailer. To him it is simply a child and he deals with it tenderly.

In the argument that the child is contaminated by the atmosphere of the Police Court there is nothing. The child is kept in a room by itself, treated kindly, fed on cake, and generally having the "time of its life." Then it is brought into an empty court, where it meets a genial old gentleman — say Mr. Kennedy at Marlborough street. The child's case is the first to be heard. The magistrate has not yet become depressed by his surroundings of crime. He beams on the child. He consults with Mr. Nelson, the Police Court missionary, and does exactly what is right and proper for the little fellow's welfare.

Quite different might be the fate of a child who appeared, twentieth on the list, before a magistrate whose entire life was spent in becoming a pessimist with regard to the morality of our children.

But the magistrates on the bench in the metropolis — selecting at random Mr. Kennedy, Mr. Curtis Bennett, Mr. Biron — ay, and Mr. Plowden — are unsurpassable for meting out justice with the proper seasoning of mercy. They are not magistrates first and men of the world . . . when their duties are over. They are men of the world during office hours.

THE EDUCATIONAL VALUE OF THE LAW. — It has been well said that there is no profession the study of which brings a man so much into contact with subjects of national interest and international importance as that of the law. Whatever topic he touches, the lawyer finds himself face to face with great questions of public policy and difficult social problems. If it is the subject of workmen's compensation, he must look at it in the light of the true relations of employer and employed — of labor and capital. If it is a money-lending case, there is the whole question of the propriety of Equity or Parliament remaking people's contracts for them. If it is a question of divorce, there enters into it the profoundly difficult problem of the relations of the sexes, and of marriage not merely as a personal contract, but as an institution vital to the welfare of the state. In comparative law he finds a still wider field in observing how other civilized nations are dealing with difficulties — political, social, or economic — similar to those of his own. It is the realization of these bearings of the law on human society which makes the really great lawyer, as distinguished from the mere practitioner. And why should not the layman participate also in this educational and elevating power of the law? How is it possible for a man to be a good citizen in the truest sense unless he knows something of the general principles of that law which has been well described as the effort of a people to express their idea of right — unless he knows something, for instance, of the system on which justice is administered, of the theory and practical working of the Constitution, and of the powers of the executive government, of his duty of care towards others, of the rights and obligations of property? Last, not least, what an immense gain it would be to the layman and to the cause of reason if he were trained to distinguish between the relevant and irrelevant, to sift and weigh the value of testimony! — *Law Journal.*

Obiter Dicta.

A UNION LAWYER. — On his professional card Henry W. Lackey, a Chicago attorney, announces that he is a "member of Bricklayers and Stonemasons' Union, No. 21, of Illinois."

A GOOD ONE. — They are having a perfectly jolly time at the national capital these days over a story in which Chief Justice Fuller figures. The chief justice, so the story runs, met an old-time friend, and, after passing the time of day, remarked: "You are looking exceedingly well. Aren't you filling out a little?" "No, indeed," replied the wag of a friend. "You probably think so because I'm looking Fuller in the face." Every time that one is told there are hearty bursts of laughter from the hearers.

USUALLY THE CASE. — In the recent case of Hinckley *v.* Casey, 88 Pac. Rep. 753, the Washington Supreme Court said: "Both parties concede that this statute is so plain that it is not susceptible of construction, and such was the language of this court in Bond *v.* Chapman, 34 Wash. 606, 76 Pac. 97. Notwithstanding this concession and adjudication, the constructions for which the parties contend are widely different."

TOLD HIS REAL NAME. — In the South Orange (N. J.) Police Court recently a prisoner on being asked his name responded, "Alias Shaheen." "Aliases don't go in this court," said Justice Roll, with some asperity. "What's your real name?" "Alias Shaheen," reiterated the accused. Of course no police justice would ever submit tamely to such foolishness as that, and the offender was standing face to face with Trouble when a police officer explained that he was a Syrian and had told the literal truth about his name. Much mollified Justice Roll extracted five dollars from Alias for peddling towels without a license and allowed him to go on his way rejoicing.

CAUGHT REDHANDED. — The following notice of the taking of animals *damage-feasant* was posted by a J. P. of Archuleta county, Colo.:

Pagosa Jct. Colo
April 20 A. D. 1907

in According with Section 1941 Notice is here by given to the public that I have held 5 Burros for security for Damages sustained on Account of such trespass together with costs of suit the said Burros been Doing Damages on our crop seberl times and if the owner not call for them or come to settle the Damages I will sell them at my office for the highest bidder the day of April 30 A. D. 1907 at the hour of 9 A M.

Jose N. Chavez
Justice of Peace

GOOD BUSINESS. — A Columbus, Ohio, attorney whose office had suffered from a fire recently sent out a lot of postal cards reading as follows:

"FIRE! WATER!! SMOKE!!"

"FIRE SALE."

Such are the advertisements of a business house after they are burnt out. Although my furniture is scorched and my books and papers are water soaked by the big fire in the Dispatch Building, I will not have a fire sale.

I have opened a law office at 49 North High Street. All Legal Work promptly done at reasonable prices.

Let me do your collecting. I have made a success of that business.

(CUT OFF ON THIS LINE AND PUT THIS IN YOUR POCKET.)

GEORGE LEWIS HOPPES
Attorney and Counselor at Law
49 North High St., Columbus, Ohio.

Bell Phone 1863 Main Room 222 McCune Bldg.

HAD THE COURT ON THE DEFENSIVE. — During the trial of an assault and battery case before a newly elected justice of the peace down in Florida, the attorney for the defense in his speech to the jury criticised rather vigorously some of the justice's rulings on points of evidence. The old fellow squirmed uneasily in his seat until he could stand it no longer, when he sprang up and shouted: "I object to that kind of argument, suh." The lawyer paused a moment and then replied with grave dignity: "Your objection is overruled, suh." The justice swallowed hard, but realizing that it was his duty to preserve the legal technicalities, he slowly subsided into his chair and announced in humble tones: "Then the State takes an exception, suh." Then meekly bowing his head he awaited the further pleasure of the attorney.

A LAWYER'S CARD. — A correspondent sends in the professional card of Edward Menkin, a Chicago lawyer, which bears on its back the following legend:

"MAN"

A man's life is full of crosses and temptations. He comes into this world without his consent, and goes out against his will, and the trip between the two is exceedingly rocky.

The rule of contraries is one of the features of the trip. When he is little the big girls kiss him, when he is grown the little girls kiss him. If he is poor he is a bad manager, if he is rich he is dishonest. If he needs credit he can't get it, if he is prosperous every one wants to do him a favor. If he is in politics it's for the pie, if he is out of politics you can't find a place for him, and he is no good for his country.

If he doesn't give to charity he is a stingy cuss, if he does it's for show.

If he is actively religious he is a hypocrite, if he takes no interest in religion he is a hardened sinner.

If he gives affection he is a soft specimen, if he seems to care for no one he is cold-blooded.

If he dies young there was a great future before him, if he lives to an old age he has missed his calling.

The road is rocky, but man loves to travel it.

If you want a Good Attorney see me.

THE TRUTH ABOUT THE MATTER. — The following notice recently appeared in a Wilmington, N. C., newspaper in connection with litigation which has rent asunder one of the colored congregations of that city:

NOTICE!

In reply to a peace came out in the Wil. dispatch on May the 8th in this present month to all whom it may concern there is no authority has been given out from the 1st Baptist Church col for that publication the said church in regular church conference realected Rev. J. H. Rhoe for their pastor indefinite — May the second of this present month vs L. W. Wheeler and Joe Cogdell has just been restored by acknowledgment to their error Charles Carroll and David Bigott and Richard Baskerville has ben turn out of this Church and never has ben restored in this said church. Deacons of said church Dea Robert Willie, Dea J. W. Williams, Dea Foster Williams, Dea Sip-Mo-Lett, Dea Hardie Miller, Dea J. W. Williams acted sect. Trustees Sip-Mo-Lett, March E. Walker.

GOING SOME. — We should like to know the lad who writes the editorials for the Lexington (Ky.) *Herald*. As a describer he occupies a pinnacle all by himself. Recently he dipped his pen in the vinegar and remarked of a local lawyer that he was an attorney at law "by the grace of Kentucky's low standard of admission to the bar and the negligence of the Bar Association in maintaining its standard of ethics." If that isn't fair to middling, we'd like to know.

AN UNCERTAIN PROMISE. — A correspondent sends in the subjoined promissory note, which he thinks may be of interest to the profession because embodying several peculiarities not usually found in such instruments:

$48.00. July 13, 1906.

Abe Sternoff after date I promise to pay to the order of Anna Britak Forty Eight ——— no — 100 Dollars with interest at 6 per cent. per annum.

Commencing Sept. 12th, 1906 I promise to pay $1.00 a wk. Value received.

No. 58327. Due Sept. 15, 1907. Abe Sternoff.

THE ONLY ONE. — The world is burdened with so many cheap and wearisome witticisms based on the theory that lawyers are a mendacious and generally rascally crew, that one cannot but learn with joy that in at least one case a member of the noble profession found due recognition. On a tablet in the Church of St. Dustan, Fleet street, London, this inscription is to be found: "Hobson Judkins, Esq., late of Clifford's Inn, the Honest Solicitor, who departed this life June 30, 1812. This tablet was erected by his clients as a token of gratitude and respect for his honest, faithful and friendly conduct to them throughout life. Go, reader, and imitate Hobson Judkins." To be sure, that was a good long time ago.

Correspondence.

A Guilty Community.

To the Editor of LAW NOTES.

SIRS: In your last May issue I noticed an item to the effect that for three successive days all the criminals arraigned in the Lauderdale County (Ala.) Court pleaded guilty and that the lawyers there were thoroughly disgusted with the behavior of the criminal classes. In this connection the criminal record of Whiteside county, Illinois, from 1880 to 1904, the term of Walter Stager as State's attorney, may be interesting. During said term of twenty-four years 871 persons pleaded guilty. During said term there was one period of two years three months and eleven days, and another period of one year eleven months and twenty-three days, and another period of one year eight months and nineteen days, and another period of one year four months and one day, and another period of one year two months and ten days, during which all criminal cases heard either in the Circuit or County Court, either on indictments found or information filed in said courts, were disposed of on pleas of guilty. J. M. S.

STERLING, ILL.

Federal Statutes and Treaties.

To the Editor of LAW NOTES.

SIR: The newspaper press of the day seems, in a majority of instances at least, to rank United States statutes and United States treaties on the same equal footing with the Constitution of the United States. For this doctrine of equality of importance they frequently quote the first part of the second section of the sixth article of the Constitution, which is in these words: "This Constitution, and the laws of the United States which shall be made in pursuance thereof; and all treaties made, or which shall be made, under the authority of the United States, shall be the supreme law of the land." The above language of the Constitution in no legal sense ranks federal statutes and federal treaties as equal to the Constitution, except as the statutes and treaties *are constitutional.* The Constitution provides that statutes shall be made in pursuance of the Constitution; and treaties shall be made "under the authority of the United States;" — and what is the supreme source of authority? — the Constitution. Federal treaty makers cannot barter away the reserved rights of the States.

SIBLEY, IOWA. J. F. GLOVER.

otes

07.

MPSON COMPANY.
LAND, N. Y.

ol of constitutional con-
af for the United States
), as abstracted in 206
the States'] powers of
boundary, and yet the
d. There is a conflict
is competent to settle."
e of the waters of the
Colorado into Kansas.
ansas is stated in the
this case on a former
allegations were that
of Kansas of all the
h the Arkansas by its
the purposes of irrigat-
case could be imagined
ne of sovereign and in-
e United States inter-
f its standing appealed
gn and inherent powers.
ls the brief (206 U. S.
decisions of the court,
well recognized. It is
ull development is of
ustice Brewer, speaking
e Moody took no part,
ind proceeded: "His
ment runs substantially
er must be vested either
rnment; no legislative
ment other than those
airs of that State; con-
onal in their scope must
the United States. But
slative powers affecting
ng to, although not ex-
in direct conflict with

the doctrine that this is a government of enumerated powers. That this is such a government clearly appears from the Constitution, independently of the amendments, for otherwise there would be an instrument granting certain specified things made operative to grant other and distinct things. This natural construction of the original body of the Constitution is made absolutely certain by the Tenth Amendment. This amendment, which was seemingly adopted with prescience of just such contention as the present, disclosed the widespread fear that the national government might, under the pressure of supposed general welfare, attempt to exercise powers which had not been granted. With equal determination the framers intended that no such assumption should ever find justification in the organic act, and that if in the future further powers seemed necessary they should be granted by the people in the manner they had provided for amending that act. It reads: 'The powers not delegated to the United States by the Constitution, nor prohibited by it to the States, are reserved to the States respectively, or to the people.' The argument of counsel ignores the principal factor of this article, to wit, 'the people.' Its principal purpose was not the distribution of power between the United States and the States, but a reservation to the people of all powers not granted. The preamble of the Constitution declares who framed it, 'we the people of the United States,' not the people of one State, but the people of all the States, and Article X. reserves to the people of all the States the powers not delegated to the United States. The powers affecting the internal affairs of the States not granted to the United States by the Constitution, nor prohibited by it to the States, are reserved to the States respectively, and all powers of a national character which are not delegated to the national government by the Constitution are reserved to the people of the United States. The people who adopted the Constitution knew that in the nature of things they could not foresee all the questions which might arise in the future, all the circumstances which might call for the exercise of further national powers than those granted to the United States, and after making provision for an amendment to the Constitution by which any needed additional powers would be granted, they reserved to themselves all powers not so delegated. This Article X. is not to be shorn of its meaning by any narrow or technical construction, but is to be considered fairly and liberally so as to give effect to its scope and meaning."

THE extracts just quoted have to do with the legislative power of the national government; for the United States, as was said by the court, "rests its petition of intervention upon its alleged duty of legislating for the reclamation of arid lands," a duty based on a claim of rights paramount to those of the individual States. This claim the court finds unsupported in the Constitution, viewed as it always has been viewed as a grant of powers. There were no extensive tracts of arid lands within the boundaries of the country when the Constitution was adopted, and naturally no provision was made for the control or reclamation of such lands. "But, as our national territory has been enlarged, we have within our borders extensive tracts of arid lands which ought to be reclaimed, and it may well be that no power is adequate for their reclamation other than that of the national government. But if no such power has been granted, none can be exercised." The case in which the government intervened, however, was a justiciable dispute between two of the United States, and the Supreme Court has jurisdiction to determine it under the grant of judicial power in the Constitution. "Whenever the action of one State reaches through the action of natural laws into the territory of another State, the question of the extent and limitations of the rights of the two States becomes a matter of justiciable dispute between them, and this court is called upon to settle that dispute in such a way as will recognize the equal rights of both and at the same time establish justice between them. In other words, through these successive disputes and decisions this court is practically building up what may not improperly be called interstate common law."

The most casual glance at the case of Kansas *v.* Colorado, coming as it does from a unanimous court, will show its great importance, the leading position it is destined to take in that series of great judgments in which the Supreme Court has explained the fundamental principles of the national government and the relations of the States to each other and to the nation under the Constitution. It comes at a moment when the national administration is chafing at the limits set by the constitutional division of powers between the States and the nation to its well-intentioned efforts at reforming all things *instanter*. It has been accepted as in some measure a reply to the theories of amending the Constitution by judicial construction and occupying by national legislation fields of law-making neglected by the States. It was recently alluded to in several notable addresses: those of ex-Attorney-General Harmon before the Kentucky Bar Association and of ex-Judge Alton B. Parker before the North Carolina Bar Association, and by Senator Knox at the Yale commencement. Mr. Harmon, after alluding to Kansas *v.* Colorado and to the present tendency in the executive and legislative departments of the government to stretch the powers of their respective departments at the expense of the States on their own interpretation of the Constitution, "which has then no safeguard or sanction except the official oath," proceeded: "We have, however, in view of the latest and most timely decision to which I have just referred, the security that any such usurpation on the ground of real or supposed necessity must now be made consciously." Senator Knox, in a speech on "The Development of the Federal Power to Regulate Commerce," said: "That the Congress of the United States has no general legislative powers but only such as are granted to it by the Constitution is not an old-fashioned and exploded notion. It has been reaffirmed with emphasis by the Supreme Court within the last sixty days in a great opinion by Mr. Justice Brewer in the case of Colorado *v.* Kansas." And the Senator quoted from the opinion some of the remarks already given above.

Judge Parker spoke at length of the same case, but perhaps its main significance for him was in the support given in a passage already quoted to his well-known hobby that the common law is adequate to remedy all the ills that flesh is heir to with the least possible assistance from statutes. He clinches his conclusion by a reference to the number of statutes produced annually in this country as compared with the number produced in five years in England. According to Judge Parker's figures there were two hundred and ninety-two acts in England in five years as against our twenty-five thousand pages of statutes annually. The comparison is obviously somewhat unfair, as the figures for America include the results of some fifty distinct legislatures, legislating for some eighty millions of people, as against the laws framed by a single body for about forty millions. Add to this that his English figures give only the number of acts while those for the United States are given in pages, and the force of the contrast is much weakened. We deplore as much as any one the excessive and not infrequently unwise activities of our law-making bodies, but we would not have our case made worse by misleading statistics.

Probably most people, and all the lawyers at any rate, will cordially acquiesce in condemning the mass of legislation poured out by our legislators. For a very large part of our annual statute books consists of freak legislation — not all as bad as the statute in a Western State determining the period during which a woman must nurse her child, or as the impertinent enactment fixing a statutory length for chorus girls' skirts, but statutes which embody the theoretical nostrums for social ills of every village wiseacre who can get a seat in the legislature. Verily we need schools of legislation, which legislators should be required to attend before taking part in the great annual or biennial game of law-making. It is said that the recent regular session of the New York legislature, which adjourned after having so neglected necessary legislation that the Governor found it necessary to call it together for the consideration of certain necessary laws, considered over 2,000 bills and passed over 500 which have become laws. Over-legislation was a subject of discussion by Mr. Adrian H. Joline, of New York, in addressing the New Jersey Bar Association. Mr. Joline complained that "unless the present harvest of legislation is stopped, no man can go to his bed at night assured that he has not broken some law that will lay him open to fine or imprisonment." He heaved a sigh of relief that some at any rate had been defeated, and he instanced "the law to place life insurance companies under the control of the federal government." A Maine paper, displeased at Mr. Joline's criticism of President Roosevelt and a remark about Governor Hughes of New York, refers to him sarcastically as "a flippant lawyer and railway director of New York, addressing the New Jersey Bar Association," and declares that "the corporation lawyers applauded the speech" — which looks a little like an attempt to appeal to the class bias whose influence in legislation the same paper deplores.

In the well-known case of Roberson *v.* Rochester Folding Box Co., 171 N. Y. 538, the court, speaking in an admirable and elaborate opinion by Chief Judge Parker, concluded that it had no jurisdiction to restrain the defendant from using in advertising the portrait of the plaintiff, a comely young lady. The judge admitted the plaintiff's grievance, and suggested legislative interference by admitting "the absolute impossibility of dealing with this subject save by legislative enactment, by which may be drawn arbitrary distinctions which no court could promulgate as a part of general jurisprudence." (For once evidently the common law was considered inadequate.) The legislature adopted the suggestion, and passed a statute to meet the evil. The opinion in this case, declaring the inability of a court of equity to protect the so-called "right of privacy," has always seemed to us an admirable piece of judicial reasoning, an impression which was not removed by the contrary conclusion reached by the Supreme Court of Georgia in Pavesich *v.* New England Life Ins. Co., 122 Ga. 190. The latter is the only case, so far as we have observed, in which the question has arisen since the Roberson case, and it is therefore with some surprise that we notice Judge Dill in the New Jersey Court of Errors, in the recent case of Vanderbilt *v.* Mitchell, going somewhat out of his way in a dictum to express his disapproval. The Georgia case is referred to as "adopting the dissenting opinion of Gray, J., and rejecting the doctrine of the majority in Roberson *v.* Rochester Folding Box Co., a case seldom cited but to be disapproved, the force of which was subsequently removed by statute" — he might have added, at the suggestion of the court itself. The New Jersey case does not, as Judge Dill admits, render necessary the discussion of the matter involved in these cases. The facts in the Vanderbilt case are peculiar. John Vanderbilt was married to Myra and they lived together as husband and wife for two months. Afterwards Myra deserted John and began adulterous relations with another. After more than two years of this intercourse, during which the husband had been excluded from access to the wife, a child was born to her. The birth certificate of this child, drawn by the attending physician in accordance with statute, recorded it as the son of John Vanderbilt and his wife. Subsequently John filed his bill setting out the facts and asking that the certificate be canceled and that mother and child be permanently enjoined from claiming for the child under the certificate the name or property rights of a lawfully begotten child. The Court of Errors holds that equity has jurisdiction to grant the relief demanded, on the ground that property rights are threatened and also upon the broader ground that a court of chancery may interfere to prevent the invasion of personal rights. Of course, if the decision is placed upon the first of these grounds, and it seems clear that it can properly be done, there is no need of placing it upon the vexed second ground. The case, which is one of first impression, suggests the grave dangers that may result from the statutory status given to such vital statistics as *prima facie* evidence of the facts involved.

An interesting circular letter to the Bar Associations of sister States, prepared by the committee on correspondence of the Alabama Bar Association, deals with the subject of granting new trials for merely technical errors. Says the letter: "The doctrine that an error of ruling created *per se* for the excepting and defeated party a right to a new trial, has obtained the ascendency in a majority of the jurisdictions of this country. That was the old English rule made in 1830, which has since been changed, so that now in England the appellate court is not called upon to reverse a case or grant a new trial if it is satisfied the verdict was just, even though the record be full of error. The result of this new rule in England is that new trials are granted in less than 3½ per cent. of the cases on appeal. There, the trial court and lawyer exert their skill and industry to shape the record so that the case may be disposed of on its merits and justice be done. . . . The zeal and skill of the trial lawyer in this country is devoted largely to getting error in the record, while the appellate court, in a majority of the jurisdictions, grant new trials for error in the record, without regard to whether the verdict was just or the error fundamental to the cause." Attention has more than once been drawn to this matter in these columns. It is one of the weighty factors in bringing about the lowered respect for law which is so ominous a feature of contemporary life. Happily this particular evil influence seems to be easily controlled. In England it has been overcome, as is pointed out above. The present English rule was adopted from the former practice in equity, the difference between which and the practice at law is explained by Lord Eldon in Barker *v.* Ray, (1826) 2 Russ. 75, 76. The rule at present is embodied in Rules of the Supreme Court, order 39, rule 6, as follows: "A new trial shall not be granted on the ground of misdirection or of the improper admission or rejection of evidence, or because the verdict of the jury was not taken upon a question which the judge at the trial was not asked to leave to them, unless in the opinion of the court to which the application was made some substantial wrong or miscarriage has been thereby occasioned at the trial; and if it appears to such court that such wrong or miscarriage affects part only of the matter in controversy, or some or one only of the parties, the court may give final judgment as to part thereof, or some or one only of the parties, and direct a new trial as to the other part only, or as to the other party or parties." The proposed amendment to the Federal Judiciary Act is in substance much the same as the first clause of this English rule. The judiciary amendment will be remembered as the result of a recommendation in President Roosevelt's message to the last Congress. The Alabama Bar Association urges on its sister associations the advocacy of similar measures, a course which has been adopted in the Maryland Association.

The New York Court of Appeals has affirmed the decision of the lower courts in declaring unconstitutional that section of the Labor Law which prohibits the employment of women in factories before six o'clock in the morning and after nine o'clock in the evening. The case, People *v.* Williams, was noticed upon its decision by the New York Court of Special Sessions by us in October last. Judge Gray, in delivering the opinion of the Court of Appeals, says: "It is clear, as it seems to me, that this legislation cannot and should not be upheld as a proper exercise of the police power. It is certainly discriminative against female citizens in denying to them equal rights with men in the same pursuit. The courts have gone very far in upholding legislative enactments framed clearly for the welfare, comfort, and health of the community, and that a wide range in the exercise of the police power of the State should be conceded I do not deny. But when it is sought, under the guise of a labor law, arbitrarily, as here, to prevent an adult female citizen from working at any time of the day that suits her I think it is time to call a halt. It arbitrarily deprives citizens of their right to contract with each other. The tendency of legislatures in the form of regulatory measures to interfere with the lawful pursuits of citizens is becoming a marked one in this country, and it behooves the courts firmly, fearlessly to interpose the barriers of their judgment when invoked to protest against legislative acts plainly transcending the powers conferred by the Constitution upon the legislative body." In the case of People v. Lochner, 177 N. Y. 145, the Court of Appeals upheld the constitutionality of an act prohibiting the employment of bakers for more than sixty hours a week, and Judge Gray wrote a concurring opinion. That case was reversed by the Supreme Court of the United States. Lochner v. New York, 198 U. S. 45. The present decision is in agreement with the determination of the Federal Supreme Court, but the Court of Appeals has never hesitated to check the legislature in undue interference with private business under the pretense of police regulation. Matter of Jacobs, 98 N. Y. 98.

A NEW prominence has been given to the question of the "unwritten law," so called, by the trial and acquittal of ex-Judge Loving for the killing of a young man named Estes, whom his daughter had accused to him of having drugged and ruined her. The young woman had gone driving with Estes, and in the conviviality of the moment had partaken too freely of his pocket flask, so that she reached home in a more or less limp condition. Being asked by her father for an explanation of her condition, she told the story of drugging and assault, which so worked on the father's feelings that he sought out Estes and killed him. The prosecution was not allowed to offer evidence of the falsehood of the girl's story, the whole issue being, in the view of the court, its effect on the mind of Loving, under his defense of emotional insanity. The verdict seems to be regarded generally as a gross miscarriage of justice, a view in which some of the leading Virginia papers join. As we suggested some time ago, a reason for not attempting to put into statutory form what is known as "the unwritten law" might be found in the essentially equitable nature of the defense, that is, its dependence on the facts and circumstances surrounding the case. If we must have it, it seemed better to have it unwritten rather than in the hard and fast form of a statute. As "unwritten," a jury might refuse to apply it where, under all the circumstances, it was merely colorable, or where, taking everything into consideration, the killing was not under the sting of unspeakable wrong to a loved and defenseless woman. The Loving verdict seems to deprive our suggestions of all weight. If "the unwritten law" is to be administered by such juries it ceases to be an excuse for a certain class of homicides committed under excessive provocation, and opens wide the doors for every instance of murder, if the murderer can connect the deed with any tale of seduction or assault, true or false, possible or impossible, told to him by some female relative. "The unwritten law" thus loses one of the two foundations on which it rested. It appealed to the instinct of vengeance, but it also rested on the conception that the victim had placed himself beyond the protection of the law by his own acts. A life for a life was a rule which no longer applied, and instinct revolted from requiring the life of a man, however culpable he might have made himself, for the life of the perpetrator of certain wrongs on woman. The creature was no longer a man, no longer entitled to the law's protection as against the avenger. All this is changed under the new "unwritten law." The loathsomeness of the person killed does not count, the single prop on which it rests is the provocation existing in the imagination of the murderer. There has been quite an outburst of the unwritten law in the older sense lately. Besides the Strother case in Virginia, there is the Bowie case in Maryland, and, across the Atlantic, the Waddington case in Belgium. So strong are the primitive instincts in civilized man. But a few verdicts like that in the Loving case will ring the death knell of "unwritten law" everywhere.

SECRETARY TAFT'S address at Iowa University contained the rather novel suggestion that the commercializing of the legal profession in this country will lead to the division of our lawyers into the two classes of barristers and attorneys, as in England. But the secretary hopes for good from the change. "I think this division will have a healthy effect in one way, because it will make the barrister look to the attorney as his employer, and not to the client of the attorney as such. The separation of the barrister from the person whom he ultimately represents in court has one effect the advantage of which cannot be too much emphasized. It prevents the barrister from so identifying himself with the cause of his client as to lead him to extremes to bring about the result which the client would have in the case." The excessive loyalty of the lawyer to his client is the cause of other evils. "One must," says Mr. Taft, "recognize that the administration of justice in this country has suffered grievously from the intensity with which lawyers have served their clients and the lightness of the obligation which they have felt to the court and to the public as officers of the court and the law to do no injustice. The almost slavish loyalty to great corporations which their regularly and constantly employed counsel sometimes exhibit in defense or preservation of interests acquired under circumstances that will not bear the light of searching inquiry is often the real occasion for the popular resentment against corporations that we know to exist. Again, the conduct of the defense of criminals in this country, and the extremes to which counsel deem themselves justified in going in preventing their clients from receiving the just judgment of the law, have much to do with the disgraceful condition in which we find the administration of the criminal law." With regard to these matters, too, he hopes for reform when, under the influence of the awakened moral conscience of the country, "the members of the legal profession will become more impressed with the weight of the obligation that they are under to the court, of which they are officers, to do no more than to see that their clients' legal rights are protected, and not so to lose their own identity as officers of the law in the cause of their clients as to resort to any expedients to win their clients' cause, however much they pervert the instrumentalities that the law furnishes them to secure justice. How this reform may be brought about, there is not now time for me to discuss, but that it is much easier to bring it about when a court is clothed with the power which an English or a federal court has than under the system prevailing in some States, in which the judge is nothing but a moderator, goes without saying."

The Secretary is careful to declare that he does not mean to reflect on the conduct of the great mass of the honorable men who are pursuing the legal profession, yet there are enough of them who have so far forgotten their obligations as to contribute to the evils arising from corporate greed and miscarriages in criminal law.

ATTACK ON CONFESSIONAL AS OBSCENITY.

With the exception of the supremacy of the Pope, there is probably no question concerning which Catholics and Protestants differ so widely as that of the propriety of auricular confession. On the one hand, confession is considered a sacrament, of which all the faithful, prince and prelate, pauper and peasant, must alike partake, not only for the purpose of obtaining forgiveness for past transgressions, mortal or venial, but also as a salutary act of self-mortification which will tend to deter the transgressor from repeating his offenses in the future. On the other hand, confession is considered at best a superstitious rite, without divine sanction, observance of which is imposed for the purpose of assuring slavish subserviency to clerical authority, and at worst as a means whereby knavish priests, sworn to celibacy, may obtain information which will enable them to disregard their vows; or, as an intermediate between these two views, it is looked upon as affording profligates, at prices based upon their financial ability and the enormity of their offenses, past and prospective, license to go and sin again.

With the comparative correctness of these opposing views we have nothing to do. It may be said that foul and vituperative abuse of the confessional is not only offensive to Catholics, but is also distasteful to most Protestants, who feel that zeal, honest though it may be, does not excuse indecency. But this also is a question with which we have nothing to do. We may, however, inquire whether such abuse is a wrong of which the law takes cognizance and for which it affords a remedy, irrespective of the good faith and intention of the person from whom it emanates.

In New York there is a statute (Penal Code, § 317) making it an offense for any person to sell, lend, give away, or show, or to offer to sell, lend, give away, or show, or to have in his possession with intent to sell, lend, or give away, or show, or to advertise in any manner, or otherwise to offer, "for loan, gift, sale, or distribution, any obscene, lewd, lascivious, filthy, indecent, or disgusting book, magazine, pamphlet, newspaper, story paper, writing, paper, picture, drawing, photograph, figure, or image, or any written or printed matter of an indecent character."

In the recent case of People *v.* Eastman, 188 N. Y. 478, 81 N. E. Rep. 459, the defendant was prosecuted under this statute for selling and exposing for sale a newspaper containing an article reading as follows:

"*The Open Door to Hell*

"Is the confessional box. It is hell's gate. The mainspring to lust. The very embodiment and focus of the virus of hell. It is the very matter and pus that runs from the corpse in hell. It is the pollution and rottenness of the decay of ages. It is the cesspool, the recipient, the reservoir of lust, of vile thought and communication, adultery, the birthplace of sexual criminality, with men's wives and young girls, and the convent is earth's terminus and hell, the lake of fire is the dumping-ground. It is the criminal college. The mother of prostitution. The author of pauperism. From it emanates poison to society, homes, our schools, and government. I speak in love. No time to trifle. The Anaconda is drawing itself over many a threshold and stinging thousands to death. Hark! A voice from the tomb, the blood of the innocent crying out, in what sense is the confessional box needed? The word of God says, in 1 John, 1, 9, If we confess our sins, He is faithful and just to forgive our sins and to cleanse us from all unrighteousness. You go direct to God Almighty through Jesus Christ to confess your sins. Not in a concealed and secluded place alone. No wife can go with her husband. Here the priest asks the vilest of questions, and of course the husband could not be present. He asks the most delicate and intimate questions. But under what obligation is any one to a priest? What business has he got to go into a box and ask delicate female questions that no minister of Jesus Christ or true gentleman on earth would ask? Right here in the confessional box many have been ruined, and many become mothers as a result; and men, you are paying your money to priests and to a church that is ruining your daughters and stealing the affections of your wife, until he knows more about her than you do. She has many secrets kept from you, husband, but not from that licentious priest. This is all true, dear reader, and can be proven by thousands of witnesses. May it not well be called the open door to hell? Last month a dear brother gave *The Gospel Worker* to some in the place where he was at work in this city. It was the January number with the article, 'Break Open the Doors and Look In,' and it caused much excitement. Bloody threats and curses were made, and two could not sleep all night, they were so stirred over the truth in it. Was any one ever benefited in any way by going to the confessional box? If it is advice you need, why go to that secret place? Dear reader, Jesus Christ never instituted the confessional. Would He call lustful, licentious, drinking men to ask such low, vile questions, which are unbecoming for any one to ask another? I am sure you say no and begin to see the awfulness of it. You might as well confess to a dead dog. The Roman Church teaches you cannot be saved unless you confess to a priest. Read this from their own teaching: 'If any one shall say that priests who are in mortal sin have not the power of binding or loosing, or that priests are not the only ministers of absolution, let him be accursed.' This does away with Jesus' blood. It makes God second to this fellow in the confessional box. They teach that every sin, the vilest and lowest, the most criminal, by man and woman, must be confessed to the priest. They do not teach it necessary to repent, but to do penance. Notice, this takes the place of repentance. Penance and confession to a wicked priest necessary to salvation? Is there any intelligent person on the earth who believes it? The following is what Margaret L. Shepard, who was for three years an inmate of the Arno's Court Convent, Bristol, Eng., says: 'In a confessional the depth of corruption and womanly degradation is reached. There the seeds of hell are planted in the soul. The thoughts of a young girl are polluted. Her heart is polluted, her mind becomes familiarized with the most revolting sins of impurity. The lessons engraved in the memory, the heart, the thought, the soul, like the sear of a red-hot iron, leaves its scar. In the confessional young unmarried and married women get accustomed to hear and repeat without a scruple things which would cause even a fallen woman to blush.' These are the words of one who has been through the above and escaped from their murderous hands. I will close with the above. It is a clincher and positive evidence and witness of all I have said. All unite with me in prayer that the above will open the eyes of many deceived Romanists and come to the blood of Christ.

"N. L. A. Eastman."

A majority of the court were of the opinion that the publication did not come within the statute. This holding was made in a brief *per curiam* opinion and was based on the following reasoning: "It is clear from the manner in which the legislature has used the word 'indecent' that it relates to obscene prints or publications. It is not an attempt to regulate manners, but it is a declaration of the penalties to be imposed upon the various phases of the crime of obscenity. The word 'indecent' is used in a limited sense in this connection and falls within the maxim of *noscitur a sociis.*"

In addition to the opinion of the court, there was a concurring opinion by Cullen, C. J., and a dissenting opinion by O'Brien, J., in the latter of which Haight, J., concurred. An examination of these opinions seems to disclose that the decision of the case not only involved a difference of opinion, but also aroused a little momentary feeling between some of the judges. That this is so is not surprising, as there are some questions of religion, patriotism, and politics about which men may differ honestly, but which the most enlightened and dispassionate men find it difficult to discuss calmly, as it is almost impossible for them to rid themselves of inborn and hereditary prejudices which insensibly influence their opinions.

It is not inconceivable that one of the opinions in this case was written by a zealous Protestant, and the other by an equally zealous Catholic, each of whom had the most implicit faith in the other's intellectual integrity and sense of justice, without being able to appreciate or understand his point of view. The passages upon which we base our surmise are as follows: "That the article is a scurrilous and vile attack on a large and respected body of Christian clergymen is unquestionable. That it is 'indecent' from every consideration of propriety is entirely clear, but that is not the indecency condemned by this section of the Code. . . . From the context of the statute it is apparent that it is directed against lewd, lascivious, and salacious or obscene publications, the tendency of which is to excite lustful and lecherous desire. That such is not the effect of the publication is clear from the fact that my brother who writes the dissenting opinion publishes it in full, and I am entirely certain that, did he believe the tendency of the article was lecherous and salacious, he would find no justification for its publication in the fact that the majority of the court, from whose decision he feels constrained to dissent, entertain a contrary view. . . . I regreat that the publication should appear in the reports of this court, not because I deem it lewd, but because I feel that the reports of this court should not be made the means of perpetuating a scurrilous and wanton slander on any class of the community." (Opinion of Cullen, C. J.)

"It would be difficult to compose any writing more indecent and more immoral. It is so indecent that, in my opinion, it is unfit to appear upon the records of this court, and it would not appear as a part of this opinion except for the contention at the bar and in the court itself that it is not indecent. Of course, if it is not, then I must be in error in supposing that it is unfit to appear in the records of this court. . . . It is true that my brethren have considered it necessary to denounce the publication in question upon almost every conceivable ground of impropriety, except the ground which presents the only question before the court, that it is an indecent publication within the statute. . . . Having arrived at the conclusion that it is not an indecent publication, it is of very little consequence what else it may be." (Opinion of O'Brien, J.) (In this connection it should be explained that the publication is set out only in the dissenting opinion.)

But, getting away from the side issue which we have just been discussing, is the publication violative of the New York statute? With all due respect to the majority of the court, it seems to us that the rule *noscitur a sociis* has been invoked to give the statute a meaning not intended by the legislature. To us it seems that the legislature intended to prohibit not only obscene, but also other indecent publications, and that this intention is disclosed by the clause forbidding "indecent or disgusting" publications. The word "obscene" has a perfectly well understood meaning, and if the legislature intended merely to prevent obscene publications, it would not have been necessary for it to have added the characterizing words "indecent" and "disgusting" in order to make its meaning clear. It is well settled that in construing a statute every word should be given effect if possible. Furthermore, if the rule *noscitur a sociis* is operative to refer the word "indecent" to the word "obscene" it is equally operative to refer it to the word "disgusting;" and it is of course true that while an obscene publication is necessarily disgusting, a disgusting publication is not necessarily obscene. As said before, the statute seems to us to prohibit not only obscene publications, but also indecent and disgusting ones. That this publication is highly indecent and disgusting is unquestionable.

But even conceding that the majority of the court construed the statute properly, we have with some hesitation reached the conclusion that the publication was obscene, and therefore within the statute. It imputes to confessors, in the plainest sort of words, the practice of asking women licentious questions for the purpose of debauching them if possible, and does all but put those questions in the words of the questioners. It leaves about as little to the imagination as does a Venus draped with a filmy scarf; and it is generally conceded that an imperfectly draped figure, or one with disarranged drapery, may be and frequently is more suggestive, and therefore more obscene, than a perfectly nude one. Besides, in all deference to

Judge Cullen, it seems to us that he takes an extreme view in holding that an obscene publication is necessarily one tending "to excite lustful and lecherous desire." Theoretically this is no doubt true. Practically, however, it seems to us clear that a statute directed against obscenity may be violated by a publication which has no tendency to excite any emotion other than anger or disgust — except in the mind of a peculiarly abnormal person. Thus the use of foul and scurrilous epithets may constitute obscenity. Of course, it is impossible for us to illustrate our meaning, but we feel that it is obvious without illustration.

There are at least two other cases (both English) involving the precise question involved in the case we have been discussing. In Reg. v. Hicklin, L. R. 3 Q. B. 360, it was held that a pamphlet entitled "The Confessional Unmasked" was an obscene publication within the meaning of 20 & 21 Vict., c. 83, and that it was immaterial that the defendant sold the pamphlet in good faith for the honest purpose of exposing what he conceived to be a corrupt practice indulged in by the professors of the Catholic faith. In that case opinions were delivered by Cockburn, C. J., and Blackburn, Mellor, and Lusk, JJ., all being positive but Mellor, J., who concurred with some hesitation.

In the subsequent case of Steele v. Brannon, L. R. 7 C. P. 261, what seems to be a somewhat expurgated edition of the same pamphlet was held to violate the statute. In the reports of those cases neither the pamphlet nor any extract therefrom is set out. It is only fair to say, however, that the publication was probably of a somewhat viler nature, so far as mere words go, than the publication involved in the New York case, as it apparently purported to set out some of the questions which it was alleged were asked of females by priests in the confessional.

If the decision of the majority of the court in the New York case is correct, the New York statute should be so amended as to broaden its scope, in order that indecent as distinguished from obscene publications may be made punishable. Cullen, C. J., suggests in his opinion that while the author of the publication could not be held liable in an action for libel, a prosecution for criminal libel could be maintained against him. The remedy suggested is, however, clearly inadequate. If it is impossible to maintain a civil action for a libel against a class, it is difficult to obtain a conviction in a criminal prosecution for such a libel.

J. C. M.

SOUND AND HEARING.

THAT a wagon was almost new (Lang v. Missouri Pac. R. Co., 115 Mo. App. 489, 91 N. W. Rep. 1012) and that a wagon moving slowly over ground soft from recent rain (Esler v. Wabash R. Co., 109 Mo. App. 580, 83 N. W. Rep. 73, and other cases) would make little noise, have been judicially noticed as possible facts. So a court declined to infer that the noise from a light express wagon drawn by a gentle and walking horse prevented the driver from effectually listening for a train upon approaching a railroad crossing. Sherwin v. Rutland R. Co., 74 Vt. 1, 51 Atl. Rep. 1089. But if the highway near a crossing had been recently graveled "a wagon in motion over it would make considerable noise." Schremms v. Pere Marquette R. Co., 145 Mich. 190, 108 N. W. Rep. 698, *per* Moore, J. In a multitude of other cases of collisions at crossings courts have had occasion to decide whether a vehicle probably did or did not make much noise, and in so doing have called attention to such facts as the speed of the horses, that the horses were not shod, that the ground was or was not frozen, that bottles, or barrels, or washboilers, rattled in the body of the wagon, etc.

The importance of such seemingly puerile cases becomes evident when we reflect that according to the rule laid down in hundreds of cases an appellate court will affirm a verdict, as far as the weight of evidence is concerned, if it can perceive that reasonable men would either concur or *differ* on the question of fact — or will reverse if a verdict was directed contrary to the appellate court's views in that behalf. Where the jury find, for instance, that a plaintiff's vehicle made so much noise that he could not well have heard a train which approached without signals, and was therefore guiltless of contributory negligence, that verdict will stand on appeal if the court will concede that the point was reasonably *arguable*.

In a very great number of cases, only a few of which can be cited in this article, the fate of a verdict — involving perhaps the issue of life or death — depended not upon a question of law, but upon the question whether the court would conclude that certain phenomena of sound or hearing raised a fairly debatable question.

A lawyer preparing a case for trial on behalf of a client who was run over at a railroad crossing will of course inform himself of the rulings of the local and other courts on the questions of law involved. But we conceive that it might not be an unimportant piece of information for him, especially if he is an Indiana lawyer, that the Indiana Supreme Court said in a late case: "A large number of telephone and telegraph wires stretched along both the highway and the railroad at the crossing made a loud roaring sound resembling the rumbling of an approaching train." Greenawalt v. Lake Shore, etc., R. Co., 165 Ind. 219, 73 N. E. Rep. 910. The amount of noise made by trains, detached cars, engines, or hand cars, running on a level track, up grade, down grade, on bridges, on frozen ground, on rails covered with snow; of noise made by electric cars under divers conditions; the sound of locomotive signals; sound of the wind, and a great variety of noises which may deaden the noise of approaching trains or cars and the sound of signals — all those matters and numberless others in the same line have been discussed and pronounced upon by the highest courts.

Was there snow on the track? We will brief that point for our readers this instant, although it consumes space we had intended for other matters:

Fresh snow on the tracks would muffle, to some extent, the noise made by a train (see Fisher v. Monongahela, etc., R. Co., 131 Pa. St. 292, 18 Atl. Rep. 1016) or a backing engine (Camp v. Chicago, etc., R. Co., 124 Iowa 238, 99 N. W. Rep. 735). There was "snow on the track, which deadened the usual rumbling sound of a moving train," said Sharswood, J., in Pennsylvania R. Co. v. Ackerman, 74 Pa. St. 265. "There were three inches of snow on the ground, which we may suppose would prevent a part of the noise usually made by the running of the train," said Downey, J., in St. Louis, etc., R. Co. v. Mathias, 50 Ind. 65, 81. The point has not been alluded to in any other reported case.

"It is quite conceivable" that the exhaust steam of a locomotive, making considerable noise, would prevent one standing near it from hearing an approaching train. Parsons v. New York, etc., R. Co., 113 N. Y. 355, 364, 21 N. E. Rep. 145. Many other courts have said the same. But along comes the Ohio Supreme Court with the admonition that the train would make a noise of a different character from that of the escaping steam, and if the volume of the latter is left shadowy by the testimony failure to hear the train can hardly be attributed to it. Baltimore, etc., R. Co. *v.* McClellan, 69 Ohio St. 142, 68 N. E. Rep. 816.

The Ohio court's comparison of the quality or pitch of sounds in determining whether one would probably suppress the other is based on every-day experience, which instructs us that concurring sounds entirely unlike are readily distinguishable by the ear. In the inquiry of the Senate Committee on Military Affairs into the Brownsville raid, a negro soldier said he heard gun reports and the sound of horses' hoofs. On cross-examination Senator Warner was inclined to cavil at this testimony.

"Jes' yo' wait right there one minute, Senator," said the darky; "let me ask yo' a question, will yo'?"

"Well, go ahead then, I'll submit," said the Senator, good naturedly.

"Now, jes' yo' s'posin' a case," the witness went on, "s'posin' youse hear a man choppin' wood 'bout three or fo' blocks from yo', and right ober here like youse hears a dawg a-barkin', don't yo' s'pose yo' can tell de difference 'tween de man a-choppin' wood an' dat dawg a-barkin'?"

In battle "it is almost impossible to hear the voice of command in the rattle of rifle fire, the explosion of projectiles, and the thunder of artillery. . . . A whistle, repeated by all the noncommissioned officers of the company, is heard best of all." Captain L. Z. Soloviev, of the Thirty-fourth East Siberian Rifle Regiment, in "Battle Action of the Infantry; Impressions of a Company Commander," July, 1906, translated for the United States Army War College.

It is universally agreed that a railroad train or the signal of a locomotive or a vessel may not be heard soon enough to avert collision, where a considerable wind is blowing from the listener toward the source of the sound. Among thirty or forty cases here are three: Malott *v.* Hawkins, 159 Ind. 127, 63 N. E. Rep. 308; Crane *v.* Michigan Cent. R. Co., 107 Mich. 511, 65 N. W. Rep. 527; The Bristol, 10 Blatchf. (U. S.) 537. Conversely, if the wind was favorable the trier of facts may feel safer in his conclusion that a reasonably attentive person should have heard the train. Schmidt *v.* Great Northern R. Co., 83 Minn. 105, 85 N. W. Rep. 935.

Portia.—I heard a bustling rumour, like a fray,
And the wind brings it from the Capitol.
Julius Cæsar, Act II., sc. 4.

The cardinal condition of accuracy of observation of sounds or of anything else made known through the senses is, Attention. On almost everything relating to that point some experienced judges are competent to instruct any professor of mental science that ever lived. The sage discussions and wealth of illustrations in the law reports cannot be matched elsewhere. Whatever diverts, divides, or distracts attention diminishes the probability of correct observation. In many collision cases between vessels where witnesses on one vessel have testified that they heard no signals from the other, the courts have been satisfied that such signals were given but not heard because, as the evidence showed, the witnesses were preoccupied with other duties (The Buffalo, 50 Fed. Rep. 630, 631; Dougherty *v.* The Steamer Franconia, 3 Fed. Rep. 397, 402, and other cases), had their attention strained in another direction (The City of Dundee, (C. C. A.) 108 Fed. Rep. 679, 683), were excited by finding the other vessel almost upon them (The Steamship Westphalia, 4 Ben. (U. S.) 404), or that the lookout was distracted by the noise of animals on deck beneath him (The Vedamore, 131 Fed. Rep. 154, 156), etc.

"It is a matter of common experience that persons do not always hear customary sounds when they are paying no attention." *Per* Grant, J., in Sanborn *v.* Detroit, etc., R. Co., 99 Mich. 1, 57 N. W. Rep. 1047. The same point is noticed in many other cases, and in James, Principles of Psychology, *in loco*. In such a case, says Locke, "a sufficient impulse there may be on the organ, but it not reaching the observation of the mind, there follows no perception; and though the motion that uses to produce the idea of sound be made in the ear, yet no sound is heard." (Essay Concerning the Human Understanding, Book II., c. ix.) For this reason the testimony of persons who live near a railroad and hear locomotive signals very frequently all day, that on a particular occasion a signal was not given, is little regarded by *judges* unless the witness had some pretty definite motive for special attention at the time. But where the court allows the negative testimony even barely to squeeze in, *juries* rarely fail to give it full face value if necessary to help out a plaintiff against the corporation, thereby sometimes eliciting expressions of impotent disgust from an appellate court. There is an old Roman maxim on evidence which says, *Unus testis affirmans plus valet quam mille negantes.* Quoted and applied in Greene *v.* Windsor Hotel Co., 26 Quebec Super. Ct. 97. And a poet tells us:

One single positive weighs more,
You know, than negatives a score.
M. Prior, Epistle to Fleetwood Shepherd.

The writer recollects cases where vessels' officers have testified that they do not ordinarily hear the signals given by the pilot when they are frequent and not alarming, and cases where locomotive firemen declared that they were unable to say whether a signal was or was not given by the engineer only a minute before their attention was first called to the matter.

"A faint sound or light is rendered louder or brighter as we attend to it," says the writer of the article "Attention," in the New International Encyclopædia. Dr. Tuke, treating of the influence of the mind upon the sense of hearing, says "that the thought uppermost in the mind, the predominant idea or expectation, makes a real sensation from without assume a different character." (Influence of the Mind on the Body, p. 47.) So when it was sought to enjoin an alleged nuisance consisting of noises produced by machinery in a factory, and some of the plaintiff's witnesses expressed the opinion that the noises which were once concededly lawful and harmless had become excessive and noxious, although defendant testified that there had been no change in the operation of the factory, Lord Chancellor Selborne, in dismissing the bill, said every one knows that "a nervous, or anxious, or prepossessed listener hears sounds which would otherwise have passed unnoticed, and magnifies and exaggerates into some new significance, originating within himself, sounds which at other times would have been passively heard and not regarded." Gaunt *v.* Fynney, L. R. 8. Ch. App. 8.

Feeble health is generally unfavorable to fixedness of attention. Still, the senses of some ill persons become preternaturally acute so that they are tortured by sounds which bring pleasing reminiscences to others. Thus the ringing and chiming of church bells was enjoined in Harrison *v.* St. Mark's Church, 12 Phila. (Pa.) 259, the court being convinced that the sounds caused real and substantial suffering to the sick and those who, though not invalids, had somewhat declined from the fortunate condition of robust health. On the other hand, when Christiana and her companions were weary and betook themselves to rest in the land of Beulah "the bells did so ring and the trumpets sounded so melodiously that they could not sleep, and yet they received as much refreshing as if they had slept their sleep ever so soundly." (Bunyan's Pilgrim's Progress, Part II.)

There seems to be some probative weight in testimony of a person in a house that he recognized the peculiar step of a man going out. See People *v.* Ciardi, (N. Y. Ct. App., 1907) 80 N. E. Rep. 925. But surely such testimony must be taken with extreme caution, for the witness will unavoidably be prepossessed by the surrounding probabilities. He would recognize the face of a familiar acquaintance if he met him in China, but we cannot believe he would confidently identify the footfall if he had every other reason to think his acquaintance was thousands of miles distant.

A witness "might easily be mistaken," said the court, in his inference that footsteps which he heard going upstairs and in a bedroom overhead were the steps of more than one person. Chancellor Zabriskie refused to grant a divorce on that testimony alone. Reid *v.* Reid, 21 N. J. Eq. 331.

The well-known aberration of sounds in fog has been the subject of much discussion in collision cases in admiralty courts, and has had influence in settling rules of navigation. The leading American case is The Lepanto, 21 Fed. Rep. 656. Occasional and unaccountable deflections of sound in clear weather, as well as "areas of silence," are phenomena known to scientists and have been judicially recognized. The Koning Willem I., [1903] P. 114, 121.

We are not aware of any authority for the statement of a certain law writer that "the air of night is more favorable than that of the day for the transmission of sound." Describing a visit to Keswick, the poet Gray says in his journal: "In the evening I walked down to the lake by the side of Cro-park, after sunset. . . . At a distance were heard the murmurs of many waterfalls, not audible in the daytime." But it is the silence of night, when beasts and birds as well as men are mostly at rest, that makes the sounds more noticeable.

The moon among the clouds rode high
And all the city hum was by.
Upon the street, where late before
Did din of war and warriors roar,
You might have heard a pebble fall,
A beetle hum, a cricket sing,
An owlet flap his boding wing
On Giles's steeple tall.
Marmion, Canto Fifth, XX.

In Wall street, New York city, on Sunday, except for the noise of Broadway or elevated cars, all sounds are heard about as distinctly as in any Northport street at night. Then, again, it is familiar knowledge that if a person is deprived of the use of one sense, the others acquire greater strength, or at least are more closely attended to.

Hermia. — Dark night, that from the eye his function takes,
The ear more quick of apprehension makes;
Wherein it doth impair the seeing sense,
It pays the hearing double recompense.
Midsummer Night's Dream, Act III., sc. 2.

Stillness of night is always a material circumstance in estimating the audibility of sounds. In State *v.* Shinborne, 46 N. H. 497, a woman's testimony that in the middle of the night she heard a carriage driven from the square near her house and that she should say *it started from somewhere near the square* was held to be admissible, against objection directed to the statement we have italicized. Judge Bellows simply said that its weight would depend upon circumstances — it might be much, or it might be little. It was observed in Buckmaster *v.* Chicago, etc., R. Co., 108 Wis. 353, 84 N. W. Rep. 845, that the noise of "a freight train in the country at midnight" cannot be unnoticed by any one on the track and possessing the sense of hearing, and would be especially significant to him if he were a railroad man. In Belford *v.* Brooklyn Heights R. Co., 86 N. Y. App. Div. 388, 83 N. Y. Supp. 836, Justice Hirschberg said that "in view of the well-known fact that trolley cars cannot be run at a high rate of speed in the silence of the night without making some noise," the probable reason why the plaintiff did not hear a car was because he was not listening.

Charles C. Moore.

THE DEVELOPMENT OF THE FEDERAL POWER TO REGULATE COMMERCE.*

There are no questions before the American people to-day of greater importance than those relating to the federal control over commerce.

That power was granted chiefly as a safeguard against commercial hostilities and reprisals between the States. It remained practically unused until comparatively recent years. It is now clearly recognized as a great affirmative and constructive power, not limited to composing differences between State laws and systems, but constitutionally capable of effective and fruitful development in a region all its own. In some respects it may be said to be the greatest power lodged in the general government, and the possibilities of its application are co-extensive with the possibilities of the expansion of the vast subject to which it applies.

Nothing, therefore, is of more consequence in our governmental affairs than an accurate understanding of the scope of the National and State powers in respect to commerce and the activities related to commerce, for no effective regulation is possible in either sovereignty if the power of the one be usurped or obstructed by the other. This will be understood and conceded, except by those who appear to think the federal government can constitutionally accomplish everything that seems good for the people and are constantly raising expectations in that direction which cannot possibly be fulfilled.

Notwithstanding the complex system of polity which prevails in this country, the American people have a complete and entire system of government with all the powers necessary to deal with every subject and situation. All governmental authority is included in one or the other, or in both, of the two sovereignties which constitute the American system.

The fact that the State governments are supreme in State affairs, and the national government supreme in national affairs does not result in the deduction that there are any affairs which may escape governmental control.

While the constitutional powers of the nation and the reserved powers of the States remain ever the same, the question as to when an act or transaction is exclusively a State affair, subject to State control, or a national matter subject to national control, is one of fact as well as law, and it can be readily understood that the facts differ at different periods of our development and under different circumstances relating to the subject.

That which in the earlier period of our history was a matter of State concern may become one of national concern by the establishment of commercial intercourse in respect to it with other States and foreign nations, or become a national concern because of conditions affecting the subject which call for the exercise of national power theretofore dormant. The power to regulate this intercourse or commerce between the States, the right to engage in which the Constitution did not create, but which existed at the time of its adoption, was given to the federal government by the Constitution.

The constitutional power of regulation having been granted to the federal government in respect of a subject naturally liable to development and change, it can be said its authors contemplated a corresponding enlargement; not, be it observed, in the power, but in its application to the expanding subject. When congressional powers are applied to new conditions it is not, as it sometimes seems to be, an extension or expansion of the power, but an indication of a change in or extension or expansion of the subject upon which the power operates. Neither

* Address of Senator Philander C. Knox to the graduating class of the Yale Law School.

the power to regulate commerce nor the conception of its scope has expanded beyond its definition by the Supreme Court when first considered, nearly one hundred years ago. It was then pronounced "complete in itself, that it may be exercised to its utmost extent and acknowledges no limitations other than are prescribed by the Constitution."

"The design and object of that power (the commercial power), as evinced in the history of the Constitution, was to establish a perfect equality amongst the several States as to commercial rights and to prevent unjust and invidious distinctions which local jealousies or local and partial interests might be disposed to introduce and maintain."

The necessity to exercise the national power over commerce arises largely out of the failure of the States to regulate wisely great corporations created by and under the dominion of the States and engaged in interstate commerce. That failure has led to well-known abuses which affect interstate commerce, and thereby created the necessity for the exercise of federal regulation to prevent the abuse.

The necessity for the exercise of federal regulation almost always springs from causes which the States could have prevented.

The national power of regulation should ordinarily be invoked only when necessity for regulation exists. Normally and honestly conducted commerce requires but little if any governmental regulation, and the failure by Congress to regulate interstate commerce is equivalent to a legislative declaration that it shall be free. Abnormal conditions in commercial intercourse caused by monopolies, preferential service, rebates, and the like, destroy the normal operations of commerce and create the demand for federal regulation to restore the rule of freedom and equality.

The pressure of the accumulated evils and abuses of many years of inadequately regulated commerce in this country culminated some few years ago in an imperative necessity for action to test the adequacy of existing laws to meet the situation, and the enactment of such additional ones as should prove to be necessary to restore and preserve freedom and equality in interstate and foreign commerce.

The combinations to control the production, distribution, and sale of commodities which were to be subjects of interstate commerce; the combinations between and the mergers of interstate railroads, designed to bring under one control the transportation business of large areas of the country; the unjust discriminations for the benefit of favored shippers and localities, both in the carrying service and the rates charged therefor; the secrecy sometimes surrounding the operations of corporations rendering service to the public, had utterly destroyed in many localities the ability of other persons and concerns to engage in commercial competition with the favored ones who enjoyed such unfair and illegal advantages.

A brief statement of how this situation was dealt with by the national government, the theory upon which the government proceeded, and some observations upon certain dangerous misconceptions as to the scope of the powers that have been successfully invoked to correct the evils I have named, will not, I hope, be uninteresting nor uninstructive.

The scope of existing laws was tested through a series of suits. These suits had for their main purpose to determine the effectiveness of existing statutes to reach new types of combination which had for their object to restrain the free play of the law of competition, and new and subtle discriminatory devices which had sprung from fertile and experienced minds instructed in the interpretations the courts had put upon the existing laws.

The purposes for which this litigation was undertaken were all accomplished. The completeness of the federal power over commerce was reaffirmed and declared to extend among other things to the holding company.

This device which had been successfully employed to establish under one control the leading productive industries of the country was declared illegal when utilized to absorb competing systems of interstate railroads, and thereby we escaped a danger to our commerce, our government, and our very liberties, the magnitude of which can scarcely be grasped.

It was likewise judicially determined, that a combination between a railroad company and a shipper, to grant the latter an unlawful rebate which results in the establishing of a monopoly, is a violation of the Sherman Act, and that a court of equity might restrain the guilty parties at the suit of the attorney-general of the United States, as well under that act as under the general jurisdiction in equity. Of almost equal importance was the decision that the operations of a monopolistic combination within a State may be so connected with those between the States as to bring the whole under the regulative power of Congress.

Notwithstanding the success which attended these suits, there was developed a number of serious defects and omissions in national legislation necessary to be remedied, if the avenues of commerce were to be kept open to all upon the same terms, and if a speedy and workable remedy for violations of the law was to be placed in the hands of the government itself to restore the rule of freedom and equality in interstate and foreign commerce.

The legislation proposed to the Fifty-seventh Congress as necessary to accomplish the restoration of the normal commercial rule, all of which was promptly enacted, was:

1st. That in respect of railroad rebates, the omission in the act to regulate commerce to punish the beneficiary should be supplied by imposing a penalty, not only upon the carrier who gave, but upon the shipper who received, such rebates, and that the power of the equity courts to restrain such practices at the suit of the United States should be made certain by statute.

2d. That it should be made unlawful to transport traffic by carriers subject to the act to regulate commerce at any rate less than such carriers' published rate, and that all who participated in the violation of such law should be punished.

3d. That a comprehensive plan should be framed to enable the government to get at all the facts bearing upon the organization and practices of concerns engaged in interstate and foreign commerce essential to a full understanding thereof.

4th. Another step in legislation which was earnestly recommended was an act to speed the final decision of cases under the interstate commerce and anti-trust law.

These laws, enacted during the short session of the Fifty-seventh Congress, were followed by the railroad rate law of the Fifty-ninth Congress, the principal feature of which is the grant of power to the Interstate Commerce Commission to fix a reasonable rate for the carriage of goods and persons.

These laws were designed to secure equality in transportation service and equality, stability, and reasonableness in transportation charges. They provide a swift remedy at the suit of the government in its own courts of equity, thereby relieving the individual sufferer from the expense and delay incident to a private suit.

All these laws have been declared constitutional except the Railroad Rate Act, and as to that act, not yet passed upon by the courts, it is believed by the great weight of legal opinion to be constitutional in respect to the power to fix reasonable rates and practices.

The public satisfaction resulting from the enactment and the enforcement of these statutes regulating commerce has induced some persons to contend that the congressional power to regulate commerce is a panacea for many other public evils, and it is proposed to utilize that power to accomplish ends not within the national jurisdiction, and having no relation to the subject of the power.

"The power to regulate is the power to prescribe the rule by which commerce is to be governed." These are the words of Chief Justice Marshall, in Gibbons v. Ogden.

This power of prescribing the rule by which commerce is to be conducted extends to commerce itself and to the instrumentalities of commerce.

By commerce itself I mean the activities and intercourse which constitute the commercial relation. By the instrumentalities of commerce I mean the animate and inanimate means used to maintain and carry on commercial intercourse.

As to these activities and intercourse which constitute commerce, Congress has from time to time prescribed certain rules; such, for instance, as the rule that commerce shall be free from monopoly and restraint effected by combinations, and that the general rule of competition shall have free play.

As to the animate and inanimate means or instrumentalities by which commerce is conducted, Congress has likewise prescribed various rules; such as contained in the Railroad Safety Appliance Act, and the act prescribing the hours of labor of employees upon railroads engaged in interstate commerce.

Over this subject of commerce among the States and with foreign nations and its instrumentalities the power of Congress is plenary. It may be exercised in the most general or minute way. For this purpose Congress possesses all powers which existed in the States before the adoption of the National Constitution, and its power when the subject is national is or may be made exclusive. The constitutions, laws, corporations, and citizens of the States are subject to this paramount authority. Congress can regulate anything, everything, any and every person, natural or artificial, in the sense that it can prohibit or prevent any use or act that will interfere with congressional control over interstate commerce, or that will injuriously affect such commerce. Congress may likewise prevent the arteries of interstate commerce from being employed as conduits for articles hurtful to the public health, safety, or morals, and may remove obstructions from the highways of commerce whether they be physical or economic, whether they may be sand bars, mobs, or monopolies.

The power of Congress may be exercised by prohibition and by prescription.

Congress has prohibited combinations in restraint of interstate and foreign trade, and has prohibited the carriage of diseased cattle, explosives, and lottery tickets, and Congress has prescribed that certain safety appliances shall be used upon railroads doing an interstate business. The one class of laws is designed to keep the channels of commerce free and unpolluted; the other is designed to secure the safety of the employees and patrons of the carriers.

I cite these acts because their constitutionality has been sustained, because they obviously bear directly upon commerce and for that reason will serve to make clear the distinction between the well-established rule to be deduced from the decided cases and the extension of the rule involved in certain pending legislative propositions of federal control, to which I shall now direct your attention.

The existing rule, as it has been judicially determined, may be restated in these words: Congress has the power to regulate interstate commerce, which includes the power to regulate the means or instrumentalities by which commerce is conducted.

The new proposition is this: Congress has the power to regulate commerce including its instrumentalities, *and likewise power* to regulate the persons by whom articles of commerce are produced in respect to matters not connected with commerce.

This addition to the rule finds expression in the suggestion to prohibit the interstate transportation of articles of value which are in themselves innocuous and which are lawfully made or produced in a State, for reasons not affecting interstate commerce.

Let us now consider whether the regulation of the business of producing articles which may in whole or in part go into interstate commerce, by denying to the owner the privileges of interstate commerce for reasons not affecting such commerce, is a legitimate regulation of commerce. In other words, is the mere production of goods commerce? If it is not, then can Congress regulate such production within a State under the constitutional power to regulate interstate commerce?

It would be difficult to overstate the importance and seriousness of the question thus presented, as upon its ultimate authoritative determination depends, it may be, the autonomy of the States in substantially all matters of internal police.

It is scarcely worth while to discuss the proposition that production is not commerce.

Mr. Justice Lamar remarked in Kidd v. Pearson, 128 U. S.:

"No distinction is more popular to the common mind, or more clearly expressed in economic and political literature, than that between manufacture and commerce. Manufacture is transformation — the fashioning of raw materials into a change of form for use. The functions of commerce are different. The buying and selling and the transportation incidental thereto constitute commerce; and the regulation of commerce in the constitutional sense embraces the regulation at least of such transportation. If it be held that the term includes the regulation of all such manufactures as are intended to be the subject of commercial transaction in the future, it is impossible to deny that it would also include all productive industries that contemplate the same thing. The result would be that Congress would be invested, to the exclusion of the States, with the power to regulate not only manufacturers, but also agriculture, horticulture, stock raising, domestic fisheries, mining — in short, every branch of human industry. For is there one of them that does not contemplate, more or less clearly, an interstate or foreign market? Does not the wheat grower of the Northwest or the cotton planter of the South plant, cultivate, and harvest his crop with an eye on the prices at Liverpool, New York, and Chicago? The power being vested in Congress and denied to the States, it would follow as an inevitable result that the duty would devolve on Congress to regulate all of these delicate, multiform, and vital interests — interests which in their nature are and must be local in all the details of their successful management."

In Veazie v. Moore, 14 How. 574, the court said:

"The phrase 'to regulate commerce' can never be applied to transactions wholly internal, between citizens of the same community, or to a polity and laws whose ends and purposes and operations are restricted to the territory and soil and jurisdiction of such community. Nor can it be properly concluded, that because the products of domestic enterprise in agriculture or manufactures, or in the arts, may ultimately become the subjects of foreign commerce, that the control of the means or the encouragements by which enterprise is fostered and protected is legitimately within the import of the phrase *foreign commerce,* or fairly implied in any investiture of the power to regulate such commerce. A pretension as far reaching as this would extend to contracts between citizen and citizen of the same State, would control the pursuits of the planter, the grazier, the manufacturer, the mechanic, the immense operations of the colliers and mines and furnaces of the country; for there is not one of these avocations, the results of which may not become the subjects of foreign commerce, and be borne either by turnpikes, canals, or railroads, from point to point within the several States, towards an ultimate destination, like the one above mentioned."

But it is claimed that as the power to regulate commerce is absolute, complete, and mainly exclusive in Congress, the right to forbid the shipment in interstate trade of any kind of goods, for any reason, comes within that power. That is to say, under the guise of a commercial regulation, not necessary for the promotion or protection of commerce, a producing regulation, which Congress could not have enacted, may be enforced; or, in other words, Congress can deny a person the right to engage in interstate commerce for doing that which Congress cannot prohibit him from doing. But, as we have seen, Congress cannot regulate production, and Chief Justice Marshall said in McCulloch *v.* Maryland:

"Should Congress, under the pretext of executing its powers, pass laws for the accomplishment of objects not intrusted to the government, it would become the painful duty of this tribunal, should a case requiring such a decision come before it, to say that such an act was not the law of the land."

In my judgment, the power to regulate commerce between the States does not carry with it the power to prohibit commerce, unless the prohibition has for its purpose the facilitation, safety, or protection of commercial intercourse, or the accomplishment of some other national purpose.

The power to regulate interstate commerce does not extend to the laying of an arbitrary embargo upon the lawfully produced, harmless products of a State, nor to the right to defeat the policy of a State as to its own internal affairs.

I concede that the national power to regulate interstate commerce carries with it the right to prohibit commerce in order to secure equality of commercial right, or to prevent restraint of or interference with commerce, but not to prohibit the shipment from the State of the innocuous products of producers who are pursuing a course sanctioned by the laws of the State and in no wise in itself interfering with interstate commerce. If prohibition of interstate trade is within the arbitrary power of Congress, it might be exercised so as to exclude the products of particular States or sections of the country. Congress then might prohibit the shipment of cotton or wheat to promote the interests of wool or corn.

There is no authority for any such proposition. The power of prohibition has never been sustained except as against articles noxious or dangerous in themselves. It is not possible to find even a suggestion that in respect to natural products which are prime necessities, Congress can prohibit commerce in them between the States in order to enforce its conception of what would be a wise police regulation of a State.

In the case of Champion *v.* Ames, 188 U. S. 321, it was held that lottery tickets are subjects of traffic, and their carriage by independent carriers from one State to another is interstate commerce, which Congress may prohibit under its power to regulate commerce among the several States, but this was specifically placed upon the character of the business. The court said, through Mr. Justice Harlan: "It is a kind of traffic which no one can be entitled to pursue as of right."

The court also said:

". . . The power of Congress to regulate commerce among the States, although plenary, cannot be deemed arbitrary, since it is subject to such limitations or restrictions as are prescribed by the Constitution. This power, therefore, may not be exercised so as to infringe rights secured or protected by that instrument."

The right of each State to regulate its domestic affairs is "secured and protected" by the Tenth Amendment reserving to the States respectively, or to the people, the powers not delegated to the United States.

In Gibbons *v.* Ogden, 9 Wheat. 111, the court said with regard to the right of intercourse between State and State, that that right was derived not from the Constitution, but from "those laws whose authority is acknowledged by civilized man throughout the world." Under the Articles of Confederation the States might have interdicted interstate trade, yet when they surrendered the power to deal with commerce as between themselves to the general government it was undoubtedly in order to form a more perfect union by freeing such commerce from State discrimination, and not to transfer the power of restriction.

In Dooly *v.* United States, 183 U. S. 171, the four dissenting justices correctly said:

"But if that power of regulation is absolutely unrestricted as respects interstate commerce, then the very unity the Constitution was framed to secure can be set at naught by a legislative body created by that instrument."

The sum of the matter then is this: For the purpose of promoting and protecting commerce, Congress may close its channels to those who are injuriously affecting it, but for the purpose of enforcing its views of public policy in respect to matters not within the jurisdiction of Congress, it has no such power.

Congress may employ such means as it chooses to accomplish that which is within its power. But the end to be accomplished must be within the scope of its constitutional powers. The legislative discretion extends to the means and not to the ends to be accomplished by use of the means.

In a word, I do not take issue with the general proposition that Congress may prohibit transportation, but I say the prohibition must have for its real object the regulation of interstate commerce and not something *dehors* the federal power.

In a recent case the Supreme Court of the United States, through the chief justice, speaking of the power and sovereignty of a State, uses this language:

"It cannot be denied that the power of a State to protect the lives, health, and property of its citizens, and to preserve good order and the public morals, 'the power to govern men and things within the limits of its domain,' is a power originally and always belonging to the States, not surrendered by them to the general government, nor directly restrained by the Constitution of the United States, and essentially exclusive."

That the Congress of the United States has no general legislative powers but only such as are granted to it by the Constitution is not an old-fashioned and exploded notion.

It has been reaffirmed with emphasis by the Supreme Court within the last sixty days in a great opinion by Mr. Justice Brewer in the case of Colorado *v.* Kansas.

The learned justice said: "That this is such a government" (one of delegated powers) "clearly appears from the Constitution, independently of the amendments, for otherwise there would be an instrument granting certain specified things made operative to grant other and distinct things. This natural construction of the original body of the Constitution is made absolutely certain by the Tenth Amendment. This amendment, which was seemingly adopted with prescience of just such contention as the present, disclosed the widespread fear that the national government might, under the pressure of a supposed general welfare, attempt to exercise powers which had not been granted. With equal determination the framers intended that no such assumption should ever find justification in the organic act, and that if in the future further powers seemed necessary they should be granted by the people in the manner they had provided for amending that act."

We cannot make progress in developing a body of substantive remedial law without an accurate appreciation of the restrictions upon both the State and Federal powers.

Like the Girondists in the French Revolution, American lawyers must submit to be condemned by the Bourbons as radicals if they stand for rational and constitutional legislation to meet new conditions and to correct the evils in the old conditions, and to be guillotined by the Reds as obstructionists if they fail to indorse the popular vagaries of the political ephemera who swarm about every great movement of reform, unappreciative of its origin, its tendency, and its purpose. Such is the fate of the profession that studies, loves, and defends the institutions of civilized government and has ever been their most powerful constructive and conserving force.

The preservation of our Constitution is not committed to the federal judiciary alone. It is the oath-bound obligation of every legislative, judicial, and executive officer both of the States and Nation, and is the highest duty of private citizenship. The Constitution is not to perish at the hands of the impassioned phrase-maker, and its defenders should not be deterred by mistaken or prejudiced clamor from performing their obligation to preserve and defend it.

The Constitution was founded upon the sacrifice of the lives and fortunes of our ancestors; it is the solemnly expressed will of the people; it has been preserved by the people through the most gigantic and tragic war of modern times, and it must endure as written and expounded until altered by the people by the means they have prescribed.

The power of the federal government cannot be increased except by new grants of power through amendment of the Constitution. The efficiency, however, of the federal government will progressively increase through the application of existing federal power to the growing complexities of social and commercial conditions.

What changes in these conditions may be in store for us no man can foretell. What social readjustments may follow the application of the federal commercial power to such changes is likewise unknown. The power is a fixed and definite factor; no one has pretended to define the boundaries of the subject upon which it operates. The distinguished present solicitor-general of the United States, an honored son of Yale, Mr. Henry M. Hoyt, in a recent argument in the Supreme Court aptly said: "The word commerce is not restricted to trade and traffic, or navigation or transportation. No one can now say definitely what movements and interactions across State lines may not be embraced within its meaning.

Human government is a human necessity. It is all the stronger and more effective in times of dire need for not having been experimented with and its fibre strained in times of tranquillity.

The way to make real progress in needful legislation, and to permanently retain each advance, is to move wisely along legitimate lines. This is a land of law as well as of liberty, and the liberty of the law-maker is subject to restraints as well as the liberty of the individual. Congress can only do what it is possible to do under the powers delegated to it by the body politic, which is the people. To do anything more would be futile usurpation; to do any less under those powers than the best interests of the people demand should be done would be neglect of duty.

It is beside the question to urge the desirability and popularity of measures if Congress has no power to enact them. Our heartiest sympathy may be enlisted in many movements and yet our judgment may be compelled to reject the means proposed for their accomplishment. I remember and am impressed by the words of President Roosevelt in his first message to Congress, that "the men who demand the impossible or the undesirable serve as the allies of the forces with which they are nominally at war, for they hamper those who would endeavor to find out in rational fashion what the wrongs really are and to what extent and in what manner it is practicable to apply remedies."

The last words of Washington and the first words of Lincoln contained a solemn admonition to us on the necessity of preserving our dual government intact.

In his farewell address to the American people, Washington said:

"If, in the opinion of the people, the distribution or modification of the constitutional powers be in any particular wrong, let it be corrected by an amendment in the way which the Constitution designates. But let there be no change by usurpation; for, though this, in one instance, may be the instrument of good, it is the customary weapon by which free governments are destroyed. The precedent must always greatly overbalance in permanent evil any partial or transient benefit which the use can at any time yield."

And in his first message to the American Congress, Lincoln said:

"To maintain inviolate the rights of the States to order and control under the Constitution their own affairs by their own judgment exclusively, is essential for the preservation of that balance of power on which our institutions rest."

And finally, Chief Justice Marshall, the great expounder of the Constitution, said, in Gibbons *v.* Ogden:

"The genius and character of the whole government seem to be, that its action is to be applied to all the external concerns of the nation, and to those internal concerns which affect the States generally; but not to those which are completely within a particular State, which do not affect other States, and with which it is not necessary to interfere, for the purpose of executing some of the general powers of the government."

Cases of Interest.

WIFE'S RIGHT TO SUE FOR ALIENATION OF HUSBAND'S AFFECTIONS. — In Keen *v.* Keen, 90 Pac. Rep. 147, the Oregon Supreme Court holds that a statute repealing "all laws which impose or recognize civil disabilities upon a wife which are not imposed or recognized as existing as to the husband," gives the wife the right to maintain an action for the alienation of her husband's affections. It was further held that a divorce secured by the plaintiff on the ground of abandonment was no bar to her maintenance of the action for alienation of affections.

FEDERAL EIGHT-HOUR LAW — WHO ARE "LABORERS OR MECHANICS." — In Ellis *v.* United States, 27 Sup. Ct. Rep. 600, the Federal Supreme Court holds that the Act of Congress of August 1, 1892, known as the "Eight-hour Law," prohibiting, except in case of extraordinary emergency, the employment of laborers or mechanics for more than eight hours a day on public works, is not repugnant to the Federal Constitution. It is further held that dredging a channel in Boston Harbor is not a "public work of the United States" within the meaning of the act, and that masters, matés, engineers, firemen, cranemen, deckhands, and scowmen employed on tugs, dredges, and scows engaged in such dredging are not "laborers or mechanics" within the meaning of the act. With this latter conclusion, Mr. Justice Moody takes issue in a dissenting opinion, in which Mr. Justice Harlan and Mr. Justice Day concurred.

INTERSTATE COMMERCE — C. O. D. SHIPMENTS OF WHISKEY. — In Adams Express Co. *v.* Kentucky, 27 Sup. Ct. Rep. 606, the United States Supreme Court has recently held that the agreement of the local agent of an express company to hold for a few days a C. O. D. interstate shipment of intoxicating liquors, to suit the convenience of the consignee in paying for such liquor and taking it away, does not destroy the character of the transaction as interstate commerce, so as to render the express company liable to prosecution for violating a State local option law. And evidence that the express company knew that the shipment of intoxicating liquors was not ordered by the consignee is immaterial on such prosecution, where the indictment alleges that the express company was engaged in the business of a common carrier of packages, and that the shipment and delivery were made and done in the usual course of its business.

Statute Requiring Production of Corporate Books. — In the recent case of *In re* Consolidated Rendering Co., 66 Atl. Rep. 790, the Vermont Supreme Court upheld the validity of a State statute requiring the production, upon notice, by any corporation doing business in the State, of all corporate books, etc., containing information concerning the proceedings or subject of inquiry pending before the tribunal from which the notice issues. It was held that the statute does not contravene the provision of the State constitution relating to searches and seizures, or that regarding self-criminating testimony, nor does it violate the federal guaranties of due process of law and equal protection of the laws. The proceedings were brought against the respondent for contempt in refusing to produce its books before the grand jury, after being served with an order of court calling upon it to produce them. The respondent was adjudged guilty of contempt and fined $3,000, which action the Supreme Court upheld.

The Virginia-West Virginia Case. — An important decision as to the original jurisdiction of the United States Supreme Court in suits between States was made in Virginia *v.* West Virginia, 27 Sup. Ct. Rep. 732. A bill in equity was filed to obtain an adjudication of the amount due to Virginia by West Virginia as the equitable proportion of the public debt of the original State of Virginia, which was assumed by West Virginia at the time of its creation as a State. The State of West Virginia demurred to the bill on several grounds, among them that the court had no jurisdiction. This was the only point on which the court gave a decision, holding against the contention of the defendant and overruling the demurrer. The decision of the question whether Virginia had been released from liability on account of the public debt in question, and objections of multifariousness and misjoinder of parties and causes of action, was postponed until the final hearing. Mr. Chief Justice Fuller delivered the opinion of the court.

Ouster of Foreign Corporations Engaged in Interstate Commerce. — The Kansas Act of 1898, known as the "Bush Act," requiring foreign corporations to comply with certain conditions, including the payment of charter fees computed upon the amount of their authorized capital stock for the privilege of doing business within the State, was upheld as a valid exercise of the police power by the Kansas Supreme Court in State *v.* Western Union Tel. Co., 90 Pac. Rep. 299, and State *v.* Pullman Co., 90 Pac. Rep. 319. The court held that as to corporations engaged in both interstate and intrastate business the statute must be taken as applying only to the latter, and to that extent was as binding on them as on foreign corporations engaged in intrastate business only. The requirement of a charter fee was held not to levy a tax upon property or franchises notwithstanding it might produce some revenue. Judgments in favor of the State were rendered ousting the two companies from the privilege of engaging in nongovernmental intrastate business within the borders of Kansas, for their failure to comply with the requirements of the act. In the case of the Pullman Co., the further point was decided that the judgment of ouster did not violate the obligation of the company's contracts with the railroads.

Viaduct in Street — Rights of Abutting Owner. — In Sauer *v.* City of New York, 27 Sup. Ct. Rep. 686, it was held that the decisions of the highest court of a State that an owner of land abutting on a city street has no easement of light, air, and access as against the public use of the street, or any structure which may be erected thereon to subserve and promote that public use, are conclusive upon the Federal Supreme Court when determining, on writ of error to the State court, whether such abutting owner has been deprived of his property without due process of law by the erection in the street of an elevated iron viaduct for general public use, under the authority of a statute which makes no provision for compensation to abutting owners. The court further holds that decisions made by the State court before the plaintiff acquired title that an abutting owner was entitled to the right of unimpaired access and uninterrupted circulation of light and air as against an elevated structure erected for the exclusive use of a private corporation, did not constitute a contract which was impaired by a contrary holding in regard to a structure for public use, the State court having carefully refrained from extending its ruling to the latter case and plainly pointed out the essential distinction between the cases.

Injunction Against Boycotting and Picketing. — A sweeping injunction against a labor union was granted by Vice-Chancellor Bergen, of the New Jersey Court of Chancery, in George Jonas Glass Co. *v.* Glass Bottle Blowers' Assoc., 66 Atl. Rep. 953. The vice-chancellor held that a boycott having for its object the compelling of a manufacturer to unionize his business and the submission of its conduct to the regulations of a labor union, was an irreparable injury to his property, the continuance of which a court of equity would enjoin. Also, that a combination or agreement to picket a manufacturing plant for the purpose of interfering with the free flow of labor to an employer, to whom labor was a necessity for the carrying on of his business, which, if successful, would prevent him from obtaining the means of pursuing a lawful occupation, and the sole purpose of which was to compel him to comply with the demands of an antagonistic power, was a conspiracy against the property rights of the employer, subjecting his property to an irreparable injury, and all parties to such compact, actors as well as abettors, would be restrained from establishing and maintaining such picket service. It was further held that a labor union could not in such a case be regarded as a competitor in the labor market.

Attorney and Client — Contingent Fees. — An important decision as to the right of an attorney to take a case on a contingent basis was rendered by the New York Court of Appeals in Ransom *v.* Cutting, 81 N. E. Rep. 324. The action was brought by attorneys to recover compensation from the defendant for services rendered, and the latter set up in defense that the agreement of retainer was unconscionable and also champertous. The facts were as follows: The defendant, having been disinherited, retained the plaintiffs to bring actions to set aside certain wills or to secure settlements thereunder. The defendant assigned to the plaintiffs forty per cent. of any and all recovery, to be reduced to thirty-three and one-third per cent. if the contemplated litigation was ended by a decision of the surrogate, and to ten per cent. in the event of a settlement realizing $50,000 or more. The plaintiffs agreed not to call on the defendant for any money to pay necessary disbursements. The plaintiffs succeeded in obtaining a settlement, received and for several yars paid ten per cent. of the annuity, of $4,000. The defendant paid over ten per cent. of the cash received and for several years paid ten per cent. of the annuity but finally refused to make further payments on account of the annuity. The court held that the agreement was neither unconscionable nor champertous.

Some Automobile Cases. — In Walker *v.* Grout Bros. Automobile Co., 102 S. W. Rep. 25, the Missouri Court of Appeals held that where a woman, being desirous of securing an automobile which she could run herself without manual labor, bought a machine from a manufacturer on his assurance that a woman could operate it, the contract of sale stipulating that the machine should be satisfactory to her, she had the right to return it to the manufacturer and demand a return of the price in case the machine was not satisfactory to her.

In State *v.* Swagerty, 102 S. W. Rep. 483, the Missouri Supreme Court held that a State statute regulating the operation and speed of automobiles on the highways of the State, constituted a valid exercise of the State's police power for the protection of the safety and welfare of society, and was not unconstitutional as class legislation, in that it discriminated against certain users of the highway.

In House *v.* Cramer, 112 N. W. Rep. 3, the Iowa Supreme Court holds that the operator of an automobile who stops his machine in the street, expecting to start again shortly, is not negligent in allowing the explosions from his engine to continue whereby horses are frightened, unless he sees that the explosions are frightening the horses, or in the exercise of ordinary care ought to see it, and by ordinary diligence may stop the engine in time to prevent a runaway.

In McCummins *v.* State, 112 N. W. Rep. 25, the Wisconsin Supreme Court holds that under an act providing that the operator of an automobile, on a signal of distress by a person driving horses, shall cause the automobile to stop all motor power and remain stationary, unless a movement forward shall be deemed necessary to avoid accident or injury, it is for the operator to determine whether a forward movement is necessary, and his determination is controlling unless he acts unreasonably or in bad faith.

In Doran *v.* Thomsen, 66 Atl. Rep. 897, the New Jersey Supreme Court holds that the owner of an automobile is not liable for an injury caused by the negligent operation by a person to whom the machine has been loaned, if it is not being used in the owner's business.

News of the Profession.

MISSOURI JUDGES TO WEAR GOWNS. — Westward the gown-wearing habit takes its flight. Hereafter the "silken, sad, uncertain rustling" of the judicial robe will accompany the movements of the judges of the Missouri Supreme Court.

NEW HAMPSHIRE JUDGE TO RETIRE. — Hon. William M. Chase, of the New Hampshire Supreme Court, will retire from the bench later in the present year on the age limit. He was born in 1838, and received his appointment to the Supreme Court in 1891.

GEORGIA SUPREME JUDGE TO RESIGN. — It is announced that Associate Justice Andrew J. Cobb, of the Georgia Supreme Court, will shortly retire from the bench and enter upon the practice of the law at Athens, in partnership with his nephew, Col. Howell C. Erwin.

RAILROAD ATTORNEY DROPS DEAD. — Charles N. Travous, general attorney for the Wabash Railroad, in Illinois, dropped dead at his home in Edwardsville, Ill., on July 2. Mr. Travous was about fifty years old and had been connected with the legal department of the Wabash for twenty-six years.

NIGHT COURTS FOR NEW YORK CITY. — On July 3, Mayor McClellan, of New York city, signed a bill providing for night sessions of the police courts. Now the round-tripper from South Bend, Ind., can get himself bailed out in time to be pinched again before the lights go out on the Great White Way.

PROMINENT PHILADELPHIAN DEAD. — George Hussey Earle, one of the best known lawyers and citizens of Philadelphia, died in that city June 18, aged eighty-four years. Mr. Earle was a personal friend of Abraham Lincoln, and was the oldest surviving delegate to the first Republican National Convention that nominated Fremont for the presidency.

HUMMEL'S LAW PARTNER DIES. — Benjamin Steinhardt, formerly a member of the defunct firm of Howe & Hummel, died in a sanatorium in New York city on June 17, of locomotor ataxia. His death marks the absolute extinction of this once notorious firm, for within the year Hummel has been imprisoned on Blackwell's Island, and Kaffenburgh, the other partner, has been disbarred. Howe died a number of years ago.

CONNECTICUT PRACTICE ACT BEING REVISED. — During the summer months a committee composed of Chief Justice Simeon E. Baldwin and Associate Justice Samuel O. Prentice, of the Connecticut Supreme Court, and Judges George W. Wheeler, Edwin B. Gager, and William S. Case, of the Superior Court, is hard at work codifying the laws of the State relating to practice in the courts.

JUSTICE BREWER THREE SCORE AND TEN. — On June 20, Hon. David J. Brewer, associate justice of the United States Supreme Court, celebrated his seventieth birthday. The justice has been a member of the court since 1889, when he succeeded the late Justice Stanley Matthews. He is entitled to retire on the age limit, but fortunately there is not much likelihood of his doing so for some time to come.

DEATH OF JUSTICE WOODARD OF MAINE. — Hon. Charles F. Woodard, associate justice of the Supreme Judicial Court of Maine, died at his home in Bangor, on June 17, as the result of an apoplectic stroke. Justice Woodard was born in Bangor in 1848, and was a graduate of Harvard College and the Harvard Law School. He practiced law in Bangor with distinguished success until Dec. 7, 1906, when he was chosen to fill the vacancy on the Supreme bench of the State, caused by the death of Chief Justice Wiswell.

NEW JUDGE FOR MAINE SUPREME COURT. — Governor Cobb, of Maine, has appointed Arno W. King, of Ellsworth, to fill the vacancy in the Supreme Judicial Court of Maine, created by the death of Associate Justice Charles F. Woodard, of Bangor. The new judge is about fifty years of age, a graduate of Colby College, and has long been well known throughout the State. At one time he was associated in practice with the late Chief Justice Andrew P. Wiswell.

AFTER PENSION SHARKS. — Secretary Garfield and Pension Commissioner Warner have recently started a campaign against dishonest pension attorneys who make a practice of swindling old soldiers and their heirs. Already they have secured the disbarment of W. E. Moses, of Washington and Denver, and orders to show cause why they should not be disbarred have been issued against Harvey Spalding & Son, of Washington, Milo B. Stevens & Co., of Washington, Cleveland, Detroit, and Chicago, and Edgar B. Gaddis, of Washington.

BAR ASSOCIATIONS NOT REPORTED. — In addition to the State Bar Association meetings reported in this column, the lawyers of the following States also held their conventions during July, reports of which will be given in our next issue: Colorado, at Broadmoor, July 5 and 6; Indiana, at Indianapolis, July 9 and 10; Ohio, at Put-in Bay, July 9–12; Iowa, at Davenport, July 11 and 12; Illinois, at Galesburg, July 11 and 12; North Carolina, at Hendersonville, July 11 and 12; Kentucky, at Bowling Green, July 11–13; Washington, at Seattle, July 13.

SAN FRANCISCO JUDGE UNDER FIRE. — An effort is being made by the bar association of San Francisco to secure the removal of Judge J. C. B. Hebbard, of the Superior Court, on charges of habitual intemperance. In regard to the charges filed against him Judge Hebbard is reported to have said: "I have done nothing worse than get drunk. What if I did? The Supreme Court has been guilty of a similar offense." On June 25 Judge Hebbard in desperation sought to end his life with a revolver, but was thwarted by a newspaper reporter who happened to be interviewing him at the time.

ROSCOE POUND GOES TO NORTHWESTERN UNIVERSITY. — At the close of the recent session of the University of Nebraska Roscoe Pound, the well-known dean of the law school, resigned to accept a professorship of law at Northwestern University. Prof. George P. Costigan was made dean of the law school. Mr. Costigan was graduated from Harvard College in 1892, and from the Harvard Law School in 1894. The vacancy in the staff of the University of Nebraska law school was filled by the election of Prof. E. B. Conant, of the law school of Washburn University, at Topeka, Kan.

WEEDING OUT THE UNWORTHY. — The vigor with which the black sheep of the profession are being harried just now is extremely gratifying. In New York city during June sentences of disbarment were pronounced against Charles Cohn, Charles E. Stern, and Abraham A. Joseph, while Dethlef C. Hansen was suspended for one year. In Boston Fayette W. Wheeler has been disbarred, the disbarment of Peter J. Casey has been affirmed, and William P. Hale has been suspended for a year. In Springfield, Ohio, United States Commissioner A. P. Linn Cochran has been suspended for two years, and out in San Francisco the bar association is hot on the trail of a number of lawyers who are under indictment for grafting and boodling.

FEDERAL JUDGE SWAYNE DEAD. — Hon. Charles Swayne, federal district judge for the northern district of Florida, died July 5 at the University of Pennsylvania hospital, in Philadelphia, where he had gone to be treated for kidney trouble. Judge Swayne's name was brought prominently before the public a year or so ago through an attempt to impeach him on charges that he did not reside in his district, that he made excessive charges against the government for expenses, and that he used his position to extort favors from railroad companies. His trial was the first impeachment proceeding before the Senate since the trial of Secretary of War Belknap, under the administration of Gen. Grant. He was acquitted by a vote that was almost strictly along party lines.

NEW JERSEY STATE BAR ASSOCIATION. — The ninth annual meeting of the New Jersey State Bar Association was held in Atlantic City, on June 14 and 15. The president of the association, Hon. Gilbert Collins, of Jersey City, presided and delivered the president's annual address. The principal event of the meeting was an address on "Certain Modern Tendencies," by Adrian H. Joline, of the New York bar. The annual banquet was held at the Hotel Windsor, Hon. Gilbert Collins acting as toastmaster. Toasts were responded to as follows: "The Supreme Court," by Hon. Thomas W. Trenchard; "The Court of Chancery," by Hon. James E. Howell; "The Outer Bar," by Adrian H. Joline; "Military Tactics of Trial by Jury," by Samuel Kalish. Officers were elected as follows: President, Willard P. Voorhees, of New Brunswick; vice-presidents, Clarence Cole, of Atlantic City, Edward M. Colie, of Newark; secretary, William J. Kraft; treasurer, Lewis Starr.

ALABAMA STATE BAR ASSOCIATION. — The thirteenth annual meeting of the Alabama State Bar Association was held in Montgomery, on June 28 and 29, with President F. G. Bromberg, of Mobile, in the chair. The meeting was opened by the president's address, in which Mr. Bromberg reviewed the important legislation and other matters of legal interest of the past year. Among the papers read during the meeting were: "The Province of Law," by Armstead Brown, of Montgomery, and "The Caricaturist as a Civic Power," by H. E. Gibson. A feature of the meeting was the attendance of the venerable Senator Pettus, who was given an ovation by the members of the association. There was considerable discussion of the necessity for reform in the matter of criminal appeals to put a stop to the reversal of convictions for mere technical errors. The second day's session was held at Jackson Lake, where a barbecue dinner was served. The officers elected for the ensuing year were as follows: President, H. S. D. Mallory; vice-presidents, Mac A. Smith, W. C. Sanders, I. A. W. Smith, W. O. Mulkey, and Tipton Mullin; secretary and treasurer, Alexander Troy. Central council, John London, L. C. Bradley, E. K. Campbell, Edward Degraffenried, C. C. Whitson. Executive committee, R. E. Steiner, C. P. McIntyre, P. H. Stern, Gaston Gunter, and Alexander Troy.

TEXAS STATE BAR ASSOCIATION. — The annual meeting of the Texas State Bar Association was held in Beaumont on July 2 and 3. The proceedings were opened by an address of welcome by President F. D. Minor, of the local bar association, which was responded to by W. L. Estes, of Texarkana. The president of the association, A. L. Beatty, of Sherman, delivered the usual address reviewing the State legislation for the past year. Mr. Yancey Lewis, of Dallas, was scheduled to deliver the annual address. Papers were read during the course of the meeting as follows: "Should the Legal Status of the Negro Be Changed?" by Edgar Watkins, of Houston; "Liability of Trusts for Private Wrongs," by W. M. Holland, of Dallas; "Legal Ethics," by John Charles Harris, of Houston; "Uniform Legislation," by Robert A. John, of Beaumont; "The Honor of the Bar," by T. H. Franklin, of San Antonio. John T. Wheeler, of Galveston, was to have read a paper on "Needed Reforms," but was prevented by illness from attending. The meeting concluded with the usual banquet. The following officers were elected for the ensuing term: President, A. G. Wilkinson, of Austin; vice-president, Yancey Lewis, of Dallas; secretary, L. Q. C. Lamar, of Fort Worth; treasurer, W. D. Williams, of Fort Worth. It was decided to hold the next convention at Fort Worth.

PENNSYLVANIA STATE BAR ASSOCIATION. — The thirteenth annual meeting of the Pennsylvania State Bar Association was held at Bedford Springs, on June 25–27, with the largest attendance in the history of the association. President Thomas Patterson, of Pittsburg, opened with the annual address, in which he discussed the important legislation of the year in the State and nation. The principal address was made by United States Circuit Judge George Gray, of Delaware, who spoke on "The New Federalism." Papers read during the meeting were: "The Legal Aspects of the Trial of Jesus Christ," by Edward J. Fox, of Easton; "The Guaranties of Liberty in the Early Law of Pennsylvania," by Hon. Michael J. Jacobs, of Harrisburg; "The History of the Law as Part of the Course of Study Required for Admission to the Bar," by Hon. John D. Shafer, of Pittsburg; and "Uniform Divorce Laws," by Walter George Smith, of Philadelphia. At the annual banquet, held on the evening of the last day, President Patterson acted as toastmaster, and toasts were responded to by the following: Hon. George Gray, of Delaware; Francis Fisher Kane, of Philadelphia; Col. Charles M. Clement, of Sunbury; W. D. Evans, of Pittsburg, and Samuel Cooper, of Philadelphia. Officers for the next year were elected as follows: President, Robert Snodgrass, of the Dauphin county bar; vice-presidents, Frank C. McGirr, of Allegheny, Mahlon S. Stout, of Bucks, Francis J. Kooser, of Somerset, T. C. Hipple, of Clinton, and John A.

Clark, of Philadelphia; secretary, William H. Staacke, of Philadelphia; treasurer, William Penn Lloyd, of Cumberland.

MARYLAND STATE BAR ASSOCIATION. — The twelfth annual meeting of the Maryland State Bar Association was held at Ocean City, on July 3-5, with President Conway W. Sams, of Baltimore, in the chair. As usual, the meeting was opened with the president's annual address, in which Mr. Sams dealt with the defects in American criminal procedure. He was followed by Hon. John S. Wise, of New York, who spoke on "Centralization by Construction," and sharply criticised the policy of President Roosevelt. Peter W. Meldrim, of Savannah, Ga., in an address on "Respect for the Bar," also took Mr. Roosevelt to task for his attitude towards judges who render decisions that fail to meet the approval of the administration. Other papers on the program were "Representative Government Under the Constitution, and the Government As It Is," by Herbert Noble, of New York; "Shall We Have a New Constitution," by William S. Bryan, of Maryland; "Some Suggested Changes in the Constitution of Maryland," by Isaac Lobe Straus, of Baltimore; "Brokers' Commissions on an Unexecuted Contract of Sale," by John Phelps, of Baltimore. The meeting was closed with a banquet, at which the chief address was delivered by Richard Randolph McMahon, of Harper's Ferry, W. Va., on "The Law in Literature, the Lawyers, and the Judge." The following officers were elected: President, L. Allison Wilmer, of La Plata; vice-presidents, Robley D. Jones, of Snow Hill, Edwin H. Brown, Jr., of Centreville, Hon. N. Charles Burke, of Towson, Hon. M. L. Keedy, of Hagerstown, F. Neal Parker, of Westminster, Edward C. Peter, of Rockville, J. Briscoe Bunting, of Prince Frederick, William S. Bryan, Jr., of Baltimore, and Walter I. Dawkins, of Baltimore; secretary, James W. Dennis, of Baltimore; treasurer, Frank G. Turner, of Baltimore.

THE COPYRIGHT QUESTION IN FRANCE. — As a result of an agitation on the part of literary producers in France, the French government has promised to appoint a committee to examine the question of prolonging and more effectually protecting literary copyright. The French laws are already very liberal in that respect, making the copyright of a literary work the property of the heirs of the deceased author during a period of fifty years after his death, but the men of letters are clamoring for more and declaring it to be iniquitous that the publishers alone should benefit by the expiration of a copyright. The Société des Gens de Lettres, through its president, M. Victor Margueritte, demands: (1) That the direct heirs of a deceased author shall continue to have the right to a certain portion of the profits arising from the publication of their ancestor's works; (2) in case of the extinction of the direct heirs that the Société des Gens de Lettres be authorized to receive the portion of the profits to which the heirs would have been entitled, such money to be devoted to the society's pension fund. One very strong objection urged against the proposal of the society is the possibility of the copyright of a literary work falling into the hands of an heir who might refuse to allow publication, and thus deprive the world of a masterpiece. The agitation on the subject was stirred up by the recent expiration of the copyright on the works of Balzac and Musset, and the near approach of the time when the literary productions of the elder Dumas will fall into the public domain.

English Notes.

A GOOD WAY TO ASCERTAIN. — A witness in one of the English courts recently testified with some vehemence that he was the sort of man who liked to take the bull by the horns to see which way the crow was flying. At any rate such a procedure would be calculated to give one a broader range of observation.

CHEERING NEWS FOR THE DECEASED WIFE'S SISTER. — It is rumored from London that the perennial deceased wife's sister bill stands a fair chance of at last getting through the House of Lords. The first man who craved from Parliament the boon of espousing the sister of his deceased wife has mouldered into dust these many years ago, and many of his successors have gone the same inevitable way, but the relentless Lords have consistently and sternly refused to remove the ban from such unions. Should the Lords recede from their position at this late day it could be taken as a sure indication that the foundations of that much vaunted — and deadly stupid — institution, the English Home, had been undermined, and the empire was tottering to its fall.

AN ADMISSION AGAINST INTEREST. — In a recent issue London *Law Notes*, while admitting the force of a criticism from some of its readers that a previous number had been "too Yankee in tone," remarked editorially: "Have our candid friends any idea how dull the English law and lawyers have grown lately? Rarely is there any legal incident in this country with a grain of fun in it. Hence we are driven to a younger country, where lawyers in common with the rest of the population still retain some boyish instincts, and are not too *blasé* with life to enjoy a joke. However, we will try to be less Yankee and more British and stodgy for as long as we and our other readers can stand it." Any one who is under the painful necessity of perusing the English legal journals will share the exasperation of that editor.

COMMONS VOTE TO LIMIT POWERS OF LORDS. — The crusade of the Liberal Ministry against the ancient prerogatives of the House of Lords has begun to take definite shape. On June 24, in the House of Commons, Premier Campbell-Bannerman introduced the following resolution: "That in order to give effect to the will of the people, as expressed by their elected representatives, it is necessary that the power of the other House to alter or reject bills passed by this House should be so restricted by law as to secure that within the limits of a single Parliament the final decision of the House of Commons shall prevail." After a debate which lasted three days, ending at midnight on June 27, the resolution was carried by a vote of 432 to 147, amid loud ministerial cheers. The Premier, on leaving the house, received a great ovation.

COMPENSATION FOR UNJUST IMPRISONMENT. — In the House of Commons recently a request was made of the Home Secretary for particulars as to the compensation paid by the government in the last twenty years to prisoners pardoned by the Home Office. In response Mr. Gladstone submitted the following summary:

Sentence.	Time served.	Compensation given.
Life	9 years	£800
Life	9 years	£800
10 years	6 months	£6
12 months	3 months	£16
6 months	3 months	£13
5 years	3 months	£10
14 days	14 days	£10
18 months	7 months	£40
6 months	2 months	£30
5 years	2 months	£3
3 years	2 months	£2
12 months	6 months	£20
7 years	5 years 5 months	£5,000
21 days	3 days	£1
2 months	2 months	£50

The largest item, £5,000, represents the compensation paid to Adolph Beck, whose conviction and imprisonment through a mistake in identity raised a storm of indignation in England a few years ago, and lent much impetus to the demand for a court of criminal appeal.

The New Workmen's Compensation Act. — On July 1 an Act went into force in England which very greatly increases the liability of employers for injuries sustained by servants in the course of their employment. It goes far beyond the previous Act of 1897, which gave compensation only in respect of accidents occurring in particular kinds of employment, and in certain defined localities. The new Act provides generally for compensation "if in any employment personal injury by accident arising out of and in the course of the employment is caused to a workman." The word "workman" is defined as meaning any person who has entered into or works under a contract of service or apprenticeship, except (1) any person employed otherwise than by way of manual labor whose remuneration exceeds £250 a year, (2) any person whose employment is of a casual nature and who is employed otherwise than for the purposes of the employer's trade or business, (3) policemen, (4) outworkers, and (5) resident members of the employer's family. The benefits of the Act are extended to seamen who are members of the crew of a British ship, when such ship is registered in the United Kingdom, or when the managing owner or manager has his residence or principal place of business therein. The right of compensation is also extended to workmen suffering from certain industrial diseases, and to their dependents. The category of "dependents" entitled to compensation is also enlarged by including therein illegitimate children dependent on the earnings of a parent or grandparent, and conversely parents or grandparents dependent on the earnings of illegitimate children. Another far-reaching change is that it will no longer be possible to set up the serious and wilful misconduct of the workman in defense when the injury has resulted in death or in serious and permanent disablement.

The Origin of Lincoln's-Inn. — In "Short Notes of Lincoln's-inn," recently written by Mr. Douglas Walker, K. C., one of the benchers of the Inn, appears the following interesting account of the origin of that famous society: "The Honorable Society of Lincoln's-inn have their origin in a group of lawyers, who between 1286 and 1310 were brought by H. de Lacy, Earl of Lincoln, to settle near his manor house in Holborn. Here they occupied a house in Shoe-lane (known in later years as Thavy's-inn), acquiring the title they still bear by being under the patronage of the Earl of Lincoln. Thence at a date previous to the death of Lord Furnival in 1383, the larger part of the society, taking their title with them, moved to Lord Furnival's two messuages in Holborn, leaving a minority to occupy Thavy's Inn as dependents of the society. By the year 1422 again a majority had moved from Furnival's-inn and are found occupying, as tenants to the bishop, the Palace of the Bishops of Chichester in Chancellor's or Chancery-lane, and holding Thavy's-inn and Furnival's-inn as dependencies. The Hospitium de Lincoln's-inn, as the heading of the first Black Book of 1422 called the Palace, has remained ever since in the possession of the society, who acquired the fee in 1580. The records of the society incidentally give details of the site. It was separated from Chancery-lane by a ditch and a mud wall, thatched with reeds; at one point a gate, near the present old gatehouse, gave access to the lane. A similar boundary marked the north and west sides of the property, and the latter was pierced in the north end by an opening to the space now known as Lincoln's-inn-fields. The west ditch and wall ran along the line of the present wall, across the present gateway to Lincoln's-inn-fields, and over the site of No. 11 and 11A New-square, till abreast of a point now marked by a white stone and inscription on the east wall of No. 11 New-square. On the south side a wall ran eastward from a point just mentioned along the line of the south front of No. 13 New-square, and continued south of the front of Old-buildings to Chancery-lane. The eastern end was at one time marked by a palisado and ditch some sixteen feet to the south of the line of buildings. A postern gate, just opposite to No. 13 New-square, gave access to Fickett's-fields, now in part New-square. Among the buildings were the Bishop's Hall, a chapel of St. Mary, and another of St. Richard, or, it may be, one building containing two chapels, and several two-story living houses built of timber and plaster, or 'dawb.' None of these buildings now exist, though their sites are conjecturable. The rest of the property to the northward was taken up by a garden bordering on Chancery-lane, and a coney garth or rabbit warren lying on the west of it. The herb or kitchen garden close to the postern gate before mentioned, of which traces still remain in the trees between the south end of Old-buildings and the north end of New-square, east side, was added to by the society of the later date of 1585."

Obiter Dicta.

How Did He Manage It? — A lawyer in Ithaca, N. Y., recently filed a petition in bankruptcy with liabilities scheduled at $149,150. Was ever lawyer so trusted?

Needs Another Crutch. — Out in Wyoming a Mr. Prop is being sued by his wife for nonsupport. She ought to get a divorce and take to herself another husband. Then she would have a brace. At times we wax too witty for anything.

For Better or For Worse. — It was decided in the New York Supreme Court the other day that snoring did not constitute such "cruel and inhuman treatment" as would warrant a legal separation. Which goes to show that matrimony is not to be entered into lightly or thoughtlessly.

A Presumption of Fact. — A Chicago judge has recently ruled that for a married woman to be on friendly terms with a Pittsburg millionaire is of itself sufficient ground for divorce. A Pittsburg police official, when informed of the ruling, grinned broadly and remarked: "I wonder who put the judge next."

Credit Where Credit Is Due. — It may be of interest to Judge Cooper, of the California Court of Appeal, First District, to know that the language quoted by him in People *v.* Yee Foo, 89 Pac. Rep. 450 (at page 454), from "the leading case" of Tucker *v.* Henniker, 41 N. H. 323, was lifted practically verbatim by the New Hampshire court without credit from the opinion of Judge Nisbet, in Mitchum *v.* State, 11 Ga. 615, 631, which case was decided eight years previous to the New Hampshire decision. The matter caused considerable discussion in the law magazines many years ago.

Punctured His Eloquence. — A lawyer in Johnstown, N. Y., while defending a little boy who had been apprehended in the act of making a surreptitious entrance under the fair grounds fence, drew for the jury a most pathetic picture of the prisoner's "poor old widowed mother with the tears streaming down her face and her gray head bowed in sorrow at the thought of her little boy being incarcerated." The youthful offender cut in at this point with "Please, sir, Mr. Lawyer, my mother ain't a widow." "Shut up, darn you," said the lawyer, "I'm trying this case, not you."

Insures Marriages for One Year. — The Hon. Zell G. Roe, the marrying justice of Des Moines, Iowa, has recently come forward with the happy idea of insuring for one year all marriages solemnized by him. At least he guarantees to refund the marriage fee in any case where a knot tied by him fails to stand the strain for a twelvemonth. In consideration of this guaranty the young couple has to listen patiently while he hands out to them all those fine moral platitudes that we all like to impress upon others when we can get them to listen. The justice's plan would seem better calculated to insure a half hour of happiness for him than a year of it for the newly wed.

JUDICIAL DEFINITION OF "ALL IN." — In the recent case of State v. Hennessy, 90 Pac. Rep. 221, the Nevada Supreme Court gives a definition of the slang phrase "All in." The question came up in connection with the admission in evidence of a dying declaration, the declarant's statement that he was "all in" being relied on to show that he was under a sense of impending death. The court said: "The expression 'I am all in' is one frequently made use of in this western country, and when used under the circumstances in question may, we think, be taken to have meant that the speaker considered his life was practically at an end."

HERESY AND SCHISM. — A matter of exceeding great importance will come before the Circuit Court of St. Louis county next September, when the action by the Bible College of Missouri against Dr. Gustave A. Hoffman on a note for $5,000 comes up for trial. Dr. Hoffman asserts in his defense that after he had given the note he discovered to his horror that the institution discredited the narrative about Jonah and the whale, and he does not propose to give up a cent to anybody who won't stand for Jonah. Inasmuch as there has long been a division of opinion on this important point, it will be as well to get a judicial determination whether the great fish really did stomach Jonah, or whether that was only the explanation he gave to Mrs. J. of his three days absent and unaccounted for.

WOULDN'T LEAVE MUCH OF SOME PEOPLE. — The grave and difficult question, whether a gentleman who expressed an intention to "whip hell out of" another thereby threatened to kill or inflict serious bodily injury on the person who was to have the hell extracted from his composition, was before the Texas Court of Criminal Appeals, in Hix v. State, 102 S. W. Rep. 405. The threatened party, it seems, was reluctant to be deprived of his hell, so he undertook to impair the threatener's physical ability to carry out the program — in which endeavor he was quite successful. Davidson, P. J., said: "As to how serious a result would have happened to appellant if the assaulted party whipped 'hell out of him can only be conjectured from the use of the language. What effect whipping hell out of appellant would have had upon him personally as to his physical condition is not shown, but we hardly think that it was of such nature as would have produced death or serious bodily injury."

LONG MISSING ANSWER FOUND. — An interesting find was recently made by Vice-Chancellor Howell, of New Jersey, when in poking about in a New York book shop he turned up the original answer in an equity suit which was instituted in the New Jersey Court of Chancery in 1751. The answer, which is in parchment, is well preserved and legible. It bears the signatures of over four hundred men, English adventurers, who early in the eighteenth century bartered a few handfuls of powder and shot and a quantity of trinkets with the Indians for the land which now comprises Newark, Elizabeth, the Orange mountains, and the intermediate country. The suit was brought by a party of English noblemen, to whom the same land had been subsequently granted by the Crown. What eventually became of the suit is a mystery, and the answer has been missing from the court records for more than a century. The present owner has set a price of fifteen hundred dollars on the ancient document, and an effort is to be made to have the New Jersey legislature authorize its purchase.

PUT THE JUSTICE DOWN AND OUT. — Justice of the Peace Gottlieb Graubert, of Wimpall, Minn., had to grapple with a legal proposition not long since which wellnigh brought him to an untimely end. A man by the name of Dipmaster gave a check for fifty dollars to one Urger on a Monday. Urger did not present the check for payment, and on the following Thursday the bank failed. Being advised that he could not hold Dipmaster liable, Urger devised a scheme whereby he could get even. He managed to get into debt to Dipmaster to the extent of seventy-five dollars, and in payment tendered Dipmaster twenty-five dollars in cash and the latter's check for fifty dollars. Dipmaster said nothing, but at once presented the check at the bank, and on payment being refused, brought an action against Urger on his indorsement. Now, that was a point calculated to put wrinkles into the brow of any honest justice of the peace. Justice Graubert found it difficult to see how a man could have a right to sue on his own admittedly worthless check, but the learned attorney for the plaintiff by dint of much arguing and expounding brought his honor at last to see the light. But the mental effort had overstrained the justice's powers of endurance. He succeeded in gasping out, "I give judgment for the plaintiff," and then fell to the floor in a dead faint.

BY DUE PROCESS OF LAW. — A correspondent, writing from Dickson, Tenn., contributes this story of a low-down trick he played some years ago on a worthy old justice of the peace. Having been requested by a local minister of the gospel to prepare a warrant for the arrest of a woman charged with open and notorious lewdness, and the papers having been drawn up, the justice was called in, who relying upon the preacher's signature to the affidavit, signed the warrant without reading it. The warrant ran as follows:

"State of Tennessee, Benton County. To any lawful officer to execute and return:

"Information having been made to me on oath that the offense of open and notorious lewdness has been committed by John Green Douglass and Mary Ann Townsend, who have been living together as man and wife and at various times and places have been guilty of open and notorious acts of adultery and fornication, in said County, and being satisfied that said offense has been committed in said County by the said John Green Douglass and Mary Ann Townsend: You are therefore commanded in the name of the State to forthwith arrest the said Mary Ann Townsend and bring her before me, W. T. Morris, an acting Justice of the Peace for said County, to be dealt with by me as she has been by the said John Green Douglass. W. T. MORRIS, J. P."

"It is needless to say," adds our correspondent, "that the warrant was never executed in its original form."

THE OIL OF JOY. — That Indiana judge who held that the State had no power to license the sale of intoxicating liquors because of the iniquitous character of such beverages was probably not familiar with the following remarks of Judge Perkins, in Herman *v.* State, 8 Ind. 545: "In Biblical history we are told that the 'vine, a plant which bears clusters of grapes, out of which wine is pressed,' so abounded in Palestine that almost every family had a vineyard. Solomon, said to be the wisest man, had extensive vineyards which he leased to tenants. Song 8, verse 12. And David, in his 104th Psalm, in speaking of the greatness, power, and works of God, says (verses 14 and 15): 'He causeth grass to grow for the cattle, and herb for the service of man; and wine that maketh glad the heart of man, and oil to make his face shine, and bread which strengtheneth man's heart.' It thus appears, if the inspired psalmist is entitled to credit, that man was made to laugh as well as weep, and that these stimulating beverages were created by the Almighty expressly to promote his social hilarity and enjoyment. And for this purpose have the world ever used them; they have ever given, in the language of another passage of Scripture, strong drink to him that is weary and wine to those of heavy heart. The first miracle wrought by our Saviour, that at Cana of Galilee, the place where he dwelt in his youth, and where he met his followers after his resurrection, was to supply this article to increase the festivities of a joyous occasion; that he used it himself is evident from the fact that he was called by his enemies a winebibber; and he paid it the distinguished honor of being the eternal memorial of his death and man's redemption."

Law Notes

SEPTEMBER, 1907.

PUBLISHED BY EDWARD THOMPSON COMPANY,
NORTHPORT, LONG ISLAND, N. Y.

CONTENTS.

WHILE American discussion of the most unsatisfactory state of our appeal practice in criminal cases has been pointing a moral by instancing the state of things in England, where no criminal appeal existed, the English Parliament has been considering a criminal appeal bill. The observations of the English *Law Times* on this measure will be of interest to our readers. The *Law Times* says: "Although many arguments can be put forward against allowing appeals on questions of fact, they do not, to our mind, carry much weight. If an appeal is to be given on criminal matters — and there is no doubt that the introduction of such a right is a 'veritable revolution' in criminal procedure — the grounds of appeal should not be restricted to points of law. Naturally the whole thing is an experiment, but we think it will prove a successful one, though we agree with the [London] *Times* that the result rests largely on the manner in which the Court of Criminal Appeals does its work at the outset. As our contemporary states: 'If it is prompt in making it understood that nothing is to be gained by appealing, unless there has been in all probability a mistake; that it will not interfere merely because on the evidence before the jury the court would have acquitted; that it is reluctant to quash verdicts or vary sentences, we shall see the good results of the new system.'" Proceeding along these lines, the English court may succeed in avoiding some of the extreme sensitiveness to technical error which has come so near to wrecking our criminal appeal system. The obvious fact that the court is for the benefit of the community, and not for the benefit of the criminal, may stand a chance of being remembered. It is worth noting that the bill provides, to quote the *Law Times*, "that judgment [meaning in English usage what we call the opinion] is to be according to the opinion of the majority of the court hearing the case, in this way following out the procedure of the Privy Council. Power, however, is to be given to the court to direct to the contrary in cases where, in the opinion of the court, the question is a question of law on which it would be convenient that separate judgments should be pronounced. In this way dissenting judgments will be avoided save in the case of points of law — a state of facts that is highly desirable."

THE impressions of the English courts formed by "a well-known American lawyer traveling in Europe" have been somewhat extensively quoted in the newspapers during the recent hot weather — and they are by no means complimentary to those who occupy the seat of British Themis. From his description the reader will probably deduce a picture of the critic as himself a man of wide acquaintance with the modern world, in business "a hustler," who has snatched a few weeks from his clients' demands to "size up" the effete old world. "The judges" of the English courts, he says, "were too advanced in age and were apparently not men of the world. They seemed insufficiently experienced in every-day life and every-day business. They simply sit in judgment and lay down the law just as it was administered hundreds of years ago. A judge elected to the bench in America is invariably a man of the world, with wide human knowledge, a man of modern life. Altogether, British legal machinery impressed one as insufficiently up to date." A sad contrast, this, between the effects of an appointive system where the judges are selected from the leaders of the bar at high salaries and our elective system where salaries are generally small and qualities other than learning may enable a candidate to secure a seat on the bench. The complaint has been that appointive judges tend to reflect the ideas of a class rather than of the whole community, and that, in some vague way, they are further removed from the people than elective judges. This is the first allegation which we have seen that they are impractical and inefficient. What idea was in our traveler's head when he asserts that they "simply sit in judgment and lay down the law just as it was administered hundreds of years ago" is hard to get at. The English judges, as everyone knows, have and exercise far more power over trials than American judges, hedged about, as the latter usually are, by statutes which forbid them to express an opinion on the weight of the evidence. The last clause of the sentence — administering law as it was hundreds of years ago — is even more mysterious. Does he mean that the substance of the law as it existed hundreds of years ago is unchanged? With the nineteenth century just closed — that century which Sir Frederick Pollock says has seen the greatest growth of the common law since the thirteenth, and wherein the statute book has revolutionized rights and duties in many directions — the idea is egregiously absurd. Does he refer to administrative methods? Within thirty-five years methods of pleading and practice have undergone the greatest change in English history.

IN an interesting paper read last year by Mr. Thomas Leaming before the Pennsylvania Bar Association, which discusses the English administration of justice with intelligent appreciation of points worthy of imitation or avoidance, it is observed: "In America litigation begins in the court room. In England it ends there. American proceedings tend to be somewhat formal, conventional, diffuse, and dilatory. Pitfalls and traps are occasionally laid by astute practitioners which embarrass the side really in the right and delay a conclusion upon the merits. Much is incomprehensible to the layman concerned except the result. English legal proceedings, on the contrary, are colloquial, flexible, simple, and prompt — thoroughly in touch with the spirit of the times and with the ordinary man's everyday life. The legal decisions of the two countries are probably of equal value, and are held in mutual respect, and neither, perhaps, could claim any superiority over the other in its legal results; but in methods, England, at present, is far in advance. This was not always so. Up to 1875 the English courts were most dilatory, expensive, and unsatisfactory in method, but in these thirty years reforms in method have been evolved, step by step, and are still progressing, by which the most important action can be tried, a judgment given, appeal taken, argued and orally decided as counsel sit down — all in ninety days. The details of these improvements are too technical for the present occasion; suffice it to say that they are characterized by the utmost simplicity, and many of them are capable of adaptation with modifications to American conditions." Mr. Leaming's observations are founded on a close study of the English courts made at London. Their results differ rather widely from those of the well-known American lawyer who is traveling in Europe.

THE Committee on Commercial Law of the American Bar Association in their report at the recent meeting of the association make some interesting announcements with regard to their attempts to secure uniform legislation on certain matters of commercial law. We alluded some months ago to the Sales Act prepared on the basis of the English Act on the same subject. In addition to this there has been prepared also a uniform act concerning warehouse receipts. The committee have sought to secure the consideration and adoption of both measures by the legislatures of States which have recently been in session. How far their efforts have been successful appears by a few sentences from their report: "The Sales Act has been actually adopted in Connecticut, New Jersey, and Arizona, or in two States and one Territory in all. It was introduced but not passed in the legislatures of Georgia, Maine, Massachusetts, Minnesota, Nebraska, New York, Pennsylvania, and Washington. The Warehouse Receipts Act has become the law of Connecticut, Idaho, Illinois (in slightly modified form), Iowa, Massachusetts, Montana, New Jersey, and New York, or eight States in all. It was introduced but did not pass in the legislatures of Florida, Georgia, Maine, Minnesota, Nebraska, Pennsylvania, and Washington. . . . The committee has been able to obtain no report on either bill from Mississippi; the last advices from Alabama indicate that the Warehouse Receipts bill is pending in the senate of that State. It will be observed that Connecticut and New Jersey are the only two States which have adopted both laws." The announcement is also made that "the Commission on Uniform State Laws have also had under consideration two other bills of great public moment, one on the law of Partnership and the other on the law of Bills of Lading." These proposed acts are not yet in such shape as to render desirable a definite conclusion in respect to them.

THE Committee of the American Bar Association on Legal Education and Admissions to the Bar in their report at the Portland meeting of the association advocate changes of a radical nature as applied to legal education in the country as a whole. The report of the committee recommend for adoption "in each State and in the District of Columbia" a bill standardizing, so to say, the requirements for the degrees conferred by institutions offering courses in law. The bill introduces a distinction between the degrees of Bachelor of Laws and Bachelor of Law. Bachelor of Laws (LL.B.) is to be conferred only by institutions which maintain a course of law for undergraduates, the course extending over three academic years of at least eight months in each year, and which require at least ten hours of class work per week. Institutions which do not come up to these requirements are allowed to confer on their graduates the degree of Bachelor of Law (L. B.). In the second class would, of course, come that large class of institutions over the country offering a legal degree as the result of a two years' course of instruction. Institutions conferring LL.B. must require as a prerequisite for admission "an education equivalent to that possessed by one who has completed a course required for graduation from a high school in this State." A number of the institutions requiring only a two years' course for the degree in law demand as a prerequisite for admission to the course the equivalent of two years of college work. Will the young man who begins his legal education with a mind disciplined by two years of college work in addition to a high school education, and then pursues a two-year course in law, be worse fited for the active work of the profession than he who goes directly from the high school to an institution offering a three years' course of legal study? Those who have had practical experience in teaching law will, we think, decide unanimously in favor of the man who has received five years of mental discipline, even though only two years were spent in technical legal study, rather than of the man with three years' training in law, imposed on a high school education. And yet the committee's bill relegates to an inferior position the institution which, it seems to us, is doing the most efficient work. Unquestionably the legal profession should lend every encouragement to raising the standard of education in law, and should strive to make the degree conferred by institutions offering a legal education represent as much as possible of sound professional training. It is no answer to cite, as is sometimes done, instances of exceptional men, who without preliminary training and by their own ability have reached positions of eminence in the profession. Genius and even talent have their own rules. The Abraham Lincolns are not so numerous that we need consider them in framing general rules, and "nature must make room where greater spirits come." If the desirability of raising the standard of legal education be granted, and we heartily grant it, the question is whether it is better to encourage in our smaller colleges and in certain parts of this large and not too homogeneous country the offering of showy courses in law, reared on meagre foundations, or the work of institutions offering thorough though shorter courses, based on solid and adequate preliminary work. The course taken by the committee seems to us unwise. They are advocating a change which some day will be of great advantage, but which should follow and not precede the requirement of more adequate general education.

MR. EDWARD M. SHEPARD'S thoughtful address before the Illinois Bar Association is mainly concerned with a proposed remedy for some of the evils of corporate greed. Mr. Shepard proposes to abolish the issuance of shares of corporation stock at a valuation nominally fixed in money, but in reality ever varying, and he would substitute a certificate stating that it is issued for a certain aliquot proportion of the value of the enterprise. There could be no watering of stock under this system, says Mr. Shepard. But it is not to advocate or oppose so seemingly fanciful a scheme that we mention this address, but for the preliminary analysis of certain present-day conditions of business and of the relation between these conditions and the standing of the legal profession. Readers of Mr. Shepard's address last fall at the meeting of the New Hampshire Bar may guess his attitude on the last question. The loss of prestige by lawyers, which now as then Mr. Shepard emphasizes and deplores, is due not to any falling off in the standard of the profession, or to distrust of lawyers as individuals, but it falls upon them as agents and advisers of corporations. "The jealousy against power," says Mr. Shepard, "and especially centralized power, which in earlier days was directed against government, the fear of executive or federal usurpation which was dominant in our own country for the half century from the end of the first Adams administration until the interests of the negro slavery dominated our politics — these to-day give place to jealousy of corporations. A good American used to dread George III.; to-day he dreads the Standard Oil Company. And it is not mere wealth, but distinctively corporate wealth, which is in his mind. Popular jealousy of enormous personal fortunes, like those of the late Marshall Field or Russell Sage or of the Astor family, is not acute. Even when they and other possessors of such fortunes do not, by profuse munificence after the fashion of Mr. Carnegie or Mr. Rockefeller, appeal for popular condonation of the offense inherent in the very fact of their wealth, even then the jealousy is tepid compared with that incurred by fortunes which, like Mr. Harriman's or Mr. Ryan's, concretely signify actual control of great corporations." But if we grant that Mr. Shepard is right in the distinction between the feeling toward corporate and individual wealth, we may feel assured that distinction will not long survive in the minds of the untrained masses. "How distinguish heretics from true believers?" was asked of the legate before the massacre of Béziers. "Slay them all," was the reply, "God will know his own." A modified form of the holy man's precept is beginning to be observed toward wealth for its own sake.

A FEW months ago Secretary Root sounded a note of warning to the States. "It may be," he said, "that such control [as was advocated for the federal government] could better be exercised in particular instances by the governments of the States; but the people will have the control they need, either from the States or from the national government, and if the States fail to furnish it in due measure, sooner or later constructions of the Constitution will be found to vest the power where it will be exercised by the national government." Perhaps this widely circulated utterance was a factor in procuring State enactments to control public enterprises which was so marked a feature of the legislation of last winter and spring. Several legislatures passed railroad rate laws, prescribing the mileage which railroads might exact from passengers. The States had been told that if they neglected these grave public duties they might find that their franchise to legislate had been forfeited by non-user, and they hastened with what wisdom they had to occupy the vacant legislative field. Some of the Southern States, notably North Carolina, Virginia, and Alabama, were among those commonwealths adopting this course. The North Carolina seal is embellished with that old maxim from Sallust, *esse quam videri*, and having gotten such a railroad rate law upon their statute books, the State authorities, acting in the spirit of the maxim, proceeded to do their best to put it in force. The result has been an exciting legal contest between the State authorities and the Southern Railroad, backed by the authority of the federal courts as represented by Judge Jeter C. Pritchard of the Circuit Court. The State and the railroad have arrived at a temporary settlement providing for the enforcement of the rate law pending the final disposition of the case by the Supreme Court of the United States. The attitude of Judge Pritchard tends to put the States in an embarrassing position. If they do not legislate to control corporations, they will, says Mr. Root, forfeit all right to legislate at all. If they do legislate, says Judge Pritchard, their laws will be enjoined, pending the final disposition of the case. Surely a dilemma worthy of consideration. A somewhat widespread misapprehension of Judge Pritchard's position is observable in the lay press. Judge Pritchard spoke of the fines levied by the State for infractions of its rate law as confiscatory in their character. His view of the case was based of course on the Fourteenth Amendment, which forbids the taking of property without due process of law. It is assumed in some quarters that his statements as to excessive fines were based on the prohibition of excessive fines in the Eighth Amendment. It is, of course, a fundamental principle that the first ten amendments limit only the powers of the national government and do not affect the States. This has never been disputed since the decision of Barron *v.* Baltimore, 7 Pet. (U. S.) 243.

JUDGE LANDIS'S unprecedented fine inflicted on the Standard Oil Company in the rebate cases has been the subject of much comment. And yet it seems as if in imposing a fine of $29,000,000 on the Standard Oil, Judge Landis was but treating that company as he would have treated an individual convicted of some wilful infraction of law. Because the cases reveal a number of deliberate wrongs instead of one, the contention seems to be that the punishment ought to have been lessened — a wholesale rate established for violating law. Now a portion of the press comes out with pleas for the innocent and unhappy stockholders who are made to suffer for the faults of others. In sentencing a man to the penitentiary for theft Judge Landis is reported to have said: "The everlasting pity is that the real punishment in cases like this falls on innocent people" — the man had a family. "It does seem as though every man who comes here has a wife and children and an old mother — babies and gray hairs." Yet the public recognizes the necessity of punishing wrong-doing, although the weight of the punishment must fall in part on the innocent. Perhaps, however, if the present fine is affirmed by the higher courts, and it is collected from stockholders, the stockholders might have a remedy over against the really guilty persons. It would make an interesting question. Capital, too, is represented as shaking in its boots and deserting our shores, on account of such vigorous punishment of corporate wrongdoing. This is something which ought to have been considered by the legislature before the law was enacted. The court's duty is to administer the laws as it finds them written on the statute books. If such punishment results in the withdrawal of capital, it only shows that in our complex civilization the wrongdoing of one set of men must affect more or less the whole community. So the overbearing and high-handed attitude in the past of certain railroads has engendered an attitude toward them on the part of the public which is leading to severe legislation, legislation which may temporarily injure the community. But the corporate and trust interests which in the days of their power were overbearing, readily find channels for such pleas for mercy when their wrongdoing finds them out.

The constitutionality of the New York law under which Mr. Hearst is seeking a re-examination by the courts of the results of the New York mayoralty election of 1905 has been affirmed by the Appellate Division, and yet we may say that the law emerges from the contest in much worse condition than it entered. The matter first came before the Appellate Division of the Second Department, in Brooklyn, and the constitutionality of the law was affirmed by a majority of one, Mr. Justice Gaynor writing the opinion of the court, and declaring that the statute did not cast upon the court ministerial duties. The re-count proceedings in New York city proper came before the Appellate Division of the First Department a few days later. That court was unanimously of opinion that the law was unconstitutional, and they approved the dissenting opinion in the Brooklyn case. Yet in spite of their views, they formally upheld the law out of respect for their brethren of the Second Department. Of course, the matter goes immediately to the Court of Appeals. In his dissenting opinion in the Second Department, Mr. Justice Jenks said: "There is no judicial power to review because there is nothing to review — the original returns are entirely superseded. There are no parties before the court asking for judicial action, which shall determine the relative rights of the litigants upon the facts, and in accordance with law expressed in a judgment or in a decree. There is no ministerial act of a board of officers up before the court for review. The proceeding does not rest upon any complaint for fraud, violation of law or statute, or dispute which is not abated so long as all of the candidates do not acquiesce in the count and canvass made. Dissatisfaction with the result thereof has led to this statute. And so the court is now called upon for reasons of convenience, and I think of public confidence, as counter and canvasser only, and not to reach a result by the exercise either of the broader powers conferred by the statute or its general judicial powers. After all, the predominant consideration is that, whatever the nature of the recount or the canvass, whether judicial or *quasi*-judicial, or ministerial, the constitution commands that the count and canvass at an election shall be made by bipartisan agents. The policy or the purpose of this legislation is not our concern, any more than the policy of any candidate who seeks or opposes this proceeding. Legal objection calls for legal adjudication, and with that made we reach our limitations."

We derive from the Milwaukee *Sentinel* the interesting details of a momentous litigation in progress in the city of Denver. Mr. Sherman Goodwin is a gentleman earning four dollars a day, and there is also a Mrs. Sherman Goodwin. Looking around for eligible accommodations, chance brought to him stories of the elegant and homelike character of the boarding-house which is the scene of these happenings — the landlady's name is omitted for obvious reasons. Perhaps previous experience in refined boarding-houses had created an atmosphere of general and gloomy suspicion in Mr. Goodwin's mind. Perhaps it was something in the appearance of this particular establishment, when Mr. Goodwin went thither to engage a room, which influenced his conduct. At any rate, on the occasion of that initial visit he was moved to declare in emphatic language his utter abhorrence of *cimex lectuarius*, his ways, and all his places of harborage. With energy the implied imputation was resented, and the landlady haughtily and recklessly offered to refund him every cent of board if he or Mrs. Goodwin found one of the horrid creatures about their bed. Relying on these representations — who could doubt in the presence of so much ingenious indignation? — he selected a room, paid a week in advance, and he and Mrs. Goodwin moved in with their trunks. In the still watches of the night, when honeyed sleep, bolstered on the landlady's fair promises, had settled over the occupants of the room, Mr. Goodwin was awakened by a detested, but, alas! a familiar sensation. He recognized it as the bite of *cimex*. Mr. Goodwin was a man of decision and presence of mind. Instantly he sprang from bed, struck a light, and turned over the pillow. He discovered, says the *Sentinel*, "thousands of the busy creatures holding a mass convention under the pillows, preparatory to advancing in force." The emergency was a time for action. Hastily arousing Mrs. Goodwin, they fled for their lives, leaving behind their trunks, and hunted up another boarding-house. Let us hope that rest for the remainder of the night was unbroken. Next day Mr. Goodwin came for the trunks and to secure the return, as per the landlady's promise, of the board paid in advance.

She refused to refund, and Mr. Goodwin is seeking balm for his wounded feelings in a damage suit for a broken night's rest, laying the damages at twenty-five dollars. The cruel suggestion is made that twenty-five dollars is an excessive amount of damages for the broken rest of a gentleman earning only four dollars a day. But the effect on his health of the shock and fright and the hasty flight by night ought to be considered, and the landlady will escape luckily if Mrs. Goodwin does not bring a similar suit.

THE practical character and importance of the issues involved in this case are carefully pointed out in the newspaper from which we have quoted. "If the contention of Mr. Goodwin is borne out by the courts it will establish a precedent which will be, must be viewed with alarm by all proprietors of lodging-houses, whether they harbor bedbugs in their sleeping apartments or not. For if a man can collect damages from his landlady for broken rest, there is no limit to the possibilities of these suits. For instance, if the star boarder is deprived of some hours of sleep by the concert of cats in the back yard, he can institute a damage suit against the landlady. If the people in the adjoining house disturb the slumbers of the young man in the hall bedroom, obviously he may sue for damages, perhaps including the neighbors as parties defendant. If the landlady's daughter insists on practicing on the piano or taking vocal exercises in the early morning hours, he will not have to change his boarding place as is done nowadays, but will promptly have his hostess summoned into court and mulcted in damages for his lost slumber." It is readily seen that this case, if contested through the courts with the determination which its importance deserves, may become as leading an authority on the relation of landlady and boarder as the other great bedbug case in the books, Smith *v.* Marrable, 11 M. & W. 5, is on the relation of landlord and tenant. That case is the leading authority on implied conditions in leases of furnished houses. Sir Thomas Marrable rented for five weeks a furnished house from Mr. Smith. The Marrables moved in, but found it impossible to sleep because of the attentions of *cimex lectuarius*. The discussion between the Smiths and the Marrables waxed hot, and, as befitted the domestic character of the issue, the gentlemen retired from the field and left Lady Marrable to pen a note informing "Mrs. Smith that it is her determination to leave the house in Brunswick Place as soon as she can take another," as all the bedrooms "are so infested with bugs that it is impossible to remain." There was a suit for the rent for the remainder of the term, and the court instructed that when one lets a house it is upon the implied condition that it shall be habitable, and the jury found for the defendant on the ground that the premises were so beset with bugs as not to be habitable. Hard cases make bad laws, they say, and this case has been distinguished and pared down again and again, and yet when a tenant moves out on account of smoky chimneys, leaky roofs, defective furnaces, etc., his lawyers always cite Smith *v.* Marrable and the doctrine of "constructive eviction."

EFFECT OF NEGOTIABLE INSTRUMENTS LAW ON LIABILITY OF THE SURETY.

A RECENT decision involving an important point on the law of negotiable instruments, as affected by the Negotiable Instruments Law, comes from the Supreme Court of Oregon. Cellars *v.* Meachem, (April 9, 1907) 89 Pac. Rep. 426. It is here held that a person who signs his name to a note as accommodation maker, adding the word "surety" to his signature, is not released by the subsequent act of the payee in making a binding agreement with the principal for an extension of time to the principal. This extraordinary conclusion is based on the ground (1) that the surety is primarily liable on the instrument, and (2) that the section of the Negotiable Instruments Law enumerating the modes by which a negotiable instrument may be discharged does not refer to the discharge of a surety by extension of time to the principal, while the section enumerating the modes by which a person secondarily liable may be discharged does mention this mode of discharge. The failure to mention this mode of discharge in the one case and the express enumeration of it in the other is taken to signify a legislative intent that such discharge shall be recognized only where the person setting up the defense is secondarily liable.

The decision will, no doubt, come as a surprise to practitioners generally, and the writer of this note is of the impression that a mistake has been made. It may be admitted that the court was right in saying that under the language of the act a surety who signs as accommodation maker is primarily liable in the sense that he is "absolutely required to pay the same;" for section 192 (as the law was originally sectionized) reads as follows: "The person primarily liable on an instrument is the person who by the terms of the instrument is absolutely required to pay the same. All other parties are secondarily liable."

The second proposition on which the decision is based is the one which is most easily subject to criticism. Section 119 of the Negotiable Instruments Law (as originally sectionized) being section 4521, B. & C. Compilation of Oregon statutes, provides as follows: "A negotiable instrument is discharged (1) by payment in due course by or on behalf of the principal debtor; (2) by payment in due course by the party accommodated, where the instrument is made or accepted for accommodation; (3) by the intentional cancellation thereof by the holder; (4) by any other act which will discharge a simple contract for the payment of money; (5) when the principal debtor becomes the holder of the instrument at or after the maturity in his own right."

Section 4522, B. & C. Comp. (being almost the same as section 120 of the original Negotiable Instruments Law) reads thus: "A person secondarily liable on the instrument is discharged (1) by any act which discharges the instrument; (2) by the intentional cancellation of his signature by the holder; (3) by the discharge of a prior party; (4) by a valid tender of payment made by a prior party; (5) by a release of the principal debtor, unless the holder's right of recourse against the party secondarily liable is expressly reserved; (6) by any agreement binding upon the holder to extend the time of payment, or to postpone the holder's right to enforce the instrument, unless made with the assent of the party secondarily liable, or unless the right of recourse against such party is expressly reserved."

The court in reaching its conclusion laid great stress on the circumstance that the defense arising from an extension of time to the principal is enumerated in section 4522, B. & C., but not in section 4521, B. & C. *Expressio unius est exclusio alterius.* The allowance of this defense to a party secondarily liable is necessarily a denial of it, so the court reasoned, to a person primarily liable. This interpretation does violence to what we believe to be the plain meaning of the statute, and it introduces, of course, a decidedly undesirable change in the pre-existing law. The court did not discuss the meaning to be given to subdivision (4) of section 119, wherein it is provided that an instrument may be discharged "*by any other act which will discharge a simple contract for the payment of money.*" What does this mean if it does not include such a discharge as has always been held to result to the surety where an extension of time is made to the principal? This subdivision was evidently inserted for the very purpose of covering contingencies that were not and could not be foreseen by the codifier. The contract of suretyship is a simple contract, and the making of a binding agreement for the extension of time to the principal debtor has long been held to be an "act" sufficient to discharge the simple contract of the surety. Clearly, we should say, this defense is as certainly included in the general language of subdivision (4) of section 4521, B. & C., as it is expressly enunciated in subdivision (6) of the succeeding section. This conclusion seems so plain and such good common sense that one is at a loss to see how a different conclusion could commend itself to the judicial mind. That the court was right in the view it took of this question we cannot believe, and yet we are confounded by the circumstance that the Supreme Court of Maryland has, in a case where the point was not necessary to the decision, expressed the same view as the Oregon court. See Vanderford *v.* Farmers' Bank, 66 Atl. Rep. 47.

The vice of interpretation exhibited in these two cases consists of what, for the sake of novelty, we may call the fallacy of imputed omniscience. This fallacy of interpretation consists of imputing to the legislative mind a power of insight, comprehension, and foresight transcending the ordinary human faculties. It is assumed not only that the legislature in passing an act foresees all the possible contingencies which may arise under the act and provides for them, but also that the legislative mind is so far omniscient as to make its expression in the legislative act square with all the petty canons of interpretation which have been wrought out by courts and legal scholars. It should on the contrary be remembered that the legislative mind consists only of ordinary human faculties striving to give expression to finite human thoughts. Rules of interpretation must not be taken to be inflexible. They are merely helpful as pointing to general truths, and they must not be arbitrarily applied. Human expression in language is an expression of the infinite variety of the workings of the human mind, and it cannot be reduced to any unchangeable canons of interpretation. In the bankruptcy proceeding of *In re* Baudouine, (1899) 96 Fed. Rep. 536, 539, 540, the court, in construing the Bankruptcy Act, refused to apply the maxim *expressio unius exclusio alterius* under conditions apparently much more favorable to its application than exist in this case.

In the light of this suggestion and in the light of common sense, it is easy to see how it happened that the draftsman of the act enumerated this defense specifically in section 4522, B. & C., but did not enumerate it in section 4521. He was simply betrayed by the deeply imbedded notion — a part of the intellectual equipment of every lawyer — that the obligation of the surety is a secondary obligation, and that when he is liable at all he is secondarily liable. Therefore it was quite natural to enumerate this defense specifically only in section 4522, without any mental advertence to the other remote provision of the statute which makes the surety primarily liable. The defense is, we insist, clearly allowable under the general language of subsection 4 of the preceding section, and there is no evidence whatever of an intention on the part of the draftsman, or, if you please, of a legislative intent, to abolish any defense on the part of the surety or any other party which the law has hitherto recognized.

A moral to be drawn from this episode — and it is a hint that may well be taken to heart by scholars or lawyers entrusted with the delicate and responsible business of drafting uniform laws — is this, namely, beware of giving general definitions to the particular terms used in the draft of the statute. It certainly looks neat and gives an appearance of precision to an enactment to have a general clause or section defining the technical terms used in the draft. The danger is that by defining the terms the legislature thereby applies a straight edge, as it were, to the whole act, and leaves no room for the play of judicial interpretation in rounding out the statute and giving it proper effect. If left alone the courts will have no great trouble in giving to each technical term the meaning proper in each particular context. T. A. S.

LIGHT AND SIGHT.

In a great number of cases appellate courts have been compelled to decide whether a judge or jury had reasonable ground to conclude that a person was or was not negligent in failing to observe an approaching train or car or an engine, because of darkness, or because smoke, steam, snow, rain, or fog, etc., obstructed his view; or in failing seasonably to perceive locomotive or electric car headlights or vessels' lights for similar reasons, or because other lights dazzled his eyes or confused him. The cases are so numerous that we will not attempt to consider them in this article, but confine ourselves to a few of the hundreds of other and miscellaneous cases relating to light and sight which are found in the books. Suffice it to say that, whereas in the trial court it is incumbent on a party having the burden of proof to convince the trier of facts of the validity of his contention, a judgment or verdict will ordinarily be sustained if it appears to the reviewing tribunal that the successful party made out a case sufficient to cause reasonable men to *differ* if they should not concur with him. And it is the tendency of the judicial mind to follow precedents even on questions of fact.

In his fascinating treatise on the "Art of Cross-Examination," Francis L. Wellman says perjury is "undoubtedly on the increase." Mr. Justice Gaynor, of the New York Supreme Court, declares that "it has grown rapidly during the past twenty years." (*Bench and Bar*, January, 1907, p. 15.)

The fact was made the subject of the annual address to the New York Bar Association by President Whitaker a few years ago. Nevertheless, no rule for weighing testimony is so frequently applied and is the parent of so many subsidiary rules as that which forbids the imputation of perjury without strong evidence of it. "That, in the course of my long experience, both at the bar and on the bench, has been the argument that I have always found to be the most powerful in obtaining a conclusion from the court and jury, according to the contention of the party urging it," said Lord Brougham. M'Gregor *v.* Topham, 3 H. L. Cas. 132, 148, 10 Eng. (Reprint) 51, 56. But where a witness is biased, no matter how exalted his character, and it is possible that he was mistaken, an experienced judge never hesitates to abate something from the face value of his testimony if necessary to reconcile it with credible testimony of neutral witnesses or with proved circumstances.

"No doubt the eyes of some witnesses are livelier than those of others, and the sense of sight may be quickened or diminished by the interest or bias of him who possesses it," said Judge Danforth, of the New York Court of Appeals. O'Neill *v.* New York, etc., R. Co., 115 N. Y. 579, 583, 22 N. E. Rep. 217. "Men are prone to see what they want to see." Ideal Stopper Co. *v.* Crown Cork & Seal Co., (C. C. A.) 131 Fed. Rep. 244, 255, *per* Brawley, D. J. In a case not at this moment at the writer's hand, Lord Stowell remarked that such witnesses "see with sharp eyes and bear with keen ears." *Per contra*, their senses are sometimes dulled in subservience to their bias; not actually, perhaps, but they very readily lose faith in the accuracy of their observation, and their testimony suffers accordingly. They become prodigiously conscientious, and do not speak affirmatively and positively unless they are absolutely certain. If they have a substantial doubt, why trouble the court with it? Better to say No outright, they reason. Judicial explanations, from a psychological viewpoint, of distortion in testimony by reason of bias not amounting to deliberate mendacity appear frequently in the reports.

Prepossession of witnesses is a kindred phenomenon. If they observed something under a strong conviction of what was the actual fact they are apt to have seen things through the medium of their belief. When the virgins in the palace Beautiful directed Christian to look towards Immanuel's Land he saw "at a great distance" not only "a most pleasant mountainous country, beautified with woods, vineyards, fruits of all sorts," but by inference naturally assumed as reality "flowers also, with springs and fountains, very delectable to behold." (Bunyan's Pilgrim's Progress.) In an article on "Illusions of Memory" (*Scribner's Magazine*, February, 1892, p. 188), Dr. Wm. H. Burnham, of Clark University, says "the researches of modern psychologists, notably those of Helmholtz, have shown how largely inference enters into perceptions of sight and hearing," and that "in fact the very woof of our perceptive life is made up of a simple form of inference." So, Polonius saw as Hamlet bade him:

Hamlet. — Do you see yonder cloud that's almost in the shape of a camel?
Polonius. — By the mass, and 'tis like a camel, indeed.
Hamlet. — Methinks it is like a weasel.
Polonius. — It is backed like a weasel.
Hamlet. — Or like a whale?
Polonius. — Very like a whale.

Hamlet, Act III., sc. 2.

It was the "bloody business" acting upon "the heat-oppressed brain" that made Macbeth exclaim:

Mine eyes are made the fools o' the other senses.

Macbeth, Act II., sc. 1.

Retroactive attention giving the same assurance of correctness of observation as primary attention has been noticed by courts in several cases. On the same principle retroactive prepossession may operate upon an observer's recollection of things seen. Thus Prescott, describing a fierce battle between Cortez and his soldiers and the Aztecs in the City of Mexico, says (italics ours): "More than one grave historian refers the preservation of the Spaniards to the watchful care of their patron apostle, St. James, who, in these desperate conflicts, was beheld careering on his milk-white steed at the head of the Christian squadrons, with his sword flashing lightning, while a lady robed in white — supposed to be the Virgin — was distinctly seen by his side, throwing dust in the eyes of the infidel! The fact is attested both by Spaniards and Mexicans — *by the latter after their conversion to Christianity.*" (Conquest of Mexico, book V, c. ii.)

Upon the question whether an engineer of a railroad train was negligent in not detecting a person walking on the track on a clear moonlight night, the circumstance that the ground was covered with snow and that the pedestrian was a tall woman dressed in black was not overlooked by the appellate court when holding that the trial court erred in withdrawing the case from the jury on the assumption that there was no negligence. Brown *v.* Boston, etc., R. Co., (N. H. 1906) 64 Atl. Rep. 194. Evidence that a child run over by a locomotive was clothed in white with red ribbons on her dress had an obvious relevancy in determining whether the engineer was careless. Dennis *v.* New Orleans, etc., R. Co., (Miss. 1902) 32 So. Rep. 914. The difference between scarlet and red, when the colors are placed in juxtaposition, is quite noticeable; ballots of the one color side by side with those of the other should be readily distinguished by official counters of votes. *Re* Sinclair and Town of Owen Sound, 12 Ontario Law Rep. 488, 504.

Whether a traveler at a railroad crossing looking up a straight track in the sunshine could distinctly see a train approaching at a distance of a mile or more might possibly depend upon the position of the sun. See Stowell *v.* Erie R. Co., (C. C. A.) 98 Fed. Rep. 520, 523. It is well known that at the famous battle of Crecy the afternoon sun shone so brightly in the eyes of the French crossbowmen as they advanced towards the English that they could not take accurate aim. Was not this historical fact overlooked by Scott when he wrote his brilliant description of the attack upon the castle of Front-de-Boeuf, in "Ivanhoe"? Rebecca is asked what device the Black Knight bears upon his shield.

"Something resembling a bar of iron, and a padlock painted blue on the black shield," she replied.

"A fetterlock and shacklebolt azure," said Ivanhoe; "I know not who may bear the device, but well I ween it might now be mine own. Canst thou not see the motto?"

"Scarce the device itself at this distance," replied Rebecca; "but when the sun glances fair upon the shield, it shows as I tell you."

If the sun glanced upon the shield, wasn't it shining in the faces of the archers? And yet they shot with such precision that "no point at which a defender could show the least part of his person escaped their clothyard shafts." It is not impossible that Scott made a slip here, for although he was a lawyer, credulity itself could hardly be imposed upon by his assertion in another part of the story that Rowena failed to recognize Ivanhoe when they were conversing face to face at Rotherwood, while she recognized him at the tournament a few days later the instant his helmet was removed! It would take a well-seasoned and hardy advocate to ask a jury to believe that.

In a case of collision in the night-time between a steamer and a steam tug which had a steamboat in tow at her side, both having regulation side lights burning, it was contended that there were no staff lights on the tug indicating her tow and no masthead lights to indicate that either was a steamer. But the testimony on these points was conflicting. The moon at the time of collision was nearly two hours high, and a distinguished federal judge said that this might possibly have made the tow lights less sharply visible, but that an approaching vessel had sufficient opportunity to see that the tug and tow were steamboats long before they were within 300 or 400 feet of each other. The Eagle, 69 Fed. Rep. 157, *per* Brown D. J.

> *Portia.* — That light we see is burning in my hall.
> How far that little candle throws his beams!
> *Nerissa.* — When the moon shone we did not see the candle.
> *Portia.* — So doth the greater glory dim the less.
> *The Merchant of Venice*, Act V., sc. 1.

It is possible that the glare of moonlight upon a man's coat may be mistaken by witnesses for color and lead them to believe that the man's dark coat was a light one. Jefferds *v.* People, 5 Park. Crim. (N. Y.) 539, where Recorder Hoffman reminded the jury that any testimony at all upon the question of identity coming from people who have merely a glimpse of a man running in the moonlight, under the exciting circumstances attending a pursuit, is to be looked at cautiously and subjected to the most careful scrutiny. However, Scott says:

> To the squire's hand the rein he threw,
> And spoke no word as he withdrew;
> But yet the moonlight did betray
> The falcon-crest was soiled wth clay;
> And plainly might Fitz-Eustace see,
> By stains upon the charger's knee
> And his left side, that on the moor
> He had not kept his footing sure.
> *Marmion*, Canto Third, XXXI.

In his essay on "Unity in Religion," Lord Bacon says: "There be also two false peaces or unities; the one, when the peace is grounded upon an implicit ignorance; *for all colors will agree in the dark.*" In the course of a university commencement address, last June, Senator Foraker characterized much of the testimony taken by the Senate committee in the Brownsville raid investigation as worthless. Continuing, he said: "Various people said they heard the shooting, went to their windows, looked out into a night of unusual darkness, and at a distance ranging all the way from 25 feet up to 150 feet saw the men who were doing the firing, and recognized them as negroes wearing the uniform of United States soldiers. All the officers of the battalion, in addition to everything else they said in favor of their men, testified that the night was so dark that it was impossible to tell a colored man from a white man without the aid of artificial light, at a distance of ten to twelve feet. Major Penrose testified that he could not tell his officers, who were white, from his enlisted men, who were colored, ten feet away from him, and that he could not tell at that distance from him anything about clothing. The testimony of every other officer was to the same effect. These officers were all intelligent, honorable, high-minded men." (*The Sun*, June 21, 1907.) It was observed in a New York murder case that the defendant immediately after entering a dimly lighted inside room used as a morgue could not have identified the features of a corpse therein, and especially not the color of an overcoat on the body; so that his exclamation professing to identify the coat as that of the deceased was highly suspicious. People *v.* Ciardi, (N. Y. Ct. App. 1907) 80 N. E. Rep. 925.

A flash of lightning on a dark night may give such a perfect view of a person as to enable another who has previously seen him to recognize him on the instant. Ackerson *v.* People, 124 Ill. 563, 16 N. E. Rep. 847.

"Stand back in the shadow. No one can see beyond the light of a fire," said Rudyard Kipling's Kim to the Lama. (Kim, c. v.) An electric arc light casting its rays across a street railway track would make it difficult for a motorman on a car to see a wagon on the track in the darkness beyond the glare of the light. Abbott *v.* Kansas City Elec. R. Co., (Mo. App. 1906) 97 S. W. Rep. 198, *per* Ellison, J.

> *Biron.* — Light seeking light doth light of light beguile.
> *Love's Labour's Lost*, Act I., sc. 1.

So, the greater glare of a torchlight on a steamer may have obscured to those on board the steamer the lesser light of a lantern on a flatboat near the river shore where the steamer was attempting to land. Culbertson *v.* The Southern Belle, 1 Newb. (U. S.) 461, 6 Fed. Cas. No. 3,462. The engineer of an engine backing in the night might not observe a lantern on the ground ahead of him at a place illuminated by the lights of a train passing on another track. Baltimore, etc., R. Co. *v.* State, 101 Md. 359, 61 Atl. Rep. 189. It is not impossible that a person at a railroad crossing on a very dark night would confuse the headlight of a locomotive coming at high speed with the light shining through the car windows of a train passing it, and thus not discover the locomotive in time to escape. Seely *v.* New York Cent., etc., R. Co., 8 N. Y. App. Div. 402, 405, 40 N. Y. Supp. 866, 868. Lights of an electric car passing another "would naturally cause some confusion to a person about to cross the track," and might cause him to overlook the one that was approaching and close at hand. Morris *v.* Metropolitan St. R. Co., 63 N. Y. App. Div. 78, 71 N. Y. Supp. 321.

In the Valley of the Shadow of Death, Bunyan's Pilgrim found "the pathway was here so dark that ofttimes when he lift up his foot, he knew not where or upon what he should set it next." So, too, "the way of the wicked is as darkness; they know not at what they stumble." Proverbs iv. 19. A passenger alighting from a train in a dark tunnel might suppose he was stepping onto a platform and not perceive that he was landing on a heap of rubbish. Bridges *v.* North London R. Co., L. R. 7 Eng. & Ir. App. Cas. 223, 227. A jury would be at liberty to infer that a stranger riding in an elevator car not brightly lighted was free from fault in failing to observe a space eighteen inches wide between the elevator floor and the wall before stepping backwards and falling into it. Gray *v.* Siegel-Cooper Co., (N. Y. Ct. App. 1907) 80 N. E. Rep. 201.

Mingled lights and shadows have been responsible for many serious accidents and resulting litigation. When alighting passengers are stepping over a space between a car and a station platform, if the station lights are in front of them the foremost passengers will cast a shadow behind so that those following will not be able to see clearly where they are stepping. Fox *v.* New York, 5 N. Y. App. Div. 349, 39 N. Y. Supp. 309.

> Shadows are but privations of the light;
> Yet, when we walk they shoot before the sight;
> With us approach, retire, arise, and fall;
> Nothing themselves, and yet expressing all.
> *Dryden, Epistle to Sir Godfrey Kneller.*

A shadow cast upon the track by an elevator in front of an electric light might prevent a person from seeing a dark train approaching. Jenkins *v.* Baltimore, etc., R. Co., 98 Md. 402, 56 Atl. Rep. 966. The fact that a defect in a sidewalk was in the shadow of a tree, although not far from a street light, might be material in determining whether a finding that a pedestrian exercised due care was supported by the evidence. North Peoria *v.* Rogers, 98 Ill. App. 355. Moonlight may throw the shade of moving box cars over another track so as to obscure a person walking thereon and prevent the engineer of an approaching locomotive from perceiving him. Shaber *v.* St. Paul, etc., R. Co., 28 Minn. 103, 9 N. W. Rep. 575.

When a person passes from light into darkness his ability to see his environments plainly will be much diminished until his eyes become gauged to the changed condition. Corcoran *v.* New York, (N. Y. Ct. App.) 80 N. E. Rep. 660, where an automobile sped from a well lighted street into a dimly lighted cul-de-sac. It is reasonable to suppose that a person coming from sunlight out of doors into the comparative darkness of a hallway could not see at all at first, although when he fell down a flight of stairs those within the building who went to his relief had no difficulty in seeing him and his surroundings. Brugher *v.* Buchtenkirch, 187 N. Y. 153, 60 N. E. Rep. 420. There are many similar cases in the reports.

Charles C. Moore.

RECOLLECTIONS OF A PRACTITIONER.

Written for *Law Notes* by Judge JOHN S. WILKES, of the Supreme Court of Tennessee.

I REMEMBER distinctly the first lawsuit that it was my proud distinction to appear in. It was in 1866. My client was charged with stealing a coat. He was arrested and carried for trial before two country justices of the peace. The evidence in the case was plain; he was seen to take the coat, and it was found upon him, and taken from his person on the public road. His only defense, on the merits, was that he had won it in a game of craps. He had no evidence on this point, however, beyond his own testimony.

The trial commenced early in the morning, and continued throughout the day. There were numerous objections to evidence and to all steps taken in the case. After a heated day's trial, in the middle of the summer, with a large audience in attendance, the case was continued until eight o'clock the next morning; and all parties separated until that time, the prisoner in the custody of the constable.

At eight o'clock the next morning the prisoner and his counsel were present, but neither the prosecutor nor his attorney had arrived. An hour passed by, and still no prosecution appeared The attorney for defendant moved for the defendant's discharge, under the statute applicable alone to civil cases, providing that neither party should be required to wait for more than one hour from the time appointed for trial. The justices, after consulting, decided that the statute applied, and the prisoner was discharged. He borrowed the constable's horse, and went at a full run down the public pike.

About the same time the prosecutor and his attorney appeared from the opposite direction, coming under whip and spur. When they arrived they were informed that the justices had waited the required time, and that the prisoner had been discharged. To this counsel and prosecutor entered vigorous protests; and thereupon the justices, after conferring together, said: "Maybe we have done wrong; but we will hear argument on it." Argument was accordingly made, which occupied some two hours. In the meantime, the prisoner, on the constable's horse, had gone some ten or twelve miles.

Counsel for the prosecutor thereupon said that, inasmuch as the prisoner had gone off with the coat, and had taken the constable's horse, and there was no way to catch him, he would dismiss the prosecution.

I received no fee in this case.

My second venture was equally notable. My client had charged his neighbor with killing one of his cows for beef purposes. The meat was found in the possession of the accused, and was brought to the trial. There was no way whatever to identify it. The defendant had a large number of friends, armed to the teeth, and they were determined that their friend should not be convicted. The trial was before one of the same magistrates heretofore spoken of. The prosecutor had no one on his side, except myself, as his friend. The situation looked "squally" for me, and equally "squally" to the justice of the peace. The magistrate took me to one side, and asked me what I was going to do, and he advised me not to go to trial. I left the matter with him, and he suggested that I convert the suit into a replevin case, and let the defendant prove and take the beef. I was more than willing to do this, under the circumstances.

Then came up the question of costs. The old justice of the peace suggested that they were all old friends and neighbors, and that he would have the beef barbecued, and there would be no costs in the case. This was also very acceptable to all parties, and the barbecue went on. In the meantime I slipped to one side and "went on" also, and left the parties to enjoy their barbecue and picnic among themselves.

I got the same fee in this case as I did in the previous one.

At that time I had my office with the sheriff of the county. He had arrested a man under suspicious circumstances. After keeping him confined for a week, he advised me to apply to the judge for a writ of habeas corpus to get him out of jail, as there was no proof against him whatever. I applied to the judge for the writ, and it was returned for a certain day before the circuit judge at Columbia, about thirty miles distant from Pulaski, where I was practicing law. The sheriff sent the prisoner, under my custody, to Columbia, and sent along by me his return upon the writ, which was about in these words: "I ain't got this man. I done give him up. And I don't want him no more." The circuit judge promptly released him. Fee same as before.

In a county not far from this, a summons was placed in the hands of a constable to execute against William Jones, alias Smith. The constable, after keeping this summons for several weeks, returned it as "duly served on William Jones, but that Alias Smith was not to be found in the county, and that no such man had ever lived in the county."

About the year 1870 or 1875 the dockets of the Supreme Court of Tennessee were very much crowded, and the judges adopted the plan of deciding all cases practicable from the bench on oral presentation of the attorneys. At the same time, no assignments of error were required, and it was altogether uncertain and problematic what would be the case when it was presented to the court. Counsel were not restricted to the points made in the court below, and wandered off on all questions that they thought might influence the court. Of course, the discussion took wide range, and was much abused.

On one occasion Chief Justice Nicholson took occasion to lecture the bar upon the wide range of their arguments and the inconsistent positions taken. After giving his lecture, in his peculiar and impressive way, he proceeded to say that the abuse had gone so far that it was very frequently impossible for the court to determine which side the counsel represented. Mr. Spurlock, a bright mountain lawyer, sitting at the bar in front of the court, arose very deferentially and said: "If the court please, is that the fault of the court or of the bar?" Mr. Nicholson had no further comments to make.

During this period of quick disposition of cases, a noted lawyer was presenting his case, which was that of damages against a railroad for running down his client with an engine without exercising any statutory or other precaution. He had lost his case in the court below, and was progressing with the presentation of his appeal, and insisting that the road should have given his client notice, by whistling or otherwise, of the engine's approach. He imagined that he was making a very deep impression upon the court, when to his surprise the chief justice announced that the judgment of the court below must be affirmed.

Thereupon counsel said to the court: "I think that you ought to have given me some notice, and not run over me, as the engine did over my client, without warning."

The chief justice replied: "We would have given the warning if we had observed any obstruction on the track."

Criminal cases were disposed of as expeditiously as civil cases, when they had no merit in them. On one occasion, a prominent lawyer from a distant State was in the court room, on the invitation of a local attorney, to see and observe the court's proceedings. A capital case was called, and, there being no merits or bill of exceptions, counsel for the defendant presented his plea for mercy, and left the matter in the hands of the court. The judgment of the court below was promptly affirmed. The chief justice thereupon called the marshal of the court to him, and whispered something in his ear, and the marshal hurriedly retired from the court room to the clerk's office.

The visiting brother by this time had become decidedly nervous, and inquired of his friend as to what they were going to do. His friend replied: "Well, they have just affirmed the case, and now they have sent the marshal out to get the rope to hang him." The visitor insisted upon leaving at once, and his friend could not prevail on him to stay. On going into the clerk's office they met the marshal with a calendar in his hand, which the chief justice had sent for in order to fix the date of execution. The visiting brother, however, continued to go, and had no desire to witness any short ceremonies that might take place.

A damage suit was on trial, and the attorney for the railway had argued that the headlight was bright, that a good lookout was kept, that the bell was rung, and in fact everything was done to prevent the collision.

Counsel, in reply, quoted the following:

"The lightning bug is a wonderful sight;
You'd think he had no mind;
He plumps about in the darkest night,
With his headlight on behind.
He hit the owl between the eyes,
And is it not strange to tell,
He began to bow and apologize,
And swore he'd rung the bell."

While the court was disposing of cases from the bench, a prominent lawyer had a very important case, involving, as he thought, a very difficult and delicate question. His adversary had presented the opposite side of the case, and had evidently made a favorable impression. Counsel was proceeding to argue the case in reply, when he was interrupted by frequent questions from one of the members of the court. He stood this for a little while, until he became convinced that the mind of the court was made up, and that he was going to lose his case. The judges had asked him several times to explain certain matters, referring to him as "learned counsel." Seeing the inevitable drift, the attorney paused in his argument and said: "If your honors please, I see that I am going to gain the appellation of 'learned counsel' in this case, while my opponent is going to gain his suit. All that I ask of your honors is that you give me anything to which I am entitled, and I shall make no further remarks." To which one of the judges replied: "That is fair; nothing remains but the costs, and you can pay that."

On another occasion a prominent and very intelligent young lawyer from Memphis had an important case before the Supreme Court. He was somewhat frightened, and not altogether sure of his ground. He had prepared his case with great care and elaboration; had his line of argument written out, and was following it very closely. He had progressed only a short way, when the chief justice interrupted him with a question. This he answered promptly, and immediately returned to the thread of his prepared argument. He had gone but little further before he was interrupted again by another question, to which he made answer, and immediately returned to the thread of his argument. In a short time he was interrupted a third time by a question, which it was difficult for him to answer; but he did make answer and explanation, and then leaned forward to the court, and said to the chief justice: "I did the best I could with that question, but I will be very much obliged to you if you won't make any further collateral attack on me while I am arguing this case." Needless to say he was allowed to have his way in the balance of his argument.

The Supreme Court sits at Jackson, for the western division of Tennessee, and for forty years had for its porter a negro named Napoleon, familiarly called "Nap." "Nap" was a typical negro, six feet and a half tall, and could neither read nor write. He never had any difficulty, however, in distributing the records among the different judges as they were indicated to go. After one of the elections, two new judges made their appearance at Jackson to be sworn in. The lawyers had assembled before the court met, and they inquired of "Nap" if he had met the new judges, and what they looked like. He said that he "had seed them, but that he hadn't sized them up yet. One of them was a good looking man, and the other one wasn't; but he couldn't tell. But both of them had brought a big lot of books with them; and he just supposed they would have to read lots, before they could ever ketch up."

For several years the marshal at Knoxville was a man who had been a farmer, a very clever, prominent, and influential man, but verging on the seventies. He never could get the formula for opening the court, and on one occasion convulsed the bench and bar by announcing: "Oh, yes! oh, yes! This Honorable Supreme Court has now met, and is ready to transact any business that it is competent to do."

Once a prisoner in the custody of the marshal made his escape while on the way between the courthouse and the jail. The old gentleman shot at him several times, but could not hit him. In coming into the presence of the court to announce the event, he remarked very solemnly: "I never had any use for a man that would treat me in any such way."

On another occasion, one of the judges of the court had rendered a humorous opinion, at which the bar was convulsed with laughter. The chief justice not being present to preserve order, the fun and noise became somewhat hilarious; when the old marshal came around in front of the bar, and, standing before the judges' desk, raised both hands, and shouted out to the audience: "Gentlemen, you must keep quiet. This is the opinion of the court, and there ain't any fun in it." This, of course, added to the uproar, very much to the mortification of the old man. At recess he came before the court and apologized for the conduct of the lawyers, saying: "I was very much ashamed of them. They had no right to make that noise, and I didn't see anything to laugh at. It looked to me like it was a good opinion, and I am ashamed of the way that they did."

The court, on one occasion, called the porter before them, and told him that if he did not stop drinking they would be compelled to discharge him. Upon being asked to make the promise to stay sober, the porter thought for a minute, and then said: "Gentlemen, I will take the case under advisement." His resignation followed later on the same day.

A very important case was pending before one of the circuit judges of this State, when the counsel on both sides were seeking every technical advantage. While the case was being presented, counsel for the prosecution saw that they were up against a knotty proposition. The court had ruled against them on various propositions, and it was very evident that, as matters were drifting, they were going to lose the case. One of the attorneys therefore arose and seriously objected to the court's proceeding further with the case; and, on being asked to state his ground of objection, he said that "The law and the constitution provided that every man should have his hearing before a judge learned in the law; and that his honor was not learned in the law; and his client was, therefore, being deprived of his constitutional rights."

This was a stunner to the trial judge; he called to one side a leading attorney, and consulted with him as to what he ought to do. The lawyer, appreciating the situation, advised him to appoint a commission, and take the testimony of all the lawyers present, and prove that he was learned in the law. To this suggestion the judge acceded, and appointed the commission; and thereupon adjourned court until the report could be made.

During the recess the judge consulted with another attorney, who advised him that the whole matter was irregular, and that he ought to fine the lawyer who had made the objection for contempt of court, and send him to jail. The judge adopted this suggestion, and immediately reconvened court. As soon as this was done, the lawyer committing the offense, finding out what had been done, and what was contemplated, arose and made an abject apology and retraction of everything that he had said in regard to the competency of the judge. The reference was thereupon set aside, and the case proceeded to trial.

The judge afterwards remarked confidentially to one of the attorneys that he was glad that the matter had taken that shape, for he didn't like the idea of that reference anyway.

One of the biggest and brainiest lawyers of east Tennessee is Colonel Y., of Sweetwater. He is as jovial and fun-loving as he is bright and able. It is his peculiar delight to get a judge "in a hole," as he expresses it, and he never lets an opportunity escape to accomplish this purpose. On one occasion he appeared before the Supreme Court of Tennessee, at a time when there were two new members recently added to the bench. These judges had been notified of Colonel Y.'s peculiarity, and warned to be on the lookout for him. He presented his case with a great deal of earnestness and ability, and noticed that one of the new judges was apparently following him very closely, and taking copious notes of his speech. When recess came, he approached the judge and said to him: "You paid my argument very close attention, and seemed to be taking full notes of it. What was there about it that so interested you?" The judge replied: "My interest was not so much in the argument as it was in a side matter. I was thinking, during the course of your argument, about how many yards of cloth it would take to make you a suit of clothes; and I was trying to figure it out on a tablet. I had gotten down twenty-five yards when you stopped your argument, and I never finished the calculation." It is needless to say that Colonel Y.'s vanity received a very severe shock, but he gave many promises that the joke should be returned with interest.

Colonel Y., on one occasion, was defending a criminal convicted of a felony. Upon the trial of the case in the court below, he introduced a witness for his client, who had theretofore been convicted of a felony, sent to the penitentiary, and rendered infamous. The State objected to his testifying, and he was ruled out as incompetent. In the subsequent progress of the case, the State put this same witness upon the stand and required him to partially undress, so as to exhibit some wounds which it was proven he had received upon the occasion of the commission of the felony. Colonel Y. objected to his being made an exhibit, and upon being required to state his ground, he said that he had been shown to be infamous, so far as his tongue was concerned, and that if his tongue was infamous he was infamous all over, and no part of his body could be made to testify.

One of the most prominent lawyers in west Tennessee was Judge B., of Memphis. Another very prominent lawyer at that bar at the same time was Colonel G. Both were learned in the law. The latter was an inveterate wag and wit, but the former did not know a joke if he met it in the public street. He was one of the most confiding and unsuspecting of men, and firmly believed that every lawyer, at least, told the truth. These two gentlemen, with other members of the bar, were, on one occasion, going on the train together from Memphis to Jackson, Tenn., to attend a session of the Supreme Court. Such trips were the occasions for all kinds of practical jokes by the lawyers upon each other. Judge B.'s wife had prepared for him an elegant lunch, as there was nothing to eat to be had between Memphis and Jackson. It was nicely packed away in a box, and carefully wrapped. Judge B. placed it for safekeeping in the rack of the passenger coach, and confided to Colonel G. what it was, and said to him that as soon as they got well under way they would take it into the back coach and enjoy it together. He then commenced to tell one of his favorite jokes to Colonel G. and the other lawyers who were gathered about him. No one could tell a joke in a more interesting manner, or get himself more completely lost in the narration of it. He had gotten fairly launched into his narrative when Colonel G. motioned to two of his companions, and they went into the rear coach and consumed the lunch with a great deal of satisfaction. They then wrapped the box up again, took it into the front coach, and put it into the rack where Judge B. had placed it. It is needless to say that nothing eatable was left in it. In the meantime Judge B. had progressed to about the middle of his narrative, when Colonel G. and his two companions resumed their places and listened to the remainder of it. After it was over, and properly enjoyed, Judge B. arose and took his box, motioning to Colonel G. to go back with him into the rear car, which he did. Judge B. then with great elaboration untied his box, and prepared a spread for the lunch; when lo and behold! there was nothing in the box to eat. Judge B. was perfectly thunderstruck, and denounced the scoundrel who had pilfered his box in unmeasured terms. After he had somewhat exhausted himself, Colonel G. said to him: "Judge B., you have forgotten. Don't you remember that we ate that lunch some time ago; that you handed it around to the lawyers in the other coach, and how much we all enjoyed it?" Judge B. declared that he had no recollection whatever of any such event; and Colonel G. offered to prove to him by the lawyers that such was the fact. He called two of them into the rear coach, and, after stating the case to them, he proposed to prove by them that they had eaten the lunch, and that they, the two associates, were present and participated in it, and that they enjoyed it very much. Judge B. thereupon, with great astonishment, asked the two lawyers if the lunch had been actually eaten as Colonel G. stated. They assured him that it had; and thereupon Judge B. arose to his feet and said: "Gentlemen, I would believe anything that a lawyer would tell me; and if you say that we ate that lunch, I will let it go at that; but I haven't the remotest recollection of any such occurrence, and I have no judicial cognizance that I have tasted a bite of it." He was, however, satisfied that the matter was as stated, and expressed satisfaction that they had enjoyed the lunch so much.

There are many events which serve to make the practice of law, and its administration from the bench, interesting and amusing; and I think that it would be well if the older members of the bench and bar would preserve many of the little episodes that take place under their daily observation.

HOWE AND HUMMEL.

Howe & Hummel were better known to the general public throughout this country than were some of the greatest lawyers of their day. The two men were better known in England than any of the famous barristers of that country were known here. Although it had some imitators, the firm was never duplicated — and never will be. It was *sui generis* and has passed away, and in its passing New York seems to have lost one of its famous institutions.

Up to 1900, when Howe & Hummel removed to the New York Life Insurance Company's building on Broadway, the former office of the firm, in the old-fashioned red brick building at the southwest corner of Centre and Leonard streets, was one of the show places of the town, standing as it did under the shadow of the old Tombs prison. Across the front and side of the building were huge signs bearing the words "Howe & Hummel."

For many years and during the days of greatest renown and prosperity, Howe & Hummel occupied the entire first floor of this building. Inside the offices there was no pretense of style. The furniture was of the plainest description, the floors were uncarpeted, and law books were scattered around on tables and chairs amid a lot of rubbish. In the front reception room was a huge old-fashioned iron safe marked "Howe & Hummel."

William F. Howe, better known as "Howe the Lawyer" and "Big Bill," would frequently gaze at this safe and laugh. On such occasions he would tell how Hummel bought the safe years ago for appearence sake, and then Howe would laugh again, Howe & Hummel had little use for a large safe. They did not keep books, and each member of the firm carried the money he collected by way of fees during the day in his pocket. At the close of each day's work — before the firm moved to the Broadway offices — it was the habit of Howe & Hummel, with the young lawyers associated with them, to gather around a table, and then each one was expected to empty out upon the table the fees collected during the day. The money was then counted, and each received his share of the total based upon the proportion of his share in the firm's business. Later, this daily division was discontinued, and the dividends were declared each Friday night. After Howe's death Hummel adopted more up-to-date business methods. But this old iron safe had its use. As recently as 1898 waiting clients on winter days were frequently astonished as well as amused to see an office boy make a rush at the old safe, throw open its ponderous doors, take from its yawning inside an antique coal bucket and dump its contents into the large stove that stood in the middle of the floor of the reception room.

Hummel occupied as his private office a good-sized room facing on Centre street. Here he received and was retained by many of the leading theatrical managers, actors, actresses, and most prominent sporting men of the day, as well as many men and women of wealth and frequently of social standing. The walls of Hummel's private office were covered with signed photographs of actresses and other celebrities. In another room Howe for years received and advised and was retained by some of the most notorious criminals of the day and was also retained by many a person charged with high crimes, from murder to the receiving of stolen goods.

The reception room in the dingy old building where Howe & Hummel did a thriving business and one that should have made millionaires of them, from 1870 to 1900 was always crowded with waiting clients, private detectives, process servers, and a small army of office boys and clerks, while cabs and carriages stood in line outside. Such a scene could not be found in any other law office in the town. Those were the halcyon days of Howe & Hummel — when Howe was in almost every leading criminal case and Hummel had a retainer in every divorce or theatrical case that was worth being in.

The firm of Howe & Hummel, says the *Evening Sun*, was feared by both men and women who burned the candle at both ends and lived the life that leads to the divorce court and were involved in intrigues that are apt to result in actions for breach of promise of marriage or for alienation of affections. A letter bearing upon it the imprint of Howe & Hummel was apt to cause the gay man — old or young "old boy" — who received it a panic and a hasty mental review of all his little affairs of the heart or of passing fancy.

Not long ago, while discussing the putting out of business of Howe & Hummel, a lawyer said: "I have a client, a gay old broker, who once told me that it was his daily prayer for years past that he might never find in his morning's mail a letter bearing the words upon it 'Howe & Hummel.' He said to me, 'Really, old chap, if I saw Howe & Hummel on a letter addressed to me, I would die of fright.'"

There is a legend to the effect that some years ago a prominent and witty business man, when he chanced to meet an old friend in the office of Howe & Hummel, said:

"So you are here, too? Hope she was a pretty girl and you didn't have to pay too high for your little experience."

But when, so runs the legend, the other fellow flushed and sighed, the first man said:

"There, don't mind! Secrets are kept here — when once paid for — and there are two things that no one who enjoys life can escape — death and Howe & Hummel!"

They of guilty conscience need fear no longer the name of Howe & Hummel, for it has passed away. Bill Howe has been in his grave for five years, and Abe Hummel will be for one year, less two months off for good behavior, "civilly dead."

Thirty-seven years ago William Frederick Howe took into partnership with him his former office boy, Abraham H. Hummel, and founded in 1870 the law firm of Howe & Hummel, which afterwards, in the language of District Attorney Jerome, became "for more than twenty years a menace to this community." Three years before the firm was formed Hummel entered Howe's office as a combination office boy and law student. Almost from the start the big lawyer began to call the diminutive little Hummel "Little Abey," and Hummel remained to Howe, until Howe's death in 1902, "Little Abey." The big lawyer's liking for Hummel was remarkable and he never wearied of telling what a bright fellow "my little Abey is." It would have been a blow to Howe, his friends have said, had he lived to see his "Little Abey" sentenced and sent to the penitentiary. But it is safe to say that he would have spent his last cent to save his "Little Abey" from a convict's cell.

The partners were in marked contrast: Howe, tall, broad shouldered, and massive, and Hummel, short, slender, narrow shouldered, but with a large head. Howe always wore "loud" clothes, fancy waistcoats decorated with gold and jeweled buttons, and an especially characteristic old yachting cap trimmed with gold braid and gold buttons. Hummel always dressed in dark-colored clothing of modest cut. Howe wore many huge diamonds, because, as he once said, "I love their glitter and sparkle." Hummel's only jewelry was a thread of a gold watch chain and plain gold cuff links. They both loved the good things of life, but were moderate in their habits. They rarely missed the racetracks, and the two partners, "Big Bill" and "Little Abey," were known to every frequenter of the turf. Howe frequently said to the persons who gathered around him on the morning after he had been to the races:

"I cannot understand it. Abey and I go to the races; on the way out we discuss the horses and pick those we are going to play for winners. Then after a while I lose sight of Abey, and when we start for home Abey has money in every pocket and I have to borrow care fare. Abey is a smart fellow."

William Frederick Howe was more than "smart." He was a great criminal lawyer, even in the days of such leaders of the criminal bar as James T. Brady, Daniel Dougherty, John Graham, William A. Beach, and many others. He was one of the last of a coterie of great criminal lawyers to survive the close of the last century. During the civil war he became known as "Habeas Corpus Howe," because of his success is obtaining the release on writs of habeas corpus of drafted men. Later he became known as the "Father of the Criminal Bar," and to the masses of crooks and criminals as "Howe the Lawyer." It has been said that during his fifty years of active practice Howe received retainers in 1,000 homicide cases. The records of the office of Howe & Hummel show that he acted as counsel for some 650 murderers. Almost from his first appearance at the bar of the city Howe took a foremost place among the criminal lawyers and he retained it for nearly a half century.

Many years ago an assistant district attorney, while summing up to a jury, warned the jurors not to be swayed by the prisoner's counsel. "Weeping Bill Howe's tears," was the phrase used. When his turn came, Howe said: "A man who ridicules me for weeping at the sorrows of this prisoner — a man charged with the murder of a woman — whether the unfortunate prisoner is guilty or innocent, is sure to come to a bad end."

Several years afterward Howe was reminded of this incident, and was asked if the assistant district attorney in question had come to a bad end. "Alas, yes," exclaimed Howe, "a most fearfully bad end. He — he — is now trying cases for a heartless railway corporation."

Another story of Howe's tears is told in connection with a case in which he appeared for the defendant before Recorder Hackett. Mr. Howe had just succeeded by his eloquence, aided by his tears, in obtaining in rapid succession the acquittal of several men charged with homicide. The recorder was somewhat disgruntled. Howe entered upon the defense of a woman charged with homicide. She was seated with her child on her knees. While Howe was pleading for her acquittal he was seen to scowl at his client. She gazed at him in blank amazement, and Howe moved up closer to her and the baby. Suddenly the baby began to cry. Howe wept as the baby's screams suddenly ceased. Recorder Hackett looked up with a smile and remarked: "Mr. Howe, you had better give the baby another jab with a pin." In telling this story, as he frequently did, Howe said: "That remark of the recorder's about the jab of the pin won a nearly hopeless case for me, for I used it against him for all I was worth and got an acquittal."

In 1900, Howe & Hummel moved from the old Centre street office to offices in the basement in the rear end of the New York Life Insurance Company's building. There the civil branch of the business under the master hand of Abe Hummel was at its best. Howe had practically retired from practice and Hummel and his associates did not find money enough in the criminal practice to engage in it extensively.

The civil end of the business, including divorce suits, matrimonial differences, breach of promise of marriage actions, suits for alienation of affections, was yielding, it is said, the large income of $300,000 a year, with office expenses of some $25,000 a year. Hummel was the representative of nearly every prominent theatrical manager, actor, and actress in the country. He was retained in all the sensational civil actions. His fame had become international. He represented many foreign managers and actors. He was the representative in the United States of the Society of French Authors. It is said that between the years 1900 and 1905, before the Dodge-Morse exposé, the firm brought about settlements of large amounts in many social scandals that never found their way into the public press.

The move from the old Centre street office seems to have brought bad luck to the firm. Shortly after the removal Hummel went abroad on a visit and was nearly killed in a cab smashup in London. In 1902 Howe died suddenly. Then came the Dodge-Morse scandal, followed by Hummel's trial and conviction.

Cases of Interest.

UNREPEATED TELEGRAM — LIABILITY FOR MISTAKE. — In Halsted v. Postal Tel., etc., Co., 104 N. Y. Supp. 1016, the New York Appellate Division, Second Department, held that the addressee of an unrepeated telegram could not recover in an action in tort for damages arising from a mistake in the message, where the message, which was sent at the request of the plaintiff, was delivered to the telegraph company on a blank containing an express exemption of the company from liability for mistakes in unrepeated messages.

EMPLOYER'S LIABILITY FOR SHOOTING BY STRIKE BREAKERS. — In Shay v. American Iron & Steel Mfg. Co., 67 Atl. Rep. 54, the Pennsylvania Supreme Court holds that a corporation is not liable for damages to a house and injuries to the owner by negligent shooting by men employed to take the place of strikers, where the shooting was directed from the defendant's premises against a mob, and was not authorized by the defendant, and was not within the scope of the employment of the persons doing it.

FAILURE TO DELIVER TELEGRAM — MENTAL ANGUISH. — In Butler v. Western Union Tel. Co., 57 S. E. Rep. 757, the South Carolina Supreme Court holds that one who sues a telegraph company to recover damages for mental anguish caused by the company's failure to deliver promptly a message, whereby the plaintiff's brother-in-law was prevented from being with the plaintiff after the death of the latter's wife to administer comfort and consolation, cannot recover unless it be shown that the company had knowledge at the time of receiving the message of the peculiarly tender relations sustained by the parties.

CORPORATE OFFICER'S LIABILITY FOR MISAPPROPRIATING FUNDS. — The meteoric career in high finance of J. Edward Addicks, the "gas man," is recalled by the case of Pepper v. Addicks. 153 Fed. Rep. 383, in which Judge McPherson, of the eastern district of Pennsylvania, rendered a decree against him for $890,000, with interest from December 1, 1897. The suit was brought by the receiver of the Bay State Gas Company, of which Addicks was an officer and director, to compel Addicks to pay over profits made by him by using the corporation's assets for his individual purposes. It was shown that Addicks absolutely dominated the board of directors and induced them to authorize the purchase of worthless bonds of other corporations in which he was interested, by reason of which he made a large individual profit.

RAILROAD STATIONS — CONSTITUTIONALITY OF STATUTES. — In State v. St. Louis, etc., R. Co., 103 S. W. Rep. 623, the Arkansas Supreme Court holds that a statute requiring railroad companies to keep waiting rooms open at all hours, to have them comfortably heated at all proper times, supplied with drinking water, and kept in a sanitary condition, and to maintain waterclosets at passenger stations for passengers and employees, is not violative of the Fourteenth Amendment. On the other hand, however, the Texas Court of Civil Appeals, in State v. Texas, etc., R. Co., 103 S. W. Rep. 653, holds that a statute imposing a penalty for the failure of railroad companies to maintain waterclosets at stations is unconstitutional as a deprivation of property without due process of law.

TOLL BRIDGE — RIGHT TO CHARGE FOR AUTOMOBILE. — In Mallory v. Saratoga Lake Bridge Co., 104 N. Y. Supp. 1025, it is held that where a bridge company, maintaining a bridge carrying a highway across a lake, is authorized by its charter to collect toll for the passage of certain specified vehicles and animals, it cannot demand tolls for automobiles, such vehicles not being within the terms of its charter. Spencer, J., said: "The fact that automobiles were not known at the time of the passage of the act can make no difference, for the reason that defendants, by accepting the franchise in consideration for the right to collect the tolls stipulated for, assumed the duty and responsibility of building and maintaining a bridge that would meet the reasonable requirements of all travelers on the public highway, including vehicles and animals then in common use by travelers, and also such as might thereafter come into common use."

SMUGGLING — WHEN OFFENSE COMPLETE. — A point of interest to globe trotters who are in the habit of importing into this country gems concealed about their persons was decided by District Judge Hough, in U. S. v. 218½ Carats Loose Emeralds, 153 Fed. Rep. 643. The importer, a South American gentleman by the name of Suarez, on arriving in the United States omitted in making his declaration to the customs officials to mention a certain package of emeralds which he had in one of his pockets, and when his baggage was examined on the dock falsely stated that he had no precious stones in his possession. The emeralds were thereupon seized and an action was brought for their forfeiture. The defense contended that the act of smuggling was not complete, as Suarez had not gone outside the customs lines established on the dock, and cited in support of such contention Keck v. U. S., 172 U. S. 434, in which it was held that the offense was not completed until the goods had left the ship and reached the shore. Judge Hough held, however, that the offense was complete when the passenger landed on the dock.

Restaurant Keeper's Liability for Assault by Waiter.—In Chase v. Knabel, 90 Pac. Rep. 642, decided by the Supreme Court of Washington, the plaintiff, a negro, entered the defendant's restaurant, and after ordering his meal proceeded to annoy a female patron of the restaurant. On being warned by one of the waiters to desist he became boisterous and profane, whereupon a couple of waiters seized him and propelled him with some violence into the street, one of them taking occasion to land a thump on his head at the moment of his exit. The plaintiff brought an action against the proprietor of the restaurant for assault and battery, and refusal of equality of civil rights. In reversing a judgment for the plaintiff the court held that it was the duty of the restaurant keeper and his employees to stop the annoyance of the female patron, and, if necessary, eject the plaintiff from the premises, in which case the defendant was liable only for the use of excessive force; and that an assault and battery by a waiter in ejecting the plaintiff, occasioned by ill-will, jealousy, or hatred on the part of the waiter towards the negro, did not constitute an act for which the defendant was liable in damages.

Interurban Railroads in City Streets.—An important decision relative to the operation of interurban railroads in city streets was decided by the Indiana Supreme Court, in Kinsey v. Union Traction Co., 81 N. E. Rep. 922. By a majority of three to two the court held that the operation by a corporation, organized under the statute providing for the incorporation of street railway companies, of interurban cars on streets of a city, with the city's permission, for the carriage of passengers, express, and light freight, was not an additional servitude on the streets, and abutting owners were not entitled to compensation therefor. The judges, however, were unanimously of the opinion that an abutting owner could sue for special damages resulting from the operation of such cars. It was shown that the company operated interurban trains of three cars, each sixty feet in length, which were run through the streets at a rate of from twenty to thirty miles an hour, and that thereby the house of the plaintiff, an abutting owner, was so shaken as to cause the fall of the plastering and ceilings and the pictures on the walls and to disturb the comfort of the plaintiff and his family. It was held that the company was liable to the plaintiff for such special damage.

Street Car Advertisements—Right to Enjoin.—A novel application for equitable relief was made in Burns v. St. Paul St. R. Co., (Minn.) 112 N. W. Rep. 412. The plaintiff, a newspaper publisher, sought to enjoin the street railway company from placing advertisements in its cars, on the ground that the defendant thereby diverted from the plaintiff a large and lucrative business in advertising and infringed upon the rights and business of the plaintiff. The plaintiff alleged that the act of the defendant company was *ultra vires* and that he, as an individual, had thereby suffered special damage. Alluding to the novelty of the application, Jaggard, J., said: "With a vivacity that is refreshing and a plausibility that is rather surprising, counsel for the plaintiff has marshaled authorities to the effect that 'this application is not a path-breaker. The path is not only broken but is well paved — macadamized with precedents.'" In addition to citing numerous cases regarding the power of equity to enjoin public nuisances or trespasses, and to restrain corporate officers from exceeding their powers, the plaintiff's counsel also quoted as follows from "Troilus and Cressida," act II., scene 2:

> "There is a law in every well ordered nation
> To curb those raging appetites that are
> Most disobedient and refractory."

The court decided, however, that even though the defendant company had exceeded its powers in the matter of the advertisements, the plaintiff's damages were too conjectural and remote to entitle him to raise the question.

Restraint of Trade by System of Contracts.—The "chain-of-contracts" scheme of the patent medicine proprietors to prevent retailers from cutting prices was dealt a severe blow by the Circuit Court of Appeals, Sixth Circuit, in John D. Park & Sons Co. v. Hartman, 153 Fed. Rep. 24. The plan was for the proprietor to sell to such jobbers only as would contract to sell to such retailers only as would contract with the proprietor not to sell below the set price. The court held that this system of contracts was in restraint of trade, its purpose and effect being to prevent competition between purchasers of the medicine, both wholesale and retail; and that, in the absence of allegations of fact showing it to be necessary for the protection of the manufacturer's business, a court of equity would not aid in the enforcement of the contracts by granting an injunction to prevent a defendant, who was not a party to such contracts, from buying the medicine from purchasers who were, and reselling the same for any price he might see fit. It was further held that an article made under a secret process or private formula was not within the exemption from the common-law rule against monopoly and restraint of trade which is extended to patented or copyrighted articles. The law will aid the proprietor in protecting his secret process or formula, and contracts against its disclosure are not in restraint of trade, because of the property right in the secret which would be destroyed by its disclosure, and because it is not in itself an article of commerce, but such considerations do not apply to the sale of the manufactured product which do not involve a disclosure of the secret.

Book Reviews.

Corporate Bonds and Mortgages. By Leonard A. Jones, A. B., LL.B. Third edition. The Bobbs-Merrill Co. Indianapolis, 1907. Pages 849.

The extraordinary increase in the use of corporate organizations in all manner of business enterprises and the complexity caused by mergers, reorganizations, holding companies, and similar devices have given rise to the necessity of a more minute development of the various branches of the law relating to corporations. Of this character is the work of Judge Jones. That he has performed satisfactorily the task which he undertook is shown by the fact that his work has sufficiently stood the test of use, the only adequate test of a law book, to warrant a third edition.

The author's experience as a writer of legal treatises has enabled him to present his subject in an orderly and logical manner, and his known ability is a guaranty of the soundness of his propositions. At times one is inclined to regret that a writer on whom reliance can be placed, and who has reviewed the decisions, should so entirely eliminate his personal judgment on close points and content himself with merely presenting the views of the court, as Judge Jones has done in this volume. After all, however, he has chosen what is probably the wiser course, as each user of the book must consider the question involved from the point of view of his particular needs, and would be hindered, perhaps, rather than helped by unauthoritative pronouncements.

There is one phase of the subject which the writer does not seem to have given a sufficiently extensive treatment, and that is reorganization as affecting the holders of corporate securities, a matter which is often of very vital interest to the bondholder. In this connection the author has committed the unusual oversight of omitting an important decision in his own jurisdiction, Child *v.* New York, etc., R. Co., 129 Mass. 170, in which it is held that where the bondholders, after foreclosure, form a new corporation in pursuance of a provision of the mortgage authorizing them to organize themselves into a corporation with a capital stock equal to the outstanding mortgage debt, the capital must be fixed at the total amount of the principal sum of the bonded indebtedness, without reference to any unpaid overdue interest.

Again, while the author correctly states the general rule that the rights of bondholders under the mortgage cannot be impaired without their consent by any scheme of reorganization, he fails to note the very important qualification that a minority bondholder, though refusing to accept the reorganization plan, will be compelled to deposit his bonds, when provision is made for the payment of his bonds, as was held in Pollitz *v.* Farmers' Loan, etc., Co., 53 Fed. Rep. 210.

While this branch of the subject is, as has been remarked, open to criticism on the ground that the author has not developed it to the extent that one would look for in such a work, the outline that he has given contains, as do the preceding chapters, a sound statement of the principles involved. On the whole, this edition will serve, as did its predecessors, as a practical help to those who have to deal with the complex questions involved in the law of corporate bonds and mortgages. The work contains a satisfactory index. The publishers have presented it in a suitable form typographically and in a substantial binding which will stand use.

The Lunacy Law of the World. By J. A. Chaloner. Palmetto Press, Roanoke Rapids, North Carolina. 1906. Pages 348.

This is a very peculiar book or monograph. One who attempts to make practical use of it will probably throw it aside as a paranoiac jumble, a hopeless confusion, badly indexed, and worse arranged. The writer is assuredly earnest, but so intemperate in his denunciation and so illogical in his deductions as to render his work generally incoherent and often incomprehensible. There is such a bitterness and such a depth of feeling exhibited as to defeat any purpose which he may have had of setting forth the unquestionable abuses to which the state of the lunacy laws has given rise, and yet the exhaustiveness of his research into the question compels admiration. An author who can work through lunacy law from the time of Emperor Conrad down to the present, and then proceed to bury it under a mass of sensational matter from the columns of the New York *Journal*, Reade's "Hard Cash," and the like, is as energetic as ill-advised.

The typography of the book is very poor and the citations are frequently inaccurate and confusing.

News of the Profession.

THE AMERICAN BAR ASSOCIATION held its thirtieth annual meeting at Portland, Me., on August 26–28. Particulars of the meeting will be given in our next issue.

CONNECTICUT COURT WILL WEAR GOWNS. — At the opening of the October term of the Connecticut Supreme Court the judges of the court will don gowns for the first time.

EX-ATTORNEY-GENERAL OF INDIANA DEAD. — Alonzo Greene Smith, ex-attorney-general of Indiana, died in Indianapolis on August 6, at the age of fifty-nine. He was attorney-general from 1892 to 1896.

MADE DEAN OF CORNELL LAW SCHOOL. — Hon. Frank Irvine, formerly a Supreme Court commissioner in Nebraska, and for several years past professor of pleading and practice in the Cornell Law School, has been appointed dean of the school.

MASSACHUSETTS SUPERIOR JUDGE DEAD. — Hon. Lemuel Le Baron Holmes, associate justice of the Massachusetts Superior Court, died at his home in New Bedford, August 4, aged fifty-five. He was appointed judge of the Superior Court in 1902 by Governor Bates.

THE INTERNATIONAL LAW ASSOCIATION held its twenty-fourth conference at Portland, Me., on August 29, 30, and 31, immediately following the annual meeting of the American Bar Association. An account of the meeting will be given in this column next month.

RETIREMENT OF JUSTICE COBB, OF GEORGIA. — On July 22, Hon. Andrew J. Cobb, of the Georgia Supreme Court, presented his resignation to Governor Smith, to take effect on October 12. Justice Cobb, who has served on the supreme bench nearly eleven years, will resume the practice of law.

EX-JUSTICE BOCKES, OF NEW YORK, DEAD. — Hon. Augustus Bockes, for twenty-nine years a justice of the New York Supreme Court, died in Saratoga on August 10, aged eighty-nine. He was appointed by Governor Clark in 1855, and, with the exception of one term, served until his retirement on the age limit in 1887.

APPOINTED TO KANSAS SUPREME COURT. — The vacancy on the bench of the Kansas Supreme Court caused by the death of Judge A. L. Greene was filled on August 1 by Governor Hoch by appointing Hon. Alfred W. Benson, of Ottawa. Judge Benson was appointed to the United States Senate to fill out the unexpired term of Senator Burton, resigned.

KANSAS SUPREME COURT JUDGE DEAD. — Hon. Adrian L. Greene, justice of the Kansas Supreme Court, died in a sanitarium at Battle Creek, Mich., July 28. He had been suffering from kidney trouble for several months. Judge Greene was born in Canton, Mo., in 1848. He was admitted to the bar of that State in 1871, and in the same year moved to Newton, Kan., where he practiced until his appointment to the Supreme Court in 1901.

ANOTHER LAW MAGAZINE. — The latest recruit to the ranks of legal periodicals is the *Oklahoma Lawyer*, which made its initial bow last month. The modest and sensible tone of its opening statement bespeaks intelligent editing, and one especially commendable, as well as unusual, feature is the giving of due credit for matters clipped from other publications. To be sure, the first paragraph under "In Lighter Vein" is not credited to LAW NOTES, in which it originally appeared several years ago, but that was doubtless an oversight.

EX-JUDGE VALENTINE, OF KANSAS, DEAD. — Hon. Daniel M. Valentine, who served in the Kansas Supreme Court from 1869 to 1893, died in Topeka on August 5, at the age of seventy-seven. He was one of the three best known justices of the Kansas court, and for fourteen years was associated with the other two — Brewer and Horton. He was a native of Shelby county, Ohio, and acquired his legal education in odd hours while teaching school. He was appointed to the Supreme Court in 1869 and retired in 1893.

DEATH OF EX-JUDGE FINCH, OF NEW YORK. — Hon. Francis Miles Finch, for sixteen years a member of the New York Court of Appeals, died in Ithaca, N. Y., on July 31. Judge Finch was born in that city in 1827, and after graduating from Yale in 1849, was admitted to practice in the following year. In 1880 he was appointed to the Court of Appeals bench, and in the following year was elected for the full term of fourteen years. Being near the age limit when his term expired in 1895, he declined a renomination, and thereafter devoted his time to lecturing in the Cornell University Law School, of which he was dean. In 1889 he was elected to the presidency of the New York State Bar Association.

THE NORTH CAROLINA STATE BAR ASSOCIATION held its annual meeting at Hendersonville, on July 11 and 12. The principal feature was an address by Hon. Alton B. Parker, of New York, on "The Common Law Jurisdiction of the United States Courts." The officers elected for the ensuing term were as follows: President, Hon. Charles A. Moore, of Asheville; secretary and treasurer, T. W. Davis, of Wilmington; vice-presidents, L. L. Smith, of Gates; W. E. Daniel, of Halifax; A. D. Ward, of Craven; T. W. Bickett, of Franklin; J. D. Bellamy, of New Hanover; W. C. Monroe, of Wayne; Stephen McIntyre, of Robinson; E. H. Gibson, of Scotland; R. R. King, of Guilford; E. P. Raper, of Davidson; Lindsay Patterson, of Forsyth; L. A. Bulkinkle, of Gaston; W. W. Barker, of Wilkes; C. F. Toms, of Hederson; W. E. Breeze, Jr., of Transylvania, and W. E. Moore, of Jackson.

THE WASHINGTON STATE BAR ASSOCIATION held its annual meeting in Seattle, on July 11-13. The principal speaker on the program was Vice-President Charles W. Fairbanks; Hon. Jas. R. Garfield, secretary of the interior, was also scheduled for an address. Other features were the annual address of President E. C. Hughes, and the following papers: "The Lawyer under Fire," by Hon. H. E. Hadley; "Community Property Law," by Frank T. Post, of Spokane; "Navigable Waters," by W. H. Abel; "Tide Lands," by H. G. Rowland; "The Lawyer the Conservative Influence of Our Government," by Hon. Jas. F. Alshire, chief justice of Idaho; "Our Sanitary Laws," by Dr. Elmer E. Heg, secretary of the State board of health. The meeting closed with the customary banquet.

THE VIRGINIA STATE BAR ASSOCIATION held its annual meeting at the Jamestown Exposition on July 31 and August 1. The principal address was delivered by John R. Dos Passos, of New York, who devoted his attention chiefly to the questions of municipal corruption and naturalization of aliens. Other addresses were: "The Province of the Court in Jury Trials," by Richard Evelyn Byrd, of Winchester, and "The Duty of the State to Diminish Divorce," by Lewis H. Machen, of Alexandria. The officers elected for the ensuing term were as follows: President, Wyndham R. Meredith, of Richmond; vice-presidents, Don P. Halsey, of Lynchburg; Richard E. Byrd, of Winchester; Charles E. Lassiter, of Petersburg; J. Norman Powell, of Bristol, and Louis C. Phillips, of Newport News; secretary and treasurer, John B. Minor, Jr., of Richmond.

COLORADO STATE BAR ASSOCIATION. — The tenth annual meeting of the Colorado State Bar Association was held at Colorado Springs on July 5 and 6, President Julius C. Gunther, of Denver, presiding. The principal address was delivered by Major F. Charles Hume, of Houston, Tex., who took for his subject "The Southern Lawyer; the Agony of the States; the Supreme Court." Papers were read during the meeting as follows: "The Law as Read Between the Lines," by W. B. Morgan, of Trinidad; "Patrick Henry, and His Contribution to the Constitution," by Lucius W. Hoyt, of Denver; "Section 34 of Insurance Laws of 1907 as to Removal of Causes to Federal Courts," by Frank E. Grove, of Denver. The meeting was closed with a banquet at the Broadmoor Casino. Officers were chosen for the next term as follows: President, James M. McCreery, of Greeley; vice-presidents, John R. Smith, of Denver, and S. Harrison White, of Pueblo; secretary and treasurer, Lucius W. Hoyt, of Denver. The next meeting will be held at Fort Collins.

INDIANA STATE BAR ASSOCIATION. — The annual convention of the Indiana State Bar Association was held in Indianapolis July 9 and 10. President Daniel Fraser, of Fowler, opened the meeting with an address on "The Courts and the Legislature." The annual address was delivered by Merritt Starr, of Chicago, who spoke on "Legislative and Judicial Development of the Law Concerning Competition Contrasted." Other papers read during the meeting were: "Our Practice," by Charles W. Miller, of Goshen; "The Value of Expert Testimony," by Charles Kellison, of Plymouth; "Are Corporations Ill Treated, and Why?" by Judge Harry B. Tuthill, of Michigan City; "Legal Ethics," by Andrew A. Adams, of Columbia City; "Our South American Relations," by John W. O'Hara, of Peru, consul to Montevideo. The meeting closed with a banquet at Maennerchor Hall. The following officers were elected for the ensuing term: President, Merrill Moores, of Indianapolis; vice-president, Dan W. Sims, of Lafayette; secretary, George Batchelor, of Indianapolis; treasurer, Frank E. Gavin, of Indianapolis.

ILLINOIS STATE BAR ASSOCIATION. — The thirty-first annual meeting of the Illinois State Bar Association was held in Galesburg July 11 and 12. The meeting was called to order by President Harrison Musgrave, of Chicago, who proceeded to address the association on the subject of recent legislation. The annual address was delivered by Edward M. Shepard, of New York, who descanted on "Corporate Capitalization and Public Morals." Papers read during the meeting were "The Municipal Court of Chicago," by Judge Harry Olson, of Chicago; "Pure Food Laws," by Albert H. Jones, of Robinson; "Some Aspects of the Pure Food Law," by Frank F. Reed, of Chicago; "The Lincoln-Douglas Debates," by Clark E. Carr, of Galesburg; "The Graduated Inheritance Tax," by Carl E. Epler, of Quincy. An interesting feature of the second day was a debate on "Railroad Rate Regulation," in which James H. Wilkerson, of Chicago, opened in favor of governmental regulation, and John M. Zane, of Chicago, opened in opposition thereto. Others who took part in the discussion were Harry S. Mecartney, Blewett Lee, and E. A. Bancroft, all of Chicago. The meeting concluded with the usual banquet. The following were chosen officers to serve during the next year: President, James H. Matheny, of Springfield; vice-presidents, E. P. Williams, of Galesburg; Edgar A. Bancroft, of Chicago, and John C. Richberg, of Chicago; secretary and treasurer, John F. Voight, Jr., of Mattoon.

KENTUCKY STATE BAR ASSOCIATION. — The annual meeting of the Kentucky State Bar Association was held in Bowling Green, on July 11, 12, and 13. Following an address of welcome by Judge John M. Galloway, of Bowling Green, came the usual address by the president, S. S. Rouse, of Covington. Papers read during the first day were: "Inheritance Taxes," by E. J. McDermott, of Louisville, and "Has the Practice of Law Become a Business and Ceased to Be a Profession," by Wilbur F. Browder, of Russellville. In the evening the annual address was delivered by Hon. Judson Harmon, of Cincinnati, whose subject was "E Pluribus Unum." The features of the second day were papers on "The Distinction Between the Judicial and Legislative Functions," by Hon. John M. Lassing, of Burlington; "Power to Enjoin Organized Interference with Property," by George R. Hunt, of Lexington; and "Professional Responsibility," by Hon. W. M. Read, of Paducah. The annual banquet was held in the evening. The third day was devoted to amusement, including a trip to Mammoth Cave. The following officers were elected: President, T. Kennedy Helm, of Louisville; vice-presidents, J. D. Mocquot, of Paducah; T. W. Thomas, of Bowling Green; James Garnett, of Columbia; E. J. McDermott, of Louisville; W. O. Davis, of Versailles; Richard Gray, of Covington, and W. M. Ayers, of Pineville; secretary, R. A. McDowell, of Louisville; treasurer, R. C. Stoll, of Lexington.

OHIO STATE BAR ASSOCIATION. — The twenty-eighth annual meeting of the Ohio State Bar Association was held at the Hotel Victory, Put-in-Bay, July 9-12. After the association had been called to order by F. J. Mullins, of Salem, chairman of the executive committee, President John C. Hale, of Cleveland, delivered an address on "Changes Required to Advance the Science of Jurisprudence and Reforms in Statute Law." The annual address was delivered by Charles Nagel, of St. Louis, who took for his theme "The Lawyer's Part in the Administration of Justice." Smith W. Bennett, of Columbus, addressed the convention on the subject of "Corporations and the Commerce Clause." An interesting feature of the meeting was a discussion of "The Initiative and Referendum," in which Atlee Pomerene, of Canton, took the affirmative, and Edgar B. Kinkead, of Columbus, the negative. An invitation was extended to the Indiana State Bar Association to hold a joint meeting at Put-in-Bay in 1908, but it was declined on the ground that to meet outside the State would cause the Indiana lawyers to lose interest in their association. The officers elected for the ensuing year were as follows: President, Thomas D. Paxton, of Cincinnati; vice-presidents, J. C. Harper, of Cincinnati; E. L. Rowe, of Dayton; E. S. Mathias, of Van Wert; S. W. Durflinger, of London; S. B. Eason, of Wooster; L. G. Gill, of Waverly; E. A. Hollingsworth, of Cadiz; Asa W. Jones, of Youngstown, and John E. West, of Bellefontaine; secretary, E. B. McCarter, of Columbus; treasurer, C. R. Gilmore, of Dayton.

IOWA STATE BAR ASSOCIATION. — The thirtieth annual meeting of the Iowa State Bar Association was held in Davenport, on July 11 and 12. J. Clark Hall, of Davenport, made an address of welcome, which was responded to by Thomas D. Healy, of Fort Dodge. President Horace M. Towner, of Corning, spoke on "Reformatory and Remedial Legislation," and Charles G. Saunders, of Council Bluffs, read a paper on "The Indeterminate Sentence Law and Parol System." The first day was concluded by a steamboat excursion tendered by the local bar association. The principal feature of the second day was the annual address delivered by Hon. Hannis Taylor, of Washington, D. C., whose subject was "The Science of Jurisprudence." Other papers read were: "Enforcing the Criminal Law," by Clifford P. Smith, of Mason City; "The Nation and Local Self-Government," by Walter I. Smith, of Council Bluffs; "Pure Food Laws," by Byron W. Newberry, of Strawberry Point; "The Legal Aspects of Primary Election Laws," by James J. Crossley, of Winterset. At the banquet in the evening the retiring president, Horace M. Towner, acted as toastmaster. Among those responding to toasts were Attorney-general Howard W. Byers, Judge Scott M. Ladd, of the State Supreme Court, Joe R. Lane, of Davenport, and Congressman Benjamin P. Birdsall, of Dubuque. The election of officers resulted as follows: President, D. D. Murphy, of Elkader; vice-president, J. W. Bollinger, of Davenport; secretary, Charles N. Dutcher, of Iowa City; treasurer, Charles S. Wilcox, of Des Moines. The next meeting will be held at Waterloo.

English Notes.

TWO K. C.'S DEAD. — On July 25, Mr. John Patrick Murphy, K. C., formerly one of the most noted members of the English bar, died at Upper Norwood, aged seventy-six. He retired from practice in 1897. On the same day Mr. R. S. B. Hammond-Chambers, K. C., died in London, at the age of fifty-two. Mr. Murphy was called to the bar at the Middle Temple in 1854, and Mr. Hammond-Chambers at Lincoln's Inn in 1879.

COST OF ENGLAND'S HIGHER COURTS. — The official returns for the year ending March 31, 1907, show that the receipts in respect to the High Court of Justice and the Court of Appeal were 499,863*l.* and the expenditures 649,396*l.* The deficit of 149,533*l.* is regarded as unduly great in England, but in comparison with the cost to the government of maintaining the judiciary in America, it seems surprisingly small.

BIRTHDAY HONORS FOR LAWYERS. — The legal profession fared well in the recent distribution of the King's birthday honors. Two of the four new privy councillors — Mr. Eugene Wason, M. P., and Mr. Spence Watson — are lawyers. Knighthoods were conferred on Mr. Nathaniel J. Highmore, Mr. Alfred Billson, M. P., and Mr. W. S. Gilbert, who, although better known as a dramatist, has been a member of the Inner Temple for more than forty-five years.

RECOVERY AGAINST RACE TRACK TIPSTER. — Persons who are accustomed to act on the advice of tipsters as to the "best bets" on horse races will be interested in a case recently before one of the lower English courts. The defendant had offered in a letter to send "six certainties for 10*l.*" The plaintiff accepted the offer, and as none of the "certainties" won, he sued to recover his 10*l.* The judge instructed the jury that the consideration for the plaintiff's money had failed and he was therefore entitled to a verdict.

SHERLOCK HOLMES FOILED AGAIN. — The efforts of Sir Arthur Conan Doyle to show that the crimes attributed to George Edalji were in fact committed by another person appear to have come to nought. On August 12 the home secretary announced that the government had been advised by the attorney-general and Sir Charles Mathews that the statements and materials furnished by Sir Conan Doyle disclosed no case, even of a *prima facie* character, against the individual indicated by him, and that consequently no action could be taken.

UNTHINKABLE. — A young Irish counsel, appearing in his first case to argue on behalf of the personal representatives of the plaintiff's grandmother, who had recently died and left a small estate, began his argument thus: "Your lordships will perceive that we stand here as our grandmother's representatives; and really, my lords, it does strike me that it would be a monstrous thing to say that a plaintiff can now come in, in the very teeth of an Act of Parliament, and actually turn us around, under color of hanging us up, on the foot of a contract made behind our backs."

STOPPING PAYMENT BY TELEGRAM. — The case of Curtice *v.* London City and Midland Bank, recently before one of the English divisional courts, involved a novel point in regard to stopping payment on a check. The plaintiff sent a telegram to the bank directing that payment be stopped on a certain check.

The telegram arrived after business hours, was dropped into the bank's letter-box, and was overlooked next morning when the box was opened. In consequence the check was paid before the telegram was opened. The court held that the bank was chargeable with constructive notice of the stopping of the check, and must make good the plaintiff's loss occasioned by its payment.

DICKENS'S JURYMAN DISCOVERED. — It is claimed by the *Pall Mall Gazette* that the original of the immortal juryman at the trial of Bardell *v.* Pickwick has been discovered. He, it will be remembered, was a chemist and had left nobody in the shop but an errand boy — "a very nice boy, my lord, but he is not acquainted with drugs; and I know that the prevailing impression on his mind is that Epsom salts means oxalic acid, and syrup of senna laudanum." The facts on which the hypothesis is based are these: In 1828, at Lancaster, a chemist's apprentice was indicted for causing the death of an infant by negligently delivering laudanum for paregoric. A mother sent a ten-year-old boy to buy a pennyworth of paregoric for her baby; the boy in the shop gave a little bottle with "Paregoric" labeled on it, but laudanum in it, the bottles of each standing side by side in the shop; he added that ten drops should be given the baby. The dose killed the infant, and the apprentice was convicted and fined five pounds. The case made some little stir at the time, as illustrating the law of manslaughter, and is reported as Rex *v.* Tessymond, 1 Lewin's Crown Cases 169. As Dickens at that time was a solicitor's clerk in Gray's Inn, it is thought likely he heard of the case and used it a few years later in "Pickwick."

AN ENGLISH COMMENT ON THE "UNWRITTEN LAW." — The traditional British inaccuracy in regard to things American is well illustrated in the second sentence of the following editorial, which appeared in a recent issue of the London *Law Journal:* "We have heard a great deal of late from America of the 'unwritten law;' but the theory has been very much in the air. Now it has received actual recognition in the acquittal of ex-Judge Loring by a Californian jury. But, briefly, the case comes to this: That a father who believes, rightly or wrongly, that his daughter has been violated is justified in killing the supposed violator. This is the particular application of the 'law.' The general principle is wider, and seems to be that in certain classes of wrongs — those touching personal or family honor — the aggrieved party may, if he deems the reparation given by the law inadequate, take the redress of his grievance into his own hands. The same idea has undoubtedly had a place in the history of our own law. A husband who takes the adulterer *flagrante delicto* might — perhaps may — lawfully slay him, and, though our law in theory condemned dueling, the man who did not vindicate his honor or that of his family by sending or accepting a challenge had to suffer social excommunication. What is important to note, however, is that these sentiments were survivals — survivals from a primitive state of society. What we to-day call crimes — theft, assault, robbery, rape — were originally, as Sir H. Maine has shown, regarded merely as private wrongs, which it was the business of the individual or his family or his clan to revenge. This law-licensed right of revenge was in time waived for a composition. Afterwards the state compelled acceptance of the composition and fixed a regular tariff, and later on a code of punishment, for injuries; but some wrongs rankled so deeply that the sufferer still held to the old rule of revenge, and society tolerated his doing so. So strong and widespread is the sympathy with *crimes passionelles* even to-day among the Latin races, that it goes far to defeat the efficacy of trial by jury. 'Extenuating circumstances' are with us the equivalent of this sympathy. Something, no doubt, must be conceded to human nature, but the object of the law is, and always has been, to curb the primitive instinct of revenge; without such a curb the world would, as Sidney Smith said, be a 'wild waste of passion.' Whatever gives a sanction to this 'wild justice,' though under the guise of honor, must be regarded as a 'throwing back' to the ages of barbarism."

Obiter Dicta.

HARD TIMES. — A Chicago lawyer has recently fasted for sixty-one days.

BEREFT. — "A 'grass lawyer' is one whose stenographer is away on her vacation." — *Canadian Law Times.*

This reminds us of a story.

AN HONORARY DEGREE. — A witness in one of the English courts was questioned as to the significance of the letters B. A. which he was accustomed to append to his signature. After some pressure he admitted that they stood for Bacon Agent.

A LAWYER'S LETTER-HEAD. — A Kansas friend contributes the following to our collection of letter-heads:

W. H. Brown, atty. at Law,
Syracuse, Kansas.
Police Judge. Practices in all the
courts of the state except his own.

EXPANDING CREDIT. — Last month we commented with surprise and admiration upon a lawyer in Albany, N. Y., who had succeeded in getting himself into debt to the extent of $149,150. Now comes an attorney in Chicago who asks the Bankruptcy Court to relieve him of liabilities aggregating $372,213. If any other lawyer has managed to owe more than that his identity is unknown to us at this writing.

LONG DISTANCE JUSTICE. — From Wyoming comes a new idea in the administration of the criminal law. On August 10, at the Bear Creek Ranch, some fifty miles from Cheyenne, Albert Bristol pulled Miles Fitzgerald off a mowing machine and dusted the contiguous territory with his person. Fitzgerald thereupon telephoned a complaint to town and a warrant was issued for Bristol's arrest. Hearing of this Bristol also resorted to the telephone, got into communication with the court, and entered a plea of guilty. Justice Carroll announced a fine of fifteen dollars and costs over the telephone, and Bristol promised to send a check for the amount by the first mail.

A STRONG PROHIBITION TICKET. — The case of Martin *v.* Wood, 4 N. Y. Supp. 208, involved a ballot for excise commissioner at a town election. The ballot read as follows: "Hear ye what the Lord saith! He that puts the bottle to his neighbor's lips is in danger of hell. From this I shall make out a temperance ticket: For supervisor, God; for town clerk, Christ; for assessor, Andrew; for justice of the peace, Simon; for commissioner, James; for collector, Zebedee; for overseer of the poor, John; for overseer of the poor, Philip; for inspector of election, Bartholomew; for constables, Matthew, Simon, Alpheus, Judas, Lebbeus; for excise commissioner, Charles Hoag." It would seem that Charles was running a bit out of his class.

WHISKEY AS RAILROAD FARE. — An action has recently been instituted in Utica, N. Y., which will require a decision on the novel question whether the giving of whiskey to a freight conductor makes one a passenger. The plaintiff, who is suing the

New York Central for damages for injuries sustained in a railroad wreck, wanted to go from Syracuse to Watertown. He was told that he might get a ride on a freight train, and on applying to the conductor, was informed by the latter that he could ride if accompanied by a pint of whiskey. The plaintiff quickly complied with this requirement, climbed aboard, and, while making merry with the conductor *en route*, was seriously injured. Of course his right to recover depends on whether he was a passenger. His counsel contends that the whiskey was accepted as fare, and the railroad company was bound by the conductor's act in accepting it as such.

INJURIA SINE DAMNO. — A correspondent writes from St. Louis that a husky Ethopian recently came into his office, and exhibiting a scalp wound about three inches long on top of his head, wanted to know if he could "git anything foh dis heah." In response to a query from the lawyer he explained: "Well, boss, it was like dis: Ah was wuking down by dis heah new buildin', an' a fo'poun' brick fell off'n de sixteenth story an' hit me smack on top do haid." "It is discouraging to be obliged to add," writes our correspondent, "that a grasping and heartless construction company, although admitting the facts and their liability, refused to pay more than ten dollars, on the ground that the evidence failed to disclose any material damage."

A GORDIAN KNOT. — The following legal problem which was much discussed at the recent meeting of the Kentucky State Bar Association is said to have actually arisen in litigation. If any of our readers can figure it out, we should be glad to be enlightened. A piece of land was mortgaged to A for $1,000, and A neglected to record the mortgage. Subsequently B, who had actual notice of A's mortgage, also took a mortgage for $1,000 and recorded it. Thereafter C, without notice of A's unrecorded mortgage, took a mortgage for $1,000 on the same land, which was duly recorded. The land was sold for $1,500, and the dispute arose over the distribution of the proceeds. A claimed priority over B because of the latter's actual knowledge of A's mortgage; B asserted a prior claim over C by reason of the record; and C contended that A's mortgage was postponed to his because of A's failure to record. It is stated that the judge before whom the matter was argued finally solved the difficulty by ordering a resale, with directions that the property must be made to bring $3,000.

CHINAMAN ADMITTED TO FEDERAL COURT. — What is believed to be the first instance of the admission of a Chinaman to practice in a federal court occurred recently in Portland, Ore., when Judge Wolverton accorded that privilege to Seid Back, Jr. His real name is Seid Gein, but he has adopted the surname of his father, one of the wealthiest of the Chinese merchants in Portland. Seid is twenty-six years old, and was recently admitted to the Oregon bar after completing a course in the Oregon Law School. A correspondent has kindly forwarded to our museum one of Seid's professional cards which is reproduced below:

砵崙柯利近

SEID BACK, JR.

薛律師天眷

ATTORNEY AT LAW

806 FIRST ST. PORTLAND, OR.

A TOO HOSPITABLE WIFE. — A sad case of an old man's darling giving him the double cross is disclosed in the recent divorce case of Duvall *v.* Duvall, (Tex. Civ. App.) 101 S. W. Rep. 521. The aged husband asked to be freed from the holy bonds, alleging that the defendant was guilty of excesses, cruel treatment, and outrages towards him, which the court summed up as being in substance "that during plaintiff's absence she would entertain other men at his home, drinking beer and other intoxicating liquors with them, which she would wheedle them into buying by fondling, kissing, and talking sweet to them when sitting on their laps, while they reciprocated in the same way, with some feeling." The young wife countered with a charge that her antique spouse entertained an inordinate and sinful affection for a young woman "not the 'bone of his bone and flesh of his flesh,' but a 'rare and radiant maiden' who was an inmate of their home." She testified that "once at night suddenly she heard a tapping, as of some one gently rapping, upon the maiden's chamber door, and that she found it was George — only this and nothing more." But the jury and trial judge seemed to have faith in George, for they granted his prayer for freedom. In affirming the judgment the appellate court said: "Evidently they did not believe in the old saying that 'Kissed lips lose no flavor, but renew themselves like the moon.' The evidence discloses another case of 'January and May,' though the scene of action was not a pear tree."

A NEW LEGAL NAPOLEON. — We have published from time to time in this column some specimens of legal advertising which struck us as rather winning, but for downright inspiration we have never seen anything to equal the following communication, which appeared in a recent issue of the El Paso, Tex., *News*:

CARLSBAD, N. M., Aug. 3. — Has Judge Gatewood, of Roswell, N. M., been employed to defend Harry K. Thaw? This is the question that is asked of Judge Gatewood and his friends every day, and as often unanswered. Judge Gatewood refuses to answer and his friends are unable to. Your correspondent knows for certain that correspondence on this subject has passed and that it will be the fault of Judge Gatewood if he is not in the case.

Your correspondent has been permitted to copy a letter written by an over-enthusiastic friend of Judge Gatewood to Harry K. Thaw, and this is supposed to be the beginning of the correspondence:

"Harry K. Thaw, Esq. My Dear Mr. Thaw. — Having an interest in your case as an American who would defend the honor of his wife, and thereby prove himself to be a man, I write you, and although a stranger to you I do not hesitate to advise you to get Judge Gatewood, of Roswell, N. M., as your leading attorney. (If you can get him.) In trying thirty-six consecutive cases he has not lost a case. This does not mean that the average murderer is cleared in the west, as lots of legal executions are had here every year. No important murder case for miles around this part of the southwest is tried without Judge Gatewood being the leading attorney. I have served on the jury in one of these cases, and I must say that his influence over that jury was bordering on a hypnotic spell. Out of a sudden burst of eloquence the jury would be spell-bound and then he would cause tears or laughter, as best suited the case. If the judge thought for a minute that any of his friends were trying to get you to employ him, money could not get him to take the case. Delmas would appear as a country lawyer in comparison to him. Jerome would meet a man who would tower above him as the tall oak does a cactus bush. Nothing would compensate the judge as much as to restore you to your beautiful wife a free man, and to vindicate your manly chivalry in removing a lecherous scoundrel from the face of God's green earth.

"If this interests you and you wish to get into communication with Judge Gatewood I will take pleasure in going to Roswell, seventy-five miles north from here, and broaching the matter to his. Wishing you much success and again offering to do anything in your behalf, I beg to remain.

Yours, etc., ——— ———"

When the judge found out this letter was written he lost no time in reprimanding the writer.

Your correspondent heard the conversation, and it was about like this: "Young man, I appreciate your friendship and your efforts for my welfare, but I would not be put in the position of wanting to represent Mr. Thaw or anybody else for ten times the fee that Mr. Thaw could pay me. I never hinted for a case in my life, not even when I was going through that stage of an embryo lawyer, struggling for bread. I am also opposed to your comparing me in the way you have done to those brilliant lawyers, who led two sides of the Thaw trial. I will also say, as much as some people think that I would grasp the opportunity to defend Mr. Thaw, I would consider the matter for some time, as it would cause me to neglect some of my clients, and while I know that to clear Mr. Thaw would be an honor to any lawyer, yet my home town and people are in the southwest, and I will never neglect them to take any case, no matter what the honor or the emoluments are."

Judge Gatewood defended some of the most difficult cases tried in this western country, and no doubt some of the eastern papers will be full of the details of these celebrated trials when the judge's name is mentioned in connection with Harry K. Thaw.

"There is one thing certain," says a leading lawyer of the Pecos valley, "if Harry K. Thaw does not employ Judge Gatewood, or some equally brilliant attorney to defend him, he will walk over the Bridge of Sighs into the electric chair."

Law Notes

OCTOBER, 1907.

PUBLISHED BY EDWARD THOMPSON COMPANY.
NORTHPORT, LONG ISLAND, N. Y.

CONTENTS.

THE meeting of the American Bar Association in Portland, Maine, at the end of August was of more than usual interest. The meeting at the same time and place of the International Law Association brought together many distinguished foreign jurists, and their deliberations had an added significance for the furtherance of orderly and peaceful international relations when we remember that the sessions of the great Peace Congress at the Hague were going forward at the same time. The address of the Hon. James Bryce, Ambassador of Great Britain, statesman, diplomat, lawyer, and accomplished scholar, gave added *éclat* to the occasion. Mr. Bryce made a happy choice of subject, the characteristics of the common law, that heritage which is common to the English-speaking nations, which has been so important a force in moulding their national characteristics, and making their institutions mutually intelligible. These points of common interest were felicitously brought out. In closing Mr. Bryce said: "The life of every nation rests mainly on what may be called its fixed ideas, those ideas which have become axioms in the mind of every citizen. Now it was mainly by the common law that these fixed and fundamental ideas were moulded whereon the constitutional freedom of America, as of England, rests. One hundred and thirty-one years have now passed since the majestic current of the common law became divided into two streams which have ever since flowed in distinct channels. Many statutes have been enacted in England since 1776 and many more enacted here, but the character of the common law remains essentially the same and it forms the mental habits in those who study and practice it. In nothing, perhaps, does the substantial identity of the two branches of the old stock appear so much as in the doctrine and practice of the law. It is a bond of sympathy, not least because it is a source of common pride. The law of a nation is not only an expression of its character, but a main factor in its greatness. What the bony skeleton is to the body, what her steel ribs are to a ship, that to a state is its law, holding all the parts fitly joined together so that each may retain its proper functions. The common law has done this for you and for us in such wise as to have helped form the mind and habits of the individual citizens as well as of the whole nation. It is all their own. They can remould it if they will. Where a system of law has been made by the people and for the people, where it conforms to their sentiments and breathes their spirit, it deserves and receives the confidence of the people. So may it ever be both in America and in England."

ARGUMENTS for and against an extension of the powers of the federal government were ably presented to the American Bar Association by President Alton B. Parker, ex-Chief Judge of the Court of Appeals of New York, and by Judge Charles F. Amidon of the United States District Court for North Dakota. Judge Amidon states with his usual clearness and frankness the reasons for extending federal powers at the expense of the States. In reading his observations, one is reminded of Lord Bacon's remark: "That courts should fence and dispute about jurisdiction is natural to humanity; the rather because of a foolish doctrine, that it is the part of a good and active judge to extend the jurisdiction of his court." The reader cannot but suspect that Judge Amidon would not have used some of his arguments in favor of what President Roosevelt, who is *not* a lawyer, has referred to with approbation as constructive statesmanship on the bench, but for the unsuspected desire, so "natural to humanity," to exalt and extend the jurisdiction of his court. Judge Amidon so frankly appeals from all recognized canons of judicial construction to a "higher law" of constitutional interpretation that one's breath is fairly taken away. He alludes to the "legal Calvinism" which would result from interpreting the Constitution to-day as having the same meaning which was given to it in the simple conditions of a hundred years ago, expatiates on the impossibility of amending it by constitutional means, and sums up for constructive statesmanship on the bench as follows: "What is needed to-day is not that the Constitution shall be construed to mean precisely what it meant to Marshall or to Miller, Field, and Bradley, but that it shall be applied to present conditions by the same method and in the same spirit wherewith they applied it to the conditions of their times." These great judges lived in the benighted times when the Constitution was believed to have a definite meaning which did not change over night, and consequently an interpretation in their spirit would not meet Judge Amidon's views. We take it that he means that the Supreme Court is to become not a body of judges construing a written instrument presumed to have one definite meaning, to be found out by the application of common sense and a settled body of canons, but a collection of "elder statesmen," deciding on contemporary needs in accordance with their own wisdom and then by deliberate casuistry importing their predetermined conclusions into the Constitution. The judges whom Judge Amidon mentions were, like all men, under the influence of contemporary feeling, and occasionally that emotion may have warped their judgment. But if this was so it was an honest warping, and not the result of a deliberate determination to read into the Constitution a meaning which they knew was never intended by its framers.

Judge Amidon continues: "Within the last fifty years economic forces have been introduced into our life that are as revolutionary of pre-existing conditions as the introduction of gunpowder was of the state of feudalism. The doctrine of *laissez faire* has been abandoned, and government is now present in all lines of business. When the state regulated but little, business was not much concerned who did the regulating; but now that all governments are competing in their zeal for regulation, whether the nation or the States do the regulating becomes a matter of paramount importance. The national government and the States cannot prescribe rules to the same instrumentality without being brought into constant conflict. This has already brought us to the verge of civil war in North Carolina, and been the occasion of the sharpest acrimony in other States. Such a conflict must in the end result in the complete supremacy of one authority or the other. The truth is that the national government has so long neglected its powers under the commerce clause of the Constitution, that now, when it tardily takes up its duties, it is charged by the States with usurpation. One hundred years ago those who opposed the adoption of the Constitution to meet the needs of our changed political condition made 'consolidation' their cry of alarm; to-day those who oppose the control by the national government of the business affairs that have become national raise the cry of 'centralization.' On both occasions the opposition has been guilty of that highest political folly which consists in hanging to a theory regardless of changed conditions. Centralization has already taken place out there in the world of commerce and industry. The only question remaining is: Shall the government take cognizance of the fact?"

It is hard to believe that these views were deliberately expressed by an American judge in an address before a representative body of lawyers. But we cannot think that Judge Amidon realizes the revolutionary nature of his own proposals. Happily he has already been answered by the unanimous opinion of the Supreme Court in Kansas *v.* Colorado, noticed in the August number of Law Notes. One more extract we must make from this remarkable address: "We are much nearer an absolute democracy now than when the Constitution was adopted, and have a correspondingly increased need of its restraining force. Triumphant democracy, having swept away all other bounds, now stands face to face with the instrument itself. Within the last twenty years there has arisen a cult who regard its limitations as productive of more harm than good. A more baneful heresy could not find lodgment among our people; and yet no method could be devised by which it would be given more substantial help than by the vigorous teaching and rigorous enforcement of the rule that the Constitution speaks the same meaning yesterday, to-day, and forever, and that those who are charged with its interpretation will be guided by this purely scholastic spirit. A constitution which fixedly restrains a people from correcting their actual evils becomes associated in the popular mind with the evils themselves. When it performs that rôle, as ours once did, it becomes, in the estimation of reformers, a 'compact with hell,' and enlightened statesmen appeal from its provisions to a 'higher law.'" It will be seen that this extract admits the need of limitations in the Constitution. We suppose he refers to its limitations on the powers of the States, for certainly he apprehends no baleful effects from disregarding the limitations on the national government. But is Judge Amidon correct in his gloomy forecast of the results of enforcing the rule that the Constitution means the same yesterday, to-day, and to-morrow? Some reasonable grounds for apprehension there might be, did that instrument, like some modern state constitutions, try to regulate in the style of a statute a multitude of details. But the Federal Constitution is confined to general principles, and those fundamental principles must be subverted in order that it may speak with a different meaning. The Supreme Court, as we have seen, is not prepared to overturn the relations which, by virtue of the Constitution, existed "yesterday" between the States and the nation, and we must be allowed to think that they are wiser in their conservatism than Judge Amidon. Revolution, whether it is brought about by bloody battles, by a *coup d'état*, or by a decision of a bench of judges, should not be tried until all orderly means have been patiently tested and found wanting.

Ex-Judge Parker, in his presidential address, is directly at issue with Judge Amidon. He believes that the Constitution has a definite meaning which is the same yesterday and to-day. After alluding to Chief Justice Marshall's famous canon of construction in McCulloch *v.* Maryland, he quotes Mr. Justice Brewer's declaration that "no unmentioned power passes to the national government or can rightfully be exercised by Congress," and his remark in discussing the grants of power to Congress and the limitations upon its powers: "The true spirit of constitutional interpretation in both directions is to give full liberal construction to the language, aiming ever to show fidelity to the spirit and purpose." The proposals to base an extension of national control on the grants of power over commerce and over post-roads do not meet his approval on constitutional grounds. "But," he declares, "the result of even an attempt on the part of Congress to seize the power of the States and deprive them of so large a measure of control would be most unfortunate. It is not my purpose to discuss the merits of the various claims for an increase of the federal power at the expense of the States. In the end such of them as are favorably acted upon by Congress will have to pass the test of constitutionality before that greatest of all courts, the Supreme Court of the United States, and such statutes will stand or fall as they show, or fail to show, fidelity to the spirit and purpose of the Constitution. The attempts, however, on the part of the federal government to despoil the States of the powers and functions belonging to them will not tend to smoothness in the working of our dual scheme of government. Already it has had its effect. The indignation of the governing forces of many of the States is already aroused. It is shown in the legislation of the year. It had not a little to do, in my judgment, with the recent conflict of judicial authority in North Carolina."

Conservatism and a calm and sure optimism speak in these sentences, evidently written with recent events in North Carolina and elsewhere in mind: "When a judge in the performance of what he undoubtedly conceived to be his duty, restrained the operation of the legislation of a sovereign State, it seemed to some, doubtless, but the culmination of a series of assaults by the federal government upon State governments. And yet we know that, by the Fourteenth Amendment, the power has been conferred upon the courts of the United States to set aside State statutes, and State constitutions as well, if they deprive any person of life, liberty, or property without due course of law. . . . Courts, both federal and State, should always bear in mind that comity which has thus far enabled the dual jurisdictions to work together so harmoniously for the public good. The abuses lying at the foundation of the earnest but sometimes reckless groping for remedies must be checked. And if it were necessary, in order to promote this result, to pass through these processes, many of which will prove destructive of the rights and interests of a multitude of innocent and honest persons — still it would be well. For the property, the services, and even the life of a citizen should be cheerfully sacrificed on the altar of the country's necessities. You cannot move legislators crazed with ambition. But the people can, and will do so when they fully understand the situation. And we need never fear they will not understand it after a time."

PERHAPS no more important paper was presented to the American Bar Association than that of Interstate Commerce Commissioner Prouty dealing with the Commission. It will be remembered that in the Maximum Rate Case, 167 U. S. 479, the Supreme Court declared that the determination of the reasonableness of established rates was a judicial function, while the prescribing of future rates was legislative in character. It is, of course, elementary that legislative functions cannot be delegated, but Congress may establish "a primary standard" and leave to administrative officers the duty of prescribing such rules as will bring about the results pointed out by the statute. Buttfield *v.* Stanahan, 192 U. S. 470, 496. The duties of the Commerce Commission belong to the three classes of administrative, legislative, and judicial, and the crux of the situation is how to reconcile these duties vested in a single body in the face of the provision for keeping separate the three departments of government. Commissioner Prouty proposes a division of the Commission. He says: "That Commission [the Interstate Commerce Commission] under the present law is charged with two sets of duties requiring diverse qualifications for their discharge. It stands, first, as representative of the government to see that these highways are in fact public. It is commanded to enforce the provisions of the act to regulate commerce. It must see that rates are reasonable and just; that the practices and regulations of railways are not oppressive; that the penalties provided by the act are enforced. In the near future its powers must be extended to the operation of the railway as well. These duties are largely executive. They can best be discharged by a single head, responsible to the executive, and answerable to the spur of popular criticism. Second, this Commission is in essence a judicial tribunal which hears and decides complaints. The qualifications of such a body are the exact opposite of the other. Its membership should be numerous so that its decisions may be the resultant of independent minds. It should be entirely withdrawn from all political and personal influences, and it should have time for the deliberate consideration of the matters coming before it. I very much doubt whether the same body can properly discharge both these functions. In the end it will either become remiss in its executive duties or will, in the zeal of those, become unfit for the dispassionate performance of its judicial functions. Whatever may have been true in the past, the time has come when the Commission should be relieved of all its duties except the hearing and deciding of complaints. There are several ways in which this might be accomplished. The Commission itself might perhaps be reorganized and its duties divided. Its executive functions could be transferred to a bureau in some department. I have myself thought that a new department should be created. Such a department would from the first have occupation in plenty. No department would be oftener applied to by all classes, nor would any be of more service to the whole public, railways and patrons alike." It is perhaps significant that some of the phrases here have an authoritative definiteness. It may be that Commissioner Prouty's remarks represent the plans of the administration.

ON the first of last month a statute went into effect in New York making adultery a misdemeanor. The common law did not treat adultery as an indictable offense, and, save as it gave the husband an action for damages against the wife's paramour, left it to be dealt with by the ecclesiastical courts *pro salute animarum*. New York is one of the numerous States which have left the common law unchanged in this respect, and it appears that the new statute was aimed not so much at the act itself as at the crying evil of collusive divorces. The only ground for divorce recognized in New York, it will be remembered, is adultery, or as the newspapers miscall it, with a sort of prurient euphemism, "the statutory ground" — as if all causes for divorce were not alike statutory. It is said to have become distressingly common for a married pair who are dissatisfied with the lottery of marriage to agree that one party shall furnish to the other the evidence necessary for a divorce, and then the proof is made and the decree granted without contest. The remedy by making adultery a criminal offense does not seem to be a very happy inspiration on the part of the legislators. Where adultery is connived at, the plaintiff will assuredly not institute criminal proceedings of his or her own volition — there is an honor even among thieves — and courts which habitually allow themselves to be hoodwinked and befooled by collusive evidence can hardly be depended upon to direct criminal prosecutions of their own motion. But the statute is certain to give rise to prosecutions instituted not to vindicate the law and outraged morals, but to gratify private revenge. And the injured party, free from all taint of connivance, who desires and is entitled to a divorce for his or her own sake and that of the children of the marriage, may well hesitate to subject the mother or father of their children to the degradation of a criminal prosecution and a possible year in prison. There are some wrongs which are best left to be dealt with by the healthy public sentiment of the people. If public morals are so debased as to excuse the wrong, it is not by legislation such as this that a reform can be effected. The statute, however, is an experiment, whose results will be watched with interest.

AN English barrister, Mr. J. Arthur Barrett "of London and New York" — so the newspapers give his residence — read before the recent meeting of the International Law Association a paper on "International Recognition of Divorce Jurisdiction," wherein he described "American migratory divorces" as a continuing source of trouble to English as well as to American courts. "I cannot," he proceeded, "too strongly emphasize the fact that, while the English courts will, of course, recognize American divorces, if duly procured and without fraud, they will decline to hold valid such divorces where there has been no *bona fide* domicil of the plaintiff in the State where the action was brought, and he or she simply resided in such State for the period required by its laws, and very soon after returned to the former domicil." The remedy which he proposed will strike the American lawyer as novel, if not practicable. "There should be a 'central registry,' say, in Washington, supported at the expense of all the States, where divorce decrees rendered throughout the United States should be recorded, and each State should enact a law providing that its decrees shall not become final and imperative until so recorded. Divorce lawyers, so called, who advertise their business should be disbarred for unprofessional conduct. It would be well if divorce proceedings were under the supervision of the attorney-general in each State." It seems almost impossible for English or foreign lawyers to grasp the intricacies of our governmental system. A registry such as Mr. Barrett describes would be of no service in rectifying the evil of "migratory divorces" unless some standard were applied to the decrees registered much more searching and severe than is permitted by the statutes of some of the States where divorce colonies now flourish. If each of the States would enact strict laws requiring *bona fide* domicil as a prerequisite to applying for divorce, there would be no need for a "central registry." As long, however, as some States virtually bid for this fake divorce business, the idea is, to put it mildly, rather absurd that they should destroy their chances of business by empowering an officer or set of officers to review the decrees of the courts and select a certain number for registration. Besides, it is difficult to imagine any scheme for a "central registry" which would not be grossly and palpably unconstitutional. It would seem that a State could not enact — and this appears to be the least revolutionary form the registry could take — that its own courts should recognize only such foreign divorces as were on record in the registry. This would seem to be depriving courts of an essential portion of their judicial power. But a score of objections must occur to any lawyer who devotes a few minutes' thought to such a scheme. The evil is a real one, and the grave abuses of fraudulent divorces should be ended, but we cannot think that Mr. J. Arthur Barrett is the happy genius who has solved the problem.

THE bill allowing marriage with a deceased wife's sister has after more than a half century of agitation become a law in England. The unlawfulness of such marriages was first established under the early Christian Roman emperors in the fourth century, though they had been previously, says Mr. Bryce, "apparently regarded with social disapproval. England is almost the only Protestant country which has retained the prohibition, a result which may perhaps have been fostered by the scruples of King Henry VIII.'s tender conscience in view of the fact that Catherine was the affianced wife of his brother Arthur. In Catholic countries, Chancellor Kent tells us, such marriages are still formally prohibited but dispensations are readily obtained. The first bill to render valid marriage with a deceased wife's sister was introduced in the Parliament of Great Britain in 1850. It passed the Commons, but was thrown out by the Lords. This was the regular history of all such attempts for nearly fifty years. It has been observed that few subjects had such power of exciting interest among the peers as the marriage with a deceased wife's sister bill; "they mustered to deal with it as if the destiny of the nation depended on its rejection." Since 1896, it is curious to note, a bill allowing such marriages, with the proviso that clergymen with conscientious scruples should not be compelled to officiate, has passed the Lords two or three times, but was blocked in the Commons without reaching a vote. Commenting on the attitude of the Church of England, whose bishops in the House of Lords have always opposed the bill, the *Nation* observes that its passage was sure to cause serious trouble. "The Archbishop of Canterbury," says this newspaper, "and the Bishop of London have forbidden their clergy to celebrate or recognize such marriages. On the other hand, the Assistant Bishop of Manchester takes a directly contrary view, holding that any kind of social or religious boycott of those who with a clear conscience take advantage of the amended law would be unjust. In case a clergyman of the Canterbury province disregarded the warning of the archbishop, he would incur no penalty but a reprimand for performing a strictly legal act. If, however, he followed the archbishop's advice, he would be within his rights, as no clergyman is bound to read the marriage service on demand. Yet it surely cannot help the Church to place herself deliberately in opposition to the law of the land."

As in several of the States of the Union, the death-penalty has become obsolete in France without having been actually abolished. Sentence of death is passed on the murderer as in former days, but for several years such sentences have been regularly commuted by the President. So completely obsolete have executions become that, it has been rumored, no appropriation has been made for the salary of M. Deibler, the executioner, or for the other necessary expenses of such occasions, as the transportation of the guillotine and the payment of assistants. But an alarming increase of murders has led to a demand for carrying out instead of commuting sentences for capital punishment, and investigation has shown that the worthy M. Deibler is still enjoying his salary, though his office is a very sinecure. Of course French murderers know that the sentence pronounced on them is a mere affair of form, and that in reality all they have to fear is imprisonment in some criminal colony. A letter to his relatives from Soleilland, the murderer of a little girl, is a curious commentary on the state of mind engendered in this class of criminals by the custom of commutation. Soleilland, who knew in advance that the penalty of death was a piece of harmless red tape, allowed himself to indulge in golden dreams of the future. In his letter he says: "On my arrival in New Caledonia they will give me plank boards to build my house on a piece of ground, my property. The almoner or pastor of the prison here has known men who had built cottages for themselves and sold them afterwards for 40,000 francs. I shall receive food during forty days, until the time arrives when I can work. There is money to be made by those who are enterprising, for every piece of work is promptly sold at high price. . . . When you (his wife and her brother) come over, two years hence, I shall have earned four francs a day and saved 2,000 francs net. All the money we shall earn afterward will be ours." It would really seem that the life of a convicted murderer is pleasanter than that of some French peasants, and the prospect holds out real charms. A different inference would be drawn from the case of the criminal sentenced a few months ago who protested against the commutation of his sentence, and insisted with energy on his constitutional right to be guillotined. *Tot homines, quot sententiæ.*

YELLOW PSYCHOLOGY.

IN other days Mr. Justice Miller and his associates on the bench of the United States Supreme Court said they found it more difficult to decide questions of fact satisfactorily than questions of law. (21 Am. Law Rev., at p. 863, *per* Mr. Justice Miller.) Many other judges have testified to the same experience. (Barrett *v.* Suttis, 17 Nova Scotia 274, 275, *per* the late Judge Weatherbe.) They are now told, however, that they may reach their goal without threading long, dark, and treacherous paths. A Northwest Passage to truth has been discovered by no less a personage than Dr. Hugo Münsterberg, professor of psychology in Harvard University. He found it in his class room, and has mapped and charted it.

In an article entitled "Nothing but the Truth," in *McClure's Magazine* for September, he says to the judges — these are his words — "Ask the psychological expert to determine the value of that factor which becomes most influential — the mind of the witness." The expert will do it in a jiffy. The judge need not exercise, nor even possess, any reasoning faculty. All he needs is faith in the expert. But there's the rub. Infidelity is rife on the bench. "Experience has caused me to have little confidence in the opinions of experts and professors, who often have more knowledge than judgment," said Mr. Justice Grier of the United States Supreme Court. Livingston *v.* Jones, 15 Fed. Cas. 8,413 (at p. 668). The same sentiment has been expressed, at one time or another, in the reported opinions of almost every court. An old Thibetan magician gave an importunate inquirer a formula which would enable him to perform miracles. Attached to the gift was this instruction: "No one is competent to use this recipe until the expiration of a period of three days during which he has not once thought of monkeys." The precedent requirement of faith in an expert's opinion in a lawsuit is a condition so difficult to fulfil that we are inclined to think the judges will continue to depend upon their own resources in searching for truth.

The author of the *McClure's* article, alluding to imperfections in human testimony, propounds this query: "Do we really all perceive the same, and does it mean to us the same in our immediate absorption of the surrounding world?" Then follows this gem: "Is the court sufficiently aware of the great differences in men's perceptions?" etc. In the last six or eight years we have read the reported opinions of judges in upwards of one hundred and fifty thousand cases, for the purpose of observing and noting what the judges have to say for themselves when announcing their conclusions on questions of fact. With equal interest — and with some profit, we trust — we have read treatises on psychology by various well-reputed writers, such as Mr. Spencer, President Porter, Dr. Ladd, Ribot, and others, and, of course, the fascinating pages of Dr. James. On almost every topic that has a proximate and practical relation to the trustworthiness of testimony delivered in court, the judges have the psychologists "beaten a mile." Why not? Antecedent probabilities all point to that conclusion. Take Judge Dillon, for instance. "I have tried literally thousands of cases with juries," he said, addressing the Yale students. (Laws and Jur., etc., Lecture IV., p. 122). A great number of these trials were in the federal Circuit Court, where the judges habitually and freely advise juries on questions of fact, as authorized by the common-law practice. The same judge has, of course, tried and decided thousands of cases without juries. Like Mr. Justice Miller, he was a practicing physician in his younger days. Were not his facilities for observation of men in every walk of life, and of their capacity as witnesses, incomparably superior to any that can be manufactured by the psychologists? Professor Münsterberg's article is devoted chiefly to an account of experiments in his class room, which we shall presently consider. A judge's class room is the court room. There, year after year, he conducts or presides over experiments of living and momentous consequence. His duty, as imperative and sacred as any that can be imposed on mortal man, demands that he shall strive to improve all these opportunities to qualify himself to execute wisely the trust confided to him. Are the judges inferior to psychologists in intellectual capacity, and less competent to utilize the information gained by their experiments? The law reports teem with opinions discussing the fidelity of human observation and memory, some of them written by men whose names will perish only with the civilization of the world. Lord Stowell and Chief Justice Marshall, for example, gave as much consideration to questions of fact involved in cases before them as to profound problems of international or constitutional law.

We never find a judge citing or quoting a psychologist. When Chief Justice Beasley spoke of "those who know from experience and reflection the laws which regulate the human memory" (17 N. J. Eq., at p. 335), he was not alluding to psychologists, and he proceeded to expound and apply some of those laws himself. A treatise on Attention and Memory that would be more voluminous than any entire work on psychology ever written, could be compiled from the opinions of judges. The most authentic instruction extant on those subjects, except where pathological conditions must be considered, is in judicial opinions. A psychologist will tell you, peradventure, that 4.1144 per cent. of eleven negro women, whom he catechised, recollected such and such a class of incidents in their childhood. But a native Southern judge knows a thing or two about the memories and mental characteristics of the negro race, and says so when occasion arises.

Professor Münsterberg says experiments in his class room reveal the fact that men differ greatly in their estimates of the length of short periods of time — a few seconds, for instance. "And yet," he remarks, "a district attorney hopes for a reliable reply when he inquires of a witness, perhaps of a cabman, how much time passed by between the shooting in the cab and a cry." Nonsense. The district attorney knows as well as the judge that "nothing is more uncertain and unreliable than the testimony of witnesses as to the time occupied in a transaction," and that "there are situations when moments seem hours, and others when time flies imperceptibly." McGrail *v.* McGrail, 48 N. J. Eq. 532, 536, and a vast multitude of other cases. The district attorney expects a reply which will be persuasive that the time was short; that is all. We challenge any one to point out, among the million and odd cases in the law reports, a single case where the decision of a court on the most insignificant question of fact was controlled by the supposed accuracy of a witness's estimate of time. Furthermore, if a witness makes a precise estimate and insists vehemently, as he sometimes does, upon its absolute correctness, the rest of his testimony is likely to be taken with caution; for gross stupidity of a witness may be as fatal to his testimony as want of integrity, and an adult witness who needs to be informed by a psychologist that estimates of time from unaided memory are pure guesswork, subjects his intelligence to just suspicion.

What would happen if a psychologist gravely informed a judge that he had discovered the fact of pronounced variations in men's judgments of lapse of time? Well, let us suppose a case or two. Imagine a man rushing up to Professor Asaph Hall, the astronomer and mathematician, and saying: "Professor, I have found that if you take a rectangular sheet of postage stamps and count the number of stamps on one side and the number on the other and multiply them together, the product will be the number of stamps in the sheet. It occurs to me that the information may be valuable in solving mathematical problems." What would Professor Hall say to his panting friend? Again, conceive a man saying to the chief engineer of the Panama Canal: "I took a quart of sand into my laboratory the other day, and with instruments of precision I find that the natural slope of dry sand is 33° 41′, or 1½ to 1, and that a few handfuls can be coquetted into standing at 1 to 1 on a table. You have so much excavating to do that I thought you would be glad to know this." If a judge spoke the dialect of the renowned John L., he would exclaim, "To the tall timbers for yours!" to the psychologist.

Professor Münsterberg also gives us the tabulated results of experiments showing that witnesses' estimates of speed are unreliable. In at least a hundred reported cases courts have discussed that topic, and shrewd comments on the absolute and relative weight of testimony of passengers, engineers, and trainmen, and outside observers as to the speed of railroad trains, electric cars, automobiles, horse vehicles, and vessels, with sage suggestions concerning the effect of various psychological influences, abound in the books.

"We hear the witnesses talking about the taste of poisoned liquids, and there is probably no one in the jury box who knows enough of physiological psychology to be aware that the same substance may taste quite differently on different parts of the tongue," says the author of the *McClure's* article. The fact is stated in at least one encyclopædia that is owned by thousands of jurymen. If a judge or juryman has not read, or cannot recollect at the moment, everything his encyclopædia contains, would an interlocutor, fresh from the book, who catches him unprepared, entitle himself to sit at the judge's elbow as a mentor in the various judicial inquiries on foot? This would indeed be "2 mutch," as Artemus Ward expressed it. A case is easily conceivable where it would be necessary for a judge to know the components of a Manhattan cocktail, but a bartender witness who enlightened him would be expected to say no more and return to his customers. The senses of taste, smell, and touch have been considered in numerous adjudicated cases. See, for example, as to taste, Ten Hogsheads of Rum, 1 Gall. (U. S.) 187, 23 Fed. Cas. No. 13,830. That was not a case of "poisoning," or of "poisoned liquids," or a "murder case," a "Bowery wrangle," or a "shooting" in a cab, matters which constitute the chief part of what Professor Münsterberg terms with amusing naïveté his "records;" it was merely a case without yellow hue where a distinguished judge of the United States Supreme Court had occasion to weigh the testimony of a witness identifying a brand of rum by its taste.

We come now to Professor Münsterberg's capital experiment, a scientific triumph. He exhibited to his class several pairs of colored paper squares, successively, and found that about a fifth of the men erroneously pronounced one of the gray squares darker than a blue one in juxtaposition with it. Then he stood on the platform behind a low desk and requested the class to watch and afterward describe everything he did for a given short period. He lifted with his right hand "a little revolving wheel with a colored disk and made it run and change its color." While the students were watching the wheel, he took several small articles out of his pocket with his left hand and deposited them on the desk. The results showed that eighteen of the hundred students had not noticed anything of all that he did with his left hand. Now mark the sentence which inexorable Science pronounces upon some of the luckless eighteen. "Of those eighteen men," says the demonstrator, "fourteen were the same who, in the foregoing experiment, judged the light gray to be darker than the dark blue. . . . The coincidence proved clearly how very quickly a little experiment such as this with a piece of blue and gray paper, which can be performed in a few seconds, can pick out for us *those minds which are utterly unfit to report whether an action has been performed in their presence or not.*" Sad, very sad. And yet they were "highly trained, careful observers," "university students, trained in observation," so we are told. Just think of it. And reflect upon the grosser incapacity of men not thus "trained," who have the temerity not to recuse themselves when they are offered as witnesses in court — the hundreds of thousands of men in this country employed in vocations where, we had supposed, their alertness of observation is all that protects the lives or limbs of themselves and their fellow workmen.

Of course, the experimenter's opinion of the unfitness of those young men, as above quoted, based upon the data which he gives, would have as little weight in a court of justice as a communication from Mrs. Pepper-Vanderbilt's little Indian spirit, Bright Eyes. It is perfectly plain that, if the experiment is to be taken as signifying anything, those eighteen young men would make exceptionally good witnesses. They testified to what they observed, upon which their attention was so closely concentrated that they frankly confessed nonobservance of collateral incidents. Mobility of attention is characteristic of children. Even the psychologists have noticed that. It is quite probable that Daniel condemned the elders, not merely because of discrepancy in their description of the trees, but because it was incredible that their attention should have been for an instant withdrawn from the principal and highly seductive proceeding. (History of Susanna, Apocrypha.)

And if the professor should offer to perpetrate those experiments upon a witness in court and let them count for what they were worth, divested of his opinion, the judge would be gifted with the patience of ten Jobs if he succeeded in keeping his temper. Among the legal profession it is familiar learning that experiments are valuable only when the conditions are fairly identical with those attending the occurrence under investigation. If the conditions are substantially dissimilar the experiments are not admissible at all, for the domain of reasoning has been passed and that of pure surmise entered. In the first place, the objects or actions to be observed in a class room or court room test would probably bear no resemblance to those in actual controversy with their manifold adjuncts of time, place, and circumstance. Next, litigated questions are seldom tried *de recenti facto*, and the trustworthiness of testimony usually depends quite as much upon the faculty of memory as upon capacity or habit of observation. Memory, however, is not a factor in the Münsterberg experiments. Again, it is a commonplace truth, noticed by all the psychologists — and by the judges of courts in numberless cases — that the bodily condition of a person pre-eminently affects the accuracy both of observation and of memory. Such conditions could not be reproduced in experiments. Professor Münsterberg did not concern himself about them at the time of his experiments. For aught he knows, he may have condemned a young man almost crazy with toothache, or another who had been all night the guest of a Boston Ancient and Honorable and just returned from copious entertainment. As to the unsatisfactory character of evidence of experiments to test the capacity of witnesses, in consequence of "varying conditions mental and physical," see West Pub. Co. *v.* Lawyers' Co-op. Pub. Co., (C. C. A.) 79 Fed. Rep. 769.

Suppose a witness declares he did *not* observe an occurrence. By what reliable means would the psychological expert test that witness in support of a theory that he did observe but has forgotten? By the way, the professor says "the witness who lies offers no psychological interest."

There is not a scintilla of evidence in the *McClure's* article that its author has ever read a single reported opinion of a judge, or that he has the remotest conception of the processes by which judges are accustomed to arrive at their conclusions. Uninformed persons, and, indeed, some lawyers (see 18 Grant Ch. (Ontario) 682, 683), greatly overrate the value that courts attach to direct testimony. It would be difficult to find a case where a question of fact has been determined solely by the statement of any witness, unaffected by the burden of proof, the requisite degree of proof, or consideration of presumptions and probabilities, number and concurrence of witnesses, or consistency of the testimony with admitted facts.

Professor Münsterberg sneers at "the primitive psychology of common sense," which, he says, is really "out of order" in the court room. Imagine him butting in with his so-called scientific experiments to appraise the testimony of a witness in competition with the following primitive common-sense utterance of the celebrated Lord Stowell: "It is a good safe rule in weighing evidence of a fact, which you cannot compare with any other evidence to the same fact, to compare it with the actual conduct of the persons who describe it. If their conduct is clearly such as upon their own showing it could not have been, taking the fact in the way they have represented it, it is a pretty fair inference that the fact did not so happen. If their actings, at the very time that the fact happened, represent it one way and their relation of it at a great distance of time represents it another way, there can be no doubt which is the authentic narrative, which is the naked truth of the matter." Evans *v.* Evans, 1 Hag. Cons. 35, 64.

CHARLES C. MOORE.

PROMISE OF IMMUNITY BY PROSECUTING ATTORNEY.

JUDGE KENESAW MOUNTAIN LANDIS, of the United States District Court, Northern District of Illinois, is credited by the daily newspapers with having stated in open court that if the district attorney had promised the Chicago and Alton Railroad Company, or its officers, immunity from prosecution for testifying against the Standard Oil Company as to the giving of rebates, the preservation of the honor of the government demanded that the promise should be redeemed. This alleged utterance has elicited considerable adverse criticism on the one hand and warm commendation on the other. The soundness of the position taken by Judge Landis depends upon whether the district attorney had a right to make such a promise. We do not understand that Judge Landis meant that the promise was absolutely binding upon the government. But the promise should confer no right, either legal or equitable, upon the promisee, if the district attorney had no power to make it. A person accused of crime is as much bound to know the law concerning the right of the prosecuting attorney to promise immunity as he is to know the law concerning any other subject. *Ex p.* Greenhaw, 41 Tex. Crim. 278.

In the Whiskey Cases, 99 U. S. 594, it was held that a United States district attorney has no authority to contract that a person accused of an offense against the United States shall not be prosecuted or his property subjected to condemnation therefor, if, when examined as a witness against his accomplices, he discloses fully and fairly his and their guilt. In its opinion the court said: "Accomplices in guilt, not previously convicted of an infamous crime, when separately tried are competent witnesses for or against each other; and the universal usage is that such a party, if called and examined by the public prosecutor on the trial of his associates in guilt, will not be prosecuted for the same offense, provided it appears that he acted in good faith and that he testified fully and fairly. Where the case is not within any statute, the general rule is that if an accomplice, when examined as a witness by the public prosecutor, discloses fully and fairly the guilt of himself and his associates, he will not be prosecuted for the offense disclosed; but it is equally clear that he cannot by law plead such facts in bar of any indictment against him, nor avail himself of it upon his trial, for it is merely an equitable title to the mercy of the executive, subject to the conditions before stated, and can only come before the court by way of application to put off the trial in order to give the prisoner time to apply to the executive for that purpose." See also U. S. *v.* Hinz, 35 Fed. Rep. 272.

In Temple *v.* Com., 75 Va. 892, the court held that a prosecuting attorney has no power to promise a person accused of a crime immunity from prosecution, basing its decision upon the following reasoning: "No implied suggestion by the court nor any implied or positive promise by the commonwealth's attorney could operate as an indemnity to the witness that he would not be further prosecuted. He had a right to stand upon his constitutional privilege, and not to trust to the chances of a further prosecution. The court, of course, could offer him no such indemnity. Nor could the commonwealth's attorney, for he might die, or be removed, or resign, and his successor might see fit to institute a prosecution against him. Or whether he did or not, a grand jury, without the advice or consent of the commonwealth's attorney, might institute such prosecution."

It has been held in several cases that a promise of immunity does not deprive a person accused of crime of his constitutional privilege to refuse to give self-incriminating evidence. *Ex p.* Irvine, 74 Fed. Rep. 954; Muller *v.* State, 11 Lea (Tenn.) 18; Temple *v.* Com., 75 Va. 892. See also Foot *v.* Buchanan, 113 Fed. Rep. 156. The reason usually given for this holding is that the prosecuting attorney has no right to promise immunity. Thus, in Temple *v.* Com., 75 Va. 892, the court said: "A man, having a privilege secured to him by the constitution, cannot be required to waive that high constitutional right upon the suggestion either by the court, who had no right to make it, or by the commonwealth's attorney, who is powerless to redeem his pledge, that *peradventure* no prosecution would be instituted against him. He has a right to stand upon his constitutional privilege, and to remain silent whenever any question is asked him the answer to which *may tend to criminate himself.*"

But while the general rule is that a prosecuting attorney cannot promise a person accused of crime immunity from prosecution, the rule obtains on the other hand that when an accomplice testifies in behalf of the prosecution and makes a full and fair disclosure as to the guilt of himself and associates, a promise is implied that he will not be punished for the offense committed by him. 1 Am. and Eng. Encyc. of Law (2d ed.) 406. In State *v.* Graham, 41 N. J. L. 15, the court stated this rule as follows, assimilating it to the obsolete practice of approvement: "When an accomplice is received by the court as a witness against his fellows, and makes a full disclosure, without prevarication or fraud, the understanding is that there is an implied promise that he will be recommended to the mercy of the crown. Such a procedure is obviously a substitute for the ancient method of approvement, which appears to have been obsolete even in the time of Lord Hale. The course in pursuing this old form was for the culprit, indicted for treason or felony, to confess the truth of the charge, and, upon being sworn, to reveal all the treasons and felonies within his knowledge, and to enter before a coroner his appeal against all his partners in crime who were within the realm. The criminal thus confessing was called the approver, or, in Latin, *probator*, and the person implicated was styled the appellee. By this confession and appeal the approver put it in the discretion of the court either to give judgment and award execution against him, or to respite him until the conviction of his partners in guilt; and if it was deemed advisable to admit him as an approver, and then if, upon being sworn, he made a full and true disclosure, and also convicted the appellee, either by his oath or on wager of battle, the king, *ex merito justitiæ*, pardoned him 'as to his life.' This practice, with its conditions that the appellee could claim a trial by battle, and that grace to the approver should be dependent on his conviction of his associate in crime, was plainly at variance with modern sentiments and habits, and the consequence was that it passed out of use; but as the purpose it served was of value to juridical administration, it was inevitable, in the ordinary development of the law, that some equivalent should take its place. That equivalent was the modern practice, before referred to, of an implied pledge that the court would recommend the criminal who made a confession and was accepted as a witness, to the royal clemency. But such an implied pledge is not a legal right, but a ground for an equitable claim only, so that under no circumstances can it supply matter for a plea in bar, or otherwise constitute a basis of a defense."

The implied promise that an accomplice testifying against his associates shall not be punished merely confers an equitable right upon the accomplice, and does not confer a legal right to immunity which he can set up as a defense to a subsequent prosecution for the same offense. Whiskey Cases, 99 U. S. 594; U. S. *v.* Hinz, 35 Fed. Rep. 272; *Ex p.* Irvine, 74 Fed. Rep. 954; State *v.* Graham, 41 N. J. L. 15; 1 Am. and Eng. Encyc. of Law (2d ed.) 407. Furthermore, it is generally considered that the equitable right conferred upon the accomplice is not to have the prosecuting attorney or the court dismiss the prosecution, but is only to receive a pardon from the executive. Thus, in the Whiskey Cases, 99 U. S. 594, the court held that an accomplice who has testified against his associates has merely an equitable title to executive mercy, of which title the court may take notice only when an application to postpone the case is made in order to give the accomplice an opportunity to apply for a pardon. See also U. S. *v.* Hinz, 35 Fed. Rep. 272; *Ex p.* Irvine, 74 Fed. Rep. 954; State *v.* Graham, 41 N. J. L. 15; Rex *v.* England, 2 Leach C. C. 767.

In Texas, however, the rule obtains that a district attorney, acting with the concurrence of the court, may make a promise of immunity which is binding upon the State, and that if the promisee faithfully complies with his part of the agreement the promise is a bar to a subsequent prosecution for the same offense. Bowden *v.* State, 1 Tex. App. 137; Hardin *v.* State, 12 Tex. App. 517; Camron *v.* State, 32 Tex. Crim. 180; Stanford *v.* State, 42 Tex. Crim. 343. *Contra*, Holmes *v.* State, 20 Tex. App. 509. In Camron *v.* State, 32 Tex. App. 180, it was held that while the prosecuting attorney's promise should be made with the consent of the court, his promise without such consent should be held binding upon the State, where the promisee acts in good faith and the court permits him to testify with knowledge of the promise.

It will be seen that the weight of authority is that a prosecuting attorney has no power to promise an offender immunity from prosecution in consideration of his testimony against other offenders, but that where an accomplice testifies in good faith against his fellows there is an implied promise that he shall not be punished, which promise gives him an equitable right to a pardon. Whatever the true rule may be in regard to prosecutions in State courts, the decision in the Whiskey Cases, 99 U. S. 594, seems to settle the following propositions, in so far as prosecutions in the federal courts are concerned: (1) A district attorney of the United States has no authority to promise a person accused of crime that he shall not be prosecuted. (2) When an accomplice testifies in good faith against his associates, and makes a full and fair disclosure of his own acts and those of his associates, there is an implied promise that he shall receive a pardon. (3) The right which such promise gives to the accomplice is equitable merely, and not legal. (4) This equitable right merely entitles the accomplice to a postponement of the prosecution against him in order that he may make an appeal for executive clemency, and the promise cannot be pleaded by him as a bar to any prosecution brought against him. It therefore appears that if Judge Landis, by his statement that the district attorney's promise of immunity should be redeemed by the government, meant that the promisee should be given an opportunity to appeal to the executive department for a pardon, he was clearly right, but that if he meant that the promise should operate to bar the prosecution without action by the executive department, the statement was unauthorized, inasmuch as it conflicted squarely with a decision of the Supreme Court of the United States.

J. C. M.

CERTAIN DEFECTS IN OUR STATUTES OF LIMITATION.

THE injustice sometimes worked by the statute of limitations, or now more properly the statutes of limitation, has often been the subject of comment at the bar, and, notwithstanding the wise and salutary purpose of these enactments, has not infrequently called forth more or less sympathetic animadversions from the bench. The unmeasured condemnation of these statutes by creditors possessed of more forbearance than the law regards as consistent with prudence, is always to be heard. That considerable adverse criticism of this branch of the law is the result of ignorance or shortsightedness or is the torrential though pardonable outpouring of the spirit by disgruntled litigants and their counsel, is quite obvious, and it is not to be taken seriously. But that some of these statutes and the interpretation given to them by the courts are in some particulars confusing, arbitrary, and illogical, and of such a character as to work hardship with but little corresponding advantage to the general cause of justice, cannot be denied; and, when the wide scope and everyday importance of these enactments are considered, some very substantial grounds for criticism become apparent. In truth the technicalities and even absurdities of many phases of the law of limitations are so numerous and well known that to include them within the limits of this article would be well-nigh impossible and would serve no very useful purpose. It is the writer's intention to point out only a few of those that appear to be the most in need of correction, with special reference to the statutes of New York. One anomaly of the statutes of limitation in some States having the "code system" is to preserve a distinction between the limitation of suits in equity and of actions at law, which, while for reasons logical enough under judicial systems supporting separate courts of law and equity, is wholly absurd in jurisdictions where the two courts are amalgamated into one with the jurisdiction of both and where there are statutes purporting to abolish the distinctions between forms of action, especially between actions at law and suits in equity. New York, the pioneer of code States, furnishes an example of this which is no less surprising than puzzling. Here the statute relating to limitation in cases of fraud stands in its antique phraseology as an awkward and unlovely monument of a day that is (or ought to be) dead. The provision referred to (N. Y. Code Civ. Pro., § 382, subd. 5) is a part of the statute stating what actions must be commenced within six years and reads as follows:

"An action to procure a judgment, other than for a sum of money, on the ground of fraud, in a case which, on the thirty-first day of December, 1846, was cognizable by the court of chancery. The cause of action, in such a case, is not deemed to have accrued, until the discovery, by the plaintiff, or the person under whom he claims, of the facts constituting the fraud."

Even more technical was the precursor of this provision in the old code, which required that the case should be one which on the date mentioned was "solely cognizable in the court of chancery" — a requirement greatly restricting the rule in equity under the Revised Statutes, which allowed limitation to run from the discovery of the fraud in cases of concurrent as well as exclusive jurisdiction. Foote *v.* Farrington, 41 N. Y. 164, 170; Mayne *v.* Griswold, 3 Sandf. (Super. Ct.) 463. And these code provisions were solemnly enacted along with a body of laws vesting in one court jurisdiction of both law and equity and declaring, though not without subsequent judicial contradiction (Gould *v.* Cayuga County Nat. Bank, 86 N. Y. 83, 84), that "there is only one form of action" and that "the distinctions between actions at law and suits in equity, and the forms of those actions and suits, have been abolished." N. Y. Code Civ. Pro. (1907), § 3339; N. Y. Code Pro., § 69. What reason existed for incorporating into a new and "reformed" judicial system this hoary relic of the days of Eldon and Kent, is as difficult to discover as is a reason for retaining it up to the present time, and the latter difficulty is increased in view of the fact that as a result of the code the principles and maxims of equity are often held applicable in actions of a purely legal character. New York Central Ins. Co. *v.* National Protective Ins. Co., 14 N. Y. 85, at pp. 90, 91; Despard *v.* Walbridge, 15 N. Y. 374; Wright *v.* Wright, 54 N. Y. 437, 442 *et seq.*; Mandeville *v.* Reynolds, 68 N. Y. 528, 545. Even more surprising is the fact that several other States in adopting the code system of New York have embodied in their statutes, apparently without hesitation or question, the same provision substantially as they found it.

The objections to such provisions as the foregoing are more than academic. Let us view the practical working of the New York statute; and in so doing begin with principles independent of the peculiarities of that law.

It is common learning that at a comparatively early date the prevailing rule in New York and elsewhere (though with regard to actions at law there soon arose respectable authority to the contrary) was that in actions based on fraud the statute of limitations when applied in courts of equity ran from the time when the fraud was discovered or might have been discovered, while in courts of law it ran from the time the fraud was committed. The common-law courts followed the statute strictly, while the courts of equity, reluctant to allow a man to "take advantage of his own wrong," and that, too, in a "court of conscience," pursued a course more in harmony with common notions of justice. See Mayne *v.* Griswold, 3 Sandf. (Super. Ct.) 463, which contains an excellent summary by Mason, J. The unquestionable and obvious injustice of the rule at law eventually led some courts to adopt the equitable rule, and in many States resulted in legislation abolishing the former and substituting the latter. But in New York both courts and legislature clung steadfastly to their ancient faith, the legislature making only one slight concession to the equitable rule, viz., to strike the word "solely" from the text of the statute which confined the rule to cases formerly "solely cognizable in the court of chancery." Carr *v.* Thompson, 87 N. Y. 160; Bosley *v.* National Machine Co., 123 N. Y. 550. And even this was curtailed by making the equitable rule apply not as formerly to "an action for relief on the ground of fraud," but to "an action to procure a judgment, other than for a sum of money, on the ground of fraud." Code Civ. Pro., § 382, subd. 5; Miller *v.* Miller, 116 N. Y. 351.

In actions of deceit the rule in New York has remained as it was before the code (Leonard *v.* Pitney, 5 Wend. 30), and the statute runs from the time the fraud was committed. Leonard *v.* Pitney, *supra;* Foote *v.* Farrington, 41 N. Y. 164, 172; Northrop *v.* Hill, 57 N. Y. 351 (*affirming* 61 Barb. 136); Miller *v.* Wood, 116 N. Y. 351 (*affirming* 41 Hun 600); Reilly *v.* Sabater, 43 N. Y. Supp. 383, 384. Such an action obviously does not come within the scope of Code Civ. Pro., § 382, subd. 5, above quoted. Miller *v.* Wood, *supra;* Foot *v.* Farrington, *supra.* Now take, for example, the common case of a purchase of corporate stock induced by the fraudulent representations of the directors, officers, or agents of the company. The defrauded purchaser has an election of several remedies. He may bring an action of deceit to recover the damages he has sustained, in which event the statute will run from the time the fraud was committed. Bosley *v.* National Machine Co., 123 N. Y. 550, 555, by Earl, J., and authorities cited above. He may declare the sale rescinded, tender back the stock and dividends received, if any, and sue for the money he has paid, in which case the running of the statute would not be postponed until the discovery of the fraud (Bosley *v.* National Machine Co., 123 N. Y. 550, 555, by Earl, J.), but might possibly date from the time of the rescission (Richter *v.* Union Land, etc., Co., 129 Cal. 367, 375). He may, however, bring an equitable action for a rescission of the contract, a cancellation of his subscription, and the removal of his name as a stockholder from the books of the company (so as to protect himself against future liability as a stockholder), and for the recovery of what he paid for the stock. Such a suit falls within the express terms of Code Civ. Pro., § 382, subd. 5, and the statute begins to run only upon the plaintiff's "discovery of the facts constituting the fraud" (Bosley *v.* National Machine Co., *supra*), or of course from his discovery of facts "from which an inference of fraud follows" (Higgins *v.* Crouse, 147 N. Y. 411). In view of the fact that in many cases the "facts constituting the fraud" or the facts "from which an inference of fraud arises" may not be discovered by the defrauded party until the statutory period has expired, the selection of the proper remedy is a matter of prime importance. But what becomes of the solemn declaration of the code (Code Civ. Pro., § 3339; Code Pro., § 69) that the distinction between actions at law and suits in equity, and the forms of such actions and suits, "have been abolished"? There can hardly be any criticism of the construction placed upon the statute by the foregoing decisions. The cases were thoroughly considered by able and accomplished judges and have never been questioned. The trouble inheres in the statute itself. It is not alone that the law is highly technical and out of harmony with the spirit of the code, but that it is woefully unjust. In this year of grace and in the State of New York, what sanctity should attach to a suit "in equity" that a man may vindicate his rights thereby when he would be precluded by lapse of time from resorting to any other remedy? And why in the name of common sense should a man thus be barred of relief by way of an action for damages when there is no impediment to his maintaining on the same state of facts a suit for rescission and cancellation and to "get his money back"? If there be any justification for such a condition of the law, verily it "passeth all understanding."

Again, the fraudulent concealment of a cause of action other than fraud did not before the code operate to toll the statute (Troup *v.* Smith, 20 Johns. 33; Allen *v.* Miller, 17 Wend. 202; Humbert *v.* Trinity Church, 24 Wend. 587), and the code has not changed the law in this particular except in a narrow class of cases embraced in section 410, subdivision 1. In order to toll the statute until discovery, fraud must be the gravamen of the action. Carr *v.* Thompson, 87 N. Y. 160. In many other States the injustice worked by this rule has been done away with either by the courts or by the legislature, so that limitation does not run while the cause of action remains concealed. What useful purpose or what theory of public policy is served by allowing a wrongdoer to cover up his tracks until the statutory period (which may be only a year or two) has expired, and then fare boldly forth unwhipped of justice? Or to deny relief on a meritorious cause of action merely because the defendant has been clever and rascally enough to keep the wool over the plaintiff's eyes for a legally sufficient space of time? Is it better that honest men be successfully defrauded of their rights than that litigation be increased! Truly this phase of the law is well designed for the confusion of the just and the delight of the ungodly. The origin of the harsh rule under discussion is merely the lack of a proper exception in the statute. This defect has been remedied in other jurisdictions; why not here?

Another odd defect in the New York statute, though less fraught with serious results, may here be noted. Although particular limitations are prescribed for particular actions and with considerable exhaustiveness of enumeration (Code Civ. Pro., §§ 381–387), and a limitation is fixed for actions not otherwise provided for (*id.*, § 388), there is no express provision made for the very common action for deceit. Within what period then must such an action be brought? The section prescribing a six-year limitation includes (*id.*, § 382, subd. 3) "an action to recover damages for an injury to property, or a personal injury; except in a case where a different period is expressly prescribed in this chapter." This does not greatly resemble an action of deceit, but the code elsewhere (section 3343, subdivision 10) defines an "injury to property" as "an actionable act, whereby the estate of another is lessened, other than a personal injury, or the breach of a contract." Here we have it. Fraud is "an injury to property." Wallace *v.* Jones, 182 N. Y. 37, 42; Hutchinson *v.* Young, 93 App. Div. 407–409; Stewart *v.* Lyman, 62 App. Div. 182; Benedict *v.* Guardian Trust Co., 58 App. Div. 302; Lanfer *v.* Sayles, 5 App. Div. 582; Campion Card, etc., Co. *v.* Searing, 47 Hun 237; Bogart *v.* Dart, 25 Hun 395, 396. The result reached may be good enough, but while the framers of the statute were about the task and were at so much pains to provide for equitable actions based on fraud, why could they not have given us something more direct and plain than this dismal and roundabout route to an action of deceit? Earlier forms of section 382 were certainly plain enough. Its authors, obsessed perhaps by a liking for profuse punctuation, apparently succeeded in compressing the whole body of civil actions within the space of less than two lines and applying thereto the six-year period. The section once read: "Within six years: 1st. An action upon a contract, obligation or liability, express or implied." Giving the provision effect according to its punctuation it clearly comprehended an action of deceit (Miller *v.* Wood, 116 N. Y. 351, 354), and might have embraced almost any other civil action. By amendment the commas in the lines quoted were omitted, and the law now reads as it perhaps was intended to read in the beginning, and provides a limitation for actions on obligations of a contractual nature (except judgments and sealed instruments).

The condition of the law of New York as above described has been all too long neglected. Its evils are serious and far-reaching, and in the interest of common justice should be remedied by proper legislation. H. T.

NEW YORK CITY.

SIR THOMAS LITTLETON.

To write a good book is one of the surest roads to immortality in the law. Certainly it is to his book on Tenures that Sir Thomas Littleton owes his fame. Had he never written it he would be remembered only as the progenitor of a distinguished family — if he were remembered at all. We learn from the preface of Coke's first Institute that Littleton came "of an ancient and fair descended family," his father being Thomas Westcote, of Westcote near Barnstaple, according to Foss;[1] his mother, Elizabeth de Littleton, whose family took their name from Littleton, or Lyttleton, in Worcestershire. Being heiress

[1] Judges of England, vol. iv, 436.

to great estates, and desiring to perpetuate the name of her family, his mother stipulated before marriage that her child, or children, who should inherit her estates should take her name, and so Thomas, the eldest of a family of eight children — four sons and four daughters — became Thomas Littleton, or Lyttleton, and bore the Littleton arms — argent, a chevron between three escallop shells, sable. He was born at the family seat at Frankley, in Worcestershire. The date of his birth is given in the "Dictionary of National Biography" as 1402, on what evidence does not appear. Where he received his early education we know not, but we have Coke's authority that he became a member of the Inner Temple, that he was appointed "reader," and that the subject of his lecture was the Statute of Westminster II., De Donis Conditionalibus. The reader was the most important man of the Inn next after the Treasurer, and he had the right to hang his escutcheon or coat of arms on the wall of the hall of the Inn.[2] That Littleton was reader is borne out by the fact that his escutcheon is the earliest there.

In the year 1445 he must have been an advocate of repute, for it appears from the Paston Letters that a suitor petitioned the Lord Chancellor to assign him as counsel in certain proceedings against the widow of Judge Paston, whom none of the "men of the law" were willing to oppose.[3] From this it would seem, says Foss, that his practice was at that time principally in the Court of Chancery, which may perhaps account for the infrequent occurrence of his name in the Year Books, in which chancery cases are seldom recorded.

In 1450 he was Recorder of Coventry, and, representing the mayor and corporation, he presented Henry VI., when he visited the city on the 21st of September, with a tun of wine and twenty fat oxen, for which, and for his "good rule and demene," he received the royal thanks.[4]

It is also recorded that in the 30th year of Henry VI. (1452), one Sir William Trussell granted him the manor of Sheriff Hales, in Staffordshire, for his life, "*pro bono et notabili consilio.*"[5]

He was made a serjeant-at-law on the 2nd of July, 1453, and about the same time was appointed steward, or judge, of the Court of the Palace, or Marshalsea of the King's Household. Two years later, on the 13th of May, 1455, he received a patent as king's serjeant, in which capacity he went the northern circuit as judge of assize.

In the first Parliament of Edward IV., which was summoned in 1461, he was named as an arbitrator in a difference between the Bishop of Winchester and his tenants, and it appears from the Paston Letters that two years later he was in personal attendance on the king with the two chief justices on one of the royal progresses.[6]

On the 17th of April, 1466, he was appointed a judge of the Court of Common Pleas, and continued to hold the office for the remainder of his life, notwithstanding the civil commotions of the time, enjoying the confidence, it would seem, of both Edward IV. and Henry VI. as they alternately occupied, or were driven from, the throne.

In the fifteenth year of Edward IV. (1475) he was, amongst others, created a knight of the Order of the Bath.

He married Joan, one of the daughters and coheirs of Sir William Burley, of Bromscroft Castle, Shropshire, and widow of Sir Philip Chetwynd, of Ingestre, in Staffordshire, whose great possessions went to swell his already ample patrimony.[7]

[2] Calendar of Inner Temple Records, vol. i., xxxiii.
[3] Paston Letters (1840), i. 8.
[4] Gentleman's Magazine (1792), Pt. II. 986.
[5] Foss, *supra*, 437.
[6] See Foss, *supra*.
[7] See Notes and Queries, 6th series, vii. 47, 312.

By her he had two daughters, who died unmarried, and three sons, William, Richard, and Thomas.

It was for the instruction of his second son, himself an eminent lawyer in the reigns of Henry VII. and Henry VIII., that he wrote his famous book, and to him it is addressed. It was written in law French, but Coke made or adopted an English translation, and most of the modern editions are in that form. Coke thought that Littleton composed it after the fourteenth year of Edward IV. (1474–1475), and that he left it unfinished, since the table of contents of an early printed edition contained the titles "Tenant by Elegit" and "Statute Merchant and Staple" after the title "Warranty," which ends the book. This appears doubtful, however, if the "Epilogue" appended to some of the editions is genuine.

Coke also thought that the book was never printed during the author's lifetime, but this, too, is a matter of controversy.[8] It is certain that it was one of the first books printed in England.

It is evident that it very soon became a work of great repute among lawyers. Coke, whose commentary on it greatly increased its fame, had the most extravagant admiration for it. He calls it "the most perfect and absolute work that ever was written in any humane science."[9]

It consists of three books; the first dealing with the various estates in land known to the English law, the second with tenures and their incidents, and the third with miscellaneous matters. There is not much skill shown in the arrangement or analysis of the subject, but it exhibits a complete grasp of the law, and its style is a model of lucidity and simplicity.

Mr. J. M. Rigg, in the "Dictionary of National Biography," says that probably no legal treatise ever combined so much of the substance with so little of the show of learning, or so happily avoided pedantic formalism without forfeiting precision of statement.

It is scarcely necessary to remind the law student that, aided by Coke's commentary, it is the source of a great part of our law of real property. For Littleton's Tenures is a book of authority — what he says is the law.

Yet the author was modest enough himself about his performance. "And know, my son," he writes in his Epilogue, "that I would not have thee believe that all which I have said in these books is law, for I will not presume to take this upon me. But of those things that are not law inquire and learn of my wise masters learned in the law. Notwithstanding albeit that certain things which are moved and specified in the said books are not altogether law, yet such thing shall make thee more apt and able to understand, and apprehend the arguments and reasons of the law, etc. For by arguments and reasons in the law a man more sooner shall come to the certainty and knowledge of the law."

Littleton died where he was born, at Frankley, on the 23rd of August, 1481, and was buried in Worcester Cathedral.

His will is dated the day previous. To quote from Coke, "he made his three sons, a parson, a vicar, and a servant of his executors, and constituted supervisor thereof his true and faithful friend John Alcocke, Doctor of Law of the famous University of Cambridge, then Bishop of Worcester (a man of singular piety, devotion, charity, temperance, and holiness of life) who, amongst other of his charitable works, founded Jesus College in Cambridge, a fit and fast friend to our honorable and virtuous judge."

No less than three peerages have been conferred on his de-

[8] See the anonymous preface to the edition of Littleton's Tenures, published by J. & W. T. Clarke in 1831. Dict. Nat. Biog., vol. xxxiii. 375.
[9] Inst. 1, Proemium.

scendants, namely, those of Lyttleton of Frankley (now united with that of Cobham), granted to a descendant of his eldest son William; Hatherton, granted to a descendant of his second son Richard; and Lyttleton of Munslow, now extinct, granted to a descendant of his third son Thomas; while a fourth, that of Lilford, is held by a descendant through the female line. — *London Law Notes.*

Cases of Interest.

COMPENSATION FOR SERVICES IN ANTICIPATION OF MARRIAGE. — In Newhall *v.* Knowles, 67 Atl. Rep. 365, the Rhode Island Supreme Court holds that, where services are rendered without expectation of compensation and only in anticipation of an intended marriage with the person for whom they are performed, there can be no recovery on account of such services if the person for whom they are performed dies before the time for the intended marriage.

LIBEL — PUBLICATION OF PHOTOGRAPH.— In Peck *v.* Tribune Co., 154 Fed. Rep. 330, the Circuit Court of Appeals for the Seventh Circuit holds that the publication by a newspaper of an advertisement containing a portrait of a woman, under which is the name of another woman, together with a statement, signed with the same name, calculated to give the impression that the woman depicted is a nurse and had personally used, and as a nurse had recommended the use of, a certain brand of whiskey as a tonic, does not constitute a libel *per se*.

SERVICES BY PHYSICIAN IN EMERGENCY — COMPENSATION. — In Cotnam *v.* Wisdom, 104 S. W. Rep. 164, the Arkansas Supreme Court holds that where a person is injured on the street by an accident which renders him unconscious, if a surgeon summoned while he is in such condition performs an operation on him in an endeavor to save his life, there is a *quasi*-contract on his part to pay a reasonable compensation for the services, and the amount of such compensation is not affected by the question of the outcome being beneficial.

RIGHTS OF SPITTERS ON STREET CARS. — In City El. R. Co. *v.* Salmon, 57 S. E. Rep. 926, the Georgia Supreme Court upheld a verdict in favor of a passenger on a street car who, in order to avoid spitting on the floor of the car, stuck his head about two inches beyond the margin of the car and was seriously injured by his head coming in contact with a pole near the track. The court said: "Many people spit when they smoke. This fact was judicially ascertained and declared by the Supreme Court in this case as reported in 124 Ga. 1056, 53 S. E. 575, and the plaintiff is so unfortunate as to belong to this class."

INDETERMINATE SENTENCE HELD CONSTITUTIONAL. — In People *v.* Madden, 105 N. Y. Supp. 554, the New York Appellate Division, First Department, held that a State statute authorizing the sentence of a first offender to the State reformatory for an indeterminate term was not unconstitutional as being an encroachment on the judicial department of the State. It was held that since it was competent for the legislature to prescribe the maximum period of imprisonment, a defendant was not prejudiced by the legislature having provided for an earlier release in the interest of first offenders. To the further objection that the statute was unconstitutional as violating the provision vesting the pardoning power in the governor, it was answered that by express statutory provision the pardoning power was reserved in the governor.

SCHOOLS — VACCINATION OF PUPILS. — In Auten *v.* Board of Directors, 104 S. W. Rep. 130, the Arkansas Supreme Court held that a rule of a city school board providing that pupils before admission to the schools should be vaccinated, adopted to prevent the spread of smallpox, and pursuant to the orders of the board of health of the city and the advice of physicians, was not an unreasonable regulation and would not be set aside by the courts; and that a provision therein that the pupils should present a certificate of a reputable physician, showing that they had been successfully vaccinated, was not unreasonable. The court said: "It is a matter of common knowledge of which the court can take judicial notice, that the great majority of medical writers and practitioners advocate vaccination as a safe and efficient means of protecting cities and thickly settled communities against the scourge of smallpox."

PEONAGE — SOUTH CAROLINA STATUTE INVALID. — In *Ex p.* Drayton, 153 Fed. Rep. 986, District Judge Brawley, of the District of South Carolina, declared unconstitutional a South Carolina statute providing that any laborer working for a share of a crop, or for wages in money or other valuable consideration, under a contract to labor on farm land, who shall receive advances either in money or supplies, and thereafter wilfully and without just cause fail to perform the reasonable services required of him by the terms of the contract, shall be liable to prosecution for misdemeanor and punished by imprisonment, etc. The statute was held unconstitutional as constituting an attempt to secure compulsory service in payment of a debt, which was not within the State's police power to create and punish offenses; as a violation of the equality clause of the Fourteenth Amendment, because limited to farm laborers, and also as a violation of the provision against slavery.

INTERFERENCE WITH CONTRACT — MALICE. — Banks *v.* Eastern R., etc., Co., (Wash.) 90 Pac. Rep. 1048, was an action by a physician against an employer of labor for maliciously causing its employees to break their contracts with the plaintiff. It had been the practice of the defendant to retain a part of its employees' wages for medical services. Certain of the employees selected the plaintiff as their physician and notified the defendant to pay their hospital dues to him, in consideration of which the plaintiff issued to them certificates entitling them to medical treatment at his hospital. The defendant refused to pay over the dues to the plaintiff, and notified its employees that such dues would be paid to a specified hospital and any employee not consenting to such payment would be discharged. It was held that the plaintiff had no cause of action; that the defendant had a legal right to take the course pursued by it; and that the fact that its action was inspired by malice against the plaintiff did not of itself warrant a recovery.

TELEPHONE COMPANY'S RIGHT TO CUT TREES IN STREET. — In Cartwright *v.* Liberty Telephone Co., 103 S. W. Rep. 982, the Missouri Supreme Court holds that a telephone company not shown to have been granted a franchise to conduct a telephone business in a city, or authorized to use the city streets, cannot defend an action for mutilating trees growing in a city street on the ground that the erection and maintenance of telephone lines is a proper use of a street, and that trees interfering with that use may be rightfully cut. The court said: "It would be no less startling than it would be novel to hold that the public service corporations have the power, right, and authority to mutilate, damage, or destroy the shade and ornamental trees growing upon the streets of our cities, at pleasure, without some authority, general or special, granted to them by the city in harmony with and recognizing the rights and interest of the property owners in and to the trees, whatever those rights may be."

TRADE SECRETS — PROTECTION BY INJUNCTION. — In Vulcan Detinning Co. *v.* American Can Co., 67 Atl. Rep. 339, the New Jersey Court of Errors and Appeals granted an injunction restraining the defendant company from using or publishing a secret process for detinning tin scrap. This process had been purchased by the complainant from a firm in Holland, and, after its success had been demonstrated, one of the complainant's original directors, who held in trust for the complainant a copy of the secret formula, became the president of the defendant corporation, and, with the assistance of certain discharged employees of the complainant, installed the secret process for the defendant. It was contended that the complainant had not acquired a title to the process that was good as against the discoverer thereof, since the Holland firm had clandestinely obtained it from the discoverer, and therefore the complainant did not come into equity with clean hands. But the court held that the doctrine of "unclean hands" did not apply to one without actual knowledge of the fraud, and that the complainant on general principles of equity was entitled, as against its wrongdoing trustee and others chargeable with notice, to protect the qualified secrecy of its process that arose from such relation of trust and confidence. An injunction was granted against the complainant's former director, against the defendant corporation, and against the discharged employees of the complainant. Swayze, Bogert, Vroom, and Green, JJ., dissented.

OKLAHOMA CONSTITUTIONAL CONVENTION UPHELD. — In Frantz v. Autry, 91 Pac. Rep. 193, the Oklahoma Supreme Court upheld the action of the recent constitutional convention. The proceeding was brought by a taxpayer against Governor Frantz and other officers of the Territory to enjoin them from issuing or publishing any proclamation proposing to submit to the electors of the proposed State of Oklahoma, either as a part of the proposed constitution or as a separate ordinance, any clause or provision dividing or purporting to divide Woods county, etc. The court vacated a preliminary injunction granted in the cause and dismissed the bill, holding that a court of equity had no power or jurisdiction to restrain or enjoin the constitutional convention, its officers or delegates, from exercising any of the rights, powers, and obligations confided to it by Congress or the people; and that the powers of the court could not be invoked to restrain or enjoin the submission of the constitution, or any proposition contained therein, to a vote of the people in advance of its adoption and ratification by the people and its approval by the President of the United States, on the ground that the proposed constitution or any of its provisions was unconstitutional, or that the convention acted in excess of its lawful powers. The majority opinion was delivered by Hainer, J. Burford, C. J., concurred in the conclusion, while Irwin, J., dissented, and Burwell, J., dissented in part and concurred in part.

ACTION AGAINST STATE — FEDERAL JURISDICTION. — In view of the clashes between State and federal governments which have recently held much of the public attention, peculiar interest attaches to the decision of District Judge Trieber, sitting in the Circuit Court for the Eastern District of Arkansas, W. D., in the case of Western Union Tel. Co. v. Andrews, 154 Fed. Rep. 95. Judge Trieber dismissed for want of jurisdiction a bill filed by the complainant against all the prosecuting attorneys of the seventeen judicial circuits of the State to enjoin them from instituting against it any proceedings for penalties for its failure or refusal to comply with the Arkansas Act of May 13, 1907, in relation to foreign corporations doing business in the State. Judge Trieber held that the State, though not named in the pleadings, was the real party in interest, since the suit was against the officers of the State to test the constitutionality of the act, in the enforcement of which the officers would act only by formal judicial proceedings in the courts of the State as its attorneys. Therefore he refused to take jurisdiction on the ground that the eleventh amendment to the Federal Constitution declares that the judicial power of the United States shall not extend to any suit commenced or prosecuted against one of the United States by citizens of another State.

Book Reviews.

GIBSON'S SUITS IN CHANCERY.

Suits in Chancery. By Henry R. Gibson, A. M., LL.D. Second edition, revised and enlarged. Large 8vo; pp. xx, 1203. Published by the author. Knoxville, Tenn., 1907.

This treatise is an ideal work on equity pleading and practice and supplies a model which future writers on this subject may strive to equal, but which they are not likely to surpass. Though the work is primarily based on the equity system of Tennessee, it will be found of value to practitioners in other jurisdictions. The author shows such a complete mastery of the subject in all its relations and is so careful to indicate just when and where the local statutes and rules come in to modify the system of equity practice as established in the High Court of Chancery in England — which system is the common basis of all equity practice in this country — that no practitioner is likely to be seriously misled by any part of the text which is based on local modifications.

The admirable plan and scope of the work, the correct working out of details, the fluent and lucid style, alike indicate the care that has been exercised in writing every part of it. The work is obviously the product of many years of loving and patient labor at the hands of a competent writer and experienced judge. Those who are familiar with the first edition of the book know its merit. The second edition, however, far surpasses the other in every respect. Indeed, it cannot be supposed that any lawyer who has the first edition can be content to remain without this when he once becomes aware of its superior excellence. This edition contains twenty per cent. more matter than the original, and over one thousand of the old sections have been rewritten or revised. It is a rare thing that as much time and effort are put into the making of a second edition as have evidently been employed here. The numerous terse and beautiful forms, happily incorporated in the body of the book, are of the greatest merit and utility.

The State of Tennessee is one of the jurisdictions in which the Court of Chancery with its particular system of practice has been constantly maintained, and by the somewhat unique course of legal development which has taken place there, the jurisdiction of this court has been so extended that it has power to entertain all sorts of suits except actions to recover unliquidated damages for injuries to person, property, or character. The statutes by which this change has been effected have merely enlarged the jurisdiction of the court as a court of equity and have not turned it into a court of law. The system of equity procedure has therefore not been abrogated. But a result of the change is that the Chancery Court in this State has drawn to itself all the most important and most profitable litigation. It has, in fact, made every Tennessee lawyer primarily an equity lawyer, and the decisions of the State courts are very rich in material bearing on points of equity practice.

The Tennessee judges and lawyers have, we believe, a well-deserved reputation for skill in this branch of the law. Judge W. F. Cooper, of Nashville, who edited the fifth edition of Daniell's Chancery Practice and who also published his own decisions as chancellor in the series of Tennessee Chancery Reports, is perhaps most widely known in this connection. The State has also furnished a number of judges to the federal bench especially learned in equity practice, and whose opinions on such matters are of the very greatest value. The late Judge Hammond may here be mentioned without prejudice to the reputation of other federal judges, living or dead. But no author or judge in Tennessee, it is safe to say, has contributed as much to the science of equity pleading and practice, or has laid the profession of that State under so heavy a debt, as the Hon. Henry R. Gibson, sometime Chancellor of the Second Chancery Division of Tennessee, also for a number of years a member of Congress from the Second Congressional District.

It may be added that the book under review is admirably gotten up, as regards typography, and it is printed on good paper. The pages are large and the type is pleasing to the eye. The book is a big one, but the matter of the treatise is so full and extensive that the author has been compelled to use compression in order to get his material into the limits of even twelve hundred large pages. The book comprises, we should say, about as much matter as would go to the making of a three-volume treatise of the usual text book size, and perhaps even more. We have read the work with pleasure and heartily commend it to the profession.

Thomas A. Street.

News of the Profession.

Prominent Cincinnati Lawyer Dies Suddenly. — Thomas F. Shay, of the well-known Cincinnati law firm of Shay, Cogan & Williams, died suddenly in that city on August 19 of cerebral hemorrhage.

Death of General Birney. — General William Birney, at one time United States attorney for the District of Columbia, died in Washington, D. C., on August 14, at the age of eighty-eight.

A Woman Trust Buster. — It is reported that Attorney-General Bonaparte has appointed Mrs. Mary Grace Quackenbos, of New York city, as special assistant in the anti-trust campaign.

Convention of Attorneys-General. — On October 1 a convention of the attorneys-general of all the States opens in St. Louis. The chief purpose of the convention is to discuss plans for co-operative effort among the chief law officers of the various States in dealing with combinations in restraint of trade.

New Massachusetts Judge. — On August 21 Governor Guild, of Massachusetts, named Robert F. Raymond, of New Bedford, to be a justice of the Superior Court to succeed Justice Lemuel Le Baron Holmes, deceased. The new judge is a native of Stamford, Conn., and is fifty years old.

Kentucky Judge Dies in Cleveland. — Hon. James Pryor Tarvin, a well-known Kentucky lawyer and politician, died in Cleveland, O., on August 20, at the age of forty-four. For six years he was circuit judge of the Covington district, but for the past four years he had been practicing in Louisville. He was senior member of the firm of Tarvin & Huggins, formerly Tarvin, Roe & Huggins.

Appointed to Georgia Supreme Bench. — Governor Hoke Smith, of Georgia, has appointed Judge Horace M. Holden, of Crawfordsville, to fill the vacancy in the Georgia Supreme Court which will occur when the resignation of Justice Andrew J. Cobb takes effect on October 12. Judge Holden is at present judge of the northern Georgia circuit. The vacancy on the circuit bench has been filled by the appointment of Colonel John N. Wooley, of Elberton.

Suicide of Two Boston Lawyers. — On August 16, Moses Lindsay Sanborn, a well-known patent lawyer of Boston, shot himself through the head with a revolver. He was forty-seven years old and had been in ill health for several years. On September 4, Robert K. Dickerman, an attorney of the same city, hanged himself with the cord of his bathrobe in a sanatorium in Salem, Mass., where he was under treatment for a tumor on the brain.

Philippine Bar Association. — At a meeting of the Philippine Bar Association, held in Manila on August 8, the following officers were elected: President, Rafael del Pau; vice-presidents, Frank B. Ingersoll, Vicente Miranda, J. Courtney Hixson, and Felix Ferrer; executive secretary, Florencio Gonzales; treasurer, Fred C. Fisher; executive committee, Alberto Baretto, Rafael Palma, Eusebio Orense, William H. Lawrence, and Thomas L. Hartigan.

Former District of Columbia Judge Dead. — Hon. Edward Franklin Bingham, formerly chief justice of the Supreme Court of the District of Columbia, died in Union, W. Va., on September 5. He was born in West Concord, Vt., in 1828, and in his youth settled in Ohio, where he became prominent, serving several terms in the State legislature, and for three terms as Common Pleas judge in the fifth district. In 1887 he was nominated by President Cleveland to be chief justice of the District of Columbia court.

Supreme Courts for Canadian Provinces. — On September 16 there went into force an act creating separate Supreme Courts for the provinces of Saskatchewan and Alberta, which have hitherto been under the jurisdiction of a single such court. The new courts are composed of a chief justice and four associate judges each, Chief Justice Sifton presiding in Alberta, and Chief Justice Wetmore in Saskatchewan.

New Mexico Bar Association. — The New Mexico Bar Association held its annual meeting at Roswell on August 24, and elected officers as follows: President, A. B. McMillen, of Albuquerque; vice-presidents, Paul A. F. Walter of Santa Fe, M. E. Hickey of Albuquerque, E. C. Wade of Las Cruces, Charles A. Spiess of Las Vegas, C. R. Bryan of Carlsbad, George B. Barber of Lincoln; secretary and treasurer, Kenneth Scott, of Roswell. Santa Fe was selected as the place of the next annual summer convention of the association.

Uniform Laws Commission. — On August 22–24, preceding the meeting of the American Bar Association, the seventeenth conference of the commissioners on uniform State laws was held in Portland, Me. President Amasa Mason Eaton, of Providence, R. I., presided and delivered an address reviewing the various fields towards which the attention of the commission is directed. The most important step taken by the commissioners was the approval of the divorce law drafted by the recent divorce congress. The officers of the commission are: President, Amasa M. Eaton, of Providence; vice-president, W. O. Hart, of New Orleans; secretary, Charles Thaddeus Terry, of New York.

Death of Ex-United States Attorney Brinker. — Hon. William H. Brinker, formerly judge of the Supreme Court of New Mexico, and later United States district attorney for the Seattle district of Washington, died in Seattle on August 21, at the age of fifty-seven. Judge Brinker was a native of Missouri, and after the civil war practiced in that State till 1884, when President Cleveland appointed him to the New Mexico Supreme Court. Six years later he moved to Washington, and in 1893 he was appointed federal district attorney by President Cleveland, which position he continued to hold during two years of the McKinley administration. After his retirement from office he practiced his profession in Seattle.

NEW YORK LAWYER TO WEAR STRIPES. — Under a decision of Supreme Court Justice Brady, of New York, handed down on August 30, Alpheus S. Frank, an attorney and a son of Major-General Frank, U. S. A., retired, must serve out a term of three years in Sing Sing for subornation of perjury. The offense was committed in connection with a fraudulent accident suit brought by Mae Herbert, an ex-circus tumbler and contortionist, against the New York City Railway Company. The woman, who it was shown was the wife of the conductor of the car from which she claimed to have fallen, used her acrobatic skill to good purpose in hurling herself from rapidly moving cars without really hurting herself. She had an old injury, received by falling from a trapeze, which she exhibited for the purpose of proving her case. It is said that she figured in several successful suits before the company discovered her identity.

TEXAS JUDGE CHARGED WITH MURDER. — On August 9 Judge S. B. Short, while holding court at Center, Tex., was arrested on an indictment charging him with the murder of Dr. Mike Paul last fall. He was engaged in trying an important civil suit, but the arrest caused a postponement until he could furnish bonds of $10,000. Dr. Paul was one of a crowd pursuing Dick Garrett, a negro. Garrett took refuge in the home of Judge Short and fired on his pursuers, killing Dr. Paul. Garrett had a preliminary trial while the court house was garrisoned with militia, and was hanged for the murder. Two grand juries have met since Dr. Paul was killed, and no indictment was returned against Judge Short until the third jury met.

EX-FEDERAL JUDGE JACKSON DEAD. — Hon. John J. Jackson, who held the record for serving the longest time of any judge who ever sat on the federal bench, died suddenly of heart disease at Atlantic City, on September 2. Judge Jackson was born in Parkersburg, Va. (now West Virginia), in 1824, and celebrated his eighty-third birthday on August 4 last. He was admitted to the Virginia bar in 1846, and from that time to the outbreak of the civil war he was prominent in the councils of the Virginia Whigs. In 1861 President Lincoln appointed him United States judge for the western district of Virginia, and on the division of the State he was made judge for the district of West Virginia. For forty-three years he served continuously, and retired in 1904, being succeeded by Judge Alston G. Dayton. During the serious labor troubles in West Virginia some years ago Judge Jackson became famous as "The Iron Judge," because of the firmness with which he issued and upheld injunctions against the striking miners. He granted the most sweeping injunctions ever issued up to that time, and won the hatred of labor unions everywhere.

INTERNATIONAL LAW ASSOCIATION. — The twenty-fourth conference of the International Law Association — the second ever held within the limits of the United States — was held in Portland, Me., on August 29–31, immediately following the meeting of the American Bar Association. Mayor Nathan Clifford, of Portland, offered the visitors the keys of the city, and Charles F. Libby extended a cordial welcome in behalf of the local bar. Lord Justice Kennedy, of the English Court of Appeal, responded. Officers for the conference were elected as follows: Honorary president, Chief Justice Simeon E. Baldwin, of the Connecticut Supreme Court; president, Right Hon. Lord Justice Kennedy; vice-presidents, Cephas Brainard of New York, Hon. Alton B. Parker of New York, Charles B. Elliott of Minneapolis, and L. J. Loranger of Montreal; secretaries, Charles C. Hyde of Chicago, and G. G. Phillimore of London. Judge Baldwin made a brief inaugural address and was followed by Dr. W. Evans Darby, secretary of the Peace Society of London, with a paper on "Intermittent Progress of International Arbitration." At the evening session Charles Noble Gregory, dean of the Iowa University Law School, read a paper on "Expropriation by International Arbitration," and J. H. Balfour Browne, K. C., of London, read one on "International Law and International Trade." A. C. Schroeder, of Zurich, had prepared a paper on "The Question of Disarmament," but was unable to be present. Walter George Smith, of Philadelphia, discussed the recent divorce congress and the question of jurisdiction in the United States.

At the morning session of the second day, over which Hon. Alton B. Parker presided, J. Arthur Barratt, of London, read a paper on "International Recognition of Divorce Jurisdiction," and papers on "Contraband of War" were read by Lord Justice Kennedy and Hon. Charles B. Elliott, of the Minnesota Supreme Court. At the evening session Everett P. Wheeler, of New York, read a paper on "Treaties as Affecting Subordinate Legislatures." A paper which had been prepared by Sir Thomas Barclay, of London, on "The Most Favored Nation Clause in Commercial Treaties," was read by Lord Justice Kennedy in the absence of the author. Judge Henry S. Dewey, of Boston, enlivened the proceedings a bit by introducing the same resolution approving of the Almighty with which he had ruffled the American Bar Association. Lord Justice Kennedy was of the opinion that it did not fall within the legitimate scope of international law, and the matter was brushed aside.

The papers scheduled for the last day of the meeting were as follows: "The Limits of Active Intervention by a State to Secure the Fulfilment of Contracts in Favor of Its Own Citizens Entered Into by Them with Other States," by Hon. Simeon E. Baldwin, chief justice of the Connecticut Supreme Court; "Diplomatic Protection of Citizens Abroad," by Gaston de Leval, adviser to the British Embassy at Brussels; "Double Imposts," by Dr. Erno Wittman, of Budapest; "The Evidence of Foreign Witnesses," by Dr. A. Hindenburg, of Copenhagen. The two last-named gentlemen being unable to attend the conference, Dr. Wittman's paper was accepted as presented, and Dr. Hindenburg's was read by Ronald Walker, of London. After adopting the customary vote of thanks the conference adjourned.

AMERICAN BAR ASSOCIATION. — The thirtieth annual meeting of the American Bar Association, in some respects the most notable convention in the history of the organization, was held in Portland, Me, on August 26–28. After President Alton B. Parker had called the meeting to order, Governor William T. Cobb, of Maine, welcomed the visitors on behalf of the State, and Chief Justice Lucilius A. Emory, of the State Supreme Court, extended a welcome from the Maine Bar. The principal event of the opening session was the address of the president on the constitutional relations of the federal and State governments. Judge Parker took a strong stand against encroachment by the federal government upon the reserved rights of the States. His address was followed by the election of eighty-five new members, election of the general council, and the reports of the secretary, treasurer, and executive committee.

At the meeting of the Association of American Law Schools, in the afternoon, the annual address was delivered by President William P. Rogers, dean of the Cincinnati Law School, and Professor Albert M. Kales, of the Northwestern University Law School, read a paper on "The Next Step in the Evolution of the Case Book."

At the evening session Hon. Charles F. Amidon, United States District Judge for the District of North Dakota, in a paper on "The Nation and the Constitution" strongly combated the States' rights views of Judge Parker. Charles A. Prouty, of Vermont, a member of the Interstate Commerce Commission, had prepared a paper on "The Fundamental Defect in the Act to Regulate Commerce," which in the absence of Mr. Prouty was read by Judge William H. Staake, of Philadelphia.

The two sessions of the second day were devoted to reports from standing and special committees. The chief interest centred round the report of the standing committee on insurance law, which was published some time ago and widely commented upon throughout the country. The two most important recommendations of the committee — that relating to federal supervision of insurance companies, and that advocating the distribution of the deferred dividend surplus on existing policies — were disapproved by the association. Something of a stir was created by the introduction of a resolution by Judge Henry S. Dewey, of Boston, to the effect that the Association indorsed the "ever-living God" and the divine "unwritten law." The resolution was squelched in short order. The report of the special committee on code of professional ethics was presented by General Thomas H. Hyde, of New York City, and unanimously adopted.

In the afternoon the Section of Legal Education held its meeting, the principal features of which were the address by Chairman Roscoe Pound, dean of the Nebraska University law school, on "The Need of a Sociological Jurisprudence," and a paper by W. R. Vance, dean of the George Washington University law school, on "Legal Education in the South."

The Section of Patent, Trademark, and Copyright Law also held a meeting in the afternoon. Chairman Robert S. Taylor, of Fort Wayne, Ind., devoted his address mainly to the proposed act to create a court of patent appeals. Arthur Steuart, of Baltimore, read a paper on "The Common-law Copyright."

At the opening of the last day's session, President Parker introduced the principal speaker, the Right Hon. James Bryce, British Ambassador to the United States. Mr. Bryce's subject was "The Influence of National Character and Historical Environment on the Development of the Common Law." An incident which caused a stir was the introduction by George Whitelock, of Baltimore, of a resolution condemning the attitude of President Roosevelt toward the decision of Federal Judge Humphreys in the Beef Trust case. The resolution was tabled.

In the afternoon the Association of American Law Schools held a session and elected the following officers: President, George W. Kirchway, of the Columbia University law school; secretary and treasurer, William R. Vance, of George Washington University law school.

The meeting closed with the annual dinner at the Falmouth Hotel, Hon. Alton B. Parker presiding. Toasts were responded to by Mr. Bryce, Mr. Justice Moody, Lord Justice Kennedy, Orville D. Baker, Sir Kenelm Digby, Louis J. Loranger, Peter W. Meldrim, Jacob M. Dickinson, F. Charles Hume, Jr.

The officers elected for the ensuing year were as follows: President, Jacob M. Dickinson, of Chicago; secretary, John Hinkley, of Baltimore; treasurer, Frederick E. Wadhams, of Albany; executive committee, besides the president, secretary, and treasurer, Alton B. Parker, Charles Monroe of Los Angeles, Ralph W. Breckenridge of Omaha, Charles F. Libby of Portland, Walter George Smith of Philadelphia, and Rome G. Brown of Minneapolis.

English Notes.

Long Vacation Ends. — The English courts opened for business after the Long Vacation on Monday, September 10.

Judge Mulholland Dead — His Successor. — His honor Judge Mulholland, K. C., of County Court District No. 26, died in Stafford, on August 23, at the age of sixty-four. He was an Irishman by birth, was called to the Irish bar in 1865, to the English bar in 1875, and took silk in 1894. He became a bencher of Lincoln's Inn in 1897, and was appointed a judge of the County Court in 1899. The Lord Chancellor filled the vacancy on the bench by appointing Mr. Alfred H. Ruegg, K. C. The new judge is fifty years of age and was called to the bar at the Middle Temple in 1877.

Criminal Appeal Bill Passed. — After much backing and filling the English Parliament on August 16 passed the bill providing for appeals in criminal cases. Under it an appeal lies as a matter of course on questions of law, and as to questions of fact an appeal may be taken either on leave of the Court of Criminal Appeal or on the certificate of the trial judge. Some of the British lawyers are wagging their heads and uttering dire forebodings as to the probable evil consequences of the measure, especially its tendency to weaken the sense of responsibility in the trial jury. However, no objections have as yet been put forward by the criminal classes.

Breach of Promise by Married Man. — In the case of Wilson v. Carneley, Lord Justice Coleridge has recently held that an action for breach of promise will lie on a promise of marriage made by a man who has a wife living at the time. A verdict for 100 guineas in favor of Miss Wilson was upheld. In deciding the case Lord Coleridge said that whatever his personal opinion might be in regard to this form of action, he shrank from holding that such a contract to marry was void as being against public policy. If he was wrong in setting a precedent he could be set right on appeal to the House of Lords.

Indian Child Marriage Upheld. — A rather peculiar nullity suit was decided by the Divorce Court recently when Miss Maria Birch was granted a decree nullifying her marriage to a man from India, on the ground that seventeen years previously he had been married to a child in accordance with the Indian custom. The husband was a student in London when Miss Birch met him, and when they were married he told her he was a widower. It was later discovered that the child-wife he had wedded when he himself was a mere tot was still living. The court held that the child marriage which took place in India, though entirely repugnant to English law and custom, was valid, and that therefore the second marriage to Miss Birch should be set aside as null and void. The nullified husband is now in India living with the bride of his infanthood.

Duty to Maintain Deceased Wife. — The question whether a husband owes a duty to maintain his wife after her death has recently come up in one of the English courts. A Hambleton man, named Broomfield, had been paying for the maintenance of his wife in Brookwood asylum for upwards of thirty years. As he was over eighty years of age an effort was made the other day to get the cost of maintenance reduced, and during the negotiations it transpired that Mrs. Broomfield had died in the asylum in October, 1901. The records of the asylum show that notification of the woman's death was made to the asylum authorities at the time, but by a curious blunder the official who collected the money from the aged husband failed to notify him of the fact. The asylum board of guardians decided that they could not legally remit the amount Broomfield had paid since his wife's death, and that the only recourse was a suit at law.

Deceased Wife's Sister Act Passed. — On August 26 the House of Lords by a vote of ninety-eight to fifty-four passed the bill authorizing marriage with a deceased wife's sister. Thus ends a remarkable legislative struggle dating back to the early history of the Church. Previous to 1532 such marriages were governed by the canon law, but in that year was passed the statute 28 Henry VIII., c. 7, making them absolutely void. In 1835 the Lyndhurst Act made past marriages of affinity valid and future marriages void. The House of Commons at first rejected the prohibitory clause regarding marriage with a deceased wife's sister, but afterward accepted it. A royal commission was appointed in 1847 to examine the marriage laws, and from 1849 to the present time attempts were made, both in the House of Lords and the House of Commons, to pass the bill making marriage with a deceased wife's sister legal. As a rule, the Commons has carried the bill by a large majority, but it has been thrown out by the Lords, through the aggressive opposition of the bishops and a few ultra-ecclesiastical lay peers, although King Edward, when Prince of Wales, set the example of voting for it. On August 20 last, after prolonged and animated debate, the House of Lords, by 111 to 79 votes, passed the second reading of the deceased wife's sister bill, the minority including the seventeen bishops who are members of the House of Lords, and as the measure had previously passed the House of Commons this session, it now becomes law. Even now, while a man may at last marry his deceased wife's sister, a woman is still forbidden to marry her deceased husband's brother.

SOLICITORS AND CLIENTS' MONEYS. — The rather frequent cases recently brought to light of embezzlement or other mishandling of clients' money by solicitors have led the English Law Society to adopt a set of recommendations for the guidance of solicitors in respect to the care of such moneys. These recommendations are in substance as follows: (1) It shall be the duty of every solicitor to keep full and accurate accounts, which shall be periodically balanced. (2) Moneys received by a solicitor on behalf of his client shall be kept separate from his own moneys, preferably by opening a clients' money bank account. (3) Moneys of clients in the hands of or under the control of a solicitor, should only be used on account and with the authority of the client. (4) Any increment in the nature of interest, income, or other profit accruing on clients' moneys should be credited to the clients whose moneys have produced such interest, income, or profit, and any solicitor who, without the authority of his client, retains for his own use any such interest, income, or other profit is guilty of professional impropriety. (5) Except under special and unavoidable circumstances, it is no part of a solicitor's business to hold money belonging to a client for a lengthened period, and it is contrary to right practice to do so. (6) In cases where a solicitor finds himself in possession of money of a substantial amount not his own, of which he cannot immediately or within a short time discharge himself, it is his duty, if he does not keep a separate clients' account at a bank — and it is desirable even if he does keep such a separate account — to pay that money into a deposit account, separate not only from his own money, but from all other money, and to earmark it by indorsement on the deposit receipt or otherwise, as belonging to the particular client or matter. The solemn promulgation of such elementary aspects of the fiduciary principle would seem to indicate that the solicitors of Great Britain have been entertaining the same fallacious ideas regarding trust funds which until recently obtained in the minds of certain high officials of American insurance companies.

SOME BRITISH FEARS FOR OUR FUTURE. — In a recent issue the London *Spectator,* commenting on the outcome of the Haywood trial, has this to say: "So many influences of corruption, of terrorism, and of class prejudice are allowed to deflect what ought to be the immutable and serene justice of the courts that their pacifying effect, and the confidence of the people in their action, are alike destroyed. It is distrust in the courts which makes the hatred of the millionaires for the workmen so bitter and the fear of them among employees so extravagant; distrust in the courts which induces the toilers to combine for purposes of menace; distrust in the courts which renders verdicts worthless as instruments for preserving or creating peace. Something of that distrust may be unjust, for there must be scores of honest judges within the Union and thousands of men who, once sworn as jurymen, would no more suppress or betray their own consciences than the best of British judges would. But allowing for that injustice, it is clear that in a great portion of the United States the judicial system fails, while it is not clear that the people, though they acknowledge the failure, will consent to any radical reform. They will not raise their judges above pecuniary temptation, they will not confine the jury-box to the classes least likely to be corrupted, and they will not accelerate the system of trial till opportunities either of corruption or of terror are reduced to a minimum. Nor, apparently, will they make crime by a combination much more penal than crime by an individual. These, however, are but suggestions, and the Americans, who are a sagacious people, could if they chose devise much more effective plans. They do not devise them, and in that failure is a cause of hopelessness, even among those who, like ourselves, reckon themselves as devoted to the Western as to the Eastern branch of our race. It is as possible to get courts beyond suspicion of postponing justice to personal considerations as to get regiments beyond suspicion of cowardice; and in neglecting to get them universally the people of the States neglect to secure the first necessity of and the best guaranty for a successful civilization. They have secured them in the Supreme Court, but they should secure them in the remotest district of their wildest State."

Obiter Dicta.

A BAD LOT. — A justice of the peace in one of the English counties recently remarked to the plaintiff in a case before him: "We consider you and the defendant as bad as one another, but you are the worst."

AN EXCLUSIVE ORGANIZATION. — At a recent convention of the International Brotherhood of Teamsters of America it was resolved that "no lawyer, saloonkeeper, or professional practitioner of any kind can be a member." Probably a case for the application of the *ejusdem generis* rule.

NO GROUND FOR DIVORCE. — A woman in Mount Vernon, N. Y., recently requested the law to release her from her husband's bed and board on the ground that he was chronically "out of a job." The lady should take counsel of the dusky bride who, when asked if her new spouse was a good provider, proudly responded, "He sholy is. He done pervide me wid six mo' people to wash for dis week."

INCREASING PROSPERITY. — In relation to our recent surprised comments on the New York lawyer who had managed to get himself in debt to the extent of $149,150, and that one who turned up in Illinois with liabilities aggregating $372,213, a correspondent calls attention to the fact that an action has been begun against a federal judge in Chicago for the neat sum of $500,000.

NOT PARTICULAR. — In most jurisdictions, as is well known, a "good" moral character is an ostensible prerequisite to admission to the bar, but in Florida, it seems, they are not so exacting, for the Supreme Court rule relative to the admission of attorneys merely requires the applicant to show that he "sustains a *fair* private and professional character." The publication of this fact ought to cause a considerable amount of immigration into Florida.

A Close Second. — A correspondent writes: "The paragraph headed 'Going Some' in your Obiter Dicta column for July, 1907, reminds the writer of an attorney of this State who is wont to characterize the district judge of his district as 'His Density ——— ———, by the grace of God and the imbecility of the suffragans of ——— County, Judge of the ——— Judicial District.'"

Who Can It Be? — The following is an extract from a letter replying to an inquiry regarding a certain attorney: "When or where or how he became a member of the bar I do not know, but it was only recently. So far as I know he has no practice, and no resources except his wits. He has at times been industriously engaged in helping me and a few others in trying to drink up all the intoxicants in town. He has not yet succeeded, but so far as I am advised is still on the job."

Often the Case.— The letter head, published in our September number, of a police judge who practices in all the courts but his own, recalls to a Sioux City correspondent the following incident which occurred in one of the local courts: The court was assigning cases for trial, and when one of them, an appeal from a justice's court, was called, a somewhat inebriated attorney asked that it be set down for trial. In response to an inquiry as to who was representing the other side, the lawyer replied that he didn't know. "Well, who appeared for the other side below?" asked the judge. "The (hic) justice of the peace," responded the attorney.

On the Safe Side. — A farmer living near Ruston, La., recently sent one of his colored hands into town with a sum of money which he had agreed to pay to one of the most prominent attorneys of the place, in the event of his successfully carrying through a certain piece of legal work. The darky strolled into the office of the clerk of court and offered to leave with him the amount of the fee. He was told by the clerk that the proper person to whom to deliver the money was the attorney, but the sable bearer would have none of it. "Naw, suh," he said, "de boss tol' me not to gib dis money to no lawyer, but to gib it to some 'sponsible white man."

Cruel and Unusual. — The Declaration of Independence to the contrary notwithstanding, the right to the pursuit of happiness has been taken away from the younger element of Highmore, S. D., for an ordinance has been enacted there which provides that it shall be unlawful for "male and female persons to loiter on the steps of any church, public building, or doorway of any store for the purpose of visiting, eating candy or peanuts, or any like thing on the street, alley, or vacant lot or other obscure place, for the purpose of flirting in the evening time." If this be a lawful exercise of the police power, then it is time for the flirting men to get together.

A Leading Question. — In a "moonshine" case which was recently tried before a United States commissioner in Alabama, the principal witness for the prosecution, locally known as "Baldy" for the reason that his crop of hair consisted of a fringe around the back of his neck, had given some very damaging testimony against the defendant. The latter, a raw-boned young mountaineer, some six and a half feet tall, being without counsel, the commissioner asked if he would like to cross-examine the witness. "Wall, jedge," he replied, "I don't reckon it air no use, but I would like to ax him one question." "All right, go ahead," said the commissioner. The defendant walked over to where Baldy was sitting, and solemnly shaking a long, bony finger in the face of the witness, said: "Baldy, don't you uns know that you uns air telling of a d—— lie, you ——— ——— ol', bald-headed ——— ——— ———!"

A Cherokee Lawyer. — The following is the letter-head of a lawyer and notary public who for more than thirty years has held sway in the Indian Territory. The hieroglyphics are in the Cherokee language.

OFFICE

WILLIAM F. RASMUS

ATTORNEY AND COUNSELOR-AT-LAW

ᎡᏗᏩᎵ, ᏗᏘᏲᎯ ᎠᎴ ᏗᎪᏪᎵᏍᎩ
ᏕᏋᎳᏗ ᏩᏔᎩ ᎠᏰᏋ ᏗᏏᏙᏍᏙᏗᏜ.

OVER CHEROKEE NATIONAL BANK, ROOMS 1 AND 2

Tahlequah, Cherokee Nation, Ind. Terry

A Titled Gentleman. — A man of varied interests is G. T. Abbott, of Thrall, a small California town some four hundred miles north of San Francisco. His business card reads as follows:

E. T. ABBOTT,
Thrall, California.

Station Agent Southern Pacific Co.
Agent Wells-Fargo Express Co.
Agent W. U. Telegraph Co.
Agent Sunset Telephone Co.
Postmaster.
Landlord Thrall Hotel.
Manager General Store.
Local Agent Pelton R. Sugar Pine Lumber Co.
Local Agent Pokegama Sugar Pine Lumber Co.
Local Agent Klamath River Improvement Co.
Weyerhaeuser Land Co.
Klamath Lake R. R. General Mgr.
Klamath Lake R. R. G. F. & P. A.
Klamath Lake R. R. Pur. A. & R. M.
Klamath Lake R. R. Chief E. & M. M.
Superintendent Schools.
Subject to R. R. Commission, Cal.
Subject to R. R. Commission, Oregon.
Subject to Interstate Com. Com.
Incidental, "keeping out of jail." Open to proposals for other positions. "Anything" I ain't "Isn't."

An Unusual Chattel Mortgage. — A correspondent sends us a complaint filed in an action before an Arizona justice of the peace. Its material allegations are as follows: "That within the past year the plaintiff became indebted to the plaintiff to the amount of: Two Hundred and Eleven Dollars and Fifty Cents ($211.50) that the plaintiff holds a contract signed by the defendant securing the defendant to that amount, that although the plaintiff has many times through his agent, demanded said payment he has never able to collect a cent of sad [*sic*] money, that the Plaintiff has in his possession a Chattel mortgage to secure the amount, wherein said document signed by the defendant, authorizes the plaintiff or his agent to sell the following property: — a stone house, measuring 20 by 14 feet, a small kitchen, 14 by 14, front of said building, as well as all the excavation thereon, and a tunnel S. E. of the said house, all being on the tract belonging to the A. C. Co. of Clifton, Arizona, on what is known as the lot No. 5 of the May Flower Addition, due N. of Chase Creek and N. of the Coronado R. R. in the town of Clifton, County of Graham, Territory of Arizona." The contest was finally terminated by the plaintiff's attorney foreclosing this remarkable chattel mortgage by a private sale at which he sold not only the house but the tunnel as well.

That Recording Act Puzzle. — A number of readers have sent in letters regarding the problem stated in this column last month. To restate the facts briefly: A held an unrecorded mortgage for $1,000; B, with actual knowledge of A's lien, took and recorded another mortgage for $1,000 on the same land; C, without actual notice of A's mortgage, took a third mortgage for $1,000. The sale of the land realized but $1,500, and the question was as to the proper distribution of the fund. Most of our correspondents reach the conclusion that each of the three should receive $500. One of them refers us to Goodbar *v.* Dunn, 61 Miss. 618, saying: "The third mortgagee would get five hundred dollars because he took his incumbrance subject to the recorded mortgage of the second mortgagee for one thousand dollars and the mortgaged property produced fifteen hundred dollars. The second mortgagee would get five hundred dollars because he took his mortgage with notice of the first unrecorded mortgage of one thousand dollars. The first mortgagee loses five hundred of his debt because that amount is taken from the fund and paid to the third mortgagee because of the failure of the first to record his mortgage." Another writes: "I find that this exact question of law has been reported twice; once in Day *v.* Munson, 14 Ohio St. 488, and once in Hoag *v.* Sayre, 33 N. J. Eq. 552; the two courts arriving at different solutions. The dissenting judge in New Jersey argued for the rule followed by the Ohio court, though without citing that case. It seems to me that the method of division followed by the Supreme Court of Ohio is much more logical than that followed in New Jersey, and according to this, A, B, and C would each receive $500 under the facts supposed." One correspondent thinks that A is entitled to nothing, and gives his reasoning as follows: "As between A and B the latter is entitled to assume that A receives from the fund the sum of $1,000 and that B will receive $500. C is entitled to the same assumption against B. Thus B and C are each vested with $500. If A's mortgage were recorded, B would now be entitled to proceed to collect his deficiency of $500 without regard to C, but is met by the proposition that C, under the valid assumption above noted, will claim that B has no deficiency. B, not in fault, equitably looks to A for redress and is therefore entitled to the remaining $500. The result is to give $1,000 to B and $500 to C, and to postpone A under all similar facts to B and C in order named. The principle laid down in the Ohio case and indorsed by the great majority of our correspondents works out peculiarly when other prices are put on the property. Thus, if the amount realized had been only $1,000, A would have taken the whole of it, whereas, if the property had brought $2,000 A would have received nothing.

SOME FINE LANGUAGE. — In Alexander *v.* Page, 101 S. W. Rep. 346, a will case recently decided by the Kentucky Court of Appeals, there was a devise to take effect only in case "reconciliation and amity" should take place between the devisees and the testator's brothers and sisters. In holding that the condition was fulfilled, Barker, J., said: "All of the participants in this ancient feud, except one, have passed away, and we may indulge in the hope that in the supernal splendor of an eternal dawn the clouds of misunderstanding which concealed their hearts from each other on earth have vanished forever. As there, so here. The ghost of this ancestral hate has been hovering about this trust fund of love for more than a generation. The chancellor has afforded it peaceful sepulture by his judgment establishing reconciliation and amity between the survivors of a noble family, and we have no inclination to roll away the stone with which he has sealed its tomb."

Correspondence.

NO TELEPHONE COURTS IN WYOMING.

To the Editor of LAW NOTES.

SIR: In September LAW NOTES there is a paragraph headed "Long Distance Justice," purporting to give the facts relating to a case alleged to have been tried in Wyoming by telephone. As the paragraph does not state the facts, and I feel that an injustice has been done Laramie county, and the State of Wyoming, I write to make this correction.

The truth is that Miles Fitzgerald came to my office and made complaint against Albert Bristol. I prepared a criminal complaint against Bristol and it was filed in the office of the justice of the peace, W. P. Carroll, and a warrant issued. Before the sheriff had time to go out to Bristol's ranch, Bristol had employed an attorney, and this attorney went before the justice of the peace and entered a plea of guilty, as he could have done if his client had been in the room, since the offense charged was a misdemeanor. The justice then imposed a fine and it was paid.

We find the telephone very useful in Wyoming, but we are not in the habit of trying our cases by telephone.

CLYDE M. WATTS.
County and Prosecuting Attorney.

CHEYENNE, WYO.

PRACTICE IN ENGLISH AND AMERICAN COURTS CONTRASTED.

To the Editor of LAW NOTES.

SIR: I read your issue of September, 1907, in which you make mention of Mr. Thomas Leaming's paper before the Pennsylvania Bar Association, in which he discusses the administration of justice in the English courts to the disadvantage of the procedure in America.

It might be of interest to your readers to hear an experience which I had in attempting to commence some partition proceedings of real estate situated on the outskirts of London.

While in England two years ago I saw several attorneys and asked them to give me, approximately, what the cost would be of these proceedings. The only estimate I could get was, that it would cost from $500 to $1,500, but they would not fix even $1,500 as the limit of the expense, claiming they were unable to tell with any degree of certainty what the expense would be. I later took up the matter by correspondence with other members of the English bar; in each case the answer was equally indefinite. Sometimes the price was more, but never less. Last summer I had a member of the New Jersey bar see three English lawyers as to the case and as to the procedure, and with his utmost endeavors he could not get them to fix a figure, nor could he get any intelligent understanding as to what the procedure might be. They would make a statement that it would probably be thus and so, but there were so many provisos that it left one skilled in our procedure at a loss to know just what their procedure consists of.

I might say, in this connection, that in New Jersey a simple partition proceeding such as I contemplated could be carried through for $200 with a profit to the attorney, and any member of the bar could and would give a figure beyond which the expense and costs would not go.

Then, again, under the English practice, I found that during the summer vacation, which was July and August, you could not even file your papers with the clerk of the court, as is done in New Jersey and practically in every State in the Union, as the clerk's office is always open for return of process whether the court is sitting or not.

The result of my attempting to partition the property in question is that I have been unable to advise my client to proceed without some definite understanding with the attorney as to the expense of such proceedings.

Then, again, while in London I attempted to look up the title and was informed that there was no office in which deeds could be recorded; that there was only one section of London where this could be done. The practice of examining a title was to go to a lawyer and hand him your paper title and depend upon his opinion, which opinion I found upon following up to be entirely dependent upon adverse possession.

I submit the above conditions for the consideration of Mr. Leaming and others who think the English practice is an improvement on ours.

Very truly,

GEO. H. PEIRCE.

NEWARK, N. J.

Law Notes

NOVEMBER, 1907.

PUBLISHED BY EDWARD THOMPSON COMPANY, NORTHPORT, LONG ISLAND, N. Y.

JAMES COCKCROFT, *President.* J. W. HILTMAN, *Treasurer.* D. S. GARLAND, *Secretary.*

CONTENTS.

THREE centuries ago Jamestown formed the only English colony in the boundaries of the United States. It was a centre of light then. To-day it is the spot to which our public men journey to give to the people lessons in wisdom. At Jamestown the sun rises each morning on some sort of "Day." It may be the "Day" of some mere State, or it may be a "Day" in which all have an interest as "Constitutional Day." The statesmen who enlightened the country on Constitutional Day were ex-Judge Parker and Congressman McCall of Massachusetts. Though these two gentlemen belong to different political parties the burden of their utterances in opposition to increase of federal power was very similar. Judge Parker's views on this subject are familiar to all. Mr. McCall directed attention to federal direction of business, and evidently his hopes of a new heaven and a new earth from this source are not sanguine. He said: "To show the extent to which this national detective system has grown, Congress, at its last session, appropriated about nine millions of dollars to inspect various kinds of business, or more than five times the amount appropriated for similar purposes ten years ago. Look at the swindles connected with federally inspected banks; at the astounding corruption attaching itself to the only railroad built under national auspices; at the horrible disasters upon the sea, due in part to the failure of federal inspectors to do their duty. National office holders are no better and no worse than are the officers of States, but as governmental functions are more and more transferred to the national authority, the number of agents subject to a single jurisdiction is increased amazingly, and the authority exercised by the man at the head of this colossal machine passes all bounds. There are, of course, certain great imperial powers that must be exercised by the national government, but the time-honored functions of the States have as a whole been well administered, and they should be permitted to remain with the States. We have had painful instances of dishonesty in connection with the government of our cities, but it is significant that they have usually been unearthed not by office holders, but by the vigilance and public spirit of private citizens." All earnest utterances on this grave question deserve careful consideration.

THE move of the attorneys-general of a number of States in meeting at St. Louis and perfecting an organization, designed to minimize as much as possible interference by the federal courts with the State courts, is interesting. The attorneys-general, who represented both political parties, have petitioned Congress for an act circumscribing the jurisdiction of inferior federal courts, when such courts interfere with the enforcement of State laws. Of course no attempt can be, or is to be, made to touch the regular appellate jurisdiction of the federal Supreme Court on appeal from the highest State tribunal. Twenty States were represented in the gathering, and it is stated that the enforcement of their corporation laws had been restrained in half of these by federal courts. The attorney-general of Minnesota declared in addressing the convention that he had already been adjudged in contempt for trying to enforce the laws of his State, and might be in danger of a prison on his return home. Whatever the merits of the immediate controversies in these States with the federal judiciary, the action of the attorneys-general assuredly indicates that their States no longer occupy an attitude of supine indifference toward the success of attempts at local corporate regulation. It is a manifestation too of the spirit of voluntary co-operation among the States, which is not the least significant of the forces at work upon our institutions. The same spirit is shown in the adoption upon certain subjects of uniform laws, and the recognition of the need of uniform legislation, even when the difficulties of securing it have hitherto proved insurmountable. Of importance as indicating the unity of interests and needs of the several States is the tendency toward the adoption of legislation controlled by and embodying similar aims, though not textually identical, and the eagerness to discover and adopt some successful solution for a common problem which some sister State may have hit upon. Unfortunately the plan adopted has not always proved successful.

THE railroad rate laws which were enacted at their last sessions by so many legislatures are meeting with no little difficulty in getting themselves observed. The effort of the State of New York to establish a two-cent rate was checkmated by Governor Hughes's veto. Where a low rate was actually enacted into a statute, it has frequently fallen a victim to United States judges and the Fourteenth Amendment. In Pennsylvania, however, the federal judges have been saved the necessity of examining the constitutionality of the two-cent fare established by law. The State Court of Common Pleas, presided over by Judges Wilson and Audenried, has held the rate confiscatory and unconstitutional. It seems that the Supreme Court of that State has established a simple test to which the rate law failed to measure up. "Public service corporations in Pennsylvania," says the Court of Common Pleas, "are entitled to look for a rate of return, if their property will earn it, not less than the legal rate of interest; and a system of charges that yields no more income than is fairly requisite to maintain the plant, pay fixed charges and operating expenses, provide a suitable sinking fund for the payment of debts, and pay a fair profit to the owners of the property, cannot be said to be unreasonable." The Pennsylvania legal rate of interest is six per cent., and so far from the Pennsylvania Railroad yielding that remuneration the court finds, after careful examination, that the company's earnings under the new law would be reduced to less than two per cent. In addition to holding the law confiscatory, it is declared that for a large part of its mileage, namely, between Harrisburg and Pittsburg, the Pennsylvania is practically immune from regulation.

FROM the other side of the continent, a hopeful year's work lies behind the Juvenile Court of Portland, Oregon. "The attractive feature of the report for the year," says the *Telegram* of that city, "is what the Juvenile Court is doing for the children. We are told that about eighty-five per cent. of those placed on probation turn out well without any further action. Out of the 614 cases before the court during the year 251 were larceny charges. Considering the matter in the average, this eighty-five per cent. statement means that more than 200 of these larceny cases represent children who were redeemed from the teachings of dishonesty. So of children accused of other offenses, it may truthfully be said that the Juvenile Court has served them as a shield, has saved them from being committed to a career of crime, as was usually the case under the old method of dealing with the child transgressor." But not all accounts of the workings of the new system are so hopeful, and we note a tendency in Massachusetts to attribute to it an increase of crime among the young. An experienced observer, however, Mr. W. F. Spaulding, secretary of the Massachusetts Prison Association, attributes the increase to other sources. Indeed, the same phenomenon is observed in a country so far removed from peculiar American influences as France, where an alarming tendency toward serious crimes among minors is observable. A French student, M. Gibon, would find the cause in the abandonment of religious education, but then we do not know on which side of the present religious struggle in France M. Gibon is arrayed, and how far he is capable of looking dispassionately at the facts. A juvenile court law recently enacted in Alabama has come to grief in the City Court of Anniston, because it was considered to be opposed to the constitutional requirement of jury trial. Pity it will be if the guaranty of jury trial, under whose banner liberty has fought so often in the past, should prove now to stand in the way of real progress in dealing with this important problem.

MR. HUGO VON KUPFFER, who recently visited the United States in the interests of the Berlin *Lokalanzeiger*, has recently contributed to his paper an interesting account of the children's courts of this country and especially of the court of New York. The article, which appears in abstract with extensive quotations in the New York *Evening Post*, is founded upon the author's own observations. Mr. Von Kupffer gives a most enthusiastic account of the court, and will welcome with the greatest hopefulness and pleasure every step undertaken by German legislation in the direction of the American procedure. "The preventive moment," says our German observer, "which plays so important a part, is certainly of decisive importance in the struggle of public order against criminality. But where could the work of moral prevention be better applied and with more hopeful prospect than with a child still capable of receiving education? For such a child makes its first step on the path of crime while still under the leading-strings of its morally poisonous surroundings." As explaining the origin of juvenile courts, he notes throughout the United States a growing sense of high responsibility on the part of the community for the moral and intellectual development of the mass of the people. Of the working of the New York court he says: "It is an interesting fact that the number of arraignments in the Children's Court for the year 1906 was only 218 more than for the year 1905, this too when the boroughs of Manhattan and the Bronx, over which the court's jurisdiction extends, had an increase in population from 2,390,382 to 2,464,432 in 1906. We may thus observe a criterion for the reformatory, or more correctly, the preventive work of this Children's Court with tolerable certainty. There is therefore no doubt that, according to the experience hitherto obtained, New York has in its Children's Court one of the most important institutions of its general administration. This tribunal tried 9,656 cases in the year 1906. These were all cases of children who, hopelessly uncared for, had come into conflict with the law, in consequence of misdemeanors committed by themselves, or through defective education and surveillance. It was demonstrated that the great majority of the children that appeared before the court were victims of bad surroundings and parental neglect. In all cases, the court proceeded on the principle of treating each case individually on the basis of humanity and human experience. The definite object of these children's courts is here strictly kept in view; namely, to preserve the child for the State, for the community. And according to the above report this object was achieved in a remarkably large number of cases." The parol system founded on the suspended sentence is especially commended. "The principle of the suspended sentence," it is said, "is based on the hope of moral improvement which humane society very justly has, or should have, for the benefit of the delinquent." It is interesting to find our sociological experiments watched with so much of interest and approval by observers from the Old World.

Too often our courts treat the naturalization of foreigners as a perfunctory matter. Provided they make the required proof of residence and take the prescribed oaths, admission is almost a matter of course. In the New York Supreme Court, Mr. Justice Miller recently reminded us how extensive are the powers of the court to refuse to grant letters of naturalization. He refused all applications for citizenship, and in explaining his action said: "We have admitted too many ignorant foreigners to citizenship already. I do not propose to admit to the franchise any person who does not know enough about the Constitution of the country to cast an intelligent ballot. I will not grant citizenship papers to any immigrant who has not a fixed intention of staying in the country and an intelligent knowledge of and patriotic interest in its form of government. An ignorant electorate tends to be a corrupt electorate, and unintelligent use of the ballot is dangerous to the success of a democratic form of government." The statutes require that it shall be made to appear to the satisfaction of the court that the person applying for citizenship during his residence in the United States has behaved as a man of good moral character, attached to the principles of the Constitution and well disposed to the good order and happiness of the country. In addition an oath, presumably intelligent, to support the Constitution is demanded upon admission to the privileges of citizenship. Proof of these facts to the satisfaction of the court, and the required oath, furnish a safeguard against undesirable citizens, and ought to render naturalization anything but a matter of course. The opinion of the court by Dallas, J., in the case of *In re* Bodek, 63 Fed. Rep. 815, years ago laid down correct principles on this subject. The applicant's oath to support the Constitution "should not be accepted in any case in which, upon examination, it appears that the applicant does not understand its significance, or is without such knowledge of the Constitution as is essential to the rational assumption of an undertaking, avouched on oath, to support it." The conclusion was said to be inevitable that "the court ought not to admit any alien to citizenship without being satisfied that he has at least some general comprehension of what the Constitution is and of the principles which it affirms." Courts too often take the requirement of attachment to the principles of the Constitution with the easy optimism of a witness whose testimony is recorded in Rodriguez's Case, 81 Fed. Rep. 337. He testified that the applicant was attached to the principles of the Constitution, and continued: "I know that he is a good man, and know that if, whatever the principles of the Constitution might be, that he would uphold them if he knew what they were."

IN an address last month before the Boston Homœopathic Medical Society, on "Medical Expert Testimony," Mr. Louis C. Southard had no good word for the present method of securing the evidence of experts. He quoted eminent judges, among whom were Mr. Justice Moody of the federal Supreme Court, and Chief Justice Emery of Maine, on the evils of the partisan expert. It is well, perhaps, to emphasize in every way the need of reform, and yet we should think every one who reads the papers or looks about him must be aware how utterly discredited the medical expert witness has become. In getting himself in that unenviable position he has had the able assistance of the gentlemen of the bar, always anxious to call as many and as eminent experts as his opponents, in order, even if the bewildered jury refuse to credit his witnesses, they may see at least that no reliance is to be placed in the experts of the other side. There is a crying need for reform, and it would seem to be the duty of the lawyer to suggest a practical way out of our present discredited system. Mr. Southard stated that France long ago adopted the plan of having expert witnesses appointed through the courts, and the results have been satisfactory. Any plan adopted in this country must take into account the temper and disposition of our people and the peculiarities of jury trial. This consideration at once excludes bills favoring "the appointment of a select board of experts whose opinions should be conclusive, barring all other experts from testifying in the case, and taxing the fees of the experts as a part of the costs." Mr. Southard proceeded: "If we cannot adopt the German or French law in its entirety, why not make one forward step and secure the presence of at least one honest and independent medical expert witness in each case? It seems to me that this can be done by having the court authorized on motion of either party, or on its own motion, to appoint one or more medical experts whenever such are needed, in substantially the same manner in which masters and auditors are now appointed in this State." This is precisely the object of the recent act of Michigan (Pub. Acts Mich. 1905, p. 242), which ought to be carefully studied by those persons seeking to reform their own laws on this subject. Another matter in this connection ought to receive the attention of legislators — the form of hypothetical questions. Questions as long and cumbersome as those asked in the Thaw case in New York serve no good purpose, and cannot convey much light to the mind of the juror or any one else. It is true they embrace all the facts upon which the expert bases his opinion, but they have no other virtue.

AN important experiment in divorce legislation is the New Jersey act excluding aliens in the courts of that State from obtaining divorces except on grounds approved in their own States. The general enactment of such a statute would go far to clear our legal atmosphere from the miasmas of our present divorce complications. The acquisition of a temporary residence for divorce purposes would be useless thereafter, and "migratory divorces" would cease to puzzle the courts. It would not, however, affect the occurrence of future cases of the type of Atherton *v.* Atherton, 181 U. S. 155, and Haddock *v.* Haddock, 201 U. S. 562, 5 A. & E. Ann. Cas. 1. An interesting attempt to reconcile these celebrated cases is made in the September number of *Bench and Bar* by Mr. Raymond D. Thurber. Mr. Thurber's article is of considerable length and closely reasoned. We give, however, a passage, which suggests the method of reconciling the Atherton case with the later adjudication: "If the jurisdiction of the Kentucky court depended on the actual fact of Mrs. Atherton's domicil in Kentucky, to reconcile the two decisions would be a logical impossibility. But that is not the case. On the contrary, the rule is that when a court has some evidence of the existence of a jurisdictional fact, its finding that the fact exists will confer jurisdiction to render a decree which will be exempt from collateral attack. Such evidence, it is believed, as to the defendant's domicil in Kentucky, is to be found in those circumstances in the Atherton case which were held to establish the jurisdiction. The parties were living there as husband and wife; and up to the time of the separation the marital status — the entire *res* — was beyond question safely housed within the State. The wife as well as the husband were both actually and constructively domiciled there; and, under a familiar rule, this status is presumed to have continued until proven to have been altered. Again, the defendant, being the wife, was subject to the presumption that her domicil was that of her husband — a presumption which could be overcome only by showing not only that had she left him, but that she had a right to leave him. Hence, by merely proving this situation, the plaintiff made out a *prima facie* case for full jurisdiction; and this would seem to put the decree beyond the reach of collateral attack." The Kentucky court "having before it a sufficient *prima facie* case of jurisdiction, it was not bound to make any preliminary inquiry, but could safely proceed without regard to the possibility that a more thorough examination, upon evidence not before it, might require it to dismiss the case. All of which tends to establish the soundness of the proposition which we started out to examine, viz., that the State of the matrimonial domicil, if the plaintiff was deserted there and still resides there, has *prima facie* jurisdiction over the marital status of the errant defendant — at least if that defendant be the wife. This, it is believed, is the only logical explanation of the consistency of the Atherton and Haddock cases.

The custom of keeping official registers of births, marriages, and deaths is said to be traceable to the middle ages and to have owed its origin to certain peculiarities of the mediæval Church. The forbidden degrees of marriage were widely extended and complex under the influence of the revenues which flowed into the Church's coffers for dispensations granted for marriages within the degrees. But by reason of ignorance of genealogies and relationships, marriages were frequently contracted between persons not entitled to marry. Thus the parties unwittingly committed grievous sin, and incidentally the Church lost valuable fees. To prevent these lamentable consequences vicars were required to keep registers of baptisms and to insert the names of the godfathers and godmothers of the children. The origin of recording marriages and deaths is quite different. Early councils forbade priests to make any charges for administering the sacraments (among which was marriage) or for burying Christian people, but they were allowed to receive any voluntary offering on such occasions. These free offerings with process of time hardened into custom, and the priests, generously extending a credit for the customary fees, in order that they might not forget to collect, began to keep lists first of the occasions upon which the parties had not paid cash, and afterwards of all marriages and deaths. From such questionable beginnings does M. Viollet in his History of French Civil Law trace the modern registries of births, marriages, and deaths, which, since the period of the Revolution, have been in the hands of the civil authorities in France. In England and America, the tendency has been to leave such matters much more largely to voluntary effort. But in respect to marriage, the necessary regulation of social relations and of property have demanded stricter rules, and most of the United States have adopted marriage license laws. It is rather surprising that the great State of New York has not sooner adopted such legislation. At last, however, a marriage license law has been adopted in that State, which goes into effect on the first of January next. The statute, like many others already in operation, depends for its enforcement on the penalties incurred by the person celebrating a marriage without license. The law requires a verified statement from the applicants, and allows the official issuing the license to require the production of witnesses to establish the identity of the parties or to testify upon any matter material to the issue of the license. The investigation required before license is issued should tend to diminish the number of marriages in New York unsuitable because of the age or circumstances of the parties. It is said that ministers and magistrates near the boundaries of the State have had the opportunity to add perceptibly to their revenues by the marriage of couples from over the borders, and that not all of them have been careful in making inquiries as to the age and condition of the parties united. The new law will put an end to this state of things.

A wave of excitement swept over the country some years ago when young Cudahy was kidnapped by Pat Crowe. Many States at the time put on their statute books severe penal provisions against the crime. Perhaps it was under the influence of the feeling and discussion engendered by this celebrated case that North Carolina enacted that "if any person shall forcibly or fraudulently kidnap any person he shall be guilty of a felony," etc. Laws N. C. 1901, c. 699, Rev. 1905, § 3634. In a recent case the Supreme Court of that State had occasion to consider the exact nature of the act so denounced. Blackstone defines kidnapping at common law as "the forcible abduction or stealing away of a man, woman, or child from their own country and sending them into another." In the case before the North Carolina court the fate of the little child abducted was not established, and the defendant asked for an instruction embodying Blackstone's definition of the offense, including as a substantive element of the offense asportation beyond the boundaries of the State. But the Supreme Court sustained the trial court in defining the crime as "taking and carrying away of a person forcibly or fraudulently." State *v.* Harrison, 58 S. E. Rep. 754. The court admitted that there was some confusion about the definition among the authorities, but preferred to follow the views of Judge Parker in State *v.* Rollins, 8 N. H. 550, which have received the approval of Mr. Bishop, who declares: "The Supreme Court of New Hampshire, more reasonably, and apparently not in conflict with actual decisions, held that transportation to a foreign country is not a necessary part of this offense." It is fortunate that the authorities admit of such a construction, for probably the necessity of taking the abducted person out of the country forms no part of the popular conception of "kidnap," nor entered into the heads of the legislators who framed this statute. Social conditions in modern times have altogether changed the emphasis in this crime from transporting out of the country to the act of stealing. Yet it may very well have been that at an earlier day a real element of heinousness was added by carrying a victim out of the country. Blackstone speaks of the atrocity "of sending any subject of this realm a prisoner into parts beyond the seas, whereby he is deprived of the friendly assistance of the laws to redeem him from such his captivity." At one time it is stated that an organized system of kidnapping prevailed on parts of the British coasts, and young lads were seized and sold into practical slavery in the American colonies. Such conditions would amply explain why kidnapping as explained by Blackstone and the older writers might become the object of severe penalties.

"YELLOW PSYCHOLOGY."

Dr. Münsterberg Replies to Mr. Moore.

The October number of Law Notes has brought an interesting and brilliant paper by Mr. Charles C. Moore, under the title "Yellow Psychology." It is a curious irony of fate that this sulphur-colored label is intended for me. Only a few years ago it was the hobby of teachers' meetings to denounce me as the most reactionary psychologist in the country. Everywhere the application of psychology to education was being preached, and I seemed for a while to stand alone with my conservative counseling against a hasty application of half-baked psychological doctrines. And now the lawyers suddenly point to my psychological radicalism and my yellow demagoguery.

But on closer inspection it becomes evident that the promising title of the article is somewhat misleading. The picturesque caption makes the reader expect to hear that I have tried with reckless boldness to carry psychology into quarters where it does not belong; but after reading the essay of my critic, he will find that my real crime is quite a different one. I have dared to carry psychology into quarters where it has been all the time! I had suggested that the methods of modern laboratory psychology might be of some service to the courts, and now my critic shows that such a proposal is superfluous, as the judges have known for a long time everything which the psychologists can possibly find out. That is certainly a grave offense on my part, but it shows rather the rosy flush of naïveté than the yellow color of the appeals to lower instincts.

My naïveté I confess frankly. I had indeed not known that the jurists of the land were so excellently versed in psychological knowledge. I have attended many a court trial and have read carefully many more reports, and have constantly been astonished by the lack of knowledge of mental facts on the part of attorneys and judges. I was continually stumbling over the questions of serious lawyers which could not have been put honestly if those men had a fair understanding of the psychology of memory and attention, of perception and judgment, of feeling and will. And a hundred times have I seen them cease from their efforts where some knowledge of the more modern and subtle psychological methods would have easily carried them forward. I have gone through scores of books on evidence in three languages, and have been astonished at the scarcity of references to the real progress of modern psychological science. I do not see what else I could have done to discover that the courts really know all that the psychologists know — and much more — about the action of the mind. My only consolation is that the lawyers and judges themselves seem not to have known that they knew it all; I can say at least that after the publication of my essays I received by nearly every mail letters from well-known lawyers and judges all over the country encouraging me in this effort and regretting the present situation.

My critic proudly says, "We never find a judge citing or quoting a psychologist;" and as to the possibility of a psychological expert, he says, "We are inclined to think the judges will continue to depend upon their own resources in search of the truth." What does this mean? The courts do not decline the aid of other sciences. If there is a suspicion of arsenic, they call a physiological chemist; if there is a brain disease, they call an alienist; if the ball of a revolver is still in the body, they call a surgeon for the diagnosis. They do not even insist that such experts shall confine themselves to "common sense" methods; they do not object to the surgeon's using his Roentgen rays. Only for the science of psychology must it remain a dogma that common sense is the last resort and that the work of the psychological laboratory shall be ignored. This country has now more than forty psychological institutes at work. Have the judges really a right to be proud of the boast of my critic that their psychology does not need the aid of modern science?

Of course, my critic himself feels sure that he is very well informed in all the most modern psychology. He has "read treatises on psychology by various well-reputed writers," and his list begins with Spencer, Porter, Ladd. But what modern laboratory psychologist would doubt that such writers are unsuited to the purpose we are discussing? They have entirely different aims. But if it were true also for the more modern experimental psychologists that the judges, as Mr. Moore says, "have beaten the psychologists a mile," it would really be a pity that they seem so unwilling to help us in our work. What a cruelty to let us perform thousands and thousands of painstaking experiments on the most subtle points of mental life, while they succeed in knowing it all so much better by common sense and instinct!

My critic adds, indeed, that the real trouble is with us. We psychologists do not know enough law. He says, "There is not a scintilla of evidence in the *McClure's* article that its author has ever read a single reported opinion of a judge." He is perfectly right. When I am discussing a topic in a popular magazine, I try to erase every trace of the technical material I have used. I am just now writing a scientific book on applied psychology, and I hope that the legal chapters of that volume will sufficiently indicate that I have devoted serious study to the literature of law. But I should have been a miserable essayist if I had dragged the material of my note books into the columns of the popular monthly. My little article in the September *McClure's* — which, by the way, filled not more than four and a half pages — was decidedly not written for judges and juristic scholars. Furthermore, it was just one link in a long chain. I have published, for instance, in the January and March numbers of the *Times Magazine* papers on the memory of witnesses and on confessions; in the October *McClure's*, on the methods of bringing out the truth; another *McClure* paper will speak of hypnotism and crime; the *Readers' Magazine* brings a paper on suggestion in court; and the *Cosmopolitan*, on emotions and crime. In short, I undertook to interest public opinion in the intimate relations between law and psychology, and the lively newspaper discussion indicates that I have fully succeeded in reaching the wider public. I knew too well that any reforms could come only through a widespread public interest. But to stir up such interest would be impossible if the presentation were to be confined to the technical statement which is suited to the legal journals.

HUGO MÜNSTERBERG.

Harvard University.

NUMBER OF PERSONS OR OBJECTS.

Estimate of Number of Persons in a Crowd.

IT is certain that estimates of the number of persons in a considerable crowd in the open air will be enormously discrepant, unless the witnesses have acquired a facility in the matter by verifying estimates made under similar conditions on other occasions. Possibly a conservative court would require that a witness should have had a slight degree of experience — very slight would undoubtedly suffice — before his estimate of a large number of persons by merely casting his eyes over them is taken as competent evidence. However, nonexpert witnesses are always allowed to give their opinions of the speed of all sorts of moving objects and of distances, and rarely, if ever, has a witness failed to qualify for that purpose; although these are subjects on which opinions would be as unreliable, we should suppose, as opinions of number in a crowd.

But a witness's opinion would be of little value if he were practically destitute of experience. Imagine a person without any practice in such observations guessing within fifty or a hundred thousand or more of the number who listened to the speech of Daniel O'Connell, "walled by wide air and roofed by boundless heaven" on the Hill of Tara, August 15, 1843! Some historians, informed by eye-witnesses, put the number as high as five hundred thousand, and careful and unsympathetic witnesses testified that the number was as great as two hundred and fifty thousand. (McCarthy, History of Our Own Times, vol. 1, p. 195.) Lord Lytton, who was one of the audience, described the human ocean spread out before O'Connell, its "wave on wave" flowing "into space away." Not unnaturally he thought "no clarion could have sent its sound even to the centre" of that crowd. Of O'Connell's voice he said:

"And as I thought, rose the sonorous swell
As from some church tower swings the silvery bell;
Aloft and clear from airy tide to tide,
It glided easy as a bird may glide.
To the last verge of that vast audience sent,
It played with each wild passion as it went;
Now stirred the uproar — now the murmur stilled,
And sobs or laughter answered as it willed.
Then did I know what spells of infinite choice
To rouse or lull has the sweet human voice.
Then did I learn to seize the sudden clew
To the grand troublous life antique — to view,
Under the rock-stand of Demosthenes,
Unstable Athens heave her noisy seas."

(LORD LYTTON, *St. Stephens.*)

Agitation of a witness is always detrimental to accuracy of observation and would especially tend to pervert the judgment. For this reason a great difference among witnesses must be expected when they testify to the number of persons in a crowd hastily collected and observed under circumstances of great excitement, said the court in a case where a mob that rescued a party of fugitive slaves was variously estimated at from one hundred and fifty to two hundred and fifty in number. Giltner *v.* Gorham, 4 McLean (U. S.) 402.

In cases where witnesses have testified to distances between vessels before collision or to speed of trains or cars before an accident, a serious element of weakness in the testimony — proverbially weak even under favorable circumstances — has frequently arisen from the fact that the estimates are made from memory of the conditions and are not actual contemporaneous estimates. Likewise a witness's recollection of the number of even a small body of persons observed when the subject was not particularly called to his attention would probably be inaccurate. Chacon *v.* 89 Bales of Cochineal, 1 Brock. (U. S.) 478, 491.

In a case where the testimony was conflicting as to the number of slaves on board a ship when she was captured, the counts and estimates ranging from ninety to over one hundred and fifty, consideration of the burden of proof and the surrounding probabilities controlled the decision of the court. The Antelope, 10 Wheat. (U. S.) 66, 128.

Count of a Stream of Persons.

In the federal Circuit Court it was held that a count of a crowd moving rapidly over a wide gang plank, on leaving a steamer, and away from the observer, could be only an approximation. Besides errors likely to occur from the displacement of positions as some turned back to return, there was the highly probable error resulting from a consciousness of that fact on the part of the observer and his effort, perhaps unconsciously, to correct it. A decree of the District Court inflicting a statutory penalty upon a steamer for carrying an excessive number of passengers was reversed because the court gave preponderant weight to such testimony as against fairly reliable evidence of a count of tickets which were supposed to represent all the passengers on board. The Columbia, (C. C. A.) 50 Fed. Rep. 441, *reversing* 39 Fed. Rep. 617.

Count of Objects.

When articles actually handled and sorted are counted under circumstances which admit of the count being made deliberately, testimony to the result by witnesses who performed the task may be accepted as at least substantially correct. See The Columbia, (C. C. A.) 50 Fed. Rep. 441.

If the count is made by persons experienced in the storage of such articles, who have observed the space usually filled by a stated number, and who actually make such quantitative observation on a given occasion after counting, it is not probable that a huge error in the count would fail to attract their attention. Cummings *v.* Zimmer, 5 N. Y. App. Div. 540, 39 N. Y. Supp. 490.

On the other hand, where a witness testified that there were 1,777 hogsheads landed on a wharf, two hogsheads short of the invoice number, but he kept no tally or account except mentally, the court said that "in so large a number it is not possible to rely upon his unsupported accuracy." Scharlock *v.* The Globe, Crabbe (U. S.) 278, *per* Hopkinson, J.

But if two or more careful persons keep tally under circumstances not conducive to error, and agree in their count, mistake is highly improbable. Backus *v.* The Marengo, 6 McLean (U. S.) 487. See also Smith *v.* Bedouin S. N. Co., (1896) App. Cas. 70.

Although the maxim *testes ponderantur non numerantur* generally prevails, very careful judges have sanctioned the practice, in exceptional instances, of deciding a controverted question of fact according to the testimony of the greater number of witnesses on the precise point. Kentner *v.* Kline, 41 N. J. Eq. 422, 4 Atl. Rep. 781. So where the clerk of a consignee of sugar testified that he went to the wharf and counted thirty-seven hogsheads of sugar, but two witnesses testified that afterwards and before the consignee's cartmen arrived they counted thirty-eight, which was the number supposed to have been consigned, the court decided that there were thirty-eight, remarking however that if the cartmen had been called and supported the clerk's count, it might have required a finding that the two other witnesses were mistaken. Struver *v.* The Roderick Dhu, 23 Fed. Cas. No. 13,552.

It is a familiar (rebuttable) presumption that an officer, agent, or servant performs his duty, and "it is not a common experience to find a disinterested employee making mistakes against his employer and in favor of" another. Hence, where a railroad company contended that its employee made gross mistakes against its interests and in favor of a contractor, who, the evidence proved, never solicited him to do so, the court said the company "ought to present very convincing evidence to sustain the burden of proof, and to overcome all these presumptions." Elliott *v.* Missouri, etc., R. Co., (C. C. A.) 74 Fed. Rep. 707, 712, *per* Sanborn, C. J.

Circumstances cropping out in the testimony of a witness may give the trier of facts a hint when weighing his testimony in a case of conflicting evidence. Suppose, for example, the witness says he counted 2664 and that *there were 44 less than 2700.* See Seymour *v.* Bradfield, 35 Barb. (N. Y.) 49.

Testimony to an actual count of articles would be far better evidence of their number than a loose estimate, The Carlotta, 5 Fed. Cas. No. 2413*a*; just as "the testimony of even disinterested and unimpeached witnesses on the subjects of measurements, distances, dates, and the like, which is based merely on memory, estimate, or casual observation, must yield to that which is based on actual measurement or reference to definite data." Busse *v.* State, 129 Wis. 171, 108 N. W. Rep. 64, and numerous other cases in the books.

A reasonable explanation of a discrepancy in the count of articles between one witness and another should readily be accepted when given by a witness in a straightforward and unequivocal manner. The Queen *v.* The Ship E. B. Martin, 4 Canada Exch. 453, 460, where the court was convinced that one of the counters of some brass and paper cartridges had made a mistake because the butts of both were of brass and identical.

Count of Ballots by Election Officers.

In a contested election case in Kentucky the number of ballots cast for the contestant, according to the official count, was less than the number found on a count in the presence of the court in the case. There was no evidence that the ballots had been tampered with since the first count. The trial court adopted the last count, although it required a finding that egregious mistakes were made in the first count. This judgment was affirmed, the court saying: "It must not be forgotten that in the count of the votes by the officers of election all do not participate in every part of the count. Usually, as the evidence shows was done in this case, one officer calls off the ballots, and another, or others, tabulate them. It requires but little familiarity with the conduct of elections to realize how easy it is for mistakes to creep into the official count at the end of the day. In the first place, the officers have been on duty for many hours and are usually weary with the duties of the day when the count commences. The judges are generally elderly men, selected for the wisdom which ought to come with age, and the count of the votes, as in the case at bar, usually takes place after dark. Often the light is poor, and under these circumstances it can readily be seen how easy it is for an old man, with dim eyes and a poor light, to overlook sporadic votes." It was also a fact that the officers had been indulging in spirituous liquors to some extent. McEuen *v.* Cary, (Ky. 1906) 96 S. W. Rep. 850.

CHARLES C. MOORE.

THE MORALS OF THE PROFESSIONS.

"A man's a man for a' that."

FOR several centuries the members of all the learned professions save one have lain under vulgar suspicion as to their morality. As to physicians, for instance, the popular idea has been that they are atheistical, or at least agnostical. Perhaps some of the more thoughtless members of the profession have taken a certain amount of pride in shocking the moral sensibilities of ordinary mortals who have had no experience in assisting people into and out of the world. Be that as it may, physicians have been generally credited (or charged) with a lack of religious faith. If our memory serves us aright, the affable and learned author of the *Religio Medici* thought it necessary to apologize in the opening sentences for writing such a treatise. He apparently thought that many people would consider the very title a contradiction of terms.

As to lawyers, it is perhaps sufficient to say that they have always been a target for popular abuse and vituperation. They have been charged with the possession of every bad trait that has ever received a name. Possibly, however, in spite of the fact that the devil is said to be their patron saint, the faults usually ascribed to lawyers are what we may call the amiable, or at least the humane, vices.

As to clergymen, the situation is quite different. The average man, whether he is religious or irreligious, is pretty apt to think of a minister of the gospel as a being who is immensely better than his fellow men; and it does not often occur to him to probe into the minister's morals.

What right has a clergyman to be immoral? We don't mean in an ethical sense; but in the eye of the law, how immoral must a clergyman be before it can be said as a matter of law that he is unfit to guide his flock along the steep and thorny path? Possibly this sounds like an irreverent question, but no irreverence is intended. To many it may seem that the question is one of ecclesiastical, and not of judicial, cognizance. No doubt the moral fitness of clergymen to perform their sacred duties is usually settled finally by the religious bodies to which they belong; but nevertheless the courts have several times been called upon to decide such questions.

One of the most recent of these judicial decisions is Moore v. Bishop of Oxford, (1904) A. C. 283, wherein the Privy Council considered charges that a clergyman was guilty of sexual immorality and of profanity. Their lordships were of the opinion that the former offense was not established. The Lord Chancellor disposed of that charge as follows, analyzing and weighing the evidence in a manner that did great credit to his sagacity: "Their lordships are of opinion that the main charge in this case has broken down. The statements of the only witness who is relied upon for the purpose of proving the charge are, in the opinion of their lordships, uncorroborated by any conduct, act, or proof, and the charge rests entirely upon the evidence of this witness, who is the accuser herself. Their lordships do not think it necessary to consider more minutely the conduct of the witness, her account of the commencement of the relations between the appellant and herself being such as probably no court would accept, and one which, so far as their lordships know, the court below did not accept as true. All the court below had to determine was whether or not immoral relations existed at any time and in any circumstances, between the parties; and on that point their lordships are unable to concur with the Consistory Court in thinking that there is any corroboration by the correspondence or otherwise in favor of the accusation which has been made. Apart from any technical rule upon the subject, it would be a most dangerous thing for any court to allow an accusation of this sort to prevail when there is no corroboration; and probably no court would be induced to do so. If that observation is true, speaking generally of an accusation of this character, it is certainly not rendered less important in this case by the fact of the witness giving an account of the commencement of the relations between herself and the accused clergyman, which (as has already been said) probably no court would accept. Brought into contact with a stranger for the first time in her life, she is ravished (according to her statement) almost instantly after being brought up into the room to inspect the repairs that had been made, and yet she made no complaint or real attempt to defend her chastity. According to her own account there was an act of violent connection with her repeated on four separate occasions, and though immediate assistance, or, at all events, opportunities of complaint were at hand, there was no loud cry for assistance on her part — no pretense of any such complaint. In those circumstances their lordships find it impossible to confirm the finding that the evidence of the witness, uncorroborated as it is, and discredited by her own version of the transaction, can be accepted as conclusive against the clergyman whom she accuses."

As to the charge of profanity, their lordships found that the reverend gentleman had sworn occasionally, but they held that he had a right to swear every now and then when the provocation was great. They probably based their opinion on the ground that a clergyman is "a man for a' that." In disposing of this point, they said:

"With regard to the other charge, of having been 'habitually guilty of swearing and ribaldry,' there is a body of evidence relating to three or four occasions, which undoubtedly establishes (as the court below has found) that on those occasions language was used which certainly could not be defended, and the use of which would be disgraceful to anybody, whether clergyman or layman. But the question upon this part of the case is, whether the defendant was, or was not, guilty of the charge made — and properly made — in pursuance of the Clergy Discipline Act, 1892, § 2, which speaks of a clergyman 'alleged to have been guilty of any immoral act, immoral conduct, or immoral habit,' the words 'immoral habit' being the words contained in the charge. Where on occasions of considerable provocation words are used, however discreditable and disgraceful to the person who used them — and certainly no words could be too severe in condemnation of language such as that found to have been used by the appellant, even allowing for exaggeration in the views of some of the witnesses who used such words themselves, and attributed them to the appellant — yet the question would still remain whether or not, the clergyman having been proved in circumstances of provocation to have used such words on three or four occasions in the course of three years, it is true to say that he is guilty of the offense contemplated by the statute. The use of language of that sort can hardly be described as an 'immoral act' in the sense in which that term is used in the Clergy Discipline Act. Immoral conduct and immoral habit are probably the same thing. What is charged — and in their lordships' opinion properly charged in accordance with the statute — is that the appellant has 'during the past five years been guilty of offenses against the laws ecclesiastical (being offenses against morality within the meaning of the Clergy Discipline Act, 1892) in that he had habitually been guilty of swearing and ribaldry.' Their lordships certainly do not mean to give any countenance to the supposed innocence of the use of such words, even on special occasions of extraordinary provocation. As has been already said, no words are too severe to condemn such language. But the view their lordships entertain is that the offense contemplated by the statute — namely, of being habitually guilty of swearing and ribaldry — is not made out. Even although the appellant may have sometimes used such language, it is not established that he has been habitually guilty of such conduct. The evidence is spread over a period of three years, and the suggestion on the appellant's behalf is that objectionable language was only used on rare occasions of great provocation. Under these circumstances their lordships are of opinion that the appeal ought to be allowed with respect to both charges."

Evidently the Lord Chancellor was relieved to find that the strictly legal view which he took of the charge of profanity did not meet with the disapproval of the ecclesiastical authorities, for in the course of his opinion he said: "It is satisfactory to their lordships to find that the views which they entertain are shared by the most reverend and right reverend prelates who have been good enough to give them their assistance on this occasion."

It also seems that it is not a very serious thing for a clergyman to get drunk occasionally, so long as he does not "get the habit." In Marriner v. Bishop of Bath and Wells, (1893) P. 145, which was a proceeding wherein a clergyman sought to compel a bishop to institute him to a certain vicarage, the court said: "Here the clergyman is applying to the bishop to be instituted, and the bishop has the right, and not only the right, but it is a most imperative duty, to see that the man who offers himself for institution is a man of good moral character, and, upon making inquiries, he finds that within a certain period, the fact not being denied, the clergyman was obliged to give up his benefice upon a charge of drunkenness. That was enough to put the bishop on inquiry. I think it was a legitimate matter of inquiry, and it is quite within the range of that inquiry to ascertain whether within one, two, three, or four years of that time the same thing had happened, because, if intoxication is a casual occurrence due to particular causes, however grave an offense it is in a clergyman, it might perhaps be looked over and pardoned, particularly after a lapse of years; but habitual intoxication is a different matter, and I think the bishop would be bound to ascertain whether this was a casual occurrence standing by itself, or whether, really, it was habitual on the part of the clergyman applying to be instituted."

But while a clergyman has the right to swear occasionally "under circumstances of great provocation," and the right to get drunk every now and then, he would better be careful how he frequents dance halls. It is said that on a certain historic occasion the Rev. Dr. Parkhurst witnessed, if he did not participate in, a game of leap frog; and it is true that the reverend gentleman has never been disciplined for his devotion to sociological studies. Nevertheless, some clergymen have gotten themselves into trouble by slumming. In Sweet *v.* Young, (1902) P. 37, the "rector of the parish of Chipstead, in the county of Surrey, and diocese of Rochester," was charged with having been drunk on numerous specified occasions, and with immoral conduct on one occasion, the particulars of the last-mentioned charge being set forth as follows: "6. On or about July 4, 1899, at about 1.30 A. M., the defendant was in a dancing room at the Alsatian Club in Oxford Street, London, with a prostitute on his knee, and behaving himself in an immoral and riotous manner with the said prostitute and other prostitutes." The defendant filed an answer admitting charge 6 of the complaint down to the word "London," and denying the remainder of that charge and all the other charges in the complaint.

The court held that the defendant was guilty of immoral conduct, saying: "It is admitted that the defendant was at the place referred to in this charge at the time charged. We consider it proved that he had a prostitute on his knee without appearing to resent it, and that he remained in this place for a considerable time, was noisy and excited, and was talking and joking with this woman and with other women of the same class. We therefore find the defendant guilty of this charge as a matter of fact.

"But I have to consider whether this is a charge properly cognizable under the Clergy Discipline Act, 1892. It has been argued on behalf of the defendant that it is not so cognizable, and if it is not, then this court, constituted as it is for this case, has no jurisdiction to deal with this charge.

"The question turns on the proper construction of certain words in the second section of the Clergy Discipline Act, 1892, which enacts that a clergyman alleged to have been guilty of any immoral act, immoral conduct, or immoral habit, or of any offense against the laws ecclesiastical being an offense against morality (not being a question of doctrine or ritual) may be prosecuted under the act.

"The word 'immoral' is susceptible of more than one meaning, and the only clue the act affords as to the meaning in which the word is therein used is in the 12th or definition section, in which it is said that the expressions 'immoral act,' etc., shall include such acts, etc., as are 'proscribed' by the 75th and 109th canons of 1603. That 75th canon is as follows:

"'No ecclesiastical person shall at any time, other than for their honest necessities, resort to any taverns or alehouses, neither shall they board or lodge in any such places. Furthermore, they shall not give themselves to any base or servile labor, or to drinking or riot, spending their time idly by day or by night, playing at dice, cards, or tables, or any other unlawful games; but at all times convenient they shall hear or read somewhat of the Holy Scriptures, or shall occupy themselves with some other honest study or exercise, always doing the things which shall appertain to honesty, and endeavoring to profit the Church of God; having always in mind that they ought to excel all others in purity of life, and should be examples to the people to live well and Christianly, under pain of ecclesiastical censures, to be inflicted with severity, according to the qualities of their offenses.'

"The 109th canon is as follows:

"'If any offend their brethren either by adultery, whoredom, incest, or drunkenness, or by swearing, ribaldry, usury, and any other uncleanness and wickedness of life, the church wardens or questmen or sidesmen in their next presentments to their ordinaries, shall faithfully present all and every of the said offenders to the intent that they and every of them may be punished by the severity of the laws according to their deserts; and such notorious offenders shall not be admitted to the Holy Communion till they be reformed.'

"The question of the scope of the word 'immoral' in this act was considered by the judicial committee of the Privy Council in Beneficed Clerk *v.* Lee, (1897) A. C. 226. The precise point in that case was whether 'simony' is 'immorality' within the meaning of the act. It was held that it was not; but Lord Halsbury, in delivering the judgment of the committee, explained the effect of the reference to the two canons I have read. He said: 'The language of these canons denounces offenses which the 109th canon sums up as "uncleanness and wickedness of life," but it goes further, and it condemns acts and conduct hardly to be considered immoral, but certainly dangerous to the reputation or unworthy of the character of ministers of religion. It appears to their lordships that in thus applying and extending the use of the term "immoral" the act shows that the intention was to confine its scope to offenses of the kind referred to in these canons.'

"I think these observations have an important application to this case.

"It is proved that the Alsatian Club was, before it was closed as a disorderly house, a well-known night club frequented by men and prostitutes, where dancing was carried on very late at night after all respectable places of entertainment had been closed.

"The defendant went there after twelve at night, at the end of an evening spent at different places of entertainment, and then, after realizing the character of the place, stayed there three-quarters of an hour, talking and joking with prostitutes and behaving himself in the manner that has been described.

"I have not to decide whether the mere fact of a clergyman being in such a place, however regrettable, would be enough to create an offense under this act. I can conceive circumstances which might explain or justify his presence. But I think that, under the circumstances proved in this case, Mr. Young's presence and action at this place constitute conduct so 'dangerous to the reputation and unworthy of the character of ministers of religion'—to quote Lord Halsbury's words—as to be contrary to the 75th and 109th canons, and therefore 'an offense against the laws ecclesiastical' as well as 'an offense against morality' within the meaning of the Clergy Discipline Act, 1892."

In Vallancey *v.* Fletcher, (1897) 1 Q. B. 265, it is held that a clergyman is a "person" within the meaning of a statute providing that "any person" who shall be guilty of riotous, violent, or indecent behavior in any church shall be liable to a penalty.

The foregoing cases are all English ones; but it is doubtful if the American courts would be any more severe on the brethren of the cloth. Indeed, the following general rule has been laid down: "The immoralities for which a parish may dismiss the minister are of the grosser sort, such as habitual intemperance, unchaste behavior, etc.; lesser offenses, such as imprudence, censoriousness, etc., are not good cause for dismissal." 24 Am. and Eng. Encyc. of Law (2d ed.) 336.

Those who are interested in the proceedings of American ecclesiastical courts would do well to read the published account of the famous trial of Bishop Onderdonk. An edition was published by D. Appleton & Co. in 1845, and possibly later editions have appeared from time to time.

J. C. M.

OBSERVATIONS HERE AND THERE.

In The Queen *v.* Viau, 7 Quebec Q. B. 362, 372, Judge Wurtele had this to say concerning the practice of "the third degree" upon alleged criminals: "It is a fundamental principle in the criminal law of this country that a prisoner cannot be compelled to give evidence against himself on his trial, and such being the case, it is highly improper and contrary to principle for detectives, policemen, and others in authority to cross-examine prisoners who are in their custody in order to extort evidence against them. I do not go to the length of saying that constables or other peace officers should be entirely debarred from holding any conversation whatever with the prisoners whom they may have under their charge, and that any admissions made to them freely and voluntarily by such prisoners should be held inadmissible; but the practice of constables and other peace officers deliberately and designedly cross-examining and harassing prisoners for the purpose of extorting confessions of guilt, or of getting evidence against them, is reprehensible and should be discouraged."

The injustice of the former disqualification of a person accused of crime to testify in his own behalf in England was demonstrated in a startling manner in Davies *v.* Brecknell, 3 L. R. P. & D. 88, decided in 1873. There the propounder of a will testified on application for probate, the issues being tried by a jury. Although other witnesses testified against him, the jury believed him and decided in favor of the will. Lord Penzance was satisfied with the verdict, and denied a motion for a new trial. Thereupon the contestants of the will procured the indictment of the proponent for perjury in regard to his testimony in the will case, and without any evidence against him other than what was given in that case, he was convicted and sentenced to twelve months' imprisonment; because the mouth of the prisoner was closed on the criminal trial, and his adversaries had it all their own way. On the basis of this conviction the application for new trial in the will case was renewed, but the court bravely stood by the former determination of the jury giving credit to the proponent, which had been sanctioned by the judge, and again refused to grant a new trial. It is to be hoped that the proponent was not compelled to serve his sentence.

Last summer there was considerable discussion in bar associations and law periodicals in favor of a statutory enactment providing that in criminal cases a judgment of conviction shall not be reversed on appeal for errors not substantially prejudicial to the defendant. That this external remedy will hardly cure the evil aimed at, and that the real difficulty is the willingness of judges to use a microscope in order to discover substantial prejudice, is indicated by such cases as State *v.* Oscar, 7 Jones L. (N. Car.) 305. In that case, which was a prosecution for murder, the trial judge instructed the jury that if they had a rational doubt they must acquit the accused. "To exclude this rational doubt," he continued, "the evidence should be such as that men of fair ordinary capacity would act upon in matters of high importance to themselves. If the evidence here did not produce this degree of belief in their minds, then they ought to acquit the defendant; if it did produce that degree of belief, it authorized a conviction." A conviction was reversed and new trial granted because of error in the foregoing instruction, and Judge Battle, speaking for the Supreme Court, pointed out the error in the following opinion: "It is to the latter part of the charge, in which his honor undertakes the difficult, if not impossible, task of giving a precise and intelligible definition of what a rational doubt is, and what is sufficient to exclude it, that the counsel for the prisoner object. They contend that the standard by which the judge attempts to measure the evidence which is to exclude a rational doubt is fallacious in itself, and perilous to a prisoner charged with a crime. They insist that men of fair ordinary capacity will often act upon very slight evidence in matters of high importance to themselves, and that the very fact of the matter being of high importance to themselves will the more readily induce them to act upon such slight evidence. Thus, they say, that if one person were to say to another, 'Sir, I fear that your house is on fire,' he would instantly rush to the spot without stopping for a moment to inquire whether the information was founded upon a great or slight assurance of truth; whereas, if the alleged threatened danger of loss was slight or insignificant, the person exposed to it would probably stop to inquire into the grounds of his informant's belief, and not act upon it at all, until he was satisfied of the great probability of its being true. It must be confessed that there is great force in the objection, thus stated and illustrated. The idea which his honor intended to convey was, no doubt, suggested to him by the following passage from a very popular and learned work on evidence: 'A juror ought not to condemn, unless the evidence exclude from his mind all reasonable doubt as to the guilt of the accused, and, as has been well observed, unless he be so convinced by the evidence, that he would venture to act upon that conviction in matters of the highest concern and importance to his own interest.' See 1 Starkie on Ev. 414. At first view, the charge of his honor may seem to be identical in meaning with this passage, but upon a more minute and critical examination of the two expressions, a marked difference between them will be observable. Mr. Starkie introduces the idea of *venturing to act*, thereby implying that the party who acts upon the proposed evidence is making a *venture*, which, one way or the other, will be of the highest importance to his own interest. Supposing him to be a man of ordinarily sound mind, and to have the usual prudential regard to his own interest, we may well take it for granted that he will require almost a moral certainty in the evidence, on which he *ventures to act*, in a matter of life or death, or the loss or gain of a large estate. This idea of a *venture*, or a putting to hazard, is not *necessarily* involved in the language used by the learned judge. He merely says that 'to exclude the rational doubt, the evidence should be such as that men of fair ordinary capacity would act upon in matters of high importance to themselves.' Now, we have seen that such men might, and probably would, act upon comparatively slight evidence in matters of the highest import to themselves, if what they did was, at the moment, prompted by their feelings or their interest, and no risk was incurred by it. But if, in the case supposed by the prisoner's counsel, the owner might by running to his house be exposed to a greater calamity than its destruction, in the event of its not being on fire, we may be sure he would require strong proof that the cry of fire was well founded before he would make the venture, and incur the risk. We think it likely that the learned judge intended to convey this idea, but his language, as reported to us in the bill of exceptions, does not embrace it; and as his charge, in this particular, may have misled the jury upon a point all important to the prisoner, it is erroneous."

LORD THURLOW.

EDWARD THURLOW — the surly Chancellor — was the eldest son of a country parson, the Rev. Thomas Thurlow, and was born at Bracon Ash, Norfolk, on the 9th of December, 1731.

The successes of his career cannot be held up as the fitting reward of a virtuous and well-spent youth. On the contrary, it must be admitted that he was a bad boy. He possessed considerable talent, but was so overbearing and refractory that his parents had very soon to send him away to school — first to Seckar's School, at Scarning, in Norfolk, and afterwards to the King's School, at Canterbury — and at both he acquired the reputation of an incorrigible.

His natural ability had determined his father to put him into the legal profession, and from school he was sent to Cambridge, where he managed to win a scholarship at Caius College. But his record did not improve, and after a university career distinguished for idleness, which, however, was perhaps more affected than real,[1] as an alternative to being sent down for insubordination he was allowed to remove his name from the books of the college, and so left the university without a degree in the spring of 1751.

He had already been entered at the Inner Temple, and, in accordance with the practice of the day, on leaving the university he proceeded to the office of Mr. Chapman, an eminent solicitor in Lincoln's Inn. Here he still affected the character of an idler, and instead of studying law he spent his time in society.

Cowper, the poet, was a fellow pupil, and Thurlow struck up a close friendship with him. Cowper introduced him to his cousin, Lady Hesketh, and at her house in Southampton Row the two spent most of their time "in giggling and making others giggle," as the poet relates, instead of attending to their work.

However, the law student of those days was not required to satisfy any test of knowledge before being admitted to practice, so that his idleness was no obstacle to Thurlow's call to the bar, which took place on the 22d of November, 1752.

But it was a long time before he began to get business; the attorneys of the day were shy of sending work to one who had the reputation of such an idle fellow. Some four years after his call, however, he was engaged in a case before Lord Mansfield at the Guildhall, in which Sir Fletcher Norton, then one of the bullies of the bar, was on the other side. Norton, as usual, expected to silence the unknown junior by his accustomed arrogance. But this kind of treatment only served to rouse Thurlow, who turned on his antagonist and completely discomfited him, to the great delight, according to Lord Campbell, of the attorneys who had long smarted under Norton's despotic rule.

From this time he began to get more work, but still his progress was slow, and it created general surprise among his contemporaries when, through influence in high places, he managed to get appointed a King's counsel in 1761 and a bencher of his Inn in 1762. Through similar influence he got elected to Parliament for Tamworth in 1765.

The decisive point in his career was the result of a lucky accident. Thurlow, like many other lawyers of the time, was accustomed to frequent a certain coffee-house near Temple Bar known as Nando's and famous for its punch. Here, one evening in 1767,[2] he chanced to get into argument with a friend about a *cause célèbre* of the day, Douglas *v.* Hamilton, on which the succession to the Douglas estates depended, and which was then under appeal from the Scots courts to the House of Lords. The friend having expressed an opinion that the decision appealed from was correct, Thurlow delivered a vigorous and powerful argument in favor of the appellant, and having studied the case more closely than his opponent, completely silenced him.

[1] Campbell, Lives of the Chancellors (3d ed.), vol. v. 485, 486.

[2] Dict. Nat. Biog., vol. lvi. 345. There appears to be a good deal of confusion about the date. Lord Campbell puts the incident down to 1761. But this seems to be an error. See Foss, Judges of England, vol. viii. 378.

Unknown to the two disputants, the appellant's law agents were sitting at an adjoining table attentive listeners to the discussion, and they were so struck with the force with which Thurlow stated their side of the case that next day they sent him a retainer in the cause. Thurlow devoted to the case, for once, the most patient industry, and when it came on in the Lords in 1769, exhibited in it, as Lord Campbell says, the finest display of his forensic powers.

From this time on his advancement was rapid. He was made Solicitor-General in 1770, and Attorney-General the next year.

As a minister he displayed, both in his speeches in Parliament and in the state prosecutions in which he was engaged, so violent and uncompromising hostility to every opponent of the king and government — being especially bitter and truculent in his vituperation of the revolting American colonists — that on Lord Bathurst's resignation of the great seal there was not a moment's hesitation in appointing Thurlow his successor. He was made Lord Chancellor on the 3d of June, 1778, being at the same time raised to the peerage as Baron Thurlow of Ashfield, in the county of Suffolk.

He remained Chancellor, with a short interval, for fourteen years. Lord Campbell's estimate of him as a judge seems substantially just. "He was tolerably well qualified," he says, "to preside in the Court of Chancery from his natural shrewdness, from the knowledge of law which he had acquired by fits and starts, and from his having been for some years in full practice as an equity counsel. But he had never devoted himself to jurisprudence systematically; he was almost entirely unacquainted with the Roman civil law, as well as with the modern codes of the Continental nations; and unlike Lord Nottingham, Lord Hardwicke, and the Chancellors whose memory we venerate, upon his elevation to the bench he despised the notion of entering on a laborious course of study to refresh and extend his juridical acquirements. Much engrossed by politics, and spending a large portion of his time in convivial society or in idle gossip with his old coffee-house friends, he was contented if he could only get through the business of his court without complaints being made against him by the suitors or any very loud murmurs from the public. Permanent fame he disregarded or despised. He was above all taint or suspicion of corruption, and in his general rudeness he was very impartial; but he was not patient and painstaking; he sometimes dealt recklessly with the rights which he had to determine; and he did little in settling controverted questions or establishing general principles. Having been at the head of the law of this country for near thirteen years, he never issued an order to correct any of the abuses of his own court, and he never brought forward in Parliament any measure to improve the administration of justice."[3]

In White and Tudor's Leading Cases in Equity, eight of his decisions are cited as leading cases; namely, Hulme *v.* Tennant (1778), deciding that a married woman can dispose of equitable separate estate as if she were a *feme sole;* Ackroyd *v.* Smithson (1780), as to the effect of a partial failure of a trust for conversion of real estate in a will; Duke of Ancaster *v.* Mayer (1783–1785), that residuary personal estate is the primary fund for payment of a testator's debts; Ashburner *v.* Macguire (1784), on the characteristics of the different kinds of legacies; Sloman *v.* Walter (1784), on the right to equitable relief against penalties; Scott *v.* Tyler (1787–1788), on conditions in restraint of marriage; Countess of Strathmore *v.* Bowes (1789), on settlements in fraud of marital rights; and Fox *v.* Mackreth (1788–1791), that a trustee must not purchase the trust property from his *cestui que trust.*

His judgment in Ackroyd *v.* Smithson is no more than an

[3] Campbell, 527.

adoption of the celebrated argument of John Scott, afterwards Lord Eldon, and that in Scott *v.* Tyler appears to be based on the learned argument of Francis Hargrave, whom he is said to have frequently called in to assist him when research was necessary.[4]

His chief claim to fame as a lawyer is perhaps his invention of the restraint against anticipation of a married woman's property, the origin of which was as follows: In 1785 one Thomas Vernon eloped with a ward of the Court of Chancery, carried her off to Scotland, and married her. She was an heiress, and one may guess that it was her fortune he was after more than her, for he was in financial difficulties, and was heavily indebted to his bankers. Her friends, however, induced him t agree, upon having part of her property, that the rest should be settled on her, and Lord Thurlow, as Chancellor, referred it to the Master to prepare a settlement.

A settlement was accordingly made, by which part of her real and personal estate were conveyed to trustees, as to the real in trust to permit her to receive the rents and profits for life, or to pay them to such persons in such proportions and for such uses as she should from time to time appoint, and in default of such appointment for her sole and separate use for life, and after her death, if she had no children, as she should appoint, and in default of appointment for her heirs and assigns forever; and as to the personal property in the same manner, except that in her power of appointment the words "from time to time" were omitted, and in default of appointment it was to go to her executors and administrators.

This settlement was executed on the 6th of May, 1785.

Thomas Vernon's bankers were Messrs. Pybus. In 1785 he had greatly overdrawn his account, and they were pressing him for security. He thereupon induced his wife to assign the property, the subject of the settlement, to them for the purpose, and accordingly, on the 15th of August, 1785, she appointed the whole of the settled property to Messrs. Pybus as security for any sums to be advanced by them to her husband, and the next day made an absolute appointment in favor of her husband, "thus," as her counsel said, "stripping herself of everything." In 1788 Vernon was made a bankrupt, and Messrs. Pybus brought an action against the trustees of the settlement for the property.

The case came before Lord Thurlow, and though the reporter says he had "a most anxious desire to find any principle of a court of equity strong enough to protect the property against the improvident act in question," the authorities were too strong for him, and he was obliged to hold that she *had* "stripped herself of everything."[5]

Thus, as Lord Eldon said in a subsequent case, although the court had settled the property in order to protect it "with all the anxious terms" then known to conveyancers, in a day or two afterwards, while the wax was yet warm upon the deed, the creditors of the husband got a claim upon it by an informal instrument; and the same judge who had made such efforts to protect her was upon authority obliged to withdraw that protection.[6]

Lord Thurlow determined to do what he could to prevent such a disaster occurring again, and when, some time afterwards, he was made one of the trustees of the settlement of a Miss Watson, he directed the insertion in the settlement of words restraining her from anticipating her interest under the settlement.[7] Lord Eldon relates that the words introduced were, "not to be paid by anticipation." "I believe these were Lord Thurlow's own words; with whom I had many conversations about it. He did not attempt to take away any power the law gave her as incident to property, which being a creature of equity she could not have at law; but as under the words of the settlement it would have been hers absolutely so that she could alien, Lord Thurlow endeavored to prevent that by imposing upon the trustees the necessity of paying to her from time to time and not by anticipation; reasoning thus, that equity, making her the owner of it and enabling her as a married woman to alien, might limit her power over it."[8]

Lord Thurlow himself never had a chance of passing judgment as Chancellor on his own invention, and it remained of doubtful validity during his time. However, Lord Alvanley, who was Master of the Rolls till 1801, seems to have thought that it was a valid clause,[9] and Lord Eldon held in 1817 that it was too late to contend against its validity.[10]

For a short time in 1783 Lord Thurlow's tenure of the Chancellorship was interrupted, for when the coalition ministry of Fox and North came into power, the former insisted on Thurlow's resignation, but on the resumption of office by Pitt in December of that year Thurlow resumed the Great Seal. For a time he was a loyal supporter of Pitt, but gradually the relations between them became strained, and his intrigues widened the breach until, although nominally Pitt's colleague in the ministry, he was almost in opposition to him. Eventually the position became intolerable, and Pitt and Grenville finally told the King he must make his choice between them and the Chancellor, and as a consequence Thurlow had to resign, which he did on the 15th of June, 1792.

He continued for a time to attend the House of Lords and to take part in its business, but latterly he suffered very much from gout, and spent most of his time at various English health resorts.

He died at Brighton on the 12th of September, 1806, and was buried in the Temple church.

In manner Thurlow was rough — often coarse — and his habit of swearing was a by-word even among his contemporaries, by whom profanity was regarded as a far more venial offense against good manners than it is now. Moreover, he was notoriously a loose liver.

He was tall, well built, and singularly majestic in appearance. His features were stern, but regular, and matched well with his black, piercing eyes and bushy eyebrows.

It was to these physical advantages, added to natural shrewdness, illimitable self-confidence, a sonorous voice, and awe-inspiring manner, that he owed his reputation and ascendancy; for all his biographers seem agreed that he was rated much above his merits. "No one ever was so wise as Thurlow looks," Fox said of him.

Mr. J. M. Rigg says, in the Dictionary of National Biography, "Though his natural powers were great, he was too indolent to master either statecraft or law;"[11] and Foss sums him up thus: "To a coarseness partly natural and partly assumed, to a presumptuous haughtiness of demeanor, to a pretended disregard for the opinion of mankind, and to a gross looseness of morals were added undoubted talents, courage under difficulties, love of literature, and natural good nature. . . . His reputation as a judge does not at the present day stand very high."[12] — *London Law Notes.*

4 See Campbell, 533; Dict. Nat. Biog., vol. lvi. 348.

5 See the reports of the case of Pybus *v.* Smith, (1791) 3 Bro. C. C. 339, 1 Ves. Jr. 189.

6 See Jones *v.* Harris, (1804) 9 Ves. 493.

7 Parkes *v.* White, (1805) 11 Ves. 221.

8 Brandon *v.* Robinson, (1811) 18 Ves. 434.

9 See his remarks in Socket *v.* Wray, (1794) 4 Bro. C. C. 486.

10 Jackson *v.* Hobhouse, (1817) 2 Mer. 488.

11 Dict. Nat. Biog., vol. lvi. 348.

12 Judges of England, vol. viii. 374, 384.

Cases of Interest.

WHAT CONSTITUTES VAGRANCY. — In Gainer v. State, 58 S. E. Rep. 295, the Georgia Supreme Court holds that the fact that a party is black and ragged, and asleep at night, and has not worked for four days, although he may have no money, will not of itself authorize a conviction for vagrancy. And where a person is arrested without a warrant, evidence that he has no money, obtained by unlawful search and seizure, is not admissible against him.

WHO IS A CANDIDATE. — In State v. Bates, 112 N. W. Rep. 1026, the Supreme Court of Minnesota was called upon to decide at what time a political aspirant becomes a candidate within the meaning of a "corrupt practices act" requiring a verified statement of the expenditures of candidates and restricting such expenditures within a certain limit. The court held that the aspirant did not become a candidate until the time of filing his affidavit of intention of becoming a candidate as provided by statute, and that items of expenses incurred or paid anterior to the filing of such affidavit need not be included in the verified statement.

ACCIDENT INSURANCE — BLOOD POISONING. — In Fidelity & Casualty Co. v. Thompson, 154 Fed. Rep. 484, the Circuit Court of Appeals, Eighth Circuit, held that, where a patient on whom a dentist was operating suddenly coughed, thereby blowing into the dentist's eye particles of septic matter, which, without abrading, penetrating, or bruising the membrane, infected it and caused blood poisoning, this did not constitute a "wound" within the meaning of an accident policy, which covered, *inter alia*, blood poison sustained by physicians or surgeons resulting from septic matter introduced into the system through wounds sustained in professional operations.

CHILD LABOR — POLICE POWER. — In Lenahan v. Pittston Coal Min. Co., 67 Atl. Rep. 642, the Pennsylvania Supreme Court holds that an act prohibiting the employment of any person under fifteen years of age to oil machinery in a coal mine is a valid exercise of the police power; and that where a boy under such age is injured while oiling machinery in motion, the employer cannot set up contributory negligence as a defense. The court said: "This exact question has not been before our courts, but it has been passed upon by the courts of many other jurisdictions, and, so far as we are informed, the rule hereinbefore stated has been unanimously followed."

ACCORD AND SATISFACTION — PART PAYMENT. — In Melroy v. Kemmerer, 67 Atl. Rep. 699, the Pennsylvania Supreme Court held that where a debtor, in contemplation of bankruptcy, offered his creditor thirty per cent. in settlement, and the creditor accepted the same and closed the account, this constituted an accord and satisfaction, the additional consideration being the debtor's relinquishment of his intention to go into bankruptcy. The court said: "The accord in this case was good on both branches. By it the creditors got a sum certain, instead of the chances of an uncertain dividend in bankruptcy. On the other hand, the debtor accepted the responsibility of paying a sum certain, whether his assets were sufficient or not, and gave up his right to a release of his future assets, and to a discharge from his whole debt, without regard to the sufficiency of his present assets."

AUTOMOBILES — CAVEAT EMPTOR. — In Morley v. Consolidated Mfg. Co., 81 N. E. Rep. 993, recently decided by the Massachusetts Supreme Court, the plaintiff sought to recover back the price paid for an automobile on the ground of breach of warranty. He purchased the machine for about half the price of a new one, and at the time was told by the agent that it had been in use as a demonstrating car and had been run about 500 miles, but that it was in first-class condition and all right. After the plaintiff had used the car about two months the crank shaft broke and damaged the engine materially. It was held that not only was there no express warranty, all that was said being seller's talk, but there was no implied warranty on which recovery could be had for the breaking of the shaft after two months' use. The court (probably having in mind the three wise men of Gotham) said: "If the shaft had been stronger, it might have lasted for a longer time."

GAMING HOUSE — SPECULATION IN FUTURES. — In Anderson v. State, 58 S. E. Rep. 401, the Georgia Court of Appeals decided the first case which has come up under the Boykin Act of 1906, which prohibits dealing in futures. The defendant was convicted of maintaining a bucket shop, and this judgment is upheld. The court holds that an assertion, although made in each transaction, by the customers of an office where futures are bought and sold, that actual delivery is contemplated and understood in all cases, will not prevent the keeper of the office from being guilty of maintaining a gaming house, if as a matter of fact the customers, throughout a continued course of dealings, do not make, tender, or accept actual delivery, but, through the proprietor of the office, settle their winnings and losses in money. The actual facts of the case must override the contradictory alleged contemplation of the parties. And the fact that the contracts are telegraphed out of the State does not affect the liability if the actual wagering or the settlement of the wagers take place in the State.

THE RIGHT OF PRIVACY. — In Edison v. Edison Polyform Mfg. Co., 67 Atl. Rep. 392, the New Jersey Court of Chancery granted an injunction to restrain the unauthorized use by the defendant of the complainant's name as part of its corporate title, or, in connection with its business or advertisements, his picture and his pretended certificate that a medicinal preparation manufactured by the defendant is compounded according to the formula devised by him; and this although the complainant was not a business competitor. Vice-Chancellor Stevens reviewed the cases at some length, and expressly disapproved the holding in Roberson v. Rochester Folding Box Co., 171 N. Y. 538, saying: "This case cannot be sustained on principle, and has been disapproved by the Supreme Court of Georgia, in Paversich v. New England L. Ins. Co., 122 Ga. 190, 50 S. E. 68, and by our own Court of Appeals in Vanderbilt v. Mitchell, 67 Atl. 97, 103. If a man's name be his own property, as no less an authority than the United States Supreme Court says it is (Brown Chemical Co. v. Meyer, 139 U. S. 542), it is difficult to understand why the peculiar cast of one's features is not also one's property, and why its pecuniary value, if it has one, does not belong to its owner rather than to the person seeking to make an unauthorized use of it."

LIFE INSURANCE — DEATH "AT HANDS OF JUSTICE." — In Supreme Lodge Knights of Pythias v. Crenshaw, 58 S. E. Rep. 628, the Georgia Supreme Court holds that an exception in a life insurance policy of death "at the hands of justice" does not cover a case where a husband slays his wife's paramour. The court said: "It is contended, not that the death of the insured was the result of the administration of punitive justice, but that it was the result of the administration of preventive justice; that the law allows the husband to kill his wife's paramour under certain circumstances, and the killing, under these circumstances, is in the administration of preventive justice within the meaning of the code. We do not think that the word 'preventive' in the code is to be given this interpretation. The word 'punitive' certainly refers to death inflicted by an officer of the law, in obedience to the commands of the law. The word 'preventive' must be construed to refer to a killing by an authorized officer of the law, or a private person standing for the time being in the attitude of a public officer; as a member of the sheriff's posse, or the like, under those circumstances where the law authorizes the taking of human life in the advancement of public justice. It cannot be properly interpreted to ever include a killing by a private person to avenge or prevent a private wrong, even though the circumstances be such that the homicide be justifiable."

EXTRADITION — OFFENSES TRIABLE. — Both the majority opinion by Shelby, J., and the dissenting opinion of Pardee, J., in Greene *v.* U. S., 154 Fed. Rep. 401 (Circuit Court of Appeals, Fifth Circuit), are rich with interest and instruction on the subject of extradition. The case was one of those growing out of the Savannah harbor frauds and the subsequent long drawn out proceedings to extradite Greene and Gaynor from Canada. The principal point decided was the contention of the plaintiff in error that the offenses charged in the indictments under which he was convicted were not the same for which he had been extradited, and that, therefore, the court had no right to try him under such indictments. In regard to this the court said: "While the extradition and the indictment must be for the same criminal acts, it does not follow that the crime must have the same name in both countries. The same crime often has different names in different countries. If the act in question is criminal in both countries and is within the terms of the treaty, nothing more is required. In deciding whether the indictment charges the same offense for which the defendants were extradited, the acts of the defendants alleged in the two proceedings must be considered. It is not a question of names. The technical niceties and distinctions recognized sometimes in criminal law as making a fatal variance cannot be applied."

RELIGIOUS SOCIETIES — JURISDICTION OF CIVIL COURTS. — The power of civil courts to review the decisions of duly established tribunals of religious societies is discussed at length by the Georgia Supreme Court, in Mack *v.* Krine, 58 S. E. Rep. 184. The case arose out of the reunion of the Cumberland Presbyterian Church with the Northern Presbyterian Church, brought about by the General Assembly at Decatur, Ill., in May, 1906. The action was brought by certain members of the First Cumberland Presbyterian Church, of Atlanta, who sought to restrain the transfer of the church and its property to the Northern Presbyterian Church. It was held that while civil courts would sometimes interfere in such cases to protect property rights and prevent an utter subversion of the purposes for which the society was formed, yet where a property right was dependent on a question of doctrine, discipline, ecclesiastical law, rule, custom, or church government, the civil courts would regard as conclusive the decision of the highest tribunal within the organization; and interference would only be had when it was manifest that what the church tribunal had adjudicated was not a difference of opinion as to doctrine or teachings, but an attempt, in the form of such adjudication, utterly to abandon the purposes for which the church was organized. In case of a schism the courts will not inquire into the existing religious opinions of those who adhere to the acknowledged organization. The action of the General Assembly of the Cumberland Presbyterian Church in uniting with the Northern Presbyterian Church was upheld.

"FAMILY" DEFINED — BENEFICIAL ASSOCIATIONS. — In Starnes *v.* Atlanta Police Relief Assoc., 58 S. E. Rep. 481, the Georgia Court of Appeals defines the word "family" as used in the constitution of a benefit association to designate the class to which the beneficiaries must belong. Hill, C. J., defined the word thus: "Where the word 'family' is used to designate the class who shall receive the benefit, any relation who is living with and dependent upon the member, or with whom the member is living and upon whom he is dependent, at the date of his death, is within the designated class and entitled to the benefit." Russell and Powell, JJ., specially concurring, gave the term a broader scope, saying: "From a review of the decisions we deduce the following order of precedence which should ordinarily be observed in determining who are entitled to take under the words 'family of the member,' or similar designations: (1) Wife and unmarried children, minor or adult; or, if no unmarried children, (2) wife alone; or, if no wife, (3) unmarried children alone; or, if no wife and no unmarried children, (4) persons related by consanguinity or affinity, living with the member in the same household; or, if none of these, (5) any person related by consanguinity or affinity, dependent on and supported by the member; or, if none of these, (7) married children, irrespective of dependency; or, if none of these, (8) father, mother, brothers, and sisters, irrespective of active household connection and irrespective of the question of dependence; and in some instances an even further extension may be made, if necessary, in order to find a beneficiary. The existence of the benefit connotes a contemplated beneficiary, and the law will find one, if possible."

News of the Profession.

PROMINENT BOSTON ATTORNEY DEAD. — Ex-Judge Hiram P. Harriman, a prominent Boston attorney, died at his summer home in Wellfleet, Mass., on September 21, aged sixty-one years.

TEXAS JUDGE RESIGNS. — On October 4 Hon. J. A. Eidson, of the Texas Court of Civil Appeals, Third Supreme Judicial District, tendered his resignation to Governor Campbell, to take effect at once. His action was forced upon him by continued ill health.

TO HONOR CHIEF JUSTICE MITCHELL. — On November 10 the Pennsylvania State Bar Association gives a reception and banquet in Philadelphia in honor of the fiftieth anniversary of the admission to the bar of Hon. James T. Mitchell, chief justice of the Pennsylvania Supreme Court.

LAWYER KILLED BY TRAIN. — John W. Gregory, an attorney of Waitsfield, Vt., fifty-three years old, was killed on September 14 by a train. He was on a high railroad bridge taking photographs of Winooski Gorge when the train struck him and hurled him into the river, a hundred feet below, killing him instantly.

THE NATIONAL PRISON ASSOCIATION held its thirty-first annual convention in Chicago, beginning on September 15. It was the largest gathering of the kind ever held in this country, delegates being in attendance not only from all the States, but from Canada, Mexico, and Cuba as well. One of the most important steps taken was the appointment of a committee to act in connection with the American Bar Association to bring about unity in the criminal laws of the various States.

APPOINTED TO NEW YORK SUPREME COURT. — On October 7 Governor Hughes appointed Hon. S. Nelson Sawyer justice of the New York Supreme Court for the Seventh Judicial District to succeed the late Justice Dunwell. Judge Sawyer was, at the time of his appointment, judge of the Wayne County Court. His appointment runs only to January 1. Judge Sawyer is the Republican candidate for the same office, which will be filled at the coming election.

EX-JUDGE BOOKSTAVER, OF NEW YORK, DEAD. — Hon. Henry W. Bookstaver, formerly a member of the New York Supreme Court, died suddenly on September 21, at his summer home near Newport, R. I. Judge Bookstaver was seventy-three years old. He was admitted to the New York bar in 1864, and in 1885 was elected judge of the Common Pleas Court. Ten years later he was transferred to the Supreme Court, where he served until 1900, when he resumed practice.

CENTENNIAL OF CONNECTICUT SUPREME COURT. — On September 23 Chief Justice Simeon E. Baldwin, of the Connecticut Supreme Court of Errors, gave a luncheon to the judges of the Supreme and Superior Courts and the members of the State bar associations in commemoration of the one hundredth birthday of the State Supreme Court. Judge Baldwin read to his guests a paper on the history of the court.

DEATH OF YOUNG ALABAMA JUDGE. — Hon. Terry M. Richardson, of Montgomery, Ala., who had the reputation of being the youngest man ever appointed to the circuit bench of Alabama, was found dead in bed at a hotel at Luverne, Ala., on September 16. His death was said to have been caused by chloroform taken to relieve a headache. He was only thirty-one years of age at the time of his death, and was appointed judge of the Montgomery circuit when he was but twenty-seven.

PEASLEE PROMOTED TO CONNECTICUT SUPREME COURT. — On October 3 Governor Floyd nominated Hon. Robert J. Peaslee, of the Connecticut Superior Court, to be a justice of the State Supreme Court in succession to Justice William M. Chase, who will retire on the age limit in December. At the same time William A. Plummer, of Laconia, was nominated to the vacancy on the Superior Court bench caused by the promotion of Judge Peaslee.

DEATH OF RANDOLPH GUGGENHEIMER. — Randolph Guggenheimer, senior member of the widely known firm of Guggenheimer, Untermeyer & Marshall, died of apoplexy at his summer home at Long Branch, N. J., on September 12. Mr. Guggenheimer was a native of Lynchburg, Va., and was fifty-nine years old. He was for years prominently identified with Tammany Hall, and has held a number of important municipal posts under Tammany administrations, including that of president of the council.

NOYES APPOINTED TO SUCCEED JUDGE TOWNSEND. — On September 19 the President appointed Hon. Walter C. Noyes, of New London, Conn., as United States circuit judge to fill the vacancy caused by the death of Judge William K. Townsend. Since 1895 Judge Noyes has been judge of the Court of Common Pleas for New London county. He is forty-two years of age, and is a native of Lyme, Conn. He is the author of two well-known text books, "The Law of Intercorporate Relations" and "American Railroad Rates."

NORTH DAKOTA STATE BAR ASSOCIATION. — The annual meeting of the North Dakota State Bar Association was held in Jamestown, N. D., on September 13, with about fifty members in attendance. The retiring president, John Carmody, of Hillsboro, delivered an address on the subject of recent legislation. A banquet was held in the evening. The following officers were elected for the ensuing year: President, S. E. Ellsworth, of Jamestown; vice-president, F. G. Register, of Bismarck; secretary and treasurer, W. H. Thomas, of Leeds.

DISTINGUISHED CALIFORNIAN DEAD. — Hon. Milton Hills Myrick, an ex-justice of the Supreme Court of California, died at his home in Santa Clara county on September 18, at the age of eighty-one. Judge Myrick was a New Yorker by birth, but migrated to California in 1854, and began practice in San Francisco in 1866. He was elected probate judge in 1871, and after serving two terms in that capacity was elected a member of the State Supreme Court in 1879, where he served until 1887. In that year he again took up practice in San Francisco in partnership with F. P. Deering, and enjoyed a large and lucrative practice until advancing age compelled him to retire a few years ago.

WELL-KNOWN ILLINOIS LAWYER DEAD. — Hon. David McCulloch, a prominent lawyer and citizen of Peoria, Ill., and formerly a member of the State Appellate Court, died in Peoria on September 17, at the age of seventy-five. A native of Pennsylvania, Judge McCulloch moved to Peoria in 1853, and was admitted to the bar of Illinois in 1857. In 1877 he was made circuit judge, and two years later was assigned to the Appellate Court, where he served until 1885. Since then he had practiced in Peoria, and for the last six years had been referee in bankruptcy. In 1880 he was president of the Illinois State Bar Association.

DETROIT'S PROSECUTING ATTORNEY DIES. — George Francis Robison, prosecuting attorney of Wayne county, Mich., died at his home in Detroit on October 5, after a brief illness. He was born in Manchester, Mich., in 1848, and was a graduate of the University of Michigan. He was first elected prosecuting attorney in 1884, and held the position for two years, after which he took up private practice and gained much reputation as a criminal lawyer. In 1906 he reappeared as a candidate for his former office, and was elected on the Democratic ticket, although most of the other candidates on the same ticket were defeated.

INTERNATIONAL MARITIME COMMITTEE. — The conference of the International Maritime Committee was held in Venice on September 25–28. The inaugural address was read by the Italian Minister of Justice, after which the officers of the conference were elected. The most important features were reports on the labors of the Diplomatic Conference at Brussels and on the work of the International Maritime Committee since the Liverpool conference, and discussions on the draft treaty on Limitation of Shipowners' Liability, the draft treaty on Maritime Mortgages and Liens, and the Conflict of Laws as to Freight.

FEDERAL SUPREME COURT IN SESSION. — On October 14 the Supreme Court of the United States convened for the October Term with all the members of the court in attendance. The chief justice stated that, owing to Mr. Roosevelt's unavoidable detention in the Louisiana canebrakes, the usual formality of a call on the President would be dispensed with, and the court would be happy to hear motions, preferably those for admission to practice. Thirty-one lawyers were admitted to practice before the court, and a number of other motions relative to pending causes were heard, the session lasting slightly more than half an hour. The calendar is said to be the largest the court has ever faced at its opening, containing four hundred and eighty-one cases.

ARKANSAS SUPREME JUDGE DEAD. — Hon. James Edward Riddick, associate justice of the Arkansas Supreme Court, died at Little Rock on October 9 of typhoid fever. Judge Riddick was born in Fayette county, Tenn., in 1849, and received his legal education in the Lebanon Law School and Michigan University, graduating from the latter school in 1872. Soon after entering upon the practice of law he was made prosecuting attorney for the second Arkansas circuit, which he relinquished in 1878 to become a member of the State legislature. In 1886 he became judge of the same circuit, and in 1894 was elevated to the bench of the State Supreme Court.

CONVENTION OF ATTORNEYS-GENERAL. — At St. Louis, on September 30 and October 1, was held a convention of the attorneys-general of the various States. Not all the States were represented, but a sufficient number of delegates were in attendance to make the meeting one of considerable significance. The papers on the programme were as follows: "The Standard Oil Trust," by Wade H. Ellis, attorney-general of Ohio; "Anti-trust Laws," by Jewel P. Lightfoot, assistant attorney-general of Texas; "Railroad Rate Regulation," by Herbert S. Hadley, attorney-general of Missouri; "Conflict Between State and Federal Courts," by Edward T. Young, attorney-general of Minnesota; "Capitalization of Public Service Corporations," by Dana Malone, attorney-general of Massachusetts; "State Regulation of Public Utilities," by William S. Jackson, attorney-general of New York. The St. Louis Bar Association tendered the visitors an informal luncheon, which was attended by more than two hundred St. Louis lawyers. The president of the association, John F. Lee, delivered an address of welcome, to which response was made on behalf of the visitors by Mr. Lightfoot, of Texas.

VERMONT STATE BAR ASSOCIATION. — The twenty-ninth annual meeting of the Vermont State Bar Association was held in Montpelier on October 1, with President F. M. Butler, of Rutland, in the chair. The afternoon session was devoted entirely to routine business. In the evening the annual address was delivered by President Butler, who discussed means for remedying delays and undue expense in legal proceedings. Max L. Powell, of Burlington, read a paper on "Twenty-seven Years of Litigation Between the Vermont and Canada Railroad and the Central Vermont," and Judge E. L. Waterman gave a sketch of the life and work of the late Judge Hoyt H. Wheeler, of Brattleboro. After the speaking the annual banquet was held, President Butler acting as toastmaster. Those who responded to toasts were Lieutenant-Governor George H. Prouty, of Newport; Hon. J. W. Rowell, of Randolph, chief justice of the Vermont Supreme Court; Hon. W. H. Taylor, of Hardwick; Hon. Henry C. Ide, of St. Johnsbury; J. W. Redmond, of Newport, chairman of the State Board of Railroad Commissioners; Hon. Frank Plumley, of Northfield; Col. J. H. Mimms, of St. Albans; Congressman D. J. Foster, of Burlington, and H. Hugh Henry, of Chester. The following officers were elected: President, Alexander Dunnett, of St. Johnsbury; vice-presidents, C. G. Austin, of St. Albans, Z. H. Albee, of Bellows Falls, and F. A. Howland, of Montpelier; secretary, John H. Mimms, of St. Albans; treasurer, Hiram Carleton, of Montpelier.

English Notes.

A PROMISING BREACH OF PROMISE SUIT. — A breach of promise case which promises to be the sensation of the Michaelmas term has been begun against the Hon. John Yarde-Buller by a Mrs. Atherton. The plaintiff is a sister of Sir Aubrey Deane Paul, and was married in 1892 to Col. Atherton, who secured a divorce from her, naming Mr. Yarde-Buller as corespondent. She is said to be a strikingly beautiful woman, and used to be well known in London society. The defendant, who is son and heir to Lord Churston, was recently married secretly to Denise Orme, an actress. A brilliant array of legal talent has been retained by each side.

INSOLVENCY STATISTICS FOR 1906. — The recently issued Bankruptcy Report of the Board of Trade shows that, while the total number of bankruptcies in England during 1906 was less by 328 than in the preceding year, and the number of deeds of arrangement was less by 198, yet the estimated total loss to creditors was greater by about a quarter of a million pounds. The number of applicants for discharge was 867, as against 800 in 1905, while more than 3,000 bankrupts did not apply for discharge. The total number of failures of women was 504, eight more than in the preceding year, and among them were fewer married and single women and more widows. Nothing of unusual interest is to be found in the statistics.

LUNACY AS GROUND FOR DIVORCE. — The question whether supervening insanity of husband or wife should be recognized as a ground for divorce has been brought to the public attention in England by some astonishing figures furnished by Mr. Richard Gates, secretary of the Divorce Law Reform Union. It seems that of the 121,979 persons certified as insane in England and Wales, over forty-five per cent. are married. They are the figures of the commissioners in lunacy, and they mean that considerably more than fifty thousand persons — many of them very young — are prevented by law from remarriage. Of course the opponents of divorce decry the movement to make insanity a cause for rescinding the marriage contract, on the ground that the insane partner needs the tender care and consideration of the other partner. But it seems fairly obvious that if the sane spouse is disposed to give the required care and consideration, he will give it regardless of the law on the subject, and if he isn't, he won't.

IMPRISONMENT FOR DEBT. — The subject of imprisonment for debt is again attracting considerable public attention in England, and the matter will probably be brought before the next session of Parliament. The statistics show that, while 4,288 debtors were imprisoned in 1876, no fewer than 11,986 were sent to jail in 1906 — a larger number than before the passing of the act by which imprisonment for debt was nominally abolished. Under the present system a man who owes a sovereign may suffer a heavier penalty than a man who steals one, and one evil result has been a harmful extension of credit-giving among the working classes. Some of the county judges are very free with commitments under the Debtors' Act, committing debtors when they think the effect of the order will be that the friends of the debtor will pay the debt for him, or that he will get the money to do so from a money lender or in some other way.

BEES AND THE LAW. — An interesting case involving the law relative to bees was before one of the English County Courts recently. In Quantrill v. Spragge (see *Law Journal* for Sept. 21, 1907, page 586), a swarm of bees left the premises of their owner and settled on an apple tree in a neighbor's garden. The neighbor, being in a surly mood, refused to admit the owner of the bees to his garden, and, while they were debating the matter rather hotly, his son went and shook down the swarm, which remained in a cluster on the ground. The neighbor having at last grudgingly assented, the owner approached the swarm to hive them, whereupon they took wing and disappeared to parts unknown. Suit being brought by the owner, Judge Mulligan held that the bees still remained the plaintiff's property after they had attached themselves to the defendant's tree, but the plaintiff had no right to go on the defendant's premises to reclaim them without the defendant's consent; that the shaking down of the bees by the defendant was a tortious act, but that, since this act did not itself cause the bees to take flight, the plaintiff was not damaged thereby; and that, as each party had trespassed against the other, but without causing damage, each should pay his own costs.

LORD HALSBURY. — The death of Lord Brampton leaves Lord Halsbury, who celebrated his eighty-third birthday during September, practically the only survivor of the notable array of lawyers who were associated with him in the earlier days of his legal career. With the sole exception of Lord Eldon, who was Lord Chancellor for the unprecedented period of twenty-four years, the Earl of Halsbury easily heads the list as to length of judicial service of holders of this office for generations if not centuries past. His first appointment as Chancellor was in the Marquis of Salisbury's first administration of 1885, but this was a relatively brief tenure, lasting only 227 days. He was again Chancellor throughout the whole of the second and third Salisbury administrations, as well as the Balfour administration, the first lasting six years and fifteen days, and the second going on continuously from July 2, 1895, till December, 1905 — roughly, ten years and a half. Thus Lord Halsbury has been Lord Chancellor for rather more than seventeen years. The tenure of office by other Chancellors in modern times has been, Lord Herschell about three and a quarter years, Lord Selborne between seven and eight years, and Lord Cairns a little over six years.

DECEASED WIFE'S SISTER ACT STIRS THE CHURCHMEN. — The anticipated turmoil over the passage of the act legalizing marriage with a deceased wife's sister has speedily developed, and the columns of the London *Times* have of late been crowded with letters from agitated gentlemen of the clerical persuasion declaring against this scandalous and indecent measure. The bishops of the Church of England, in particular, are aghast at the iniquity, and the Archbishop of Canterbury has let it be known in a public letter that such sinful unions are not to be solemnized in church. The Bishops of London, of Exeter, and of Southwark have also emitted cries of horror which would lead one to believe that the deceased wife's sister is altogether the most fearful menace that has ever threatened the United Kingdom. On the other hand, some of the prominent laity and a few of the minor clergy with liberal tendencies have returned the fire of the bishops quite effectively. Canon Henson, of Westminster Abbey, fired a shot at the Bishop of London in a letter to the *Times* which concludes with the following sentence: "I know no reason why a Christian Englishman should not be conscientiously convinced that the Parliament of his country in 1907 is a more efficient and morally respectable instrument for expressing the mind of the divine society of the church than the convocation of 1604."

LORD CHANCELLOR VISITS CANADA. — The Lord Chancellor, Lord Loreburn, who visited Canada during September for a short vacation, is the only Lord Chancellor who has crossed the Atlantic during his term of office. In connection with this fact, the London *Globe* remarks that America is better acquainted with the Lord Chief Justice than with the Lord Chancellor. Lord Coleridge, accompanied by Lord Bowen, Lord Hannen, and Sir Charles Russell, made a triumphant tour through the United States in 1883, and Lord Russell of Killowen, accompanied by Sir Frank Lockwood, was the guest of the American Bar Association for a second time in 1896. But the Woolsack is not without American associations. Lord Lyndhurst was born in Massachusetts in 1772, a grandson of the Boston merchant who was the consignee of the famous tea chests that were emptied into Boston harbor. While one Lord Chancellor was born in the United States, another has died there. Lord Herschell, who, after he had ceased to be Lord Chancellor, was appointed a member of the Anglo-American Commission, died at Washington in 1899. The United States government offered a battleship for the conveyance of his remains across the Atlantic, but Lady Herschell had already accepted Lord Salisbury's proposal that the body of her distinguished husband should be brought home in a British man-of-war.

LORD BRAMPTON DEAD. — Lord Brampton, better known as Sir Henry Hawkins, died in London on October 6. Only a few weeks ago he celebrated his ninetieth birthday, at which time he received congratulations from all over the world. Lord Brampton did not achieve unusual success when first called to the bar, and his income for the first few years was meager, but after he was made a Queen's Counsel at the age of thirty-one he quickly acquired a very large and lucrative practice. Probably the most noted litigation with which his name is connected as a practitioner was the Tichborne case, in which his rare skill as a cross-examiner was largely instrumental in exposing the fraudulent nature of the claimant's pretensions. In 1876 he was appointed to the bench, and up to the time of his retirement a few years ago was always one of the most conspicuous members of England's judiciary. His severity in dealing with hardened criminals earned for him the soubriquet of "the hanging judge." An anecdote illustrative of the terror he inspired in the breasts of evildoers runs as follows: At the Old Bailey a policeman, who was giving evidence against a prisoner on trial before Judge Hawkins, was asked what the man had said when he was first charged. The constable whipped out a pocket book and read, without a smile: "Prisoner said when charged, 'God grant I be not tried before 'Awkins, or he will bring down my hairs in sorrow to the grave.'"

CUTTING PRICE OF PATENTED OR COPYRIGHTED ARTICLES. — A question which has recently received considerable attention in the United States courts — the right of the owner of a patented or copyrighted article to control the price thereof after it has come into the hands of a retailer who is under no contractual obligations to the owner — was before Mr. Justice Parker, sitting as vacation judge, in National Phonograph Co. *v.* Pedesta. The plaintiff company had made agreements with all their retail customers by which the records manufactured by them could not be sold below a certain price; but the defendant, who had managed to secure a quantity of these records in some indirect way at a much reduced price, was offering them at lower figures, and was so able to undersell the plaintiff's customers. The plaintiff sought to enjoin this, and the defendant claimed that as he had no contractual relations with the plaintiff, he was entitled to sell the records at any price he chose, which was the view taken by one of the United States courts recently. In England, however, the law appears to be otherwise, though the point was not decided in the present case. Judge Parker dismissed the application for an interim injunction upon the defendant's giving an undertaking not to sell below the prices set by the plaintiff till the trial of the action. The *Law Journal* thinks "there can be little doubt as to the ultimate conclusion of the matter," and cites several cases in support of the proposition that the owner of a patent or copyright has an overriding right which entitles him to fix the terms on which the patented or copyrighted articles shall be used or distributed.

EXCLUSION OF IMMIGRANTS. — Commenting on the recent troubles on the Pacific coast over Japanese immigrants, the *Law Journal* of recent date says editorially: "Grave constitutional questions are being raised by the action of the political mongers on the Pacific coast who are asserting the right of the 'self-governing' colonies and dominions of the Crown to exclude immigrants 'undesirable' to them, though unobjectionable or even desirable in the general interests, regardless of the treaty obligations which concern the whole empire. There is already talk of imitating the historic precedent of casting imported tea chests into the sea by expelling *vi et armis* these human bundles of goods who have come by invitation under the protection of the King; and this demagogic chatter does not stand alone as a symptom of disaffection and want of regard for the larger imperial considerations. The mobs at Vancouver who have attempted the destruction of the harmless Japanese settlement have their counterpart in the South African agitators who insist on the exclusion of our Hindu fellow subjects from their unpeopled lands; and the fisherfolk of Newfoundland who object to the introduction of American competition, and protest against our refusal to recognize their attempts at restrictive legislation, have the larger example before them of the Australian colonies who have discriminated, not only against Asiatics and other aliens, but against even British immigrants, and have thus created a dividing wall within our own native-born populations. The principle of exclusion has been admitted, unfortunately, even into the legislation of the mother country, and the Aliens Act of 1905 has sanctified views and methods with reference to immigrants previously foreign to our constitutional system and inimical to our position as one of the largest centres of emigration and colonization. The Prime Minister recently expressed his strong disapproval of this reactionary legislation; and the inclination of the 'self-governing' colonies and dependencies to improve on the evil example which it offers affords an additional reason for immediate action by the government to remove this blot from our statute book. We must set our own house in order before we can hope to control the action of fellow subjects to whom the privileges of self-government have been accorded, or to influence effectively even those who are entirely dependent on us for guidance and support."

Obiter Dicta.

NOT ALWAYS IN FACT, THOUGH. — The New York artist who recently gave the newspapers so much to talk about by firing his wife in order to make room for his "affinity," whom he had run across on a steamer, may be surprised to learn that in law "affinity" means relationship by marriage.

RETRIBUTIVE JUSTICE. — Mayor Bennett, of Fort Dodge, Iowa, who brought himself into the public eye about a year ago by announcing that all bachelors who did not wed within the year would be fined, has recently had his faith in his own theory put to the test quite forcibly. On October 6 Nolan Snow, a chauffeur, eloped with the mayor's daughter, just in time to escape the fine.

READY FOR CUSTOMERS. — The following advertisement, clipped from a Baltimore newspaper of recent date, certainly seems entitled to a place in our collection of curios:

> W. H. LOGUE JR., 931 North Broadway, having been assigned to jury duty in the Criminal Court, EARNESTLY REQUESTS THE PATRONAGE OF HIS FRIENDS AND ACQUAINTANCES. 824-3tp

QUANTUM MERUIT? — An action, based on the following rather unusual state of facts, was recently begun against a citizen of Danville, Ind. The citizen in question, being desirous that a certain mare owned by him should reproduce, sought the good offices of a jack belonging to the plaintiff, and agreed to pay the plaintiff $12.50 in the event of issue. In course of time the mare brought forth, not one, but two foals, and the plaintiff is now suing to recover $25, or twice the amount of the stipulated fee.

A WIDE OPENING. — Referring to our comment last month on the rule of the Florida Supreme Court which requires applicants for admission to the bar to show that they sustain a "fair" character, an esteemed correspondent calls attention to the fact that the Supreme Court of the United States is even less exacting in its requirement. The rule of that court merely requires that the applicant's private and professional character "shall *appear* to be fair." This moderation is perhaps based on the fact that the average lawyer's character has been pretty well thumbed before he ever has occasion to appear before that court. And, by the way, another esteemed correspondent writes from Florida protesting that we owe an apology to that State, inasmuch as by the Laws of Florida, c. 5650, § 2, every candidate for admission is required to be a man of "upright character."

A LAWYER'S CARD. —

MOVING PICTURES

It would have been cheaper to move to the Court-house than to pay rent; but I am now permanently located at

OTT & CO.'S
ASSAY OFFICE
Nevada City, Nevada County, California.

P. F. SIMONDS
ATTORNEY AT LAW
Late Nominee for
District Attorney
Of Nevada County, California
UNION LABOR NOMINEE

COULDN'T BE BLUFFED. — A correspondent sends in the following account of an incident which occurred in his presence in a Kentucky court room.

Under the laws of Kentucky, the penalty for gaming is a fine of from twenty to fifty dollars. Judge W. W. Jones was holding a term of Circuit Court, and when the case of the Commonwealth of Kentucky against Daniel Cross was called, he asked Daniel if he had a lawyer to defend him. Daniel said he had not, and Judge Jones asked him what he wanted to do about his case, which was a charge of gaming. "I don't know, hardly, Judge," said Daniel, "I thought I would just pay it off." "Were you actually playing?" said the Judge. "I guess we were," Daniel replied. "About how much were you playing for, Daniel?" the Judge asked. "Oh, nothing much," said Daniel, "just a nickel or dime on the corner." "Well, Daniel," said the Judge, "I will see your dime and raise you twenty dollars." Daniel looked rather crestfallen for a moment, but, catching the force of the Judge's remark, he quickly looked up at the Judge and said: "Well, Judge, I am satisfied that you have got me beat, so I'll not raise you, but I guess I will have to call you."

AN EXPERT WITNESS. — A rather amusing bit of expert testimony was involved in the case of McDonald *v.* Triest, 103 N. Y. Supp. 1041. The plaintiff, a young woman employed in a vanilla warehouse, had suffered severely from an eruption of the skin, resembling that caused by poison ivy, which she claimed to have contracted in handling vanilla beans. She sued her employer on the ground that he had failed to notify her of the dangerous nature of the work. On the trial her attending physician testified that in his opinion the eruption was caused by "an oil secreted by an insect known as the 'anacardium occidentale,'" which ferocious insect "is found in connection with vanilla beans, and is sometimes known as the elephant louse." In reversing a judgment in favor of the plaintiff, Judge Jenks, in a mild, almost diffident manner, stated that he had examined a number of medical dictionaries, and that all of them described the anacardium occidentale as a tropical tree, commonly known as the cashew-tree. He said: "Speaking with all seriousness, here are books, technical and general, of high standard, which describe that which the physician says repeatedly is an insect as a tree or shrub. The doctor and the dictionaries disagree. It may be that in the march of scientific knowledge he is ahead."

AN UNWARRANTED STRICTURE. — In the case of Cagle *v.* Shepard, 57 S. E. Rep. 946, recently before the Georgia Supreme Court, the appellant, against whom a verdict had been recovered for injuries caused by his automobile, made the statutory pauper's affidavit that he was unable to pay the costs. In granting a new trial upon technical grounds, the court animadverted upon this fact as follows: "Not only do we grant to the plaintiff in error a new trial, but we also extend to him our condolence in the sad loss of fortune which has occurred to him during the pendency of the suit. We say 'sad loss of fortune which has occurred to him during the pendency of the suit,' for we are led to believe from certain indicia appearing in the record that such misfortune has overtaken him. In the beginning of the case he was the owner of an automobile, a circumstance which of itself imports wealth. At the first term he caused to be stricken by demurrer a paragraph of the petition which alleged that he was 'well circumstanced with worldly goods,' by inference raising the presumption that he was afraid to allow the jury to hear proof as to his financial condition, lest it tend to enlarge the verdict. In the evidence it is shown that he is a skilled machinist, and that he lived in a fashionable portion of the city of Macon; and yet there is filed with the recorder a statutory pauper's affidavit, made by him to escape the payment of the costs. It is therefore charitable to him to conclude that, pending the suit, he has had financial backset." The skepticism of the learned court as to the alleged poverty of the appellant evidences a considerable unfamiliarity with the pains and penalties incident to the ownership of an automobile.

"A SPRY LADY." — The following is a copy of a letter on file in the office of the State's attorney at Centralia, Ill.

March tHe 19 date 1907.
Baxter Springs Kanas
Mr Polece Joug at Salom
Will you plece do me a FaveR tHat is too see iF al Hotz and ORgia England is Keeping House tHar in your sity if oRgia and Hotz is Keeping House tHar tHa aRe liven ing in a dult Re i am oRgia England man By law and se Hase not got Hene devorse Fum me and Hotz Hant got Hene devorse Fum Hise Wife and iF oRgia England and Hotz is Keeping House Rest tHam at onCe For oRgia Englend mi Wife Hase not got Har devorse Fum me and al Hotz Hant got Hene devorse Fum Hise WiFe and tHe laSt cont i Hat oF tHam tHa Wose live ing in YouR Sity in a Dult Re oRgia England is alady a Bout 4 Feet and 4 incH Hi BlacK Har and BlacK ise and darK complex and too Heve sed Wate a Bout 90 Ponds and a dempel in Face and Hi FoRe Hed and am a Bad caR-RectaR Her move fast and aM a Spry Lady tHis lady oRgia England mi wiFe leFt me too KeeP House For tHis man aL Holtz and now daRe Frend Will You Be So Kind too looK tHis Matter uP as i dont Wont tHis lady a live ing in a dult Re with a Man with mY littel gurls tHis man Hotx Work For tHe Frickko RR C'O and i tHinK you may Fin tHam in YouR Sity iF you Fin tHam Rite and tell me on Retun mail and iF tHa Hant tHar Rite on Retun mail Woot You Hav Fond out BacK all mail to Wm. England Baxter Springs Kanas tHis lady leFt me at sentelmo Ills a Bout 5 montHs a go and tooK all oF Hor House Hold goods and i HaFe Fond out tHat tHis lady and tHis man went to Your sity too live.
so Good BY
iooF

A SEVERE ARRAIGNMENT OF THE DOG. — In the case of *Ex parte* Ackerman, 91 Pac. Rep. 429, recently before the California Court of Appeal, Third District, Hart, J., discussing the validity of an ordinance regulating the licensing of dogs, said: "Much has been written and spoken of the dog and his many noble qualities. It may truthfully be admitted that innumerable instances of the unflinching loyalty and faithfulness of that quadruped to his master or to a friend to whom he has become attached are recorded, and have justly inspired writers of intense and ardent natures and of vivid and lively imaginations to soar to supernal heights of eloquence and of poetic fancy in their descriptive song of the noble attributes of the dog. There can be nothing farther from the purpose or disposition of the writer of this opinion to detract from or underestimate the worth of a good, conscientious, law-respecting dog — a canine content to remain at all times within the limits of his own bailiwick and there regale himself in an atmosphere of perfect ease and comfort, with frequent delightful excursions to the land of Hypnos, and at the same time ever alert to the highest interests of his master, and, generally speaking, scrupulously faithful to all the pacific and innocent pursuits which have come within the curriculum of his education. There can be no doubt that many dogs, for their acts of heroism in saving human life or preventing injury to their masters when surrounded by appalling circumstances of danger, deserve a conspicuous place in poetry and song; but there is no inconsistency between this observation and the suggestion that when the poet, as, under the entrancing spell of ethereal dreams, in winged boat, he flits 'from mount to mount through Cloudland,' permits fancy to get the upper hand of fact, and thus unconsciously wanders from concrete cases to abstractions in his perfervid panegyrics upon the canine, he slips far over and beyond even the boundary line established and tolerated by poetic license. It is, we think, safe to say that those writers who have written such glowing tributes to the dog in the abstract have never had any actual experience with a monstrous canine of the bull family, to which they were strangers. There is neither poetry nor sentiment in the dog, as a rule, especially when one meets him upon what he conceives to be his own preserves, for such an occasion is generally conceded to be an appropriate time to cast song and sentiment to the winds and to get busy by moving with all possible haste a comfortable distance beyond the danger line. But it must be admitted that there are really some good-tempered, well-behaved dogs, which are, it may be granted, quite useful in their way. But the other kind become good dogs only when they have ceased to be able to exercise the power of respiration.

"At the common law the dog was classed in the category of animals *feræ naturæ*, and many of them should be so classed now. We are safe in going further and declaring that the very best of them can, with less effort and in a shorter space of time, make themselves more of a nuisance to the square inch than any other domestic quadruped of which we have any knowledge. Even those having the good fortune to have received the fullest measure of civilizing care, nursing, petting, and general disciplinary domestication, from puphood to the danger point of maturity, have not had the instincts of savagery inherited from their distinguished ancestral relative and implacable enemy of the human race, the wolf, so mollified as to render them altogether disposed to maintain uniformly peaceful relations with the human family. For it may be accurately declared that nearly all dogs are friendly only with their masters and immediate family, and that strangers, however honest and peaceful their intentions may be, are almost invariably treated by them as intruders, having no rights that a dog is compelled to respect. In these observations, though rather *dog*-matically asserted, we think no one of ordinary experience of the common, all-around affairs of this mundane sphere will hesitate to *concur*."

The italics in the last sentence, which are the judge's own, will cause no little grief to the judicious.

Law Notes

DECEMBER, 1907.

PUBLISHED BY EDWARD THOMPSON COMPANY.
NORTHPORT, LONG ISLAND, N. Y.

CONTENTS.

THE second Hague Peace Conference, which came to an end on the 18th of October last, has been a disappointment to the enthusiastic friends of the movement. Almost every phase of the problems of international law has been discussed in one or another of its sections and committees, but the result of all this collected learning reminds one of the mountain and the mouse. Of constructive work there is not much to show. And yet from the larger point of view of the ages there is every reason for hopefulness. Analytical jurists have denied to international law the characteristics of law at all, and some of the leading statesmen of the nineteenth century, for instance Prince Bismarck, were accustomed to treat it with rather cynical contempt. Lord Salisbury declared that it "depends generally on the prejudices of the writers of text-books," and that "it can be enforced by no tribunal," and to call it law is misleading. At the end of a period dominated by ideas such as this, it was no small achievement to get the nations to consent to come together and discuss the rules of international law in a rational spirit, looking to the preservation of the world's peace. This unheard-of thing in history has now been accomplished in two successive conferences. The movement is probably proceeding as rapidly as, looking at such faint parallels as other ages supply, could be hoped. How long a period was necessary to evolve the powers of parliament and to establish parliamentary government! The *Nation,* summing up the achievements of the second Conference, observes: "The establishment of an international [appellate] prize court; the extension of the Geneva convention to warfare by sea; the limitation imposed upon the collection of contractual debts, with some of the regulations about submarine mines and bombardments, and the pious vow in favor of arbitration, all have their merit and promise." So distinguished an authority on international law as Sir Thomas Barclay, summing up in the *Fortnightly Review* the results of the Conference a short time before its break-up, said: "To have begun turning the rules of international law, hitherto sneered at as a body of theorists' notions, into a written code, accepted by all mankind, is so new to men's minds that the public has hardly yet realized the immensity of such an undertaking. . . . The Hague conferences are bringing order, precision, and civilized methods into matters in which only a few years ago the very idea of codification was too remote to be seriously considered. The Declaration of Paris was still, in 1899, the only case of any rules of law which had been adopted by any international enactment as 'law' in the sense of the late Lord Salisbury. To understand the value of the work of 1907 we need only compare with this short declaration of what (after all) was already the practice of the leading states, the vast groundwork of international legislation which will have been laid down by the present Conference. There has, indeed, been no justification for the fear that it would do too little and thus discourage public opinion. The danger, on the contrary, has been that in undertaking so much it would turn out carelessly drafted work, and this probably will be the case as regards a good deal of it." M. Bourgeois, the head of the French delegation at The Hague, alluding to the tendency to sneer at the small results accomplished by the second Conference, said: "Let the skeptics laugh, but we who labored at The Hague as faithful servitors of justice can bear testimony that we heard in the Hall of Knights the whispering of the universal conscience — the first slow but regular and distinct beatings of the heart of humanity."

WHEN does a voluntary agreement between the States become obnoxious to that provision of the Federal Constitution which forbids a State without the consent of Congress to "enter into any agreement or compact with another State"? The Supreme Court has told us several times what is not such an agreement, and has in doing so declared in a general way when it considered that the Rubicon would be crossed in such matters. The words "agreement" and "compact" are sufficiently broad to relate to all kinds of subjects, said Judge Field, in Virginia *v.* Tennessee, 148 U. S. 503; "to those to which the United States can have no possible objection or have any interest in interfering with, as well as to those which may tend to increase and build up the political influence of the contracting States, so as to encroach upon or impair the supremacy of the United States, or interfere with their rightful management of particular subjects placed under their entire control." It is the latter class that the prohibition is aimed at. "If," he said further, "the bordering line of two States should cross some malarious and disease-producing district, there could be no possible reason, on any conceivable public grounds, to obtain the consent of Congress for the bordering States to agree to unite in draining the district, and thus removing the cause of disease. So in case of threatened invasion of cholera, plague, or other causes of sickness and death, it would be the height of absurdity to hold that the threatened States could not unite in providing means to prevent and repel the invasion of the pestilence without obtaining the consent of Congress, which might not be at the time in session." Story, in commenting on the Constitution, directs attention to the absolute prohibition to States to enter into "any treaty, alliance, or confederation," and suggests that this may apply to treaties of a political character, and that the terms "agreement or compact" may very properly apply to such as regarded what might be deemed mere private rights of sovereignty, such as "questions of boundary, interest in land situated in the territory of each other, and other internal regulations for the mutual comfort and convenience of States bordering on each other." See also Stearns *v.* Minnesota, 179 U. S. 223. All these observations are merely the dicta of eminent jurists, and they do not appear harmonious. Judge Story seems to think that all the possible agreements of a State fall either in the class entirely prohibited as "treaties," etc., or in that of "compacts." Judge Field admitted a third class not requiring the consent of Congress. The difference might be vital, as he suggests, in view of a sudden emergency. On the last occasions on which we have been threatened with an outbreak of yellow fever, the State authorities have, we believe, found it advantageous to place the situation in the hands of federal officers, but this might be, to adopt a suggestion of Mr. Justice Brewer made in a different connection in Stearns *v.* Minnesota, only an agreement between one of the States and all the States, constituting as one body the nation. So viewed it would equally require, perhaps, the consent of Congress. The last quarter of a century has been teaching us, through trusts and corporations, a great object lesson of the power of voluntary combinations and "gentlemen's agreements." There are many indications that the States of the Union mean to shoot these monsters with a dart from their own quiver, and to try the force of voluntary concerted action against them. It is only interesting speculation at present, but perhaps before very long it may be more than mere speculation, how far the States are permitted to go in combination for such an end. Mr. Justice Field's words were, "any combination tending to the increase of political power in the States, or interfere with the just supremacy of the United States." Would a combination of two or more States to establish a uniform and prearranged system of railroad rates for definite ends in a struggle with the railroads which in their interstate aspects are subject to Congress, under the commerce clause, fall in this description? At any rate we may meet other applications of the concerted action plan.

UNDER the mystifying and misleading title, "Is the Supreme Court Constitutional?" Chief Justice Clark, of North Carolina, not long ago published in the *Independent* a striking plea for the election of the members of the Federal Supreme Court for a limited term as a substitute for their appointment for life. His point of departure is the power which, he declares, the court has illegally assumed, to declare invalid, as opposed to the Constitution, acts of Congress which have been duly passed. This momentous power has been so long acquiesced in by the co-ordinate departments of government, that he admits it may be perhaps established on the principle *communis error facit jus*. But it is, in Chief Justice Clark's view, intolerable that this prerogative should be lodged in the hands of "five elderly lawyers selected by influences naturally antagonistic to the laboring classes and whose training and daily associations cannot incline them in favor of restrictions upon the power of the employer;" a "body of men without supervision or control by other authority," who, because the judges are practically irremovable, possess a veto power which is "irresponsible" upon the actions of the other departments. In place of this undemocratic method of government, the chief justice would substitute a bench composed of judges elected for a term only, who periodically would come before the people for indorsement. The proposal, reasoned out upon the lines laid down, is surely radical and startling. The court is to be made elective, so that if its decisions are not in accord with the popular sentiment of the time, the people may elect other judges who will heed the demand for new policies. This is frankly the proposal, and, if the plan is to be effective, the substituted judges must treat the decisions of their predecessors as mere political essays, overruling them whenever the sentiment of the moment demands some more "progressive" doctrine. The judges are thus to become political personages rather than interpreters of law. The reports of the court will become a mere collection of State papers. All this is so radical a change in present conditions, that the coming of the golden age of constructive statesmanship on the bench will be viewed by some of us with considerable apprehension. How, for instance, will the habits that judges thus acquire in dealing with political questions react on their more routine duty of determining in the light of precedents the law between man and man?

THE present Supreme Court, like all American and English courts, of course recognizes the principle of *stare decisis*. If a decision on ordinary subjects shows a rule of law not harmonious with the usages or needs of society, a change in the law is effected by statute through the legislature. As to ordinary matters of law, a judicial decision is only operative until the legislative branch of the government shall establish a different rule. In the construction of the State constitutions somewhat the same consequences follow judicial interpretation. If the machinery for amending the constitution is in working order, and the judgment of the court announces an undesirable rule, the machinery may be set in operation and a better rule produced. The difference is only that in the case of the constitution the change, as is proper in respect to the fundamental law, is a graver and more deliberate process than in the case of a simple statute. But in either case, if the popular sentiment really demands the change, the demand can be satisfied. The decision of the court in either case is, to phrase it so, merely a suspensive veto, and popular sentiment, taking effect over the court's judgment, may respond to the new mode of thought of the times. And this can be accomplished in a way which is thoroughly in accord with the genius of our institutions, and without overturning the very idea of the functions of judges and courts to which our whole civilization has adjusted itself. If the method provided for amendment to the Federal Constitution was in a functioning condition, so that one or two slight changes might be introduced, there would be no need to feel dissatisfaction with the prerogative of the court to declare statutes unconstitutional, or to propose the plan of having judges elected on platforms composed of legal propositions which the candidate is pledged to carry out. But apart from theoretical views, has the introduction of judges elected for terms in place of judges appointed for life made the difference in the character of the opinions of the courts which the advocates of a federal elective judiciary would lead us to expect from the change? In the older States which have had a considerable history under the appointive system, are there, since the election of judges, any noticeably different views on the part of the bench on large economical questions and matters of public policy? The reader may answer these questions for himself. Occasionally radical men may be swept in as a result of popular sentiment, but even in such cases they usually become much like their brethren of the bench, and conclude after all to decide cases by musty old precedents, rather than by their own enlightened reason.

BUT it is an obvious truth that the machinery for amending the National Constitution is sadly rusted and out of order. A method which was workable with only thirteen States seems hopeless with something like four times that number. The real reformer should invent and get adopted a method to amend the Federal Constitution. In the absence of such a discovery, the plans outlined above are being advocated as cutting the Gordian knot. Thus Dean Bruce, of the Law School of the University of North Dakota, tells us in the *Green Bag* that organized labor is now in bitter and relentless opposition to the idea of life-term judges. Labor argues, says he, "that the judge, even though not so when first elected, soon becomes far removed from the common people; that he takes up his residence in an exclusive district; that his wife and children move in an exclusive society; that he has as a rule been a corporation lawyer before his elevation to the bench, especially if in the first place he has been appointed and not elected; that he knows but little of and consequently comes to care but little for the upward struggle of the great masses of men. It argues that the longer and more stable his term of office, the more aristocratic will he become. It lays down as a cardinal principle that in a democracy such as ours, in which the judge can set aside legislative enactments and determine great social and industrial policies, he should understand, sympathize with, and be responsive to the great social and industrial movements and ideals of the day, and should above all be made to feel that he owes his position to the ballots of the people." As showing that the successful experience of England (might he not have added our New England States?) with judges appointed for life is no guide under our present conditions, he says: "If it were true in America, as it is in England, that our judges did not have imposed upon them or had not assumed to themselves the decision of all our great political questions and economic and industrial policies, the case would be very different. As long, however, as the contrary is the case, that is to say as long as our written constitutions are looked upon as the fundamental law of the land, their amendment is so difficult as to be almost impracticable, and their interpretation is entrusted to our judiciary, the judicial office must of necessity be more or less political, and permanence of tenure and appointment as opposed to election will be vigorously assailed by a large portion of the American people."

THE English Constitution, to which the critic of our Supreme Court point us, is the majestic growth of a thousand years. The greatest conservative force in human society, the force of custom, guards it from rash or revolutionary change. With no venerable traditions surrounding our Constitution, with all the history of the nation before us and nothing to look back on, it was our inestimable good fortune, if it was not the wisdom of the fathers, that placed the Supreme Court as the final interpreter of the Constitution, and saved us from the anarchy of three independent constructions of our fundamental law. The Supreme Court has given to the Federal Constitution the stability which could have come otherwise only after ages of use. It must be in error now and then, but occasional error should not blind us to the great and beneficial part that it has played in our history, and it stands to-day a bulwark to protect our institutions from impulsive experiment and innovation. It is to be hoped that the men who sit on that august bench will never consciously allow themselves to be swayed by motives of policy and expediency. The words of Lord Mansfield, applied to an English court, are worth repeating: "The constitution does not allow reasons of state to influence our judgment. God forbid it should! We must not regard political consequences, how formidable soever they might be; if rebellion was the only consequence we are bound to say *Fiat justitia, ruat cœlum.* We are to say what we take the law to be; if we do not speak our real opinions we prevaricate with God and our consciences."

A NEW JERSEY jury has found a Christian Science father and mother guilty of manslaughter for failing to provide medical attention for their child of seven who died of meningitis superinduced by pneumonia. The New Jersey act declares that parents must provide food, clothing, education, and "medical attendance" for their children. The jury comprised six church members, two of whom were Roman Catholics. Now and then a prosecution is brought against parents under similar circumstances, but very rarely is a conviction had. The jury, seeing the grief-stricken parents, whose fault is not in the heart but in the head, are usually so moved by sympathy and pity that they are unwilling to bring in a verdict of guilty. The defendants in the New Jersey case, Mr. and Mrs. Watson, have appealed, so the end is not yet. A somewhat similar case occurred in England a few years ago. Reg. *v.* Senior, (1899) 1 Q. B. 283. The defendant there was not a Christian Scientist, but a member of a sect calling themselves the "Peculiar People." They based their doctrines as to the treatment of the sick on a passage in the Epistle of James. "Is any sick among you? Let him call for the elders of the church, and let them pray over him, anointing him with oil in the name of the Lord. And the prayer of faith shall save the sick, and the Lord shall raise him up, and if he have committed sins, they shall be forgiven him." Senior treated his infant child by prayer and anointing for a case of diarrhœa and pneumonia. The child died and the father was indicted and convicted of manslaughter. The judge instructed that to convict, the jury must be satisfied of three things: first, that death was caused or accelerated by the want of medical attendance; second, that medical assistance was so essential that reasonably careful parents would have provided it; and, third, that the father's means reasonably permitted him to do so. The conviction was sustained. In the case of People v. Pierson, 80 App. Div. (N. Y.) 415, 176 N. Y. 201, the defendant was a member of the Christian Catholic Church of Chicago, and held, like Senior, the precepts of the Epistle of James. The result was the same so far as concerned his infant daughter, affected with that form of mental trouble (she was only sixteen months old) which physicians call whooping-cough. Pierson was indicted and convicted, not for manslaughter, but for the misdemeanor under section 288 of the New York Penal Code of wilfully omitting without lawful excuse to furnish medical attendance to his child. In all these cases, as in others where the defense was the religious opinions of the defendant, the court held that belief is no excuse for a deliberate violation of the law, and the criminal intent is the intent to violate the law, without looking to motive. Reynolds v. U. S., 98 U. S. 145. It is creditable to the New Jersey jury that they were logical enough to look beyond the misguided creatures before them to the larger interests of society involved in the case. Experiment should stop when the subject of it is a helpless child.

THE case of *Ex p.* Collins, (Cal.) 90 Pac. Rep. 827, presents a rather interesting point in the law of extradition. While it is definitely settled that between the States of the Union, a prisoner surrendered for one offense may be tried for another and different offense, Lascelles v. Georgia, 148 U. S. 537, yet as between independent nations, whose right to demand and receive the surrender of criminals is dependent upon the terms of treaties, a criminal extradited for one crime may not be tried for any other offense than that mentioned in the demand for his surrender, until he has had an opportunity to return to the country from whose asylum he has been taken. U. S. v. Rauscher, 119 U. S. 234. In the Lascelles case the court observed: "To apply the rule of international or foreign extradition to interstate rendition involves the confusion of two essentially different things, which rest upon entirely different principles. In the former the extradition depends upon treaty contract or stipulation, which rests upon good faith, and in respect to which the sovereign upon whom the demand is made can exercise discretion, as well as investigate the charge on which the surrender is demanded; there being no rule of comity under and by virtue of which independent nations are required or expected to withhold from fugitives within their jurisdiction the right of asylum." In the Collins case, Collins had been extradited from Canada on one charge and afterwards had committed another crime for which he was convicted. He sought to obtain his freedom on habeas corpus on the ground that he was entitled, before being tried for the last offense, to an opportunity to return to Canada under the doctrine of the Rauscher case. The court held that the principle invoked applied only to offenses committed before the date of extradition. A curious state of affairs would have attended a contrary decision. An extradited person might murder every one who came within his reach, and yet before he could be tried he would have the right to return freely to perhaps a distant country. The correctness of the decision seems beyond all question.

THE view of the offenses of children upon which is based the new legislation on this subject was well stated recently in an address by Mr. Warren F. Spalding, secretary of the Massachusetts Prison Association. After alluding to the state of things which used to exist, when the same kind and degree of punishment was dealt out to adults and to children, Mr. Spalding stated in substance that the offenses of children are different from those of adults, even when the act is the same. Comparatively few of them indicate criminality of character. Many of them are very petty. Why do boys do wrong? In the cities, partly because they cannot play as they do elsewhere. Bad homes are another cause. Boy nature, too, is partly responsible — the surplus vitality, the activity and restlessness which wants to have something "going on." The gang instinct of boys is another cause. The lack of playgrounds another. The new method does not ignore the offense, but it does not deal with it as a crime, to be punished. The process is not a criminal one. The boy is charged with being a "delinquent child." He is not asked whether he is guilty, for "delinquency" does not imply "guilt." He is not "convicted;" he is not "punished." But the power of the court is not materially lessened. It can do whatever needs to be done for the boy, but solely with the purpose of reclaiming him. New powers are given to the court. It may compel restitution, when the boy has stolen, or reparation when person or property has been injured. Probation has a large place in the new system. This gives volunteer service a new place. When a boy is to be reformed, the aid of good men and women must be secured. The old system depended upon power — to restrain a boy from doing the bad things he wants to do. The new system aims to so change his character that he will not want to do the bad things. This depends not upon power, but upon influence. "The only hope of the bad is from loving contact with the good," and this is especially true of bad boys.

THE practical advantage of this method of dealing with youthful criminals is that it frequently gives the State a law-abiding citizen, whereas under the old method the trial, conviction, and term in prison was almost certain to produce a member of the criminal classes who would never cease to be a menace to society, and when detected in his crimes would become a burden upon the taxpayer. But the advantages of reform as contrasted with punishment pure and simple need not be confined entirely to young criminals, and the indeterminate sentence promises to extend the beneficent influences of the new penology to other classes. The interesting letter of Governor Hoch, of Kansas, to the district judges of that State, urging upon them care in sending young criminals and first offenders to the penitentiary, contains some striking confirmation and illustration of these views. Governor Hoch says in part: "My experience as governor has greatly enlarged my vision as to the prison problem and greatly intensified my interest in it. It is a great problem. Perhaps the trend of civilization toward better things is nowhere more manifest than in the realms of penology. Students of criminology know that many men convicted of crime are not bad men at heart, that many of them are victims of sudden temptations, or great provocation, of evil associates, or the drink habit, and of countless other concomitants of crime. Prison life may confirm these men in crime or it may help to reform them and restore them to society and relieve the State of the burden of their care. Especially is all this true of young offenders. In harmony with these views Kansas was one of the first States to establish a reformatory (in 1895) for the incarceration of offenders between the ages of sixteen and twenty-five years, that they might be separated from older and more hardened and hopeless criminals. But few States preceded Kansas in this good movement, and I believe even as yet only about a dozen have joined in it. The experiment is amply vindicated here and elsewhere by the logic of results. Our reformatory, located at Hutchinson, has nearly as many of its young men out on parole as are within its walls, and the record of their reformation is gratifying indeed. Only about eight per cent. violate their parole and are returned to the institution. This institution has reform methods not possible perhaps in a penitentiary, such, for instance, as a day school, the need of which is evidenced by the fact that over fifty per cent. of the inmates must enter the first and second readers, an alarming showing, by the way, as to the relation of ignorance to crime. To keep the penitentiary brand off of men when possible is a matter of tremendous concern, not only to them, but also to the State, for it is a brand that won't rub out, and it is vastly more difficult for an ex-penitentiary convict than for an ex-reformatory inmate to 'make good,' and every one who fails becomes a menace again to society and a burden to the State." The time is coming, we believe, when the impersonal, yard-stick method of punishment, to call it so, will seem as curious a relic of barbarism as the burnings, quarterings, and mutilations of the middle ages.

SOME RECENT EXTRADITION PROCEEDINGS.

Two cases involving the principle of extradition, both of exceptional general interest and legal importance, have claimed the attention of "foreigners" dwelling in the Orient during the past three months.

The first arose out of the murder of Gertrude Dayton, an American prostitute, in Hongkong, and the arrest of Walter Adsetts, an American citizen, charged with the crime, at Chefoo, China. On Aug. 10, 1907, the strangled body of Dayton was discovered in a Saratoga trunk in the baggage-room of the C. P. R. trans-Pacific steamer "Monteagle" at Hongkong, and subsequent police investigations connected Adsetts with the crime besides showing conclusively that the deed had been done in the Hongkong Hotel, Hongkong. Hongkong, it will be observed, is a British colony, under British law. Adsetts, however, had secured two or three days' start by the time suspicion had definitely settled upon him, and had fled, but was finally apprehended at Chefoo, a treaty port on the North China coast, the arrest being made by a British constable (consular) assisted by a pugilist. Adsetts, who himself had some training and experience as a prize-fighter, resisted arrest by assaulting and flooring the British constable, and was in turn floored and taken by the pugilist assistant. He was then incarcerated in the British jail, whence he escaped the same day by climbing through a small window situated high above the floor. The two persons who had originally taken him, however, effected his recapture, and it was arranged that he should be sent south to Hongkong the evening of the same day on a British ship bound for that port.

At this point, however, the American consul-general at Chefoo intervened and took official control of Adsetts as an American citizen, though up to this time, in the absence of official knowledge of his citizenship, he had been treated by the British authorities as a British subject. By direction of the American consul-general, he was sent on board the United States third-class cruiser "Galveston," then lying in Chefoo harbor, for safe custody.

Having got thus far, the dilemma was at once apparent to all. Had the American consul ignored Adsetts's status as an American citizen, the British authorities would have proceeded to the fulfilment of their original intention to treat Adsetts as a British subject and would have dispatched him to Hongkong, as proposed, on a British ship; but the American consul having expressed officially his knowledge of Adsetts's citizenship, the British authorities needs must at once relinquish their control of his person. It must be said that probably the refusal of recognition to Adsetts by the American consul would have subjected that official to criticism from Americans. At all events, the United States now having Adsetts, the problem to be confronted was, how, in the absence of an extradition law, to effect his delivery to Hongkong, where alone he might be tried for the atrocious crime with which he was charged. The American authorities could not now withdraw from the position assumed and release Adsetts either in Chefoo or Shanghai, with the expectation of the British authorities retaking him, because this the British authorities plainly stated they would not do. Moreover, Adsetts had committed no crime for which he was amenable to an American jurisdiction, and it might well be feared he should succeed in suing out a writ of habeas corpus in the United States Court for China at Shanghai, and thus obtain his liberty, contrary to common sense and common justice, but in conformity with existing law.

Two courses appeared to be open. Adsetts had committed an assault upon the British constable at the time of his arrest. For this offense, committed in China within the jurisdiction of the United States Court for China, he might be held to answer before that court at Shanghai. If convicted and sentenced to imprisonment, the Department of State could order that his sentence be served in Manila or San Quentin, California, whence he could be legally extradited under existing treaties. It will be observed that every step in this course would have been strictly legal, though the delay would have been great and the general impression produced in the Orient probably unfavorable. The alternative course was, to order the "Galveston," with Adsetts on board, to proceed direct to

Manila, whence he could be extradited at once. Technically, it appears that this course is open to the criticism that, in strictness, Adsetts's rights are violated by his forcible transportation by the United States government, without legal warrant, from Chefoo to Manila — in fact, a species of justifiable kidnapping. Moreover, if Adsetts's rights are to be disregarded (whatever those rights might be and to whatever extent they should be allowed to protect him) why go through the forms of extradition at all? Hongkong being less distant than Manila, why not order the "Galveston" to put into Hongkong, where Adsetts might be put off the ship?

It was decided by the State Department to adopt the latter of the two alternatives, namely, to send Adsetts on the "Galveston" to Manila and thence allow extradition. Meantime, be it said, Adsetts had again been transferred from the "Galveston" to the shore, where he was confined under a guard of Chinese soldiers. He was accordingly again put on board the ship, she proceeded to Manila, as instructed, and Adsetts was extradited by Hongkong on his arrival and duly handed over to the Hongkong authorities.

Though the spread-eagle home lawyer, accustomed to a painfully technical criminal procedure, would no doubt stand agape and aghast and denunciate blatantly at this apparent juggling with the "rights of an American citizen," nevertheless those familiar with Oriental conditions in connection with extraterritorial rights are as one in the opinion that the United States government as a nation in this affair has acted well, and has blazed a way for other nations to follow in the future. No real or substantial rights have been violated. On the other hand, justice, even though to be administered in a foreign forum, has been well and expeditiously served, and in so straightforward and direct a manner as to excite the approving admiration of sister nations.

The other and later case involving an extradition proceeding to which I will refer is more important as presenting an instance wherein the doctrine of comity in extradition has been pushed to its very limits, and applied in a manner for which there are only a few rare precedents in international relations.

One McKinley, wanted by the United States government in Oregon in connection with the Oregon land frauds, has been resident in Mukden, Manchuria, for the past two years. He was of course cognizant of the fact that there was no extradition treaty between the United States and China, and had expressed to friends his feeling of safety and security.

He had reckoned, however, without a full appreciation of the resources of Secretary Root as a lawyer and diplomat.

Mr. Root, through the American minister at Peking, brought the matter of McKinley's extradition before the Chinese government as a special case, and requested the Chinese government, as a matter of comity, to accomplish his arrest and allow his extradition on this legal basis; but it was frankly stated by the American State Department that the American government could not reciprocate in like manner should it be asked by the Chinese government, and hence the plain question was put to the Chinese government, Was China willing to do America this favor with the full understanding that it would not be reciprocated in kind?

It may be noted that accused persons charged with crimes not included within the terms of extradition treaties covering certain enumerated offenses are occasionally given up to their national authorities upon request, as matter of comity. The already existing treaty, however, forms the basis of the request. It is an extension of the terms of the treaty which is granted as matter of comity, although it is true that there have been rare instances where criminals have been given up in the entire absence of a treaty. In this case, however, there was not only no treaty on which to found the proposal, but it was distinctly stipulated that the reciprocity, usually necessarily inferred from the principle of comity on which the proceeding is founded, was to be in terms eliminated. Obviously, the proposal could not conceivably have been made to any strong or self-respecting government, and probably to no other government but China. The Chinese government made no difficulty about the matter. Accustomed to yield to diplomatic pressure substantial advantages, it probably seemed a small and reasonable request, the importance of which in American eyes considerably outweighed the sacrifice involved on China's part, and hence a request to which wise diplomacy might readily accede. The American consul at Mukden, apparently in the capacity of interpreter only, accompanied a file of Chinese soldiers to McKinley's residence. McKinley was taken by the soldiers and conveyed to the Chinese magistrate's "yamen," where at this date he remains in custody pending the arrival of a marshal from Oregon.

Whatever may have been the motives controlling the Chinese government in its decision, whether assignable to mere weakness and a desire to please, or a common-sense minimization of the importance of the whole question, the fact remains that a remarkable precedent has been established in modern international relations. Viewed apart from circumstances and in itself, the proceeding is gratifying in its untechnical and liberal application of the great principle of international comity. Without the necessity of a departure from strict theory, a perceptible advance in civilization is achieved by the withdrawal from the fugitive criminal of another harboring place, while international law is simplified and enriched by the addition of a humane precedent.

JOSEPH W. RICE.

Tientsin, China.

DROPPING INTO POETRY.

THE habit of dropping into poetry neither originated nor died with the late lamented Mr. Wegg — if, indeed, it can be said that that ingenious gentleman has passed away. Many judges have indulged in the habit, to the pleasure of the reader weary of law books and the making thereof. The poetry quoted by the judges ranges from grave to gay, from serious to frivolous, from classical to nonsensical, and from good to bad, as will be seen from the few specimens reproduced below.

In Boon v. Wethered, 23 Tex. 675, 684, Bell, J., in discussing the impeachment of a witness, said: "No one can be so bold as to deny, that if a man be worthy of credit under oath, notwithstanding a general bad character in other respects, then no person to whom his testimony is of value should be robbed of it upon any ethical theory concerning the kindred nature of vices. It may be only in the verse of the poet who has drawn with inimitable power the character of the piratical chief, that we find one virtue linked with a thousand crimes.

But if, without taxing our credulity to that extent, it can be asserted to be indeed true that a man may preserve his veracity amid the general wreck of his character; if,

'All other virtues gone,
Not guilt itself could quench this loveliest one;'

then the law could not claim to be the perfection of reason, if it should withhold its respect from that virtue, which had preserved its integrity when deprived of every support."

In Stanbro *v.* Hopkins, 28 Barb. (N. Y.) 265, 270, it was held that the credibility of a witness may be tested by inquiry as to his religious belief, the court saying, *per* Balcom, J.: "I think, inasmuch as the barrier against admitting unbelievers in anything heavenly or divine to testify has been thrown down in this State, witnesses may be compelled to disclose, on cross-examination, their opinions on matters of religious belief; for however awful their opinions may be, they are of their own choosing. This rule only carries out that doctrine of the common law which permits the laying open, as far as possible, the minds of witnesses to those who are compelled to pass upon their evidence. I have no fears that this rule will encourage parties to scandalize truly religious witnesses by imputations that they profess the worst of creeds. For so long as no religious test shall be required for judges and jurors, parties will be loath to cross-examine witnesses as to their opinions on matters of religious belief, unless they are well assured the opinions of the witnesses are very obnoxious to the sentiments of citizens who say with Pope,

'For modes of faith let graceless zealots fight,
His can't be wrong whose life is in the right.'"

In Smith *v.* Adams, 6 Paige (N. Y.) 435, 443, which was a suit to enjoin the diversion of spring water from its natural channel, to the injury of the complainant, Chancellor Walworth said: "In this case I find no evidence from which it can fairly be inferred that the complainant has sustained any injury whatever on the ground that the water which flows through the defendant's half-inch quill is not suffered to run in its accustomed channel across the corner of the spring lot. The defendant might therefore say to the complainant, in the language of Latona to the Lycian clowns,

'What rudeness water for my use denies,
Whose endless store the common world supplies?
Nor light nor air did Heaven create for one,
Nor gentle streams.'
(*Ovid's Met.* 4.)"

Harrison, J., said in Roller *v.* Paul, 106 Va. 214, 218, in discussing the necessity of disinterestedness in a receiver: "It is of the utmost importance that, in his character as receiver, he should have no personal interest but that flowing from the accurate and faithful discharge of his duties.

'If self the wavering balance shake,
It's rarely right adjusted.'"

In Thompson *v.* Thompson, 21 Barb. (N. Y.) 107, 121, which was a will contest, Clerke, J., dissented from the opinion of the majority of the court that the testator was competent to make a valid will, but he made the following admission as to the effect of religious delusions upon testamentary capacity: "A man may, peradventure, believe in all the abominations and 'wanton rites' of ancient Greece and Rome, and worship in sincerity 'fanatic Egypt's wandering gods, disguised in brutish form;' he may hope to obtain salvation, like the poor Hindoo devotee, by standing for a lifetime on one leg, with the other elevated towards the skies, or by throwing his emaciated or lacerated body under the car of Juggernaut; he may believe in

'Moloch, horrid king, besmeared with blood
Of human sacrifice, and parents' tears;'

he may 'turn atheist, as did Eli's sons;' he may even be a howling dervish, and rave, and gash his naked body, thinking the while he is doing God service; and yet he may not be destitute of the ability to transact the affairs of life, or to dispose suitably of his property."

In Ellis *v.* Newbrough, 6 N. Mex. 181, 189, 27 Pac. Rep. 490, Freeman, J., confessed himself to be "a native of the land of Dixie, that

'Fair land of flowers,
And flowery land of the fair.'"

In Brentwood School District No. 2 *v.* Pollard, 55 N. H. 503, 505, Foster, C. J., in holding that the word "inhabit" does not convey the idea of permanent residence, said: "To dwell, or to abide, does not indicate permanency of location or of time; for the angels abode with Lot one night, and the Arabs dwell in tents, but they

'fold their tents like the Arabs,
And as silently steal away.'"

That case held that the minor children of paupers, supported at a county poor farm, have the right to attend the public school in the district in which the county farm is located. The chief justice said, concerning this question: "It need not be denied that there may be authority and power vested in the county commissioners to establish a school within the limits of the county farm, for the special uses and necessities of the children located there; but the law does not require it, and the commissioners have not done it; and if these children are denied the privileges of schooling in the district school, they are denied altogether. They are in as woeful plight as Wordsworth's sorrow-burdened 'traveler on the skirt of Sarum's plain:'

'And homeless near a thousand homes he stood,
And near a thousand tables pined and wanted food.'"

Taft, C. J., held, in Baker *v.* Sherman, 71 Vt. 439, 445, that the age of a tree may be ascertained by counting the concentric layers in its grain, saying: "It is argued that the age of a tree cannot be told by counting the rings in its grain, and the case of Patterson *v.* McCausland, 3 Bland's Ch. (Md.) 69, is cited. However ingenious and learned the reasoning of the court in that case may be, it fails to convince us that mankind has lived under an hallucination in that respect for centuries. Almost every one acquainted with the subject treats it as true, that the age of a tree can be approximately told by counting the concentric layers in its grain, one of which, as a general rule, is made annually. Even the tree itself, in 'The Talking Oak' of the late poet laureate Tennyson, voices the popular belief when it says,

'That though I circle in my grain
Five hundred rings of years.'"

In State *ex rel.* Crandall *v.* Chicago, etc., R. Co., (Neb. 1904) 101 N. W. Rep. 23, 24, which involved the question whether a carrier of goods had discriminated between rival shippers, the court made the following remarks, winding them up with a paraphrase of Gay's famous couplet: "We are further convinced that no intention on the part of the respondent's agents or officers to discriminate unfairly against Mr. Crandall has been shown, and that they have been placed in the difficult position of trying to do business with two active and jealous competitors in such a manner as to remain upon good terms with both, a task almost beyond human power.

'How happy could' they 'be with either,
Were t'other dear charmer away!'"

In State *v.* Wisdom, 119 Mo. 539, 24 S. W. Rep. 1047, the court refused to reverse a conviction of murder in the first degree for the admission of evidence that the defendant had refused to touch the body of the deceased when requested to do so. This holding was based on the ground that the evidence, though immaterial, was harmless, the court saying, *per* Gantt, P. J.: "The request to touch the body was evidently prompted by the old superstition of the ordeal of the bier in Europe in the middle ages, which taught that the body of a murdered man would bleed freshly when touched by his murderer, and hence it was resorted to as a means of ascertaining the guilt or innocence of a person suspected of a murder. This superstition has not been confined to one nation or people. It obtained among the Germans prior to the twelfth century, and is recorded in the Nibelungenlied, the great epic poem of that country, in the incident in which the murdered Siegfried is laid on his bier, and Hagen is called on to prove his innocence by going to the corpse, but at his approach the dead chief's wounds bleed afresh. That it dominated the English mind is attested by the passage of Matthew Paris that when Henry II. died at Chinon in 1189, his son and successor came to view his body, and, as he drew near, immediately the blood flowed from the nostrils of the dead king, as if his spirit was so indignant at the approach of the one who caused his death that his blood thus protested to God. And Shakespeare voices the same superstition in Richard III. (Act I., scene 2), thus:

'O gentlemen, see, see! dead Henry's wounds
Open their congealed mouths, and bleed afresh.'

And so does Dr. Warren, in Diary of a Late Physician (vol. 3, p. 327). That it was a prevalent belief in Africa and Australia in another form, see 17 Enc. Brit., pp. 818, 819. This superstition has come to this country with the emigration from other lands, and, although a creature of the imagination, it does to a considerable degree affect the opinions of a large class of our people."

In State *v.* Benson, 110 Mo. 18, 29, the court, in reversing a conviction for obtaining money under false pretenses, said, *per* Thomas, J.: "The defendant made shipwreck of his business. He proceeded in a loose way. He was improvident. But improvidence is no crime. He bought the hay expecting to be able to pay for it when delivered, and if his business had prospered as he anticipated he would have paid for it. Hay badly baled and damaged was sent to market, and of course was sacrificed. When his creditors came upon him he paid out all he had, and then he was sent to jail because he had nothing more to pay with. This record discloses the same old story of a hard-hearted, merciless creditor on one side, and a helpless, unfortunate debtor on the other. A Shylock always presses his victim,

'Unmindful tho' a weeping wife
And helpless offspring mourn.'"

Poor *v.* Poor, 8 N. H. 307, was a libel by a wife seeking a divorce on the ground of extreme cruelty. Richardson, C. J., in recounting one of the little passages at arms between the loving pair, said: "In the skirmish which ended in his taking the crowbar from her, she seems to have encountered some of

'the perils that environ
The man that meddles with cold iron,'

and to have been rather roughly handled. But, considering the irritable temper of the husband, it seems to us that she escaped with quite as little injury as she could have had any right to expect in such an attempt to take his castle by storm."

In State *v.* Moore, 101 Mo. 316, 330, a prosecution for larceny, Sherwood, J., said: "Evidence of flight, etc., is admissible on the ground that it commonly betrays a consciousness of guilt and this induces endeavors to escape. Nothing is more common in criminal prosecutions than the introduction of such evidence, though the flight occurred not only before any prosecution was threatened, but before the community became aware that any crime had been perpetrated. So true it is that

'Suspicion always haunts the guilty mind;
The thief doth fear each bush an officer.'"

In Katz *v.* Walkinshaw, 141 Cal. 116, 128, the court, in discussing conflicting claims to water rights in an arid country, said: "The application of the rule contended for by the defendants will tend to aggravate these difficulties rather than solve them. Traced to its true foundation, the rule is simply this: that owing to the difficulties the courts will meet in securing persons from the infliction of great wrong and injustice by the diversion of percolating water, if any property right in such water is recognized, the task must be abandoned as impossible, and those who have valuable property acquired by and dependent on the use of such water must be left to their own resources to secure protection for their property from the attacks of their more powerful neighbors, and, failing in this, must suffer irretrievable loss; that might is the only protection.

'The good old rule
Sufficeth them, the simple plan,
That they should take who have the power,
And they should keep who can.'"

Two of these lines were quoted by Wagner, J., in Anderson *v.* St. Louis, 47 Mo. 479, 485, which case involved an illegal exercise of the power of eminent domain.

In State *v.* Harriman, 75 Me. 562, wherein it was held that a dog was not a domestic animal, Appleton, C. J., in a dissenting opinion, quoted from Otway as follows:

"They are honest creatures
And ne'er betray their masters, never fawn
On any they love not."

In State *v.* Kelly, 71 Kan. 811, 830, 81 Pac. Rep. 450, Greene, J., in holding that a statute providing for the establishment of a State oil refinery was unconstitutional, said, in reference to a message of the governor's urging the passage of the statute and denouncing the Standard Oil Company: "The indictment of the Standard Oil Company in the message is no doubt true, and the provocation was very great, but

'We must not make a scarecrow of the law,
Setting it up to fear the birds of prey.'"

The word "honesty" has been said to be synonymous with chastity under some circumstances. Thus, in State *v.* Snover, 63 N. J. L. 382, 384, Garrison, J., said: "The word 'honesty,' from the Latin *honestus*, is essentially a word that takes its meaning from its context. Primarily it means 'suitable,' 'becoming,' or 'decent' — meanings that obviously lend themselves to diverse contexts. In moneyed transactions it means financial integrity; in affairs of state it means loyalty; in matters of friendship it means steadfastness; and so on. In sexual relations it imports chastity. This is an accepted signification. In Webster's International Dictionary it is said to mean 'chastity, modesty.' As early as 1385 Chaucer so used it, saying,

'Why lyked me thy yelow heer to see
More than the boundes of myn honestie.'

In 1621, Burton, in the 'Anatomy of Melancholy,' wrote: 'It was commonly practiced in Diana's Temple for women to go barefoot over hot coals to try their honesties.' Shakespeare constantly so used it, notably in the phrase 'Wives may be merry and yet honest too.' Merry Wives, IV., 2. In 1661, Pepys, in the Diary of August 11, gives it this sense. In 1711, Steele, in the 'Spectator,' No. 118, paragraph 2, says: 'The maid is *honest*, and the man dares not be otherwise.' In Fletcher and Rowly's 'Maid of the Mill' it is said: 'Her honesty was all her dower.' In 1749, Fielding, in 'Tom Jones,' xv., viii., writes: 'Miss Nancy was, in vulgar language, soon made an honest woman.' And Scott, in 'St. Ronan's Well,' chapter 25, gives it a like meaning."

In State v. Burns, 119 Iowa 663, 671, Weaver, J., in speaking of the latitude allowed counsel in argument, said: "It is his time-honored privilege to

> 'Drown the stage in tears,
> Make mad the guilty and appall the free,
> Confound the ignorant, and amaze, indeed,
> The very faculties of eyes and ears.'"

In Jumpertz v. People, 21 Ill. 375, 423, Breese, J., in dissenting from a judgment reversing a conviction for murder, paid the following somewhat dubious compliment to the skill of the trained advocate: "There is not in my judgment a single prominent fact in this case, consistent with the innocence of the prisoner, but

> 'In law, no plea so tainted or corrupt,
> But, being seasoned with a gracious voice,
> Obscures the show of evil.'

His counsel, who have managed this case with signal ability, have argued his innocence, as it was their duty to do. There is in every mind a strong tendency to weave for itself a theory out of the minute incidents surrounding a transaction, itself shrouded in some mystery, and to bend everything to its support; it is not strange, therefore, that able and enlightened counsel, having been assured of the fact itself by their client as he desired to establish it, should find in everything a tendency to prove their theory true."

In Maril v. Connecticut F. Ins. Co., 95 Ga. 604, 613, Atkinson, J., in discussing the question whether a written statement in a fire insurance policy as to the subject of the insurance is controlled by an inconsistent printed condition, referred in the following words to a verse which most of us learned with our A, B, C's: "A rule which permitted the printed conditions to control the written statement of the subject upon which the insurance was issued would place the insurance company in the peculiar condition of saying, in effect: I issue you this policy; I accept your money in satisfaction of my demand for premiums; I insure your property to be used in your business, but if you use it your policy is void. A parallel case, and one which alone adequately expresses the peculiar paradox in the case supposed, is to be found in the sage advice given to her youthful daughter when an affectionate but over-cautious mother, in reply to the simple request,

> 'Mamma, may I go out to swim?'

said to her:

> 'Yes, my darling daughter;
> Hang your clothes on a hickory
> But don't go near the water.'

In Warlick v. White, 76 N. Car. 175, 179, the court used the following quotation from one of the Epistles of Horace as an argument in favor of exhibiting a child to the jury in an action involving the legitimacy of the child, which was alleged to be of mixed blood: "On general principles it would seem that when the question is whether a certain object is black or white, the best evidence of the color would be the exhibition of the object to the jury. The eyes of the members of the jury must be presumed to be as good as those of medical men. Why should a jury be confined to hearing what other men think they have seen, and not be allowed to see for themselves?

> 'Aut agitur res in scenis, aut acta refertur,
> Segnius irritant animos demissa per aurem,
> Quam quae sunt oculis subjecta fidelibus, et quae
> Ipse sibi tradit spectator.'
>
> HOR. *Ad Pisones*."

In Aikman v. Edwards, 55 Kan. 751, 763, Allen, J., in philosophizing on the necessity of vigilance on the part of the people to prevent the loss of their rights, rights that are easy to lose and hard to regain, quoted as follows from the Æneid (liber vi., 126–129):

> "Facilis descensus Averno;
> Noctes atque dies patet atri janua Ditis;
> Sed revocare gradum, superasque evadere ad auras,
> Hoc opus, hic labor est."

Some of the judges show a familiarity with sacred poetry. In Knorpp v. Wagner, 195 Mo. 637, 662, Lamm, J., laid down the rule that a master cannot delegate his primal duties as master by a general order or rule and thus avoid responsibility. In so doing he said: "If the courts would tolerate such ready-at-hand scheme of easy avoidance, then the employer of men might well add a new and worldly significance to the lines of the good old hymn:

> 'This is the way I long have sought,
> And mourned because I found it not;'

for a cure-all for not a few of his ills lies in a stroke of his pen."

In some cases the courts have cited poets as authorities, practically. Thus, in Groom v. Thomas, 2 Hagg. Ecc. 433, Sir John Nicholl, in passing upon the sanity of a testator, said: "Let it not, however, be supposed that the court holds change of mind and interlineations in a testamentary instrument to be, *per se*, a proof of insanity; but coupled with the previous insanity and the general description of the deceased's conduct, they are circumstances carrying symptoms of disorder into the act itself. What says the great poet of nature and master of the passions upon the subject? What is one of the tests of madness that he suggests? Hamlet, being charged with 'coinage of the brain,' answers,

> 'It is not madness
> That I have uttered; bring me to the test,
> And I the matter will re-word; which madness
> Would gambol from.'

Madness, then, varies and fluctuates; it cannot 're-word'—if the poet's observation be well founded; and though the court would not at all rely upon it as authority, yet it knows from the information of a most eminent physician that this test of madness, suggested by this passage, was found by experiment in a recent case to be strictly applicable, and discovered the lurking disease."

It will be observed that, while the learned judge expressly disavowed any intention of relying upon the passage as an authority, he called attention to the fact that the test of madness suggested therein had been found to be effective in actual practice.

CRUEL AND UNUSUAL MODES OF PUNISHMENT.

THE frequent reference to the fine recently imposed by Judge Landis on the Standard Oil Company as a "cruel and unusual punishment" renders of interest at the present time an investigation of the meaning of the term and a review of its application by the courts.

The provision in the Federal Constitution prohibiting such punishment was taken from the Act of Parliament of 1688, entitled "An Act Declaring the Rights and Liberties of the Subject and Settling the Succession of the Crown," in which certain of the grievances of the people were set forth, and a provision made that "excessive bail ought not to be required, nor excessive fines imposed, nor cruel and unusual punishments inflicted." Mr. Justice O'Brien has pointed out that this statute was intended to be little more than a declaration of the rights of the subject. The English people were about to place upon the throne, made vacant by revolution, a foreign prince whose life had been spent in military pursuits rather than in the study of constitutional principles. The opportunity was accordingly considered a favorable one to enact in solemn form a declaration of the principles upon which the people desired the government to be conducted. People v. Durston, 119 N. Y. 569.

When the statute was made part of the Constitution of the United States the word "shall" was substituted for the word "ought." Though the prohibition in the Federal Constitution did not affect the States, nearly all of them have incorporated similar provisions in their own constitutions.

Whether or not a punishment comes within the prohibition depends both on the nature of the crime and the circumstances of the punishment. It has been held that the provision is aimed more at the form or character of the punishment than at its severity in respect to duration or amount. Sentences have, however, in a number of cases been annulled on the ground that their duration in view of the nature of the offense made them "cruel" within the meaning of the Constitution. The Supreme Court of Alabama distinguished in one case between a punishment that was "cruel" and one that was "unusual," holding that the two were not synonymous; that a cruel punishment was not necessarily unusual nor an unusual punishment necessarily cruel. Turnipseed v. State, 6 Ala. 664. "But be this as it may," said the court, "there may be punishment that is both cruel and unusual; thus if a slave should be punished, even without bodily torture, in a manner offensive to modesty, decency, and the recognized proprieties of social life, the offender would be chargeable."

The Supreme Court of the United States has held that a punishment is cruel and unusual when it involves torture or a lingering death. *In re* Kemmler, 136 U. S. 436. It has also been held that the constitutional prohibition applies to such punishment as would shock the mind of every man possessed of common feeling, such as drawing and quartering the culprit, burning him at the stake, cutting off his nose, arms, or limbs, starving him to death, or throwing him into boiling water for the crime of poisoning. State v. Williams, 77 Mo. 310.

Except for this prohibition the power of the legislature over the subject of punishment is absolute. It may graduate the punishment according to its own discretion. But where a statute attempts to except a small part of a State from the general law and gives to a local magistrate within that jurisdiction the power to inflict double the punishment for the same crime when committed therein, such statute is plainly unconstitutional. *In re* Bayard, 25 Hun 549.

Where no particular punishment has been fixed by statute for the commission of an offense, it is the duty of the judge "in the exercise of his legal discretion to fix upon the term of punishment suited to the case, without restriction save that in the constitution which forbids cruel or unusual punishments to be inflicted." State v. Pettie, 80 N. C. 367, 30 Am. Rep. 88. The degree of punishment "ought to be left to the judge who inflicts it, under the circumstances of each case, and it ought not to be interfered with except when the abuse is palpable." Driver's Case, 78 N. C. 423. It is the general rule, though not without exceptions, that where the punishment for an offense is set at imprisonment for a term of years to be fixed by the judge, it should not extend beyond the average life of persons confined in prison. People v. Murray, 72 Mich. 10.

It would certainly seem that putting a person to death as a punishment for an offense, if not unusual, was certainly cruel, within the meaning of the constitutional provisions. But it has been held from the earliest times that the infliction of the death penalty is legal. "Whoso sheddeth man's blood, by man shall his blood be shed." The practice was thus justified by Sir Matthew Hale (1 Hale P. C. 13): "When offenses grow enormous, frequent, and dangerous to a kingdom or state, destructive or highly pernicious to civil societies and to the great insecurity and danger of the kingdom or its inhabitants, severe punishment and even death itself is necessary to be annexed to laws in many cases by the prudence of lawgivers." The New York Court of Appeals said on this point: "Punishment by death in a general sense is cruel, but as it is authorized by a law adopted by the people as a means to the end of the betterment of society, it is not cruel within the sense and meaning of the constitution." People v. Kemmler, 119 N. Y. 580. The legislature may also change the punishment formerly inflicted for the commission of a particular crime and make it capital. The mere fact that such change is made does not render the new mode of punishment cruel and unusual within the meaning of the constitution. Territory v. Ketchum, 10 N. M. 718, 65 Pac. 169.

When electrocution first came into vogue as a method of inflicting the death penalty, the objection was strenuously urged that it was both cruel and unusual. In a frequently cited case decided in New York, testimony was taken by a referee in regard to the use of electricity as a means of producing death. The court examined the testimony of the referee and found "but little in it to warrant the belief that the new mode of execution is cruel within the meaning of the constitution, though it is certainly unusual. On the contrary we agree with the court below that it removes every reasonable doubt that the application of electricity to the vital parts of the human body, under such conditions and in the manner contemplated by the statute, must result in instantaneous and consequently in painless death." People v. Durston, 119 N. Y. 569.

It has been everywhere held that imprisonment for a length of time commensurate with the gravity of the offense is not objectionable. It has even been held in Kentucky that imprisonment in the penitentiary for gambling is legal; that if it requires such a sentence to put a stop to gambling it is the duty of the legislature to enact such a law, that body being the judge of the adequacy of the punishment. Harper v. Com., 93 Ky. 290. It has been held that the legislature may make the payment of costs a part of the punishment and add to the sentence in the event that they are not paid, without violating the constitution. Nelson v. State, 46 Ala. 186. The modern indeterminate sentence by which the term of imprisonment is made to depend on the action of the prison directors has also been upheld. Miller v. State, 149 Ind. 607.

Prison regulations may be of such a character as to come within the constitutional prohibition. An early ordinance passed in San Francisco provided that all prisoners in the county jail should have their hair clipped to a uniform length of one inch from the scalp. A case involving the ordinance at last reached the Supreme Court of the United States. As Mr. Justice Field there pointed out, the ordinance was intended only for the Chinese of San Francisco. "The ordinance is known in the community as the 'queue ordinance,' being so designated from its purpose to reach the queues of the Chinese, and it is not enforced against any other persons." The justification for the ordinance was that nothing else than a fear of the loss of his queue would induce the Chinese to pay their fines. But as Justice Field remarked, "probably the bastinado, or the knout, or the rack would accomplish the same end, and no doubt the Chinaman would prefer either of these modes of torture to that which entails upon him disgrace among his countrymen and carries with it the constant dread of misfortune and suffering after death." Ho Ah Kow v. Nunan, 5 Sawy. 552. But where such regulations are reasonable and enforced without discrimination they will be upheld.

In addition to being sent to the penitentiary a person may be put to hard labor, without violating the constitutional provision. But when a statute provides for imprisonment only as the punishment for an offense, the additional punishment of hard labor will not generally be allowed. The physical condition of a prisoner may also at times make a sentence of imprisonment at hard labor illegal. The court in such case should at least postpone the latter requirement. State v. Smith, 5 Day 175.

Fines imposed may at times be so severe as to be improper. The necessity of limiting the power of the courts in this regard was recognized as early as the time of Magna Charta. It was provided in that instrument that "a free man shall be amerced for a small offense only according to its measure, and for a great offense only according to its magnitude, saving his land, and the merchant in the same manner saving his merchandise, and a villein shall be amerced in the same manner saving his wainage." Blackstone states that in his time it was "never usual to assess a larger fine than a man is able to pay without touching the implements of his livelihood, but to inflict corporal punishment or a limited punishment instead of such fine as might amount to imprisonment for life." 4 Com. 380. In accordance with this doctrine it was held in an early Connecticut case that the common law can never require a fine to the extent of an offender's goods and chattels or sentence of imprisonment for life, such punishment being both uncertain and unnecessary as it is not more difficult to limit the imprisonment of an atrocious offender to an adequate number of years than to prescribe a limited punishment for minor offenses. State v. Danforth, 3 Conn. 112.

An Iowa statute provided for a fine of not less than one thousand nor more than five thousand dollars for a first violation of any of the provisions of the statute which provided for the establishment of a joint through rate of transportation upon railroads, and of not less than five thousand nor more than ten thousand dollars for a subsequent violation thereof. The constitutionality of this statute was assailed, but it was upheld by the Supreme Court of that State on the ground that "the fines are intended to enforce obedience to the law by corporations having great incomes and controlling vast properties. The legislature, in the exercise of its discretion, fixed penalties which if imposed upon individuals might appear excessive, but when imposed upon the corporations would be esteemed no greater than necessary to enforce obedience to the State. The railroad companies have a ready and efficient way of avoiding these severe penalties, namely, by obeying truly the laws of the State. If they do not they are in no condition to complain of the laws." Burlington R. Co. v. Dey, 82 Iowa 312, 31 Am. St. Rep. 477. But in another case involving a statute which prohibited any discrimination in freight rates and imposed as the only penalty for the violation thereof a forfeiture of all the offending company's franchises, which, as was pointed out, would sometimes amount to a fine of a million dollars, the Supreme Court, though basing its decision on another ground, said: "Is not this a violation of the spirit of the constitutional provision which says in terms that all penalties shall be proportioned to the nature of the offense? Is it not also a violation of the spirit of the very clause of the constitution under which this Act was framed, and which requires the legislature to pass laws to prevent unjust discrimination and extortion by railroad corporations, 'and enforce such laws by adequate penalties to the extent, if necessary for that purpose, of forfeiture of their property and franchises'? Would it not be better to enforce the law by a series of considerable and increasing fines before imposing the final penalty of forfeiture?" Chicago & A. R. Co. v. People, 67 Ill. 11, 16 Am. Rep. 599. The test of whether or not the court has abused the discretion intrusted to it was thus expressed in a Wyoming case: "It is evident that much latitude must be accorded to the legislature in prescribing the degree of punishment for crime, as well as to the courts in imposing sentence, and that to be held excessive in any case it should be so out of proportion to the offense as to shock the moral sense of the people." Fisher v. McDaniel, 9 Wyo. 457, 64 Pac. 1056.

R. L. McWILLIAMS.

SPOKANE, WASH.

OBSERVATIONS HERE AND THERE.

"UNNATURAL PERSONS" is United States Circuit Judge McCormick's definition of corporations, or at least of those of "omnivorous character." McConnell v. Camors-McConnell Co., (C. C. A.) 152 Fed. Rep. 321, 332.

"One method of proving that a thing is not black is by proving that it is white," said Lord Penzance, in Railroad Co. v. Slattery, L. R. 3 App. Cas. 1177.

"Those who have struggled up from very small beginnings in the profession will not soon forget the feelings of gratitude, almost emotional, towards those clients who early intrusted them with business." Conmee v. Canadian Pac. R. W. Co., 16 Ontario 639, 653, *per* Rose, J.

"Men are not in the habit of looking at their wills after once they have summoned up courage to make them. It is not a document which men generally like to gaze at." Bessey v. Bostwick, 3 Grant Ch. 279, 299, *per* Chancellor Van Koughnet.

"It is often assumed that people with red hair have ungovernable tempers, but the assumed relation would hardly justify proof that a man had red hair, for the purpose of contradicting evidence of his peaceable and quiet disposition." Smith v. Johnson, 16 Ohio Dec. 43, 45, *per* Hosea, J.

Judge Coxe says that "the code of morals which commands the defendant who has had his coat taken in replevin, to give his cloak also to the successful plaintiff, is from an ethical point of view without a flaw, but it has never been followed in a single reported case." Mfg. Co. v. Enameling Co., 108 Fed. Rep. 79.

With respect to criminal punishments in general, and capital punishments especially, it is commonly said that it is better that ten guilty persons should escape than that one innocent person should suffer. "But there are bounds to that principle," said Lord Cranworth; "it is not better that ten thousand guilty persons should escape than that one innocent person should suffer." Rorke v. Errington, 7 H. L. Cas. 617, 630.

Lord Justice Brett (Viscount Esher) was not an Irishman, but he perpetrated the following: "But on mature consideration, all I can say is that I differ on this question from those judges, and I feel bound to say that when I do differ from two such judges, I entertain much more doubt as to the propriety of my decision than of theirs." Blake v. Blake, L. R. 7 P. D. 102, 114.

On October 10, 1846, a pedestrian on a public thoroughfare in Boston had in his hand a lighted cigar. He was arrested and convicted for violation of a statute of 1817, which provided that "every person who shall smoke, or have in his or her possession, any lighted pipe or cigar, in any street, lane, or passage-way or any wharf in said town [of Boston] shall forfeit and pay, for each and every offense, the sum of two dollars." Com. v. Thompson, 12 Met. (Mass.) 231.

Judge Bliss, author of Bliss on Code Pleading, was something of a philosopher withal. "There is a vast difference in the temper of men on the down-hill of life," said he, in Gupton v. Gupton, 47 Mo. 37, 44. "Some show the brightness and serenity of the clear evening sky, while many, as reason grows dim, seem given up to petty jealousies and passions. The former may be hoped for, yet the latter may be expected."

In Missouri the court takes judicial notice that while the remark, "You would be the first one to kick if anything should happen," if spoken jocularly, "would perhaps be entirely harmless, yet if the parties were strangers and the one thus spoken to was making a request within his legal rights, to say it in an angry and contemptuous manner . . . might have proven sufficiently offensive to provoke a breach of the peace." Knight v. Quincy, etc., R. Co., (Mo. App. 1906) 96 S. W. Rep. 716, *per* Johnson, J.

In Hopper v. Com., (Ky. 1906) 96 S. W. Rep. 838, where Hopper was convicted of murder, we get a glimpse of life on Cumberland mountain, near the Tennessee line, in Bell county. "On the particular night in question in this case some one had fired into Hopper's house [blind tiger]. Hopper, believing the shot was fired from Shackelford's establishment [blind tiger], went over to investigate it. . . . Hopper did not find out who it was that fired the shot. In a few hours, but after midnight, Shackelford, with some of his friends, returned Hopper's call. . . ."

Cases of Interest.

What Constitutes a Cigarette. — In State v. Goodrich, 113 N. W. Rep. 388, the Wisconsin Supreme Court holds that under the State statute outlawing "cigarettes," the word must be taken to mean a well-known, recognized, and definite article, consisting of tobacco of a peculiar kind, distinguished by its light color and mildness, rolled in a paper wrapper. The term does not include an article consisting of a cylindrical roll of cigar leaf tobacco, where the leaves are cut in strips the length of the roll and rolled in a section of wrapper leaf tobacco; such articles being generally known as cigars at the time the act in question was passed.

Railroad's Liability for Cutting Fire Hose. — In Clark v. Grand Trunk, etc., R. Co., 112 N. W. Rep. 1121, the Michigan Supreme Court holds that where, there being no other efficient way to carry water to extinguish a fire, the hose is laid across the tracks of a railroad, and employees in charge of the train know of the presence of the hose, and there is no occasion for haste, and they can stop the train, but, instead thereof, they run over the hose, thereby causing such delay in procuring water that the property is destroyed, the railroad company is liable for the loss. But the railroad cannot be charged with negligence in not looking for and discovering the hose laid across its tracks.

Railroads — Care Required at Stations. — In Atchison, etc., R. Co. v. McElroy, 91 Pac. Rep. 785, the Kansas Supreme Court held that, where a railroad company stopped a passenger train in such a position that other tracks lay between it and the station platform, the rights of people having business with such train, and the duty of the company toward them, were the same as if all the intervening space between the train and the depot constituted the platform. Under such circumstances the ordinary rule of "look and listen" was held not to apply, as persons rightfully there had a right to assume that the company would protect them from danger, and any such person injured by a train passing on the intervening tracks at a high rate of speed and without blowing the whistle or ringing the bell is entitled to recover against the company.

Wife's Right to Be Mistress of House. — In Brewer v. Brewer, 113 N. W. Rep. 161, which was an action by a wife for separate maintenance, the Nebraska Supreme Court holds that a wife does not forfeit her right to be supported by her husband where she is forced to leave the common home to escape the domination of her mother-in-law. The court said: "Every wife is entitled to a home corresponding with the circumstances and condition of her husband, over which she shall be permitted to preside as the mistress. . . . Whatever his filial obligation may be, a man may not bring his mother to preside in his new home. That place belongs to the wife. Neither may he, without her consent, take her to the home of the mother, there to be under her domination and control, and when the wife objects to this she does not thereby forfeit her right to support and maintenance."

State's Right to Restrict Use of Artesian Wells. — In *Ex parte* Elam, 91 Pac. Rep. 811, the California Court of Appeal, Second District, holds that a landowner is not deprived of his property without due process of law by a statute declaring an artesian well not provided with appliances for preventing the flow of water therefrom to be a nuisance, and one who maintains it or permits water unnecessarily to flow from such well, or to go to waste, to be guilty of misdemeanor; defining an artesian well to be an artificial opening in the ground through which water naturally flows from subterranean sources to the surface of the ground, and defining waste to be permitting the flow from an artesian well to run into a bay, pond, or channel, unless used thereafter for the beneficial purposes of irrigation or domestic use, or onto land, unless it be used for irrigating it, or for domestic use, or for the propagation of fish.

Rebates — The Standard Oil Case. — In United States v. Standard Oil Co., 155 Fed. Rep. 305, is reported the famous decision of Judge Landis finding the defendant guilty of receiving unlawful rebates and sentencing it to pay a fine of $29,240,000. In arriving at the amount of the fine Judge Landis held that, since the published rate was on car lots, and the reduced rate was granted on the same basis and a separate charge made for each car, therefore, in the absence of evidence to the contrary, each car must be taken as constituting a separate shipment and a separate violation of the law. The defendant contended that, as its concession from the railroad remained in force for a year at a time, all shipments made in a year constituted but a single offense; or, failing that, that the rendering of monthly bills by the railroad made all shipments in each month a single offense; or, at worst, that where several car lots were shipped at the same time, the shipment constituted but one offense. But all these contentions were waved aside by Judge Landis.

Monopoly — Restraint of Trade. — In Locker v. American Tobacco Co., 106 N. Y. Supp. 115, the New York Appellate Division, Second Department, holds that an agreement whereby the American Tobacco Company constituted the Metropolitan

Tobacco Company its sole selling agent in the city of Greater New York is not illegal as creating a monopoly or being in restraint of trade. The plaintiffs alleged that the Metropolitan Tobacco Company had refused to sell to them on any terms, and claimed to have sustained damages to the amount of $100,000. The court holds that any one may legally refuse to maintain trade relations with another for any reason or without any reason; that a producing corporation may lawfully authorize a selling corporation to sell, or refuse to sell, its products to any persons, and to establish the price and terms of sale thereof; and, at most, the court could only declare such an agreement invalid, and could not compel the sale of defendant's products to the plaintiffs.

Telephones — Use of Other Company's Wires. — A decision of considerable interest to the independent telephone companies is Billings Mut. Telephone Co. *v.* Rocky Mountain Bell Telephone Co., 155 Fed. Rep. 207, decided by District Judge Hunt, in the United States Circuit Court for Montana. The constitution of Montana provides that any telephone company within the State shall have the right to connect its wires with other lines, and authorizes the legislature to pass laws giving effect to such provision. By statute it is provided that in case one company refuses to allow another to connect with its lines, the acquiring of the right by the one to use the lines of the other may be had by condemnation proceedings. Judge Hunt holds that under such provisions a telephone company operating a local exchange, on payment of compensation to be ascertained as provided by the statute, can require another company operating long distance lines to permit a connection with such lines, and also their "use," by receiving and forwarding messages through such connection from subscribers of the other company substantially as it did messages tendered by its own local subscribers.

Testamentary Capacity — Belief in Spiritualism. — In an extended and interesting opinion the Illinois Supreme Court, in Owen *v.* Crumbaugh, 81 N. E. Rep. 1044, considers the question whether a belief in spiritualism is such a monomania or insane delusion as to deprive its possessor of the power to make a will, and comes to the conclusion that it is not. The testator, it seems, was another ward of that industrious spirit, "Bright Eyes," who figured so prominently in a recent Brooklyn trial. He was fond of relating how "Bright Eyes" had acted as his guardian angel on a number of occasions when he was in jeopardy, and he was a very ardent advocate of the tenets of spiritualism, and directed that the bulk of his property be applied to the erection of a spiritualistic church. Otherwise he was shown to have been an industrious, economical, and successful business man, and handled his ordinary business affairs in an intelligent and orderly manner. The authorities on this question, all of which support the decision in the present case, are collected in 28 Am. and Eng. Encyc. of Law (2d ed.) 89.

Voting Machines — Statute Authorizing Use Held Invalid. — In Helme *v.* Board of Election Commissioners, 113 N. W. 6, it was held by the Supreme Court of Michigan that a state statute authorizing the use of voting machines was unconstitutional, as violating the right of the elector to vote a secret ballot, and that such machines could not be used unless absolute secrecy were secured. It was shown that the names of candidates could not be so arranged on the machines as to permit a voter to vote for certain combinations of candidates, and that, where a voter desired to vote for such a combination, he must apply to the election inspector for a paper ballot, which, after being prepared and folded, was dropped by the inspector into a receptacle in the machine, to be counted if it were found that the combination could not otherwise have been voted by the use of the machine. The court said: "It is obvious that a voter cannot ask for and vote such a ballot without indicating that he does not vote for his full party ticket, and, to the degree that he is reluctant to have his want of party fealty known, it acts as a deterrent to his voting for the persons of his choice, and operates against his independence as a voter." On rehearing, the court stated that "it was not intended to hold or intimate that the voting machine in question was open to objection in any election in which the choice between candidates can be expressed by the use of the machine, or by any other method which does not disclose to the inspector or others the purpose of the voter."

Fraternal Society Liable for Injuries in Initiation. — That a secret fraternal society is liable for injuries inflicted by its members on a neophyte while he is being initiated into the mysteries of the order, is held by the New York Court of Appeals in Thompson *v.* Knights of Maccabees, 189 N. Y. 294. The plaintiff sued the Supreme Tent, a Michigan corporation, for injuries sustained during his initiation into one of the subordinate tents, and it was shown that the act which caused such injuries was one prescribed by the ritual issued by the defendant to its subordinate tents. The court held that the officers and members conducting the initiation ceremonies acted as the lawfully constituted agents of the defendant within the scope of the authority vested in them, and that the action was maintainable. In concluding the opinion, Haight, J., said: "We are not disposed to criticise the defendant on account of its being a secret society. Its main object is the insurance of its members against disability and death, and as such we recognize the fact that it has accomplished much good. Coupled with the mutual benefit of its members through insurance is the social and fraternal feature, which, through the secret ritual of their lodges, has enabled them to keep their members in touch with each other and interested in the work of the tents. We think, however, that other acts might be prescribed by the ritual, from which the importance of the work of the tent might be impressed upon the mind of the applicant without resorting to violence."

State Regulation of Railroad Rates. — The decision of United States Circuit Judge Pritchard, which stirred up such a fine hornets' nest in North Carolina a few months back, is reported in *Ex parte* Wood, 155 Fed. Rep. 190. The petitioner, a ticket agent, was indicted on a charge of violating section 4 of the recent North Carolina statute prescribing the maximum rates to be charged by carriers of passengers within the State, and making it a misdemeanor for any agent to charge a higher rate. Judge Pritchard had previously granted a preliminary injunction restraining the State officers from enforcing the statute until its constitutionality could be determined, and ordering the companies to issue coupons to purchasers of tickets for the difference between the rate charged and that prescribed by the statute. On habeas corpus he discharged the petitioner, holding that he had acted in pursuance of an order of a federal court. At the same time Judge Pritchard held that the statute was unconstitutional as a denial to the railroad companies of the equal protection of the laws by subjecting them to excessive and ruinous penalties if they exercised their right to contest the validity of the law in the courts. Other federal decisions under similar statutes which have been reported at this writing are St. Louis, etc., R. Co. *v.* Hadley, (Mo.) 155 Fed. Rep. 220, decided by District Judge McPherson; Poor *v.* Iowa Cent. R. Co., (Iowa) 155 Fed. Rep. 226, decided by District Judge McPherson; Perkins *v.* Northern Pac. R. Co., (Minn.) 155 Fed. Rep. 445, decided by District Judge Lochren; Southern R. Co. *v.* McNeill, (N. Car.) 155 Fed. Rep. 756, decided by Circuit Judge Pritchard; Seaboard Air Line R. Co. *v.* Railroad Commission, (Ala.) 155 Fed. Rep. 792, decided by District Judge Jones.

Book Reviews.

NATURE AND FUNCTION OF LAW.

Law: Its Origin, Growth, and Function. By James C. Carter, LL.D., of the New York Bar. G. P. Putnam's Sons. New York and London.

This posthumous contribution to the science of theoretical jurisprudence is worthy of the name of its gifted author. It consists of a series of lectures prepared, just before Mr. Carter's death, for delivery before the Law School of Harvard University. They were to be delivered in the spring of 1905, and the manuscript was completed only a few days before the author was stricken with the brief illness which resulted in his death. When he realized that the lectures would never be delivered, he expressed a wish that they be published by his executors.

The material embodied in these lectures is not merely the result of an effort on the part of a mature and brilliant thinker rightly to comprehend the nature and function of law and to give expression to his thoughts on that subject for a temporary purpose; it is really a product of the experience and thought of his whole professional life, and its value is much greater for that reason. The subject is one that for a great many years exerted a powerful influence over his mind and possessed for him an unusual attraction. The field of inquiry covered in these pages was therefore not new to him. This was no doubt partly due to the peculiar philosophic bent of his mind, but it was also due in a measure to the accident, or circumstance, that he had been actively concerned for many years in opposing the adoption, in the State of New York, of the Civil Code of which the late David Dudley Field was the author. This task and the inquiries which it led Mr. Carter to make were pursued by him with keen and unflagging interest.

The incident has considerable biographical significance, and we therefore quote a passage in which Mr. Carter has himself spoken of this chapter in his life and in which he has incidentally cast an interesting light on the personality of his distinguished opponent. The passage is taken from some words of Mr. Carter written "by way of a possible preface" to the book now before us. "It happened to me many years ago to be appointed by the Association of the Bar of the City of New York upon a committee charged with the duty of opposing a bill which had been introduced into the legislature of that State, entitled 'An Act to establish a civil code.' This proposed code purported to be the work of a legislative commission which had been created by an act of the same legislature, adopted many years before, and at the head of which was the late David Dudley Field; but it was in fact, as he often declared, entirely his own work. This eminent lawyer was a man of great intellectual audacity, the worthy disciple in that particular of Jeremy Bentham. He would not tolerate the suggestion that there was any insurmountable difficulty in reducing into statutory form the entire body of the law which governs the private transactions of men. He insisted that the whole of it could be embraced in a volume of very moderate size, and that its adoption would substantially supersede the necessity of consulting that prodigious record of judicial precedent which fills so many thousand volumes and has been hitherto deemed an essential part of the furniture of every complete law library. Moved by the high incitements of conferring upon society a benefit so prodigious, and, as we may suppose, of achieving for his own name a renown like that bestowed upon the great lawgivers of mankind, he threw himself into the enterprise of procuring the enactment of his proposed code with the greatest energy and prosecuted it for years with the utmost persistency. This made the task of opposition extremely laborious, and the chief burden happened to fall upon myself."

The arguments of Mr. Carter led to the final rejection of the proposed code. His views are in a measure familiar to the profession, as several pamphlets were published by him, and two important addresses were made, one of which was delivered before the American Bar Association, "The Ideal and the Actual in the Law" (1890).

After his retirement from active practice he continued to devote his attention to the same line of inquiry, and so in the end we have these lectures. The thesis maintained in these pages is that *Law is not made, it grows.* A more powerful exposition of the theory that law is the product of custom could not well be penned. Law is not so much a dictate of force as an expression of order, and, says he, that which has governed the conduct of men from the beginning of time will continue to govern it to the end. Legislation, of course, is conceded to have its place, but its true function is to supplement and aid the operation of custom, not to supplant it. A passage in which he depicts the futility of all attempts at codification is impressive. It ends thus: "A judiciary law will grow up around the code and will eventually replace the written enactment, and the law actually administered will be that which conforms to the customs of men. *Naturam expellas furca, tamen usque recurret.*"

The author's views of the nature of the unwritten law naturally lead him to combat the theories of the utilitarian philosophers, and in particular does he repudiate the Austinian definition which considers law to be a command imposed by the sovereign. The skill with which Mr. Carter has presented his theory and the learning which he has brought to play on the subject make the book an interesting and very valuable addition to legal science. It is not a temporary piece of controversial literature, it is a profound contribution to the theory of law. As a comprehensive study of the origin and development of law and of its influence and function as a powerful force in the civilization of mankind, we know of no work more worthy of attention.

Expert Testimony as to Handwriting. By Albert S. Osborn, Rochester, N. Y.

In three pamphlets, reprinted in the main from the Albany Law Journal, Mr. Osborn treats in an interesting manner of the nature and value of expert testimony as to handwriting. Mr. Osborn, who is himself an expert of repute in this field, gives a demonstration of the manner in which the expert arrives at conclusions, accompanying it with illustrations of the apparatus employed and very interesting examples of the tests in certain cases. He also sets forth a very strong argument as to the admissibility and value of this class of expert testimony, and against "expertphobia," citing in his support a number of decisions.

The pamphlets will be of service to the practitioner in cases where handwriting and documents are in dispute.

News of the Profession.

THE MISSOURI STATE BAR ASSOCIATION will hold a meeting in Kansas City on December 12 and 13.

APPOINTED TO QUEBEC SUPERIOR COURT. — Hon. Auguste Tessier has been appointed a judge of the Quebec Superior Court for the district of Rimouski, to succeed Judge Larue, who recently resigned.

NOTED BOSTONIAN DEAD. — Thomas Riley, one of the best known members of the Boston bar, died in that city on November 7, at the age of sixty-one. In addition to being an able lawyer, Mr. Riley was a noted wit and a man of broad scholarship.

NEW VICE-CHANCELLOR IN NEW JERSEY. — Chancellor Magie, of New Jersey, on October 29, appointed Edwin Robert Walker, of Trenton, to succeed Vice-Chancellor Bergen, who was recently promoted to the bench of the Supreme Court. The new vice-chancellor is a native of Rochester, N. Y., and is forty-five years old.

THE OLDEST JUDGE. — Hon. Charles Field, of Athol, Mass., is probably the oldest judge actively exercising judicial functions in this country. Although in his ninety-third year, Judge Field sits regularly in the First District Court of Northern Worcester, holding sometimes as many as five sessions a week.

TO BUY AMERICA'S FIRST LAW SCHOOL. — The Litchfield (Conn.) County Bar Association has under advisement a plan looking to the purchase and preservation of the Topping Rieve Law School, at Litchfield, which was the first law school in America. The building was recently purchased by D. C. Kilbourn, clerk of the Superior Court.

YOUNGEST WOMAN LAWYER IN FRANCE. — The youngest woman lawyer in France and the first to be admitted to the bar at her age is Mlle. Helene Mirapolski, a girl twenty years old, who recently took the barrister's oath before the First Chamber Court of Appeals and is now entitled to practice before the courts. She is of Polish origin, but a Parisian by birth.

DEATH OF DISTINGUISHED TEXAS LAWYER. — Hon. John L. Henry, for many years one of the best known and most distinguished members of the Texas bar, died in Dallas on October 21, aged seventy-six years. He was a native of Virginia, but moved to Texas in 1852. Up to two years ago he was a member of the Dallas law firm of Leake, Wellborn & Henry.

SHOT HIS FORMER COUNSEL. — On October 23 Judge Charles W. Brammell, a prominent lawyer and politician of Laramie, Wyo., was shot by William Lepper, an old resident of that place, who immediately thereafter killed himself. Judge Brammell had once acted as Lepper's counsel, and the latter believed that his interests had not been properly looked after.

PROMINENT BROOKLYN LAWYER DEAD. — Hon. Abram H. Dailey, former surrogate of Brooklyn, and for many years one of the foremost lawyers of that city, died there on November 3 of pneumonia. Outside his profession he was widely known as a defender of the doctrines of spiritualism, and recently he came into public notice as the defender of Mrs. May Pepper Vanderbilt of "Bright Eyes" fame.

A CORRECTION. — Through a slip of the pen it was stated in this column last month that Hon. Robert J. Peaslee had been appointed to the Connecticut Supreme Court, and that he was succeeded on the Superior Court bench by William A. Plummer. The statement was all right, except that the venue should have been laid in New Hampshire instead of Connecticut.

EDDYITES CONVICTED OF MANSLAUGHTER. — On October 10, at Mount Holly, N. J., a jury returned a verdict convicting Mr. and Mrs. Edwin M. Watson, of Moorestown, of manslaughter in failing to provide medical treatment for their seven-year-old son, who died on May 26 last, one day after a physician was called in. The verdict was accompanied by a recommendation for mercy. The death was caused by meningitis, superinduced by pneumonia.

WELL-KNOWN GEORGIAN PASSES AWAY. — Hon. John W. Akin, president of the Georgia senate, lawyer, author, and one of the most prominent men in the public life of his State, died in Cartersville on October 18, at the age of fifty-three. At the early age of nineteen he was admitted to the bar and quickly won success in his profession. For ten years he served as secretary of the Georgia State Bar Association, and was afterwards its president.

KARL HAU'S SENTENCE COMMUTED. — The death sentence pronounced upon Karl Hau, a professor in the George Washington University Law School, who was convicted in Germany for the murder of his mother-in-law, has been commuted to penal servitude for life. The Grand Duke of Baden, who has just succeeded to the throne, was unwilling to begin his reign with so sinister an event as the signing of a death warrant.

REFUSED A RAISE OF SALARY. — One of the strangest tales on record comes from Mt. Pleasant, Mich. It is stated that Circuit Judge Peter F. Dodds, who holds sway over the counties of Clare, Midland, and Isabella, has recently refused an increase of salary because there were some dissenting votes among the supervisors of Isabella county. He gave notice to the supervisors that he would not accept an increase unless they were unanimous in voting it.

THE ONLY INDIAN WOMAN LAWYER. — Miss Julia St. Cyr, a Winnebago Indian, is said to be the only lawyer of that race and sex in the United States. When tried recently before a federal court in Omaha on a charge of accepting too large a fee for securing a pension for a member of her tribe, she conducted her own defense and secured an acquittal. She was educated at Hampton, Va., and was later in charge of an Indian school on the Kickapoo reservation.

TO REORGANIZE CONNECTICUT BAR ASSOCIATION. — In accordance with a resolution passed by the Connecticut State Bar Association at its recent meeting in New Haven, President Charles E. Perkins has appointed a committee to consider the reorganizing of the association. It seems that the organization has of late years lost much of its influence among the Connecticut lawyers, and its ranks have grown thin, and the present movement is designed to reawaken the interest of the profession in the body and secure a larger membership.

PROCEEDINGS OF ILLINOIS BAR ASSOCIATION. — We are in receipt of a copy of the proceedings of the thirty-first annual meeting of the Illinois State Bar Association, which was held at Galesburg on July 11 and 12, 1907. It is a handsomely gotten up volume of some four hundred pages, and contains a number of interesting papers, chief among them the widely discussed address of Edward M. Shepard on "Corporate Capitalization and Public Morals." The editor, John M. Voight, Jr., secretary of the association, is entitled to much praise.

MARYLAND'S CHIEF JUSTICE DEAD. — Hon. James McSherry, chief justice of the Maryland Court of Appeals, died at his home in Frederick on October 23, of angina pectoris. Judge McSherry had been ill since early in the year, but of late his health had been improving and his sudden death was a surprise. He was born in Frederick in 1842. He was admitted to the bar in 1864, and practiced until 1887, when he was elected to the Court of Appeals. Nine years later he was made chief justice of the court, and served in that capacity until the time of his death.

EX-JUDGE HAWLEY DIES. — Hon. Thomas P. Hawley, former United States District Judge for Nevada, died in San Francisco on October 17 at the age of seventy-seven. Judge Hawley was a native of Indiana, but went west as a young man and was admitted to practice in California in 1857, remaining there till 1868, when he moved to Nevada. In 1872 he was elected a justice of the Nevada Supreme Court, which position he held until 1890, when he resigned to accept the federal judgeship, which was tendered him by President Harrison. When the Circuit Court of Appeals was organized in 189[illegible], Judge Hawley was made a member of it. He retired June 30, 1906.

Death of Judge McComas. — Louis Emory McComas, associate justice of the Court of Appeals of the District of Columbia, former United States senator and representative from Maryland, died November 10 at his home in Washington of heart failure. Justice McComas was a native of Maryland and sixty-one years of age. After a successful career at the bar and as a member of Congress, he was appointed to the District of Columbia Supreme Court by President Harrison. In 1898 he was elected United States senator from Maryland to succeed Senator Gorman. On the expiration of his term he was appointed by President Roosevelt to the bench of the Court of Appeals of the District of Columbia.

A Centenarian Law Suit Ended. — A case which has been in the Virginia courts for more than a century was ended during October by the entry of a decree in the Circuit Court at Staunton, showing all disbursements in the case of Peck *v.* Borden and Borden *v.* Borden. Over $100,000 was involved, and the beneficiaries, now numbering nearly four hundred, are scattered all over the country. One heir, originally represented as an infant, died some years ago at the age of ninety-six. Nearly every lawyer at the Staunton bar for the last hundred years has been employed in the case, and the papers were so voluminous that nobody was acquainted with all of them.

Supreme Courts of Saskatchewan and Alberta. — The personnel of the recently organized Supreme Courts of the Canadian Provinces of Saskatchewan and Alberta has been announced. The Saskatchewan court has for its first chief justice the Hon. E. L. Wetmore, formerly associate justice of the Supreme Court of the Northwest Territories. The other judges are the Hons. H. W. Newlands, J. E. P. Prendergast, and T. C. Johnstone, formerly puisne judges of the Territories, and the Hon. J. H. Lamont, who was attorney-general for Saskatchewan up to the time of his appointment. The chief justice of the Alberta court is Hon. A. L. Sifton, who was chief justice of the Supreme Court of the Territories, and his associates are the Hons. D. L. Scott, Horace Harvey, and C. A. Stuart, of the old court, and N. D. Beck, K. C., of Edmonton.

Comparative Law Bureau. — We are in receipt of a copy of the laws and regulations of the Comparative Law Bureau of the American Bar Association, which was organized at the annual meeting of the association held last August in Portland, Me. The purpose of the bureau, briefly stated, is to bring the legal profession and legislators in this country in touch with the important laws of other nations. An annual bulletin of legislative titles and general bibliography of foreign laws covering the preceding twelve months is to be published. The officers of the bureau are as follows: Director, Simeon E. Baldwin, of New Haven, Conn.; treasurer, Eugene C. Massie, of Richmond, Va.; secretary, William W. Smithers, 1100 Land Title Building, Philadelphia. The managers are Edwin A. Jaggard of St. Paul; James Barr Ames, of Cambridge, Mass.; Charles E. Littlefield, of Rockland, Me.; Edgar H. Farrar, of New Orleans; Clifford S. Walton, of Washington, D. C.; John H. Wigmore, of Chicago; William Draper Lewis, of Philadelphia; George W. Kirchwey, of New York, and Andrew A. Bruce, of Grand Forks, N. D.

English Notes.

Lord Brampton's Estate. — The estate of Lord Brampton, formerly Sir Henry Hawkins, who died during October last, is valued at something over seven hundred thousand dollars, which is doing pretty well for a judge.

Death of a King's Counsel. — Mr. William Pearson, K. C., formerly one of the foremost practitioners at the chancery bar, died in London on October 15, aged eighty-three. He retired from practice more than fifteen years ago.

Reopening of the Courts. — On October 12 the courts opened after the Long Vacation, the ceremony being as usual preceded by a service at Westminster Abbey, which was attended by the lord chancellor and nearly all the judges, with a large number of king's counsel and members of the junior bar.

The Last of the Serjeants-at-Law. — The recent death of Lord Brampton leaves Lord Lindley the only surviving serjeant-at-law in England. Before the suspension of the Order of the Coif judges on the common-law side were made serjeants before the election to the bench, and the coif was a part of the judicial wig. The last judges who wore the coif on the bench were Lord Field and Lord Lindley. Lord Brampton was the last judge who appeared on the bench in a powdered wig.

Compulsory Evening Clothes. — The question whether a restaurant proprietor can exclude persons on the sole ground that they are not in evening dress is likely to come up in the English courts before long. Recently an earl and his wife, both prominent socially, went for dinner to the Savoy hotel, in London, and the proprietor declined to serve them because of his rule requiring all guests of the hotel to appear in evening dress. The incident has caused some discussion, and even though the noble gentleman who was cast out because of his lack of a wedding garment does not take up the matter with the proprietor, some other martyr to principle is very apt to do so. Otherwise the British character has been greatly misrepresented.

Lord Coleridge Appointed to King's Bench. — Lord Coleridge, K. C., has been appointed to fill the additional judgeship in the King's Bench Division of the High Court of Justice. The new justice is the son and grandson of a judge. His grandfather, Sir John Taylor Coleridge, was forty-five years of age when he succeeded Mr. Justice Taunton as a judge of the King's Bench in 1835; his father, who was lord chief justice for fourteen years, was fifty-three when he succeeded Sir William Bovill as chief justice of the Common Pleas in 1873. The present Lord Coleridge is fifty-six years old. He was called to the bar at the Middle Temple in 1877, was created a Q. C. in 1892, and elected a bencher of his Inn in 1894.

The Rights of an Understudy. — The Court of Appeal, in the case of Newman *v.* Gatti, has recently decided a point of considerable interest to theatrical folk. The question in dispute was whether the plaintiff, who, by the contract involved, was engaged for the run of a certain play "to understudy Miss Edna May," was entitled, when that lady gave up her part before the end of the run, to take it for the rest of the run. The court found that the word "understudy," as used in theatrical circles, did not involve the idea that the understudy was entitled to the principal's rôle when the principal gave it up. The plaintiff also relied on a collateral verbal agreement giving her the right to succeed Miss May in her part, contained in a conversation between the parties before the contract was signed, but the court held that evidence thereof was not admissible to vary the written contract.

Talked Back at the Parson. — In one of the London police courts recently Thomas Quelch was charged with the violation of a statute prohibiting riotous or indecent behavior in places of worship, and disturbance of ministers preaching or conducting service therein. The accused had answered aloud during the sermon some remarks of the preacher, and had later in the service at All Saints', Peckham, cried out, "Ladies and gentlemen, I stand before you as a second Lazarus." It did not appear of which of the two of that name the defendant claimed to be a reincarnation; but the substance of his defense was that the preacher at the service had discussed the contents of a Socialist leaflet, circulated at the church door at the conclusion of a harvest festival service, which reflected on the churchgoers, and that, being more used to political meetings than churches, he had been swept away by his enthusiasm. The magistrate, however, convicted him.

CODIFICATION IN ENGLAND. — Since the presentation in 1867 of the first and only report of the Royal Commission on Codification, appointed in 1866 at the instance of Lord Westbury, little has been heard of the codification of the English law, and very little has been done, says the *Law Journal*. Only in the domain of commercial law has any codifying at all been done in England. Four codifying acts have been passed — the Bills of Exchange Act, 1882; the Partnership Act, 1890; the Sale of Goods Act, 1893, and the Marine Insurance Act, 1906. These acts have admittedly proved successful codifications of their respective subject-matters, and what has been done in these four branches of law might very well be done in other branches of commercial law. This argument can be extended. If commercial law can be successfully codified, why should not property law be also treated in the same way, and so on with other heads of law? A partial attempt has, indeed, been made with patents and designs by the Patents and Designs (Consolidation) Act, 1907, but this can scarcely be called a code, as it is incomplete without the judicial authorities which constitute a large part of the existing law on the subject. With the Indian codes as examples, the work of shaping most branches of law into statutory form would be almost half done when once begun in earnest. Leaving the ambitious project of a general code to take care of itself, steady progress might well be made towards that ideal by simply continuing the system of codification by compartments. But the rate of progress must be accelerated if anything resembling an approach to the ideal is to be secured in our generation.

THINKS POORLY OF THE ENGLISH BENCH. — That chronic dyspeptic, the *Saturday Review*, had this to say in a recent issue regarding the judges now on the English bench: "The distinction of the bench has unfortunately gone down considerably during recent years. There is a high general average of lawyer-like, professional ability, but the bench is singularly destitute of outstanding figures. None of the judges has had a brilliant career, even at the bar, comparable with that of Lord Brampton. They recall nothing in their careers except that some of them have had large practices and others none to speak of. The bench is barren of great reputations in Parliament, in any branch of public life, in science, or in letters. Not many years ago on the puisne bench there were Grove, famous in science, and Stephen, of note as a jurist and as a vigorous writer in criticism, history, and philosophy. One need not go far back to recall Cairns, Selborne, Cockburn, Coleridge, Bowen, Fry. All these were names and personalities that meant something more to men in other walks of life than those of successful practitioners in a merely professional sphere. It seems as if the law had lost its intellectual pre-eminence relative to other professions. Though lawyers go into Parliament in even greater numbers than they used to do, fewer stand prominently before the public as representative intellectual men of the time. More doctors than lawyers make extra-professional reputations. Forensically the bar is very much on about the same level of average though rather high mediocrity as the bench, so that it must be confessed the government would have had considerable difficulty in adding to the prestige of the bench by any appointment possible at present. This dearth of distinction may be only a passing phase. Perhaps it is common to the nation, to Parliament, to the bench, and all other institutions, to have periods of depression and revival, and we may always hope for a renewal of past lustre even when we do not see any prospect of it. In the meantime, however, such an appointment as this of Lord Coleridge is not encouraging. Several more judges will probably have to be appointed in the near future. It would be a scandal if this necessity were turned into an opportunity for appointing to the bench other Radicals as insignificant politically as they are professionally."

THE DRUCE CASE. — Rarely, if ever, has the manufacturer of melodrama imagined a more thrilling plot than that involved in the Druce case, which is now before the English courts. The facts of the case in brief are as follows: T. C. Druce, the keeper of a commercial bazaar in Baker street, London, after rearing a family of children, ostensibly died and was buried in 1864. The fifth Duke of Portland, one of whose residences was located in the vicinity of the Druce bazaar, died in 1879, a bachelor, and the bulk of his large property went to his sister. Thereafter some of the descendants of T. C. Druce laid claim to the Portland estates, alleging that Druce was in fact the Duke of Portland in disguise, and that the coffin in which Druce's remains were supposed to lie was in reality filled with two hundred pounds of sheet lead. The contest was thrown out of court some ten years ago on the testimony of Herbert, second son of T. C. Druce, who swore that he had seen his father's dead body in the coffin. There the matter rested until the recent litigation was instituted by George Hollamby Druce, grandson of T. C. Druce, against his uncle Herbert, to prove that the latter had sworn falsely in the former proceeding, the implication being that he was bribed to do so by the present holders of the Portland estates. The chief witness for the claimant is one Robert Caldwell, of New York, who has sworn that he knew the fifth Duke of Portland; that the duke and T. C. Druce were one and the same man; that, to his personal knowledge, the duke had a coffin made and filled with two hundred pounds of lead; and that he assisted at the obsequies over the lead-filled coffin in 1864. But more striking even than the story of this witness is the fact that in June, 1906, workmen uncovered a secret passage leading from the duke's residence in Cavendish square to the site of the old Baker street bazaar. At this writing considerable doubt has been raised as to the truthfulness of Caldwell's story, but that underground passage has not been explained away. Both sides profess to be anxious to have Druce's coffin opened, and any other termination of the sensational case would, of course, be sadly disappointing to public curiosity.

THE KING AND THE MIDDLE TEMPLE. — By the death of Lord Brampton the king, whose birthday is celebrated to-day, has become the senior bencher of the Middle Temple, says the *Law Journal* for November 9. He was admitted, called to the bar and to the bench on Oct. 31, 1861. After the formalities in the Parliament Chamber, the prince and a distinguished company proceeded to declare open the new library. A service followed in the Temple church. In the evening there was a conversazione, when the terrace was arranged with flowers and the fountain illuminated. The efficiency of the library is an important factor in the popularity of an inn of court. The addition made to the Middle Temple library in the summer of last year has improved considerably, both internally and externally, the building opened by the Prince of Wales in 1861. Perfection must not be sought in a library, for

> Who hopes a perfect library to see,
> Seeks what nor is, nor was, nor e'er shall be.

The Prince of Wales did not visit the inn again until 1874, when he dined on the Grand Day of Trinity Term (June 11) in the presence of a distinguished gathering, which included chancellors and high officers of the Universities of England,

Scotland, and Ireland, together with leading members of the Council of Legal Education.

After the opening of the law courts on Dec. 3, 1882, when Lord Selborne received his earldom, the benchers of the Middle Temple invited some two thousand guests to luncheon. The Prince of Wales was then accompanied by the Duke of Cambridge, Prince Christian, and the Duke and Duchess of Teck.

When next the Prince of Wales visited the inn it was to second the resolution for the admission of his eldest son, the late Duke of Clarence, and his call to the bar. Archbishop Benson was present on the occasion, and entered in his diary: "Dined Middle Temple on their great Grand Day. Very striking, 430 in hall. Prince Edward made a bencher. According to their custom, sat above Prince of Wales, whose guest I was supposed to be, and next to the treasurer, the Master of the temple being the chief guest on the treasurer's right."

The Jubilee year of 1887 was marked by two visits, for in it his royal highness consented to act as treasurer, with Sir Peter Edlin as deputy. The date of Grand Day in Trinity Term was fixed as near as possible to the national commemoration, in consideration of the Prince's numerous engagements. The second visit was at the conclusion of his year of office on the last day of Michaelmas Term. Since an entire departure from precedent has been made in favor of the last representative of the United States in this country, it may be interesting to recall that on this occasion a quite unusual course was taken by requesting Mr. Phelps, then United States ambassador, to propose the toast of the health of the prince, which he did in a felicitous speech. The prince himself did a similar thing when he dined on Grand Day in May, 1893 — the third occasion within six years, as he had taken his place at dinner on April 9, 1891. In 1893 Sir Henry Hawkins, who was a close personal friend of the king, marked the jubilee of his call to the bar, so the prince took the opportunity to propose the health of the well-known judge. The last occasion on which, as Prince of Wales, his majesty visited the Middle Temple Hall was on Dec. 21, 1893, at a smoking concert of the Inns of Court Volunteers.

It is not necessary to recall the details of the memorable day in 1903 when the king dined in the Middle Temple Hall. It was the first occasion on which a sovereign of the realm has taken his place by right of his position as a bencher. The event has been commemorated for perpetuity by the addition of an elaborate silver-gilt loving-cup and four massive salt-stands to the plate of the society. *Vivat Rex!*

Obiter Dicta.

Against Public Policy. — The Iowa Supreme Court has recently held that a woman's stocking is not the proper place to carry her money.

A New One on Us. — A well-known law publishing company announces the publication of the annotated rules of the federal courts, "by William Whitwell Dewhurst, member of the Supreme Court of the United States."

A Candid Judge. — In the case of Runkel *v.* Winemiller, 4 H. & McH. (Md.) 429, 449, Chase, J., began his opinion by rehearsing what had taken place "at a former sitting, when the court was full."

Unencumbered. — In the course of an examination of a negro witness in the Jackson, Miss., Chancery Court a few weeks since, the attorney asked, "Are there any incumbrances on your land?" "Naw, suh," responded the witness, "nothin' but pines."

A Failure of Proof. — The case mentioned in this column last month of the owner of a jack suing to recover double compensation because the defendant's mare bore twins is, according to a correspondent who writes from Kewanee, Ill., "about equaled by one brought here by an old lawyer of forty years' practice, who was a law book writer and an ex-member of the State legislature. He commenced two prosecutions at the same time against the same man for bastardy because the woman had twins. He was beaten on the merits because she was a married woman."

A Decree Pro Confesso. — The following, except for the names, is a true copy of a decree rendered by a Louisiana justice of the peace:

"Personally appeared before me the undersigned legal authority Sarah Jones, who being sworn deposes and says that she is the wife of George Jones and that she has not lived in accordance with the marriage laws of the State, having had three children by another man, thereby forfeiting her marriage contract, which entitles her husband to a divorce.

This done, read and signed in open Court on the 2nd day of Jan., 1906.

(Signed) Amos Brown, J. P.

A Valuable Form. — The following is a copy of an instrument (except in the matter of names) attached to a bill for separate maintenance in a suit now pending in the Circuit Court of Cook county, Ill.:

Exhibit A.

STATE OF ILLINOIS, }
County of Cook. } *ss.:*

December 17th, 1906 of the City of Chicago County of Cook and State of Illinois being duly sworn, doth depose and say, that I, William Schmidt and Ester Schmidt both as husband and wife of the City of Chicago — hereby agree to appoint Mr. Brown of Number 69 Howe Place of the City of Chicago to be the holder and trustee of three hundred (300.00) Dollars as a guarantee that the over said William Schmidt will in no way, manner or form ill tread his wife Ester Schmidt for the term of one year from this date, should William Schmidt fail to hold this agreement than and only then must the holder of the three hundred (300.00) Dollars give over said money to both parties, William & Ester Schmidt. It is agreed and understood that this agreement is null and void, and the money to be returned to William and Ester Schmidt one year from this date.

And further this deponent says not.

(Signed) S. Lederer,
Notary Public.

Subscribed and sworn to before me this 17th day of December, A. D. 1906.

(seal) Wm. Schmidt.

A Professional Card. — A correspondent writing from Ohio sends in the following specimen for our museum with the comment, "Let not the East be omitted in the exhibition of business cards."

When you want to get married call and see me	**Henry Bosset.** **Justice of the Peace.**
When you want a divorce call on me	Notary Public Commissioner of Deeds **Office 103 Market St.**
Fire Insurance	Near Washington St Room 21. Office Tel NEWARK, N. J. Residence 7 Boston St Tel
All legal papers carefully drawn	Marriages performed while you wait.

The Worst Ever. — The attention of prosecuting attorneys is respectfully called to the fact that Justice Riddell, of Ontario, has recently fined the Michigan Central Railroad $25,000 for allowing a carload of dynamite to explode in Essex county, Ontario. Perhaps the railroads will be more careful when they realize that it is criminal to spread such reports.

First Aid to the Injured. — Out in Wichita, Kan., recently a man was knocked down by colliding with a buggy. A Hibernian gentleman who kept a nearby popcorn emporium ran to him and asked, "Are ye hurted much? Do ye want a docther?" "A doctor!" exclaimed the man who was down, "I've been run over. What I want is a lawyer."

Cosmopolitan Tribunals. — They must have a pretty variegated assortment of litigants down in Mississippi. In the recent case of Hampton *v.* State, 88 Miss. 257, Judge Calhoon said: "Mulattoes, negroes, Malays, whites, millionaires, paupers, princes, and kings, in the courts of Mississippi, are on precisely the same exactly equal footing." We hadn't heard of any crowned heads figuring in the courts down that way of late. Maybe, though, the king and the duke who voyaged with Huckleberry Finn have been up to some of their old tricks.

The Desired Information. — An Oregon law firm recently wrote to a resident of South Omaha, Neb., as follows:

Dear Sir: We understand that you have made an assignment for the benefit of creditors, and would be pleased to have you advise us of the name of the assignee and the terms of the assignment. Kindly favor us with a prompt reply.

Yours truly.

The following reply was received:

Dear Sir: I made assingment for the benetif of cridoters to Shear and Shear alike. Yours truly.

An Austere Man. — A correspondent sends us the following excerpt from a deed which is on record in Tarrant county, Texas:

"This conveyance, however, is made for the purpose of building a church house by the said grantee for the Worship of God after the Apostolic order, as recorded in the New Testament Scriptures, and in case this property is used for any other purpose, even the use of instrumental music in the worship, or in the house or society work of any human origin, such as W. C. T. U. work and conventions, lectureships, or church festivals, or ice cream suppers, old maid conventions, and such like, political meetings or discussions, or lodge gatherings of any character, then this property is to revert back to the said T. W. Phillips, his heirs or assigns."

"It is evident," writes our correspondent, "that the grantor was a 'Firm Foundationist,' and the peculiar provisions of his deed, the consideration being $1,500, are, perhaps, attributable to the fact that the old gentleman at one time attended an old maids' convention and got stuck on and married an old maid and was disappointed. Hence his everlasting protest against old maids' conventions. Or perhaps he had his leg pulled at a church festival, or overate himself at an ice cream supper."

The Correct Procedure. — A correspondent sends us this from Rhode Island:

"During a recent epidemic of scarlet fever in one of our suburban towns, a certain physician was prosecuted under the town ordinance for failing to report a case. The local health officer, who essays a use of legal and medical phraseology somewhat beyond his understanding, delivered himself of the following dissertation: 'This 'ere hypodermic ain't handled right. The town oughter have a inlaid hospital just for such cases. Now they've persecuted this doctor under the town audience. It won't amount to nothin'. There'll be a bunch of doctors as witnesses, all agin each other. The alpathetics will swear one way; the homepathetics the other. Now I'd a got a good smart lawyer to get an order from the legislater to change the venus of the case, and if the judge wouldn't allow it I'd have him peached. The judge is a friend of the doctor anyway, so what's the use? Even if he don't know nothin' about the dinosis of cases the judge will let him go. Then he'll get all the cases in town, put on a good front, and have a shef to drive him round in his auto. He'd oughter be arranged by the Torney General, and all the dispositions of the witnesses should be wroten out so they couldn't go back on 'em.'"

A Friend of the Court. — The taxation of costs by collection agencies is growing to such an extent that the courts may ere long be in a large measure relieved of that burden. A correspondent sends us the following circular which a Boston agency is accustomed to forward to a justice of the peace with a request that he sign his name and mail it to the delinquent debtor:

COMPLAINT AGAINST

....	Amount due	$2.40
....	Fees	
....	Cost	1.00
	Total amount due....	$3.40

The above claim has been placed in the hands of the Justice of the Peace in your town to collect from you $2.40 with costs, making the total amount $3.40.

The evidence is as follows:

About one year ago The Friend Soap and Supply Co., of Boston, Mass., expended large sums of money in advertising their goods. In response to one of their advertisements, they have your written order for $2.40 worth of their goods to be sold at a premium. The Company honored said order and sent you twenty-four pieces of their goods, valued at ten cents each, on their regular terms, to be sold and paid for within thirty days, or the goods were to be returned. The result has been that you have kept the goods many months beyond the stipulated time, without paying for or returning them. You have repeatedly ignored all letters notifying you that the contract had expired and that no further delay would be tolerated, also telling you that action would be taken for recovery of their value.

It is the law of every State that any person receiving or making use of any article is liable for payment of same, and under this law can begin action.

Please make note of the fact that these goods were not sold, only consigned to you, and therefore remain the sole property of The Friend Soap and Supply Co., of Boston, Mass., until paid for.

A failure to settle for goods shipped on consignment constitutes an act of embezzlement, punishable by law, but using the United States mails for obtaining goods illegally is fraud and is punishable by imprisonment; minors are not exempt. Ask your postmaster to read to you section 505, page 237, Postal Laws and Regulations.

It is our purpose to see that justice is done and to punish all offenders and when necessary to send the constable with writs of execution.

Now, therefore, take notice that this account must be settled at the office of the justice of the peace mentioned below, on or before ten days after the date affixed below on this complaint. The law is severe in suppressing all wrong-doing. Unless you pay the amount due the law will be enforced.

The total amount due, including costs, is $3.40. If the claim is paid within ten days from date, we will accept $2.40. If not, additional cost will be added for prosecution of the claim.

WHITNEY-PARSONS COLLECTION BUREAU.
41 Holmes Building, Boston, Mass.

Dated this .... day of ...., 1907.

Please call at my office at once and pay the above claim and avoid extra cost.

.........................,
Justice of the Peace.
Town.....................

Law Notes

JANUARY, 1908.

PUBLISHED BY EDWARD THOMPSON COMPANY,
NORTHPORT, LONG ISLAND, N. Y.

CONTENTS.

THE decision of the Supreme Court of the United States in the suit by the Commonwealth of Virginia against the State of West Virginia will probably settle some interesting questions as to the jurisdiction and powers of that court, and the relation of the several States to the Union. The State of West Virginia was created out of a portion of the territory of Virginia at a time when the last-named State was deeply in debt. The first constitution of the new State provided that it should assume an equitable proportion of such debt and that the legislature should proceed to ascertain such equitable proportion as soon as possible and provide for its liquidation. Afterwards the legislature practically repudiated this obligation, and when the constitution was amended the provision relating to the Virginia debt was omitted. West Virginia now denies liability for any part of this debt. The bill in the impending suit seeks to compel West Virginia to perform the obligations assumed by her first constitution. On demurrer to the bill the Supreme Court held that it had jurisdiction, and in answer to the proposition that there was no power to enforce a decree against the State, if one should be rendered, the chief justice observed that "it is not to be presumed on demurrer that West Virginia would refuse to carry out the decree of this court. If such repudiation should be absolutely asserted, we can then consider by what means the decree may be enforced."

THE Federal Constitution gives the Supreme Court jurisdiction "in all cases . . . in which a State shall be a party," and, having jurisdiction to hear and determine the controversy, it cannot be imagined that the power to enforce a decree is wanting. It can only be supposed that the decree, if in favor of Virginia, will be promptly obeyed by the defendant State, but should it prove otherwise it is a matter of great interest as to what subsequent proceedings the court would adopt. The State has little or no property that could be taken under execution, and the legislature might neglect to provide for the finding of the amount decreed. There can be no doubt that it would be the duty of the State legislature to perform the decree, but performance could not be enforced by any direct process. Decrees of the federal courts have been enforced by aid of the military power of the United States, and it is not improbable that such aid would be invoked against a contumelious State as well as against a mob. The view might be taken that a State refusing to obey the mandate of the Supreme Court and resisting its officers is in rebellion against the United States. At all events the members of that court do not seem to doubt their power, and, as the chief justice has said, they will probably find a way to enforce their decree.

IT has been said in regard to judicial decisions that there is no very great probability of the court of last resort reaching more correct results in point of theory than the court below, but that the court of last resort simply has the last guess at the question; and counsel who lose on appeal a case which they had won in the trial court often console themselves with this reflection. Under the judicial organization in some States, and notably New York, the saying has a peculiar force, as may be seen from a consideration of the constitution of the several courts, and by following a case from the court of first instance to the Court of Appeals. Thus, a case is tried at a Special Term of the Supreme Court before one judge. On appeal to the Appellate Division of the First Department the decision of the trial judge is unanimously affirmed by the five judges of that court. The case is then taken on appeal to the Court of Appeals, where the decision of the Appellate Division is reversed by four of the seven judges of the Court of Appeals, three being for affirmance, and that decision settles the law and becomes a precedent to be followed in future cases. But note this: As to the judicial personnel, the case was heard by thirteen judges. These judges differed as to the law, *nine* of them taking one view and *four* of them taking another view. And yet the opinion of the four determines what the law is.

To carry the matter still further, it would be easy to suppose a case involving the same question of law, pending in each of the five judicial departments of New York. Supposing the same conclusion to be reached in each department, we have thirty judges who are agreed as to the law. These cases then come, one by one, before the Court of Appeals, and are reversed, the judges of that court standing four to three. This is not an impossible case, but it shows that the law may be established by a very insignificant number of judges against nearly the whole current of judicial opinion. It is curious to observe what striking results would be obtained by two of these judges exchanging places. Suppose one of the judges who voted for reversal in the Court of Appeals had been in the Appellate Division, and one of the Appellate Division judges had been in the Court of Appeals. In that event the decision of the Special Term and the Appellate Division would have been affirmed by a vote of four to three, thus establishing a diametrically opposite rule of law by nine judges as against four. It is perfectly obvious that such adventitious circumstances often make the law, because it is not an uncommon occurrence for a vacancy in the Court of Appeals to be filled from the Appellate Division. But it is not necessary to resort to the imagination. Such cases have actually occurred. In Roberson *v.* Box Co., 171 N. Y. 538, the decision of the Special Term was affirmed by the Appellate Division, consisting of four justices, and the decision of the Appellate Division was reversed by the Court of Appeals on a vote of four to three. In this case we have the law established by four judges against the opinion of seven others of presumably equal learning and ability. Such a decision, while undoubtedly a precedent, cannot be convincing. It is closely analogous to a decision by a divided court; that is, it disposes of the case in hand, but does not settle the law, except as applicable to the exact facts of that case, and as an authority in another jurisdiction it would be entitled to very little consideration. The Roberson case is a striking instance of the unsatisfactory results of such a judicial system. It was not received with favor by the profession, and other courts have refused to follow it. It was first disapproved by the Superior Court of Georgia in the well-considered case of Pavesich *v.* New England Life Ins. Co., 122 Ga. 190, and later by the Court of Chancery of New Jersey, in Edison *v.* Edison Polyform Mfg. Co., 67 Atl. Rep. 392, as not sustained by principle. The editor of the *American Law Review* (vol. 36, p. 634) says: "From first to last there is a decisive majority of the judges who have dealt with the case against the final conclusion announced by the Court of Appeals. It cannot therefore be regarded as settling anything except for the guidance of inferior judicatories within the State of New York. It should not be followed as authority in other jurisdictions."

THE action of the board of education of New York prohibiting the usual Christmas exercises in the public schools on the ground, it seems, that they are improper and inappropriate because "this is not a Christian nation," has provoked considerable discussion. Bishop Satterlee, of Washington, D. C., says that the Supreme Court of the United States has decided that "this is a Christian nation." The case to which the bishop refers is doubtless Holy Trinity Church *v* U. S., 143 U. S. 457, in which Mr. Justice Brewer (at page 471) uses the phrase quoted. Substantially the same expression is to be found in a number of other cases cited in the opinion of Mr. Justice Brewer, but it is true only in a limited or qualified sense. It is true in the sense that Christianity is a part of the common law derived from England, and also that it is the religion of by far the greater part of our population. Being a part of the common law, blasphemy, which consists in wantonly uttering or publishing words casting contumelious reproach or profane ridicule on the Christian religion, is a common-law offense, and may be punished as such. Nevertheless the Christian religion is not a civic or political institution in this country, and no rights are dependent on professing it. A Mohammedan or an atheist would not, by reason of his religious belief, be disqualified to hold any public office, and the privilege of religious freedom does not permit the teaching of any religion in the public schools. But singing Christmas carols is no more in the nature of religious instruction than the giving of the Christmas holiday. Of course the board of education had the power to make the order in question, but it was not a wise act. The objection to reading the Bible in the public schools presents quite a different question, and even those who personally might favor the practice can sympathize with the view of the objectors. A taxpayer whose money helps to support the schools has a right to object to the teaching of any particular religious creed, and the courts have generally sustained such objections. But the opposition to a harmless musical performance appropriate to the season which is a legal holiday has no reasonable foundation, and suggests a desire to suppress a long-established custom merely because it is not acceptable personally to members of the board of education.

THE new law in Minnesota permitting a person accused of crime to plead guilty at once without waiting for the action of the grand jury is said to operate in a highly satisfactory manner in that it gives him an opportunity to begin to "do time" without unnecessary delay. It might well be doubted that any great number of criminals are in a special hurry to expiate their crimes, but they might improve in this respect if the encouragement given by the Minnesota law should be afforded by other States. After all, is such a statute necessary? It is true that the State constitutions generally provide that no person shall be held to answer a criminal charge except on an indictment or presentment by a grand jury, but since this provision is designed for the benefit of the person by giving him definite information as to the charge he is required to answer, it would seem that his rights would be fully protected by permitting him to specify the crime with which he charges himself and to plead guilty to such self-made accusation. As to the technical requirement of an indictment or presentment by a grand jury, no reason is perceived why that could not be waived as effectually as a trial by jury is waived when a prisoner pleads guilty to an indictment.

THE compilation of the code of ethics of the various State Bar Associations which have adopted such canons, printed in another column, should command attention. It has been prepared by the Committee on Code of Professional Ethics of the American Bar Association as a working basis for a code which such committee, it is understood, will present to the association for consideration at the next annual meeting. The subject is an important one — indeed, scarcely any subject is of more real importance to the well-being of the profession. As Judge Sharswood observed in his famous essay on professional ethics: "Counsel should ever remember how necessary it is for the dignified and honorable administration of justice, upon which the dignity and honor of their profession entirely depend, that the courts and the members of the courts should be regarded with respect by the suitors and people; that on all occasions of difficulty or danger to that department of government, they should have the good opinion and confidence of the public on their side. Good men of all parties prefer to live in a country in which justice according to law is impartially administered."

THE TWO-YEAR COURSE IN SOUTHERN LAW SCHOOLS.

In this paper something will be said about the two-year course in law and, more especially, about that course as it affects the policy and future of Southern law schools. The writer is constrained to give expression to his views because they are apparently somewhat different from those generally held at this time.

To begin with, it appears to be taken for granted among the legal educators of the country that the two-year course in law is hopelessly out of date and should be abandoned in every college where it is possible to substitute a longer course in its stead. The colleges of the North and East have generally adopted the three-year course, and the associated law schools are assiduously striving to bring all law schools in the country to the same standard. The Southern colleges, for the most part, hold out against the change and generally maintain the two-year course. Judging from expressions that have come from men connected with the faculties of those law schools, we suppose that those in authority there are anxious to hasten the day when the three-year course will prevail in Southern colleges also. Their present attitude is that of acquiescence in local conditions which they hope ere long to see changed. Evidently the three-year course has come to be considered, in the mind of most legal educators, the minimum period that should be devoted to the study of law in a college in any part of the country; and the giving of such a course has thus come to be a true badge of respectability among colleges maintaining schools of law.

As opposed to this current opinion of the legal educators, we have a conviction that, speaking with particular reference to the South, the two-year course in law is the proper one to give in the law schools of that section; and we hope to see the experiment of the two-year course continued in those law schools for another generation, at least. We must not be understood to mean that those schools should be maintained without improvement on their present footing. Certainly every effort should be made to strengthen the courses and enlarge the teaching faculties, not indeed that the student may be overwhelmed by crowding the work of three years into two, but that he may have more careful teaching and may get a better insight into fundamental principles.

It is a necessary part in the scheme of legal education here contemplated, that the student, before beginning his course in law, should be a well-educated man; that he should in fact, if possible, have an academic degree. Appreciation of the vital importance of this factor supplies, indeed, the chief reason why a preference has been expressed for the continuance, for the present, of the two-year course in the law schools of the South. If we had the responsibility of deciding such a matter in a Southern college, and efforts were made to induce us to change from the two-year course to a three-year course, we should unhesitatingly meet the proposition with a firm No. Instead of extending the law course for an additional year, we should increase the requirements for admission to the law school. It is not, in our judgment, enough that the candidate for admission into the school of law should be equipped with a regular high school training or its equivalent. It is not enough that such training should be supplemented by one year or two years in a regular college course. Every candidate for admission into a law school ought to be a well-educated man — well educated, that is, according to the standards that prevail in this day and time — and this means that he ought to have at least as much schooling as is represented by the A. B. degree conferred by American colleges.

And this, we submit, is an ideal that the Southern law schools may well keep before themselves for a long time yet to come. It is, in our opinion, a better and higher ideal than that which would be reached by the adoption, at the present time, of the three-year course in law. When it has been brought to pass that candidates for the law degree are, on the whole, either college graduates or otherwise well-educated men, then and not until then will it be time to consider the advisability of adopting a three-year course in the Southern law schools.

The suggestion above made is based on a deep-seated conviction that, to the future lawyer, a sound general education is of far greater value than the knowledge gained in an additional year in a law school. It is better, in our opinion, to build a modest edifice on a sound basis than to put up a more pretentious structure on a less solid foundation. This statement may seem trite and commonplace. Nevertheless it apparently runs counter to the views now entertained by many legal educators, for chief emphasis appears to be laid on the importance of the three-year course. This is entirely in line with current tendencies in all lines of education. It is very much in vogue nowadays among professional educators in technical schools to lay emphasis on their special branches at the expense, too often, of the broader foundation to be obtained in the ordinary collegiate courses. This tendency very naturally results from the fact that, as each art and science develops, those who are engaged in teaching it find a larger and ever larger sphere for their work. But it is a tendency that nevertheless should be constantly tested and at times checked by the practical experience of every-day life.

If it be true, as the Board of Visitors recently said about army officers, that they should first of all be educated gentlemen, how much more true this is of the members of the legal profession. One does not have to argue that the law is the profession that, above all others, demands that its members should be broad-minded and should have the widest possible range of intellectual horizon. There is hardly any branch of human knowledge upon which at times the lawyer does not have to levy contribution. Therefore it is important that he should start with the best practicable equipment in the way of general education. To our mind the man who has a full collegiate education and who then gets some sort of a start in law, such as may be had in an honest two-year course, will be found to be much better off in the long run than the man who either cuts his collegiate education out or truncates it in the middle, in order to take three full years of professional instruction.

Always, in considering the needs of purely professional training in the law, it should be borne in mind that when a serious man embarks in the legal profession, he thereby dedicates the faculties of his whole mature life to that calling. In the course of years, as his experience widens and as opportunities present themselves, the man and the lawyer develop. All the powers of his nature are concentrated on the one branch of learning. The danger here is, not so much that the lawyer will become too little versed in the technical learning of his science, but rather that he will become narrowed by running too long in the same grooves.

It is also to be remembered that, after all, practical experience is the great school in which to learn the science of law. You cannot turn out a finished lawyer at the end of a two-year course. Not a whit more can you do so at the end of a three-year course. We have an idea that it takes five, or six, or ten years, according to the capacities and opportunities of the individual, to develop such a product as that. And many, very many, never reach the stage of the finished lawyer at all, simply because they are incapable of reaching it. We repeat, only the school of experience can turn out the finished lawyer.

There is another consideration that would, in our judgment, under present conditions, mark the adoption of the three-year course in many law schools of the country as a hasty and unadvised step. In order to be profitable, the three-year course presupposes and requires a large equipment and an extensive faculty such as many of our law schools do not now, and cannot soon, supply. The law student should not be kept too long under the tuition of the same instructors. In the three-year school the teaching faculty should be large in order that, at the different stages of his professional studies, the student may be brought into contact with different minds. He should learn not to judge things by the standard of any one man or set of men. Always it should be said of him,

"Nullius addictus jurare in verba magistri."

The law course should not be a mere extended collaboration of study between the student and a limited set of teachers. Better for him to get out in the world and be in actual contact with mankind and the profession at large. In the great universities, located in or near large cities, it is no doubt practicable to supply a faculty large enough and varied enough to meet the defect we have mentioned and thus make the extension of the course in these universities to three years desirable and proper. But what can be done there cannot be done everywhere. Those universities simply have exceptional facilities and advantages for which they should be duly thankful. We should be slow indeed to advise any young man of parts to put himself for three full years under the tuition of the law faculties of many of our schools as they are at present constituted or as they can be constituted at any early day. This is no reflection on the personnel of those faculties. However fine the qualities of an instructor may be, there is a limit to the stimulative effect he is capable of exerting, and unless the faculty is large and the equipment of the school quite complete, it is better, as was said above, for the young man to get out and seek the intellectual prod elsewhere.

But it is said that lawyers have great responsibilities, that large interests are committed to them, and that therefore the public must be protected from the ignorant and incompetent, just as it should be protected from quackery in the medical profession. A consideration of the conditions under which the young lawyer is placed at the outset of his practice will show that the necessity for such protection is not so great in the case of the legal profession as one might superficially suppose. It is often said that the law is a jealous mistress; but, if this be true, it is also true that the law is a very kind mistress, especially to the beginner. The young lawyer is really an apprentice. This is recognized by the public, by other lawyers, and, best of all, usually by himself. At the beginning he is not often given the management of complicated affairs. He is put to do things that an apprentice in the business may well be trusted to do. If, perchance, important things come his way, he does not usually have to act at once. There is an appreciable interval of time for consideration and thought before the critical steps have to be taken. The young medical practitioner may be confronted on the first day of his work with the most difficult and complicated case that could arise. The exigency may be such as to require immediate action, and the issue may be that of life or death. The lawyer is not thus placed. Usually he does not have to be hasty. He has time to plan and, in a measure, feel his way before him. In a pinch he will find the more experienced practitioner to help him with friendly counsel and advice. This is a great advantage in his favor, and it is a reason why the public welfare is not so much jeopardized by the existence of a somewhat lower standard of purely professional education in law than in other professions. However, we are no advocate of low professional standards. We are an advocate of the highest practicable standard of preparatory collegiate work, and believe that in the end this will prove to be the best means of raising the professional standard in the law.

Legal education should preserve a just balance between the collegiate and the professional, and when we commit ourselves to the proposition that there must, at all events, be at least three years of technical legal schooling and that these three must be had even at the sacrifice of the later years of collegiate work, then all sense of due proportion seems to be lost. Rather than to have such overaccentuation of the technical learning, it would be better to give the intending lawyer the benefit of the full collegiate course and then, as was said above, just some sort of a start in law. We think that, in a very short time after getting into actual practice, such a young man would be found to be fully on a par with another who, with a less extended collegiate course, may have had the benefit of the entire three years in law. And that the college graduate would have much the best chance for larger development in the long run, we do not doubt. Is not this conclusion corroborated by the observation and experience of lawyers at large and by the history of the legal profession in England and America for hundreds of years? The law school, as we now know it, is a very modern institution, and it is, we may add, an institution almost peculiar to this country. What a young lawyer does not learn in such a school he may learn later; but, when he quits the collegiate course in the arts or sciences, what he leaves behind is, as a general rule, gone forever. No doubt the relative values of general collegiate training and professional training in a school of law will be found to differ in different men; but if there is found, in a particular person, any element capable of the finer finish that can be obtained only from the general course in arts or sciences, it is far better for that person to finish the college course than to stop sooner in order to take three full years of instruction in law.

That the purport of this paper may not be misunderstood, we wish to say that we believe a three-year course, or even a longer course, in law to be a very fine thing, especially when it follows, as it does in Harvard, upon the heels of a full collegiate course. But in considering the status and policy of schools where only two years of work are required and where the conditions of admission are far below the high standard set by Harvard, it is necessary to choose between the two lines of advancement. These schools must decide whether it is best to begin at the top or at the bottom. For our part we think it better to begin at the bottom.

We close this paper with a reference to a fact that has a peculiar bearing on the problems now before Southern educators. It is an observed phenomenon in nature that all forms of life develop more quickly in warm climates than in the cold regions. Plants are more rapid in their growth in tropical places, and humankind is there more precocious, both physically and mentally. Now, somewhere between the equator and the pole, this fact may rightfully be taken into account in determining the period of training to be required of those intended for professional work. Certainly, in a southern country, it may well be expected that the period of school and college work shall end at a somewhat earlier age than in a country farther north. Upon the point as to how great this difference in time should be, we express no opinion. However, we may be permitted to suggest that by future experience it may be discovered that the climatic difference between, say, the States of Massachusetts and Alabama, is rightly interpreted, in matters of education, by putting it at about a year. If there be anything in this suggestion, it cannot be considered unreasonable that the colleges in that extensive region from the Potomac and Ohio to the Rio Grande should be slow to extend the professional course in law over another year. For our own part we certainly hope to see the problem of legal education in the South solved by some other means than the too precipitate adoption of the uniform three-year course.

THOMAS A. STREET.

PSYCHOLOGY IN THE COURTS.

IN my article on "Yellow Psychology" in the October number of LAW NOTES I said that "on almost every topic that has a proximate and practical relation to the trustworthiness of testimony delivered in court, the judges have the psychologists 'beaten a mile.'" Replying in the November number, Professor Münsterberg says: "I had, indeed, not known that the jurists of the land were so excellently versed in psychological knowledge." It would be very remarkable if one with an earned reputation for learning on two continents had found time to read thousands of volumes of law reports. But in no other way could he gain the information which he lacks. Text treatises and digests give us nothing worth mentioning concerning the methods of judges in solving questions of fact; upon such and such evidence "it was held" so and so, that is all. The investigator must read law reports page by page. Accordingly I have read in that way something like 2,000 volumes of reports, including every case in New Jersey, every case in the sixty-seven volumes of the Atlantic Reporter — perhaps 25,000 — every case in the "Federal Cases" series — upwards of 18,000 — every case in 120 volumes of the "Federal Reporter" and nearly all the other cases in that set, nearly every case in the United States Supreme Court reports, every case in the 189 New York Court of Appeals reports and some tens of thousands of other New York cases, hundreds of volumes of State reports, about 300 volumes of Canadian reports in the various provinces — also the Prince Edward Island and Newfoundland reports — all the Hawaiian reports, thousands and thousands of English cases, and scattering volumes of Bombay, Australian, and New Zealand reports. Of course I did not do all this reading as a mere pastime. Some of the results will soon appear in book form. Meanwhile, perhaps I am entitled to say that I speak by the card when I describe the attainments of judges in the science of psychology.

Samuel Rossiter Betts was a judge of the United States District Court for the Southern District of New York, from Dec. 21, 1826, to May, 1867 — forty years on the bench in the busiest of federal districts. Probably the great majority of his reported opinions, especially in equity and admiralty cases, discuss questions of fact as well as of law. It is said that during his first twenty years on the bench no appeal was taken from any of his decisions, although the most eminent lawyers in America practiced in his court, and although a judge's finding on questions of fact in equity and admiralty cases is reviewable *de novo* on appeal. For forty years he was an experimental psychologist, presiding over experiments in his court room conducted under the tremendous advantages of cross-examination, checked and counterchecked by the zeal and ingenuity of great lawyers in forensic struggles, and concerning real and not mimic occurrences. And yet it has been strongly urged that if such judges would use colored paper squares in testing witnesses there might be greater assurance of accuracy in their conclusions!

Professor Münsterberg showed to a class of students some pairs of colored paper squares. About one-fifth of the students erroneously judged that the gray was darker than the dark blue. In the next experiment nearly all of the students who thus erred failed to notice what he was doing with his left hand while he held up in his right hand a revolving wheel, which was made to change its color, and towards which he eagerly turned his eyes. His deduction was as follows (italics mine): "The coincidence, therefore, proved clearly how very quickly a little experiment such as this with a piece of blue paper, which can be performed in a few seconds, can pick out for us *those minds which are utterly unfit to report whether an action has been performed in their presence or not.*" That is to say, a witness's inability to distinguish shades of color instantly, a matter involving at least a slight degree of judgment, is to be used as a factor in determining the trustworthiness of his sworn statement that he saw, for example, a traveler within three rods of him stop and look up and down a railroad track before attempting to cross it. An "*occurrence* in his presence" — and a colorless occurrence, too — is to be put in juxtaposition with something that was not an occurrence!

As to Professor Münsterberg's last experiment, it showed *non*observation by the unfortunate one-fifth. But in the supposed case of a traveler at a crossing the witness has *mis*observed or else he has lied. His conviction of error in the experiment would be utterly irrelevant to either alternative. If one-fifth of the Harvard undergraduates are, as Professor Münsterberg asserts, "unfit to report whether an action has been performed in their presence," they ought, for their own sakes, to be forbidden to go upon the public highways unattended. If they cannot observe accurately enough to "report," they are incompetent to observe for the protection of their lives or limbs on thoroughfares traversed by automobiles and other vehicles or crossed by railroad trains, for all these are "actions in their presence" to which "they are blind and deaf and idiotic," as the professor says. Am I to be reproved for terming this sort of hyperbole "Yellow Psychology"?

Under the pretentious title "What Is the Value of Evidence?" the *Strand Magazine*, September, 1907, Professor Ed. Claparede, director of the psychological laboratory at the University of Geneva — experimental psychologist, mark you, and would-be instructor of judges — proclaims his discovery that testimony elicited by leading questions is apt to be untrustworthy! Surely in these pages comment would be superfluous. Again, speaking of one of his experiments, he says: "It shows us, in the first place, how great is the confidence each of us places in his own memory. When we have no recollection of an object about which we are questioned, we are inclined to deny the existence of that object rather than question the faithfulness of our memory. Rather than say 'I do not know,' we are ready to deny." The learned professor declares that "a result such as this is very instructive." Certainly; it is instructive to the learned professor. Would it be instructive to Judge Dayton, of the New Jersey Supreme Court, whose judicial experiments had taught him that "this rash mode of swearing does not alter the legal nature of the evidence, which is positive or negative in its character according to the facts sworn to, and not according to the phraseology of the witnesses"? Den *v.* Matlack, 17 N. J. L. 86, 114. Similar statements occur in other reported cases.

A naive inquiry by Professor Claparede is (italics mine), "whether evidence given by men of good faith really deserves the confidence with which it is usually accepted, *and which is expressly accorded to it by the codes of every country.*" It is to smile.

Psychologists incessantly remind us that recollection involves a process of inference, and that an inference may be incorrect. "The researches of modern psychologists, notably those of Helmholtz, have shown how largely inference enters into perceptions of sight and hearing. . . . Likewise, in recollection we remember parts of series of events, we infer others. Even the filling in of imagined details is largely a matter of inference." Dr. William H. Burnham, in "Illusions of Memory," *Scribner's Magazine*, February, 1892, p. 188.

Judges have greater familiarity with these vagaries of memory than any psychologist. While the latter refers to his "researches" as the source of his knowledge, the judge, without conveying any idea of profundity, merely alludes to "the day's work" in his court room for ten, twenty, or, as in the case of Judge Betts, for forty years. Thus, in Pierce *v.* Brady, 23 Beav. 64, 70, Sir John Romilly, M. R., speaking in 1856, said: "In the examination of the evidence of witnesses, great difficulties of various sorts arise, and one of the difficulties and dangers with which the court has constantly to deal, in examining the evidence of witnesses who are perfectly honest and give their evidence perfectly *bona fide*, arises from their turning inference into recollection." Any federal judge who has sat long in the Second Circuit — Wallace, Lacombe, or Coxe, for instance — could write a manual on "Memory of Witnesses in Patent Suits." An admiralty judge acquires a great store of knowledge concerning the strength and weakness of honest testimony in collision and salvage cases. Having read every reported admiralty case of any kind in the United States and Canada and nearly every one in England, I have written a chapter of thirty pages on "Course and Bearing of Vessels," and another of twenty pages on "The Weather," consisting entirely of classified observations of English, Canadian, and United States judges — observations on the weight of direct and circumstantial evidence, of weather bureau predictions and reports, etc., made in the course of their judicial "experiments."

Superiority of testimony to the performance or nonperformance of an act by the witness himself was remarked by Cicero in his speech for Archias, the poet, when he told the judges he would prove conclusively that his client was enrolled as a citizen of Heraclea. "There is a man present," said he, "a most scrupulous and truthful man, Lucius Lucullus, who will tell you not that he thinks it, but that he knows it; not that he has heard of it, but that he saw it; not even that he was present when it was done, but that he did it himself." And in a great number and variety of cases courts have applied the rule, to which I have given the appellation "The Actor Rule," and by force of which the actor's testimony is awarded greater probative weight than the testimony of mere observers or inconclusive inferences from facts proved. There is a strong presumption that his recollection will be more definite and trustworthy than that of any one else, because of the higher degree of attention and interest which he bestows upon his own acts. One of numerous examples occurs where it is contended that the required locomotive signals were not given when a train approached a crossing; "the best evidence of the fact in dispute would be the testimony of those persons who, on the particular occasion in question, had the custody or management of the bell or whistle." Greany *v.* Long Island R. Co., 101 N. Y. 419, 5 N. E. Rep. 425, *per* Danforth, J. As far as my knowledge goes — of course I may be mistaken — no experimental or speculative psychologist has done or pointedly said anything that would assist a judge in arriving at such a conclusion or fortify his opinion. Professors of psychology delight in reaction-time experiments, which some of them have carried out on an elaborate scale. Probably the judges do not know the exact fractions of seconds that appear in the tabulations. Possibly they don't care. Very likely the judges have not learned the fact which Professor Jevons laboriously brought to light, that "by counting instantaneously beans thrown into a box . . . the number 6 was guessed correctly 120 times out of 147, 5 correctly 102 times out of 107, and 4 and 3 always right." James, Principles of Psychology, vol. 2, p. 406 *et seq.* Again I say perhaps this specific information would not greatly interest the judges. By their own experiments, however, judges have found that the man whose hands moved the helm of a vessel knows and remembers whether or not her course was changed before a collision, better than witnesses on other vessels who testify from observation of her course. The knowledge thus acquired has been applied in at least half a hundred reported cases. There are some exceptions and qualifications to the Actor Rule, and in respect of these the judicial experiments have guided to satisfactory conclusions in legal controversies.

Where the engineer and fireman of a locomotive give warning signals for crossings at short intervals throughout every day, their testimony from unaided memory that this was done at a specified crossing days or weeks before, when nothing whatever occurred to fix their attention upon the fact, is regarded as extremely weak evidence. State *v.* Kansas City, etc., R. Co., 70 Mo. App. 634, 643. In the case cited I suppose Judge Gill might very properly have quoted Professor James's statement that "habit diminishes the conscious attention with which our acts are performed." Principles of Psychology, vol. 1, p. 114.

But in a case where a man was struck and killed at a crossing the court said: "After the accident occurred the train was stopped, and it was very natural to suppose the events made a very deep impression on the mind. It was the duty of the engineer and fireman to give the usual signals, and the events were such they would certainly remember whether the signals had been given. When in the presence of the dead they must have remembered whether they gave the usual signals just a few moments before, and, if so, no lapse of time would efface it from their recollection. It is true, then, the usual signals were given, or else these witnesses have deliberately sworn to falsehoods. It was not possible for them, under the circumstances, to have been mistaken." St. Louis, etc., R. Co. *v.* Manly, 58 Ill. 300, 309, *per* Mr. Justice Scott. What psychologist has ever deigned to notice specifically this common phenomenon which I, a layman, would term "retroactive attention," and which has been recognized by judges in many similar cases?

Dr. Burnham, of Clark University, has written an interesting monograph on "Retroactive Amnesia." *American Journal of Psychology*, July–October, 1903, pp. 118–132. The importance of the subject has by no means escaped the attention of judges. For example, "sudden and extreme pain drives from the memory what immediately preceded it, to a greater or less extent," said Judge Vredenburgh, in New Jersey R. Co. *v.* Palmer, 33 N. J. Law 90, 92. In another case of severe accidental injury the court speaks of "unconsciousness, which renders the sufferer unable, in most instances, to recollect anything that occurred." Griffith *v.* Baltimore, etc., R. Co., 44 Fed. Rep. 574, 576, *per* Sage, J. See also Jones *v.* Morton Co., 14 Ont. Law Rep. 402, 409. In such a case, the injured person's admission of contributory fault, which is strong evidence against him in ordinary cases, might prejudice him very little. See Curtis *v.* Central R. Co., 6 McLean (U. S.) 401, 6 Fed. Cas. No. 350 (at p. 1004), *per* Mr. Justice McLean, instructing a jury.

The foregoing references to decided cases are given only as some "evidence of good faith" — I have cited thousands in my books — when I say that judges' bellies are not altogether filled with the east wind. "From the experience we have in this place, we know," etc., said Sir John Nicholl, in Reay *v.* Cowcher, 2 Hag. 249, 4 Eng. Ecc. 109, 112, alluding to certain frailties of memory and observation. And so it is with judges everywhere.

A former trial judge, and judge of the highest of one of the State courts, now one of the foremost law school professors in this country, writes to me as follows in regard to the Münsterberg experiments: "I have no hesitation in saying that if I were a judge I would not permit any 'experimental psychology' whatever to be practiced in my court room. I can imagine nothing better designed to confuse issues and to distract attention from real tests of credibility, etc., based on the experience of mankind." One of the most successful trial judges in New England, who has served twenty years on the bench at *nisi prius*, and is now a judge of a court of last resort, says he concurs in those sentiments. For some remarks on the embarrassment that would be caused by collateral issues if such experiments were entertained, see Bell *v.* Rinner, 16 Ohio St. 46; Goodwyn *v.* Goodwyn, 20 Ga. 620. In Heath *v.* State, 93 Ga. 446, 21 S. E. Rep. 77, the trial judge was sustained in his refusal to allow the power of vision of a witness under cross-examination to be tested by requiring him to go to the window and look at an object on the street not visible to the judge and jury from their positions in the court room. It is not at all improbable that the ordinary constitutional guaranties would protect a witness from a compulsory inquisition which would expose his physical infirmities, such as color blindness or other defect in vision, when they are absolutely irrelevant to any issue in the case. See Goodwin *v.* State, 114 Wis. 318, 90 N. W. Rep. 170, 171.

Would a psychological expert be allowed to supplement his tests by expressing his opinion that a witness is or is not a trustworthy observer? Not until Dr. Doyle (Sherlock Holmes) is allowed to testify to his opinion of the guilt or innocence of a defendant in a criminal case — not until then. Expert testimony has already become so scandalously degraded that in the last several years medico-legal societies, bar associations, and legislators have been striving to find some means to relieve the courts from its enormities.

In the November LAW NOTES Professor Münsterberg argues that the psychological expert should be called, like any other scientist, to the assistance of courts. "If there is a brain disease, they call an alienist," etc. When and where did an alienist ever undertake to pass judgment on a single person by "a little experiment . . . performed in a few seconds" which sufficed for Professor Münsterberg's conclusion that one-fifth of the Harvard undergraduates ought not to be allowed to go at large without a keeper? If an alienist should make such an attempt in court, he would not retire unscathed.

CHARLES C. MOORE.

ROGUES' GALLERY LAW.

IT is generally conceded that the police may photograph criminals for the purpose of making their identification easy in the event they escape or continue to break the law. The police department of every city of any size in the United States has its "Rogues' Gallery." But when may the right to photograph be exercised? Does arrest give the right, or does indictment, or is it necessary to wait until the accused has been convicted?

This question has been raised recently in Brooklyn, N. Y., by one William Gow, who is under indictment on a charge of having participated in certain alleged frauds in connection with the management of a bank. It is obvious that the question is one of great importance, and it is remarkable that it has been raised so seldom. It is possible, if not probable, that police officers, in their efforts to detect crime, have frequently overstepped the bounds of their authority and invaded the rights of real or suspected criminals.

In the Gow case, which has not yet been reported except in the daily newspapers, it appears that Mr. Gow, after having been indicted and arrested, was photographed and measured under the Bertillon system. He thereupon filed a petition in the Supreme Court for a writ of mandamus compelling the police commissioner to remove from the police department all photographs and measurements taken of him. According to the New York *Times*, the petition was denied on the ground that mandamus was not the proper remedy, but the court asserted that the action of the police was criminal in character, and that they were liable to prosecution for assault, and also to a civil action for damages. The court declared that the police power was dependent upon legislative enactment, and that it was necessary for them to show legislative authority for the acts complained of. "No statute has been found," said Mr. Justice Burr, "which in express terms authorizes any member of the police force of this city to deprive any person of his liberty of action or invade his right of personal immunity to the extent of requiring him to submit to having his photograph taken and measurements and impressions of his body made for the purpose of preserving them in the criminal records of this department, simply because such person has been indicted charged with a criminal offense." The court pointed out that the police asserted that implied authority for their acts was to be found in two provisions of the city charter, and in an amendment to the Penal Code adopted by the last legislature. The police commissioner was thus required to make such rules, orders, and regulations as might be reasonably necessary to effect a prompt and efficient exercise of all powers conferred upon him by law. But if no power was conferred upon him by law in this regard, any rule he might promulgate respecting the same was utterly void. "The exercise of any such extreme police power as is here contended for," continued the justice, "is contrary to the spirit of Anglo-Saxon liberty. The construction contended for by the police department is in direct conflict with the provisions of the charter itself, which makes it the duty of every member of the police force, under the penalty of a fine or dismissal from the force, immediately upon an arrest to convey the offender, not to police headquarters to be photographed and measured, but 'before the nearest sitting magistrate,' that he may be dealt with according to law."

In Owens v. Partridge, 40 Misc. (N. Y.) 415, it was held that a person who has been arrested upon suspicion of having committed a crime, and whose photograph and Bertillon measurements have been taken by the police department, is not entitled to a mandatory injunction ordering the destruction or surrender of the photograph and the measurements, notwithstanding the fact that when he was arraigned before a police magistrate he was discharged for lack of evidence that he had committed a crime. The court held that the remedy of such person, if any, was at law. It also held that he was not entitled to relief upon the ground that his right of privacy had been invaded, as no such right exists in the State of New York. In that case the court, in discussing the question as to whether it is lawful for the police to take photographs of a person who is merely suspected of crime, said: "It is a well-known fact, however, and admitted by the defendant, that the Rogues' Gallery contains, as well, the photographs of persons merely suspected of crime. How far this may be justified as a police measure may be a question not easy of solution. Professor Tiedeman intimates that where the suspicion is well founded the right exists. 1 Tiedeman 157, 158. But what is a well-founded suspicion? Where the person photographed is not an habitual criminal, or has never been convicted of crime so that preventive measures might be justified, or where the suspicion, directed to a particular case, has not sufficient legal basis in fact to warrant some criminal proceeding — the definition of a 'suspicious person' becomes vague and shadowy, varying with the circumstances of each case, and measures like those under consideration may approach dangerously near an arbitrary interference with personal rights. In this case the arrest has nothing but suspicion to support it, and were it necessary to inquire into the foundation of the suspicion, it would, on the facts disclosed, be found to rest on hearsay merely. The sworn statement of several detectives that the plaintiff was known to them for years as a common cheat and gambler, as an associate of criminals and disreputable persons, without the disclosure of any fact showing the source of such knowledge, can hardly be deemed sufficient."

It has been held recently in Louisiana that the photographing of a person accused of crime should be postponed until he is convicted, unless it is evident that the photograph should be taken before conviction for the purpose of identification or for the detection of the crime. Itzkovitch v. Whitaker, 115 La. 479, 117 La. 707; Schulman v. Whitaker, 115 La. 628, 117 La. 704. In each of those cases the person seeking relief was a pawnbroker whose photograph had been taken after he had been arrested for having received stolen goods. The police contended in each case that the accused had been conducting a "fence" where thieves might sell stolen property without being asked embarrassing questions, and that he had been arrested repeatedly. The court, however, granted an injunction in each case, on the ground that the accused had not been convicted, and that the taking of his picture constituted an invasion of his right of privacy. In Schulman v. Whitaker, 117 La. 704, the court, in the course of its opinion, said: "After his conviction, it will be time to determine whether or not his picture should be taken and placed in the Rogues' Gallery; not before, in this particular case, for, while from all appearances plaintiff must have engaged in a pretty active business in his line, the proper place to inquire into the violations of the criminal law in connection with that business is before a tribunal having jurisdiction in the premises. Before that is done, his picture should not be taken."

In State v. Clausmeier, 154 Ind. 599, a person who had been arrested for forgery, and acquitted, brought an action on the official bond of the sheriff who had arrested him to recover damages for the sheriff's action in taking his photograph and placing it in the Rogues' Gallery. The court, in holding that the sheriff's action did not constitute a breach of his official bond, whether or not it rendered him liable to an action of libel, said: "It is the duty of a sheriff to confine in jail and safely keep all persons in his custody awaiting trial on a charge of crime until lawfully discharged, and, if they escape, to pursue and recapture them. A sheriff, in making an arrest for a felony on a warrant, has the right to exercise a discretion, not only as to the means taken to apprehend the person named in the warrant, but also as to the means necessary to keep him safe and secure after such apprehension until lawfully discharged; and he has the right to take such steps and adopt such measure as in his discretion may appear to be necessary to the identification and recapture of persons in his custody if they should escape. Unless this discretion is abused through malice, wantonness, or a reckless disregard for and a selfish indifference to the common dictates of humanity, the officer is not liable. . . . It would seem, therefore, if in the discretion of the sheriff he should deem it necessary to the safekeeping of a prisoner, and to prevent his escape, or to enable him the more readily to retake the prisoner if he should escape, to take his photograph, and a measurement of his height, and ascertain his weight, name, residence, place of birth, occupation, color of his eyes, hair, and beard, as was done in this case, he could lawfully do so. The complaint does not charge that any physical force was used to induce the relator to have his negative taken, or to furnish the sheriff the information above mentioned not obtainable by observation."

In People v. York, 27 Misc. (N. Y.) 658, it was held that a person who has been convicted of an assault and has been sentenced therefor to the city workhouse, who has frequently been arrested, and who is an associate of criminals, is not entitled to a mandamus compelling the police commissioner to remove his picture from the Rogues' Gallery, the court saying: "It is well settled that a mandamus will issue only to compel a public officer to perform a duty imposed upon him by law. There is no duty in respect to the matter now before the court imposed upon the police commissioners. If the police commissioners have wronged the relator at all, that wrong is in the nature of a libel, for which he has an adequate remedy at law."

In Molineux v. Collins, 177 N. Y. 395, it was held that one confined in a State prison under sentence of death is a criminal so long as the sentence remains in force, that his photograph and measurements, made and recorded in the manner prescribed by statute, are properly made and constitute public records, and that the fact that upon a subsequent trial he is acquitted does not entitle him to a mandamus to compel the superintendent of State prisons to remove such records and deliver them to him. In the course of its opinion in that case the court said: "The measurements and record, therefore, were made by authority of law and became the property of the State, which paid 'the necessary expenses incurred' for the purpose. L. 1896, c. 440, § 2. They were public records and were beyond the control of the superintendent of prisons, except for preservation and use. He had no power to destroy them or give them away, or surrender them even to one who, although under judgment of death when they were made, was finally adjudged not guilty. The custodian of a public record cannot deface it or give it up without authority from the same source which required it to be made. The statute directed the superintendent to make the record, and when he made it the State made it, and it has not authorized him to destroy it under any circumstances, not even to relieve a citizen from an unjust reflection upon his character. It would be usurpation of power for him to surrender the record or for the court to direct him to do so. If the position of the defendant is sound, where is the destruction of public records to end? What may become of the indictment, the minutes of the clerk recording the verdict of guilty, and the judgment of conviction? May the death warrant be withdrawn from the custody of the warden, although it is the only authority he had for the imprisonment of Molineux while he was awaiting execution? Even the courts, which have control of their own records, do not direct one made through error to be physically destroyed, although they vacate it and direct that it shall be held for naught. Our order of reversal and the judgment acquitting the defendant are public records, open to the inspection of all, which neutralize every legal presumption against him arising from the judgment of conviction."

On principle as well as authority it would seem that the police should not be allowed to take photographs or measurements until after the conviction of the accused in a court of competent jurisdiction, and not then unless the crime is one of violence or one involving moral turpitude. To permit the accused to be photographed before he has been convicted is virtually to permit the police to usurp a judicial function and say that he is guilty. It is no answer to this objection to say that it is well understood that every Rogues' Gallery contains pictures of suspected as well as of convicted criminals. That is simply begging the question. If a Rogues' Gallery may be filled with the photographs of persons suspected of crime, why not fill our prisons with such persons themselves? It is, of course, of the first importance that the police shall not be hampered by unreasonable restrictions in their efforts to detect and prevent crime; but it is of at least equal importance that citizens shall not be deprived of rights secured to them by the law. The question of the advisability of photographing persons who are merely accused of crime is a legislative and not a ministerial one. If the legislature sees fit, it may confer that power upon the police, but the grant should be coupled with such restrictions upon its exercise as will protect accused persons from the overzeal of somewhat cynical officials who are apt to think, and honestly think, that a person accused of crime is a person guilty of crime.

It would seem to be just, also, to destroy the photographs of a person who, after having been convicted of a criminal offense, is acquitted on a subsequent trial. It is difficult, however, to see how this can be done, in the absence of a permissive statute. It may be remarked here that such a statute has been passed in New York since the decision in the Molineux case was handed down.

The decisions in the Louisiana cases, cited *supra*, are based upon the ground that the photographing of an accused person before his conviction is an invasion of his right of privacy. With all respect to the able judges who compose the Supreme Court of Louisiana, the reason given for the decisions is hardly a satisfactory one. Waiving all consideration of the moot question of whether the law recognizes an invasion of the right of privacy as an actionable wrong, the decisions might well have been placed on the ground that photographing before conviction constitutes a violation of the due process clause of the Federal Constitution. The action of the police in photographing a person who is merely accused of crime is tantamount to a finding that he is guilty, before he has been found guilty by a competent tribunal proceeding in the manner prescribed by law.

J. C. M.

COMPILATION OF THE CODES OF ETHICS ADOPTED BY THE STATE BAR ASSOCIATIONS IN ALABAMA, COLORADO, GEORGIA, KENTUCKY, MARYLAND, MICHIGAN, MISSOURI, NORTH CAROLINA, VIRGINIA, WISCONSIN, AND WEST VIRGINIA.[1]

THE Code of the Alabama State Bar Association, as it is the foundation of all the other codes, is made the basis of this compilation. All concurrences therein, additions thereto, or eliminations and material alterations therefrom are noted. The Missouri Bar Association, alone of all the others, has incorporated synoptic headings with each canon adopted by it; in this compilation these headings are noted in italics in front of all the canons to which they are applicable.

At the commencement of the Alabama Code are the following introductory statements:

[Paragraph I.] The purity and efficiency of judicial administration, which under our system is largely governmental itself, depend as much upon the character, conduct, and demeanor of attorneys in this great trust, as upon the fidelity and learning of courts, or the honesty and intelligence of juries.

[Paragraph II.] "There is perhaps no profession, after that of the sacred ministry, in which a high-toned morality is more imperatively necessary than that of the law. There is certainly, without any exception, no profession in which so many temptations beset the path to swerve from the lines of strict integrity; in which so many delicate and difficult questions of duty are constantly arising. There are pitfalls and mantraps at every step, and the mere youth, at the very outset of his career, needs often the prudence and self-denial, as well as the moral courage, which belong properly to riper years. High moral principle is the only safe guide; the only torch to light his way amidst darkness and obstruction." — SHARSWOOD.

[Paragraph III.] A comprehensive summary of the duties specifically enjoined by law upon attorneys, which they are sworn "not to violate," is found in section 791 of the Code of Alabama. These duties are:

"First. To support the Constitution and laws of this State and the United States.

"Second. To maintain the respect due to courts of justice and judicial officers.

"Third. To employ for the purpose of maintaining the causes confided to them such means only as are consistent with truth, and never seek to mislead the judges by any artifice or false statement of the law.

"Fourth. To maintain inviolate the confidence, and at every peril to themselves to preserve the secrets, of their clients.

"Fifth. To abstain from all offensive personalities, and to advance no fact prejudicial to the honor or reputation of a party or a witness, unless required by the justice of the cause with which they are charged.

"Sixth. To encourage neither the commencement nor continuance of an action proceeding from any motive of passion or interest.

"Seventh. Never to reject, for any consideration personal to themselves, the cause of the defenseless and oppressed."

[Paragraph IV.] No rule will determine an attorney's duty in the varying phases of every case. What is right and proper must, in the absence of statutory rules and an authoritative code, be ascertained in view of the peculiar facts, in the light of conscience, and the conduct of honorable and distinguished

1 Prepared by the Committee on Code of Professional Ethics of the American Bar Association. The committee is distributing this compilation in order to receive advice and comments to assist it in framing a code of ethics to be submitted to the next meeting of the association.

attorneys in similar cases, and by analogy to the duties enjoined by statute, and the rules of good neighborhood.

[Paragraph V.] The following general rules are adopted by the Alabama State Bar Association for the guidance of its members:

"Craft is the vice, not the spirit, of the profession. Trick is professional prostitution. Falsehood is professional apostasy. The strength of a lawyer is in thorough knowledge of legal truth, in thorough devotion to legal right. Truth and integrity can do more in the profession than the subtlest and wiliest devices. The power of integrity is the rule: the power of fraud is the exception. Emulation and zeal lead lawyers astray; but the general law of the profession is duty, not success. In it, as elsewhere in human life, the judgment of success is but the verdict of little minds. Professional duty, faithfully and well performed, is the lawyer's glory. This is equally true of the bench and of the bar." — RYAN. (Wis.)

The oath of office prescribed by law, "I do solemnly swear that I will support the Constitution of the United States and the Constitution of this State, and that I will faithfully discharge the duties of the office of attorney and counselor-at-law, and solicitor and counselor in chancery, according to the best of my ability," includes within its terms all the duties formerly declared in the oath itself, viz.: "To behave himself in the office of attorney according to the best of his learning and ability, and with all good fidelity, as well to the court as to the client; that he will use no falsehood, nor delay any man's cause for lucre or malice." (Mich.)

Fidelity — to the court, to the client, to the claims of truth and honor — summarizes the duty of the lawyer. (Mich.)

Duties of Attorneys to Courts and Judicial Officers.

1. *Respect for Judicial Officers.* — The respect enjoined by law for courts and judicial officers is exacted for the sake of the office, and not for the individual who administers it. Bad opinion of the incumbent, however well founded, cannot excuse the withholding of the respect due the office, while administering its functions. (Ala., Ga., Va., Mich., Colo., N. C., Wis., Md., W. Va., Ky., Mo.)

2. *Criticisms of Judicial Conduct.* — The proprieties of the judicial station in a great measure disable the judge from defending himself against strictures upon his official conduct. For this reason, and because such criticisms tend to impair public confidence in the administration of justice, attorneys should, as a rule, refrain from published criticism of judicial conduct, especially in reference to causes in which they have been of counsel, otherwise than in courts of review, or when the conduct of a judge is necessarily involved in determining his removal from or continuance in office. (Ala., Ga., Va., Mich., Colo., N. C., W. Va., Md., Ky., Mo., Wis.)

3. *Using Personal Influence on the Court.* — Marked attention and unusual hospitality to a judge, when the relations of the parties are such that they would not otherwise be extended, subject both judge and attorneys to misconstructions and should be sedulously avoided. A self-respecting independence in the discharge of the attorney's duties, which at the same time does not withhold the courtesy and respect due the judge's station, is the only just foundation for cordial personal and official relations between bench and bar. All attempts by means beyond these to gain special personal consideration and favor of a judge are disreputable. (Ala., Ga., Va., Mich., Colo., N. C., Wis., Md., W. Va., Ky. And see Mo. Code, § 3.)

4. *Defending the Courts Against Popular Clamor.* — Courts and judicial officers, in the rightful exercise of their functions, should always receive the support and countenance of attorneys against unjust criticism and popular clamor; and it is an attorney's duty to give them his moral support in all proper ways, and particularly by setting a good example in his own person of obedience to law. (Ala., Ga., Va., Mich., Colo., N. C., Md., W. Va., Ky., Mo. See Wis. Code, § 4.)

5. *Candor and Fairness.* — The utmost candor and fairness should characterize the dealings of attorneys with the courts and with each other. Knowingly citing as authority an overruled case, or treating a repealed statute as in existence; knowingly misquoting the language of a decision or text-book; knowingly misquoting the contents of a paper, the testimony of a witness, or the language or argument of opposite counsel; offering evidence which it is known the court must reject as illegal, to get it before the jury, under the guise of arguing its admissibility; and all kindred practices, are deceits and evasions unworthy of attorneys.

Purposely concealing or withholding in the opening argument positions intended finally to be relied on, in order that opposite counsel may not discuss them, is unprofessional. Courts and juries look with disfavor on such practices, and are quick to suspect the weakness of the cause which has need to resort to them.

In the argument of demurrers, admission of evidence, and other questions of law, counsel should carefully refrain from "side-bar" remarks and sparring discourse, to influence the jury or bystanders. Personal colloquies between counsel tend to delay, and promote unseemly wrangling, and ought to be discouraged. (Ala., Colo., Wis., Mo. See also Va., § 5; N. C., § 5; W. Va., § 5; Md., § 5; Ga., § 5; Mich., § 5; Ky., § 5.)

6. Attorneys owe to the courts and the public whose business the courts transact, as well as to their own clients, to be punctual in attendance on their causes; and whenever an attorney is late he should apologize or explain his absence. (Ala., Ga., Va., Mich., Colo., N. C., Md., W. Va. See Wis. Code, § 6; Ky. Code, § 6.)

7. *Display of Temper.* — One side must always lose the cause; and it is not wise or respectful to the court for attorneys to display temper because of an adverse ruling. (Ala., Ga., Va., Mich., Colo., N. C., Wis., Md., W. Va., Ky., Mo.)

Duties of Attorneys to Each Other, to Clients, and the Public.

8. It is a mark of proper respect, and a practice worthy of adoption in all courts of record, for attorneys to rise and remain standing while the judges enter and take their seats upon the bench. (Wis.)

9. *Upholding the Dignity of the Profession.* — An attorney should strive at all times to uphold the honor, maintain the dignity, and promote the usefulness of the profession; for it is so interwoven with the administration of justice that whatever redounds to the good of one advances the other; and the attorney thus discharges not merely an obligation to his brothers, but a high duty to the State and his fellow man. (Ala., Ga., Va., Mich., Colo., N. C., Wis., Md., W. Va., Ky., Mo.)

10. *Disparaging Members of the Profession.* — An attorney should not speak slightingly or disparagingly of his profession, or pander in any way to unjust prejudices against it; and he should scrupulously refrain at all times, and in all relations of life, from availing himself of any prejudice or popular misconception against lawyers, in order to carry a point against a brother attorney. (Ala., Ga., Va., Mich., Colo., N. C., Md., W. Va., Ky., Mo.)

11. *How Far an Attorney May Go in Supporting a Client's Cause.* — Nothing has been more potential in creating and pandering to popular prejudice against lawyers as a class, and in withholding from the profession the full measure of public esteem and confidence which belong to the proper discharge of its duties, than the false claim, often set up by the unscrupulous in defense of questionable transactions, that it is an attorney's duty to do everything to succeed in his client's cause.

An attorney "owes entire devotion to the interest of his client, warm zeal in the maintenance and defense of his cause, and the exertion of the utmost skill and ability," to the end that nothing may be taken or withheld from him, save by the rules of law, legally applied. No sacrifice or peril, even to loss of life itself, can absolve from the fearless discharge of this duty. Nevertheless, it is steadfastly to be borne in mind that the great trust is to be performed within and not without the bounds of the law which creates it. The attorney's office does not destroy man's accountability to his Creator, or lessen the duty of obedience to law, and the obligation of his neighbor; and it does not permit, much less demand, violation of law, or any manner of fraud or chicanery, for the client's sake. (Ala., Ga., Va., Mich., Colo., N. C., Md., W. Va. See Wis. Code, § 10; Ky. Code, § 10; Mo. Code, § 10.)

12. *Exposing Corrupt Attorneys.* — Attorneys should fearlessly expose before the proper tribunals corrupt and dishonest conduct in the profession; and there should never be any hesitancy in accepting employment against an attorney who has wronged his client. (Ala., Ga., Va., Mich., Colo., N. C., Wis., Md., W. Va., Ky., Mo.)

13. *Attitude of State's Attorney Toward Innocent Prisoner.* — An attorney appearing or continuing as private counsel in the prosecution for a crime of which he believes the accused innocent, forswears himself. The State's attorney is criminal, if he presses for a conviction, when upon the evidence he believes the prisoner innocent. If the evidence is not plain enough to justify a *nolle prosequi*, a public prosecutor should submit the case, with such comments as are pertinent, accompanied by a candid statement of his own doubts. (Ala., Ga., Va., Mich., Colo., N. C., Wis., Md., W. Va., Ky., Mo.)

14. *Defending One Whom Advocate Believes to Be Guilty.* — An attorney cannot reject the defense of a person accused of a criminal offense, because he knows or believes him guilty. It is his duty by all fair and honorable means to present such defenses as the law of the land permits, to the end that no one may be deprived of life or liberty but by due process of law. (Ala., Colo., Mo., Ga., Va., Mich., N. C., Md., W. Va. See Ky. Code, § 13; Wis. Code, § 13.)

15. *Maintaining Harassing Litigation.* — An attorney must decline in a civil cause to conduct a prosecution, when satisfied that the purpose is merely to harass or injure the opposite party, or to work oppression and wrong. (Ala., Ga., Va., Mich., Colo., N. C., Wis., Md., W. Va., Ky., Mo.)

16. It is bad practice for an attorney to communicate or argue privately with the judge as to the merits of his cause. (Ala., Ga., Va., Mich., Colo., N. C., Wis., Md., W. Va., Ky.)

17. He should avoid all unnecessary communications with jurors, even as to matters foreign to the cause, both before and during the trial. (Md.)

18. *General Rules as to Professional and Unprofessional Advertising.* — Newspaper advertisements, circulars, and business cards, tendering professional services to the general public, are proper; but special solicitation of particular individuals to become clients ought to be avoided. Indirect advertisement for business, by furnishing or inspiring editorials or press notices, regarding causes in which the attorney takes part, the manner in which they are conducted, the importance of his positions, the magnitude of the interests involved, and all other like self-laudation, is of evil tendency, and wholly unprofessional. (Ala., Colo., N. C., Wis. See also § 16 of Codes of Ga., Va., Md., W. Va., Ky.; Mo. Code, § 45; Mich. Code, § 51.)

19. *Newspaper Discussion of Pending Litigation.* — Newspaper publications by an attorney as to the merits of pending or anticipated litigation, call forth discussion and reply from the opposite party, tend to prevent a fair trial in the courts, and otherwise prejudice the due administration of justice. It requires a strong case to justify such publications; and when proper, it is unprofessional to make them anonymously. (Ala., Ga., Mich., Colo., N. C., W. Va., Md., Mo., Wis., Ky.)

20. It is better that all newspaper reports be taken from the records and papers on file in the court. (Wis., Ky.)

21. *Where Attorney Becomes Witness for His Client.* — When an attorney is a witness for his client except as to formal matters, such as the attestation or custody of an instrument and the like, he should leave the trial of the cause to other counsel. Except when essential to the ends of justice, an attorney should scrupulously avoid testifying in court in behalf of his client, as to any matter. (Ala., Ga., Va., Colo., N. C., Wis., Md., W. Va., Ky., Mo. See also Mich. Code, § 38.)

22. *Impersonality of the Advocate.* — The same reasons which make it improper in general for an attorney to testify for his client apply with greater force to assertions, sometimes made by counsel in argument, of personal belief in the client's innocence or the justice of his cause. If such assertions are habitually made they lose all force and subject the attorney to falsehoods; while the failure to make them in particular cases will often be esteemed a tacit admission of belief of the client's guilt, or the weakness of his cause. (Ala., Colo., Wis. See also Codes of Mich., § 39; Ga., § 19; Va., § 19; N. C., § 19; Md., § 19; W. Va., § 19; Mo., § 19.)

23. *Stirring Up Litigation.* — It is indecent to hunt up defects in titles and the like, and inform thereof, in order to be employed to bring suit; or to seek out a person supposed to have a cause of action and endeavor to get a fee to litigate about it. Except where ties of blood, relationship, or trust make it an attorney's duty, it is unprofessional to volunteer advice to bring a lawsuit. Stirring up strife and litigation is forbidden by law, and disreputable in morals. (Ala., Ga., Va., Mich., Colo., N. C., Wis., Md., W. Va., Ky., Mo.)

24. *Confidential Communications.* — Communications and confidences between client and attorney are the property and secrets of the client, and cannot be divulged except at his instance; even the death of the client does not absolve the attorney from his obligation of secrecy. (Ala., Ga., Va., Mich., Colo., N. C., Wis., W. Va., Md., Ky. And see Mo. Code, § 16.)

25. *Accepting Adverse Retainers.* — The duty not to divulge the secrets of clients extends further than mere silence by the attorney, and forbids accepting retainers or employment afterwards from others involving the client's interests, in the matters about which the confidence was reposed. When the secrets or confidence of a former client may be availed of or be material, in a subsequent suit, as the basis of any judgment which may injuriously affect his rights, the attorney cannot appear in such cause, without the consent of his former client. (Ala., Ga., Mich., Colo., N. C., W. Va., Md., Ky. See Mo. Code, § 17.)

26. *Attacking His Own Instruments or Conveyances.* — An attorney can never attack an instrument or paper drawn by him for any infirmity apparent on its face; nor for any other cause where confidence has been reposed as to the facts concerning it. Where the attorney acted as a mere conveyancer, and was not consulted as to the facts, and unknown to him the transaction amounted to a violation of the criminal laws, he may assail it on that ground, in suits between third persons, or between parties to the instrument and strangers. (Ala., Mich., Mo., Ga., Va., N. C., W. Va., Md., Ky. See Wis. Code, § 23.)

27. *What Influences an Attorney May Use.* — An attorney openly, and in his true character, may render purely professional services before committees, regarding proposed legislation, and in advocacy of claims before departments of the government, upon the same principles of ethics which justify his appearance before the courts; but it is immoral and illegal for an attorney so engaged to conceal his attorneyship, or to employ secret personal solicitations, or to use means other than those addressed to the reason and understanding to influence action.

(Ala., Ga., Va., Mich., Colo., N. C., Md., W. Va., Mo. See also Wis. Code, § 22; Ky. Code, § 24.)

28. *Representing Conflicting Interests.* — An attorney can never represent conflicting interests in the same suit or transaction, except by express consent of all so concerned, with full knowledge of the facts. Even then such a position is embarrassing, and ought to be avoided. An attorney represents conflicting interests within the meaning of this rule, when it is his duty, in behalf of one of his clients, to contend for that which duty to other clients in the transaction requires him to oppose. (Ala., Va., Mich., Colo., N. C., Wis., Ky., Mo., Ga., W. Va., Md.)

29. "It is not a desirable professional reputation to live and die with — that of a rough tongue, which makes a man to be sought out and retained to gratify the malevolent feeling of a suitor, in hearing the other side well lashed and vilified." (Ala., Ga., Va., Mich., Colo., N. C., W. Va., Ky.)

30. *Ministering to Prejudices of His Client.* — An attorney is under no obligation to minister to the malevolence or prejudices of a client in the trial or conduct of a cause. The client cannot be made the keeper of the attorney's conscience in professional matters. He cannot demand as of right that his attorney shall abuse the opposite party or indulge in offensive personalities. The attorney, under the solemnity of his oath, must determine for himself whether such a course is essential to the ends of justice and therefore justifiable. (Ala., Ga., Va., Mich., Colo., N. C., Wis., W. Va., Ky., Mo.)

31. *Ill-feeling and Personalities Between Advocates.* — Clients and not their attorneys are the litigants; and whatever may be the ill-feeling existing between clients, it is unprofessional for attorneys to partake of it in their conduct and demeanor to each other, or to suitors in the case. (Ala., Ga., Va., Mich., Colo., N. C., Wis., Md., W. Va., Ky., Mo.)

32. (See synoptic heading to section 31, *supra.*) In the conduct of litigation and the trial of causes, the attorneys should try the merits of the cause, and not try each other. It is not proper to allude to, or comment upon, the personal history, or mental or physical peculiarities or idiosyncrasies of opposite counsel. Personalities should always be avoided, and the utmost courtesy always extended to an honorable opponent. (Ala., Ga., Va., Mich., Colo., N. C., Wis., W. Va., Ky., Mo.)

33. *Right of Attorney to Control the Incidental Matters of the Trial.* — As to incidental matters pending the trial, not affecting the merits of the cause, or working substantial prejudice to the rights of the client, such as forcing the opposite attorney to trial when he is under affliction or bereavement; forcing the trial on a particular day to the serious injury of the opposite attorney, when no harm will result from a trial at a different time; the time allowed for signing a bill of exceptions, cross-interrogatories, and the like — the attorney must be allowed to judge. No client has a right to demand that his attorney shall be illiberal in such matters, or that he should do anything therein repugnant to his own sense of honor and propriety; and if such a course is insisted on, the attorney should retire from the cause. (Ala., Ga., Va., Mich., Colo., N. C., Md., W. Va., Ky., Mo.)

34. Where an attorney has more than one regular client, the oldest client, in the absence of some agreement, should have the preference of retaining the attorney, as against his other clients in litigation between them. (Ala., Mich.)

35. *Making Bold Assurances to Clients.* — The miscarriages to which justice is subject, and the uncertainty of predicting results, admonish attorneys to beware of bold and confident assurances to clients, especially where the employment depends upon the assurance, and the case is not plain. (Ala., Ga., Va., Mich., Colo., N. C., Wis., W. Va., Ky., Mo.)

36. *Promptness and Punctuality.* — Prompt preparation for trial, punctuality in answering letters and keeping engagements, are due from an attorney to his client and do much to strengthen their confidence and friendship. (Ala., Ga., Va., Mich., Colo., N. C., W. Va., Ky., Mo.)

37. *Disclosing Adverse Influences.* — An attorney is in honor bound to disclose to the client, at the time of retainer, all the circumstances of his relation to the parties, or interest or connection with the controversy, which might justly influence the client in the selection of his attorney. He must decline to appear in any cause where his obligations or relations to the opposite parties will hinder or seriously embarrass the full and fearless discharge of all his duties. (Ala., Ga., Va., Mich., Colo., N. C., Wis., W. Va., Ky., Mo.)

38. *Expressing a Candid Opinion as to the Merits of a Client's Cause.* — An attorney should endeavor to obtain full knowledge of his client's cause before advising him, and is bound to give him a candid opinion of the merits and probable result of his cause. When the controversy will admit of it, he ought to seek to adjust it without litigation, if practicable. (Ala., Ga., Va., Mich., Colo., N. C., Wis., W. Va., Ky., Mo.)

39. Where an attorney, during the existence of a relation, has lawfully made an agreement which binds his client, he cannot honorably refuse to give the opposite party evidence of the agreement, because of his subsequent discharge or instructions to that effect by his former client. (Ala., Mich., Colo., Md.)

40. *Dealing with Trust Property.* — Money or other trust property coming into the possession of the attorney should be promptly reported, and never commingled with his private property or used by him, except with the client's knowledge and consent. (Ala., Ga., Va., Mich., Colo., N. C., Wis., Md., W. Va., Ky., Mo.)

41. *Business Dealings with the Clients.* — Attorneys should, as far as possible, avoid becoming either borrowers or creditors of their clients; and they ought scrupulously to refrain from bargaining about the subject-matter of their litigation, so long as the relation of attorney and client continues. (Ala., Ga., Va., Mich., Colo., N. C., Wis., W. Va., Ky., Mo.)

42. Natural solicitude of clients often prompts them to offer assistance of additional counsel. This should not be met, as it sometimes is, as evidence of want of confidence; but after advising frankly with the client, it should be left to his determination. (Ala., Ga., Va., Mich., Colo., N. C., Wis., W. Va., Ky.)

43. *Keeping Agreements with the Client.* — Important agreements, affecting the rights of clients, should, as far as possible, be reduced to writing; but it is dishonorable to avoid performance of an agreement fairly made, because not reduced to writing, as required by rules of court. (Ala., Ga., Va., Mich., Colo., N. C., Md., W. Va., Mo., Ky.)

44. An attorney should use his best efforts to prevent his clients from doing those things which the attorney himself will not do, particularly with reference to their conduct towards courts, officers, jurors, witnesses, and suitors. (Mich.)

45. *Taking Advantage of Opposite Counsel Without Notice to Him.* — An attorney should not ignore known customs or practice of the bar or of a particular court, even when the law permits, without giving opposing counsel timely notice. (Ala. See Codes of Va., § 39; N. C., § 39; W. Va., § 39; Md., § 32; Ga., § 39; Mich., § 7; Mo., § 37; Colo., § 40; Ky., § 39.)

46. (See synoptic heading to Compilation, section 45.) An attorney should not attempt to compromise with the opposite party, without notifying his attorney, if practicable. (Ala., Ga., Va., Mich., Colo., W. Va., Wis. See Codes of Ky., § 40; Md., § 33; Mo., § 37.)

47. In any matter, controversy, or action, where the opposite parties are represented by attorneys, the attorneys of the re-

spective parties shall confer and negotiate with each other and not with the clients. (N. C.)

48. When attorneys jointly associated in a cause cannot agree as to any matter vital to the interests of the client, the course to be pursued should be left to his determination. The client's decision should be cheerfully acquiesced in unless the nature of the difference makes it impracticable for the attorney to co-operate heartily and effectively; in which event, it is his duty to ask to be discharged. (Ala., Ga., Va., Mich., Colo., N. C., Md., W. Va., Ky.)

49. *When Association with Other Attorneys Is Objectionable.* — An attorney coming into a cause in which others are employed should give notice as soon as practicable, and ask for a conference, and if the association is objectionable to the attorney already in the cause, the other attorney should decline to take part unless the first attorney is relieved. (Ala., Mich., Colo., Wis., Md., Mo.)

50. When an attorney has been employed in a cause, no other attorney should accept employment as his associate, without previously ascertaining that his employment is agreeable to the attorney first employed. (Ga.)

51. (See synoptic heading to Compilation, section 45, *supra.*) An attorney ought not to engage in discussion or arguments about the merits of the case with the opposite party, without notice to his attorney. (Ala., Va., Mich., Colo., N. C., W. Va. See Codes of Ga., § 43; Wis., § 33; Md., § 33; Ky., § 40; Mo., § 37.)

52. *Explicit Understanding as to Compensation.* — Satisfactory relations between attorney and client are best preserved by a frank and explicit understanding at the outset as to the amount of the attorney's compensation; and where it is possible, this should always be agreed on in advance. (Ala., Ga., Va., Mich., Colo., N. C., Wis., W. Va., Ky., Mo.)

53. *Suing a Client for a Fee.* — In general it is better to yield something to a client's dissatisfaction at the amount of the fee, though the sum be reasonable, than to engage in a lawsuit to justify it, which ought always to be avoided except as a last resort to prevent imposition or fraud. (Ala., Ga., Mich., Colo., Wis., Md., Ky., N. C., W. Va.)

54. *Fixing the Amount of the Fee.* — Men, as a rule, overestimate rather than undervalue the worth of their services, and attorneys in fixing their fees should avoid charges which unduly magnify the value of their advice and services, as well as those which practically belittle them. A client's ability to pay can never justify a charge for more than the service is worth; though his poverty may require a less charge in many instances, and sometimes none at all. (Ala., Mich., Colo. See also Mo. Code, § 41.)

55. (See synoptic heading to Compilation, section 54.) An attorney may charge a regular client, who intrusts him with all his business, less for a particular service than he would charge a casual client for like services. The element of uncertainty of compensation where a contingent fee is agreed on justifies higher charges than where compensation is assured. (Ala., Mich., Colo., Wis. See also Mo. Code, § 41.)

56. *Elements to Be Considered in Fixing the Fee.* — In fixing fees the following elements should be considered: 1st. The time and labor required, the novelty and difficulty of the questions involved, and the skill requisite to properly conduct the cause. 2d. Whether the particular case will debar the attorney's appearance for others in cases likely to arise out of the transaction, and in which there is a reasonable expectation that the attorney would otherwise be employed; and herein of the loss of other business while employed in the particular case, and the antagonism with other clients growing out of the employment. 3d. The customary charges of the bar for similar services. 4th. The real amount involved and the benefits resulting from the services. 5th. Whether the compensation be contingent or assured. 6th. Is the client a regular one, retaining the attorney in all his business? No one of these considerations is in itself controlling. They are mere guides in ascertaining what the service was really worth; and in fixing the amount it should never be forgotten that the profession is a branch of the administration of justice and not a mere money-getting trade. (Ala., Mich., Colo., N. C., Md., W. Va. And see Codes of Ga., § 46; Va., § 45; Ky., § 44; Mo., § 42.)

57. *Contingent Fees.* — Contingent fees may be contracted for; but they lead to many abuses, and certain compensation is to be preferred. (Ala., Ga., Va., Mich., Colo., N. C., Wis., W. Va., Ky., Mo.)

58. *Compensation for Services Rendered to Another Attorney.* — Casual and slight services should be rendered without charge by one attorney to another in his personal cause; but when the service goes beyond this, an attorney may be charged as other clients. Ordinary advice and services to the family of a deceased attorney should be rendered without charge in most instances; and where the circumstances make it proper to charge, the fees should generally be less than in cases of other clients. (Ala., Ga., Va., Mich., Colo., N. C., Wis., Md., W. Va., Ky., Mo.)

59. *Treatment of Witnesses and Parties to the Cause.* — Witnesses and suitors should be treated with fairness and kindness. When essential to the ends of justice to arraign their conduct or testimony, it should be done without vilification or unnecessary harshness. Fierceness of manner and uncivil behavior can add nothing to the truthful dissection of a false witness's testimony and often rob deserved strictures of proper weight. (Ala., Ga., Va., Mich., Colo., N. C., Wis., Md., W. Va., Mo., and see Ky. Code, § 47.)

60. *Attitude Toward Jury.* — It is the duty of the court and its officers to provide for the comfort of jurors. Displaying special concern for their comfort, and volunteering to ask favors for them, while they are present — such as frequent motions to adjourn trials, or take a recess, solely on the ground of the jury's fatigue, or hunger, and uncomfortableness of their seats, or the court room, and the like — should be avoided. Such intervention of attorneys, when proper, ought to be had privately with the court, whereby there will be no appearance of fawning upon the jury, nor ground for ill-feeling of the jury towards the court or opposite counsel if such requests are denied. For like reasons, one attorney should never ask another, in the presence of the jury, to consent to its discharge or dispersion; and when such a request is made by the court, the attorneys, without indicating their preference, should ask to be heard after the jury withdraws. (Ala., Ga., Mich., Colo. See also Codes of Md., § 40; Mo., § 8; Ga., § 50; Va., § 49; N. C., § 49; W. Va., § 49; Ky., § 48.)

61. All propositions from counsel to dispense with argument should be made and discussed out of the hearing of the jury. (Ga., Va., N. C., W. Va., Md., Ky.)

62. Treating jurors after the rendition of a verdict in favor of one client is disreputable. All like practices are disreputable, and should be scrupulously avoided. (Mich.)

63. *Conversing Privately with Jurors.* — An attorney ought never to converse privately with jurors about the case; and must avoid all unnecessary communication, even as to matters foreign to the cause, both before and during the trial. Any other course, no matter how blameless the attorney's motives, gives color to the imputing [of] evil designs and often leads to scandal in the administration of justice. (Ala., Ga., Va., Mich., Colo., N. C., Wis., W. Va., Ky., Mo. See also Md. Code, § 15.)

64. An attorney assigned as counsel for an indigent prisoner ought not to ask to be excused for any light cause, and should

always be a friend to the defenseless and oppressed. (Ala., Ga., Va., Mich., Colo., N. C., W. Va., Ky.)

65. The lawyer should study the law with the constant purpose to do what he can to amend and perfect it. (Ky.)

66. Except upon the ground that a moral principle is involved, an attorney ought never to counsel or approve the infraction or evasion of a valid law. The fact that the end to be gained is a political one will not justify any departure from this rule. (Ky.)

67. While an attorney should speak respectfully of the judiciary and of all lawfully constituted authorities, and in the trial of causes and in all his dealings with the court should demean himself towards it with deference and respect, he has, on the other hand, a right to expect and exact from the court the same demeanor towards himself. It is unfortunate for the cause of justice when the judge forgets his dependence on the bar and forgets to pay it the deference and respect which is its due. (Ky.)

68. The qualities desirable in a judge are courtesy, affability, even temper, patience, conscientiousness, legal learning, sound sense and judgment, the moral courage to meet an issue squarely, and an impartial mind. (Ky.)

69. The bar should never permit political considerations to outweigh judicial fitness in selecting material for the bench, and it should earnestly and actively protest against the appointment or election of those who, in the general estimation of the bar, are unsuitable for the bench. (Ky.)

70. The enumeration of the foregoing duties shall not be construed to deny the existence of other duties equally imperative, though not specifically mentioned herein. (Ky.)

Cases of Interest.

AUTOMOBILE — DUTY TO STOP WITHOUT SIGNAL. — In Strand *v.* Grinnell Automobile Garage Co., 113 N. W. Rep. 488, the Iowa Supreme Court holds that the driver of a restive horse, on approaching an automobile, is not required under all circumstances to give a signal to the chauffeur to stop, in order to free himself from contributory negligence. The fact that the plaintiff, when approaching an automobile with a restive horse, does not signal the chauffeur to stop, is held not to relieve the latter from his duty to exercise ordinary care to avoid an accident and to stop the automobile until the plaintiff's horse can pass, if such precaution appear to be reasonably necessary.

THEATRE — EXCLUSION OF CRITIC. — In People *v.* Flynn, 82 N. E. Rep. 169, the New York Court of Appeals has recently decided that an agreement among members of a theatrical managers' association to refuse a dramatic critic admission to their theatres, made to protect themselves from public articles reflecting on their personal integrity, and as a protest against attacks on their patrons and members of a particular religious faith, and not as an attack on his right to exercise his calling as a dramatic critic, does not constitute a criminal conspiracy to prevent another from exercising a lawful calling. The case grew out of a concerted action on the part of a combination of New York theatre managers to exclude from their theatres Mr. Metcalfe, the dramatic critic of *Life*.

ROLLER SKATING ON STREET — ORDINANCE AGAINST. — In Billington *v.* Miller, 67 Atl. Rep. 935, it was held by the New Jersey Supreme Court that an ordinance prohibiting roller skating as a sport on a portion of a certain street was not objectionable as infringing the right of the public to travel on the street on roller skates, the sport of roller skating on such portion of the street having reached a point where it constituted a serious injury to abutting property owners. The court said: "Whether there is a right to use the public streets of a city for the purpose of mere sport is a question which has never been decided in this State, nor is it necessary now to determine it. If there be such a right, it must be subject to regulation by the city authorities, and as long as the restrictions imposed upon it are reasonable, for a public purpose, and not arbitrary, the courts ought not to interfere."

FRAUDULENT REPRESENTATIONS — KEELEY CURE. — In Memphis Keeley Institute *v.* Leslie E. Keeley Co., 155 Fed. Rep. 964, the Circuit Court of Appeals, Sixth Circuit, holds that where the proprietor of a medicine or remedy made in accordance with a secret formula knowingly makes false and fraudulent representations to the public as to the ingredients of such remedy through his advertisements and labels, he cannot maintain a suit in equity to protect from invasion and injury by another his business of selling or administering such remedy. The evidence was held to establish that the complainant, the proprietor and manufacturer of a secret remedy for the cure of the opium, liquor, and tobacco habits, which was represented to the public as having as its chief and most valuable ingredient chloride of gold or "double chloride of gold," was chargeable with fraudulent misrepresentations, in that such remedy did not contain any gold or chloride of gold.

CARRIERS OF PASSENGERS — MAXIMUM RATE LAW. — In Kansas City Southern R. Co. *v.* Brooks, 105 S. W. Rep. 93, the Arkansas Supreme Court holds that where a person boards a train to go from a point within the State to one without it, and pays the amount demanded therefor, not wishing or offering to break up the continuous passage by paying to the last station within the State, the transaction constitutes interstate commerce, and a State statute fixing the maximum passenger rate does not apply; but where one, though bound for a point outside the State, offers to pay his fare to the last station within the State, expecting to get off the train there and purchase a ticket for the remainder of his journey, this constitutes an intrastate transaction within the operation of the State law, and if the railroad charges him more than the statutory rate it becomes liable to the penalty fixed by the statute.

EJUSDEM GENERIS — "OTHER IMMORAL PURPOSE." — A rather strained application of the *ejusdem generis* rule of construction was made in U. S. *v.* Bitty, 155 Fed. Rep. 938, by Judge Hough, in the Circuit Court for the Southern District of New York. The defendant was indicted for importing from England an alien woman for the purpose of having her live with him as his concubine. The statute under which the indictment was found prohibits the importation of any alien woman or girl "for the purpose of prostitution or for any other immoral purpose." Judge Hough holds that the words "any other immoral purpose" must be construed with reference to the preceding word "prostitution," and to relate only to a like immoral purpose, and, so construed, cannot be held to include concubinage. He said: "I do not think that the mistress is near enough to the prostitute to be included by general words in a statute directed against the latter unfortunate class."

INNKEEPER'S LIEN ON GOODS OF THIRD PERSON. — In Horace Waters Co. *v.* Gerard, 82 N. E. Rep. 143, the New York Court of Appeals holds that a statute giving an innkeeper a lien on goods of a third person in the rightful possession of a guest is merely declaratory of the common law, does not extend or enlarge the innkeeper's lien, and is not in violation of any constitutional right. In the opinion, Chase, J., said: "So long as public policy requires that an innkeeper be held to the extraordinary and severe responsibility prescribed by the common law, the same considerations of public policy require that the rule of the common law be retained in its entirety, and that the innkeeper have a lien upon the luggage and goods in the possession of the guest for payment of his reasonable charges." The court reviews the authorities at considerable length and quotes from 16 Am. and Eng. Encyc. of Law (2d ed.) 548 *et seq.*, where numerous cases on the subject are collected.

MONOPOLY — CONTROL OF COMPETING CORPORATION. — In Bigelow *v.* Calumet & Hecla Min. Co., 155 Fed. Rep. 869, it was held by Judge Knappen in the Circuit Court, W. D., Michigan, N. D., that the control by one mining corporation organized under the laws of Michigan, of another similar corporation engaged in a competing business in interstate and foreign commerce, by a majority of its stock, or in part by acquiring stock and in part by securing proxies from other stockholders with the purpose of eliminating competition and obtaining a monopoly of trade in their products, either partial or complete, is in violation of the federal anti-trust law, which makes unlawful every combination in restraint of interstate or foreign commerce; also that such proceeding violates thè Michigan statute prohibiting all combinations entered into for the purpose and with the interest of establishing and maintaining a monopoly; nor is such transaction relieved of its invalidity by a Michigan statute which authorizes mining corporations of the State to purchase and own stock in other similar corporations.

BASEBALL CONTRACTS. — In Kelly *v.* Herrman, 155 Fed. Rep. 887, Judge Thompson, sitting in the Circuit Court for the Southern District of Ohio, W. D., holds that the provisions of the "national agreement for the government of professional baseball," adopted by the so-called "major" and "minor" leagues in 1903, and of the rules of the national commission created thereby, which give to a club having a player under contract with it the right to reserve such player for the ensuing season or to sell him to another club, in the absence of a stipulation to the contrary in the contract, are not binding upon a player who continued during succeeding years to play with a club under a contract entered into prior to the adoption of such agreement or the promulgation of the rules, and who did not thereafter make any new contract under or with reference to the same, and such club has no power to sell him without his consent, nor has the commission the right to enforce the prescribed penalties because of his refusal to recognize such a sale.

Book Reviews.

Criminal Investigation: A Practical Handbook for Magistrates, Police Officers, and Lawyers. Translated and adapted from the System der Kriminalistik of Dr. Hans Gross, Professor of Criminology in the University of Prague, by John Adam, M. A., Barrister-at-Law, and J. Collyer Adam, Barrister-at-Law. The Specialist Press, Limited. London, 1907. Pp. xxviii and 889. Appendices, xlvii.

This work of Dr. Gross is intended, as is indicated by the title, to serve as a practical manual of instruction for all engaged in investigating crime, and not only to deal in detail with subjects coming directly within the province of a criminal investigator, but also to guide him in resorting to expert assistance. Throughout, the book is characterized by the patient and wonderful elaboration of detail which is nearly always the hallmark of the products of European, and especially German, scholarship, the lack of which characteristic so often makes the pretentious fruition of the West seem superficial and amateurish.

The author begins with a general discussion of the duties of the investigating officer, and review of some of the qualities that are essential to such an official, which is rather of general than of professional interest.

The following chapter deals with the examination of witnesses and of the accused and must prove of great value to the lawyer at the criminal bar. Dr. Gross does not classify all men as liars, but shows that some men are unwittingly liars. He says: "Fear, terror, pain, produce all sorts of mistakes on their own account; all the more will they do so when people find themselves in a condition practically equivalent to the morbid state. They suffer real hallucinations and hear words which have never been pronounced. Thus, they hear voices of people pursuing them, and threats which have never been uttered; and at the same time they hear the voices of persons offering them assistance, although there is no one in the neighborhood." He also finds that strong feeling materially varies the quality of a man's evidence. He was present at an execution at which for some reason or other the executioner wore gloves. After the execution he asked four officials who were present what was the color of the executioner's gloves. Three replied, respectively, black, gray, white; while the fourth stoutly maintained that the executioner wore no gloves at all. Yet all four were in close proximity to the scaffold; each replied without hesitation, and all four are still perfectly confident that they made no mistake. A railway accident furnishes an example of what a man in a state of terror can see and hear. A brewer, a veritable Hercules, in the prime of life and in no way nervous, having jumped from a smashed carriage, took to running across the fields to the neighboring town, three-quarters of an hour's distance, in the full belief that he saw and heard the locomotive of the train puffing and blowing after him.

Dr. Gross finds that between the state of a person who desires to speak the truth and that of another person who does not so desire, there are what may be called intermediary positions; such is the case where a person, not having at a given moment the intention of lying, yet under the influence of habit presents his facts in such a manner that their falsity becomes at once apparent. This he terms "pathological lying."

Another chapter of interest to the profession is that which deals with the consultation of experts. Recourse to such aid, within proper limits, he considers advisable. To quote the words of his introduction: "We of course foresee and meet on the threshold the charge of encroaching upon the province, and thereby attempting to dispense with the help, of specialists. Nothing could be more harmful than such advice, nothing could so expose the investigator to mistakes as such fancied independence. But there is a vast gulf between permitting an investigating officer to undertake work beyond his sphere, and instructing him how to recognize when he ought to resort to experts, what experts should be chosen, and what questions must be submitted to them; just as an attorney requires long training and much knowledge of law to be able to state his case effectively for the opinion of the advocate. *Cuilibet in sua arte perito credendum est.*" That he is no "expertophobe," to adopt Mr. Osborn's coinage, is shown by the numerous instances which he sets out of the invaluable aid which they have rendered him in his practical experience. Also he advocates expert aid in many callings from which help is rarely sought by lawyers in this country.

It appears from the results of the use of finger-prints to aid in the detection of criminals that members of that profession must become "kid glove gentry" if they wish to protect themselves. In one instance the offender was detected by means of the photograph of a finger print which he had incautiously made on a beer bottle, another one by a finger print on a drinking glass. Thus, by the law of compensation, one vice leads to the punishment of another, the moralist will probably conclude.

Another chapter is devoted to serious accidents and boiler explosions, showing how investigation should be conducted in such cases and dealing with the true and false theories as to the causes of accidents and explosions.

It will be seen readily that the book is filled with matter of importance to lawyers, and not only is the matter of lively interest, but the form of treatment is so careful and so exhaustive as to render the book a very valuable working adjunct, containing matter elsewhere inaccessible.

Among the difficulties which beset the way of the transgressor and one which is not generally known is the fact that, by certain processes which Dr. Gross sets forth, burnt paper can be preserved and deciphered. Also casts can be made of footprints. To the average reader these and similar measures which the author advises may seem a species of Sherlock Holmes histrionics, but it must be recollected that the author is not merely theorizing but is stating the methods employed, largely by him, in actual cases. In fact, the work rather inclines one to regard the Doyle creation in the light of an amateur.

One objection to the book is that in the hands of the educated professional it will prove a very dangerous guide. On the other hand, it certainly should be accessible to every officer whose duty it is to investigate crime.

The typography, binding, and illustrations are not of the quality to which a book of such dignity and of such expense is entitled. In future editions a more careful recension will also be desirable.

News of the Profession.

The West Virginia State Bar Association opened its annual meeting in New Martinsville on December 31. Details of the meeting will be given in this column next month.

Death of Prominent Louisville Attorney. — Judge Asher G. Caruth, one of the most eminent members of the Louisville bar, died in that city on November 25, aged sixty-three.

New Hampshire Judge Retires on Age Limit. — On December 28 Judge William M. Chase retired from the bench of the New Hampshire Supreme Court, having reached the age limit.

Lincoln's Law Partner Dead. — Colonel Haviland Tompkins, an eccentric recluse eighty-four years old, who once practiced law in partnership with Abraham Lincoln, died on his farm near Fairfield, Ill., on December 1.

New York Lawyer Cut His Throat. — Marcus Hirschfield, a lawyer of New York city, formerly of Buffalo, committed suicide in New York city on November 23 by cutting his throat with a razor.

Made United States Attorney for New Mexico. — Captain David J. Leahy has been appointed United States District Attorney for New Mexico to succeed Major W. H. H. Llewellyn, who has accepted a position with the department of justice.

Well Known Oregonian Dies. — Hon Arthur L. Frazer, judge of the Circuit Court and Juvenile Court of Multnomah county, died in Portland, Oregon, December 3, aged forty-seven. He was a lecturer in the University of Oregon Law School.

Oklahoma and Indian Territory Lawyers Meet. — On December 19 and 20 the annual meeting of the Oklahoma and Indian Territory Bar Association was held in Oklahoma City. An account of the proceedings will be given next month.

Distinguished Kentuckian Dies. — Hon. Joseph I. Landes, one of the most distinguished lawyers in western Kentucky, and a former member of the State Court of Appeals, died on December 1, at his home in Hopkinsville, aged seventy-one years.

The New York State Bar Association will meet in New York city on January 24 and 25. The business meetings will be held in Carnegie Hall, and the banquet will be at the Waldorf-Astoria on the evening of the 25th. Hon. James Bryce will be the principal speaker.

Well-known Massachusetts Judge Dead. — Hon. Joseph Tucker, for thirty-four years judge of the District Court of central Berkshire, Mass., died at his home in Pittsfield, on November 28, at the age of seventy-five. He was lieutenant-governor of Massachusetts from 1869 to 1873.

Made Chief Justice of Nova Scotia. — Hon. Charles Townshend, puisne judge of the Supreme Court of Nova Scotia, has been appointed chief justice of the court to succeed Chief Justice Weatherbe, resigned. The vacant puisne judgeship has been filled by the appointment of Frederick A. Lawrence, K. C., M. P., of Colchester, N. B.

Judge Howe Resigns Federal Attorneyship. — Hon. William Wirt Howe, United States attorney for the Eastern District of Louisiana, has sent in his resignation, to take effect on January 1, 1908. He was first appointed to the post by President McKinley in 1899, and was reappointed by President Roosevelt in 1904.

Justice Harlan Has Served Thirty Years. — On November 29 Mr. Justice Harlan celebrated the thirtieth anniversary of his appointment to the Supreme Court of the United States. He is seventy-four years old, but is still hale and hearty, and frequently plays golf as a recreation. The imperishable rumor that Judge Harlan is about to resign is once more afloat.

Widely Known Missouri Attorney Dead. — Judge Edmund Orlando Brown, senior member of the firm of Brown & Mooneyham, died at his home in Carthage, Mo., on December 8, aged sixty years. Judge Brown was one of the best known lawyers in Missouri, having practiced in the State nearly forty years, and at one time served as judge of the twenty-fifth circuit.

Mexico's Most Prominent Lawyer Dead. — Pablo Martinez del Rio, of Mexico City, probably the most prominent of the Mexican lawyers, died on November 14, at San Antonio, Texas, of heart failure. For twenty years he was the leading corporation lawyer of his country, and about a year ago he gained especial prominence through his work in arranging the merger of the Mexican railway systems.

Michigan Bar Not to Meet This Year. — It is announced that no meeting of the Michigan State Bar Association will be held this year. The reasons assigned are that the constitutional convention will occupy the time of many of the members and that the Grand Rapids members wished a postponement in order that they might be able properly to entertain the delegates at the next meeting.

Death of Colorado Supreme Judge. — Hon. Charles F. Caswell, associate justice of the Colorado Supreme Court, died in Denver, November 21, of paralysis of the heart. Judge Caswell was born in Stafford, N. H., in 1851, and was a graduate of Dartmouth, class of 1874. He was admitted to the bar of Massachusetts in 1877, and practiced at Lynn for four years, after which he migrated to Colorado. He was elected to the Supreme Court in 1906 on the Republican ticket.

Appointed to Colorado Supreme Court. — Hon. Joseph Church Helm, of Denver, has been appointed by Governor

Buchtel to the vacancy on the bench of the Colorado Supreme Court occasioned by the death of Justice Charles F. Caswell. Judge Helm was born in Chicago in 1848, and settled in Colorado in 1875, after completing his legal education at the Iowa University. He was elected to the Colorado Supreme Court in 1881 and re-elected in 1892, but resigned to run for governor against David H. Waite, who defeated him. Since that time he has been practicing his profession in Denver.

OLDEST PRACTICING LAWYER DEAD. — Albert Ware Paine, believed to have been the oldest practicing lawyer in the United States, died December 3 at his home in Bangor, Me., aged ninety-five years. He was graduated in 1832 from what is now Colby College, and was admitted to practice in 1835, since which time he has resided and practiced his profession in Bangor. He is said to have originated the law permitting prisoners to testify in their own behalf, having procured the adoption of a statute to that effect in Maine in 1864.

JUDGE MCSHERRY'S SUCCESSOR. — Judge A. Hunter Boyd, chief judge of the Fourth Judicial Circuit of Maryland, and by virtue of his office a member of the Court of Appeals of Maryland, has been appointed by Governor Warfield chief judge of the latter court to succeed the late Judge James McSherry. Judge Boyd is fifty-eight years of age and a native of Virginia. The vacancy in the chief judgeship of the Sixth Circuit, comprising the counties of Frederick and Montgomery, has been filled by the appointment of Mr. Glenn H. Worthington, of Frederick. By virtue of this office Judge Worthington will have a seat in the Maryland Court of Appeals. He is forty-nine years old.

CHICAGO PIONEER DEAD. — Hon. James B. Bradwell, one of the first settlers of Chicago and one of the best known figures in the life of that city, died there November 29, of pneumonia. He was born in England in 1828 and was brought to this country as an infant. Seventy-three years ago he arrived at Chicago with his parents, who had crossed the continent in a covered wagon. He practiced law with former Governor John L. Beveridge, and was afterwards president of the Chicago Bar Association, of the Illinois Bar Association, and the Press Club of Chicago. For eight years he served upon the Cook county bench.

SUCCESSOR TO JUDGE MCCOMAS. — The vacancy in the Court of Appeals of the District of Columbia, caused by the death of Judge McComas, has been filled by the appointment of Hon. Josiah A. Van Orsdel, of Wyoming. Judge Van Orsdel was born in Pennsylvania in 1860 and went West in 1888, at first locating in Nebraska, but moving to Cheyenne, Wyo., three years later. After holding a number of other offices he was appointed attorney-general of Wyoming in 1898, which position he held until 1905 when he was made an associate justice of the Wyoming Supreme Court. On Feb. 1, 1906, he was appointed assistant attorney-general of the United States.

RHODE ISLAND STATE BAR ASSOCIATION. — The tenth annual dinner of the Rhode Island State Bar Association was held in Providence on December 2. After a brief business meeting the members sat down to dinner. Neither of the two invited speakers, Asa P. French and Sherman L. Whipple, both of the Massachusetts bar, was able to attend. President William A. Morgan delivered an address, in which he scathingly criticised "the Anglo-Saxon antiquated and cumbersome system of trial by jury." Amasa M. Eaton read a paper on "Thomas W. Dorr and the Dorr War." Officers for the ensuing year were elected as follows: President, William A. Morgan; vice-presidents, Dexter B Potter and Oscar Lapham; treasurer, James A. Price; secretary, Howard B. Gorham.

English Notes.

MR. JUSTICE KEKEWICH DEAD. — Sir Arthur Kekewich, senior judge of the Chancery Division, died at his home in London, on November 22, after having been operated on for appendicitis.

JAPANESE JUDGES VISIT OLD BAILEY. — Two distinguished Japanese judges, K. Sazuky and K. Heranuma, visited the Old Bailey recently and sat on the bench in Mr. A. T. Lawrence's court watching the proceedings with interest.

THE LORD CHANCELLOR MARRIED. — On December 3 Lord Loreburn, Lord Chancellor of England, was married to Miss Hicks-Beach, niece of Lord St. Aldwyn. This is the first time that an occupant of the woolsack has been married during his term of office.

QUERY? — At Southwark County Court recently Judge Willis, K. C., remarked: "Women are the best witnesses. They describe exactly what takes place, which is what so many men altogether fail to do." This would be important, if true.

DEATH OF A COUNTY COURT JUDGE. — Hon. Arthur Russell, judge of County Court Circuit 45, died on November 22, following an operation for appendicitis. He was forty-six years old. From 1890 to 1900 he was editor of the Law Times Reports, and in the latter year was made a County Court judge.

EDALJI ONCE MORE A SOLICITOR. — George Edalji, the young solicitor who was convicted of maiming cattle and whose pardon was secured by the efforts of Sir Arthur Conan Doyle, has had his name restored to the roll of solicitors, and can now resume the practice of his profession and appear in the English courts. The Home Secretary has taken no action as yet on the petition for compensation on account of his wrongful imprisonment, but Edalji's friends are still active in bringing pressure to bear on the Home office, and it is probable that he will eventually receive a fuller measure of reparation for the miscarriage of justice.

REFUSED ADMISSION TO THE BAR. — The benchers of Gray's Inn, exercising a power that is rarely used, recently refused to call one of their students to the bar. From their refusal the student appealed to the judges, but his appeal was dismissed. Ordinarily it is not a difficult matter for students at the inns to secure admission, and so far as examinations are concerned, those who aspire to be solicitors have a much harder task. At the recent final examinations for the bar only 18 out of 106 candidates were unsuccessful, whereas at the final examination for admission to the ranks of the solicitors 99 failed out of 206 candidates.

NEWSPAPER — LIABILITY FOR LOSS CAUSED BY ADVERTISEMENT. — In the recent case of De La Bere v. Pearson, noted in the *Law Journal* for November 30, at page 739, the Court of Appeal rendered a decision of considerable importance to newspaper proprietors. The defendants published in their newspaper called M. A. P. the following notice: "M. A. P. in the city. Spare cash and advice. Readers of M. A. P. desiring financial advice in these columns should address their queries (with full name and address) to the City Editor, 17 Henrietta Street, Covent Garden, W. C." The plaintiff answered the advertisement, stating that he wished to invest £800, and asking the defendants to name some good stockbroker. The defendants handed the plaintiff's letter to one Thompson and requested him to answer it. Thompson was not a member of the stock exchange, but an outside broker, and was an undischarged bankrupt. He wrote to the plaintiff, introducing himself as the broker recommended by the defendants, and succeeded in getting hold of £1,400 of the plaintiff's money which he converted to his own use. The plaintiff thereupon brought an action against the proprietors of M. A. P., claiming

£1,400 damages for breach of a contract whereby the defendants promised to give the plaintiff financial advice, and for negligence in the performance of the contract. The plaintiff recovered judgment for the full amount, and the Court of Appeal has now affirmed it, holding that the contract was that the defendants should name a "good stockbroker," which meant *prima facie* a member of the stock exchange; that they had not been reasonably careful in the selection of a broker, and that the measure of damages was the whole loss sustained by the plaintiff.

A COMPLIMENT TO AMERICAN LEGAL EDUCATION. — In a recent issue the *Law Times* says editorially: "In the matter of legal education England has much to learn from her kin beyond sea in the United States. In the American law schools the completeness of the equipment for teaching not only legal principles, but the method of dealing with concrete cases, has long been the envy of those in this country who have the subject much at heart. How wide the scope of the teaching of the American schools is, may be gathered from the fact that at Yale University regular instruction is given in the German Civil Code. In this country all studies that do not fall within the category of those that 'pay' are regarded with scant favor. American authorities do not adopt this narrow attitude towards legal studies, and have wisely included in their curriculum a course of lectures on the monumental work of the German jurists, which the late Professor Maitland justly termed 'the most carefully considered statement of a nation's laws that the world has ever seen.' Of the code there have already appeared four French, one Spanish, one Italian, one English, and two Japanese translations. A Chinese rendering is also expected at no distant date. Perhaps some day, still a long way off, and probably too late to make a conquest of the legal world, the English people may see fit to reduce 'the lawless science of their law' into a well-ordered code."

MARRIAGE AND CONFLICT OF LAWS. — During November the Court of Appeal decided the case of Ogden *v.* Ogden, which has been the cause of much comment in the English press. The facts of the case were as follows: An Englishwoman resident in England contracted a marriage there with a Frenchman temporarily residing in England. The consent of his father had not been obtained, and therefore, he being under the age of twenty-five years, the marriage was by French law voidable by the father. The latter accordingly obtained a decree in France annulling it. Subsequently the young man, who had returned to France, married again there. The English wife then sought to obtain a divorce in the English court, asking in the alternative for a declaration that the French decree of nullity was valid; but Sir Francis Jeune refused to entertain the suit, on the ground that if she was a lawful wife the matrimonial domicil was French, and therefore the English court had no jurisdiction, and he also declined to make any declaration as to the validity of the French decree, though he said, somewhat rashly, that it was *prima facie* good. The lady afterwards contracted a second marriage in England, which the second "husband" sought to have annulled in these proceedings. The result is an exhaustive and unanimous judgment of the Court of Appeal that the prior marriage, being valid according to the English law, was not rendered invalid by the fact that the husband had not complied with certain formalities which the law of his own country required. Here we have a conflict of law with a vengeance, and if Sir Francis Jeune was right, the position of a woman situated like this unfortunate lady is a hopeless one. The English law says that she is a wife, but that the English court has no power to dissolve the marriage; the French court cannot pronounce a divorce because of the fact that in France there is no marriage at all.

Obiter Dicta.

LIKELY. — "It may be assumed that a man can recognize his mother-in-law when he sees her." *Per* Hirschberg, P. J., in *In re* McInnes, 104 N. Y. Supp. 149.

WELL WORTH IT. — In St. Louis, etc., R. Co. *v.* Stamps, 104 S. W. Rep. 1114, the Arkansas Supreme Court holds that $500 is not excessive damages for the mental and physical suffering of a person who is struck by a train, thrown off a bridge, and drowned in the river below.

A COMMON FAILING. — It is told of the late Mr. Justice Ferguson, of Canada, that, finding some difficulty in reading an affidavit, he inquired of the lawyer who drafted it what a certain figure was, and was told that it was a five. "Can't you make a better five than that?" asked the judge with some petulance. "Well, your lordship," responded the counsel, "some days I find it very difficult to make a five at all."

WORSE AND WORSE. — A Texas correspondent states that a difficulty has sprung up between two of his neighbors because a hen belonging to one of them wandered onto the premises of the other and there laid an egg. Both parties have asserted their title to the egg with some heat, and our correspondent prays for enlightenment as to the legal rights of the claimants. Just offhand we should say that the case is governed by the law relating to mislaid property.

WOMEN MAY WEAR HATS IN CANADIAN THEATRES. — In a Montreal police court, on November 21, Judge Piche held that there was no law in Canada giving to proprietors of theatres the right to compel feminine patrons to remove their hats. The ruling was made in connection with a charge of assault laid against a constable for ejecting Miss Robertine Barry, an authoress, from a moving picture show because she resolutely declined to remove her headgear, though often requested so to do.

TOO CASUAL. — In concluding the opinion in Southern R. Co. *v.* Wiley, 88 Miss. 825, Whitfield, C. J., animadverted rather scathingly upon the pernicious carelessness displayed by corporations in regard to the lives and limbs of their own employees, closing with this refreshing sentence: "The 'God-damn-it,-Johnnie,-go-ahead-anyhow' style of attention to the nondelegable duty of the master to supply to employees safe machinery and appliances can meet at the hands of this court nothing short of the sternest condemnation."

NO ROBBERY — MAYBE. — The ingenuity of some of the legal brethren in advertising their wares has been the subject of frequent comment in this column, and from time to time particularly admirable specimens have been reproduced, but we believe that nothing that has hitherto appeared contained quite as much of novelty as the following which was clipped from the "For Exchange" column of the *Philadelphia Inquirer:*

HAVE YOUR WILL LEGALLY DRAWN BY a bachelor of laws, who will make it for anything useful. H-144, Inquirer office.

AN AMBIGUOUS LICENSE. — The following was published in a recent issue of the Nauvoo (Ill.) *Rustler:*

IMPORTANT NOTICE.

Notice is hereby given that any one who has legal business with the heirs of J. C. Louvier estate are hereby authorized to go on said premises and remove the same.

LUCY LINGE } The Heirs.
LUCIAN LOUVIER }

Now to Hon. States Attorney, Geo. V. Helfrich:

We desire to express our sincere thanks for your kindness in advising us as to what is our rights concerning said estate, that has been abandoned to ruin and destruction.

Very Respectfully, THE HEIRS.

THE LIMIT IN LAWYERS' CARDS. — A correspondent forwards the subjoined "lawyer's card," with the remark that he had supposed our collection was complete until he encountered this one:

CEDAR RAPIDS, IOWA
VINCEL DRAHOS
LAWYER
Magnetic Healing

He has, by magnetic power, produced wonderful results. It is simply a marvelous and wonderful gift that can not be explained by himself or anybody else. — Cedar Rapids Evening Gazette, Dec. 22, 1906.

Office Rooms 6 and 7 Jim Block
S. U. I. 1883-4

A DIFFICULT POINT. — Magistrate Hughes, of Philadelphia, had a case of first impression in his court recently when two youngsters were before him charged with setting fire to the whiskers of Abraham Bender. It seems that Bender had been industriously cultivating his beard for the last fifty years, and had coaxed it to such great length that he could tuck it into the tops of his boots while standing erect. One day during November he was approached by the lads, who asked him for a match. "Sure," said Bender, handing a match to one of the boys, who immediately scratched it, thrust the flame into the cherished beard, and struck out for the back country on his high speed, leaving Bender blazing as merrily as a Christmas tree in a Sunday school. A bystander hurriedly turned in a fire alarm, but the beard was a total loss before any apparatus appeared on the scene. The difficulty which confronted Magistrate Hughes was whether to hold the culprits for assault or arson, and, to our regret, we have never learned what his decision was.

ONE WAY TO ESCAPE JURY DUTY. — In reference to a note published in this department of our November number, a correspondent writes from Baltimore:

"Referring to your reproduction of the advertisement of W. H. Logue, Jr., of 921 N. Broadway, who having been assigned to jury duty in the Criminal Court recently, requested the patronage of his friends and acquaintances, I feel constrained to say that it is the opinion of divers and sundry folk in these parts that this advertisement was a good scheme upon the part of the enterprising Mr. Logue to get out of serving on the jury. And it worked all right, because on the afternoon of the appearance of the advertisement he was summarily dismissed as a juryman. So it seems that there are more ways of fighting what some people think is the devil than with fire."

EXAMINED FOR ADMISSION TO HIS OWN COURT.— A novel sight was witnessed at Muskogee, Ind. Ter., recently when Hon. William R. Lawrence, of the United States Court for the Western District of Indian Territory, was examined for admission to the bar of the court over which he was then presiding. Judge Lawrence, who is a learned member of the Illinois bar, was appointed judge of the Territorial Court some three years ago. With the advent of statehood his court was to be abolished, and as, under the law in force in the Indian Territory, no license to practice law in any other State was accepted in lieu of an examination, it was necessary for him to be examined if he wished to secure a license from that court. Accordingly he summoned his colleague, Judge Sulzbacher, and startled him with the announcement that he wished to be examined for admission to the bar. On the appointed evening, with Judge Sulzbacher presiding and before an examing board of his selection, Judge Lawrence and three other candidates were "quizzed" in open court, the examination covering the usual range of topics. All four candidates were admitted to practice.

A RECENT EXTENSION OF THE "POLLARD PLEDGE." — If success crowns a recent venture into the realm of preventive justice by Judge William Jefferson Pollard, of the Second District Police Court of St. Louis, then the name of that distinguished jurist is destined to rank high in the list of the great benefactors of the human race — if not at the very top. A few years back, as our readers will doubtless remember, Judge Pollard was brought prominently into public notice by the success of a system inaugurated in his court whereby gentlemen and ladies who had been gazing too intently on the wine when it was red were enabled to escape fine or imprisonment by signing a pledge to abstain from the seductive beverages for the space of one year. Encouraged by the results of his efforts with the "booze artists," Judge Pollard has now turned his attention to a more pernicious class of malefactors, and has put into operation an anti-nagging pledge, which, if successful, must necessarily go further toward ameliorating the pains and penalties of existence than would the total extinction of the Demon Rum. Recently there was brought before him a woman charged with so scolding, browbeating, and bullyragging her spouse as to demolish completely the peace and dignity of the neighborhood. Judge Pollard promptly fined the lady $25 — which apparently gave the husband no joy whatever — and then offered her the alternative of signing the anti-nagging pledge for one year. She seized the opportunity with alacrity, and after apologizing to her husband and promising to report to the judge once a week for a month, was allowed to go on her way. The outcome of this momentous experiment will no doubt be awaited with breathless interest not only by criminologists but by oppressed husbands the world over. Here's Judge Pollard's health, and a long life to him.

Law Notes

FEBRUARY, 1908.

PUBLISHED BY EDWARD THOMPSON COMPANY, NORTHPORT, LONG ISLAND, N. Y.

JAMES COCKCROFT, *President*. W. M. MCKINNEY, *Vice-President*.
D. S. GARLAND, *Secretary*. J. W. HILTMAN, *Treasurer*.

CONTENTS.

Mr. Justice Brewer's Criticism of the President.

THE general opinion seems to be that a justice of the Supreme Court of the United States ought not to criticise anything that the President says or does. This is said to be because the justice "is a member of the co-ordinate branch of the national government, the duty of every member of which is to pass on litigated causes which come before him, some of which occasionally construe the lawful or unlawful acts of the President," and also because it is "bad taste." As to the last it may be observed that it is very much a matter of opinion as to what is and what is not bad taste. In regard to the possibility of the Supreme Court being called on to "construe the lawful or unlawful acts of the President," it is apprehended that the court would not be led astray by the views of one of its members as to the President's style of play in the game of politics. The only effect that Mr. Justice Brewer's now famous speech could have would be to strain somewhat the personal relations between the two men, and the President would naturally be all the more irritated if he really was playing hide and seek with the American people on the subject of the presidential nomination. The remark may have lacked decorum according to former standards, but this is a new era of freedom of speech, and men in high places now speak very plainly about other men in high places and are fond of using "language which goes straight home to the hearts of the people." If a United States judge in the discharge of his judicial duty declares unconstitutional a statute which the President wishes to enforce, the President does not hesitate to say wrathful things about the judge, because he has the "courage of his convictions," and his convictions are of a very positive sort. It is not surprising, therefore, that a judge should feel at liberty to comment on the President's methods in politics. But whatever may be the merits of the matter from the point of view of decorum, the people should be as indulgent with Mr. Justice Brewer as they are with Mr. Roosevelt, for the learned justice is also a versatile man and is able to turn his attention to many things outside his official duties.

The Revision of the United States Statutes.

THE commission appointed in 1897 to "revise and codify" the laws of the United States did not prove an entire success. After nearly ten years' continuous work they succeeded in covering the entire field of the permanent and general laws and made their report to Congress. The commission went out of existence Dec. 15, 1906. The work was performed with great care and labor, but unfortunately the result was not wholly satisfactory. Not having legislative power, the proper functions of the commissioners were to report the existing laws with suggestions for such amendments and additional legislation as in their judgment might be required, but instead of taking this course in accordance with the act pursuant to which they were appointed, their codification was composed in a large part of substitutionary provisions without showing the existing enactments. Hence, much of the proper work of revision has not yet been done. Congress cannot intelligently pass on any of such new provisions without a view of the present statutes, and since the commissioners did not supply that information, the burden falls on Congress or on one of its committees of performing the principal duty of the commissioners. This has been partly accomplished by the committees on revision of the laws, and a new penal code may soon be promulgated; but the penal code, though important, is a very small part of the whole, being less than four hundred sections out of a total of about nine thousand, and the completion of the work does not seem to be alluringly near at hand.

IT IS greatly to be regretted that the results of the expenditure of so much time and money are so meagre, but this is not surprising when the character of the work is considered. Legal compilation is work of a special character. Ability and learning as a lawyer are not the only requisites. It requires both special aptitude and special training, and this has been demonstrated many times. The efficiency of specialists in this line of work is strikingly illustrated by the fact that the whole ground covered by the commissioners appointed to codify these laws and which occupied them for nearly ten years was covered by private enterprise in a very small fraction of that time. One publisher in three years compiled and codified all the general laws of the United States, with exhaustive notes showing how each section had been interpreted and applied by the courts. Another publisher in a still shorter time compiled the same laws, omitting however the feature of complete annotations. There is food for thought in this. When the enormous expenditure and the unreasonable delay in this work are considered it would seem that a much better plan could be devised than the appointment of a commission which, in the nature of things, must be an experiment, and perhaps a very costly experiment. There are many persons in the country who are specially qualified for such work, and if the commissioners had been selected from those known to have such qualifications, or if the work had been let by contract, the entire revision would have been completed and Congress would have acted on it years ago. The statutes of the States are, perhaps, without exception compiled and revised by private enterprise, and their revisions are both thorough and prompt. The result is that the State statutes are nearly always complete and up to date. The experiment in one State of a legislative committee on codification has proved a failure, and Congress has not fared much better. The federal statutes are yearly becoming more voluminous, and of more general interest and more extensive application, and the good of the public requires that they should be revised more frequently, but there can be no hope of this if the plan of the last effort is followed.

J. C. Bancroft Davis as a Reporter.

THE death of the late Judge J. C. Bancroft Davis recalls the fact that the last of the many important public offices held by him was that of reporter of the Supreme Court of the United States from 1882 to 1902, during which time he issued volumes 108 to 186, inclusive, of the Supreme Court Reports. Referring to this one of the daily papers has said: "Mr. Davis proved to be an excellent reporter. He was prompt and businesslike, accurate, and painstaking. He was one of those rare men who possess the gift of book-making, that is to say, he knew instinctively how a volume can be made attractive in appearance. Being an excellent lawyer, as well as a felicitous writer, he uniformly served the court in a manner most acceptable to the justices and to the profession." Undoubtedly Judge Davis was a man of unusual attainments. He achieved distinction as a jurist and a statesman, but not as a reporter, and it is a mere obituary euphemism to say that he "proved to be an excellent reporter," or that "he was prompt, businesslike, accurate, and painstaking." The cases were seldom published until many months after they had been decided, and such was the inconvenience to bench and bar resulting from the delay that an unofficial series of the Supreme Court reports was commenced during the period of his reportership and proved a success solely on the ground of prompt service. When it is considered that the Supreme Court decides only about two hundred and fifty cases in a year, such delays seem unreasonable and unnecessary, especially in view of the fact that these cases are now reported generally within a month after the opinions have been handed down. The most serious objection, however, to the work of the late reporter is the incompleteness of the headnotes or syllabi. It was his almost invariable practice to omit from the headnotes in these reports one or more of the points decided in each case. Consequently such points are not indexed in the reports, and they are thus practically lost. A concrete instance of the extent of this is afforded by an examination of volume 124 of the Supreme Court reports. In this volume the reporter has omitted to index nearly a hundred points. As to the quality of the headnotes, also, much might be said, but it is sufficient here to observe that many of them entirely fail to show what the court decided, as for instance in the case of Andrews *v.* Hovey, 124 U. S. 694, the headnote of which merely says: "The question of the proper construction of the second clause of § 7 of the patent act of March 3, 1839, 5 Stat. 354, as affecting the validity of a patent, considered."

A REPORTER'S duties are plain. He is to report faithfully the decisions of the court, and thoroughly index them. To do this he must state in his headnotes each point decided. He is not expected and should not be permitted to determine that particular points which the court has taken the pains to decide may be neglected as of no value. His judgment in this respect may be perfectly good as far as he and others equally learned are concerned, but every point that a court decides is of value to some one, and besides the court often needs to refer to its rulings on particular questions. It is a great mistake to suppose that the qualities which go to make the successful lawyer or the efficient statesman demonstrate capacity for the humbler work of law reporting. A selection made on that basis is as likely to prove a failure as a success, and this has been proved by experience. It may sound paradoxical, but it is a fact that the compensation attached to the office of reporter of the Supreme Court is so out of proportion to the service required, exceeding as it does the salaries paid the justices, that it practically precludes a selection on the ground of known efficiency. The office is desirable and the duties light, and the usual result of such a condition generally follows.

Impeachment of Judges for Incompetency.

MINNESOTA courts and lawyers are greatly agitated and embarrassed by the action of Capt. Francis B. Hart, a member of the bar of that State, in making a formal accusation that the judges of that court are grossly incompetent to perform the duties of their high office, and, in effect, that their decisions are often a travesty of justice. The charges were formally presented to the governor of the State, with a request that they be examined with the view of impeaching the judges and removing them from office. They contain three specifications selected, as he says, "as fair samples of what the court has now and then done and is doing, and not because they stand alone or are worse than others," and the author adds that "if no proper motive for the decisions can be gathered from the decisions themselves, it seems to me that impeachment would be proper, leaving the senate free to make inquiry as to motive outside of the decisions, and I am constrained to think that not a little evidence can be adduced relevant thereto." At the same time he disclaims any imputations of personal dishonesty on the part of the judges, but asserts that they must in law be regarded as corrupt, if it appears that a fatally erroneous decision was intelligently made, excluding the hypothesis of mistake, because they are conclusively presumed to be learned in the law. Thus, in a dignified manner and in due form, but without mincing matters, Mr. Hart alleges that the judges of the court of last resort in the State either cannot or will not do justice in the causes which they are called on to decide, and offers to prove it before the proper court. If it is a ground of impeachment that the decisions of a court are "illogical, illegal, and unjust; that they are not good sense, not good law, not justice," then he makes a strong case. It is claimed, however, that no cause for impeachment is stated, and that Mr. Hart, in asking that the judges be impeached, is guilty of a grave offense for which he must answer. Accordingly the State Bar Association has taken the matter in hand and passed resolutions declaring him "guilty of misconduct in his profession" and recommending that he be disbarred on that ground. The action taken wholly ignores the question of the truth of the charges against the court. The determination of that question is of the first importance. The mind of the public must be satisfied. As has been pertinently said, "the question of the competency of the court having been raised, it cannot be settled by the court asserting that it is competent, nor by the bar association announcing any such thing as a fact without investigation nor even the pretense of investigation." The question of a possible violation of legal "ethics" is of no interest to the people at large. If their highest court is one that is not capable of deciding causes according to law, they want to know it, and since that allegation has been made, the court should see to it that there is prompt investigation.

THIS matter involves some interesting and difficult questions. There are only two grounds on which proceedings can be taken against Mr. Hart; one that he has committed a contempt of court, and the other that he has violated his duty as a counselor at law. On the first ground, if found guilty, he might be imprisoned, or fined, or disbarred. On the second ground he could be punished only by disbarment. It is difficult to see how a charge of contempt of court could be successfully maintained. He has merely exercised the right which every citizen has of procuring or seeking to procure the impeachment of public officers for malfeasance in office. Possibly the grounds which he assigns for such action are insufficient, but that is another question, for there can scarcely be any doubt of his good faith, and if his charges are true, he has not only done what was his right as a citizen but his duty as a member of the bar. If the judges are corrupt or so incompetent as to be unable to perform their functions, the court ought to be purged, and in order that this may be done it is necessary that some one should take the initiative. The rules of law which protect the dignity and uphold the authority of the courts can never be invoked to protect the individual judges from the penalty of their own wrongdoing. But it is by no means clear that under the State constitution a judge could not be impeached for deciding causes contrary to law, if the hypothesis of ordinary judicial error be excluded. There are at least three cases in American history in which this very thing has been done. In two cases, one in Rhode Island in 1786 (Trevett *v.* Weedon, referred to in Arnold's Hist. R. I.), and the other in Ohio in 1807 (see "Sketch of Hon. Calvin Pease," 5 West. L. Mo. 3), judges were impeached for refusing to enforce unconstitutional laws. In the third case, which arose in Pennsylvania in 1788 (see 1 Dall. 329), the Supreme Court adjudged Eleazer Oswald guilty of contempt of court and sentenced him to pay a fine of ten pounds and to be imprisoned for one month and until the fine should be paid. Through an error in the direction of the justices as to the day on which the month would expire (the legal month in Pennsylvania at that time being twenty-eight days) Oswald was detained a day or two beyond the expiration of the legal month. After his discharge Oswald brought impeachment proceedings against the judges, on the grounds that his sentence had been illegally protracted and also that the sentence was unlawful.

IN THE present case of Mr. Hart it is probably not necessary to inquire whether a judge is "corrupt" because he is ignorant of the law. It is, to say the least, a debatable question whether a judge may not be impeached under the constitution of Minnesota on the ground of incapacity. The provision is that "the judges of the Supreme Court and District Courts may be impeached for corrupt conduct in office, or for crimes and misdemeanors." The phrase "crimes and misdemeanors" in this connection is one that has long been in use and is well understood as including not only crimes for which an indictment may be brought, but also maladministration, neglect of duty, arbitrary and oppressive conduct, and even gross improprieties by judges and high officers of state. If the well-settled interpretation of this phrase was adopted with the phrase itself, as must in the nature of things have been done, then the judges of the Supreme Court of Minnesota are subject to impeachment, and the only court that can try the question is the senate of the State. It cannot be determined collaterally in any proceeding to disbar Mr. Hart or to commit him for contempt. As to his possible disbarment, of course that is a matter that is in the hands of the court whose reputation is at stake, and from which he cannot appeal. It is true that special judges have been assigned to hear the case, but if they disbar the respondent they will greatly imperil their own reputation by subjecting themselves to the imputation of endeavoring to shield their brethren, and any such course would probably result in a searching investigation by the legislature when it next assembles.

The Proposed Copyright Law.

PERSISTENT efforts during the last two years to procure the passage of a new copyright law have resulted in the introduction from time to time of several bills, none of which have passed but three of which are now pending in Congress. The bill first offered contained provisions of such doubtful constitutionality and such undoubted impropriety that its rejection was almost a matter of course. It is generally conceded that the law requires amendment in certain respects, but it could scarcely be claimed with any show of reason that it is wholly inadequate. The copyright law in substantially its present form has been in force for more than a hundred years, and its efficiency for the purpose which it was intended to accomplish is fully attested by the progress which "science and the useful arts" have made under its protection, and the great prosperity of the business which it has fostered. It also has the merit of the certainty that comes with long practice under it and the frequent interpretation of its various provisions by the courts. Under these circumstances no change is desirable unless some useful purpose is to be accomplished. The present law involves four central ideas, namely, (1) registration of copyrights in a public office, (2) a definite term of protection, (3) the deposit of two copies of each copyrighted work in the library of Congress, and (4) a notice of copyright showing the date of registration and the name of the proprietor. By the requirement of registration the copyrighted article is completely identified, and the fact of copyright as well as the exact period of protection and the name of the proprietor becomes a matter of public record, and it is important that such information should be accessible to all who desire it. The requirement of the deposit of the two copies in the library of Congress is not a hardship on the copyright proprietor, but only a small return for the protection which he receives from the government. It is obviously of great importance that new books should be found in the national library at as early a date as elsewhere, and no other method so effective for the purpose could possibly be devised.

It is now proposed by the so-called copyright revision to abrogate these requirements. The necessity of registration is to be dispensed with, and copyright is to be secured by publication with a notice of copyright; instead of a fixed term of years the period of copyright is to be made indeterminate, that is for the lifetime of the author and a certain number of years after his death; and the deposit of copies is in effect to be left to the option of the copyright proprietor. It is believed that the policy of such a law is altogether bad and at variance with the fundamental law which permits copyright only for "limited times." With no record to mark the commencement of the term there will, of course, be no means of ascertaining the time of its expiration, and copyrights would be practically perpetual. As an illustration of this the case of a painting may be taken. Under the present law, the artist may enter his painting for copyright, and the term begins to run when the record has been made. Under the proposed law he obtains copyright on his work "by publication thereof with the notice of copyright." This may seem plain, but it is not. It has been held that placing a painting in an art gallery for public exhibition, or even a sale of it, is not a "publication," and what does constitute publication is altogether uncertain. The proposed law further provides that nothing therein contained "should be construed to annul or limit the right of an author or proprietor of an unpublished work, at common law or in equity, to prevent the copying, publication, or use of such unpublished work without his consent, and to obtain damages therefor." According to these provisions the painter of a picture could keep it on exhibition for an indefinite period or sell it, and yet without a copyright, and before the copyright term begins to run, may have all the protection that a copyright could give. This, of course, would be nothing more or less than perpetual copyright. The proposed law also forbids the importation, without the proprietor's consent, of foreign copies of a book, though the foreign publication was with the consent of the proprietor. It would be entirely proper to make such foreign copies dutiable under the customs laws, but such absolute prohibition of importation could only be intended to protect the domestic publisher against competition with the foreign publisher, or, in other words, to regulate the market, and not to protect the copyright.

One of the few really debatable questions raised when the revision of the copyright law is considered, and the principal one, relates to the musical copyrights. As the law now stands, the purchaser of sheet music which has been copyrighted may perform it on any musical instrument either privately or in public for profit, or he may make perforated rolls, disks, and the like, which by aid of mechanism will automatically reproduce the music to the ear. It is claimed that this is injurious to the composer by depriving him of a large part of the profits of his compositions. It is strenuously claimed, and with some show of reason, that this is merely an attempt to confiscate the private property of one person for the benefit of another; but however that may be, it is plain that the inventors of automatic musical instruments and appliances would be seriously injured. They invented and perfected their devices at a time when it was legal to make and use them. There is certainly a conflict of interest here, but is not one class as meritorious as the other? The real difficulty with the situation is that the different subjects of copyright cannot be advantageously included in one bill, and there should be a separate enactment for each. There should be one bill for musical copyrights and another for works of art and the like, and with these subjects separately presented the needs of each could be more justly understood. It would then doubtless be perceived that the law of literary copyright requires but little change.

The Identification of Criminals.

Apropos of the article on Rogues' Gallery Law in the January Law Notes, a Canadian correspondent calls our attention to a statute which has been in force in the Dominion since 1898, known as the "Identification of Criminals Act." This statute appears to meet squarely the difficulties which confront the courts in the United States in dealing with the rights of persons arrested. Under it, any person charged with, or under conviction for, an indictable offense, may be subjected to the measurements and processes "practiced under the system for the identification of criminals commonly known as Bertillon Signaletic System, or to any measurements, processes, or operations sanctioned by the Governor in Council having the like object in view." The signaletic cards and other results may be published for the information of legal and administrative officers.

EMPLOYER'S LIABILITY AS A SUBJECT OF FEDERAL REGULATION.

The long looked for decision of the Supreme Court of the United States on the validity of the Federal Employers' Liability statute of July 11, 1906 (Fed. Stat. Annot., Supp. 1907, p. 68), has been rendered, and, upon a division of five to four of the justices, the act has been declared unconstitutional. (*Howard v. Illinois Cent. R. Co.; Brooks v. Southern Pacific Co.*) But, unlike some other leading cases involving the construction of the United States Constitution in which the division of the court was close, the fundamental question in this case was decided with an authority which leaves the main question open to no doubt.

As an analysis of the statute, we use substantially the

language of Mr. Justice Moody in the dissenting opinion, wherein he said that the remedy afforded by it is more generous to the employee than that given by the common law in several respects. (1) The common law recognized no recovery of damages for death resulting from negligence; by the statute damages are recoverable for death as well as for injury. (2) The common law allowed no recovery against the employer for the neglect of a fellow servant engaged in a common employment; by the statute the employer is held responsible for the negligence of any of its officers, agents, or employees, even though the guilty person is a fellow servant of him who is injured or killed. (3) The common law denied to one who by his negligence had contributed to his own injury the right to a remedy for the neglect of another which had been a concurring cause; by the statute the negligent sufferer may recover if his negligence be slight, and that of the employer gross in comparison, though the contributing negligence must be taken into account in reduction of the damages. (4) The common law, as adjudged by that court, permitted the employee to enter into a contract renouncing his right to damages in case he incurred injuries in the course of his employment; the statute forbids such a contract.

There were two main objections to the statute presented for the consideration of the court: First, that the relation of master and servant is a matter purely of State concern, and that as the statute was solely addressed to the regulation of the relations of the employer to those whom he employs and the relation of those employed by him among themselves, it deals with subjects which cannot under any circumstances come within the power conferred upon Congress to regulate commerce; second, assuming that the statute was upon a subject within the power of Congress to regulate, it was nevertheless invalid because it included within its operation the relation of interstate carriers to all their employees and was not limited to the relation of such carriers to their employees actually engaged in interstate business. It will readily be seen that the first of these contentions was the important point in the case, and that, deciding against it, the second objection can easily be remedied if, upon reconsideration, Congress may deem it wise to re-enact the statute in limited terms in order to bring the subject-matter within the constitutional power of Congress to regulate.

Although upon the whole case the statute was held to be invalid by a majority of five to four, there was no positive dissent to the holding that Congress may legislate upon the subject-matter of the statute. The four dissenting justices, Harlan, McKenna, Holmes, and Moody, necessarily so held, and Mr. Justice White, who wrote the opinion of the court with which Mr. Justice Day fully concurred, was definite in his pronouncement that Congress has power to pass a statute upon the subject provided it is properly limited in terms to the relation between interstate carriers and their employees actually engaged in interstate business. The other three, Chief Justice Fuller and Justices Brewer and Peckham, while intimating doubt as to this part of the decision, were satisfied to rest their conclusion upon the part of the opinion which decided that as to traffic or other matters within the State, the act was unconstitutional, and that it could not be separated from that which was claimed to be valid as relating to interstate commerce. This part of the case, sustaining the power of Congress to legislate upon the subject, does nothing more than affirm beyond doubt a conception of the power of Congress clearly to be inferred from previous cases. State statutes respecting civil liability, and declaring, modifying, or abrogating common-law rules of liability of common carriers to their employees, have frequently been attacked upon the ground that, as applied to interstate carriers, they were invalid in imposing burdens upon and regulating the business of interstate carriers. But it has uniformly been held that "in the absence of legislation by Congress," such State statutes have operated under the State police power upon interstate carriers in their interstate relations. Said Mr. Justice Moody: "It is difficult to conceive how legislation may effectively control the business if it cannot regulate the conduct of those engaged in the business, in every act which is performed in the conduct of the business. . . . Of course the power to regulate commerce does not authorize Congress to control the general conduct of persons engaged therein, but, unless it is an idle and useless power, it authorizes Congress to control the conduct of persons engaged in commerce, for that is commerce itself. It would seem, therefore, that when persons are employed in interstate or foreign commerce, as the employment is an essential part of that commerce, its terms and conditions, and the rights and duties which grow out of it, are under the control of Congress, subject only to the limits on the exercise of that control prescribed in the Constitution." So that it may now be considered as clearly settled that under its power to regulate interstate commerce, Congress may enact legislation affecting interstate instrumentalities in all their interstate relations, and that so far as such interstate instrumentalities may be engaged in interstate business they are subject to the operation of State law.

As has been said, however, the case was really decided and the statute held to be invalid on a question of construction of the statute. The act extended to every individual or corporation who might engage in interstate commerce as a common carrier, and the subjects stated all came within the statute when the individual or corporation was a common carrier who engaged in trade or commerce between the States. So that, the court said, the statute dealt with all the concerns of the individuals or corporations to which it related if they engaged as common carriers in trade or commerce between the States, and did not confine itself to the interstate commerce business which might be done by such persons, and as the act, by its terms, related to every common carrier in interstate commerce and to any employees of every such carrier, thereby regulating any relation of a carrier engaged in interstate commerce with its servants and of such servants among themselves, the court was unable to say that the statute would have been enacted had its provisions been restricted to the limited relations of that character which it was within the power of Congress to regulate. On the other hand, it was insisted by the minority that the statute might properly have been applied to that commerce which Congress may regulate, namely, foreign and interstate, and that which is within the District of Columbia and the Territories. Voicing the opinion of the dissenting justices, Mr. Justice Moody said: "The natural meaning of the words of the statute considered together, each word receiving significance from those with which it is allied, the respect which is due to Congress, the belief which I hold that it would not intentionally overstep the clearly defined limits of its authority, and the principles of construction heretofore acted upon by this court, lead my mind to the settled conviction that the statute can be interpreted, and ought to be interpreted, as affording the remedy therein prescribed only to the employees of foreign, interstate, and territorial carriers, who are themselves engaged in some capacity in such commerce in some of its manifold aspects. If this meaning be attributed to the words of the law, it is apparent that in the opinion of a majority of the court the law, in its main features at least, would be constitutional."

The wisdom or expediency of the statute was, of course, not a judicial question, but the court, though recognizing and affirming this principle, significantly enumerated the objections on this ground that had been urged against it. It was said that the statute inordinately extended the power of Congress and unduly diminished the legislative authority of the States, since it sought to exert the power of Congress as to the relation of master and servant, a subject hitherto treated as being exclusively within the control of the States; and that in practice its execution would cripple the State and enlarge the federal judicial power, since its effect would be to cause every action concerning an injury to a servant employed by a common carrier who may engage in interstate commerce to cease to be a matter of State jurisdiction and to become cognizable in the federal courts. Moreover, it was said, the statute would create confusion and uncertainty as to the rights of those dwelling within the States, that it would operate injuriously upon all who chose to engage in interstate commerce as common carriers, since those who so did would have become subject to the liability which the statute created, to be tested by the rules of negligence which the statute embodied, although such rules be unknown to the laws of the several States. Besides, the statute, it was urged, discriminated against all who engaged as common carriers in interstate commerce, since it made them responsible, without limit as to the amount, to one servant for an injury suffered by the acts of a coservant, even in a case where the negligence of the injured had contributed to the result, hence placing all employers who were common carriers in a disfavored, and all their employees in a favored, class. Indeed, it was insisted the statute proceeded upon contradictory principles, since it imposed the increased responsibility just stated upon the master presumably in order to make him more careful in the selection of his servants, and yet minimized the necessity for care on the part of the servant by allowing recovery although he may have been negligent. Especially has the wisdom of the provision declaring the doctrine of comparative negligence been questioned. See Street on Foundations of Legal Liability, vol. 1, p. 147. However this may be, Congress will have another opportunity to determine the advisability of enacting such a statute, and we may rest assured that the interests to be affected will see that these and many other considerations are not overlooked.

T. H. CALVERT.

Raleigh, N. C.

GOVERNMENT UNDER THE CONSTITUTION.[1]

By JOHN M. HARLAN, *Associate Justice of the Supreme Court of the United States.*

THERE are some who think they see dark clouds upon the horizon of our future, and express grave apprehension as to the stability of the government ordained by the people of the United States and established by the Constitution. In a population of ninety millions of people we must expect to find some who indulge in gloomy forebodings as to the future of the country, and who seem to cultivate the habit of predicting disaster. Such persons are quite unhappy when the facts do not justify them in believing that everything is going wrong. But there is no occasion for alarm. The American people, knowing that eternal vigilance is the price of liberty, will take care that no harm comes to the country. At all times since the organization of the government they have shown themselves equal to every emergency, however sudden or startling, which involved the safety of our institutions. They may seem at times to tolerate false, visionary, and mischievous views, but in the end they will surely recognize the dangers of the situation whatever they may be, and will do what prudence and patriotism require at their hands. Their final, deliberate judgment upon public questions is quite certain to be the best for all concerned.

What, let me ask, are some of the grounds upon which the pessimist of these days bases his fears for the safety of our institutions? He persuades himself to believe that the trend in public affairs is towards the centralization of all governmental power in the nation and the destruction of the rights of the States. If this were really the case the duty of every American would be to resist such a tendency by every means in his power. A national government for national affairs and State governments for State affairs is the foundation rock upon which our institutions rest. Any serious departure from that principle would bring disaster upon the American system of free government.

But the fact is not as the pessimist alleges it to be. The American people are more determined than at any time in their history to maintain both national and State rights, as those rights exist under the Union ordained by the Constitution. I say the people of the United States, for although the Constitution was accepted by the separate action of the people in their respective States, they moved together, in a collective capacity, as one people, in creating a nation for certain specified objects of general concern. They will not patiently consider any suggestion or scheme that involves a union upon any other basis. They will maintain at whatever cost, and in all their integrity, both national and State rights.

The best friends of State rights, permit me to say, are not those who habitually denounce as illegal everything done by the general government, but those who recognize the government of the Union as possessing all the powers granted to it in the Constitution, either expressly or by necessary implication; for, without a general government possessing controlling power in relation to matters of national concern, the States would have no prestige before the world and would be in perpetual conflict with one another. With equal truth it may be said that the best friends of the Union are those who hold that the States possess all governmental powers not granted to the general government, and that are not inconsistent with their own constitutions or with the Constitution of the United States or with a republican form of government. The people of the United States cherish, and will compel adherence to, the funda-

[1] Extracts from the recent address of Mr. Justice Harlan at the banquet given in his honor by "The Kentuckians" in New York, on Dec. 23, 1907.

mental doctrine that the States are vital parts of the American system of government; and they will insist with no less determination upon the recognition of the just powers of the States — to be exerted always in subordination to the supreme law of the land — as essential to the preservation of our liberties. The Supreme Court of the United States has again and again declared, upon full consideration, that a close and firm union is necessary for the happiness of the American people, and that "without the States in union there could be no such political body as the United States."

If then the matchless government devised by the fathers and ordained by the people of the United States is to be preserved and handed down intact to posterity, national power and State power must go hand in hand in harmony with the Constitution. If those powers clash, the paramount authority of the Union within its prescribed sphere of action must prevail. Such is the express mandate of the Constitution, and such our common sense and experience tell us must always be the case, if liberty regulated by law is not to perish from our land. The nation being supreme within the sphere of its action as defined by the Constitution, its authority, when legally exerted, binds every State as well as all individuals within the territory of the United States. The glory of the Republic is that its affairs are regulated by a written Constitution — the fundamental law which distributes the powers of government among three separate, co-equal, and co-ordinate departments, each exerting the authority, and only the authority, conferred upon it — and which Constitution, until amended in the mode prescribed by itself, must be deemed supreme over the Congress, over the President, over the courts, over the States, and over the people themselves.

The pessimist is misled by the declaration of some, happily few in number, who hold that whatever the words of the Constitution that instrument should be so construed as to make it mean what a majority of the people think, at a given time, it should mean. He is also misled by the theory advanced by those who hold that Congress must be permitted to exert any governmental power whatsoever, not expressly *denied* to it, if that body deems that its exercise will promote "the general welfare." But such theories of constitutional construction find no support in judicial decisions or in sound reason, least of all in the final judgments of that tribunal whose greatest function it is to declare the meaning and scope of the fundamental law. The national government, it should ever be remembered, is one of limited, delegated powers, and is not a pure democracy, in which the will of a popular majority as expressed at the polls at a particular time becomes immediately the supreme law. It is a representative republic, in which the will of the people is to be ascertained in a prescribed mode, and carried into effect only by appointed agents designated by the people themselves, in the manner indicated by law. It would be a calamity unspeakable if our institutions and the sacred rights of life, liberty, and property should be put at the mercy of a majority unrestrained by a written supreme law binding every department of government, even the people themselves. The pessimist — indeed all — may take courage in the fact that it has become a recognized rule of construction that the Constitution is to be taken as meaning what its words in their natural, obvious sense import, and, if the people desire it to mean something different, that instrument must be amended in the manner, and only in the manner, prescribed by itself. The dispute among statesmen has not been so much in reference to the general principles that should govern constitutional construction as to the application of those principles in determining the extent of the powers granted to the national government. Early in the history of the nation some insisted upon a narrow, literal interpretation of the Constitution which, had it been approved, would have made the general government a rope of sand, wholly inadequate to the great purposes for which it was established. But long ago that view was rejected by the Supreme Court of the United States, and its rejection has been universally approved.

There are some who would deny to Congress all powers that are not, in words, specified in the Constitution as belonging to the legislative branch of the government. They would eliminate altogether from our jurisprudence the long-established doctrine that Congress may exercise powers that are plainly incidental to those expressly granted and not prohibited by the Constitution, that is, powers necessarily implied because embraced by those enumerated, and without which the government would be unequal to the objects for which it was avowedly established, and would become, to use the words of Marshall, "a splendid bauble." If the views of the latter class of constitutional critics should gain the approval of the American people the country would be carried back to that period of its history when distinguished politicians gravely argued that the Supreme Court of the United States could not, without violating the Constitution, review the action of a State court which, by its final judgment, denied or destroyed rights plainly secured to the citizen by the supreme law of the land. Such critics are politically of kin to those who affirm that the courts may not declare a legislative enactment void, even when it is in plain violation of the Constitution.

It is true that national power, as now exerted, covers a wider field of action than it did in the early days of the Republic; but that does not prove, as the pessimist would have us think, that the government has usurped powers that do not belong to it and has entered the domain reserved by and for the States. It proves only that the nation has from time to time, as the public interests demanded, brought into active operation powers which Congress had not previously chosen to exert. So vast has been the increase in our population and so diversified and extended have become our industrial interests, that occasions must necessarily arise, from time to time, for a more intimate connection between the government of the Union and the commercial and other affairs of the people than perhaps the fathers ever dreamed of. Hence, if modern problems, as connected with the operations of government, are to be solved in the interest and for the benefit of the people, and if the nation is to keep abreast with advancing civilization, new fields of legislation must be occupied. While new legislation must always be closely scrutinized and care be taken that it is not inconsistent with the Constitution, we must not be so unwise or suspicious or timid as to reject a new policy or a new law simply because it is new, or simply because it may cover areas not consciously within the mental vision or the thoughts of the framers of the Constitution. That wonderful instrument, the Supreme Court has said, was intended "to be adapted to the various *crises* of human affairs." The wise men of the constitutional period deemed it unnecessary to go further than to specify the general objects to be accomplished by the national government, and to enumerate the powers that may be exerted by it, leaving to Congress — under its responsibility to the people and under its authority to pass such laws as were necessary and proper to carry into effect the powers enumerated and granted — to employ such means not expressly or impliedly prohibited as are appropriate to the particular object designed to be accomplished. The supreme judicial tribunal of the nation has spoken with distinctness upon this point. Its words in a great case — all its members concurring — are: "The Constitution unavoidably dealt in general language. It did not suit the purposes of the people, in framing this great charter of our liberties, to provide for minute specifications of its powers, or to declare the means by which those powers should be carried into execution.

It was foreseen that this would be a perilous and difficult, if not an impracticable task. The instrument was not intended to provide merely for the exigencies of a few years, but was to endure through a long lapse of ages, the events of which were locked up in the inscrutable purposes of Providence. It could not be foreseen what new changes and modifications of power might be indispensable to effectuate the general objects of the charter; and restrictions and specifications which, at the present, might seem salutary, might in the end prove the overthrow of the system itself. Hence its powers are expressed in general terms, leaving to the legislature, from time to time, to adopt its own means to effectuate legitimate objects, and to mould and model the exercise of its powers, as its own wisdom, and the public interests, should require." Thus was the nation armed with authority to meet new conditions that might arise, and which permitted or required governmental action. Is a proposed new law embraced by any general power granted? Has it any reasonable connection with the specified objects, or any of them, to which, under the Constitution, the power of the nation extends? If these questions be answered in the affirmative, then it will only remain for the law-making department of the government to determine whether the proposed law will be conducive to the public welfare. And that determination will not be one of law, but simply one of policy. Granted the power to legislate in reference to a particular matter, Congress can employ any means, not forbidden nor inconsistent with the Constitution, that may be germane to the end proposed to be accomplished.

Therefore let the country gather up all the strength that comes from the patriotism and loyalty of the American people and go forward in its marvelous career, holding to the confident belief, justified by the words of the Constitution and by judicial decisions, that the checks in our governmental system will suffice in the future, as they have sufficed in the past, to guard our institutions against insidious attacks upon the fundamental principles of free government, or against the exercise of arbitrary or usurped power. Keeping within the scope and broad lines of the Constitution, we may walk safely and without fear. We need not hesitate to build on the foundations laid by the forefathers. Those foundations are broad and deep, and so long as new measures and policies are tested by the plumb line of the Constitution and we keep well within its wise limitations, we may safely rear whatever superstructure our welfare and greatness as a nation may require.

Let us then move on in the "old paths, where is the good way" marked out by the fathers. Let us not give our approval to any interpretation of the Constitution that will either cripple the nation's authority or prostrate the nation at the feet of the States, or that will deprive the States of their just powers. Let us hold fast to the broad and liberal, and yet safe, rules of constitutional construction approved by the fathers and established by judicial decisions. In so doing we will sustain our dual system, under which the government of the Union is forbidden to exercise any power not granted to it expressly or by necessary implication, while the States will not be hindered or fettered in the exercise of powers that have not been surrendered by them to the Union, and not inconsistent with the Constitution.

JAMES HAMILTON LEWIS VERSUS WOMEN.

Are Women Less Trustworthy Witnesses than Men?

Early in January it was reported in some of the newspapers that in the course of an address to the students in the Northwestern University Law School, Colonel James Hamilton Lewis, now of Chicago, charged women with habitual mendacity in the following language: "Remember, an oath means nothing to a woman, and as Horace has so truthfully expressed it, 'when a woman starts out to perjure herself all Hades cannot keep her record.' . . . A woman has no idea of the sanctity of an oath, and a woman will repeat when on oath anything which she will say when not on oath."

But Colonel Lewis promptly denied that he had been correctly quoted. "I never made such an assertion in my life," he said. "I had referred analytically to different kinds of witnesses. I divided women witnesses into classes. After defining the method to be employed as to women witnesses generally, I concluded with the last class — the few who bring suits against men for money for certain well-known alleged reasons. It was this last class of whom I said that revenge or cupidity was their purpose — and the oath a useless thing. They were there to accomplish their object. Of all women I spoke in the terms that honorable and Christian men employ referring to good women." All lawyers are well aware that a person's oral statements are constantly garbled and perverted, even by honest witnesses, and Colonel Lewis's explanation may be accepted without the slightest hesitation.

At least one eminent philosopher has expressly sanctioned the notion which Colonel Lewis was reported to have indorsed. Schopenhauer maintained that habitual dissimulation is a fundamental defect in women. He asserted that perjury in a court of justice is more often committed by women than by men, and deemed it indeed generally questionable whether women ought to be sworn at all. Like the unenlightened observers of the epileptic and the insane in former days, he ascribed women's actual shortcomings, physical and intellectual, to fundamental and innate characteristics. But in "Sex Equality," by Emmet Densmore, M. D., the author recalls the fact that the observations of Schopenhauer were made in Germany, where the status of women is still much lower than it is in England and the United States. Spencer, who found his data in England, advances reasons for believing that the physical and mental infirmities of women are the outcome of environment and heredity, not of fundamental differences based on sex. Darwin expressed the same opinion, which he placed upon a strictly scientific basis. It is quite clear that neither of those eminent *savants* would have concurred in the gross aspersion upon women by the morose, pessimistic, and empirical Schopenhauer. Of course, that consummate logician, John Stuart Mill, would have made short work of him. As for the courts, we have not seen a single case where a judge has said anything in disparagement of the testimony of women, although several judges of the highest eminence, whom we could name, were much given to philosophizing whenever occasion arose, and they had abundant opportunities in connection with weighing the testimony of female witnesses.

In Gaines *v.* Relf, 12 How. (U. S.) 472, 551, Mr. Justice Catron said: "The distinguished Sherlock says, without any satirical intention or meaning to say that women are inferior to men, 'Whilst she trusts her instinct she is scarcely ever deceived, and she is generally lost when she begins to reason.' And I need not tell my brethren, as evidence rests upon our faith in human testimony, as sanctioned by experience, that the conclusion of the great divine is that of the law, and that the testimony of women is weighed with caution and allowances for them differently from that of men, *but never with the slightest suspicion that they are not as truthful.*" What are the "caution and allowances" of which the justice speaks is not clear. It may be conjectured that he refers to a tendency of women — due to their inexperience — to indulge in inferences instead of adhering closely to facts derived from personal knowledge as men might be more apt to do. However, he impeaches Schopenhauer.

"In my opinion, women are as reliable witnesses as men, and often give better testimony on some points," said Judge Fisher, of the Supreme Court of New Brunswick, in Napier *v.* Ferguson, 18 N. Bruns. 415, at p. 430.

"Women are the best witnesses; they describe exactly what takes place, which is what so many men fail to do," said Judge Willis, K. C., at Southwark County Court, England, as reported in the *Law Journal*, London, Nov. 23, 1907, at p. 731.

It is well known that evidence sufficient to prove the contents of a lost document, in order to found a right thereon, must be highly convincing and of very pure quality. Nevertheless, the lost will of Sir Edward Sugden (Lord St. Leonards) was established by the testimony of his daughter, who "was the daily companion for many years of one of the greatest lawyers that ever lived," although she was the principal beneficiary in the will. "Of her integrity there can be no doubt," said Sir James Hannen; "that has been stated with even greater force by those who represent the defendants than by the learned counsel who represent Miss Sugden herself." Again he said: "Trusting as I do, completely, to the integrity of Miss Sugden, and so excluding the possibility of invention on her part, it happens," etc. Speaking of the deep pecuniary interest of Miss Sugden, Chief Justice Cockburn said: "I am glad to think that it has not occurred to any one to say, or to suggest, that upon that ground Miss Sugden has intentionally departed one hair's breadth from the truth." Sugden *v.* Lord St. Leonards, 1 P. Div. 154, 177, 178, 198, 223.

In Turner *v.* Hand, 3 Wall. Jr. (U. S.) 88, 113, 24 Fed. Cas. No. 14,257, at p. 362, a contested will case, Mr. Justice Grier, instructing the jury and commenting upon the testimony of the principal male witness, said that he was "proved to have been a talking, babbling man, whose statements of facts are not much to be relied on, and if the fact of the execution of this will depended on his testimony alone, the jury might well consider it insufficient to satisfy their minds as to any doubtful matter." But in speaking of the testimony of that witness's wife and daughters in the same case it is patent that he meant the jury to understand he would set aside a verdict if it were rendered against their testimony. In Grant *v.* Bradstreet, 87 Me. 583, 33 Atl. Rep. 165, a highly intelligent housekeeper's testimony prevailed against that of a man of substance and high character, for reasons stated with great earnestness by Chief Justice Peters. The foregoing cases are not cited as evidence that women are generally entitled to superior credit, but only to show that there is no recognized presumption against them.

In Campbell *v.* Campbell, 22 Grant Ch. (U. C.) 322, 357, a husband's suit for divorce, Vice-Chancellor Blake cites as authority Solomon's observation in Prov. xxx. 20. But it is generally suspected that the distinguished personage whom Sergeant Ballantine refrained from cross-examining testified in obedience to a well-known precept current among "gentlemen."

Has any woman attained the celebrity of Titus Oates, Majocchi, the Tichborne claimant, Pigott, and numerous other artistic male perjurers? In his History of Crime in England, vol. 2, pp. 15, 465, Pike speaks of the time when perjury was "the most thoroughly ingrained of all the English crimes, . . . one of the most ineradicable of offenses in England."

If it had been asserted by any one entitled to notice that "Amelia," Sophia Western, Elizabeth Bennet, Amelia Sedley, or Eugénie Grandet, was capable of committing the vulgar and odious offense of perjury, can it be imagined that those famous oracles Fielding, Jane Austen, Thackeray, and Balzac would not, respectively, have resented the imputation? And it was a lawyer who created Jeanie Deans.

But Colonel Lewis was also reported to have said to the students: "A woman always comes to testify as a witness for one of two reasons; either through a sense of affection or duty to those whom she loves, or to satisfy what she regards as a perfectly legitimate feeling of resentment. If it is the first, she will come through fire and water to testify, and she will see things as her friend views them. Sincerely and earnestly she will testify that things are as she thinks they ought to be, and you may cross-examine until you have exhausted the vocabulary, and you will get nothing from her but her ideas of what they ought to be."

Let us see if a man is not apt to "see things as his friend views them," and let us see how much can be gained by cross-examining *him*. Judge Sneed of the Supreme Court of Tennessee is speaking: "The lawyer who has practiced long in jury causes cannot have failed to observe that the practice of permitting witnesses to hear each other's testimony has often resulted in a great and gross abuse of public justice. Human nature is frail, and that frailty is as often illustrated in the witness-box as elsewhere. The witness in an excited litigation often becomes the mere partisan of the litigant whose cause he represents. His solicitude in the cause, and his anxiety to win the verdict, are often no less than those of his friend and summoner, whose life, liberty, or property may depend upon that verdict. He comes to regard the adverse party and the adverse witnesses as his adversaries, and often, with scarce a consciousness of the serious obligation that is upon him, lapses into the conviction that the scene before him is a mere tilt and tourney in which he enters to overturn and countervail the testimony of the adverse party. He has heard the evidence of his own party in regard to the transaction, and perhaps he remembers it somewhat differently; but a conflict would be fatal, and he often reasons his flexible conscience into the opinion that his own memory is at fault, and the statement of his confederates is the true version, and he therefore corroborates it. He has heard the testimony of the adverse party, and his ingenuity is taxed at once to strike it where it is vulnerable, and to destroy it. A brief and whispered conference behind the bar, and he finds one of his own party who saw the transaction as he saw it, and the thing is done. Of what value is the cross-examination, that most efficacious test of truth, under such circumstances? The witness who is disposed to ignore the truth may now defy the onset of the most skilful cross-examination. And even he who would fain lean toward an honest story finds himself confounded, and often yields his own conviction, to adopt the strong, emphatic statements of another." Rainwater *v.* Elmore, 1 Heisk. (Tenn.) 363, at p. 365.

In patent infringement suits, testimony of witnesses to prove "prior use" in order to defeat the patent is always "subjected to the closest scrutiny" because of "their proneness to recollect things as the party calling them would have them recollect them," among other reasons. *Per* Mr. Justice Brown, in Barbed Wire Patent, 143 U. S. 275, 284, 12 U. S. Sup. Ct. Rep. 443, 447.

In Dysart *v.* Dysart, 1 Rob. Ecc. 106, 127, a suit for divorce *a mensa* on the ground of cruelty, Dr. Lushington declared that the experience of the oldest practitioner could not furnish an instance of a lady's maid deposing in such a case who had not a bias in favor of her mistress. Mark, however, that the decision in that case was reversed on appeal in Dysart *v.* Dysart, 1 Rob. Ecc. 470, where Sir Herbert Jenner Fust said (at p. 535): "If it be considered that [the maid] has a bias in favor of Lady Dysart, it may be said with equal confidence that [the man servant] is biased in favor of his lordship, and is as likely to misrepresent what did take place." By the way, in a similar case the husband's sister testified in favor of his wife, and her statements were awarded great weight because, said Dr. Lushington, she would be "the last person to take part unjustly with the wife." Saunders *v.* Saunders, 1 Rob. Ecc. 549, 563.

There is no judicial authority for an assertion either that women are peculiarly addicted to perjury or that they are exceptionally predisposed to testify with a bias.

Charles C. Moore.

PREFACES TO LAW BOOKS.

When we read a novel, a history, a book of travel or of poetry, we unconsciously gain a more or less definite idea of the personality of the author. Who of us will confess to being so dull that we cannot guess that the novel which we have nearly finished, though a masculine name appears on the title page, was really written by a woman, if, of course, the author does not happen to be a George Eliot? So, too, in books of this character the author's age, temperament, religious, social, and sometimes political convictions are more or less clearly revealed. The reader would be lacking in perspicuity, indeed, could he lay down Tom Watson's Life of Napoleon without the conviction that the author, in spite of his laudation of Napoleon the emperor, is a man of ultra-democratic ideas.

All this is different with law books. The writer of these books is hedged about on every side so that there is almost no chance for his personality to find expression in his work. His course is marked out by precedents. He may, it is true, weigh authorities, and boldly declare this or that case to have been wrongly decided, or this or that view to be wrong, but even in doing this he is guided and circumscribed by principles which have been established by precedents. His reasoning must be the "reasoning of the law," as Bishop called it. Even his language must be the language of the law. The result of this is that the typical law book, with its judicial weighing of the evidence of the law, its severe, unimpassioned reasoning, and its stilted phrasing, lacks that personal interest which is possessed by most of the other books which the lawyer reads.

It is only in the preface that the writer of a law book may be himself. It is in the preface that the personality of the author may be revealed. Therefore, however interesting a law book may be to the reader as a lawyer, it is only the preface to the book that can be of interest to him as a man who is interested in the personality of his fellows.

This truth, which, it is believed, is now for the first time expressed in written words, has induced the writer of this article to make an exhaustive study of the subject of prefaces to law books with a view to ascertaining some of the rules which should control the writing of law-book prefaces in order that they may be models of their kind.

The writer is aware that some people entertain an unreasoning prejudice against prefaces. "Who ever reads a preface?" he once heard a superior person say. "Most prefaces," said Sir Roger L'Estrange, "are effectually apologies, and neither the book nor the author one jot the better for them. If the book be good, it will not need an apology; if bad, it will not bear one; for where a man thinks, by calling himself noddy in the epistle, to atone for showing himself to be one in the text, he does, with respect to the dignity of an author, but bind up two fools in one cover."

But, for the reason that has been suggested, it is to be hoped that prefaces will not be omitted at least from law books. And there need be little fear that this is a vain hope; for, as Robert Louis Stevenson very truly said: "A preface is more than an author can resist, for it is the reward of his labors. When the foundation stone is laid, the architect appears with his plans, and struts for an hour before the public eye. So with the writer in his preface: he may have never a word to say, but he must show himself for a moment on the portico, hat in hand, and with an urbane demeanor."

Since, then, prefaces should and will continue to be written, let us proceed with the appointed task of outlining the form and contents of the model law-book preface.

A formula for preparing a preface, which shall not violate the traditions of preface writing, would call for just about three essential ingredients. First comes the apology for having written the book at all. Then comes a commendation of the book, disguised under a seemingly frank statement of the scope, plan, and purpose of the book. After the author has in this modest way shown how very valuable his book must be, its merits are generously submitted to the judgment of an indulgent profession, coupled, perhaps, with the pious hope that the author has in some measure discharged the duty which every lawyer owes to his profession. These are the elements out of which the orthodox preface must be compounded. It may of course be seasoned with other things to suit the taste, and these elements may be so disguised that they cannot be readily identified, but when carefully analyzed every normal preface will be found to contain these ingredients.

The *apologia* assumes many forms. Usually it points out the need of a work on the subject treated, coupled, belike, with a regret that the task has not been undertaken by an abler hand. Not unfrequently it appears that a realization of the long felt want was brought home to the author in the course of his own practice, and the reader is left to infer, if he is not actually told, that this practice has been quite extensive. Occasionally the author tries to throw dust in the eyes of the reader by boldly declaring that no apology is needed for printing a book on the subject treated. This is rather an effective way in which to disguise the apology, still it is only a different, though a bolder, way of saying that the book fills a long felt want, which is ever a large part of the burden of the apology part of the normal preface.

A closer approach is made toward doing away with the apology when the author disowns responsibility for having undertaken the work, and throws the blame on some one else, as was done by John S. Wise in the preface to his recent book on Citizenship, wherein it is stated that idea of writing the book was not conceived by the author, but that he was incited thereto by the publishers. Another example of this expedient is found in the preface to the 1795 edition of Runnington on Ejectment. There the learned author protests that the responsibility for the work rested upon Mr. Justice Gould — the "late" Mr. Justice Gould — who, to quote from the preface, "cordially and repeatedly requested me to revise and enlarge" the earlier work. "The request of that venerable character (a character which will not easily be deprived of the esteem of posterity, while learning has any reverence, or integrity any respect, among the professors of the law) had the influence of a command; a command which, at every interval of leisure, I cheerfully set myself about to obey." It seems a pity that the learned justice did not live to enjoy the results of the labor which he had so effectually commanded, and to which he was made to give his posthumous i 'orsement, for the book must have been one of surpassing merit since the author so cheerfully placed the responsibility for it upon one who was no longer in a position to defend himself. While this shifting of the responsibility for a book may not be, strictly speaking, an apology, it is nevertheless an implied admission that an apology may be due from some one. But even so, this device is not to be commended. It is a frittering away of one of the fundamental rules governing preface writing, and, therefore, a dangerous innovation which may in time lead to the omission of the apology from all prefaces. And goodness knows most law books need to be thoroughly apologized for by some responsible person.

A reason for publishing which will be appreciated by every lawyer who has had his time taken up in giving, or evading the giving, of gratuitous advice to fellow members of the bar, is advanced by Sir James Burrow, in the preface to the first volume of his reports, wherein he says: "It may naturally be asked why I publish *at all?* . . . I found myself reduced to the necessity of either destroying or publishing these papers (which were originally intended for my own private use, and not for public inspection). For as it was become generally known 'that I had taken some account (good or bad) of all the cases which had occurred in the Court of King's Bench for upwards of forty years,' I was subject to continual interruption and even persecution, by incessant applications for searches into my notes; for transcripts of them; sometimes for the note-books themselves (not always returned without trouble and solicitation); not to mention frequent conversations upon very dry and unentertaining subjects, which my consulters were paid for considering, but I had no sort of concern in. This inconvenience grew from bad to worse, till it became quite insupportable; and from thence arises the present publication."

Still another reason for writing a book is that the author was in jail, and needed some occupation by which to pass the time. In the preface to his work on the Bankruptcy Law of America, Thomas Cooper said: "The present compilation originated from a desire of being engaged in some professional pursuit during the latter months of a tedious imprisonment to which I had the honor of being sentenced, for exposing some few among the errors of a weak, a wicked, and a vindictive administration." This imprisonment was for a violent newspaper attack upon President John Adams. The author was tried under the Sedition Law, and convicted of libel.

The reader who does not belong to that unfortunate class of petty souls who are ever on the alert to discover egotism in others, will usually condone the very natural tendency of an author to claim more for his book than the unbiased mind will concede. Still it is well for the writer of a preface not to overtax this indulgence. Few authors can afford to imitate the preface to the fifth edition of Dr. von Ihering's Struggle for Law when the learned doctor says: "I still consider the fundamental idea of the work so undoubtedly true and irrefutable that I look upon every word said in opposition to it as lost."

Prefaces should be truthful; for experience has shown that the writer of a preface who departs from the truth sometimes diggeth a pit for himself. The author of a certain work on corporations stated in the preface that "previous experience and researches incident to a somewhat extensive practice, principally in this branch, has been of great assistance" in writing the book. This statement was well calculated to make an impression upon the reader; but, unfortunately for the author, a reviewer pointed out that it "may possibly excite attention" among the members of the bar in the city of the author's residence to learn that the author had become qualified for the writing of the work by a "somewhat extensive practice" in corporation law. In North's Life of Lord Guilford (vol. 1, p. 110, ed. 1826) is this account of the preface to Pollexfen's Reports: "By way of remark to show how faction will get the better of common sense and truth, even in men great pretenders to both, I must add that Pollexfen, an arguer for Sir Samuel Barnardiston, since the Revolution, published (or fitted for the press) a book of reports, as they are called, consisting chiefly of his factious arguments; and particularly in this case (Barnardiston *v.* Soame); but most brazenly and untruly in his preface tells how 'he had carried the cause, if the Lord Chief Justice North had not solicited the judges to give a contrary judgment' — or to that effect. This book and preface was shown to the then Lord Chief Justice Holt, who did a singular piece of justice to his lordship's memory and honor; for he sent for the bookseller to answer it before him, and had suppressed the book, if he had not promised to change the preface, and leave out that scandal — which was done; but some copies had escaped before." "Reader," appeals the editor of Latch's Reports in pompous and lying solemnity, "the testimonials of many sages of law, the judges, his contemporaries, give you an assurance, above all that I can express, that the original of this impression was all written by that worthy person's own hand." But, unfortunately for the author of these reassuring words, we find, in the preface to Palmer's Reports, the following: "Why there are so few [cases] in King Charles the First's time is, because the author lent his book to Mr. Latch, in whose reports, now extant, there are above 120 cases transcribed; (which although corruptly enough) yet that the reader should not be encumbered with repetitions are here purposely omitted."

The author may wish to put something in his preface to disarm criticism. Bellewe has supplied an excellent model in the preface to his report, wherein he quaintly says to the reader: "Beseeching you that where you shall find any faults, which either by my insufficiency, the intricateness of the work, or the printer's recklessness, are committed, either friendly to pardon, or by some means to admonish me thereof." Or, if it is not desired to be quite so gentle, a suggestion is afforded by the preface to Bendloe's Reports, which concludes with the following very proper advice to the reader: "Wherefore accept in good part the author's pains, and bestow your own in the perusal of them, before you proceed to censure, and then no doubt you will find very good advantage thereby." But neither of these extracts is satisfactory if the author wishes to pay his respects properly to that numerous class of critics who do not know that books, as everything else, can only be fairly judged by a balancing of the good and the bad — those mightly hunters in hunting for motes, who need only to find one or two faults in order to condemn. For critics of this kind, here is something from the preface to Parke's History of the Court of Chancery, which is at once a defiance and a threat: "It is anticipated that in such a work as the present, embracing periods of history by no means satisfactorily explored, numerous omissions and errors may be pointed out by those who make it more their business to detect them than to appreciate the contribution to the common stock of knowledge. He will no further notice or answer any disingenuous criticism than by perfecting and extending a future edition of his work."

While there is often much of interest in prefaces, they sometimes degenerate into the trite. This may be because the author has become completely exhausted by the writing of his book (or reading the proof), and is incapable of another effort, but whatever the reason it is certainly true. To illustrate: The commencement of the preface to the third volume of Modern Reports, p. xiv, is as follows: "Gentlemen, All human laws are either natural or civil." In commenting upon this solemn utterance, a writer with pretensions to humor has said: "This puts us in mind of a humorous introduction to death, which we have somewhere read:

'Death is common to all,'
It occurs but once.'"

A more happy classification of the law may be found in the preface to Fortescue's Reports, wherein we are given this information: "The grand division of law is into the divine law and the law of nature; so that the study of law in general is the business of men and angels. Angels may desire to look into both the one and the other; but they will never be able to fathom the depths of either." T. M.

Cases of Interest.

Privilege Tax on Coca-Cola Upheld. — In Coca-Cola Co. *v.* Skillman, 44 So. Rep. 985, the Mississippi Supreme Court holds that a state law imposing a privilege tax on the bottling, distribution, and sale of coca-cola and certain other kindred beverages, violates no provision of the State or Federal Constitution, though there may be other proprietary drinks on which no privilege tax is imposed.

SUNDAY CLOSING STATUTE — CONSTITUTIONALITY. — In State v. Herald, 92 Pac. Rep. 376, the Washington Supreme Court holds that a statute forbidding the keeping open of any playhouse or theatre on Sunday does not prevent the opening of such buildings for religious or other quiet, legitimate, and orderly exercises, and, therefore, is not violative of the constitutional provisions forbidding the passage of laws granting special privileges or immunities to any citizen or class of citizens.

INTOXICATING LIQUORS — POLICE POWER OF STATE. — In De Grazier v. Stephens, 105 S. W. Rep. 992, the Texas Supreme Court holds that a statute requiring that an applicant for a retail liquor license must be a citizen of the State and a resident of the county wherein the license is sought is not a mere guise to evade the provisions of the Federal Constitution prohibiting discrimination by a State against nonresidents, but is calculated to aid in regulating the liquor traffic, by rendering the licensee subject to process where suit is brought on his bond, and by facilitating the determination of his other qualifications to exercise the license.

MONOPOLY — HOLDING COMPANY. — In Burrows v. Interborough Metropolitan Co., 156 Fed. Rep. 389, Judge Holt, in the Circuit Court for the Southern District of New York, held that the acquisition by a corporation of a controlling interest in the stock of the corporations owning or controlling and operating all of the street railway lines in the boroughs of Manhattan and the Bronx in New York city, including the underground, elevated, and surface lines, was unlawful as creating a practical monopoly of the means for transportation of passengers in the city, in violation of the provision of the New York stock corporation law that "no domestic stock corporation and no foreign corporation doing business in this State shall combine with any other corporation or person for the creation of a monopoly or the unlawful restraint of trade, or for the prevention of competition in any necessary of life."

RAILROAD COMMISSIONERS — ACT CREATING UPHELD. — In State v. Missouri Pac. R. Co., 92 Pac. Rep. 606, the Kansas Supreme Court upholds the validity of the State statute creating a board of railroad commissioners. The act was attacked on the grounds that it attempted to delegate to the board legislative authority; that it conferred upon the board a combination of legislative, executive, and judicial powers; that it conferred upon the State Supreme Court legislative and nonjudicial powers not within the jurisdiction granted to the court by the constitution; that it deprived the defendant of its property without due process of law; that the constitution did not specifically grant to the legislature the power to create a board of railroad commissioners, and that the act placed upon a political commission the entire control and regulation of railroads and deprived the owners of all control and regulation, except to finance the companies to which the roads belonged. Each of these contentions was examined by the court and held to be untenable.

TICKET SCALPING — INJUNCTION AGAINST. — In Bitterman v. Louisville, etc., R. Co., 28 Sup. Ct. Rep. 91, the United States Supreme Court holds that carrying on the business of buying and selling nontransferable reduced-rate excursion railroad tickets for profit, to the injury of the railroad company issuing such tickets, is an actionable wrong, although actual malice in the sense of personal ill will may not exist. The court held that in such a case injunction relief would not be denied on the ground of there being an adequate remedy at law, where the ticket brokers admitted past dealings and avowed their purpose to continue the practice, and where the number of such tickets issued was large, the risk to be incurred by the steps necessary to prevent their wrongful use was considerable, and numerous suits would be necessary if redress was sought at law. An injunction was granted restraining the defendants generally from dealing in such tickets, whether already issued or thereafter to be issued.

SLEEPING CARS — POWER OF STATE TO REGULATE. — In State v. Redmon, 114 N. W. Rep. 137, the Wisconsin Supreme Court holds that a statute providing that the upper berth in a sleeping car shall, when unoccupied, at the option of the occupant of the lower berth, be closed, is unconstitutional and void. The court holds that the mere fact that the legislature has disguised such an act as an exercise of the police power does not make it such in fact, and that the giving to the occupant of the lower berth the option to say whether the upper berth be closed or not, manifestly suggests that it is for private rather than for public interests. After an extended and interesting discussion of the limits of the police power, Marshall, J., reaches the conclusion that the statute in question "is clearly unconstitutional, both because the subject as dealt with is not within the scope of police power, but is a mere matter, as to the persons sought to be benefited, of individual concern, and because if it were otherwise the character of the remedy, under the circumstances, is not within the boundaries of reason and so is an interference with constitutional rights of property."

STREET RAILWAYS — HALF FARE FOR SCHOOL CHILDREN. — In Interstate Consolidated St. R. Co. v. Massachusetts, 28 Sup. Ct. Rep. 26, the United States Supreme Court affirmed the judgment of the Massachusetts court (187 Mass. 436), holding that a street railway company whose charter subjected it to "all the duties, liabilities, and restrictions set forth in all general laws now or hereafter in force, relating to street railway companies," was bound by the requirements of a statute previously enacted, that street railway companies shall transport school children at half fare, regardless of whether the statute was constitutional as to corporations existing at the time of its enactment. Mr. Justice Holmes, who wrote the opinion, went further and asserted his individual belief that such a statute was constitutional irrespective of any disabilities to object to its terms. Mr. Justice Harlan thought that the constitutionality of the act was necessarily involved in the determination of the case, and joined in the affirmance on the sole ground that he did not regard the act as vulnerable to the constitutional objections urged against it.

BOYCOTT — INJUNCTION AGAINST. — In two very recent cases injunctions have been granted against labor unions restraining them from boycotting employers whom they had pronounced "unfair." In Shine v. Fox Bros. Mfg. Co., 156 Fed. Rep. 357 (Circuit Court of Appeals, Eighth Circuit), the defendant unions attempted to coerce the complainant into discharging the nonunion men in its employ, and on its refusal to accede to their demands they issued circulars stating that union workmen would not be permitted to work upon materials put out by the complainant. By this means, and by threatening and in some instances calling strikes, they compelled a number of contractors who had been customers of the complainant to sign agreements not to buy from it in future, and in other ways undertook to make it impossible for the complainant to do business unless it acceded to their demands. This was held to constitute an unlawful interference with the complainant's business, warranting an injunction. In Buck Stove & Range Co. v. American Federation of Labor, 35 Wash. L. Rep. 797, the Supreme Court of the District of Columbia reached the same conclusion on a substantially similar state of facts, and granted an injunction *pendente lite* restraining the defendants from boycotting the complainant's business.

SOME AUTOMOBILE CASES. — In Lewis *v.* Amorous, 59 S. E. Rep. 338, the Georgia Court of Appeals holds that the owner or keeper of an automobile is not liable for a negligent homicide committed with the machine in a public street by a person old enough to be discreet and responsible in the eyes of the law, where such person takes the machine, without the knowledge of the owner, from a garage where it had been left, notwithstanding the leaving of the automobile at the garage furnishes the opportunity whereby such person gets possession of it. To the same effect is Jones *v.* Hoge, 92 Pac. Rep. 433, wherein the Washington Supreme Court held that where the defendant's chauffeur, without authority, took the defendant's automobile from the garage without his knowledge or permission, and while using it on a personal errand of his own ran over the plaintiff, the accident occurred while the chauffeur was acting beyond the scope of his employment, and hence the defendant was not liable.

In Mahoney *v.* Maxfield, 113 N. W. Rep. 904, the Minnesota Supreme Court held that a statute requiring the driver of an automobile to stop on signal from one driving a horse did not impose upon the operator of an automobile the absolute duty to stop his engine also upon such signal being given, in addition to stopping the vehicle itself. Whether the failure to stop the motive power is negligence must be determined by the circumstances of each case.

FOREIGN CORPORATIONS — POWER OF STATE OVER. — An important decision regarding the power of a State to exclude a foreign corporation or impose conditions on its admission was rendered by the Circuit Court of Appeals, Eighth Circuit, in Butler Bros. Shoe Co. *v.* United States Rubber Co., 156 Fed. Rep. 1. The court held that the broad statement in Paul *v.* Virginia, 8 Wall. 168, that a State may exclude a foreign corporation, or impose such conditions as it deems proper on the right of such corporation to do business within the State, has been qualified by subsequent decisions of the federal Supreme Court, and the following exceptions to it are established: (1) Every corporation empowered by the State of its creation to engage in interstate commerce may carry on that commerce in sound and recognized articles of commerce in every other State in the Union. Every prohibition, obstruction, or burden which the other States attempt to impose upon such business is unconstitutional and void. (2) Every corporation of every State which is in the employ of the United States has the right to exercise the necessary corporate powers and to transact the requisite business to discharge the duties of that employment in every other State in the Union, without let or hindrance from the latter. (3) Every corporation of every State has the absolute right to institute, maintain, and defend in the federal courts, and to remove to those courts, its suits in any other States in the cases and on the terms prescribed by the Acts of Congress. The court held that the constitution and statutes of Colorado, prohibiting any foreign corporation from doing any business whatever, from exercising any corporate power, and from prosecuting or defending any suit in that State unless it file certain writings, pay certain fees, etc., were unconstitutional so far as they attempted to limit the exercise in that State by a foreign corporation of its right to engage in interstate commerce and to institute and defend in the federal courts suits arising out of that commerce.

MAXIMUM RATE LAW — SUIT AGAINST STATE. — In an extended and carefully considered opinion the North Carolina Supreme Court, in State *v.* Southern R. Co., 59 S. E. Rep. 570, denied the power of the federal courts to enjoin the enforcement of the State maximum passenger rate law. One ground on which the decision was based was that, under the general principle of the law of injunctions that equity courts are without jurisdiction to interfere by injunction with other courts in the due course of administering and enforcing the criminal laws, a federal court had no power to enjoin a criminal prosecution for a violation of the act. But the greater stress was laid on the point that the suit in the federal court, being against the North Carolina Corporation Commission, the attorney-general, and the assistant attorney-general, was a suit against the State, and, therefore, within the Eleventh Amendment to the Constitution of the United States, declaring that the judicial power of the United States shall not extend to any suit against a State by a citizen of another State. The majority of the court held, however, that under the language of the act the railroad corporation was merely subject to a fine of $500 for each violation of the statute and was not indictable either as principal or as accessory of the agent who sold a ticket in violation of the act. On this point, Clark, C. J., dissented vigorously. In the course of his dissenting opinion he said: "It has not only always been human law that he who causes another to commit crime is equally as guilty as he who does the act, but it is the divine decree in the first recorded judgment. The serpent received no part of the fruit. It did not compel Eve to eat. But because it suggested and encouraged the violation of the law it received the heavier sentence. Here the railroad both compelled the act to be done and received all the profits of the crime. Adam did not procure the violation of the law, but only received part of the fruit. Yet was he also punished."

Book Reviews.

A Treatise on the Modern Law of Banking. By Albert S. Bolles. Philadelphia: George T. Bisel Co., 1907. 2 vols., 1124 pp.

Dr. Bolles, as a college lecturer on commercial law and banking, and as a prolific writer on subjects connected with banking, seems to have been qualified to produce the rounded treatise which the Bisel Company have brought out in two handsome canvas-bound volumes.

The Trial of James Stewart (the Appin Murder). Edited by David N. Mackey. Canada Law Book Co., Toronto.

The lovers of Stevenson's "Kidnapped," who remember the Stewarts of Appin and their enmities with the Campbells, will read and be fascinated by this stirring account of the strange doings in the Argyle country, and the story of the tragedy at Lettermore in 1752 and its grim sequel at Inveraray and Ballachulish. The book is one of the delightful series of "Notable Scottish Trials."

Toxicology: the Nature, Effects, and Detection of Poisons. By Cassius M. Riley, M.D. Third edition. Philadelphia: P. Blakiston's Son & Co., 1906.

A convenient manual for ready reference, primarily written for physicians, but of undoubted usefulness to prosecuting attorneys and to lawyers who undertake the defense of persons accused of committing murder in the Borgian manner.

Analytical Index of Louisiana Personal Injuries Cases. By H. H. White. Alexandria, La., 1907. 96 pp. $7.50.

This little book is a novelty. In eight columns the author has analyzed every reported personal injury case in Louisiana under the heads, Title, Cause of Action, Defense, How Tried, Judgment of Lower Court, Judgment of Upper Court, Date, Report. There is also a table of amounts awarded for various classes of injury. Confined to a single jurisdiction, such a scheme is practical and the result as worked out by Mr. White is of real value. There are other groups of cases which might well be analyzed in the same manner.

An Essay on Professional Ethics. By George Sharswood. Fifth edition. Philadelphia: T. & J. W. Johnson Co., 1907.

This work was first published in 1854, and is now reprinted as a part of the Reports of the American Bar Association, in conformity to the action of the Association taken upon the report of the Committee on Code of Professional Ethics. A half century has not lessened in a particle the keen force of Judge Sharswood's comments on professional conduct and manners.

The Raid on Prosperity. By James Roscoe Day, LL.D., D. C. L. New York: D. Appleton & Co., 1907.

"Are cases to be known in this country as President's cases?" asks Chancellor Day. "If so, how will such cases stand in the courts?" Well, the Supreme Court has just held the Federal Employers' Liability Act to be unconstitutional, in spite of executive scoldings at the inferior judges who first reached that conclusion, and in spite, too, of a presidential decree that the act "must be kept on the statute books in drastic and thoroughgoing form."

Memoirs of Sir Edward West, Chief Justice of King's Court during its conflict with the East India Company. By F. Dawtry Drewitt. London and New York: Longmans, Green & Co., 1907.

The lot of a king's judge in India in the first quarter of the last century was a singularly hard one. There was constant collision with the "Company" and its officials, who seemed to regard the sovereignty of India as their private property. Sickness and death were rife; the average length of the lives of the judges after reaching Bombay being less than four years. The crown gave scant support to the judges sent by it to enforce English justice. Amid such trying surroundings Sir Edward West did his duty and died "a champion of judicial integrity." As a picture of life in Bombay in the days of George IV., and a story of the fight made by one courageous lawyer against the forces of greed and injustice, Mr. Drewitt's contribution to legal memoirs is well worth reading.

News of the Profession.

The Kansas State Bar Association met in Topeka on January 30 and 31. Details of the meeting will be given in this column next month.

The South Carolina State Bar Association held its fifteenth annual meeting in Columbia on January 15 and 16. An account of the meeting will be given in our next issue.

The New York State Bar Association held its thirty-first annual meeting in New York city on January 24 and 25. An account of the meeting will be given in this column next month.

Death of Prominent Tennessee Lawyer. — Col. Arthur S. Colyar, one of the leading members of the Tennessee bar, died at his home in Nashville, on December 13, in his ninetieth year.

American Bar Will Meet in Seattle. — At a meeting held in Chicago on December 28 the executive committee of the American Bar Association decided to hold the next meeting of the association in Seattle, beginning on August 25.

Death of Judge Henderson, of Texas. — Hon. John N. Henderson, for the last thirteen years a judge of the Texas Court of Criminal Appeal, died December 22 at his home in Dallas, aged sixty-four.

New Judge for Manitoba. — John Donald Cameron, K. C., of Winnipeg, has been appointed to fill the recently created additional judgeship on the Court of King's Bench, of Manitoba. He was formerly attorney-general of the province.

Ex-Judge Thomson, of Colorado, Dead. — Hon. Charles I. Thomson, one of the ablest judges of the Colorado Court of Appeals prior to the abolition of that court in 1905, died on December 31 in Denver, aged seventy-one. He was appointed to the Court of Appeals in 1892 and served until that court was merged into the State Supreme Court.

New Brunswick's Chief Justice Resigns. — On January 8 Chief Justice Tuck, of New Brunswick, tendered his resignation to the prime minister. Justice Tuck is seventy-six years old and has sat on the bench of the New Brunswick Supreme Court since 1885. He was made chief justice in 1896.

Judge Chase Retires. — On December 28 Judge William M. Chase, of the New Hampshire Supreme Court, reached the age limit of seventy years and retired from the bench after a service of nearly seventeen years. He is succeeded by Hon. Robert J. Peaslee, of Manchester, former judge of the Superior Court.

Death of Senator Mallory. — United States Senator Stephen R. Mallory, of Florida, died in Pensacola, on December 23, at the age of fifty-nine. He was admitted to the Louisiana bar in 1873, but removed to Pensacola the following year. Very soon thereafter he rose into political prominence, and it was rather as a politician than as a lawyer that he was known.

Michigan's New Chief Justice. — On January 1 Associate Justice Claudius B. Grant, of the Michigan Supreme Court, became chief justice of the court, succeeding Hon. A. V. McAlvay. Justice Grant is the oldest member of the court, being seventy-two years old. He has served eighteen years, and before that was a circuit judge for eight years. His term has two years more to run.

Well-known Connecticut Lawyer Dead. — Samuel Fessenden, widely known as "plain Sam Fessenden" and the originator of the famous phrase "God Almighty hates a quitter," died at his home in Stamford, Conn., on January 7, at the age of sixty. He was for many years one of the most prominent factors in Connecticut politics and was several times a candidate . the office of United States senator.

Distinguished New Yorker a Suicide. — Suffering from the combined effects of an attack of grip and the loss of his fortune, Ernest G. Stedman, a wealthy real estate lawyer of New York city and a relative of the banker-poet Edmund Clarence Stedman, committed suicide on December 26 by throwing himself in front of a subway train. The recent failure of the J. C. Lyons Building and Operating Company swept away his entire fortune of more than a million dollars.

Appointed to Wisconsin Supreme Court. — On January 4 Governor Davidson appointed Robert M. Bashford, of Madison, an associate justice of the Wisconsin Supreme Court to fill the vacancy created by the death of Chief Justice Cassoday. Judge Bashford is a native of Wisconsin, and is sixty-two years old. He has long been prominent in his State, both as a lawyer and a politician. By reason of length of service Justice John B. Winslow has become chief justice of the court, to which he was appointed in 1891. The new chief justice, although the senior member of the court, is comparatively still a young man, being but fifty-six years of age.

J. C. BANCROFT DAVIS DEAD. — J. C. Bancroft Davis, reporter of the United States Supreme Court from 1882 to 1901, died at his home in Washington, D. C., on December 28, aged eighty-five years. He was a native of Worcester, Mass., and was a son of Governor John Davis, of Massachusetts. He was graduated from Harvard in the class of 1840, and after studying law in an office was admitted to the bar in 1843. He was secretary of the United States legation in London from 1849 to 1853, and was assistant secretary of state from 1869 to 1871 and from 1873 to 1874, in the latter year being appointed minister to Germany, in which position he served for three years. In 1878 he was appointed a judge of the Court of Claims, serving until 1882, when he was made reporter of the Supreme Court.

PROFESSOR GARDNER A VICTIM OF CANCER. — After a lingering illness Professor George Enos Gardner, of the Boston University Law School, died of cancer at his home in Worcester, on December 17. He was forty-two years of age. In 1885 he was graduated from Amherst College, and was admitted to the Massachusetts bar in 1887. After practicing for a year or two he became a teacher in the Worcester high school, where he remained till 1897, when he became an instructor in the Illinois Law School, going the following summer to Bangor, Me., to take the position of dean of the University of Maine Law School, which he held until 1902. In that year he was elected professor of law in the Boston University Law School. Professor Gardner was the author of a textbook on Wills.

SOUTH DAKOTA STATE BAR ASSOCIATION. — The eighth annual meeting of the South Dakota State Bar Association was held at Watertown, on January 8 and 9. The annual address was delivered by Justice Edwin A. Jaggard, of the Minnesota Supreme Court, on the subject "The Study of Comparative Law." The president's address was delivered by President Joseph W. Jones, judge of the second judicial circuit. Papers were read before the association as follows: "Trial by Jury," by Judge James H. McCoy, of Aberdeen; "The Police Power — Its Importance and Development," by Hon. Philo Hall, of Brookings; "The Manufacture of Prejudice," by Hon. H. C. Preston, of Mitchell; "Ought Not Changes to Be Made in the Law with Reference to Jury Trials in Civil Cases?" by Hon. Robert B. Tripp, of Yankton. The meeting was concluded with the annual banquet.

NEW HAMPSHIRE STATE BAR ASSOCIATION. — The annual meeting and banquet of the New Hampshire State Bar Association were held in Concord, on December 12, with about two hundred members in attendance. The president, Hon. James A. Edgerly, of Somersworth, was prevented by illness from attending, but the address which he had prepared was read by Leslie P. Snow, of Rochester. The annual address, which was delivered by ex-Gov. Frank S. Black, of New York, aroused great interest and has since been widely published because of the speaker's severe arraignment of some of the Roosevelt policies. The banquet was held in the evening and the new president acted as toastmaster. Among those who responded to toasts were ex-Gov. Black, Hon. Oliver E. Branch, Hon. Henry F. Hollis, and Hon. James W. Remick. The officers elected for the ensuing term were: President, Edwin F. Jones, of Manchester; secretary and treasurer, A. H. Chase, of Concord.

DEATH OF WISCONSIN'S CHIEF JUSTICE. — Hon. John B. Cassoday, chief justice of the Supreme Court of Wisconsin, died at his home in Madison, on December 30, from the effects of an operation for gallstones. Judge Cassoday was born in Herkimer county, N. Y., in 1830. His academic education was had in Pennsylvania schools, after which he attended the University of Michigan for one year and then studied law in the Albany Law School. Afterwards he moved to Janesville, Wis., and was admitted to the bar of that State in 1857. He was elected a member of the Wisconsin legislature in 1865, and two years later was made speaker of the house. In 1880 Governor Smith appointed him an associate justice of the State Supreme Court, and in 1895, on the death of Chief Justice Orton, he became chief justice of the court. At one time he was professor of constitutional law in the University of Wisconsin. He also did considerable law writing, his best known work in that line being Cassoday on Wills. While not a man of especially brilliant parts, Judge Cassoday was a good lawyer and a good judge, and served his State well in the high office to which he was called.

WEST VIRGINIA STATE BAR ASSOCIATION. — The twenty-third annual meeting of the West Virginia State Bar Association was held in New Martinsville, on December 31 and January 1. President J. Hop Woods, of Philippi, delivered an address on "The Evolution of the Law of Options." The annual address was delivered by Professor William Herbert Page, of the Ohio State University, who took for his theme "The Crisis in the Development of the Law." Other papers on the program were: "Habits and Customs of Bench and Bar," by P. J. Crogan; "Our System of Forfeiting Land Titles," by W. W. Hughes; "The Justice of the Peace; What Is the Remedy?" by Charles McCammick. The meeting was concluded with the customary banquet, at which John W. Davis, of Clarksburg, acted as toastmaster. Responses were made by General Alfred Caldwell of Wheeling, E. Wood Daily, Charles E. Hogg, E. L. Lickolf, and W. P. Hubbard. The following officers were elected: President, George Tucker Brooke; vice-presidents, Harvey W. Harmer, Boyd Faulkner, T. M. McClintic, Walter Pendleton, W. W. Hughes; secretary, Charles McCammick; treasurer, C. A. Kreps. The next meeting is to be held in Huntington.

MISSOURI STATE BAR ASSOCIATION. — The twenty-fifth annual meeting of the Missouri State Bar Association was held in Kansas City, on December 12 and 13. After a few words of welcome from R. J. Ingraham, president of the Kansas City Bar Association, and a response by W. J. Haliburton, of Carthage, President Sanford B. Ladd delivered the usual address, reviewing the important statutes enacted during last year, concluding with an exhortation to give the corporations a fair chance. The annual address was delivered by Federal Judge Peter Grosscup, of Chicago, who discussed the trust problems and the causes for the financial troubles of the country. Other addresses were: "Commerce under Our Dual System of Government," by Charles Nagel, of St. Louis; "The Spirit of the Law," by Judge Samuel Davis, of Marshall. The meeting closed with the annual dinner, at which Judge J. McD. Trimble officiated as toastmaster. Among those who responded to toasts were General John W. Noble, Judge J. B. Gantt, and Colonel L. H. Waters. The officers elected for the next year were as follows: President, Robert T. Railey, of Harrisonville; secretary, Lee Montgomery, of Sedalia; treasurer, R. E. Ball, of Kansas City. The judges of the various circuits serve as vice-presidents.

OKLAHOMA STATE BAR ASSOCIATION. — The annual meeting of the Oklahoma State Bar Association was held in Oklahoma City, on December 19 and 20, with President Jackson presiding. After a reception to the state and federal judges the president delivered his address on the noteworthy legislation of the past year, and the balance of the morning was taken up with reports of officers and committees. The feature of the meeting was the annual address by Hon. Joseph M. Hill, chief justice of the Arkansas Supreme Court, whose subject was "The Evolution of the State." Other papers on the program were: "A Code of Laws for the New State," by United States District Judge R. E. Campbell; "Land Tenures in That Part of the State Recently Known as Oklahoma Territory," by United States District Judge J. H. Cotteral; "Land Tenures in That

Part of the State Recently Known as Indian Territory," by W. H. Kornegay; "Our Judicial System," by Judge J. R. Keaton; "A Form of Legislative Jurisdiction," by E. E. Blake; "Corporations Continuing Business After Statehood, Their Rights and Powers," by C. J. Wrightsman; "Exemptions," by T. J. Womack; "The Enforcement of Judicial Decrees," by G. A. Brown; "Revenue and Taxation," by W. J. Horton; "Municipal Corporations in the New State," by J. E. Humphrey; "The Initiative and Referendum," by John Embry; "The Corporation Commission and Its Powers," by W. E. Utterback. On the evening of the second day the annual banquet was held in the Threadgill Hotel. Officers for the ensuing year were elected as follows: President, Frank Wells, of Oklahoma City; secretary, F. H. Kellogg, of South McAlester; treasurer, S. S. Lawrence, of Guthrie.

English Notes.

Lord Halsbury Sits in Court of Appeal. — During December Lord Halsbury, ex-Lord Chancellor of England, sat in the Court of Appeal during the absence of Lord Justice Vaughn Williams on the Welsh Church Commission. Lord Halsbury is now in his eighty-third year.

New Judge in Chancery Division. — The vacancy on the bench of the Chancery Division created by the death of Mr. Justice Kekewich has been filled by the appointment of Mr. Harry Trelawney Eve, K. C., M. P. The new judge is fifty-two years of age. He was called to the bar at Lincoln's Inn in 1881, and fourteen years later was made a Q. C. The appointment has been cordially welcomed by the profession, as the appointee is one of the most popular as well as one of the ablest men practicing at the chancery bar.

Condition Against Military or Naval Service Illegal. — In a recent case, *In re* Beard, decided during December, Mr. Justice Swinfen-Eady decided what appears to be a point of first impression regarding the avoidance of a condition on the ground of public policy. The case involved a devise containing a condition subsequent whereby the devisee was to forfeit his interest in the testator's property if he should enter the naval or military service of the country. The judge ruled that such a condition was void as being against public policy.

Promise to Marry Made During Spouse's Lifetime. — The question whether a promise of marriage is actionable when at the time it was made one of the parties had, to the knowledge of the other, a husband or wife living, was recently decided for the first time in England by the King's Bench Division, in Spiers *v.* Hunt, noted in 42 L. J. 792. The promise of marriage was made at a time when the defendant's wife, as the plaintiff knew, was living. Relying on this promise, the plaintiff established meretricious relations with the defendant, and, on his refusal to fulfil his promise after his wife's death, brought an action against him for breach of promise. Mr. Justice Phillimore held that the contract was void as against public policy, and gave judgment for the defendant. Another case, Atherton *v.* Yarde-Buller, which involved the same question, except that it was the woman who was married, was terminated by settlement.

The Druce Case. — With the exhumation of the coffin of T. C. Druce, and the finding therein of the remains of a man instead of a quantity of sheet lead, the sensational claim to the Portland estates which has excited so large an amount of interest during the last few months practically collapsed. The witness Caldwell, who testified that he personally knew Druce and the fifth Duke of Portland to be one and the same person, and that he assisted in the burial of the lead-filled casket, was completely discredited. He fled to America, but was arrested on his arrival at New York and held for extradition on a charge of perjury. The proceeding by the claimant against his uncle, Herbert Druce, for perjury in swearing that he had seen the dead body of T. C. Druce in his coffin, has been dropped, but it is stated that the civil proceedings to get possession of the Portland estates will be carried on. However, it is not likely that the stockholders of the corporation which was organized to push the Druce claim will realize any dividends on their investment.

One Tangible Result of the Hague Conference. — That the popular impression that the recent Peace Conference accomplished nothing is not justified by the facts, is the tenor of a recent article in the *Fortnightly Review*, from the pen of Sir Thomas Barclay. He points out that while the nations have not yet agreed to beat their swords into pruning hooks, or to settle their disputes by wars of words, they have at least laid a foundation upon which in the future may be reared an edifice of real international law. What has hitherto been known by that name is not "law" in a strict sense, but rather a system of ethics to which right-minded nations are supposed to conform. Something more tangible, says Sir Thomas Barclay, is being given to the world by the Hague Conference. It is laying down a vast groundwork of international legislation upon which future conferences will be able to work. A written code of international law will be the possession of future generations, and whether or not the conference fails of its object, to secure the peace of the world, this much, at all events, will stand to its credit, and to the profit of the nations.

The Chartreuse Case. — In the proceeding brought to restrain the unauthorized use of the word "Chartreuse" the Court of Appeal has recently unanimously reversed the decision of Mr. Justice Joyce and restored to the Carthusian monks the sole right to the name attached to their world-famous product and all the privileges associated with it. The court held that the word had acquired the secondary meaning of a liquor made by the Carthusian monks; that the defendant French company were trying to make the public believe that their liquor was the same as the original product of the monastery, and that in fact their liquor was not the same. The French government seized the place of manufacture and the materials stored there, but it could not seize the incorporeal process and the secret. The government disposed of the business, and in France the product of the new company is sold with the old familiar labels and peculiarly shaped bottles, while the product of the monks will, with the same bottles and labels, be sold as "Chartreuse" in England, where the sale of the liquor of the French company in that form and under that name will be restrained.

Check — Stopping Payment by Telegram. — An important point regarding the countermanding of a bank check was decided by the Court of Appeal in the case of Curtice *v.* The City and Country Bank, noted in 42 L. J. 787. The plaintiff after business sent a telegram to the bank to stop payment on a check. The telegram was put in the letter-box at the bank, but was overlooked by the cashier when he cleared out the box next morning, and the check when presented was paid. In the Divisional Court it was held that the telegram constituted notice to the bank, but with this view the Court of Appeal disagreed. In the opinion the Master of the Rolls said: "Countermand is really a question of fact. It means much more than a change of purpose on the part of the customer. It means, in addition, the notification of that change of purpose to the bank.

There is no such thing as a constructive countermand in a commercial transaction of this kind. In my opinion, on the admitted facts of this case, the check was not countermanded in fact, although it may well be that it was due to the negligence of the bank that they did not receive notice of the customer's desire to stop the check. For such negligence the bank might be liable, but the measure of damages would be by no means the same as in an action for money had and received."

ENGLISH LAWYERS AGAINST TORRENS SYSTEM. — Ever since the Land Registry Act was put in force in London the legal profession in England has been crying out against it, and recently the council of the Law Society has come out with a lengthy paper protesting against the further extension of the system and citing a mass of statistics to show its iniquities. Of this pronouncement the *Law Journal* says editorially: "The facts and figures which it discloses are positively alarming in their importance, and they should be enough, when realized, to dispose of the wild scheme now being put forward to extend compulsory registration of title over the whole of England and Wales, to promote which a government committee has been appointed — in Scotland! The experimental trial of the system initiated ten years ago in the administrative county of London has proved a gigantic failure, and it is proposed now, in order to offer fresh inducements for the registration of absolute titles, to raise a public loan — charged on future land registry fees — to meet initial expenses. Yet the evidence is overwhelming that the growth of expenses incident to compulsory registration is greater than any fees to be obtained from the enforcement of such a system without imposing a crushing burden on the owners of house and landed property; and the position now is that with an income of over £50,000 per annum there is still a large deficit every year which has to be borne by the treasury. This deficit contrasts badly with the profit of £10,000 a year derived from the Middlesex Registry under the system in vogue before the adoption of this new departure in experimental legislation. The loan necessary to defray the initial cost of the extended experiment is estimated at no less a sum than twenty millions sterling, and the annual charge for salaries of officials and other expenses at local registries in every county at two millions, while the provision of offices and fireproof buildings would cost another million per annum. These accumulated charges would inevitably impose an intolerable burden on the public exchequer, for they could not be met by any scale of fees which could conceivably be imposed in dealings with land without destroying that freedom of transfer which it is the professed object of the whole system to develop. The financial side of the question is not the only one on which the Law Society depends in its exhaustive discussion of the proposals boldly put forward to cover the failure of the land registry, but it is sufficient in itself to dispose of the whole bad scheme, and, it may be hoped also, to bring to an end the present experiment in compulsory registration, which has led to such unsatisfactory results."

Obiter Dicta.

SURE. — In Carrithers *v.* Shelbyville, 104 S. W. Rep. 744, the Kentucky Court of Appeals says: "Of course, a woman is a person, and so is a corporation."

REAL THOUGHTFULNESS. — A Kansas City law book company, in a recent advertisement of second-hand sets of the National Reporter System, says: "We refrain from quoting our price on the above sets out of respect for other houses that are selling these sets for more than we ask."

AN INSPIRATION. — Our attention has just been called to a new legal periodical which came into existence last year in Madras and is entitled *The Criminal Law Replenisher.* It is edited by P. C. Subrahmanyam Pillai, B. A., B. L., and if Mr. Pillai is the genius who christened the magazine, we hereby make him our most respectful obeisance.

A TRIBAL CUSTOM. — In People *v.* Soloman, 106 N. Y. Supp. 1110, which was a prosecution for intoxication in a public place, the court said: "The fact that the defendant was an Indian ought to have made the court even more careful than usual to observe the rules of evidence." The humor in this will of course be apparent to such persons only as are familiar with the latter-day significance of the word Indian.

AN EX PARTE COPYRIGHT. — In its January number our old friend *The American Lawyer* makes its appearance in a new form and gayly bedight with illustrations. At the head of the table of contents is a statement that "the articles and pictures in this magazine are copyrighted and must not be reprinted without special permission," but one may search in vain for any copyright notice, wherefore we are inclined to the opinion that any one so minded may at pleasure "lift" from the contents of the January number of *The American Lawyer* without fear, albeit not without reproach.

A STRIKE OF LAWYERS. — All the lawyers in the French town of Thonon, on the Lake of Geneva, went on strike during December, and at last accounts were still "out." Their discontent was caused by the fact that the last judge in the place retired recently, and no successor having been appointed, each of the lawyers has in turn been compelled for the past few months to discharge the judicial duties — presumably without compensation. Meanwhile the court has remained closed, notwithstanding the numerous cases awaiting judgment, and the lawyers have been happily whiling away the time in yodeling, making cuckoo clocks, and indulging in the other pastimes indigenous to that region.

PRESERVED THE PROPRIETIES. — A correspondent writes that during a recent trial for cattle stealing in one of the eastern counties of Colorado, the attorney for the defense, a man noted for his great ability and Chesterfieldian manners, asked a female witness, who had testified for the prosecution as to a certain conversation with the defendant: "Then you and the defendant were simply engaged in a social tête-à-tête?" Before the witness could answer the judge sternly interposed with, "Mr. ———, I want you to understand right here that this court will tolerate no vulgarity."

A PROFESSIONAL CARD. — The following is clipped from a Susquehanna, Pa., newspaper:

Look Here

Over forty years of experience says I can do you better shoeing than any carpenter or mule shoer from the mine; the price will be right. Come and see me. I have a few drag breakes for light wagons and surreys. Will put them on cheap; they are right. I Keep Hanford Balsam of Myrrh. Head quarters to get your deeds and mortgages written and acknowledged. I write contracts; also make papers for Bounty on Fox, etc.

W. P. Tallman, Thompson,
Practical horse shoer.

SOMETHING NEW UNDER THE SUN. — The new year brought into the unstable ranks of legal periodicals a new one called *Law and Lawyers*, which is published at White Plains, N. Y., by the Law Press Company. This fact alone would probably not cause King Solomon to revise his opinion, but we believe the worthy old gentleman would sit up and take notice if perchance his eye could fall upon the following sentence in the opening editorial of *Law and Lawyers*: "We know of no magazine published on the lines of a pure law magazine, and it has often been a matter of wonderment that such is and has been the fact." The motto of this long felt want is "Knowledge is the fountain of liberty."

NOT SO MANY AFTER ALL. — In the case of Nixon *v.* Wright, 146 Mich. 231, the court, speaking of a decree for alimony, remarked *obiter* that "many courts hold that it is not such an one as may be assigned." Less than two weeks later the same court, being called upon to pass directly on the point in Fournier *v.* Clutton, 146 Mich. 298, said, *per* Carpenter, C. J.: "The briefs of counsel and my own research have enabled me to find but two cases touching the question of the assignability of decrees for alimony." Sometimes things don't seem so well settled when we get right down to cases. However, a diligent search would have turned up at least two other authorities on the point — Watkins *v.* Watkins, (1896) Pro. 222, and Lynde *v.* Lynde, 64 N. J. Eq. 736.

A NEW PERIL. — A divorce suit recently instituted in France by an Englishman who resides near Paris reveals what we believe to be the prize hard-luck story of the age, and also contains a warning for those whom it may concern. The plaintiff was happily whiling away an hour at a moving-picture show, when, to his great astonishment and indignation, who should saunter across the canvas but his own wife leaning fondly on the arm of a "gentleman friend." The ruthless cinematograph had stored up the evidence against the erring spouse, and capricious fate had contrived to bring the husband to that particular show at the very time when that particular picture was exhibited. Needless to say the irate Briton proceeded with all convenient speed to unloose the holy bonds. And thus cold, relentless science continues to encroach upon the right to pursue happiness. With the rapid multiplication of these new-fangled snares for the feet of unwary pleasure-seekers it is obvious that before long life will be stripped of all its innocent amusements.

A CHAMPION OF THE J. P. — So often has the justice of the peace been held up to ridicule in these columns that it is but fair to give equal prominence to the following encomium on that much derided official, which is taken from a brief handed up by an attorney of Conconully, Wash., who was endeavoring to uphold a judgment rendered by a justice of the peace:

"Let us give the poor J. P. all that is coming to him. Every court in the land seems to take pride in pouncing upon him at the slightest provocation, and with a vehemence nearly equal to mob violence. He is worse persecuted than ever were the Jews. He has ever been a martyr to his views of the law, as were the saints to the Christian religion. So constantly and steadfastly has he held to his convictions, that, like Daniel of old, he has refused to eat of the king's meat, or to drink of his wine; and notwithstanding royal decrees to the contrary, he has preferred to set his face toward Jerusalem, and make his petitions to the source of greater wisdom; while those courts which happen to be constituted above him go about in a sort of half-sacrilegious way, consoling their feelings and justifying their actions by saying to him: 'How often would I have gathered your children together, even as a hen gathereth her chickens under her wings, and ye would not.'"

IS IT DEMURRABLE? — A rather novel method of campaigning for a seat on the supreme bench of a sovereign State has been resorted to by Mr. T. H. Humphreys, who desires to be substituted for Mr. Justice Wood, of the Arkansas Supreme Court. The candidate has distributed posters, or handbills, bearing on the upper half a portrait of himself, and below the following statement of his cause of action:

IN THE

PEOPLE'S COURT OF ARKANSAS,

March Term, 1908.

T. H. HUMPHREYS, *Plaintiff*, *against* C. D. WOOD, *Defendant*. } *Complaint.*

Now comes the plaintiff, T. H. Humphreys, and for his cause of action against defendant C. D. Wood states:

1. C. D. Wood has held office 25 years.
2. C. D. Wood will have been on the Supreme Bench over 15 years when his present term expires.
3. C. D. Wood has been paid about SIXTY THOUSAND DOLLARS ($60,000.00) for his services as an office holder.
4. C. D. Wood did not believe in life-tenure on the Supreme Bench in 1904, when he ran for Governor. All of a sudden he has come to the conclusion that the great interest of the State demands that he remain on the bench f-o-r-e-v-e-r.
5. And as matter for affirmative relief, the plaintiff further states, that the lawyers and people who know him best will bear witness that said T. H. Humphreys is qualified for the office of Associate Justice of the Supreme Court.

Wherefore the premises considered, the said plaintiff, T. H. Humphreys, prays that all Democrats in Arkansas cast their respective votes for plaintiff, the said T. H. Humphreys, and against the defendant, the said C. D. Wood, in the March primary, and will ever pray.

T. H. HUMPHREYS, Plaintiff.

A PHILANTHROPIST. — In the interest of progress it has long been our practice to call to the attention of the profession such new developments in advertising methods as seem to us to mark a distinct advance in the art. The latest genius in this line to come under our notice is Mr. Jesse L. Rogers, Jr., of Knoxville, Tenn., who has distributed circulars among the laboring men of that city, bearing, among other attractive features, a most winsome picture of himself and the following engaging proposition:

Opportunity for 1,000 Laboring Men.

Have you any civil suits to file or contracts to execute? Do you expect any one to bring suit against you? Have you wrongfully had your *wages attached*? Have you received *letters* from *collecting agencies* not fit for a dog to get, much less a man to receive? Have you been bluffed into doing things which proved detrimental to you, which you would not have done had you known your rights? One or more of these occur in the year of nearly every one's life. All corporations, firms, and a good many individuals employ counsel by the year for a certain stipulated amount, and these counsellors attend to the business of the corporation, firms, or individuals, let it be little or much. *I will attend to all your civil matters, instituting and defending you in all civil matters, executing all contracts and consultations*, one year from date of agreement, for a fee of $5.00, *payable in advance, or for* $6.00 per year payable $3.00 every six months in advance. This fee includes *my services for one year*, whether you have one hundred suits or none. I have an agreement which I will enter into with you to this effect, and this will include civil suits filed, prosecuted, and defended in all City, State, and United States Courts in the city of Knoxville. Do you know there are two or half-dozen agencies or organizations in this city which will bring suit against you for 25c, attach your wages, place all the cost possible on you; not only this, but will report you to every merchant or individual of like business belonging to the agencies of the fact, not being satisfied with receiving the principal and cost, but trying to hurt your credit. I believe in paying all just and honest debts, but do not believe in paying them twice and some cost added.

Both Rhymed and Reasonable. — In the District Court of Pocahontas county, Iowa, January Term, 1907, the court charged the jury in the case of H. C. Dorton *v.* S. S. Martin as follows:

Gentlemen of the Jury:

The plaintiff Dorton as his claim and cause of action against the defendant Martin says:

That Martin told Dorton one day,
"If you will turn Thompson my way,
And I to him sell,
Your pocket I'll swell
With eighty good plunks for your pay."

That Dorton told Martin, "Agreed, —
Take Thompson and take him with speed,
And if he should buy,
It's settled that I
Shall have eighty plunks, which I need."

That Martin sold Thompson the place,
But soon he grew pale in the face,
When to him it came
That Dorton would claim
The plunks with an agent's grimace.

And Dorton comes here to allege
That Martin is trying to hedge,
To wiggle and squirm
And eke disaffirm
That he owes him a cent on his pledge.

And Martin for answer replies
That all Dorton says he denies,
And says unto you
No commission is due
To any man under the skies.

That Dorton agreed on that day,
Before he should get any pay,
To get as a price,
No less should suffice,
One hundred twelve fifty per a.

That Thompson he never would buy
For the price Martin had in his eye,
So Martin took less,
And hence the distress,
And our having the case here to try.

And you are required to decide
The disputes which these neighbors divide;
Give each one his due
As seems right to you,
And let the tail go with the hide.

If you believe Dorton, I say,
Give Dorton the plunks right away;
If you believe Martin,
It's equally "sartin"
That Martin should not have to pay.

In some matters you are the judge;
As to these I now give you a nudge;
Whether witnesses say
What is true here to-day
Or only are paying a grudge.

Now you to your room will repair,
The jury room, which is your lair;
Whatever you say,
One man will feel gay
And the other go up in the air.

Decide by the evidence plan —
Agree to it every man;
The court keep in awe,
Remember the law,
And do us the best job you can.

Correspondence.

THE TWO-YEAR COURSE IN SOUTHERN LAW SCHOOLS.

To the Editor of LAW NOTES.

SIR: We have read with great interest the article contained in the January issue of LAW NOTES, entitled "The Two-year Course in Southern Law Schools," by Thomas A. Street. While Mr. Street is very clever in modifying nearly every assertion, we believe the article as a whole is not productive of the good that the author evidently intended.

We first take issue with Mr. Street in his contention that the young man applying for admission to a law school "ought to have at least as much schooling as is represented by the A. B. degree conferred by American colleges," and that he should "have an academic degree," and the implication that a "well-educated man" is one holding an academic degree. Not only do we believe these positions unfair, but not well founded in fact. There is a modern tendency to overestimate the value of an A. B. degree. The public generally, and those not knowing what small value the article really possesses, are most prominently committed to this grave error.

Mr. Street would have only such men as are laden with blanket knowledge eligible to the law school course, and yet our experience has led us to believe that a youth can go to college year after year and grasp little of the permanent and essential things of life, and leave the college centre without being a "well-educated man" and wholly unfit to take up the study of law. Our opinion is, that it is not the A. B. degree which makes the man, but man that makes the A. B. degree. The commonwealth should encourage progress, ambition, and aspiration, wherever and whenever found. The best preparation for the law which a young man can have is a good high-school education, supplemented by contact with the business world for a length of time, and a determination to study and master a three-year course in any well-equipped law school. Mr. Street asserts, "Only the school of experience can turn out the finished lawyer," and yet lays no emphasis upon that experience which makes the man. The mature lawyer is not the product of an inexperienced man, no matter how much theoretical knowledge he may possess.

We next take issue with Mr. Street in his statement that the "public welfare is not so much jeopardized by the existence of a somewhat lower standard of purely professional education in the law than in the other professions." We can see no reason why there should be a lower standard in the law than in any other profession, and believe a standard three-year course would do much to make the remark quoted ridiculous. Mr. Street knows that the day of specialization has arrived; that division of labor is greater than ever before, and that to do one thing and do it well is not only masterful but necessary.

If legal educators believe that the best interests of the law student are not subserved by spending three years at one institution, and that the student would gain by meeting faculties of different colleges, we suggest a coalition of law schools; that a uniform course of study be adopted, covering three years; that each school recognize and honor the credits of the other standard schools. Under such a dispensation, a student might graduate with honor after taking a year each in, say, Illinois, New York, and Tennessee. A uniform curriculum and period of study would do much for the student. The advantages are obvious.

We believe the best interests of all parties concerned demand that the Southern law schools adopt the three-year course, but that neither the profession nor the public will gain by imposing an A. B. degree barrier or its equivalent between the hoping, struggling young men of America and the honorable profession of the law, which, when obtained, opens the broad avenues of unlimited opportunities to serve the people of the Republic, and to be of some permanent good to the world.

HARRY E. HUNT.

DETROIT.

Law Notes

MARCH, 1908.

PUBLISHED BY EDWARD THOMPSON COMPANY, NORTHPORT, LONG ISLAND, N. Y.

CONTENTS.

An index to volume 11 of LAW NOTES, which is completed by this number, is being prepared and will be sent free to subscribers on application to the publishers.

TO THE READERS OF LAW NOTES:

We are desirous of making LAW NOTES as useful and entertaining to the profession as possible, and shall appreciate the courtesy if you will lend us your assistance by writing a letter to the editor of LAW NOTES answering the following questions and making such other suggestions for improvement as may occur to you:

1. Do you prefer articles of the kind that now appear in LAW NOTES, or do you prefer articles of a more technical nature; and why?
2. Is there any part of LAW NOTES that you are in the habit of reading first; and if so, what?
3. Which of the regular departments of LAW NOTES — *Editorial, Cases of Interest, News of the Profession, English Notes, Obiter Dicta* — do you prefer; and why?
4. Can you suggest any new department or feature that, in your judgment, would make LAW NOTES more readable and valuable; and if so, what is your reason?

A prize consisting of books of our publication, to the value of $25, will be awarded to the reader whose answer, in the judgment of the editor of LAW NOTES, affords the most helpful suggestions. The winner of the prize may, at his election, either select books to the value of $25, or order books valued at a greater sum and have $25 applied as a credit on the purchase price. In awarding the prize, no answers will be considered other than those reaching Northport on or before May 1, 1908. The name of the winner will be announced in the June, 1908, issue of LAW NOTES.

In answering the questions, it will be sufficient to refer to them by number, without repeating the questions themselves.

EDWARD THOMPSON COMPANY.

An Unconstitutional Labor Law.

THE labor unions have had their way for a long time. By means of boycotts, strikes, and other more or less violent proceedings they have forced capital to a very lively realization of their power, and have obtained many concessions in the interest of the laboring man. Their influence has also been felt in politics, and many laws have been passed in their favor. But a lack of moderation in their claims and in their methods of enforcing them has had the inevitable result. Class privileges can end in but one way, whatever the favored class may be. Therefore the decision of the Supreme Court of the United States in *Adair v. U. S.*, declaring unconstitutional section 10 of the Erdman Act (4 Fed. St. Ann. 787), which forbids common carriers to discriminate against members of labor organizations or to dismiss them from service because of such membership, will meet with general approval as an affirmance of the inviolability of the constitutional right of liberty to contract. The question involved is made very clear in the opinion of Mr. Justice Harlan, as follows:

"The right of a person to sell his labor upon such terms as he deems proper is, in its essence, the same as the right of the purchaser of labor to prescribe the conditions upon which he will accept such labor from the person offering to sell it. So the right of the employee to quit the service of the employer, for whatever reason, is the same as the right of the employer, for whatever reason, to dispense with the services of the employee. It was the legal right of the defendant, Adair, however unwise such a course might have been, to discharge Coppage because of his being a member of a labor organization, as it was the legal right of Coppage, if he saw fit to do so, however unwise such a course on his part might have been, to quit the service in which he was engaged because the defendant employed those who were not members of some labor organization. In all such particulars the employer and the employee have equality of right, and any legislation that disturbs that equality is an arbitrary interference with the liberty of contract which no government can legally justify in a free land."

Equal Justice.

THE most serious calamity, however, that has happened to organized labor was the application of section 7 of the Sherman Act (7 Fed. St. Ann. 345) to boycotts. The Supreme Court has just handed down a unanimous decision in the case of *Lowe v. Lawlor,* holding that a boycott, when of interstate proportions, is a combination "in restraint of trade or commerce among the several States" in the sense in which those words are used in that Act, and that a labor union, by boycotting a manufacturer, incurs the liability of threefold the damages sustained in consequence, together with the costs of the suit, including a reasonable attorney's fee, just as the manufacturer would have been liable had he entered into a combination with other manufacturers in violation of the Act. The effect of this decision is to deprive the unions of their most effective weapon, because practically all articles manufactured in the United States are subjects of interstate commerce. The correctness of the decision cannot be questioned, but it is a curious fact that the Sherman Act was primarily designed to prevent combinations of the very class of persons who are now declared to be within its protection, and probably Congress had no other object in view.

The Supreme Court and Constitutional Rights.

THERE is material for comfortable reflection in these decisions. Popular impulse often carries legislation too far in righting wrongs, and efforts to relieve the oppressed sometimes infringe the legal rights of the oppressors, but it becomes more evident each year that the Supreme Court stands fast for the rights secured by the Constitution and deals out equal justice to all. It may be that just and wholesome statutes must sometimes be declared unconstitutional, but if this works injustice the answer is that the people hold in their own hands the power to remedy the evil. The opinion seems to be growing that there are several subjects of legislation now denied to Congress which should be within its power, but the States are still jealous of their rights, and the federal government, for some time to come, will probably have to do the best it can with the "interstate commerce" and "general welfare" clauses of the Constitution.

Physicians as Witnesses.

BOSTON physicians have become sensitive as to the esteem in which medical expert witnesses are regarded by the public. They say that conditions have come to such a pass that a respectable physician might well hesitate to appear on the witness stand, as he could hardly fail to be conscious that he was looked upon as mercenary; that his opinions would be considered as having been bought and paid for by the party who summoned him, and that neither court, jury, parties, nor the public in general would give him the credit of being honest, sincere, or unbiased. They therefore propose to remedy the matter by asking the legislature to authorize the courts to appoint official experts who shall be delivered from temptation by having their compensation fixed by the court and paid by the county. This is all very well and good for the medical profession, at least from the point of view of those of its members who think that the reputation of the profession generally will be safeguarded thereby, but it does not take into consideration the rights of the individual whose life, liberty, or property may depend on some fact which can be ascertained only by the aid of the testimony of medical experts. It is perfectly true that in most of the important cases in which such testimony has been given there have been two sets of physicians, each testifying squarely in contradiction of the other, but this is not astonishing when the nature of the subject of the testimony is considered. In a matter of insanity, for instance, the physician does not testify to any fact; he merely says that in his opinion a certain person is sane or insane as the case may be. It is pure opinion evidence as to a matter concerning which opinions naturally differ. Indeed, it would be remarkable if there were not a difference of opinion. A party interested in such an inquiry should have the right to call any competent and credible witness whose views are in his favor, with the same right in the opposite party, so that the jury may exercise their proper function of deciding the fact involved. It is questionable, to say the least, whether the plan proposed would not infringe one of the most important of the rights of persons accused of crime, viz., the right of impartial trial and of having compulsory process for the attendance of witnesses. If opinion evidence is to be received at all, it would be manifestly unjust for the law to say that the court should receive the opinions of particular individuals only and that all others should be excluded however eminent they might be in their special department of science. Opinion evidence is necessarily less satisfactory than the testimony of a witness who testifies as to facts, and conflict of opinion is generally unavoidable, but it would be an amazing thing to undertake to eliminate the conflict by the appointment of official experts and the exclusion of the testimony of equally or better qualified persons who might hold different views.

A Fool and His Money.

IT is hardly within our province to take any part in the crusade against patent medicines, further than to condemn violations of the written law concerning their manufacture and sale. We cannot refrain, however, from calling attention to a startling statement made by Judge Archbald in *Jayne v. Loder*, 149 Fed. 21. In that case the Circuit Court of Appeals for the Third Circuit held that the so-called "tripartite agreement" between the Proprietary Association of America, the National Wholesale Druggists' Association, and the National Association of Retail Druggists, which was entered into for the purpose of preventing "aggressive cutters" from cutting the prices of proprietary remedies, was a combination in restraint of trade within the meaning of the Sherman Act (7 Fed. St. Ann. 336 *et seq.*). The opinion was delivered by Judge Archbald, and in the course of it he said: "It seems incredible, except as the trade in patent medicines is known to be incredible, but it is confidently asserted, by those having the right to speak, that the cost to the country of the tripartite agreement amounted to $90,000,000 in six years." One of our versatile young friends who has a taste for statistics and some knowledge of the inside workings of the patent medicine business, tells us that these figures indicate that in six years the public spent from $350,000,000 to $400,000,000 for the nostrums made by the parties to the tripartite agreement. He also tells us that many makers of proprietary medicines are not parties to that agreement, and that therefore the figures just named do not represent the total amount spent. It is quite apparent that those ingenious and enterprising gentlemen who proceed upon the theory that "there's a sucker born every minute" do not confine their activities to mining schemes and wireless wire-tapping.

Ambulance Chasers.

THE class of lawyers facetiously termed "ambulance chasers" are now standing in the limelight, though not by their own procurement. The American Bar Association opened the matter by condemning them and others who seek to stimulate their business and increase their earnings by drumming up litigation where none existed before, and it has since been taken up in several of the States. In Minnesota it is proposed to remedy the evil by the appointment of a claim agent, or at least such an officer has been appointed in the city of St. Paul to protect the city against claims for pretended injuries. In New York a bill has been prepared for the consideration of the legislature imposing stringent restrictions on contracts between attorney and client respecting the prosecution of claims for death or injury caused by negligence. The methods of these gentry are very reprehensible, and many of them, no doubt, are unfit to be members of the profession; but it may be something of a question whether chasing the ambulance is the real evil. The great difficulty in the now overstocked profession of the law is to get business. As to this it is said that of 175,000 lawyers in the United States, about half of them earn less than $1,200 per year. Now getting business by dubious methods is one thing, and trickery and fraud in the trial of cases is another thing entirely. A retainer may be secured by solicitation and yet the client may be dealt with fairly and the trial may be conducted on strictly honorable and professional lines. But the complaint seems to be directed not so much against the solicitation of business as against bringing actions for injuries caused by negligence. As Mr. Justice Woodward, of New York, said in a recent address, this class of practice is not only as old as the law itself, but is rendered particularly important by modern conditions. "The oft-repeated and sneering reference to that branch of the legal profession who gain a livelihood in the prosecution of negligence cases as 'ambulance chasers,'" he says, "has served to create a popular impression that this line of practice is essentially disreputable, and even the courts, it may be feared, are not free from the prejudice."

The Des Moines Plan.

THE practical working of the Des Moines plan of municipal government will be observed with interest by the reformer and the grafter alike — the one with hope and the other with fear and misgiving. If the plan proves a success, the pernicious activities of the ward politician will cease and he will pass away as pirates and others of like predatory habits have done. Briefly stated, the plan is to place the municipality on the basis of business corporations, by committing its affairs to a few responsible heads of departments, to be selected without regard to political parties. They are to be paid adequate salaries for their services, and are given ample powers to secure efficiency of service, while provision is made for a simple method of removal from office in case of incompetency or unfaithfulness. Under its new charter the affairs of the city of Des Moines are to be administered by a mayor and four councilmen, each of whom is made the head of one of five departments, with plenary executive and administrative powers in such department. All the officers in the several departments are to be appointed by the council by a majority vote and may be removed at any time by a majority vote, except that clerks, employees, and others occupying subordinate positions are to be governed by civil service rules. The council is authorized to grant franchises and enact ordinances, but no grant of a franchise is to be operative until it has been submitted to a popular vote at an election ordered for the purpose. A majority of the votes cast is necessary to ratify the grant of a franchise. Ordinances enacted by the council are not to be subject to veto by the mayor, but he or two of the councilmen must sign them. They are not to take effect until ten days after their passage, and during the ten days they are subject to protest and referendum. If a protest against an ordinance with a demand for a referendum signed by twenty-five per cent. of the voters is filed within ten days after its passage, such ordinance must be submitted to a vote of the people and requires a majority vote to sustain it. It is also provided that if twenty-five per cent. of the voters petition for the passage of an ordinance, the proposed measure shall be submitted to the voters. The mayor and councilmen are to be nominated at a primary election, the names of the candidates for mayor and councilmen respectively being printed in alphabetical order on the ballots. The two candidates for mayor and the eight candidates for councilmen receiving the highest number of votes are to be the nominees. The nominations are all to be made from the city at large (wards are abolished) and without any designation of political parties, and the final elections are to be conducted in the same manner. At any time, on a petition signed by twenty-five per cent. of the voters, an election may be held to remove the mayor and councilmen or any of them. This plan seems to be admirably designed to secure a competent administration, because the salaries will induce capable men to undertake the management of municipal affairs as a business and not for the "pickings" that they may be able to get out of it, and the provisions for referendum give the voters a voice at all times. The requirement of the signatures of twenty-five per cent. of the voters in case of a petition for a referendum would seem to be scarcely practicable in a large city, but the idea is a good one and experience will probably perfect it. At any rate it aims in a fairly practical way to give a system of municipal government under which honesty will not depend entirely on the personnel of the city officers, and by which the temptation to corrupt practice is largely removed.

Educational Qualifications of Lawyers.

THE opinion generally prevails throughout the United States that admission to the bar should be conditioned on educational qualifications to be ascertained by careful and thorough examination, and it is not to be supposed that any one would question the soundness of the proposition involved. It is therefore somewhat astonishing to find that in one State the right to practice law has been classed among the unqualified rights of citizenship. The constitution of Indiana (article 7, section 21) provides that "every person of good moral character, being a voter, shall be entitled to admission to practice law in all the courts of justice." The theory of this probably is that the incompetents will soon be weeded out by natural selection, but the theory is unsound because of the harm that unqualified lawyers may accomplish before they are weeded out. Many citizens who have to seek legal advice are poor judges of the qualifications of a lawyer, and it is this class in particular that should be shielded from legal incompetents. It is a singular circumstance that in this age of progress and improvement such a condition should continue to exist, but it is still more singular that its effects on the bar of the State should not be noticeable. This may, perhaps, be accounted for by the fact that candidates for admission to the bar are examined as to their legal attainments, though doubtless those who are voters could demand admission as a right on proof merely of good moral character.

The President and the Judges.

CRITICISM of the judiciary is not the least important subject dealt with by the President in his famous message of January 31. He considers both the criticism which "our opponents" have pronounced upon the judges who acted in the Standard Oil and Santa Fé Railroad cases, and that which he and his administration expressed in relation to the judges whose decisions "resulted in immunity to wealthy and powerful wrongdoers." Most of the extended comment on the duties of judges and the right to criticise their judicial action is unexceptionable. "The judge who does his full duty well stands higher . . . than any other public servant." "Untruthful criticism is wicked at all times; . . . it is peculiarly flagrant iniquity when a judge is the object." "No man should condemn a judge unless he is sure of the facts." "All honor cannot be rendered him [the upright, wise, and fearless judge] if it is rendered equally to his brethren who fall immeasurably below the high ideals for which he stands." "No servant of the people has a right to expect to be free from just and honest criticism." Like most of the President's generalizations on moral and ethical questions, these observations are as sound as they are vigorous and will meet with the approval of the lawyers of the country. The respect which is due to the high office of judge, and especially to a judge of one of the United States courts, is not exaggerated in the minds of the legal profession. Lawyers believe in intelligent criticism of judges, but they know that much which passes for criticism is only clamor against decisions which do not meet with popular or administrative approval.

Opening the Judge's Eyes.

A JUDGE'S duty is simply to administer the law as he finds it. He is bound by his oath to abide by the law, and that however much he may disapprove or dislike it. In determining what is the law, he answers solely to his own conscience. With questions of political policy or the plans of a government administration he has nothing to do. We regret that these simple and accepted doctrines are not echoed in the President's message. There is much there about the need for weight of public opinion to bear on the judge "if he clearly fails to do his duty by the public in dealing with law-breaking corporations." Does this refer to Judge Humphrey's decision in the beef trust case? If Judge Humphrey ruled according to the law — and we have yet to find a good lawyer who says he did not — what other duty had he "to the public"? Does it refer to Judge Evans, who fell under executive censure because of his decision holding unconstitutional section 10 of the Labor Act of June 1, 1898; or to Judge McCall, who declared one of the President's pet measures, the Employers' Liability Act, unconstitutional? Can it be said that these judges did not do their duty to the public in first refusing to give force to congressional enactments which the Supreme Court has since declared to be in violation of the Constitution? How are judges to understand the President's assertion that those who fall below the "high standard . . . of sympathetic understanding" should "have their eyes opened to the needs of their countrymen"? If the Constitution, the statutes, and the rules of the common law do not provide for the needs of the people, how can the sympathetic understanding of a judge help matters? Two courses alone are open to him: to administer the law as he finds it or to violate his oath. "A *popular* judge," said a celebrated English lawyer, "is an odious and pernicious character." Lord Bacon put it in even stronger words when he said: "A popular judge is a deformed thing."

Lord Mansfield on Judicial Popularity.

JOHN WILKES was a malefactor who had been prosecuted relentlessly by the British Government. He had withdrawn to France, and a judgment of outlawry had been pronounced against him. Coming over to England in 1768, he appeared in person in the Court of King's Bench asking that the judgment of outlawry be reversed. Lord Mansfield was chief justice, and, on a technical point which had escaped the counsel for defendant, he gave judgment against the crown and declared that the outlawry should be reversed. The nation was frenzied by faction. Abuse and threats of personal violence were heaped upon the chief justice. Crowds thronged the hall where he sat. Amid such surroundings, in his address from the bench, Mansfield gave utterance to these memorable words: "If, during this king's reign, I have ever supported his government, and assisted his measures, I have done it without any other reward than the consciousness of doing what I thought right. If I have ever opposed, I have done it upon the points themselves, without mixing in party or faction, and without any collateral views. I honor the king, and respect the people; but many things required by the favor of either are, in my account, objects not worth ambition. I wish popularity, but it is that popularity which follows; not that which is run after. It is that popularity which, sooner or later, never fails to do justice to the pursuit of noble ends by noble means. I will not do that which my conscience tells me is wrong, upon this occasion, to gain the huzzas of thousands, or the daily praise of all the papers which come from the press. I will not avoid doing what I think is right, though it should draw on me the whole artillery of libels; all that falsehood and malice can invent, or the credulity of a deluded populace can swallow."

Not Now.

IN his speech at the dinner given to the Pennsylvania delegation in Congress a short time ago, Senator Knox, in praise of the present national administration, said:

> "It is gratifying to say of this administration that I have never known it to make a recommendation that has become a law, or to place an executive construction upon an existing law affecting largely the general welfare, that its position has not been sustained in the Supreme Court when it has reached that tribunal."

A fine compliment, but one which, alas! is not now available.

"LAW grows, and though the principles of law remain unchanged, yet (and it is one of the advantages of the common law) their application is to be changed with the changing circumstances of the times. Some persons may call this retrogression, I call it progression of human opinion." — Lord Coleridge, Reg. *v.* Ramsey, (1883) 1 Cababé and Ellis Q. B. D. 135.

REGULATION OF CONTEMPT PROCEEDINGS IN INJUNCTION CASES.

In the President's last message to Congress, speaking of injunctions in labor cases, he says "the process should be surrounded by safeguards," etc. A much needed safeguard is a simple statutory provision that proceedings to punish alleged violators of an injunction shall not be heard by the judge who granted the injunction. Such a provision should receive the ready assent of lawyers, for they are peculiarly qualified to appreciate its salutary character.

An action was brought in a Michigan court by the City of Detroit against the Detroit City Railroad Company. There was strong public feeling against the defendant. The judges of the State court held their offices by popular election, were candidates for re-election, and most of the electors were citizens of Detroit. On application of the defendant the United States Circuit Court ordered the removal of the case from the State court to the federal court on the statutory ground of "prejudice or local influence" and inability "to obtain justice" in the State court. This order was affirmed by the Circuit Court of Appeals, Judge William H. Taft, then on the bench of that court, writing the opinion. Judge Taft said that "we must presume a human weakness" in the judges of the State court; that "men may be unconsciously influenced by personal motives, and public policy will not trust any judge, however great and pure, when such motives are present." "At common law," he continued, "the ownership of a single share of stock in a corporation, which is party to a suit, absolutely disqualifies a judge to hear it. . . . It is held by some courts that where a judge is a taxpayer of a county he cannot hear a case in which the county is interested. No one claims that in many of such cases the judge is not able to discard utterly from his consideration of the merits of the case every motive of pecuniary interest, but *the policy of the law forbids that litigants should be exposed to the possibility of bias* arising therefrom." City of Detroit *v.* Detroit City R. Co., 54 Fed. Rep. 1, 19, 20.

Now, when a person is charged with a criminal contempt and deprived of a right of trial by jury, does not public policy loudly forbid that his liberty shall be "exposed to the possibility of bias" of a single judge "however great and pure," especially of a judge whose finding of guilt is not reviewable on appeal?

There cannot be the slightest doubt, from the viewpoint of lawyers at the bar or on the bench, that a judge who has issued an injunction in a labor controversy where much feeling has been engendered, whose writ has been flouted, and himself, very likely, fiercely reviled by striking workmen, has "a human weakness" to relish the exercise of power to retaliate by inflicting the penalties of the law. It is a cardinal rule in weighing the testimony of biased witnesses, no matter how upright they may be, that their testimony in matters of opinion, judgment, or estimate "should be received with great caution." See Gilooley *v.* Pennsylvania R. Co., 10 Fed. Cas. No. 5448*b* (at p. 418) *per* Choate, D. J. No sensible judge would hesitate to distrust a biased lawyer's testimony in court on a question of law, or his opinion, if it were admissible, on a question of fact. By what process does the opinion of a biased lawyer delivered from the bench become more trustworthy?

In Tyler *v.* Hamersley, 44 Conn. 393, parties acting on the written advice of five of the best lawyers in the State (set forth at p. 395, note, of the report) had refused to obey a writ of mandamus, because, as advised by their said counsel, their writ of error had operated as a supersedeas to execution of the writ. According to four of the five Supreme Court judges, the legal advice of those five lawyers was erroneous. Probably the lawyers continued to think that the judges themselves — "hot under the collar" maybe — were mistaken. Possibly they were.

Courts know very well "how deceptive and unsatisfactory" is the testimony of a party that he has made diligent search for a lost writing which it is not for his interest to find and produce. Porter *v.* Wilson, 13 Pa. St. 641, 649, *per* Rogers, J. Can it be expected that a resentful judge will prosecute a diligent search for precedents that will make doubtful the validity of a proceeding on which he has already embarked, or will diligently search the evidence for circumstances pointing to the innocence of accused contemnors of himself and his writ? At any rate, is there no "possibility of bias"?

A writ of injunction is, of course, open to construction like any other process. Will any candid lawyer contend that a man who has undertaken to express his sentiments in writing is a trustworthy interpreter of that writing? Prepossessed, as the man necessarily would be, by the recollection of his intention, of course he would more readily perceive adequate expression of that intention in the writing than one whose judgment was not thus tutored from an extraneous source. Again, "an injunction order must, like penal or criminal statutes, be construed strictly in favor of the person charged with violating it." Wisconsin Cent. R. Co. *v.* Smith, 52 Wis. 140, 143, *per* Lyon, J. The judge who granted an injunction, and whose ire is naturally aroused by turbulent acts which he knows he intended to prevent, is not a person who can be depended upon to construe his order strictly. Public policy founded on elementary knowledge of human nature forbids that the duty of strict construction should be entrusted to him.

Lastly, alleged violators of an injunction may be brought before a judge notoriously irascible in his judicial demeanor in all litigations — there are such judges; before a federal judge whose extreme age would disqualify him by the State statute from sitting as a trier either of law or of facts — has not this occurred? or before a judge whose judgments on questions of law or of fact in ordinary cases are commonly reversed on appeal, and sometimes indeed pronounced absurd by the appellate tribunal — do not lawyers know of such judges? It is possible that all these infirmities might coexist in one judge. Surely to them should not be added the possibility of bias of a judge passing upon the validity and construction of his own process and upon conflicting evidence of guilt, and with no power in any other tribunal to review his finding on the facts.

It may not be wise to give the right to a jury trial in these cases, although it is to be observed that a man who should murder an officer serving an injunction would obtain a jury trial.

C. C. M.

CRIMINAL PROCEDURE IN FEDERAL COURTS.

The compilation of the criminal laws of the United States which has been undertaken by Congress is a much-needed work. At the present time these statutes are not only scattered through a great many volumes, but some of them are hidden in the mass of statutory matter in such a way that it is almost impossible to find them. When it is remembered that it is now thirty years since there has been a revision of the statutes of the United States it is easy to imagine, without actual knowledge, what the condition must be. The carrying out of this much-needed revision is being hampered not a little by the insistence of some members of Congress on changes in the substance of the laws which give rise to controversy. It seems that it would be better to be satisfied, at this time, with a bringing together and a logical arrangement of the present laws, making no other changes in the language than such as are necessary to remove redundancies, inconsistencies, and obscurities. Possibly this course will have to be adopted if we are to have the compilation completed within a reasonable time. But if this is not done, and if radical changes are to be made in the substance of the laws, there will be an excellent opportunity to effect certain desirable changes in the criminal procedure of the United States courts.

During the last few decades a few steps have been taken to simplify and improve criminal procedure. Indictments have been purged of much useless verbiage, such as the expressions "against the statute in such cases made and provided," "against the peace and dignity of the State," and "with force and arms." The common-law rule requiring that an indictment for perjury should set forth the pleadings and proceedings in the action in which the perjury was committed has been abolished. Merely formal objections to an indictment must be made at an early stage of the case. These and other changes are to be commended. But after all they are mere surface changes. The task of the criminal pleader is made more easy, and purely technical irregularities are less fatal, but much that is no real protection to an innocent defendant, but which hampers, and sometimes renders ineffectual, the prosecution of the guilty, has been allowed to remain. That criminal procedure is sadly in need of a systematic recasting has long been felt, and often pointed out, by legal and sociological writers. But in late years the subject has been taken up anew and with increased vigor. Perhaps the cause for this revival of interest in a subject which is by no means new, is to be found in the conditions which have been shown to exist in some of our larger cities, resulting in apparent miscarriage of justice, in criminal cases which have attracted public attention throughout the country. In view of these conditions it is not strange that the public press should be filled with attacks upon the technicalities of the criminal law. Neither is it strange that the reform of criminal procedure should have been made a subject for discussion before bar associations and elsewhere by lawyers of eminence.

But, whatever may be the cause, all this is as it should be. The severity of the old criminal law, the inability of the defendant to testify on his own behalf, the denial of counsel, and other causes, not unnaturally led to the throwing of so many safeguards around the prisoner, that now, when his privileges have been greatly extended, he is given an unreasonable advantage. It is not a cause for wonder that the guilty who are well supplied with money, so often escape punishment. It is, at this day, difficult to agree with the opinion of Mr. Justice Stephen, expressed in his great work on the criminal law of England, that the State can well afford to accord a prisoner the special privileges and safeguards which the law gives him, because society in the aggregate is so much more powerful than any single individual that the contest between organized society on the one hand, and an accused on the other, would otherwise be unequal and unfair. The view expressed by Mr. Justice Stephen is rejected by some very eminent American lawyers and judges. Not long since Mr. Justice Brewer, in his Yale lectures, declared that it seems sometimes as if legislation were conceived in the spirit of obstruction to the punishment of criminals, and of indefinite postponement thereof "by appeal, writ of error, and habeas corpus. Appellate courts have a wonderfully quick eye for detecting fine technical errors in criminal proceedings, and back of all stands a tender-hearted executive responding to the appeals of relatives and friends of the criminal." And Everett P. Wheeler, Esq., in an article in the *Columbia Law Review*, entitled "Reform in Criminal Procedure," says: "In this country, as well as in England, the old severity of penal legislation has been altogether reformed. But the old traditions of criminal procedure remain. They are totally inapplicable to existing conditions and require revision as much as the sanguinary penal code of a century ago. They have developed in large cities a certain number of criminal lawyers of whom it may be said as Trollope said of the Old Bailey attorneys of his day, that they existed 'for the manumission of murderers or the security of the swindling world in general.'" Mr. Wheeler then cites half a dozen instances where, in his opinion, the procedure in criminal cases can be changed to the advantage of society, without injustice to a prisoner. The most important of these proposed changes are the following: First, change the rule that the jury should be satisfied of the guilt of a prisoner beyond a reasonable doubt, and substitute the preponderance of evidence rule; second, modify the grand jury system, when possible, so as to do away with the rule which does not permit a trial except upon indictment; third, abolish the rule which gives persons who are jointly indicted for a particular crime the right to separate trials; fourth, limit the right to new trials for erroneous rulings upon the evidence.

At the present time, we do not necessarily accept each of the conclusions of Mr. Wheeler in the article to which reference has been made. But we do not hesitate to say that the members of the legal profession who, like Mr. Wheeler, have directed their attention to the problem of reforming our criminal procedure deserve the gratitude of every citizen. And it is to be hoped that the example which they have set will not be lost upon the enlightened and influential members of the profession; for it is to them that the people must look for the necessary reforms. The lay press, by intelligent criticism, can do, and is doing, much to bring the general public and also the bar to a realizing sense of something being wrong; but the tasks of pointing out just what is wrong, and of finding and applying the proper remedies, must devolve upon those who are versed in the law. Only those who are acquainted with the history of, and the reasons which underlie, the rules which govern criminal procedure, can reasonably be expected to be able to distinguish between that which is essential to the proper administration of the law, and that which may advantageously be discarded or modified. Criminal procedure should be reformed without doing anything which is reactionary.

How these much-needed reforms can be accomplished is not easy to determine. Shall it be done by comprehensive enactments or by changing specific rules? Sometimes a general and sweeping provision can be formulated which will have the effect of doing away with a number of abuses. But more often such general measures are either dangerous or ineffective. Mr. Wheeler quotes section 542 of the New York Code of Criminal Procedure, which provides as follows: "After hearing the appeal the court must give judgment without regard to technical errors or defects, or to exceptions which do not affect the substantial rights of the parties." He says that "this provision should be applied to all appellate courts." Perhaps it might be objected that an act of this kind is not sufficiently specific to be effective. The difficulty is that no rule is given for determining what constitute "technical errors or defects" or "exceptions which do not affect the substantial rights of the parties." That this is a real difficulty is shown by the number of citations annexed to the provision in a certain edition of the New York code. Perhaps, as a general rule, those excrescences in the criminal law which are properly denominated technicalities can best be gotten rid of by a process of gradual elimination.

If Congress undertakes to make any radical changes in the criminal law, it could very profitably devote some time to reforming criminal procedure. If this were wisely done the influence of the federal laws on State legislation in the same direction would probably be great. T. M.

A CENTRAL REGISTRY FOR MATRIMONIAL DECREES.

THE comments which LAW NOTES (October, 1907) made on my paper on "Jurisdiction in Divorce," read before the International Law Association at Portland, while apparently just, apparently proceed upon an incomplete report. My suggestions were (1) that all matrimonial decrees (divorce, nullity, or separation) should be recorded, not only in the office of the clerk of the county where the judgment was rendered, but also in the office of the secretary of state of the State in which such county is situated, and that it is also desirable that a copy of the summons or writ should be filed in such secretary of state's office immediately after service. (2) All such matrimonial actions should be under the supervision of the attorney-general of the State and his assistants, who would be able to intervene in cases of fraud, in much the same way that the king's proctor in England may intervene, and of his own motion take steps to prevent the decree *nisi* being made final in the States where decrees *nisi* are granted. It would also be well if he had power to ascertain whether the necessary jurisdictional facts existed before allowing the action to proceed. (3) The creation at Washington, or some central place, of a central registry for the recording of all such matrimonial decrees throughout the United States — to be done at the expense of the several States agreeing to use such registry.

These are the three main points to which I desired to direct attention, so that something might be done to prevent the numerous secret decrees which are procured by the plaintiff going to some out-of-the-way State, and then, before his spouse can ascertain where he has gone, procuring a bogus decree of divorce and marrying again. We get numerous applications in England from women whose husbands have deserted them and gone to the United States and returned, after a considerable time, with an American divorce. They desire to know where they can ascertain quickly whether such actions have been brought, so as to be able to intervene or reopen the case, and we are obliged to reply that the only method is to search the records in every county clerk's office in every State of the Union.

As these three points are entirely on matters of procedure, it is competent for the several States each to pass a statute providing that the matrimonial decrees of that State shall not be deemed final and operative unless and until a copy of the summons or writ has been filed in the office of the secretary of state of that State, and likewise a copy of the decree, and unless the attorney-general has been properly cited. There can be no constitutional objection to such a course, for if by statute of the State in which the decrees were rendered it would not be deemed a valid final decree until recorded as above stated, no other State would under the Constitution be obliged to give it "full faith and credit" unless so recorded. Each State can regulate its own procedure, and no judgment is a valid final judgment unless entered in accordance with such procedu e.

I think, therefore, this meets one of your objections, viz., that such a course would "deprive the courts of an essential portion of their judicial power." Whether the requirement that the judgment before being deemed "final" should also be entered in the central registry would be open to such objection, is a more difficult question.

Any such central registry will, of course, not be easy of accomplishment, but none the less I think some constitutional method of creating it could be devised. We ought to get rid of the notion in the United States, that because of our constitutional system nothing can be done as is done in other countries. By a search in one office in London, all matrimonial decrees affecting forty millions of English people can be searched in a short time. The same is true of both Scotland and Ireland by a search in Edinburgh and Dublin. Why cannot there be (in time) one such office in the United States?

There is the further very serious question, which is rarely touched upon with reference to divorce decrees, viz., their effect upon titles to real estate and inheritance. As matters now stand in the United States, Mr. A. on selling his real estate may offer a deed purporting to be signed by Mrs. A., who may or may not be, in law, his wife. If he has been divorced he will perhaps offer a divorce decree which may turn out to be regular, but he may at the same time conceal the fact that he was the defendant in prior divorce proceedings in which a decree was rendered, which for lack of jurisdiction is void, leaving him still married to his former spouse. At present there is no earthly practicable way of searching for such decrees throughout the United States. Again, Mr. B. dies leaving children who claim to inherit his estate. It may be that he was the defendant in some bogus divorce suit in a far away State, subsequently married again, and that these children are not entitled to inherit at all. Such registries would greatly facilitate search, and the fact that they existed would help to diminish the number of these secret divorces.

Of course States which make a bid for divorce business cannot be expected to spoil their business by agreeing to any such registries, but anything that can be done by legislation throughout the United States to lessen the number of places in which it is necessary to search is an immense gain, for it would facilitate the reopening of fraudulent divorce decrees by innocent persons before it is too late, would tend to settle titles to real estate, and to put the United States more on a par with the judicial systems of other countries.

I am aware, of course, that such central registry must be supported by voluntary action of the several States desiring to use it, and at their expense, and that it will not be a matter of federal regulation at all. There are also other difficulties and objections in the way, but I see none that are insuperable. Moreover, is it not time that there should also be a central registry for births, marriages, and deaths throughout the United States? At the present time it is practically an impossible task to ascertain the place of birth, marriage, or death of any one whose descendants may be entitled to foreign real estate, unless his foreign relatives know where he settled or lived, which very frequently they do not. It is easier in States where these records are duplicated in the secretary of state's office; but in many of them there are no such duplicate records, and so those of each county or city must be searched. Such a registry in time would probably be partly if not wholly self-supporting, and the initial expense of it would be very small when divided amongst several States. J. ARTHUR BARRATT.

Temple, London.

THE BUGABOO OF ETHICS.

[The following contribution is given space in our columns, not because it represents, in any degree, our views, but merely to show in what manner the legal profession is being involved in the political whirlpool and also to give an illustration of the more or less popular conception of the functions of a legal adviser. — *Editor Law Notes.*]

A DISTINGUISHED gentleman who is at the same time a distinguished lawyer, in fact, no less a person than the Hon. Joseph H. Choate (*stet nominis umbra!*), said to the New York Bar Association that if Mr. Roosevelt had knowledge that any eminent lawyers were sitting up nights steering their clients through devious channels to avoid and evade the laws of the country, he would be glad to learn their names and would with equal cheerfulness present them for investigation, etc. Probably Mr. Choate means this, and is to such a degree ignorant. It is to be hoped he does and is. At the same time, to dwell for a moment in the rarefied atmosphere in which "constitutional and eminent" lawyers (the classification seems to be regulated by the size of their fees) hold forth, can it be possible that he has forgotten the way in which David Dudley Field fought the fight of righteousness for Gould and Fisk while their presses were working overtime turning out Erie stock? Does he not remember how Elihu Root was befooled into believing that Boss Tweed was upright and unduly oppressed, to that degree that he litigated enormously and expensively for the Boss? These instances are taken from Mr. Choate's own State. If these gentlemen, whose reputation as astute lawyers seems well earned, did not recognize the fact that they were piloting lawbreakers through shoals which their lawbreaking had created, then their professional instinct blinded them to what was patent to the press and people.

But the objection is made that "Ethics" demands that no lawyer shall refuse to aid a man accused to secure a fair presentation of his side or cause. To the layman, this "Ethics" is a peculiar institution. It seems to be devised and manipulated to protect the lawyer rather than the client, to sting the public and elicit the elusive fee. Otherwise, its chief field is as a text for bar association addresses or talks before law students. Futile piffle! "Ethics" did not figure largely when Parsons engineered the Sugar Trust. To have been ethical, the late Mr. Dodd, of the Standard Oil outfit, should have spent his time defending petty damage suits instead of building up an illegal combination which all of the government's lawyers can't overthrow.

To the casual observer it seems that if any man or set of men are capable of recognizing an infraction of the law, it must be the trained sleuths of the profession. (The Lord knows the average citizen does not even know what the law is, maxims to the contrary!) Therefore, have these gentlemen any cause for complaint when they are designated as undesirable citizens for creating lawbreakers, as the courts daily prove they are doing? Mr. Roosevelt is showing unaccustomed mildness when he does not go at them vigorously for furthermore increasing their offending by seeking to yank their creatures to safety through back alleys of construction and loopholes left for just such emergencies. Then, too, who are the lobbyists, the "friends up the river;" who are the legislative patrons who provide a semblance of legality for these creations of legal intellect? The question carries its own reply. And the still small voice of "Ethics" is never stiller and smaller than when these sworn officers of the court are gumshoeing their way through legislature and Congress.

"Ethics" is not confined to the aristocracy of the profession, the "a v fi" bunch. It permeates the whole tribe. The professional code of honor does not prevent the acceptance of a case, no matter how unjust or shady. Lawyers nowadays hear with wonder, mixed with contempt, how Lincoln would not take a case which he believed to be improper.

On the other hand, it is an accepted convention that one cannot take a client at a lower fee than that upon which a brother lawyer has fixed when offered the same case. Very good. But take the case, and "Ethics" does not prevent you from so steering it as to bring it up before a judge whose sister-in-law is a cousin of your wife, or on whom you have some equally weighty claim. Or, it is justifiable strategy to bribe his secretary, or pass word to him through his political patron. That's a part of the game. If you go before a referee, you can earn a reputation for legal acumen by doubling the reference fees allowed by statute. It may not bring results, but it doesn't do any harm. "Ethics" is conveniently blind. In choosing a jury, it is not ethical to prefer a man of known uprightness and intelligence to one whose chief characteristic is a bias in favor of your client.

So the thing goes. The trail of the serpent is along the whole way. The lawyer acts as midwife, nurses the infant criminal through its most perilous time, going even so far as to distribute boxes of cigars and small bills amongst court officials and tipstaffs, anywhere they will do the most good. In fact he employs every antiseptic to ward off the poison of investigation and prosecution until his client becomes strong enough to have his own senators and legislators, generally effective safeguards against corporate ills. And should ill befall his client's more mature years, this superserviceable physician is ever at hand to ward off the penalties that should follow the violations of the law, to aid his patient to evade the consequences of his own misdeeds.

In the name of the prophet, figs! No lawyer, however able and honest, can disguise in a fog of "unctuous rectitude" the fact that there never was an illegal corporation organized, stayed and shored when attacked, or knocked out for its illegality, but that some eminent lawyer was its guiding hand.

Why not be honest and drop all of this hypocritical twaddle about "Ethics"? Admit that these things are done, but done at the behest of the very people whose laws they are infringing. "Ethics" as now known and understood doesn't fool the people, doesn't fool the client, and least of all does it fool the lawyer himself.

A BILL FOR DIVORCE.

THE following bill for divorce was recently filed in the Chancery Court at Memphis, Tenn. The defendant appears to be the star bigamist Witzhoff who was recently caught in England and sentenced to seven years penal servitude.

Your complainant, Mrs. G. L. Cavendish, or Miss L. G. Simmons, respectfully represents and will show to the court that she is and has been a citizen of Shelby county, State of Tennessee, for more than two whole years next preceding the filing of this suit, and that the said defendant, J. C. Cavendish, *alias* Lord Douglass, *alias* Lord Alfred Percival Scott, *alias* Count De Ramey, *alias* Count De Germain, is a nonresident of the State of Tennessee, and his address is to her unknown.

Your complainant states and will show to the court that while she was on a visit to friends at Hot Springs, Ark., during the month of October of 1905 she met the said defendant, who was then going under the name and was known as Lord J. B. Cavendish; that he was a free spender, seemingly wealthy, a man of about forty years of age, five feet seven inches in height, his eyes an alluring blue-gray, his hair iron-gray, his features well chiseled and scholarly, well made physically, caparisoned as becomes a heart-breaker, and undeniably aristocratic in his bearing and tastes; that said defendant then and there proposed marriage to her, and after a few days' consideration of his proposal and being overcome by his personality and being extremely fascinated and believing herself in love with him, consented to marriage. Said defendant then procured a marriage certificate from the clerk of the court, and her marriage to said defendant was performed on the 24th of October, 1905, at Hot Springs, Ark. Complainant and defendant then went on their honeymoon and an extensive bridal tour of the West, finally reaching the Republic of Mexico, where humiliation, disgrace, and untold trouble began.

She then for the first time learned of the deceit and fraud that had been practiced upon her by said defendant. The picture of the man she had married appeared in the newspapers, and he was heralded all over the country as one of the greatest deceivers, frauds, and perhaps the most accomplished bigamist in the United States or North America, and he immediately deserted and left her. It was then for the first time that she was advised that said defendant, under one or the other of the above titles or names, had married a Miss Hood, of a very wealthy and prominent family, of New Iberia, La., and that their marriage was perhaps the greatest social event that was ever known to the town that produces tobasco sauce and handsome women. That during the year of 1904 said defendant appeared at Ft. Worth, Texas, having conceived the idea that "if you want to succeed, young man, go West," and later met a wealthy and prominent widow, Mrs. A. S. Anderson, whom he handed a fine brand of romance, with the title with which he was threatened, and his Othello-like adventures in various parts of the world.

She believed him, and complainant is advised she became his wife by marriage certificate and performance of ceremony, and after relieving her of a nice sum of money he seemed to migrate to Columbus, Texas, where he got in trouble with another woman and landed in jail, but woman-like, Mrs. Anderson, or Cavendish, paid the penalties and costs and redeemed her title and supposed husband. Complainant avers that she is advised and believes that said defendant has since their marriage married a Miss Hopps, of Norfolk, Va.; Mrs. Scott, of South Bend, Ind.; Miss Duncan, of Reno, Nev.; Miss Belle Warner, of Niles, Ind.; and several women in North Carolina. He courted and wed with the fine distinction of a connoisseur and with discrimination of a man who likes variety. Widows and maids! It was all the same to his lordship. Like the hero of Kipling's "Ladies," he "took his fun where he found it, and rogued and ranged in his time; and he has had his pickings of sweethearts."

Complainant avers that she is advised and believes that there has been a syndicate formed in North Carolina to finance the hunt for "my lord," that they may have him put away where there are no marriages on the moving-picture plan, and that justice may be dealt out to him for "hitching up," as expressed in the sagebrush district; but all complainant asks for is that the court cancel and annul her marriage or grant her a divorce if she be legally married to said alleged accomplished bigamist, for she has had an elegant sufficiency of said defendant and alleged "lord."

Complaint avers that she acted in good faith all along and considered herself the lawful wife of said defendant, and did not know of his many wrongs and misdeeds until after he left her at San Luis Potosi, Mexico, on or about the — day of December, 1905; and that said defendant has knowingly entered into a second marriage, or several of them, since his marriage to her, and that he was a married man and had a living wife at the time he practiced fraud and deceit upon and married her.

Complainant asks that her maiden name be restored to her.

No children have been born to her.

The premises considered, your complainant prays the court to permit her to file this bill against said defendant, and that the proper process issue by publication as provided by law in such cases of nonresidents; and that said defendant be commanded to be and appear at the next rule day of this court and answer this bill under oath; and that on the final hearing of this cause the court decree her status, and that if it appear that she be lawfully married to said defendant that she be given a decree of absolute divorce, absolutely dissolving the bonds of matrimony subsisting between them forever, and her maiden name, Miss L. G. Simmons, be restored to her, but if it appear that she be not married by reason of some lawful barrier, that the court so decree and cancel and annul the marriage existing between her and the said defendant, which is a matter of record, and which she is advised is *prima facie* a marriage according to law.

Complainant prays for such other further general relief, orders, references, and decrees as she may be entitled in law and equity under this bill. And in duty bound will ever pray.

JUDICIAL WISDOM AND SENTIMENT.

"KNOWLEDGE is never ignorance." *Per* Prentice, J., in Breach *v.* Osborne, 74 Conn. 405, 413, 50 Atl. Rep. 1019.

"*Post hoc* is not necessarily *propter hoc.*" *Per* Sanborn, C. J., in Missouri, etc., R. Co. *v.* Byrne, (C. C. A.) 100 Fed. Rep. 359, 362.

"Corporate monopoly and socialism are twin children of despotism." *Per* Douglas, J., in Jones *v.* Com'rs, 130 N. Car. 451, 470.

"It is often a narrow line which separates right from wrong." *Per* Peters, C. J., in Coolidge *v.* Goddard, 77 Me. 578, 1 Atl. Rep. 831.

"Some men can drink twice as much as others without showing it." *Per* Paxson, C. J., in Com. *v.* Cleary, 135 Pa. St. 64.

"The law does not indulge in revenge." *Per* Vice-Chancellor Van Fleet, in Una *v.* Dodd, 39 N. J. Eq. 185.

"Example is always contagious, especially vicious example." *Per* Hughes, D. J., in Mercer *v.* Steamer Florida, 3 Hughes (U. S.) 488, 490, 17 Fed. Cas. No. 9,433 (at p. 30).

"Men are generally more careful in dealing with their sons-in-law than with their own sons." *Per* Sharswood, J., in Weaver's Appeal, 63 Pa. St. 309, 312.

"It is not in human nature patiently to submit to expressions denoting contempt." *Per* Dr. Lushington, in Williams *v.* Hall, 1 Curt. Ecc. 611.

"Our experience teaches that men very much resemble each other, not only in their good qualities, but their bad." *Per* Vice-Chancellor Blake, in Campbell *v.* Campbell, 22 Grant Ch. U. C. 322, 332.

"We have no right, unless there is clear proof it is so, to ascribe a bad motive for a good act." *Per* Mr. Justice Davis, in Gaines *v.* New Orleans, 6 Wall. (U. S.) 642, 708.

"It would be arrogant in any nation to claim a state of morals superior to those of England and especially to Scotland." *Per* Justice Cowen, in Cole *v.* Goodwin, 19 Wend. (N. Y.) 251, 272.

"Visiting a woman frequently, and kissing her at parting, are things that often occur without a promise of marriage having been made or expected." *Per* Cameron, C. J., in Costello *v.* Hunter, 12 Ont. 333, 339.

"It is not enough that the doors of the temple of justice are open; it is essential that the ways of approach be kept clean." *Per* Mr. Justice Brewer, in Hatfield *v.* King, 184 U. S. 162, 168.

"Emphatic modes of speech are largely the result of temperament, and impulsive minds, which are much addicted to them, are frequently less obstinate than those that are more cautious and self-sustained." *Per* Durfee, C. J., in Kaul *v.* Brown, 17 R. I. 14, 17.

"The moral growth of a community depends on its churches, schools, and teachers, and the influence of a healthy and comfortable home life, and not on the police." *Per* Mr. Justice Gaynor, in People *v.* Summors, 40 Misc. (N. Y.) 384, 82 N. Y. Supp. 297, 298.

"The prudent man is not the man who never forgets anything, who is never guilty of any inattention, who never fails to think of any possible danger to which he is exposed." *Per* Stafford, J., in Kirkpatrick *v.* Grand Trunk R. Co., 52 Atl. Rep. 531, 536.

"It is an old remark of political economists, that employments like fishing and hunting, pursued for the pleasurable excitement they afford, by persons in easy circumstances, are the hardest of any for those who are destined to gain their living by them." *Per* Ware, D. J., in The Echo, 3 Ware (U. S.) 289, 8 Fed. Cas., p. 286.

To declare that "because the world gets wiser as it gets older, therefore it was foolish before," would be a barbarous proposition, said Baron Bramwell, in Hart *v.* Railway Co., 21 Law Times [N. S.] 261, 263, quoted with approval by Mr. Justice Gray, in Columbia, etc., R. Co. *v.* Hawthorne, 144 U. S. 202, 208, and by Carpenter, J., in Aldrich *v.* Concord, etc., R. Co., 67 N. H. 250, 29 Atl. Rep. 410.

"Madame De Stael once said with biting, yet truthful, sarcasm, that 'the more she saw of men, the more she admired dogs.' For there is no animal among the brute creation that treats the mother sex with as little respect and as great brutality as brutal man." *Per* Dent, J., in Ball *v.* Stewart, 41 W. Va. 654, 24 S. E. Rep. 632, 633.

"No law can be enacted nor system be devised for the control of human affairs that in its enforcement does not produce some evil results, no matter how beneficial its general purpose may be." *Per* Circuit Judge Shiras, in U. S. *v.* Trans-Missouri Freight Assoc., 58 Fed. Rep. 58, 94, quoted in same case on appeal, 166 U. S. 290, 337.

"It can hardly be said that a business man who sues for injury to his standing and reputation in the community where he lives, but who confesses himself to be a gambler for large stakes, and who visits gambling places in company with women, should be regarded by the jury as necessarily having a reputation above reproach." *Per* Bunn, D. J., in Best *v.* Kessler, (C. C. A.) 130 Fed. Rep. 24, 27.

"We all know that prejudices become more inveterate as they ripen by age and in the soil of ignorance. We seldom recollect the particular facts and arguments which have led our minds to particular prejudices. The impressions gather strength and take deeper root, the longer they remain unremoved. The sooner, therefore, the attempt is made to remove them, the better." *Per* Mr. Justice Washington, in Hurst *v.* Wickerly, 1 Wash. (U. S.) 276, 12 Fed. Cas. No. 6,940.

"Whenever any effort is made in the interest of humanity to lessen the hours of toil and give a breathing spell, a chance, however small, for the enjoyment of life to the employed, a protest is always made on the ground stated by Judge Field (113 U. S. 703) that 'it deprives a man of the right to work at all times.' This objection means simply that it deprives the objector of the right to work 'the other fellow' at all times, without stint or limit." *Per* Chief Justice Clark, in State *v.* Rey, 131 N. Car. 825.

"The frequency of a physician's visits must depend very much, I imagine, on the timidity, nervousness, and inexperience of those who employ him. Some people send for the doctor at the slightest cause of alarm; others scarcely ever. The length of such visits, I suppose, would depend much on the number of the doctor's patients, and the sluggishness or activity of his habits. Some never, or seldom, sit down; others never want to get up, and can never go anywhere without staying all day, if any one will keep their company." *Per* Van Dyke, J., in Berckmans *v.* Berckmans, 17 N. J. Eq. 453, 458.

"It may be said truthfully, that the man is yet to come who, in all emergencies, has not blundered, whether he be lawyer, juror, or judge, major-general, minister, governor, crowned head, or president. . . . Experience, the master teacher, often demands the occurrence of more than one incident to prepare and instruct, and rarely contributes to success, to great achievements, to grand results, except after many impressive events. In the language of a distinguished author, 'experience, like the light in the stern of a vessel, illumines only the path that is past.'" *Per* Justice Brady, in People *v.* Fire Com'rs, 43 Hun (N. Y.) 554, 558.

"The affection of a dog for his master, and for the members of the household in which he dwells, is proverbial. Not only is he their friend, but often he is their protector. His resenting an intrusion by a stranger upon the premises of which he conceives himself to be the guardian is an evidence of his loyalty to those to whom he owes allegiance. It is common knowledge that the dog which is looked upon with distrust and fear by the neighborhood may be handled, even misused, with impunity by the children in the family of which he is a member. It is equally well known that with a change of the ownership of the dog comes a transference of his affections. Not that he ever entirely forgets his old master, and the latter's family, but he is loyal to the hand that feeds him. He recognizes promptly his obligation to those among whom he makes his home, and repays it with affection and devotion." *Per* Gummere, C. J., in Emmons *v.* Stevane, 73 N. J. L. 349, 251, 64 Atl. Rep. 1014, 1015.

"This case affords one among many examples of the failure of the so-called 'reform procedure' to accomplish anything towards the brevity, the clearness, the accuracy, or the convenience of legal forms. So long as the fundamental principle of our remedial jurisprudence shall be that upon conflicting evidence the jury shall ascertain the facts, and upon ascertained facts the judges shall pronounce the law, so long will it be a cardinal rule of pleading, by whatever name 'pleading' shall be called, that the line of distinction between facts and the evidence to prove them shall be kept clear and well defined. The notion of the reforming enthusiast that the average litigant or his average lawyer can make a shorter, clearer, or less redundant statement of his case, if left to his own head, than if directed and restrained by the settled forms, sifted, tested, and condensed as they have been by generations of the acutest intellects ever devoted to a logical profession, is as vain as that of any other compounder of panaceas." *Per* Mitchell, J., in Hubbard *v.* Tenbrook, 124 Pa. St. 291, 16 Atl. Rep. 817.

Cases of Interest.

COLORADO TORRENS LAW UPHELD. — In People v. Crissman, 92 Pac. Rep. 949, the Colorado Supreme Court upholds the Torrens Land Law of 1903. It was contended that the act was unconstitutional because it authorized the taking of property without due process of law, because it devolved executive duties on the courts, and because it created a new county office which was filled neither by appointment nor election as required by the constitution.

BANKRUPTCY — WHAT NOT A PREFERENCE. — In Macon Grocery Co. v. Beach, 156 Fed. Rep. 1009, it was held by Judge Speer, in the District Court for the Southern District of Georgia, N. D., that the payment by an insolvent, whose indebtedness amounted to $13,000, of the sum of $2.75 in settlement in the usual course of a current bill at a grocery store for soda water, lemonade, a bar of soap, and one dressed doll did not raise a presumption that the debtor intended to prefer such creditor sufficient to overcome his testimony that the payment was not made with any such intention.

CUSTOM AS AFFECTING CONTRIBUTORY NEGLIGENCE. — In Beck v. Southern R. Co., 59 S. E. Rep. 1015, it is held by the North Carolina Supreme Court that when it has been a custom for ten years, with the knowledge of a railroad, for its employees to pass from their place of work to their homes across a large number of the company's tracks, and, when necessary, to pass through, over, or under cars blocking the way, an employee, who in taking the customary way home was killed while passing between two cars which blocked the way, was not negligent as a matter of law. Brown, J., dissented.

MENTAL ANGUISH — FAILURE TO DELIVER CORPSE PROMPTLY. — In Beaulieu v. Great Northern R. Co., 114 N. W. Rep. 353, the Minnesota Supreme Court holds that, in the absence of wilful or malicious misconduct, damages cannot be recovered against a carrier for mental anguish in an action for breach of a contract to transport a corpse to a particular point and there deliver it to an intersecting carrier, the breach consisting in the negligence of the company's agents and servants in carrying the corpse beyond the connecting point, thus causing a delay of twenty-four hours in the funeral arrangements.

TURNTABLE DOCTRINE DISAPPROVED IN OHIO. — In Wheeling, etc., R. Co. v. Harvey, 83 N. E. Rep. 66, the Ohio Supreme Court, after an extended review of the authorities, expressly disapproves the doctrine of the Turntable Cases, and holds that a railroad company is not liable to an infant who comes upon its premises without invitation, and who is injured there while playing with a turntable without the knowledge of the company. The court distinguishes the case of Harriman v. Railroad Co., 45 Ohio St. 11, which has hitherto been regarded as supporting the turntable doctrine, on the ground that in the latter case the person injured was a licensee.

MASTER AND SERVANT — POSITION OBTAINED BY FRAUD. — A novel point in the law of master and servant was decided by the Virginia Supreme Court of Appeals, in Norfolk, etc., R. Co. v. Bondurant, 59 S. E. Rep. 1091. The action was brought to recover for the death of a student locomotive fireman. The railroad company showed that its rules prohibited the employment of minors for train service, and that the deceased had secured his position by falsely representing himself to be above the age of twenty-one, when in fact he was a minor. The court held that the knowing misrepresentation as to his age by the deceased prevented the establishment of the relation of master and servant; that he was a trespasser, or at most a bare licensee; and that consequently the railroad was not liable for his death in a collision, since it could be held liable only for injuries wilfully or wantonly inflicted on him.

FRAUD AND DECEIT IN PROCURING MARRIAGE. — In Sears v. Wegner, 114 N. W. Rep. 224, the Michigan Supreme Court holds that a good cause of action for fraud and deceit is set up by a declaration which alleges that the defendant, fraudulently intending to damage and ruin plaintiff and bring upon her pain and suffering of mind and body, paid his attentions to her as a suitor; that he fraudulently represented that, though he was married, the marriage was void; that the plaintiff, relying on his representations, entered into the marriage relation with him, lived with him for years as his wife, and had children by him; that she desired a public ceremony, and that he promised to have the same performed; that thereafter the defendant refused to keep his promises, and on obtaining a divorce from his former wife married another woman, and deserted the plaintiff and refused to support her and her children.

LIBEL — PUBLICATION BY LABOR UNION IN "UNFAIR LIST." — In Labor Review Pub. Co. v. Galliher, 45 So. Rep. 188, the Alabama Supreme Court holds that it is not libelous to publish of a person that he has been placed on the "unfair list" by a labor union. In the course of the opinion McClellan, J., said: "Applying our common knowledge to this publication, which emanates from organized labor and is borne to the public through a paper identified therewith, it must be concluded that the word 'unfair,' when coupled with the word 'list,' is an idiom of the language of that organization. It has in a sense coined the descriptive term composed of the two words, and thereby given to the couplet a meaning as distinctive as any in our language — a meaning not imported by the separated words when reference is had either to the lexicon or the usual understanding of the public." The court holds that the meaning of "unfair list" is a list of persons unfriendly to organized labor or rebellious against its rules, and that the use of the term in reference to a person does not impute to him dishonesty, faithlessness to contract, unreliability, or that he is undeserving of confidence.

BLOODHOUND TESTIMONY. — In State v. Dickerson, 82 N. E. Rep. 969, the Ohio Supreme Court had occasion to pass for the first time on the admissibility of evidence of the conduct of bloodhounds in trailing or following the tracks of one accused of crime. After reviewing the cases on the subject the court stated the circumstances under which such evidence might be received, as follows: "It is apparent that, before the acts and conduct of the dog can be shown, a proper preliminary foundation must be laid, and to establish such foundation it must be shown that the particular dog used was trained and tested in tracking human beings, and by experience had been found reliable in such cases; that the dog so trained was laid on the trail, whether it was visible or invisible, at a point where the circumstances tended clearly to show that the guilty party had been, or upon a track which the circumstances indicated to have been made by him. In addition to this, the reliability of the dog must be proved by a person or persons having personal knowledge thereof. This foundation may be strengthened by proof of pedigree, purity of blood, or the exalted standing of his breed in the performance of such peculiar work."

INJUNCTION AGAINST BULL-FIGHT. — In State v. Canty, 105 S. W. Rep. 1078, the Missouri Supreme Court holds that an arena erected for the purpose of conducting a bull-fight, and in which one is actually carried on, is a public and common nuisance which equity has power to abate by injunction as being injurious to the public safety and good morals; and this notwithstanding that no property rights are involved and that the offenders are also amenable to criminal prosecution for conducting such bull-fight. In a concurring opinion, Valliant, P. J., said: "A court of equity will not undertake to enforce the criminal law. Therefore, it will not enjoin the commission of a threatened act merely because the act would be a crime, but, on the other hand, neither will it withhold its equitable relief in a case in which, for other reasons, it has jurisdiction merely because the act when committed would be a crime. An act displayed before a public audience which is debasing in its character, debauching in its influence on public morals, and brutalizing in its effect on the spectators is a public nuisance, which a court of equity has jurisdiction to enjoin, and the court is not robbed of its jurisdiction merely because the act besides being a nuisance is also a crime. In such case a court of equity will give its attention to the public nuisance, and ignore the criminal character of the act."

Theatre Ticket Speculation — State's Power to Prohibit. — In People *v.* Steele, 83 N. E. Rep. 236, the Illinois Supreme Court holds that Laws 1907, p. 269, prohibiting the sale of theatre tickets not having thereon the words, "This ticket cannot be sold for more than the price printed hereon," and prohibiting the demanding and receiving for a ticket a price in excess of the printed rate, is invalid as an unjustifiable restriction on the business of conducting a theatre and the brokerage business of selling theatre tickets at a profit, the restriction not being required for the public welfare. The privilege of contracting, says the court, is both a liberty and a property right and is protected by the constitution; and the right of every man to choose his own occupation, provided it does not conflict with the public welfare, is included in the constitutional right to the pursuit of happiness. In the course of the opinion it is said: "The business of the broker in theatre tickets is no more immoral or injurious to the public welfare than that of the broker in grain or provisions. If he does not make the price satisfactory to intending purchasers, they are under no compulsion to buy. They have no right to buy at any price except that fixed by the holder of the ticket. The manager may fix the price arbitrarily, and may raise or lower it at his will. Having advertised a performance, he is not bound to give it, and having advertised a price, he is not bound to sell tickets at that price. It is immaterial to determine whether a theatre ticket is either transferable or revocable. The fact is that the bearer of the ticket is admitted to the performance. The business of dealing in theatre tickets is carried on to some extent, at least, and the right to do so and to contract in regard to such tickets is a right in which those who use it are entitled to be protected."

New Books.

Thayer's Essays.

Legal Essays. By James B. Thayer, LL.D., late Weld Professor of Law, Harvard University. 1 vol., cloth, $3.50 net. Boston: Boston Book Co., 1908.

In this volume is found a collection of fourteen essays by Professor Thayer, now brought together from the pages of the different periodicals in which they first appeared. Six are from the Harvard Law Review; two from the Atlantic Monthly; two from the Nation; and one each from four other periodicals, as the American Law Review and University Law Review. The principal subjects treated are: "The Origin and Scope of the American Doctrine of Constitutional Law;" "Advisory Opinions;" "A People without Law" (the American Indians); "Gelpcke *v.* Dubuque (Federal and State Decisions);" "Our New Possessions;" "International Usages, A Step Forward;" "Dicey's Law of the English Constitution;" "Bedingfield's Case, Declarations as a Part of the Res Gesta;" "A Chapter of Legal History in Massachusetts;" "Trial by Jury of Things Supernatural;" "Bracton's Note Book;" "The Teaching of English Law at Universities."

It now makes accessible to the body of the legal profession some papers that have exerted a good deal of influence on the thinking of those who have already read them. The most important ideas here presented have to a great extent already percolated into legal thought and legal literature and have thus been absorbed; but it is good even for those already familiar with those ideas to be able to renew the impression first made by the papers in question.

Perusal of the volume will cause the reader to regret — as many have done before — that the learned author accomplished no more permanent work than he did. He was professor in the Harvard Law School for twenty-eight years; and in addition to writing the "Preliminary Treatise on the Law of Evidence," compiled "Cases on Evidence" and "Cases on Constitutional Law."

But, on the whole, his career as an author was lacking in completeness. The two books that would have given him the most enduring fame were never written. What a pity it is that his contemplated single volume on the principles of the Law of Evidence was never written! If Professor Thayer had given us that treatise, the profession could no doubt have dispensed, for another generation at least, with the four or five big volumes that are now considered necessary to the complete treatment of the subject in text-book form. Again, what value would not his contemplated treatise on Constitutional Law have had in this day, when so much thought is being given to the subject of the limits of the power of the central government! Regret that those two books were not written is poorly compensated by a realization of the fact that the learned scholar was too much absorbed in teaching to do the finest work of which he was capable.

The essays in question are concerned mainly with the two themes to which we have referred. Those on constitutional questions comprise much of the material that would have gone into the proposed treatise on Constitutional Law. The first essay (that on the Origin and Scope of the American Doctrine of Constitutional Law) was delivered as an address before the Congress on Jurisprudence and Law Reform at the World's Fair in Chicago. In it the writer treats the question, How did our American doctrine, which allows the judiciary the power to declare legislative acts unconstitutional, and to treat them as null and void, come about, and what is the true scope of it? Confessedly the doctrine is a most remarkable one. Professor Thayer points out that the mere fact that a constitution is an organic writing which the judges are sworn to uphold is not a sufficient reason to account for it. In a Lowell Institute lecture recently delivered by another Harvard professor, we note that this doctrine is spoken of as "the envy and marvel of the rest of the civilized world." Marvel it certainly is, as fully appears from Professor Thayer's dissertation, but as to any feeling of envy on the part of those who live under a different system of law, we may be allowed to doubt.

The practice of allowing the judiciary to declare legislation void on the ground of its repugnance to the constitution was mainly the result, as Professor Thayer informs us, of historical experience. The colonists had long been governed under charters, and these furnished the conception of a fundamental constitutive document that could not be abrogated by local ordinances. Each charter was in effect a written constitution, and its efficacy was enforced even as against the colonial legislatures. When the colonies severed the tie that bound them to England, the constitutions of the several commonwealths were naturally conceived as taking the place of the earlier charters. The idea that they could not be overridden by mere legislative acts thus came quite naturally into the heads of American judges and lawyers.

In his review of Dicey's Law of the Constitution, Professor

Thayer makes some instructive observations on the nature and conception of constitutional law, with more particular reference to the historical forces that have shaped the English Constitution. His first sentence in this paper shows so deep an insight into the processes of English constitutional growth and is so finely expressed that the reader will be grateful for its reproduction here. "When one scrutinizes the English Constitution," says he, "it is like looking at the nests of birds or at the curious and intricate work of beavers and insects; its strange contrivances seem not so much the ordered and foreseen result of human wisdom as a marvelous outcome of instinct, of a singular political sense and apprehension, feeling its sure way for centuries, amid all sorts of obstacles, through and around and over them, with the busy persistence of a tribe of ants."

Perhaps none of these essays are more interesting than that on the Teaching of English Law. It was read before the Section on Legal Education at the American Bar Association in 1895. A logical, forceful, and even eloquent plea it is for higher education in the professional schools of law. How splendidly the law schools have responded to his call, the history of the work done and advances made in the fourteen years that have passed since that address was delivered abundantly show.

The Nation and the States.

Federal Usurpation. By Franklin Pierce, of the New York Bar. New York: D. Appleton & Co., 1908. $1.50. 427 pp.

This is a timely, strong, and thought-stirring book. The author thinks clearly and writes well of a problem which looms big in the public affairs of to-day. Year by year Congress is extending its activities, and the government at Washington, with its multitude of departments, commissions, boards, and bureaus, is constantly coming into closer touch with the life and affairs of the people. With increasing ingenuity, ways are found to put in motion the processes of the federal courts against state laws. The hand of the national government is laid on a score of matters to-day where a generation ago it touched but one. It is openly stated by the secretary of a great department, that if the Constitution stands in the way of this advancing tendency, sooner or later constructions of the Constitution will be found to vest the unexercised powers of the states in the national government. The President has said that the power of the federal government should be increased "through executive action . . . and through judicial interpretation and construction of law."

Is this really alarming, and does it bode ill for our country? Mr. Pierce, Dean Henry Wade Rogers, of the Yale Law School, and a number of other thoughtful writers and speakers, are convinced that it is a real menace to a democratic republic. Nevertheless, it seems almost sure that the federal power will continue to grow. A strong central government which does things, and especially the things which the states have not done or have done badly, is liked by the masses of the people. The administration which has stood for a wider exercise of federal power is popular beyond any in recent times. If a constitutional convention were to be held in this year 1908, who would say that Congress would not emerge with increased powers and that the number of subjects of federal legislation and regulation would not be vastly augmented?

Lectures on the Constitution.

The American Constitution. Lowell Institute Lectures delivered at Boston, by Frederic Jesup Stimson. New York: Charles Scribner's Sons, 1908.

On page 2 Professor Stimson administers his first whack to the President. He refers to the Brownsville incident and reminds us that "we have seen our President dictate what was little else than an executive bill of attainder — a thing which was hardly, if at all, attempted by the Stuart kings." On page 3 he refers to the report that the President recently promised to suspend or withhold the operation of the anti-trust laws in case the United States Steel Corporation were to take over the property of the Tennessee Coal and Iron Company. But he says this is "probably" not true. This looks like bringing Mr. Roosevelt into a study of the American Constitution rather early, but if the author carries him into the book early, he does not allow him to go until the finish, and it is a rare page which does not take a fall out of him. Cromwell "in his later despotic years," Napoleon III., and the Czar fall in line (page 87) with the Stuart kings, as fit comparisons for our present executive. We have heard before of "the rights of the people . . . that domain of sovereign power which President Roosevelt seems to think was all surrendered by the people to the federal government when they formed the Union;" of the Presidential threat "to enforce the Constitution when it represents the people's rights and not when it represents the people's wrongs;" of the censure of Judge Humphrey for his celebrated beef trust decision "sustaining the people's liberties," *et cetera;* but this is a new one: "A certain judge — a higher judge — was approached by the President or his agent and asked whether he would affirm this [Judge Humphrey's] decision if it were appealed and came before his court, and made the same answer that the great Coke made to King James: 'Sir, when that case comes before me for judgment, I will consider it as becometh a just judge.'" Too bad for the good point it illustrates, the author concedes that this story has "happily proven false."

There are other things in the American Constitution than a catalogue of what Professor Stimson thinks President Roosevelt doesn't know and doesn't care about the Constitution. Made up as it is of popular lectures, it is hardly a book for lawyers or even for law students. For popular reading it is instructive, interesting, and its style is spirited. On the great and debatable questions of constitutional interpretation, Professor Stimson's attitude is that of a sound lawyer, and his words breathe the true spirit of State rights and individual liberty.

News of the Profession.

Premier of Prince Edward Island Dies. — Hon. Arthur Peters, K. C., premier and attorney-general of the province of Prince Edward Island, died at Charlottetown on January 29.

The Youngest Chief Justice. — Hon. Samuel Hays, recently elected chief justice of the Oklahoma Supreme Court, is the youngest man who ever held such an exalted position in this country. He is but thirty-two years old. Judge Hays is a native of Arkansas and a graduate of the University of Virginia.

Col. Finlay, of Memphis, Dead. — Col. Luke W. Finlay, for more than forty years a well-known member of the Memphis bar, died there on January 26, aged seventy-seven years. Colonel Finlay was a graduate of Yale, and served with distinction as a Confederate officer.

United States Attorney Cranston Resigns. — During January it was announced that Earl M. Cranston, of Denver, had tendered to the President his resignation as United States District Attorney for Colorado, to take effect as soon as arrangements could be made to replace him.

Franklin B. Lord Dead. — Franklin B. Lord, head of the well-known New York law firm of Lord, Day & Lord, died on January 27 at his home in New York city. Mr. Lord was fifty-seven years old, a graduate of Columbia, and was admitted to the New York bar in 1873.

American Law Register Changes Name. — In its January number our esteemed contemporary, the *American Law Register*, appears under a new title, and henceforward will be known as the *University of Pennsylvania Law Review*. The old name will be carried as a sub-title.

The District of Columbia Bar Association held its annual meeting on the evening of January 14 and elected the following officers for the ensuing year: President, Nathaniel Wilson; vice-presidents, John B. Larner and Frederic D. McKenny; secretary, H. Prescott Gatley; treasurer, Charles H. Cragin.

Ex-Justice of Iowa Supreme Court Dead. — Hon. Josiah Given, who was for thirteen years a member of the Iowa Supreme Court, died in Des Moines on February 3, aged eighty years. He was appointed to the Supreme Court in 1889 by Governor Larrabee, having previously held many public posts of honor.

Officers of Arizona Bar Association. — The annual election of officers of the Arizona Bar Association, held in Phœnix on January 15, resulted as follows: President, John Mason Ross, of Prescott; vice-president, George J. Stoneham, of Globe; secretary, Paul Renan Ingles, of Phœnix; treasurer, E. W. Lewis, of Phœnix.

Made Chief Justice of New Brunswick. — On January 27 an order in council was passed at Ottawa promoting Justice Barker, of the Supreme Court of New Brunswick, to the chief justiceship of the court to succeed Chief Justice Tuck, retired. At the same time Hon. A. S. White, ex-attorney-general of the province, was appointed as one of the puisne judges of the court.

Death of ex-Justice Lovely. — Hon. John A. Lovely, a member of the Minnesota Supreme Court from 1898 to 1905, died at Albert Lea on January 28 at the age of sixty-four. He was a native of Burlington, Vt., but removed to Wisconsin in 1863 and was admitted to the bar of that State in the following year. In 1867 he located in Albert Lea, Minn. For more than a year past he had been in failing health.

Prominent New Brunswick K. C. Dead. — George V. McInerny, K. C., a leading barrister of St. John, N. B., and widely known as one of the most eloquent public speakers in eastern Canada, died on January 12, aged fifty years. He acquired his legal education at Laval University, Harvard, and the Boston University Law School, receiving from the last named the degree of LL.B.

New Federal District Judge in Pennsylvania. — On January 14 President Roosevelt appointed Judge James S. Young, of the Pennsylvania Common Pleas Court No. 2, to be United States District Judge for the Western District of Pennsylvania in succession to Judge Ewing who resigned to become a member of the Pennsylvania State railroad commission. Governor Stuart has filled the vacancy on the Common Pleas Court by appointing John C. Haymaker.

A New York Supreme Court Judge Dead. — Hon. George B. Abbott, a justice of the New York Supreme Court, died at his home in Brooklyn on February 12 of blood poisoning. Justice Abbott was fifty-seven years old, and a native of Vermont. He was a graduate of Williams College and of the Columbia Law School. He was appointed surrogate by Governor Hill in 1889 and held office for twelve years. He was elected to the Supreme Court in 1906.

Court Dress in Illinois. — The Supreme Court of Illinois has recently gone a step further than any other American tribunal in prescribing sartorial styles, for not only have its members themselves donned silk robes, but the court has also prescribed that henceforward all attorneys appearing before it must be attired in frock coats. No exception is made in favor of women lawyers. The matter has furnished considerable ammunition to the humorous paragraphers, some of whom maintain that a frock coat would cause a riot in some parts of Illinois.

Ex-Chief Justice of Ohio Dead. — Hon. Franklin J. Dickman, formerly chief justice of the Ohio Supreme Court, died of heart disease on February 12 in Cleveland, of which city he was one of the best-known residents. He was eighty years old and a native of Petersburg, Va. In 1867 he was appointed United States attorney for the Northern District of Ohio by President Johnson and held the position for two years. He was appointed to the Ohio Supreme Court in 1886 by Governor Foraker and served until 1895.

Utah State Bar Association. — The tenth annual meeting of the Utah State Bar Association was held in Salt Lake City on January 13. President Parley L. Williams occupied the chair and delivered an address. Papers read were "The Board of Pardons," by Judge J. E. Frick, and "Our Laws of To-day," by William D. Riter. The annual banquet was held in the evening with E. B. Critchlow as toastmaster. Officers were elected as follows: President, W. I. Snyder; secretary, W. D. Riter; treasurer, William M. McCrea.

Professor Strobel Dead. — Edward Henry Strobel, Bemis Professor of Law in the Harvard Law School from 1898 to 1906, died in Bangkok, Siam, on January 15 at the age of fifty-two. He was graduated from Harvard College in 1877 and from the Harvard Law School in 1882. After practicing law for a few years he entered the diplomatic service of the United States and in 1893 was made third assistant secretary of state. Subsequently he was successively minister to Ecuador and to Chili. He became professor of international law at Harvard in 1898, and five years later was made legal adviser to the King of Siam. In 1906 he resigned his professorship and removed to Siam.

Montana State Bar Association. — The annual winter meeting of the Montana State Bar Association was held in Helena on January 14. In his annual address President W. S. Hartman, of Bozeman, reviewed the work of the association during the past year, and among other things recommended the adoption of a code of ethics. After the business meeting the usual banquet was held. Officers for the ensuing year were elected as follows: President, T. J. Walsh, of Helena; vice-presidents, W. T. Pigott, L. P. Sanders, Edward Scharnikow, R. A. O'Hara, Edwin Norris, Dan Yancey, Sydney Sanner, Ransom Cooper, George Y. Patten, R. Von Tobel, C. W. Pomery, T. E. Crutcher, W. M. Johnson; secretary, Charles F. Word, of Helena; treasurer, Frank D. Miracle, of Helena.

Nebraska State Bar Association. — The eighth annual meeting of the Nebraska State Bar Association was held in Omaha on January 8 and 9. The only feature of the first day was President T. J. Mahoney's address on "A Popular Judiciary," the rest of the time being taken up with committee reports and other business. The annual address was delivered on the second day by Robert C. Smith, K. C., of Montreal, whose theme was "Some Modern Tendencies." Papers were read on "The Ethical Side of the Case," by Charles J. Ryan, and "Influence of Roman Law upon the Common Law," by Arthur C. Wakeley. The meeting concluded with the usual banquet, at which Mr. Mahoney presided. Officers for the ensuing year were elected as follows: President, C. C. Flansburg, of Lincoln; vice-presidents, Samuel Rinaker, John A. Eberhardt, and William F. Gurley; secretary, George P. Costigan, Jr., of Lincoln; treasurer, A. G. Ellick, of Omaha.

KANSAS STATE BAR ASSOCIATION. — The twenty-fifth annual meeting of the Kansas State Bar Association was held in Topeka on January 30 and 31. The president's address on "An Incident of State Control of Foreign Corporations" was delivered by W. P. Dillard, of Fort Scott. The annual address was made by Gardiner Lathrop, the general counsel of the Atchison, Topeka, and Santa Fé system at Chicago. Mr. Lathrop spoke on the subject of "Conservatism." Other papers read during the meeting were: "The Abatement of Public Nuisances," by E. W. Grant, of Emporia; "Lord Coke," by Judge J. S. West; "The Power of Congress to Create Corporations," by A. C. Mitchell, of Lawrence; "The Old Ninth Judicial District — Incidents and Suggestions," by Judge S. R. Peters, of Newton. The meeting wound up with the customary dinner, at which Harry J. Bone presided. Following are the newly elected officers: President, J. B. Larimer, of Topeka; vice-president, George A. Vandeveer, of Hutchinson; secretary, D. A. Valentine, of Clay Center; treasurer, J. G. Slonecker, of Topeka.

SOUTH DAKOTA STATE BAR ASSOCIATION. — The eighth annual meeting of the South Dakota State Bar Association was held in Watertown on January 8 and 9. President Joseph W. Jones, of Sioux Falls, presided and delivered the customary address. The principal feature of the meeting was the annual address by Hon. Edwin A. Jaggard, of the Minnesota Supreme Court. Judge Jaggard's subject was "The Study of Comparative Law." The papers on the program were "Trial by Jury," by Judge James H. McCoy, of Aberdeen; "The Police Power, Its Importance and Development," by Congressman Philo Hall, of Brookings; "The Manufacture of Prejudice," by H. C. Preston, of Mitchell; "Ought Not Changes to Be Made in the Law with Reference to Jury Trials in Civil Cases?" by Hon. Bartlett Tripp, of Yankton, former United States minister to Austria. The following officers were elected: President, Judge Charles S. Whiting, of DeSmet; vice-presidents, John B. Hauten, of Watertown, and James M. Lawson, of Aberdeen; secretary, J. H. Voorhees, of Sioux Falls; treasurer, L. M. Simons, of Mitchell. The next meeting will be held in Pierre.

DEATH OF MR. JUSTICE WILKES. — Mr. Justice Wilkes, of the Tennessee Supreme Court, died at his home in Pulaski on February 2. This announcement will undoubtedly be read with genuine regret by many who knew him only by reputation, but to whom he was a flesh and blood personality and not merely a name. Judge Wilkes was not only an able lawyer, but his literary style was excellent, and he had the happy faculty of injecting into his opinions matters of human interest. His gentle humor has done much to entertain the profession and to enrich its literature. He is said to have been very popular with the bar and especially with the younger members, who had frequent occasion to be gratified for his kindliness and thoughtfulness. John S. Wilkes was born in Maury county, Tenn., March 2, 1841, and was graduated from Pleasant Grove Academy and Florence Wesleyan University. He served in the Confederate army throughout the Civil War, and was a member of the Tennessee Supreme Court from 1893 to the time of his death. Probably his last contribution to any periodical was "Recollections of a Practitioner," which appeared in the September, 1907, issue of LAW NOTES.

SOUTH CAROLINA STATE BAR ASSOCIATION. — The fifteenth annual meeting of the South Carolina State Bar Association was held in Columbia on January 15 and 16 with about two hundred members in attendance. After President Joshua H. Hudson had called the meeting to order he delivered a brief address of a reminiscent nature. The only prepared speech delivered during the meeting was the annual address by Hon. Wendell P. Stafford, of the District of Columbia Supreme Court, who spoke on the subject of "The Lawyer." At the annual banquet on the evening of the second day toasts were responded to by Governor Martin F. Ansel, Federal Judge Hemphill, Hon. Wendell P. Stafford, Hon. George E. Prince, Hon. Robert Aldrich, Gen. Milledge Bonham, Hon. J. C. Sheppard. The election of officers resulted as follows: President, John C. Sheppard, of Edgefield; vice-presidents, T. M. Raysor, of Orangeburg, George H. Bates, of Barnwell, T. G. McLeod, of Bishopville, W. F. Stackhouse, of Marion, N. G. Evans, of Edgefield, J. S. Brice, of Yorkville, J. C. Otts, of Gaffney, W. N. Graydon, of Abbeville, B. H. Rutledge, Jr., of Charleston, and H. H. Watkins, of Anderson; secretary, John T. Earle, of Columbia; treasurer, M. S. Nelson, of Columbia.

NEW YORK STATE BAR ASSOCIATION. — The thirty-first annual meeting of the New York State Bar Association was held in New York city on January 24 and 25 with Hon. Joseph H. Choate presiding. At the morning session of the first day, besides committee reports and other routine business, papers were read by Daniel S. Remsen, of New York city, on "Safe and Sound Wills — A Lawyer's Obligation," and Elbridge L. Adams, of Rochester, on "Certain Phases of Civil Procedure in England." The afternoon session began with the president's annual address, in which Mr. Choate told the association something about the work of the recent Hague Conference. Afterwards the Right Hon. James Bryce, the British ambassador, was presented to the delegates, and on motion Hon. John F. Dillon was unanimously elected an honorary member of the association. A paper on "Some Faults in Legal Administration" was read by Elon R. Brown, of Watertown. In the evening the annual address was delivered at Carnegie Hall by Mr. Bryce, who took for his subject "The Methods and Conditions of Legislation." The principal features of the second day were a paper by William D. Guthrie, of New York city, on "The Eleventh Article of Amendment to the Constitution of the United States," and one by Harry Pegram, of New York city, on "Land Title Registration — Torrens and Other Systems." In the evening the annual banquet was held at the Waldorf-Astoria, Mr. Choate acting as toastmaster. Responses were made by Governor Hughes, Mr. Bryce, Judge Werner, of the New York Court of Appeals, Federal Judge Holt, and Talcott Williams. In the election of officers for the ensuing year Francis Lynde Stetson was chosen president. The vice-presidents are Paul Fuller, William C. De Witt, Lewis E. Carr, Edward C. Whitmyer, William Nottingham, Theodore R. Tuthill, John M. Davy, Daniel J. Kenefick, Frank B. Lown.

English Notes.

DEATH OF A KING'S COUNSEL. — Mr. William Ambrose, K. C., died in London on January 18, aged seventy-two.

APPOINTED TO COUNTY COURT. — Mr. R. H. Amphlett, K. C., has been appointed to fill the vacancy on the County Court bench created by the death of the Hon. Arthur Russell.

ENGLISH LAW BOOKS FOR 1907. — During last year an unprecedentedly large number of law books were published in England, 243 in all, more than twice as many as were published in the four preceding years together. Of these 168 were new books and seventy-five new editions.

APPOINTED SOLICITOR-GENERAL. — Mr. Samuel Thomas Evans, K. C., M. P., has been appointed solicitor-general of England in succession to Sir William Robson. He is forty-eight years old, was called to the bar at Gray's Inn in 1891, and was appointed a Q. C. in 1901.

Anxious but Polite. — In one of the English county courts recently during the trial of an action by a tailor against one of his customers the following letter from the plaintiff to the defendant was read in evidence: "I have to-day issued a writ against you for the amount of your bill. Trusting for a continuance of your esteemed favors, I remain," etc.

The New Attorney-general. — Sir William Snowdon Robson, K. C., M. P., has been appointed attorney-general of England to succeed the late Sir John Lawson Walton. The new attorney-general is fifty-six years old, was called to the bar at the Inner Temple in 1880, and was made a Q. C. in 1892. When the present government came into power he was made solicitor-general, which position he had filled with a high degree of success down to the present time.

Cutting Down Arrears in English Courts. — American lawyers and legislators may find food for thought in the fact that when the English Court of Appeal opened during January for the Hilary term, there were only 152 appeals on its list, but few of which were entered for hearing earlier than October last. A year ago the list numbered 345. In the King's Bench Division there was a decrease of 269 causes, and in the Chancery Division sixty-two. In the House of Lords but ten appeals were pending, all but one of which had been entered for hearing within three months.

Finger-print Identification. — At Scotland Yard the finger-print system of identifying criminals has been brought to a high state of efficiency, due largely to the classification of Sir Edward Henry, the chief commissioner. Detective-inspector Collins has recently been quoted as stating that more than 31,000 identifications had been effected by this means, and that Scotland Yard was in possession of no fewer than 1,200,000 prints. The inspector has examined hundreds of thousands of impressions, and says he has never known two finger tips to agree in ridge characteristics.

As Others See Us. — Commenting on the outcome of the Thaw case, Sydney Brooks, the English reviewer, remarks that, with the exception of Mexico, no other civilized country has so many murders as the United States, and the chances are more than seventy to one against any murderer being executed. "Beyond everything else," he concludes, "the breakdown of the American criminal law is to be found in the worship and perversion of procedure; just as Americans have over-elaborated the machinery of politics until democracy is bound and helpless in its toils, so they have magnified the technicalities of the law until justice has been thrown into the background and lost sight of."

Juvenile Offenders. — The beneficial results of the policy of segregating juvenile prisoners and first offenders from the company of the older and more depraved criminals, which has been steadily gaining ground in England during the last few years, are shown by the fact that during the year 1907 the number of juvenile commitments was only 728, as against 1,688 in 1897. The number of prisoners between the ages of sixteen and twenty-one also showed a similar decrease. The question of juvenile offenders is receiving a constantly increasing amount of consideration from men prominent in public affairs, and it is probable that the present Parliament will adopt measures for the further extension of the policy.

Owner's Liability for Torts of Cat. — A case which bade fair to produce some new law was recently before Judge Woodfall, in the Westminster County Court. The plaintiff, who owned a picture gallery, on opening it one morning found blood stains on the draperies and chair covers, a hole in the skylight, and a cat with cut feet. Having ascertained the owner of the cat (if anybody can be said to own a cat) he brought an action against him for damages. The defendant stated that there was no hole in the glass at the time he was informed of the occurrence, and as to the blood stains he was quite willing to wash the affected articles. The plaintiff, however, wanted new ones. Unfortunately the judge found it unnecessary to pass on the liability of the owner for the tortious deeds of his cat, and on the facts of the case decided that the plaintiff was not entitled to recover in any event. It would be really interesting to know whether any one can be held liable for the breaches of the peace and other disorderly conduct to which cats are so prone in the dead vast and middle of the night.

England's Attorney-general Dead. — Sir John Lawson Walton, attorney-general of England, died at his residence in London on January 18 of pneumonia. He was born in Ceylon in 1852, but went to England when a boy and acquired his education there. He was called to the bar in 1877, and in 1890 was made a Queen's Counsel. Within five years after taking silk he won to the front rank of the bar. The *Law Journal* said of him editorially: "The sudden death of Sir John Lawson Walton while still in the prime of life and in the very plenitude of his powers has evoked public expressions of grief not confined to the profession of which he was the titular head. The last attorney-general who died in office was Follett, whom he resembled so much alike in the manner of his life and in the circumstances of his death; and it will not be forgotten that the general sympathy which was then felt found permanent expression in the erection of the great advocate's statue in Westminster Abbey. The late attorney-general may not have had all Follett's remarkable powers and unique opportunities, but he lacked none of his persuasive eloquence, and this was accompanied by a feeling of conviction and a fairness in argument which won him many notable victories, both forensic and political. When the party to which he belonged came into power there was no question as to his pre-eminent fitness for the post of its chief law officer, and he lent distinction to the honorific professional office to which he thus succeeded as leader of the English bar."

Obiter Dicta.

An Ecclesiastical Case. — In Wardens of Church of St. Louis *v.* Blanc, Bishop, 8 Rob. (La.) 51, Canon was of counsel on one side and St. Paul on the other. Soule also appeared.

An Expert Opinion. — It is told of Lord Wensleydale, formerly of the English Court of Exchequer, that coming home from church one day he was heard to soliloquize with regard to the sermon: "A good case. No reply. The court with him. And what a mess he made of it!"

How True! — In Philips *v.* Curtis, 38 Pac. Rep. 405, the Idaho Supreme Court remarks: "Neither American politics nor politicians have as yet, even among the most Utopian organizations, reached that stage of purity which will warrant or excuse the removing of all legal restraints from them."

A Poet of the Bench. — In gaining an able jurist in the person of Judge Bleckley, of Georgia, the world doubtless lost a great poet. Even so stale and unpromising a subject as the proposition that an objection cannot be taken for the first time in the appellate court, he could turn to favor and to prettiness. In Cleveland *v.* Chambliss, 64 Ga. 352, he said: "The point appears here in its virgin state, wearing all its maiden blushes, and is therefore out of place."

Powerful Profanity. — In an action recently brought in the District Court of Ada, Okla., to recover against a railroad company for certain injuries sustained by a carload of mules, one of the witnesses for the plaintiff testified that he was a passenger on the same train with the mules and saw everything that went on. He stated that most of the time the conductor "was up at the engine cussin' the engineer." "What effect, if any, did this have upon the mules?" he was asked. "It brought them to their knees and skinned them up," responded the witness.

A Grave Question. — In Tunis v. Hestonville, etc., R. Co., 149 Pa. St. 70, wherein the question as to what were the voting rights of executors upon the stock of deceased in the corporation was involved, Paxson, C. J., concluded his opinion as follows: "It is not needed for the purposes of this case that we should speculate as to the rights of a man to control, from his grave, the election of directors of a corporation. No such question is legitimately raised by this record. It will be time enough to decide this grave question when it arises."

To the Longest Liver. — The following *habendum* clause in a deed which one of our California readers had occasion to examine recently would indicate that there are some advantages to a long liver:

"To have and to hold, all and singular the said premises, together with the appurtenances, unto the said second parties and to the longest liver of them for and during their natural lives, and the natural life of such longest liver; and upon the death of such longest liver to revert to the said first parties, their heirs and assigns forever."

Had Been in Serious Trouble. — During the selection of a jury in a murder case in Milwaukee recently, District Attorney McGovern asked one of the talesmen, a man some sixty-five years old, "Have you ever been in any trouble?"

"Yes, sir," was the unexpected reply given without hesitation.

"Was it a shooting affray?"

"It was, sir." This answer was also given without hesitation and with almost a ring of defiance in the juror's voice.

Mr. McGovern hesitated. The man's replies indicated that if he had been in trouble he was an innocent party, and he feared to ask some questions that would wound his feelings.

"Er-how long ago was this shooting?" he inquired gently.

"About forty-six years ago." The audience was becoming interested, and all sat up expectantly, waiting to catch the answers.

"Well-er-" the district attorney was treading upon dangerous ground. "Who did the shooting?"

"The rebels, sir."

A Breeder of Trouble. — The Philadelphia *Record* tells this story on a young lawyer of that city who some time ago migrated to a developing Western town in quest of fortune and of fame. At first he located in a large storeroom, where other enterprises were conducted, and had a space partitioned off for his office. He made friends rapidly, accumulated business, and was regarded highly as a counsellor. But one day friends looked at him strangely and hurled all manner of derisive threats at him. He was accused of degrading his profession, introducing get-rich-quick methods into the community, and discouraging the efforts of men to conduct themselves and their business affairs honestly. The young attorney was startled, he says, on making an investigation. A tailor who had leased space in the storeroom had placed his sign beneath the lawyer's. It read as follows:

"James B——, attorney at law.

"New suits made to order."

Of Interest to Manufacturers. — The following is a verbatim copy of Senate Bill No. 179, introduced at the present session of the Massachusetts legislature:

"It shall be unlawful to manufacture, offer for sale, or exhibit in schools, libraries, museums, theatres, halls, streets, or other public places any nude person, or any picture, photograph, statue or cast that tends to shock the young or inexperienced, or any souvenir, toy, image, vessel, ornament, picture, photograph, print or other thing that represents or suggests lawful acts which are necessary for health but which pertain to private seclusion."

The correspondent who calls our attention to this measure inclines to the opinion that such a statute would be held invalid on the ground that it puts undue restraints on our infant industries.

A Scintilla of Evidence. — In Hicks v. State, 57 S. E. Rep. 958, an appeal from a conviction of gaming recently before the Georgia Supreme Court, Chief Justice Hill said: "A social gentleman, fond of company and a glass, vocation unknown, who lived and slept in a room upstairs over a bar, the door to which he kept locked, with a peephole to look through and a slide to hide the hole, and who cautiously moved the slide, to look through the hole, in order to ascertain the identity of the knocking visitor before unlocking the door, and who had in his room, besides two beds, two tables, one a round poker table and the other a stud poker table, behind which a dealer sat with many cards, and white, red, and blue chips, which cost from one dollar to five dollars a stack, and which chips were kindly cashed by the genial host, who invariably remembered the 'takeout' for the purpose of paying expenses, and who furnished to his playing guests, from a refrigerator, beverages that cheered as well as intoxicated, whenever the varying chances of the game rendered them despondent or reckless, and who employed an Italian Ganymede to wait on his guests, may or may not have been guilty of keeping a gaming house. A verdict of guilty, based on these facts and inculpatory circumstances, seems to the inexperienced mind of the court not unwarranted by the evidence."

Ghosts Judicially Ignored. — In view of the recent assertion of Sir Oliver Lodge that he and his confreres of the Society for Psychical Research on the one side, and certain industrious shades on the other, have pushed the tunnel under the river Styx to a point so near completion that the two gangs can now hear the sound of each other's picks, it is of interest to note that at least one court has taken judicial notice of the nonexistence of ghosts. In Nagy v. Manitoba Free Press Co., 16 Manitoba 619, the plaintiff sued the defendant for slandering his house by publishing a statement that the said house was haunted. The defendant insisted that in order to recover it was necessary for the plaintiff to show that there were in fact no restless spooks hanging about the premises. On this point the court said: "It is urged that the plaintiff has not proved that the article is untrue and that the house is not haunted. It is of course impossible to prove such a matter by evidence in the ordinary way. The very nature of a ghost, as understood by superstitious people, is that of a phantom appearing at rare intervals. Unless therefore we hold that courts should take judicial cognizance of the fact that ghosts do not exist, the falsity of the statement could never be absolutely proved. I think that the members of a court may, and as educated men should, assume that there are not such things as ghosts and that therefore the statement is necessarily false." A judgment in favor of the plaintiff was affirmed in 29 Can. Supr. Ct. 340. An action involving the same point (Barrett v. Associated Newspapers, 23 Times L. R. 666) was tried in England in March, 1907, and the jury awarded the plaintiff substantial damages. Apparently no appeal was taken from the judgment.

A Lawyer's Card. — We are indebted for the following contribution to our collection of lawyers' cards to a correspondent who regards it as "advertising some:"

JOHN A. LAWING
ATTORNEY AT LAW
AND NOTARY PUBLIC

Attention Given to Collections
Claims for Pensions, Bounty, Etc.,
a Specialty

Rooms 1 and 2, 618½ Market St.
Phone 2852 Chattanooga, Tenn.

A Righteous Worker. — A Tennessee correspondent is of the opinion that, while most lawyers do a great deal of work for which they will have to look for their reward to the sweet by and by, it is not often that a lawyer, in addition to receiving his fee, gets heavenly blessings showered upon him in the manner disclosed by the following letter, which came to a Memphis attorney whose name is not really Smith:

"We have your check for $75.84, representing the balance, net, collected in the claim of Doe *v.* Roe. Allow us to extend our supreme commendation to you for your faithful, persistent effort in securing this money. When you have gained the fair shores of eternal felicity St. Peter will, with one of his most winsome smiles, say to you, 'Smith, your uncompromising loyalty to a true purpose, while down in that murky sphere, entitles you to a place among the chief priests and high rulers of this grandest of worlds; come up high and survey what the righteous workers deserve.'"

A Justice's Dictum. — The following is a copy of a transcript of record of a learned police magistrate of Boulder county, Colo.:

Defendant arrained and plead not guilty. S. C. French, Town Marshall, sworn and testified, that upon Sunday July 7th A D 07, he saw the defendant: Fred Jorgenson leave his saloon and enter the Lyons Livery Stable. with several bottles in his pockets. witness followed him into the livery stable., and saw him standing face to face. with Harry Craver. with a bottle of beer in his hand: extended towards said Craver. Defendant seemed to be flustrated and excited at seeing the Marshall. dropping the beer upon the floor. then picking it up and dropping it into the watering trough. witness advanced and took the bottle of beer. from the watering trough: and noticed that Defendant had several other Bottles upon his person. Harry Craver sworn. admitted the facts as sworn to by S. C. French, but denied receiving any beer: from Defendant. admitted being a customer of Defendant: and patronizing his saloon. but denied all knowledge of the transaction. denied having ordered or received any beer at the specific time and place, The court held that Defendant did directly: or indirectly give and dispose of the said bottlé of Beer. by dropping the same into the watering trough. said watering trough being in and belonging to the Lyons Livery Stable a building in the control of and under the management of said Harry Craver.

Wherefore it was by the Court here ordered and adjudged that for said offense the said defendant be fined in the sum of fifty $50 dollars and costs of action and in default of payment of the same that the said defendant be imprisoned in the Town Calaboose of Lyons. until said fine is fully satisfied, not to exceed Twenty Seven and one half days.

Defendant took a appeal and
Fine $50 Executed a Bond in the Sum of $125.

Total $55.55.
Judgment rendered $55.55
a mistake of the Court of one Dollar.

W. H. H. Lewis,
Police Magistrate.

Remarks. had the Defendant returned the beer to his own pocket. no action could have been maintained

Correspondence.

Election of Federal Judges by the People.

To the Editor of Law Notes.

Sir: I read with interest your comment on the election of Supreme Court judges for limited terms by the people direct. It seems to me that you fail to give due prominence in those comments to a very important point.

Legislatures are supposed to make the law, and judges to interpret and apply them, and your remarks seem to take it for granted that this theory is actually carried out in practice. I believe that not only has the theory failed to work out in practice, but it must fail. I do not believe it possible for human beings acting as judges to simply interpret and apply laws made by others. In every litigated case there is some question of fact or law. There is, in the decision of every question, more or less room for honest difference of opinion. In determining which side of this difference of opinion is the correct one, each man starts out from his own point of view. That point is fixed and determined by that man's life, consisting of hereditary tendencies, environment, home training, schooling, business experiences, political affiliations, and a thousand and one things which are not the same in any two lives. Consequently no two men do or can approach a proposition from the same point, or in the same light, be they laymen, practitioners, or judges.

Differences of opinion among judges are, then, it seems to me, not simply possible, but more than probable wherever there is a question allowing any appreciable room for such differences, which is the case in a large part of the litigation. As I see it, the result of this fact is and must be a large and constantly increasing mass of judge-made law.

If the judges on the bench cannot get each other's viewpoint sufficiently to enable them to render a unanimous opinion as to the interpretation of a law, much less can they get the viewpoint of the framers of the law; and if they fail to get that viewpoint, then they fail to understand the intent and meaning of the law; and in just so far as they do this, their so-called "interpretation" is not interpretation, but is new (judge-made) law.

We must recognize the fact that the training and habits of a lawyer before going onto the bench are, perhaps, the chief factor in determining the point of view from which he will approach questions after he becomes a judge, and, therefore, his training and habits are entitled to great weight in determining the nature of the (judge-made) laws that he will frame.

You treat the matter as if it were simply a question between interpretation and application of existing laws (either statute or case) on the one hand and the arbitrary making of laws by judges governed by political influences on the other hand.

To me it seems that the laws are undergoing constant, though perhaps gradual, remaking and changing by the judiciary, and that the tendencies, previous training and experiences, etc., of the judges are having and must have their influence in that remaking, and that it is time to quit trying to avoid such influences and, rather, devote ourselves to ascertaining just what brand of influence we desire, and then getting it.

L'ENVOI.

The United States Supreme Court is supposedly made up of the greatest lawyers in the land; and the fact that decision after decision of that court on important questions is by a divided court, many times almost evenly divided, and frequently with each of the judges on each side assigning a different reason for his concurrence or dissent, also your January editorial on the results of differences of opinion among judges under the New York judicial system, seem to me to illustrate my point very clearly and to furnish much food for thought along this line.

CARLE WHITEHEAD.

DENVER, COL.

To the Editor of LAW NOTES.

SIR: The judicial department of the Federal (or State) government is but one branch of our government which is supposed to be a government by the people. Why, then, should not this department as well as the others be responsive to popular sentiment? If a consistent responsibility of this kind cannot be predicated, then it must follow that a popular form of government is a failure. That such is not the case the writer, and probably the editor, will be averse to admitting.

Man being primarily a social being, and as an individual being constantly brought into contact with other individuals and having interests that may conflict with those of others, finds it necessary to establish government and lay down rules of conduct, as it were, in order to insure to each individual the greatest measure of freedom consistent with the rights of other individuals. This set of rules, or law, as it may be termed, is determined from various social or economic factors prevalent at any particular stage in civilization, or at least it should be so determined. When, however, social or economic relations change, as they are bound to do, then they give rise to the necessity of altered rules of conduct, or amended law. There is nothing sacred about law. Simply because laws that one state of civilization found adequate and proper were enforced, there is no reason why the same laws should be enforced in another state of civilization which they do not fit or toward which they are anachronistic. It is the belief of the writer that the principle of *stare decisis* is much overworked. If by that principle is meant only the uniform enforcement of legal principles for the present or for any one period, that is, impartial decision, then the principle is a healthy one; but to attempt to enforce legal principles that were applicable to a civilization of several generations ago, in a modern and radically changed economic system, and one to which they are not applicable, is the height of absurdity. But *do* the courts observe the principle? What about the income tax decisions and other well-known decisions of the same court?

The related question concerning the frequent decisions declaring unconstitutional laws that have with the expenditure of great effort been enacted for the purpose of regulating changed economic conditions, should not be passed over lightly. Though the people are often *mis*represented in their legislatures, still sometimes laws suitable to the times are passed, even in spite of adverse and special interests. This manner of making the laws is the best we have at present. Why should officials not responsive to the people be permitted to abrogate those laws? An amendment to the Federal Constitution is practically an impossibility. Therefore, popular will is nullified without chance of remedy.

Take a specific case — that of the new so-called Employers' Liability Act. An analysis of facts and conditions clearly shows that this law was passed to partly meet changed economic conditions. The last-mentioned conditions arise from the incontrovertible fact that the employee is no longer free to work or not work or to select the material conditions under which he works. He must work for what he can get or starve. Industry is concentrated and is becoming centralized. The employee must seek the chance to work for a firm, corporation, or trust, and must accept the conditions imposed upon him. In the light of these changed conditions, the old principle that the employee accepts all risks, except that the employer must furnish a safe place in which work is to be done, is a pure anachronism. Even the safe place is often not provided, and this, too, with impunity. The employee must work or starve, whatever be his opinion of the place, or however negligent his co-workers, over whom he can exercise no care, may be. The aforesaid act, whatever be its exact provisions, was undoubtedly passed to remedy in part the injustice just referred to. How soon, however, do some irresponsible federal judges say it is unconstitutional (probably in view of laws and principles applicable to an economic state of one hundred or more years ago)! The principle to be emphasized is no less cogent, whatever the highest court does with the act.

In short, an economic system is one of dynamics, of active progressive forces. The body of the law should not be static, it should progress and not lag centuries behind changed conditions in our social and economic fabric. It should keep step, or, to use the engineering term, if it gets out of phase it will produce no beneficial results, and there is no excuse for its existence. A change of administrative faculties which will make the law also, as interpreted and enforced, a living, progressive force and one keenly responsive to the proper governing elements, is to be commended.

CYRUS D. BACKUS.

WASHINGTON, D. C.

"THERE are frequently things sworn to which are so improbable that one does not believe them. It is one of the commonest things in the world in a criminal case to have the most positive oral evidence given on oath to establish a matter which neither the jury nor the judge can believe, although it is sworn to." — Lord Blackburn, Gardner *v.* Gardner, (1877) L. R. 2 App. Cas. 738.

Law Notes.

VOL. XI.] Entered at the Post-office at Northport, N. Y., as second-class matter. Copyright, 1907, by Edward Thompson Co. [No. 1.

Subscription $1.00 per year. NORTHPORT, NEW YORK, APRIL, 1907. *Issued Monthly.*

The American and English Annotated Cases

is a *new series* of leading current cases of general importance, selected from the official State, Federal, English, and Canadian reports, ***each case exhaustively annotated*** by members of our editorial staff of long experience.

This work was begun in January, 1906, and five volumes are now issued.

We shall publish four volumes a year. The volumes will contain an average of 250 cases each, and every case will be exhaustively annotated.

The *price* is $5.00 per volume, $20.00 annually for 1000 current cases, annotated, or ***only 2 cents a case***, and the annotations contain ***from fifteen to sixteen thousand citations of cases to the volume***, making this work the ***least expensive*** and ***best*** of its kind.

The *binding* is full law sheep or English buckram as preferred.

In the American and English Annotated Cases we are giving the profession a work superior in every respect to any other series of selected cases.

The celebrated case of Haddock v. Haddock (201 U. S. 562) exhaustively annotated will be sent free on request. It is a fair sample of our work in the AMERICAN AND ENGLISH ANNOTATED CASES and we ask that you send for it. There will be NO CHARGE.

Edward Thompson Company

PUBLISHERS

NORTHPORT, LONG ISLAND, NEW YORK

Law Notes.

VOL. XI] Entered at the Post-office at Northport, N. Y., as second-class matter. Copyright, 1907, by Edward Thompson Co. [No. 10.

Subscription $1.00 *per year.* NORTHPORT, NEW YORK, JANUARY, 1908. *Issued Monthly.*

Spotted something that isn't quite right?

Let us know and we'll fix it for future reprints. And as a thank you for your diligence, we'll send you a free Sothis book of your choice.

publisher@sothis.press